STRAIT PRESS

STRAIT PRESS

A History Of News Media On The North Olympic Peninsula

BILL LINDSTROM

STRAIT PRESS
A HISTORY OF NEWS MEDIA ON THE
NORTH OLYMPIC PENINSULA

iUniverse books may be ordered through booksellers or by contacting:

iUniverse
1663 Liberty Drive
Bloomington, IN 47403
www.iuniverse.com
1-800-Authors (1-800-288-4677)

ISBN: 978-1-5320-5905-6 (sc)
ISBN: 978-1-5320-5903-2 (hc)
ISBN: 978-1-5320-5904-9 (e)

Print information available on the last page.

iUniverse rev. date: 12/04/2018

ABOUT THE BOOK

No author has attempted to write the history of all the newspapers on the North Olympic Peninsula — until now. Strait Press: A History of News Media on the North Olympic Peninsula does that.

There have been books that detailed the newspaper history in Clallam County; two books covered the media history in Jefferson County. Now, Strait Press encompasses both counties.

This book not only is about newspapers, but radio stations and even television.

The reader will learn which president came to Port Angeles in 1937 and was instrumental in establishing Olympic National Park. Creating that park was perhaps the most divisive issue in the history of the Port Angeles newspapers. You will discover why.

Learn which newspaper owner in Sequim arrived and vowed to run the Sequim Press out of town — and did it; find out what well-known author spent a night in a Port Townsend jail on his way back from gold-panning in the Klondike; in Forks, the reader will learn which newspaper owner became part of a quad-marriage in which four sisters were wed in the same ceremony; the history of each area is discussed; learn about mastodons, the Great Blowdown, devastating fires, oil spills and how each paper handled 9/11.

And, whenever possible, the author infuses the discussion with humorous anecdotes.

So, pull up a chair and start your education of North Olympic Peninsula news media.

On the front cover

The first issue of the Port Angeles Evening News on April 10, 1916; Below, Port Townsend Leader publisher Ray Scott sits at the Linotype in this file photo from the 1950s. Behind him, from left, are printers Fred Willoughby and Claude Mitton and managing editor Dick McCurdy. The microphone is a symbol of early-day radio at KONP in Port Angeles. Cover design by Melanie Reed-Arrington, Sequim.

"I couldn't put it down. Strait Press gave me a fascinating view of our news in print and on the air."

Michael Dashiell, editor
Sequim Gazette

CONTENTS

FOREWORD

This book you hold in your hand has been three years in the making.

I grew up the fifth-generation member of a newspaper family dating back to the Gold Rush days of California. The power of the press and the importance of news coverage has been my life. My great-great grandfather, James McClatchy, an immigrant orphan living in New York City, was told by Horace Greeley in 1849 to "go west young man and cover the great Gold Rush of California". He did so, covering the Gold Rush for Greeley's *New York Tribune* and later became the editor of the *Sacramento Bee*.

I've embraced the importance of the print and broadcast media my entire life. The very preservation of our democracy depends on the freedom of the press and the journalists, reporters and broadcasters who are given the freedom to do their job.

While this book is about the media on the North Olympic Peninsula, it also chronicles and brings to life our local past. Inside you will find details on the creation of Olympic National Park, the Northern Tier Pipeline story, the sinking of the Hood Canal Bridge and the great Forks fires and timber blow downs.

Remember the Arco Anchorage oil spill? How much do you know about the founding of Port Townsend, a very ambitious railroad plan and two (1880 and 1937) presidential visits to our peninsula?

So, why do this book?

I like history — and history has to be preserved. In my view there's no greater window into the past than the press that covers history as it unfolds. Coincidentally, it was in 2015, the 100th anniversary of the *Peninsula Daily News* that I chose to take on the task of preserving as much of our two-county media history as possible. This history covers both print and broadcast.

Thank you to the countless people who have contributed greatly to make this book possible, however none more so than Bill Lindstrom.

Thousands of miles driven, hundreds of interviews, multiple dozens of trips to the state library in Olympia and thousands of hours were needed to make this happen.

My hope is that you enjoy reading *Strait Press, A History of News Media on the North Olympic Peninsula* as much as I enjoyed making it possible.

Brown McClatchy Maloney
Sequim, Washington
November, 2018

INTRODUCTION

When the idea for a book on the "History of News Media on the North Olympic Peninsula" first came up, it didn't appear to be that imposing of an undertaking.

After all, today there are four basic newspapers on the peninsula. In Clallam County, there is the *Peninsula Daily News* in Port Angeles; in Sequim, the *Gazette* and in Forks, the *Forum*. In Jefferson County, there is the *Port Townsend and Jefferson County Leader.*

The Leader is the oldest continually operating newspaper on the Peninsula, having printed its first edition in 1889; the *Daily News* began as the *Port Angeles Evening News* in 1916; the *Forum* started in 1931, while the *Gazette* is a young publication with its first issue coming in 1976 as the *Shopper*, then the *Jimmy Come Lately Gazette.*

But, newspapers are not the only media on the peninsula.

Port Angeles has had a radio station (KONP) since 1945; KSQM has operated in Sequim since 2008; Forks had KVAC, starting in 1967; and KPTZ first went on the air in Port Townsend in 2011.

There were two television stations providing local access on the peninsula. Groundwork for PTTV in Port Townsend started in the early 1990s and the station first went live in 1997. In Port Angeles, Northland Cable started in 1992, but local access didn't begin until the Public News Network (PNN) was established in 2001.

Yet these media only scratch the surface of print and broadcasting history on the North Olympic Peninsula. In fact, none of the aforementioned publications were the first in their community. Far from it.

Long before the *Port Angeles Evening News* was established in 1916, Port Angeles was the site of the Puget Sound Cooperative Colony, which was chartered on May 10, 1887. The colony published the *Model Commonwealth* newspaper with its first issue on Aug. 5, 1887.

This was only one of more than 20 newspapers in Clallam County before the first issue of the *Evening News* hit the streets 29 years later.

Port Townsend had the first newspaper published on the peninsula when the *Port Townsend Register* was circulated in 1859, eight years after the city was incorporated. Through the next 30 years, 14 newspapers came and went before the *Morning Leader* initially was published.

A distinction that envelops each of the main newspapers in each county's city, is family ownership.

From its founding in 1916 until Esther Webster sold it in 1971, the *Port Angeles Evening News* was owned entirely, or in part, by the Webster family. The Websters also established KONP in 1945 and owned it, at least in part, until 1969.

In Port Townsend, it was the McCurdy clan from 1906-1967, and in Forks, Jim Astel owned the *Forum* from 1940-1966 when first Jim died, and Marion, his second wife, died the following year.

The Sequim Press was founded in 1911 and had family ties from 1916 to 1949 when the paper was operated first by Angus Hay, then upon his death, it reverted to his wife, Vesta, and her second husband, Jack Yoakum.

The first step in an exhaustive amount of research was a visit to the Washington State Library in Olympia, which has in its microfilm files every newspaper in the state from its very first issue to the last, or in some cases, the current.

After 52 trips to Olympia from Aberdeen, where this author lived at the time, every single newspaper in the two-county area was accounted for; every publisher and a majority of editors also were found after exhaustive hours searching microfilm from newspapers, starting in 1859 to the present. This resulted in more than 1,800 digital files to research.

Several books provided a wealth of information. Most notably were *Olympic Leaders: The Life and Times of the Websters of Port Angeles*, by Helen Radke and Joan Ducceschi; *Jimmy Come Lately*, the history of Clallam County; *Story of Port Angeles*, by G.M. Lauridsen and Arthur A. Smith; and *Port Townsend: An Illustrated History of Shanghaiing, Shipwrecks, Soiled Doves and Sundry Souls*, by Tom Camfield. The bibliography is far more extensive, but these works provided a bulk of information.

Next, I formulated a list of individuals to interview, either in person, via email or telephone. I obtained contact information for previous publishers and owners for each of the existing papers. Another list included individuals who were long-serving on their newspapers. I did the same for the radio stations and a couple of television studios.

Early day newspapers are a fascinating study. James G. McCurdy provides a descriptive view of the role of newspapers in his book *By Juan de Fuca's Strait*, written in 1937.

Newspapers resemble individuals in many particulars. Some have their lines cast in pleasant places; others find a hard and stony pasturage. Some at once attain to a popularity that continues with them for indefinite periods; others meet with shafts of suspicion, enmity and open hostility.

Some have a long, eventual existence; others under-nourished and unappreciated, are doomed to an early death.

A community without a newspaper is to a certain degree lacking in leadership. While only exceptionally strong periodicals mold public opinion to any great extent, nearly all solidify and stimulate collective thinking.

What about radio? Some say it's a dying industry; people are not listening to radio that much unless they are in their cars.

Radio is not dying as you will see when reading "Voices from the Peninsula in *Strait Press*." But it is changing, and the local stations are mostly successful in staying in tune with what is happening.

When KONP in Port Angeles celebrated its 50th anniversary in 1995, announcer "Big Jim" Borte was asked to write about his decade with the radio station. In that newsletter he describes what radio has meant to him. He is speaking about the history of KONP, but what he says applies to all community radio stations.

Radio has always been part magic and part reality. As I like to say, you have to see it to understand it. Part of the magic is that each one of us must participate in the moment.

It is a medium of the mind that allows everyone to personalize it as they wish. It can be interactive or passive, depending upon the individual listener. ... In a sense, radio is an expression of democracy that permits each of us to formulate our own thoughts and ideas.

Most of us can remember or associate certain events and moments in our lives with certain songs. We can recall where we were and what we were doing when major news stories happened.

For the past fifty years, KONP has served the community by providing information and entertainment. Its history is intertwined with that of Clallam County and points beyond. In a sense, it has grown with individuals, families, business and the entire community.

When the idea for the book was first broached in March 2015, it was, in part, to celebrate the 100th anniversary of the *Port Angeles Evening News (Peninsula Daily News)* on April 10, 2016. By September of 2015, it was apparent that wouldn't happen due to the massiveness of the project. Health issues forced a five-month delay, then I moved to Olympia in April 2016.

Thirteen trips to the North Olympic Peninsula followed until the book was ready for the publisher.

I have tried to write this book with an infusion of anecdotes that added humor, hopefully making it interesting for anyone on the Olympic Peninsula, not just those involved in the news media.

Bill Lindstrom
October 2018

ACKNOWLEDGEMENTS

A project of this scope requires a great deal of help from many people. I apologize in advance if I have overlooked anybody.

First, a huge vote of gratitude to Brown McClatchy Maloney for initiating the idea, believing in me and enduring months of patience to complete this project. Heartfelt thanks to John Brewer, now retired *Peninsula Daily News* publisher, for tireless editing, commiserating and suggestions throughout the process; to Sue Ellen Riesau, who helped shepherd the book toward printing and Patricia Morrison Coate for copy-editing.

I am most appreciative to the following for graciously allowing me to interview them and/or for providing photos:

Port Angeles: Brewer, Frank and Joan Ducceschi, Ralph Langer, Rex Wilson, Paul Gottlieb, Keith Thorpe, Mark Morey, Martha Ireland, Kathy Monds, Barb Maines, Scott Price, Jim White, Peter Horvitz, John McClelland III, John Hughes, Steve Perry, David Black and Rick O'Connor.

KONP: Maloney, Todd Ortloff, Scooter Chapman, Sandy Keys, Jim and Terry MacDonald.

Sequim: Maloney, Riesau, Michael Dashiell, Troye Jarmuth, Bob Clark, Judy Reandeau Stipe, Linda Paulson, Barb Adams, JoAnne Booth, Ross Hamilton, Dave Gauger, Ron Smith, Melanie Reed-Arrington and Hillary Steeby.

KSQM: Jeff Bankston and board.

Forks: Lorraine Jacobson, Christi Baron, Chris Cook, Lonnie Archibald, Nedra Reed and Lora Malakoff.

KVAC: Randy and David Otos, Mark Lamb.

Port Townsend: Frank Garred, Scott and Jennifer Wilson, Patrick Sullivan, Fred Obee, Tom Camfield, Dick McCurdy Jr., David Simpson and Lloyd Mullen.

KPTZ: Colin Foden, Larry Stein, Robert Ambrose.

PTTV: Gary Lemons.

PART I

Port Angeles

CHAPTER 1

Clallam County newspapers

I t is not an exaggeration to say that probably no county of its size in the nation ever produced such a remarkable crop of newspaper ventures in a short amount of time as was seen in Clallam County.

Some had success, others did not. Local newspaper history is strewn with corpses of journalistic ventures and adventures.

Indeed, from 1892-1900, it appeared just about everybody who was anybody either owned a newspaper, was starting one, worked for one or had just gone broke on one.

"It is a tradition within the craft that scarcely ever is a man bitten with the virus of political advancement that he does not at the same time develop the mistaken notion that he must own or control a newspaper," newspaper owner Arthur A. Smith said in *Story of Port Angeles*, he co-wrote with Port Angeles businessman G.M. Lauridsen.

Every time there was an election, a fledgling newspaper emerged. If the prevalent publication was run by (or called) Democrat, a Republican-based paper sprung forth. And vice versa. In short order, after the election, if the candidate backed by the new newspaper failed, the newspaper generally folded.

Washington became the 42nd state of the Union in 1889, and in the first few years after statehood, every county was aflame with political ambition. This resulted with tumultuous shouting of personal and party fights, most feverishly waged for the control of offices — be it congressional, state legislature or municipal. Where best to wage these wars than on the front pages of the local newspaper?

In those days, members of the U.S. Senate were chosen by state legislators, and the struggle for control of that body by the higher-ups in the political arena reached down to the local precincts, where party-named delegates controlled the situation. Often the newspaper was the puppeteer maneuvering the strings.

Newspapers emerged not only in Port Angeles, but also in Clallam Bay, Port Crescent, Sappho, Quileute and Forks on the West End and in Dungeness and Sequim in the East End.

The eight-year period from 1892-1900 was the high-water mark for newspapers.

As many as four or five existed at one time in a town of less than 5,000 inhabitants. Most of them were weeklies, but in January 1916, the first daily paper, the *Port Angeles Daily Herald,* emerged.

Four months later, on April 10, 1916, Edward Barton Webster and Smith started the *Port Angeles Evening News.*

These newspapers waged war on the editorial pages and in their front offices until 1923 when the *Evening News* became the sole newspaper in Port Angeles.

The newspaper was owned all, or in part, by the Webster family for 55 years from 1916-1971 when the final heir, Esther Webster, sold it to John McClelland Jr., with Longview Publishing Co., as the holding company.

McClelland promptly changed its name to the *Daily News.*

In 1986, McClelland sold it to the Persis Corp. It changed the paper to its present name, *Peninsula Daily News,* in 1987 and owned it until selling to Peter Horvitz in 1994. Horvitz then sold the newspaper and its affiliates to Sound Publishing Inc. in 2011.

Newspapers in the Clallam County area began before there was an incorporated city of Port Angeles.

Port Angeles' early days

The earliest residents of the area were Native Americans, such as the S'Klallam ("Strong People") and Makah Indian tribes, both sustained by the region's abundant natural resources.

The first official non-native sighting of the peninsula was made by an explorer named Juan Perez on Aug. 10, 1774, and the first confirmed report of the sighting of the Strait of Juan de Fuca was made by Capt. Charles Barkley in 1787.

A Greek named Apostolos Valerianos, who had a reputation for "tall tales," claimed to find the strait in 1592 but it was Barkley, master of the Austrian East India Company ship *Imperial Eagle*, who named the strait in 1787.

Port Angeles has had several different names since its "discovery." In 1791, Lt. Francisco Eliza, a Spanish explorer, called it "El Puerto de Nuestra Señora de los Angeles" as it provided a haven from the stormy passage through the strait. A year later, it was shortened to Porto de los Angeles. Later it was called "False Dungeness," then "Cherbourg" as someone who had been to France wanted to name it. Finally, on June 6, 1862, the city officially was named Port Angeles.

The official settling of the city began in the 1850s after the establishment of the boundary between Canada and the United States in 1846. Victor Smith is regarded as the city's founder when, in 1862, he moved the Customs House and Port of Entry from Port Townsend to Port Angeles, where he had purchased land.

Coincidentally, the very next day Abraham Lincoln signed an order setting aside more than 3,500 acres of land at Port Angeles as a military and lighthouse reservation; this area is now known as Lincoln Park.

Unfortunately, with the passing of Victor Smith in 1865, the Port of Entry was returned to Port Townsend and Port Angeles became little more than a ghost town until the 1880s.

The railroad brought Port Angeles back to life, opening the Pacific Northwest to homesteading. All those choosing to move west found a little bit of paradise.

Settlement of the Port Angeles region started with the Puget Sound Cooperative Colony. The colony was established in Seattle on Nov. 15, 1886. The official organ of the colony was the *Model Commonwealth* newspaper.

The next year, its members moved the colony to a site on Ennis Creek in Port Angeles and the newspaper came with it.

The first issue of the *Commonwealth* that was circulated on the North Olympic Peninsula was printed on April 8, 1887.

MODEL COMMONWEALTH

The Puget Sound Cooperative Colony originated with Peter Good, a former New York judge who opened a law office in Seattle in 1886.

He had visited a colony settlement in Guise, France, and decided to try the concept in the United States.

George Venable Smith founded the Puget Sound Cooperative Colony in Seattle in 1886. It moved to Port Angeles the following year. The *Model Commonwealth*, the first newspaper in Port Angeles, was founded in 1886. *(Courtesy of the North Olympic History Center)*

His goal was to establish it on Puget Sound, and he did to some extent; he died before he could witness it.

An attorney, George Venable Smith, was assigned as administrator for the colony and articles of incorporation were filed on May 10, 1886. Smith and Laura Hall, a distant cousin of Good, were on the board of trustees.

The articles called for capital stock of $1 million to be raised from the sale of 100,000 shares at a value of $10 per share, which could be purchased in cash, labor, services or property.

The cooperative colony engaged in manufacturing, mining, milling, wharfing, docking, mechanical, mercantile and construction.

Chairmen were appointed to handle and manage law, public utilities, public safety, commerce, manufacturing, education, law, finance, agriculture and health.

George V. Smith was the first chairman. The colony was the Utopian idea Good envisioned.

According to the colony's public records and constitution bylaws, Port Angeles was chosen because of its temperate climate, good fishing, abundance of timber, productive soil, excellent harbor and its natural beauty.

A $50 membership fee entitled a subscriber to one 50-foot by 140-foot lot, which the colony was to purchase. The colony purchased 10-acre sites from the U.S. government for lots and other subdivisions.

There would be no private enterprise in the cooperative colony. The company, through its officers, owned and controlled all business enterprises, factories and other matters such as traffic, production and distribution within the company.

The beach at the mouth of Ennis Creek, later the site of now-demolished Rayonier pulp mill, was selected as the center of the colony.

The colony was widely promoted throughout the nation. Smith went on speaking tours to arouse interest.

The earliest known edition of the *Model Commonwealth* was April 8, 1887. This issue was printed in Seattle and was listed as Vol. I, No. 24, indicating the first issue was published about six months previously, or about Oct. 1, 1886.

The April issue lists the articles of incorporation and talks about moving the colony to Port Angeles. It lists Smith as the general managing agent and Laura Hall as editor.

By Nov. 18, 1887, Venier Voldo is the editor and E.B. Mastick Jr. is business manager. In that issue, the subscription rate — payable in advance — is listed as $1 a year, 50 cents for six months and 25 cents for three months.

Less than a year later, on May 4, 1888, Freeborn S. Lewis is the editor and Thomas Malony executive editor. By August 1888, Malony was the sole editor. The Nov. 2 issue of that year showed still another editorial switch with the colony leasing the paper to Lewis, who would return as editor and E.B. Mastick Jr. as publisher. At the same time, the paper became simply *The Commonwealth*.

Malony was variously the paper's editor, business manager, president, executive editor and secretary.

It wasn't beyond *The Commonwealth* to spend two or three pages or more avenging a cause its editors felt was worthy. The issue of Nov. 18, 1887, is a good example.

Most interesting in this issue is the headline: "The Anarchists Dead," followed by a bit smaller second deck: "Strangled Upon the Gallows," and yet another deck, "They Died with Great Fortitude and Bravado." Voldo's editorials were outlined in black borders, drawing attention to what he says is the "execution of innocent men."

The incident in question was the public square death by hanging of the four anarchists accused in Chicago's Haymarket Riot.

Voldo dedicates nearly four full pages to the appeal that one of those hung presented prior to having his neck stuck in the noose.

We herewith give in full the appeal of A.R. Parsons to the American people. It not only has a pathetic interest at this time as being among the last utterances of a murdered man, but is instructive, withal, as being a presentation of the case from the standpoint of naked truth.

This certainly seems like overkill on an incident that occurred in Chicago, not Port Angeles. But it wasn't to Voldo.

"Hang the Anarchists" is printed too many times to count, spouting the belief of those who wanted the four men hung. In the middle of the page is a 2-column by about 8 inches deep advertisement in much larger type than the body copy.

OBITUARY
DIED AT CHICAGO
Nov. 11th, 1887
FREE SPEECH!!!
FREE PRESS!!!

Rights of Americans Peaceably to Assemble

And Discuss Their Grievances!!!

Rights of Americans Against Unreasonable

Search and Seizure Without Warrants!!!

Rights of Americans to a Fair Trial

And Impartial Jury!!!

FOR THESE WE MOURN!!!

And he wasn't done yet. Starting on Page 6 is an in-depth report on the hanging, describing the "dark brown gallows." The description detailed what each of the four had for their last meal, then the slow walk down the hall and up the steps to greet the hangman.

In subsequent issues, the paper reported on such issues as the rise of "Girls as Journalists," and "The Dangers of Chewing Tobacco."

By 1890, the colony had management problems exacerbated by a slumping economy.

Internal struggles continued to plague the colony. In 1904, its assets were liquidated. Despite its ultimate failure, the colony was one of the greatest factors in the growth of the city of Port Angeles.

Before the colony was dismantled, it had constructed the city's first sawmill, contracted to build the first schoolhouse, the first Protestant church, the First Congregational Church; constructed the first office building and the first opera house.

In 1889, the press was moved from its first home on Ennis Creek to a building constructed for it at Front and Chase streets. In 1889, A.H. Howells, a newcomer to Port Angeles, took over *The Commonwealth* lease from Lewis and Mastick. He changed the name to *The Port Angeles Times* and its politics to Republican. Howells' printer was a young man named A.J. Cosser and we'll see him pop up among other newspapers.

PORT ANGELES TIMES

Howells was a Canadian by birth and a Congregational minister by trade — and at various times a school teacher, publisher, editor, reporter, business manager, politician, lecturer and tidelands appraiser.

He ran the *Times* plant for about a year, then sold it in June 1890 to two newcomers, Horace White and Arthur A. Smith. White came west after abandoning his post with the Chicago Press Association and became business manager. Smith had published the *Greencastle* (Indiana) *Times*, leaving the paper to his younger brother.

Smith, better known as A.A., graduated high school at age 16 in Greencastle and immediately went to work as a reporter for the *Columbus Daily Republican*. When he was 20, he became city editor. The next year he purchased the *Times* and became owner and publisher, positions he held until he was 29, and left for Port Angeles.

Smith and White apparently knew each other in the Midwest and agreed to come west together.

On June 20, 1890, Howells announced the purchase of his lease by Smith and White. In a few months, they were in undisputed possession of the local newspaper field.

However, it wouldn't be long before an epidemic of newspaper wars would be waged. In short order, clamorous times would be afield.

In the September 1891 issue, White announced his retirement after 18 months with the paper. At the time, White was the city clerk under Mayor Brumfield. A few years later, White would become mayor.

Meantime, Smith, a vital cog in the local newspaper field, would do much to mold public thought and opinion; he continued to steer the *Times* alone until April 1892 when he went to Alaska. He would return six years later.

THE PORT ANGELES TRIBUNE

The Port Angeles Times and the *Port Angeles Tribune* butted heads for years. The *Tribune* was started by Col. R.H. Ballinger and his son, Joe, in the fall of 1890 when they arrived from Port Townsend. The *Tribune* building was at the corner of First and Oak streets in the former post office building.

Ballinger was something of a "scrapper in his own right," according to a description of the paper in *Story of Port Angeles*.

Ballinger got himself in hot water when he developed a dislike for T.J. Patterson. He ran the local weather bureau and Ballinger tried to have him ousted in favor of a man he preferred. This didn't sit well with Patterson's friends, who burned the colonel in effigy.

Ballinger apparently lost interest in the paper and retired. Before he left, he hired a young printer, C.D. Ulmer Jr. who was working in Astoria, Ore. Ulmer not only came to Port Angeles, but he summoned his father and five other family members — all of them printers — to leave Kansas and work at the *Times* in Port Angeles.

Father and son would become a formidable family in local newspapers until 1897. The senior Ulmer was owner, president and publisher, while his son was editor, also in charge of the printers with five siblings under him.

In midsummer of 1892, they established *The Daily Tribune*, a 5-column folio sheet they published through the election campaign of that year.

When the election was over, so too, was the *Tribune* and the paper was put to sleep on Jan. 1, 1893, two months after the candidates they supported were defeated.

The *Tribune* was the first daily newspaper in Port Angeles, and was printed on the area's first cylinder press, which arrived with the *Commonwealth* from Seattle. The press was shipped back to Seattle when the Ulmers retired in 1897.

It was later shipped to Alaska during the Klondike Gold Rush of 1896-1899 and was in operation well into the 1930s.

PORT ANGELES HERALD

On Feb. 11, 1891, the *Port Angeles Herald* emerged along the muddy streets of the growing community.

Two newly elected county officials, auditor B. John Baker and deputy auditor William R. Hoole, announced in their first edition that the policy of the paper would be Republican, but that they would, at all times, "fearlessly denounce any political chicanery" whether perpetuated by their party or another.

In September 1891, control of the *Herald* went to John W. Troy and R.A. Grimes. Troy was a member of a Dungeness pioneer family. Grimes and Troy hired an upstart young Mississippian, F.M. Runnels, as editor.

Not only did the *Herald* change ownership with Troy and Grimes at the helm, the newspaper's political leaning switched to Democrat. In the paper's Sept. 16, 1891, edition, Runnels wrote that the *Herald* would be a paper "whose voice would ever ring out in opposition to the powers that are now crushing the life blood of the American people."

Unfortunately, before the paper could do this, Runnels scooped up all the money in the paper's coffers and left town. The *Herald* collapsed soon after.

THE TRIBUNE-TIMES

The election campaign of 1890 resulted in a mixed set of county officials and a badly disrupted Republican party. Local party officials believed their cause would be served best with only one newspaper and pushed for the *Times* and *Tribune* to combine forces.

Under ownership of the Port Angeles Printing & Publishing Co. the paper fared well through 1897. Its leading competitor, the *Democrat,* which later became the *Democrat-Leader,* was established at about the same time.

The printing plant of the *Times* was moved and merged with the *Tribune* on the D.W. Morse property facing the wharf approach on Laurel Street. In 1894, the company built a new home, called *Tribune-Times* Building on the Front Street extension, west of Oak Street; thus, it became the first newspaper in Port Angeles to own its newspaper building. Later, when the Front Street extension was abandoned, the building was switched to face First Street.

The years of 1893-1896 were tough times for the *Tribune-Times* with M.J. Carrigan and J.P. Fisher taking over. Carrigan previously had established the *Port Crescent Leader* and was the editor.

In 1898, after being out of the printing business for six years, A.A. Smith returned from Alaska in July to find his old paper with a new name and in new hands. He had no trouble purchasing the paper as the new owners were struggling and wanted to sell.

In 1903, Smith absorbed the *Clallam County Courier,* which he formed into a stock corporation to handle the transaction. Stockholders included Carrigan, Fisher, Smith, Thomas Aldwell and Major R.R. Harding. Ben T. Smith, the *Courier* publisher, became plant foreman and Louis Flowers was advertising manager and typesetter.

Smith put the *Tribune-Times* back on its feet and ran it successfully until 1916 when he merged with E.B. Webster to form the *Port Angeles Evening News.*

THE PORT ANGELES DEMOCRAT

One month after the collapse of the *Herald,* its owners, Troy and Grimes, established the *Democrat,* using the *Herald's* plant. Its first issue hit the streets on Oct. 7, 1891.

Troy was editor and publisher. It was a vigorous newspaper from its inception and a fierce competitor for the Republican *Tribune-Times.*

DEMOCRAT-LEADER

Grimes retired in December 1891 and Troy remained as editor, publisher and president until March 1893.

A few months later, the *Democrat* consolidated with the *Leader,* then owned by A.H. Howells, to become the *Democrat-Leader.* A.J. Cosser, who had been with Carrigan at the *Leader* as a printer, joined the paper in that position and later became a proprietor.

In the March 17, 1893, edition, the publisher explains the consolidation was a business decision:

"There has been a surfeit of newspapers in Port Angeles, some a disgrace, and the town could undoubtedly support two good newspapers, but that more was utter imbecility." In that same issue, Troy defined progressive journalism as "bringing the people the news and leading in thought and public movement."

Cosser bought the paper from Troy in 1896. Troy stayed on as editor through the fall election campaign. Cosser became editor and publisher later that year. He continued until he sold to the Webster family in 1906.

Troy went to Alaska and established the *Alaska Daily Empire* in Juneau.

With their mergers, the *Democrat-Leader* and the *Tribune-Times* dominated the local newspaper scene for several years. But this didn't stop the many ambitious politicians, would-be newspapermen and businessmen from entering the media scene.

PORT CRESCENT STAR

The paper was established on the West End as part of the Port Crescent Improvement Co. in late 1890 or early 1891. Port Crescent is about 18 miles west of Port Angeles.

B. John Baker, a land claim owner at Sappho, was editor and publisher and later became county auditor. Baker would team later with W.R. Hoole to establish the *Herald.* The *Star* was absorbed at Port Crescent by M.J. Carrigan's *Leader.*

PORT CRESCENT LEADER

Abandoning two newspaper properties at Chillicothe, Ohio, M.J. Carrigan was lured to the Olympic Peninsula by the Lutz Brothers, John, a lieutenant in the Coast Guard, and Harry of neighboring Circleville, Ohio.

The brothers were associated with Cyrus Clapp, a capitalist and timberland owner in Port Townsend, who had established the Port Crescent Improvement Co. to create a community on the bay to rival Port Angeles.

Carrigan was "one of the most-spirited and capable newsmen to leave his mark on Clallam County's affair," according to Smith in *The Story of Port Angeles.*

"M.J. was a writer of much grace and charm, and many of his stories were masterpieces of description." Notable among them was one telling of the peak performance of the improvement company, which exploded dynamite on the mountainside to form a west-wing breakwater for the proposed harbor.

In the summer of 1892, Carrigan and his partners in the improvement company had a disagreement and he moved the paper to Port Angeles in the old *Times* building. A few months later, he accepted a cash offer from Howells and retired.

The *Port Crescent Leader* didn't die immediately. After Carrigan left, Harry Lutz launched a new *Leader,* which he controlled for a few years. By the early 1920s, Port Crescent was a ghost town after its sentinel, the Markham Hotel, was destroyed by fire.

THE PEOPLE

This newspaper was established as one "Devoted to the Interests of the Republic and its Toiling Millions," according to the one lone issue that exists, that of Oct. 10, 1891. It lists this issue as Vol. 4. J.A. Power is the editor; there is no indication of its ownership.

The paper had a 7-column format, set all in 6-point size (the type size usually seen today on classified pages or in baseball box scores). Power seems to have been a prolific writer as he produced two long editorial columns.

Randomly throughout the paper, he shoved in poetry. When the paper folded is not known.

PEOPLE'S PUBLISHING CO.

About one year after *The People* debuted, George W. Vail, James Forsland, A. O'Brien, J.M. Grant, C.J. Grant and F.S. Lewis teamed to establish the People's Publishing Co., in Port Angeles.

A short item in the *Tribune-Times* on Sept. 1, 1892, notes the publishing company as the name of the paper, noting that Grant was the editor and the paper supported the Populist Party. No files for the paper are available.

THE DUNGENESS BEACON

Papers not only sprung up in Port Angeles but at Groveland (Dungeness), about 20 miles east of Port Angeles.

R.C. Wilson, who was a stockholder with the *Democrat* a year earlier, joined with Col. Ballinger (*Port Angeles Tribune*) and G.K. Estes to form the *Dungeness Beacon* on June 24, 1892.

In January 1893, the paper published an editorial by Estes, announcing a move from Dungeness to Port Angeles, much to the chagrin of those in the East End.

The paper was politically orchestrated by Wilson, who was a candidate for state senator in the ensuing election. After his unsuccessful campaign, Estes sold his interest and, four papers later, the *Beacon* was absorbed by the *Tribune-Times* in 1901.

CLALLAM BAY RECORD & CLALLAM BAY PRESS

In 1890, Port Townsend resident George W. O'Brien established the *Clallam Bay Record*. He enjoyed some success for a few years but discontinued the weekly in 1907. Clallam Bay, about 50 miles west of Port Angeles, was without a paper for two years when O'Brien returned and established the *Clallam Bay Press*, which published about a year before folding in 1911.

O'Brien would continue in the newspaper field, establishing the long-running *Sequim Press* on April 8, 1911. That paper would serve Sequim for 74 years before its final issue in 1985. We'll talk about the *Press* in detail in the Sequim section of the book.

THE REPUBLICAN

In May 1892, the *Tribune-Times* under Ulmer sent some printing machinery to Clallam Bay to work with George O'Brien's *Clallam Bay Record*. The new paper was called the *Republican* and functioned only a few months before quietly dropping out of the picture after the November election.

THE BEAVER LEADER

The first *Beaver Leader* arrived in 1889, though its founder is not known. A year later, two elected officials from Port Angeles, auditor B. John Baker and deputy auditor William R. Hoole, took over the paper after they sold the *Port Angeles Herald*.

William H. Sparks, a brother-in-law to Hoole, owned the paper with his wife Betty as clerk/reporter in the earliest existing *Leader* (1895). Two years later, the Sparks brothers were owners. Sometime after 1895, the paper moved to Sappho, but still retained the *Beaver Leader* name. Sappho and Beaver are about 45 miles west of Port Angeles.

After the *Port Crescent Leader* moved to Port Angeles later in 1892, the West End of the county belonged to the *Leader* for several years before it too folded after 1897.

PORT ANGELES SIMOON

In June or July of 1894, E.E. Seevers, a wealthy Port Angeles businessman, established the *Port Angeles Simoon*. The paper was the organ of the Populist Party and was believed to have emerged from the People's Publishing Co. The *Simoon*, named after a hot, dry, desert sand storm, was owned and edited by Seevers, who aspired to be a state legislator and was his party's nominee in the fall election.

He won by a mere two votes and turned the operation of the paper over to E.M. Bonhall and S.P. Carusi.

The *Simoon* lasted until January 1896 when it was passed to new ownership and got a new name — *Clallam County Courier*.

THE TYPHOON

In his book *The Story of Port Angeles*, Smith writes that "a freak in the newspaper field appeared here toward the close of the bitterly fought 1894 political campaign."

Appearing on Oct. 27 in 4-column format, one week before the election, *The Typhoon* was perhaps a left-handed salute to the *Simoon*.

Sponsored by John F. Church, this paper consisted wholly of a 4-page roast of R.C. Wilson, the Republican nominee for state senator for the district that included Clallam and Jefferson counties.

The paper charged that "Wilson had captured the county and district conventions by unethical methods to the dissatisfaction of a portion of party followers." But Wilson won and served for four years as the state's second senator from the joint district.

The Typhoon had one more issue, then went out of business.

THE DAILY POP

In early 1896, a tiny paper emerged for an indefinite period during the high tide of the Populist party. It was called *The Daily Pop*.

But to call it a daily and to call it a newspaper is going a long way. The 4-page paper was two columns of type on 6-by 8-inch pages, a little more than one-quarter the size of a standard newspaper page. It was produced on a job press.

Its ownership emerged from the former The People's Publishing Co., with E.E. Vail the editor, and its contents were brief local items and party propaganda.

On May 26, 1896, the *Pop* printed an "Extra" recounting a disaster in Victoria, B.C., the day before during the annual celebration of Queen Victoria's birthday.

A tram car carrying 100 persons plunged through the Port Ellice bridge into the bottom of Victoria harbor. "Many were killed and more injured, but thankfully none of the Port Angeles contingent attending the event were hurt."

Vail continued as editor well into 1897 before the paper's name became the *Daily News*. How long it lasted isn't known — the date of the dissolution of the *News* isn't recorded, nor was it a daily.

CLALLAM COUNTY COURIER

The paper came into existence on the last day of January 1896 when Harry E. Lutz purchased the *Simoon* and immediately changed the name to *Clallam County Courier*.

Lutz promptly proclaimed on the paper's front page that the policy would be Republican, naming himself editor and Louis R. Cole as city editor (the editor who handles local news) and business manager.

Cole was a freelance newspaperman, having contributed to many papers in the area. Under Lutz's set-up, the *Courier* ran through the fall election campaign and for a year or two after that. Lutz and Cole both retired and control of the paper was turned over to Ben T. Smith, a longtime job printer who for a time was associated with the *Democrat-Leader*.

By 1902, the paper was in financial trouble and absorbed by the *Tribune-Times* in 1903.

THE QUILLAYUTE NEWS

With the West End paperless for a couple of years after the *Beaver Leader* ran into hard times in 1898, W.H. Willis founded the *Quillayute News* in April of 1901.

Based in Forks, about 60 miles west of Port Angeles, the paper's owner, publisher and editor was Willis, but its life was short, existing only until the last of the land claim notices for the area were printed in October.

QUILEUTE NEWS & QUILEUTE CHIEFTAIN

These two papers, both tribal newspapers, emerged one after the other at La Push, serving the needs of the Quileute tribe and the Shaker religion. W.H. Hudson was the editor of both, first the *News*, which was established in 1908, the *Chieftain* in 1910. It is not known how long they existed.

THE OLYMPIC AND OLYMPIC LEADER

E.B. Webster first arrived in Port Angeles in 1900, coming from Cresco, Iowa. He opened a small print shop, then in 1902, he moved to Port Townsend, where he worked on the *Morning Leader* and operated a print shop, publishing a legal paper, *Town Topics*.

But E.B. liked being in association with the Olympic Mountains, where he could enjoy his love of nature.

He moved his family back to Port Angeles in December 1904. E.B. and Will Bassett established a weekly paper, *The Olympic*.

Bassett only lasted a few weeks before retiring. About the same time, Webster's father, W.B. sold the *Republican* and journeyed west to join his son at *The Olympic*.

Early in 1906, Webster made a deal with A.J. Cosser for the name and plant of the *Democrat-Leader*, then moved the *Olympic* to the Warren Morse Building. They established the Webster Publishing Co., then changed the name of the weekly paper to *Olympic-Leader*.

THE DAILY LEADER

Webster was looking to gain an edge on his main rival, A.A. Smith, and on Feb. 16, 1915, began printing *The Daily Leader*, using the *Olympic-Leader's* press.

It was a full-sized, 8-page format, but apparently it proved too much work for Webster and only lasted five issues.

PORT ANGELES EVENING NEWS

Throughout 1915, neighboring rivals, Smith and Webster, knew the public wanted a daily newspaper. The two competitors buried their hatchets after realizing they could accomplish their goals better as partners.

They merged their operations, establishing Smith and Webster Printers Inc. to handle commercial printing, then, after moving into a new building, operated their two weeklies — Webster's *Olympic-Leader* and Smith's *Tribune-Times* — side-by-side until April 10, 1916, when the first issue of the *Port Angeles Evening News* debuted with Smith and Webster as partners.

The newspaper continues today, serving thousands of print and online readers in Clallam and Jefferson counties as the *Peninsula Daily News*.

THE BEE

In August 1913, Dr. Albert Davis arrived in Port Angeles with $25,000, established the Bee Publishing Co., and subsequently *The Bee*, a full-sized, 8-page weekly newspaper.

He set about taking on the "gang" of Smith's *Tribune-Times* and Webster's *Olympic-Leader*.

As Smith later wrote in *The Story of Port Angeles*:

"Davis might have been a good doctor, but he knew nothing whatever about the newspaper business; and less about how to transmit intelligent English to copy paper; and how he ever happened to become editor and publisher of a newspaper was never revealed."

Smith says the only good thing *The Bee* ever did was bring young William D. "Billy" Welsh to Port Angeles.

Welsh soon saw *The Bee* was not going to be around and found a job with Smith's *Tribune-Times*, where he became a fixture in Port Angeles journalism for the next 26 years.

Despite two fires, *The Bee* continued to publish until the early 1920s when its operations became part of the *Evening News*.

THE (SECOND) HERALD

The Bee Publishing Company also published another weekly, *The Herald*, an 8-page weekly. in 1913. The paper published until early 1915.

PORT ANGELES DAILY HERALD

While Smith and Webster continued negotiations for a merger of their papers, the *Port Angeles Daily Herald* appeared the first week of December 1915, created from the former *Herald* office.

The full-size paper was published every evening, except for Sunday, and printed by the Bee Publishing Co. It subscribed to the Associated Press service, but its masthead listed no owners, no editors, no managers.

Early in 1916, the real ownership was revealed.

A syndicate of timberland owners were financing the paper with a goal to drive the *Tribune-Times* out of business.

Smith had butted heads with the syndicate, which controlled the lumber mills in and around Port Angeles.

The syndicate was, according to Smith, "trying to buy up property and thus avoid taxation within the county. The ownership installed Arthur V. Watts from Bellingham as editor, and Jack Campbell from Everett as business manager. Both were veterans in their field."

This sudden emergence of a daily accelerated Smith and Webster toward their merger and subsequent founding of the *Evening News*.

The Herald fell on difficult times as its management began to desert the ship. Campbell was the first to leave, moving back to Everett; Watts decided to retire, leaving the publication of the paper in the hands of his wife.

Mrs. Watts was described by Smith as a "two-fisted woman who kept a piece of light artillery on her desk. She displayed courage, determination and capacity as an editor and business manager, and kept the paper afloat until a fire in the plant temporarily put it out of business."

Elmer E. Beard, one of the best old-timers in the Washington state newspaper field, according to Smith, pulled *The Herald* temporarily out of its doldrums in 1920. He ran it for a couple of years before it "passed" into the *Port Angeles Evening News* organization. *The Herald* — like *The Bee* — was absorbed into the *Evening News'* organization.

THE PENINSULA FREE PRESS

Still another newspaper emerged in Port Angeles in the fall of 1913 when George Boomer, a Socialist party writer and lecturer, established the *Peninsula Free Press*.

Aided by his wife, Alice, a printer and Linotype operator, they published the paper in a small building on Front Street.

The paper was a full-size, 8-page weekly published on Saturdays.

Printing primarily local news and Socialistic propaganda, it existed for about a year and half.

Boomer died only a few months after starting the publication, and his wife ran the paper until a fire destroyed the building.

In December 1915 Alice Boomer was hired to oversee job printing at Smith and Webster. She later became a Linotype operator at the *Evening News*.

SPRUCE

During the latter years of World War I, the *Spruce* sprung to life serving those who were diligently cutting in the woods, primarily spruce trees to build airplanes for the war.

Managed and edited by Richard Kilroy, this little paper emerged as a 4-pager in Aug. 7, 1918. It expanded to 8 pages for the third edition. Its last known edition was Oct. 12, 1919. The paper was published by the Siems Carey and H.S. Kerbaugh Corp.

* * *

Since 1923 when the *Evening News* absorbed the *Daily Herald*, only a few papers have challenged it, all of them weeklies, according to the *Jimmy Come Lately*, a book produced by the Clallam County Historical Society in 1971.

The first was the *Clallam County Journal*, established in December 1934 with Clarence L. Vaughn as editor. It was founded to support the rights of organized labor, but it survived only a year.

The *Port Angeles Union Spokesman* came out July 3, 1936, with T.B. McCready as editor. It was succeeded by the *Independent*, neither of which lasted over a year.

In 1946, three local newspapermen established the weekly *Peninsula Herald*. A year later they sold it to Arthur and Ruby Poolton, who published it until 1970 when they sold the paper to Russell and Jean Fulcher of Olympia.

On Dec. 12, 1971, Gordon Otos, owner of Forks Broadcasting Co., purchased it; in 1975 he merged the paper with the *Forks Forum*, which was published as *Forks Forum* and *Peninsula Herald* until 1995 when the *Peninsula Herald* was dropped.

It was a typical neighborly weekly, livened up for many years with Poolton's tongue-in-cheek column, "By Founden Flore."

By far the most successful challenge came on Jan. 19, 1961, when Del Price angrily left his job as advertising director at the *Evening News* and debuted the weekly *Clallam County Shopping News*.

Price, John Schweitzer, Dave Partridge and Lorraine Ross, all former *Evening News* employees, made up the braintrust for the new paper.

It became the *Shopping News and Chronicle* in February 1963, then became simply the *Chronicle* in September 1963. In the beginning, it wasn't much of a paper in the traditional sense. It carried very little news but was stacked with advertising. It was successful in luring several big accounts away from the *Evening News*.

The weekly improved its news content and competed against the daily for 31 years before Price retired, putting the final issue of the *Chronicle* to bed on June 24, 1992. *The Chronicle*, and *Sequim Sun*, developed by Price, then passed their best days, were purchased by Brown M. Maloney, then folded.

CHAPTER 2

E.B. Webster

Edward Barton Webster — E.B. to his friends — was the patriarch of the family and the first in a line of Websters to operate a newspaper in Port Angeles.

His career as a printer and newspaper owner might not have happened if it weren't for a fire in his hometown of Cresco, Iowa.

Born in Cresco on Oct. 29, 1868, E.B. learned his trade from his father, William Barton Webster, who had been a printer before the Civil War, then was assigned as a foreman in the government printing office of the Union Army.

From childhood, Ed became interested in nature and, as a youngster, was widely known as an expert in birds. When he was 19, he began publishing *Hawkeye Ornithologist and Oologist,* a monthly publication, which some considered to be the leading ornithological journal of the Western states.

He printed the magazine in his father's shop from January 1888 to September 1889, and he might have become a leading ornithologist and not a newspaperman, if not for the devastating fire that destroyed most of Cresco.

Included in that tragic event was the print shop of W.B. Webster, destroying all the printing equipment. Also, going up in flames were research materials precious to E.B. That was the end of the ornithological magazine. But he remained a serious student of birds for the rest of his life.

The Websters switched gears and decided to establish Cresco's first newspaper, the *Cresco Republican*, a weekly. The first issue came off the press on Oct. 29, 1889, on E.B.'s 21st birthday.

Hired to work in the shop was a young woman named Jessie Trumbull. Her job was to set type, but she had a habit of holding the type in her mouth as she worked. She had to quit that job when she developed lead poisoning.

Miss Trumbull then became a school teacher, but she didn't forget E.B. They formed a friendship that would lead to the altar when he gave his love interest his prized possession — an owl he stuffed.

Jessie was the ninth of 12 children, born to Scottish immigrants in 1872 in Cresco.

When Jessie married E.B. in the home of her parents on June 21, 1893, the family newspaper described them as "... one of Cresco's most charming daughters ... intelligent, lovely in feature and disposition, self-reliant and hopeful. ... the groom is highly esteemed as one of our more reliable young men of whom only good is spoken," according to

Edward Barton Webster, 24, and Jessie Trumbull, 21, were married in the home of her parents in Cresco, Iowa, in 1893. *(Courtesy of the North Olympic History Center)*

Olympic Leaders: The Life and Times of the Websters of Port Angeles, a book about the Websters written by Helen Radke and Joan Ducceschi, wife of Frank Ducceschi, *Peninsula Daily News* publisher from 1981-1998.

The couple married when E.B. was 24 and Jessie, 21.

Two years later in 1895, Mae, the first of the couple's four children, was born, and in 1898, Beth entered the world.

E.B. worked at the *Republican* until 1900 when he and Jessie followed other members of her large family to the state of Washington, where he co-founded the *Evening News* in 1916. The move to the West Coast likely was prompted by the prospects of a railroad boom and the possibility to provide printing for the railroad.

In 1903, the couple's only son, Charles, was born in Port Townsend, where they had moved. The next year, when they returned to Port Angeles, the last of the children, Dorothy, was born.

E.B. was owner and publisher of the *Port Angeles Evening News*, but he also was well-known for sojourns into the Olympic Mountains.

When he wasn't working in the print shop, Edward could be found in the nearby Olympic Mountains, a vast difference from the flat plains of Iowa.

There he found the perfect location to cultivate his life as a naturalist, hiking the Olympics' many trails, fishing in the clear, ice-blue lakes and rivers and observing wildlife, particularly the hundreds of bird species.

E.B. wrote four books on the geology, plants, birds, fish and other animals of the Olympics.

Life in Iowa

Little was known about when the elder Webster's passion for flora and fauna was developed until his son, Charles, then owner and publisher of the *Port Angeles Evening News,* revealed it in his newspaper in 1954, 18 years after his father's death.

The 20-article installment about his early life in Iowa was written by E.B. and published in 1931 as a gift for his first grandson, Verle Duckering.

The series doesn't include anything about E.B.'s vocation as a journalist, newspaper owner and publisher, but it does help reveal what made him kind-hearted, loved by everybody he encountered, particularly individuals involved with his passion for gardens, birds and other wildlife.

His family would have picnics in the spring and summer, and E.B. would question his parents on the names of the flowers in the meadows. In another article, he talks about learning all he could about butterflies.

At various times, he tended to domesticated crows, horned owls, short-eared owls, plovers, flying squirrels, chickens and cats. But, E.B.'s favorite was Billy the crow, which he acquired when the bird was young, and he bottle-fed it to maturity. E.B. swore that Billy, who became a house pet, could talk.

In another article, E.B. shares that he learned his dedicated work ethic from his father early in life. While, it was a tough job for a young child, he worked hard at log-splitting and stacking until he finished, often after dark.

His compassionate spirit might have been borne from his contact with a big, barking dog in the neighbor's yard that bolted from the porch and approached young E.B. and his school chum. "We thought he had come to eat us up. But, a woman came out and called the dog to come" and the boys "ended up petting the dog," he wrote.

"Half of life's troubles are like that; they may seem terrible, but just hold out your hand to scratch their ears and you will find they aren't troubles at all."

Move to Port Angeles

When the Webster family arrived in Port Angeles, they found a raw-boned timber town with a business district built right up to the waterfront. High tides played havoc with the town's buildings, and at low tide, raw sewage gave the town an awful odor. Horses and even cows roamed free, adding to the town's health issues.

The few roads were primarily dirt or mud. What sidewalks existed were planked. A few housing developments began to spring up on the hillside.

E.B. established a small office in an upstairs room of the old McKay building on Front Street, primarily printing legal briefs for attorneys, including two of Jessie's brothers, John and Tom.

Other members of the Trumbull family had settled in Port Townsend, another burgeoning development about 50 miles east of Port Angeles. In 1900, the Websters moved to Port Angeles and set up a printing shop, publishing legal notices and briefs.

In 1902, the family moved to Port Townsend, where E.B. worked for the town's daily newspaper, the *Morning Leader*. He also published a booklet, called *Town Topics*. It contained important information from the town's leaders and was a good conversational piece.

A desire to be a newspaper owner, led him back to Port Angeles in 1904, where he established *The Olympic*, a full-size weekly, which he printed in an office above a cigar store on Front Street. The four-page publication debuted on Dec. 23, 1904.

Meanwhile, across the street, Arthur A. Smith, owner and publisher of the weekly *Tribune-Times,* did not welcome the new paper. He proclaimed his opinion in an editorial on Dec. 30, 1904.

Port Angeles has about as much a use at this time for a third newspaper as a cart has for three wheels. There

The front page of A.A. Smith's weekly *Tribune-Times* touts the lucrative lumber industry on the peninsula in a May 15, 1914, Prosperity section. Two years later, Smith merged his paper with E.B. Webster's *Olympic-Leader* to establish the *Port Angeles Evening News.*

is neither any reason for its establishment, nor any room for maintenance. The community has but escaped, within the past eighteen months, and much to the relief of businesses and political interests, from a long siege of the third-newspaper curse. … All well-regulated county seat communities have two newspapers, and no more, one representing each of the two great political parties.

The politics of the new paper, so far as we are advised, is not fixed, or at least not stated. Certain it is, however, that neither of the big political parties, has set up any demand for its advent. The local Democratic field, which is a sadly enough circumscribed one, is more than filled by the Democrat-Leader, *which has, for the past ten years, given its party a better support than it has had in return. And the Republican field, by no means a bonanza itself, is being fully served, we have reason to believe, by the* Tribune-Times.

The next day, A.J. "Andy" Cosser, owner and editor of another rival weekly, the *Democrat-Leader,* added fuel to the fire by writing his own editorial, echoing the same tone that Smith had opined a day earlier. Cosser claimed the ads in the new paper were copied from the *Tribune-Times* and not paid for or even authorized.

Cosser was highly regarded as a newsman and a gentleman, even by his political opposites. In 1914, when he was a Democratic candidate for Clallam County Clerk, it was the Republican *Olympic-Leader* that wrote the strongest endorsement. He was one of three Democrats elected in that campaign.

Webster, pretty much a "David" as far as journalism was concerned on the Olympic Peninsula, was butting heads with the veteran Smith, a "Goliath" in the business.

Much of Smith's life was identified with the incubated newspaper history and growth of Port Angeles. A high school graduate at 16, he worked as a reporter, city editor and publisher for several Indiana newspapers for 13 years before moving to Port Angeles.

Arriving at the same time in June of 1890, was Horace White. Together, Smith and White purchased *The Port Angeles Times,* which had been leased to A.H. Howells by the Cooperative Colony. Howells' printer was Cosser. The *Times* was the county's only newspaper at that time. White left the business in 1891 and later became mayor of Port Angeles.

Under Smith's editorship, the paper led the charge for moving the Clallam County seat from Dungeness to Port Angeles. Thus, the city of Port Angeles became incorporated and legal notices appeared in the *Times*. Late in 1891, *The Port Angeles Tribune* was established.

During the political campaign of 1892, a consolidation between Smith's *Times* and the *Tribune* occurred. The new *Tribune-Times* also absorbed the *Port Angeles Weekly Herald*.

Smith left the peninsula and spent the next six years in Alaska before returning to Port Angeles in July 1898, to purchase the *Weekly Tribune-Times* from M.J. Carrigan and F.P. Fisher. In 1902, Smith dropped Weekly from the name.

In 1916, Smith and E.B. Webster, publisher of the *Olympic-Leader,* settled their differences, merged their assets into the firm of Webster & Smith Inc. and established the *Port Angeles Evening News* as a daily newspaper.

In 1915, Smith was elected state senator for the 24th District, which then comprised Clallam, Jefferson and San Juan counties. The next year, after he and Webster founded the *Evening News*, he was elected president of the Washington State Editorial Association, which is today the Washington Newspaper Publishers Association.

Smith sold his interest in the paper in 1919 and moved to Portland.

Even though he left the North Olympic Peninsula, Smith didn't forget where he had come from.

In 1937, he and Port Angeles businessman G.M. Lauridsen collaborated to write *The Story of Port Angeles*, a 276-page book of early history of the city and Clallam County. He returned to Port Angeles while writing the book, living in the city for several months. He died on Aug. 4, 1944, in Portland, at 83.

While Cosser and Smith lamented (and probably feared) a third paper in Port Angeles, E.B. Webster had a different take on it with an editorial, espousing his reasons on April 7, 1905.

We realized that a newspaper really conducted in the interest of the people would be a novelty so well appreciated that success was certain to follow. ... Prior to our launching, the newspaper field was occupied by a close (sic) corporation ... this newspaper combination trained their batteries upon us.

E.B.'s new partner

E.B. acquired a partner when his father, William Barton Webster, and his wife, Marietta, joined him. In April 1905, W.B. sold the *Republican* in Cresco, Iowa, ending an ownership of the town's only paper that began on E.B.'s 21st birthday in 1889.

By July, he was with his son on the *Leader*. The paper's masthead listed Webster & Webster, editors and proprietors. Jessie Webster was the local editor, contributing social and local items, generally writing from home and sending the material to the office.

Only a few months after *The Olympic* first appeared, Webster bought out another rival weekly, the *Democrat-Leader* and soon renamed his paper, *The Olympic-Leader.*

Two different banners for the *Olympic-Leader* show the Roosevelt elk and the Olympic Mountains.

E.B. and his father worked side-by-side to produce their new paper. The eight-page *Olympic-Leader* debuted July 14, 1905, with a front-page "Salutatory:"

We take up the conduct of the Olympic-Leader *with no misgivings. The field is wide, the people are fair, the labor is congenial and the goal is a noble one.*

We have no hobby. Our central aim is the welfare of Clallam County in general, and incidentally, of Port Angeles. With our best friendships, largely, yet to be made and a high sense of duty, it is almost idle to assert that we shall travel the conservative path. No scores to settle and no collars to wear, leaves us just where we are proud to be, viz: free to aid.

The *Olympic-Leader* became a family operation, not only with the two Webster men in the editing and operation of the paper and Jessie, now a mother, writing local items, but also with the children participating.

According to the book, *Olympic Leaders,* "Charles and his three sisters worked right along with the parents in a variety of jobs. Tomboy Mae — who grew into an elegant woman — delivered the weekly *Olympic-Leader* in a business district, which still had many of the rough edges of the frontier.

In an interview, which appeared in the *Evening News* in 1941, Mae wrote from her home in Santa Cruz, Calif., saying she thought she was the *Leader's* first carrier. Her main difficulty was delivering to the saloons.

"At first, I threw the paper in the door," she said, "but that was not satisfactory to the subscribers, so I timidly took it into the counter. Then somebody thought the job was more suitable for a boy."

Mae and Beth fed the *Olympic-Leader* press, "Notorious for its cranky old gasoline engine, operating the press would stop as often as on the old-fashioned motorboat, making the paper late. We were very much excited when there was a new newspaper press at the old office on Front Street," Mae said in that interview.

Continuing in the *Evening News* article, Mae said, "I believe every time Dad got a new piece of equipment, Grandpa said Dad was always wanting to change things, and Mother said Dad put all the money into the office and she would never get a new house."

She and Beth also took turns assembling and folding the newspaper. "That was entirely a hand-job," Mae continued. As the two girls grew older, they were introduced to the job printing.

Mae wrote that the "most exciting part of newspapering in the early days was the contents of the paper. Dad had ideas and expressed them vigorously."

An article, "An Editor 30 Years Ahead of His Time," in the *Evening News* 60th anniversary special in 1976, talks about Charles as a teenager.

"As a young boy, Charles was the janitor at the weekly and helped melt lead type from which new castings were made. After the *Evening News* was established when Charles was 13, he became a carrier — likely the daily's first — covering the downtown and lower Cherry Hill, delivering the paper until he graduated from high school and departed Port Angeles for a time."

The youngest daughter, Dorothy Webster Wenner, who was born in 1906, later became involved — sort of. In the same 1976 anniversary edition, she talked about her earliest recollection:

"The newspaper shop (at First and Chase streets) next to an oriental store, was on stilts and we went swimming in the bay in back. Around 1910 or 1912, an accident involving hot lead partially blinded (Dad)," said Dorothy.

She said she wore a bright red coat that her dad could easily see and would walk with him along the raised sidewalks. She said she had to be careful, so he wouldn't fall off. She also recalled a time when the printing press was moved outside under an apple tree.

Dorothy also wrote society items for the *Evening News* and had a column briefly after her father died.

E.B. was a founding member of the Booster Club of Port Angeles, which was chartered on Oct. 6, 1905, by the city's business leaders to promote, not only the city's interests, but also that of the county.

He was a whole-hearted supporter of the city and its expansion, and often took to challenging a competing newspaper, *The Bee,* which he claimed as a "knocker," chiding its editorial comments that were critical of the town's leading citizens and the efforts they were making.

The *Leader* repeatedly wrote articles and editorials, championing Clallam County's unspoiled beauty, natural resources and agricultural opportunities as the key to the county's growth.

Cheated death

It almost came to a tragic end for E.B., when in March 1912, he escaped death in an accident at the Elwha Power plant at the Elwha River. Two men, power company employees, Walter "Shorty" Richter and John Berg, were swept to their death and Webster suffered bumps and bruises, and a severe cut several inches long over his eye.

In the *Leader* story of March 12, 1912, the reporter said E.B., Jessie and 9-year-old Charles had, moments before, stepped off the same ledge where the two men met their death when a supporting cable snapped and threw a derrick toward the men, knocking them into the river.

Neither Jessie nor Charles were injured, though both were quite shaken by the close call.

The Mergenthaler Model 10 Linotype was an innovation for the *Olympic-Leader* in 1913.

The Websters prided themselves on being innovative and progressive. This came to the front, particularly, on Jan. 3, 1913, when a front-page headline "*Olympic-Leader* Always First — Never Next" and first deck headline: "Leads Van of Progress for 1913 for installing on First Day of New Year First Linotype Ever Brought Into the County."

The paper expounded on the efficiency

of their new technology — Mergenthaler Linotype "Model Ten," but also noted that "readers could care less whether type is set by hand or a line-casting machine. They are interested chiefly in the extent to which the paper covers the local news field."

The Linotype reduced a full-day's work of typesetting to about three hours. The machine was complicated and expensive, consisting of 4,500 pieces.

It arrived from Baltimore, Md., after several weeks in transit in eight boxes, the largest weighing just over a ton and was 6 feet tall and 4-feet square. It was so big, a large section of the building had to be cut away to get the boxes through to the assembly room.

In the *Leader* article, Webster was asked if the Linotype was paving the way for the *Olympic-Leader* to become a daily newspaper. "It certainly is," he responded, "as soon as someone else attempts to occupy the field, but we trust that will be several months yet. A good weekly can make a better showing than six issues of a mighty poor daily."

Then he substantiated his reasoning for the new machine: "… It will save us money in the cost of composition, not for the purpose of publishing a daily in advance of a demand therefore."

In *Story of Port Angeles*, Smith wrote that he continued to stay ahead of Webster. "I discounted the future several years by not only bringing in a Linotype machine, but also a new cylinder press and folder."

On Jan. 31, 1913, Webster published a front-page article headlined "Herald The New Slogan" with a second deck: Clallam — The Healthiest Place in the World."

Any less astute publisher would have taken the news from the County Health Dept. report that Clallam County had 58 deaths in 1912 as "that's nice" and likely not do a story on it.

But Webster sent his staff to work to find out what that number meant. After due diligence and a great deal of research, they found out:

Precisely this, that Clallam county is one of the healthiest places in the world, if not THE healthiest. The figures given indicate, taking Clallam's population right at 7,000, that our death rate is a trifle over 8 in a thousand. Seattle's figures are 8.58 per thousand. Sydney, Australia, comes as near as any place in the world, but even they have to take a back seat. Clallam leads them all at 8.30 per each 1,000 inhabitants.

Laurel Street, looking north, before the regrade, likely about 1910, shows *Olympic-Leader* building about halfway down on the left. The Kirschberg Clothing Store on the left, faces First Street. *(Courtesy of the North Olympic History Center)*

... *All of which goes to demonstrate that the excellent showing is due to inherent conditions. The mild and uniform climate of Puget Sound and the Strait of Juan de Fuca, the beneficent effects of their bracing sea breezes, coupled with the presence of a water supply with few peers and no superiors in the world — these are the things which make for health and longevity of its citizens. "The healthiest county in the world" is a wonderfully fine slogan. It strikes a note that will attract instant attention when the assertion is backed by statistics which cannot be questioned.*

A mess Downtown

Two years later, 1914 was a significant one for Port Angeles (and the *Olympic-Leader*).

An extraordinary regrade began downtown, included sluicing First and Front street hills with water from the bay so the dirt could be used as fill to raise the beach-level streets. One block at a time, the streets were elevated 6-12 feet. Lincoln Street was extended north to the beach by cutting through the hill. A concrete sewer was built to redirect Peabody Creek, so it no longer meandered down Front Street.

What a mess it was. Downtown was in turmoil. The second floor of many old buildings were converted to street level and the first floors became basements. Other buildings were torn down and replaced with fireproof buildings.

The *Leader* didn't escape. On June 26, it had to move to make way for the new two-story concrete Warren Morse building at the corner of Laurel and First streets.

Generally, when a business moves, it packs up the equipment and transports it to the new building. In this instance, the Websters decided to take the building with them.

E.B. and printer John Schweitzer cut up the old building and moved it in sections in a horse-drawn wagon up the hill to a lot on Laurel, between Third and Fourth, near the Websters' home, which was on Fifth Street, between Lincoln and Laurel. It was a necessary, though only temporary location.

Before they could reassemble the building, a new issue of the *Olympic-Leader* was due. The papers were cranked off the press in the open under an old apple tree.

The *Leader* eventually would have a new home, but construction was nearly a year away.

Webster also led, what he called, "an almost single-handed campaign to build the Olympic Way," the completion of a section of a highway from Lake Crescent to Forks. The county and the City of Port Angeles had balked at the project.

Webster wrote a series of articles, extolling the project, then he and a reporter, mounted horses and took a two-week trip to explore the route. In September 1914, the road was completed, the final link in a highway (today part of U.S. Highway 101) between Port Angeles and Forks.

In an editorial, advancing the opening of the new road, Webster wrote:

"The *Olympic-Leader* knows of no work it would rather have had a part in, however humble, than the building of the Olympic Way and the several equally splendid side roads."

In a longer article a few days later, when the first section was officially opened, Webster turned to his roots and his pastime to describe the road:

Imagine if you can, a road many miles long, straight as a section line, level as a South Dakota prairie, smooth as the crushed rock highways of Iowa and Illinois and bordered on either hand with the close-set trunks of 200-foot trees, the whole canopied with the spray-like, airy foliage of the hemlock — and you have the Crescent-Forks section of the Olympic Way, now nearing completion.

Throughout this period when Port Angeles was beginning to stretch its wings, Webster consistently promoted civic improvements, including upgrades in fire protection, repairing sidewalks, correcting the deplorable conditions of Front Street and the backwash of raw sewage.

He encouraged residents to patronize the new City Light plant by getting rid of their oil lamps and having their homes wired for electric power.

After some initial rock-throwing, the competition between Smith and E.B. had been largely friendly. In October 1914, the *Olympic-Leader* endorsed Smith for state senator for the 24th District, noting that since the state senate would be Republican, the district would be better served with a Republican senator.

… It will be conceded that as a politician, able to hold his own … A.A. Smith is easily the peer of any man in the county, or in the district, for that matter. His wide acquaintanceship among men of the state, and particularly of Western Washington, will make his efforts effective from the first day of the session.

In December 1915, the endorsement of the previous year likely paved the way for a new alliance, and in short order, a daily newspaper in April 1916.

In 1915, the fledgling *Port Angeles Evening News* print shop moved into this building on Lincoln Street that was built by businessman G.M. Lauridsen. The *Evening News* began operation in 1916 and operated in this building for 53 years until moving to its present site at 305 W. First St. in 1969. *(Courtesy of the North Olympic History Center)*

Webster and Smith first decided to merge their commercial or "job" printing business (a mainstay of most newspapers) when they moved into a new building that they had contracted businessman G.M. Lauridsen to build specifically for printing.

According to the *Olympic Leaders book:*

The new print shop, Smith & Webster Printers, was located in the building's center. The Olympic-Leader *and the* Tribune-Times, *which were both printed on the new business's printing presses, occupied separate editorial and business offices on either side. They had the largest, most costly and best-equipped publishing and printing plant ever operated on the Olympic Peninsula, it being equipped for doing all kinds and any amount of printing ... with two Linotype machines, two new cylinder presses and four job presses, and all the other machinery, type and fixtures that go to make a modern printing plant.*

Since 1892, there had been newspaper wars throughout Clallam County, often as many as three or four at a time. But in 1915, the last of these editorial and financial battles flared when the *Port Angeles Daily Herald* was started, Clallam County's first somewhat successful daily.

The paper was started in January 1916 by Michael Earles of Seattle and Jack Campbell of Everett and proudly proclaimed to print the "news on the day it happened."

It soon boasted a circulation "never before achieved by any newspaper in this city — larger than any two other papers combined."

A daily for Port Angeles

This prompted action by E.B. and Smith.

The April 5, 1916, edition of the *Olympic-Leader* made the long-expected announcement that the *Port Angeles Evening News* would debut "on or about April 10, 1916."

The Evening News *is the logical development into a daily edition of the two pioneer weekly newspapers of the city and county, the* Olympic-Leader *and the* Tribune-Times, *long owned and operated by the Websters and Mr. Smith, and while it will be "conducted as a daily, newspaper separate and apart from the two weekly newspapers, it will be allied thereto, and is designed to inherit such prestige and strength as may come to it by reason of this relationship."*

The first edition rolled off the Babcock press with eight pages and a circulation, E.B. and Smith claimed was "upwards of 1,000, not bad for a community of 7,000."

The partners had a two-month introductory price of 1 cent a copy, 5 cents per week. 20 cents a month. This beat the *Herald's* monthly rate of 30 cents.

The *Evening News* was serviced by United Press International, receiving 15-minute telegraphs from its Portland office twice a day. The *Herald* subscribed to The Associated Press, which likewise was an abbreviated report.

Webster and Smith took aim at the newcomers with its first editor, George O'Brien, blasting the paper on its editorial pages for being run by "outsiders" and financed by Puget Sound timber businessmen. The edition's opinion page hammered home on this for its readers.

The front page of the first *Evening News* printed three different stories on World War I, featuring the Battle of Verdun in the main article. The 6-column headline read: "Battle Most Furious Since Verdun Smash Began."

The United Press report from London began: "The greatest battle in history has entered upon its fifteenth day this afternoon with the Germans launching mighty blows around Verdun, and today is witnessing the most furious fighting since the smash began. The estimated losses on both sides exceed 200,000."

The front page of the first *Port Angeles Evening News* on April 10, 1916, provided World War I news on a daily basis. *(Peninsula Daily News archive)*

Also, on the front page was a poorly written, confusing article that went for several columns on how "Two Jims" didn't buy a steamroller.

Another story was devoted to the business of the county commissioners and a brief noted that 114 "liquor permits" had been issued; in a short article, Mayor E.J. Walton proclaimed Port Angeles cleanup week a success.

There was a report about the notorious Pancho Villa, saying troopers were hot on the trail of the Mexican bandit.

Young reporter William D. "Billy" Welsh wrote a story on port shipping, calling the activity report for April "brisk," noting that the city was awaiting the arrival of the barkentine *S.N. Wilder*.

Welsh began a long and storied career in Olympic Peninsula journalism with the floundering *Bee* in 1913. A recap of the *Bee* in Lauridsen and Smith's *Story of Port Angeles* wasn't kind to the paper but was glorious in its description of Welsh.

The only thing the Bee *did for the community was to bring (Welsh) to town. "Billy," although a lean and always hungry kid printer at the time, knew even before he got here, why it is that rats want to get out of a ship, and within a few weeks he had deserted* The Bee *for a job on the* T-T *(Tribune-Times).*

… He could write stories, lay out a page as quickly as an average "print" would handle a column; he never walked, but ran about the shop on press day; he had no more than one bad habit (which is saying an awful lot for a printer), and as that was forgotten and forgiven early it will not be recorded against him here.

In short, he served his shop with cheerful ability; required trust and confidences with loyalty and respect; and, as the years went by, stood ready to grab from under "the boss" the editorial chair when the time came for it be relinquished.

Born on Sept. 26, 1890, at Rat Portage, Ontario, Canada, Welsh was one of the more beloved editors and reporters for the *Evening News*. He began his career at the *Cranbrook Herald*, then worked at Ellensburg, Wash., for the *Dawn*, then the *Daily Localizer*, which became the present-day *Record*.

In 1913, Welsh went to the *Roslyn Miner*, then to the *Tacoma News-Tribune*. Later that year, he came to Port Angeles.

Beacon Bill

Billy Welsh, center in fireman's hat, poses with members of the Port Angeles police and fire departments to promote Beacon Bill, a fundraising campaign that began in 1922 to raise money for the less fortunate. Its goals are mirrored today in the Peninsula Home Fund, the *Peninsula Daily News'* "hand-up, not a handout" community assistance program which in recent years has raised more than $250,000 annually. Welsh was reporter, editor, and part-owner of the *Port Angeles Evening News* from 1913-1939. *(Courtesy of the North Olympic History Center)*

His first job in Port Angeles was not with the *Tribune-Times*, but with the *Bee*, but he wasn't there long and was hired by Smith, owner of the *Tribune-Times*, who recognized his experience and style would be invaluable to his newspaper.

Welsh stayed with the paper through its transition to the *Olympic-Leader* and subsequently the establishment of the daily *Port Angeles Evening News* under the ownership of Smith and E.B. Webster.

Welsh was the lead reporter for the *Evening News* until Smith retired in 1919. He then became a part-owner with Webster and John Schweitzer;

Welsh was installed as the editor. He remained in that capacity until 1939 when he left the news business and went to work for Crown Zellerbach Corp. as director of public relations for the company.

An able writer with a keen sense of humor, Welsh was known as "Squire Billy" and his front-page column was called "Rarebits," which gave him his nickname, "Mr. Rarebitter."

Welsh also started and ran "Beacon Bill," the newspaper's annual Page 1 fundraiser for local charities. Its goals are mirrored today in the Peninsula Home Fund, the *Peninsula Daily News'* "hand-up, not a handout" community assistance program which in recent years has raised more than $250,000 annually.

He retired from Zellerbach in 1955, returned to live at Lake Crescent and died in 1974. He was 84.

Schweitzer, as a printer's devil, set type and handled the printing and machine maintenance. He was co-owner of the *Evening News* until he sold his shares in 1949. He remained on staff as an advertising salesman, leaving in 1961 to join Del Price's rival start-up Port Angeles newspaper, the *Chronicle*, that challenged the Webster family. He died on Nov. 4, 1985, at 90.

Another mainstay on the first *Evening News* was Jack Henson, who started in the business in 1906, working for Webster on the *Olympic-Leader*. He later would hold numerous positions with the *Evening News* and earned his title "The Wandering Scribe," a column he wrote until his death on May 5, 1964. He wrote his last column from his hospital bed. He was 80.

Inside that first edition of the *News*, was a Charlie Chaplin comic, a story on future Hall of Fame baseball player Tris Speaker traded by Boston to Cleveland for the exorbitant price of $20,000 and two players; a report on the Commercial Club meeting; three deaths of pioneer homesteaders were noted; and a short article noted that Dr. Taylor and three others forded the Dungeness River to attend a boxing and wrestling "smoker" at the East End Athletic Association at Dungeness.

Romance entered the picture as well in an article headlined "Another Good Fellow Gone Wrong." This sign greeted Ralph Davis when he returned to work at the treasurer's office after his honeymoon. His co-workers had festooned the archway in his office with red, white and blue bunting.

Among the advertisers in the first issue was H.H. Beetle's Rexall Drug's nearly full-page ad, highlighting a shaving cream special — buy one for 25 cents, the second tube for 1 cent. The Leader Department's store ad featured Easter millinery; Thomas Aldwell Co. offered 30 acres of farm land for sale; The Toggery advertised it as the finest suits available, but it was in competition with Kirschberg Clothing Co. "Home of Good Goods" which touted its slogan in a half-page ad that featured a men's Spring suit sale for $17.

Another men's furnishing store, Fillion Brothers tailors, advertised "summer clothes of character" and carried a sketch, showing "flaring lapels, knife-edge trousers, wing collards and bow tie."

Two silent-movie theaters in town advertised: "The Ransom of Julia Dean" was playing at the Star, while "Peggy," starring Billie Burke, was featured at the Dream.

When one month elapsed in the life of the *Evening News,* Smith thanked his readers and advertisers for their support.

With this issue, the Evening News *concludes its fourth week of its existence and is glad it is alive. … It has done better than pay its way financially from the day of its birth, and its friends are kind enough to tell us that as a purveyor of the daily news — its one object on earth — it has been more than a success.*

The paid circulation has grown steadily and surely until the end of the first month, it has reached a figure that its publishers did not expect to reach within six months. … The Evening News *has carried more advertising every day that it has been published, than any other daily paper printed on the Olympic Peninsula, and with this announcement, it makes its most appreciative acknowledgement to the business community. …*

The Evening News *is here to stay, grow and prosper, and to serve the community which is giving it maintenance. Its publishers promise that it will grow bigger and better as it grows older, and will endeavor to merit in every way the generous reception and support that has been accorded it.*

Meanwhile, the war between the *Evening News* and the *Herald* continued on the editorial pages.

The warfare continued until 1923 before the *Herald* brass mysteriously gave up the chase and deserted the ship. The paper was absorbed by the *Evening News.*

One significant result of the acquisition of the *Herald* was the purchase of The Associated Press news service. Until then, the weaker United Press serviced the paper. From 1923 until today, the AP supplies regional, national and international news to the paper.

State news in the paper rapidly improved with AP having a bureau in Seattle and an office at Olympia. UP's closest office was in Portland.

The *Herald's* acquisition also included five Linotype machines, which were in use until the 1970s.

E.B.'s direct editorials

As they were with the *Olympic-Leader*, editorials in which the newspaper gave its opinion, were a staple of E.B. Webster's *News*. In a 1941 article in the *Evening News*, Mae Webster Duckering told the reporter her dad had ideas and expressed them vigorously, crusading for city causes in the early days.

In several editorials, E.B. was on the side of temperance in the "wet vs. dry" argument over liquor sales. This debunked the city council's view, emphasizing the newspaper "was not astraddle of the fence."

In the early 1920s, after Smith retired and Webster brought in Welsh and Schweitzer as co-owners, E.B. moved into semi-retirement and had more time to hike the trails and lake shores of his beloved Olympics, often extolling them in his newspaper.

E.B. Webster co-founded the *Port Angeles Evening News* in 1916 and ran it until his death in 1936. *(Courtesy of the North Olympic History Center/ Port Angeles Evening News)*

The *Olympic Leaders* book said Webster "loved to hob-nob with the deer, elk and bear of the mountain's parks and to study the wildlife of the Olympics."

His apparel at the office usually was a pin-striped suit with a bowler or top hat, but away from the office it was gardening or hiking attire in short or long pants, depending on the season.

He eschewed cigarettes, but often smoked a pipe, and in later years, an occasional cigar.

By the 1920s, even when he was in his 50s, E.B. didn't stick with the shorter trails, but gravitated to the upper routes. He scaled the 6,554-foot Mount Angeles, the highest mountain in the Hurricane Ridge area, many times. One of its peaks was later named after Webster.

Shortly after moving back to Port Angeles from Port Townsend, Webster hooked up with a group of mountain climbers from Seattle, the Mountaineers.

He liked the Mountaineers, organized in 1906, because their vision was "to explore, study, preserve and enjoy the natural beauty of the outdoors."

The club chose Mount Olympus for its first climb and Webster joined them. He not only hiked with them, but in the *Olympic-Leader* he wrote a series of articles, starting with the preparation prior to the climb, then described the scaling of the peak for his newspaper readers.

Eight years later, on March 4, 1915, he teamed with bank president Ben Phillips to form the Klahhane Club, which still exists today as a Port Angeles mountain climbing group.

During the last 10 years of his life, E.B. Webster spent an increasing amount of time developing flower gardens and an aerie of birds he always loved. This started with the collection of birds he kept at the Klahhane Club's clubhouse site on the hilltop above Front and Lincoln streets in Port Angeles. Before going home each night, Webster would climb the hill to feed and water the birds.

The birds subsequently were moved, first to the Klahhane Gardens at Lake Crescent (now Camp David Jr. Park), then eventually to Heart o' the Hills, which became the government-owned E.B. Webster Memorial Gardens.

The gardens were maintained until the early 1950s; sadly, no remnant of them exists today.

A flower, native to the Olympics and a member of the aster family, the *Senecio websteri*, was first catalogued by E.B. and named after him.

E.B. passed on his love for the mountains to his children. On weekends, he could be found hiking an Olympic trail with his kids in tow. In later years, Tom, a collie, was his constant companion.

E.B. the author

In his last years, E.B. turned to book-writing. This phase of his life started in 1917 when he wrote his first of four books, *The Friendly Mountain*, his pet name for Mount Angeles.

This book served as a guidebook for Klahhane Club members, describing the craggy mountain's features that reflect on the geology and botany of the mountain. E.B. knew its wildflowers and mountain trails as well as he knew his own gardens.

Contributing to the small book's charm were illustrations by Thomas Guptill in the original version, based on photos that E.B. had taken, and

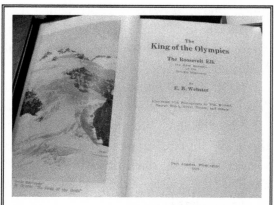

E.B. Webster wrote four books. *The King of the Olympics: The Roosevelt Elk and Other Mammals of the Olympic Peninsula*, **published in 1920, was his most popular.** *(Bill Lindstrom/ North Olympic Library System)*

added in a 1921 revision by Annette Chaddock Swan, a Klahhane Club member.

His second book, *Ferns of the Olympics*, was published in 1918 and subtitled "Nature's Lacework," with illustrations by Guptill. In this small, 26-page booklet, he meticulously identifies seven species of lowland ferns, nine mountain ferns and two alpine species. He also tells where in the Olympics you can find them.

Webster's best-known book was published in 1920 and dedicated to his mother: *The King of the Olympics: The Roosevelt Elk and Other Mammals of the Olympic Peninsula.*

It describes the Olympics' 37 mammals, from the elk, bear and cougar to the mountain beaver, marmot and sea lion.

The 227-page book is illustrated with 52 photos by Webster and others. It is infused with Webster's dry humor and in it he writes about many individuals whom he hiked and camped with through the early years.

E.B. wrote the book after discovering there had been no books about the Roosevelt elk, which was named by naturalist C. Hart Merriam.

The *Olympic Leaders* book describes how Merriam came to name the elk in the 1890s.

"It is my privilege to name this species after Theodore Roosevelt. It is fitting that the noblest deer of America should perpetuate the name of one who, in the midst of a busy public career, has found time to study our larger mammals in their native haunts and has written the best account we have had of their habits and chase."

Webster's columns in the *Olympic-Leader*, even in the early days, advocated for the protection of this "noblest animal."

In a Feb. 3, 1905, article headlined "vigorous prosecution of unprincipled scamps responsible for the slaughtering of elk and deer in order to sell their horns and teeth." Today, many of the animals are preserved and protected on the North Olympic Peninsula.

E.B.'s final book *Fishing in the Olympics*, was published in 1923. The 26-page book is a lighthearted look at what he called "the greatest of all sports," and identified the Olympics as "paradise of the angler."

E.B. never lost his interest in birds and mentioned them although he never wrote a book about them.

His son, Charles, years later commissioned a noted naturalist and close friend of his father, E.A. Kitchen, to write a book about the birds of the Olympic Peninsula. Several chapters were published in the *Evening News*.

In the late fall of 1935, E.B. suffered a stroke. On Jan. 7, 1936, he died at 67.

His good friend and managing editor Billy Welsh wrote this tribute:

The Ed Webster we love to remember is not a man with type-stained hands. Rather the lovable soul whose office was always cluttered up with peacocks, parakeets, guinea hens and Gila monsters shipped here from far-flung places ... who was as tender as a flower petal ... loved and missed by everyone in this newspaper office, from the carriers on up. The community mourns a man who left it far better than he found it.

Jessie Trumbull Webster

Jessie Webster helped on the newspaper and was involved in civic activities. She helped found the Carnegie library and established city parks. *(Courtesy of the North Olympic History Center)*

Jessie was involved both in the newspaper and among civic organizations. Her accomplishments in the community were as substantial as her husband's.

From the *Olympic Leaders,* we learn more about Jessie:

"... A diminutive woman, she was large in the force of her personality. Strong and determined, she was a leader, a manager. Civic improvements claimed her attention throughout her life. ... her leadership, her far-sightedness, and her persistence were responsible for seeing many causes through to a successful result," was a tribute written about her when she died. *"Here was a woman who headed straight for an objective and never swerved from it until it was accomplished."*

Through Jessie's efforts a public library was built in Port Angeles and a city park system established. As a member of the Women's Auxiliary to the Commercial Club (forerunner of the Chamber of Commerce), she worked for fire protection and beautification of the town, including the planting of flower gardens and hawthorn trees. She promoted city cleanup days, so important in the early 1900s when there was no garbage pickup. This effort eventually led to the city's first garbage collection service.

When she wanted to establish a park system, she was met with discord from city fathers, who argued that much of the peninsula already was forested, but she maintained that was outside the city and she eventually won the argument.

She also helped organize the local council of Campfire Girls and was known as "Mother Jessie" to hundreds of girls through the years.

From her obituary in the *Evening News* on Feb. 12, 1940, just shy of her 68th birthday, we learn much about this woman's involvement with the paper:

"With untiring persistence, she turned out thousands of small items about this person or that, this club or that — the innumerable minor events which get scant attention in big city papers, but which are the lifeblood to a small-town paper."

The *Olympic Leaders* book notes early in her career, she wrote about surprise parties, entertainment, socials, club notes, weddings, church dinners and duplicate whist games. She exuded a flowery style, so prevalent on social pages of early newspapers. Brides were "beautiful," grooms were "serious, steady young men," homes were "lovely" or "charming," and refreshments were "delicious, bountiful or tempting."

When her youngest child, Dorothy, started school, she joined her husband full-time at the paper. She was a corporate member of the Webster Publishing Co., serving as bookkeeper and local news editor.

She also wrote a column on food recipes and another titled "The City News," in which, according to the *Olympic Leaders*, "advertising and social items were presented in a delightful mix, designed no doubt, to attract readers, but also to direct them to local shops."

In 1928, the Websters took their youngest daughter, Dorothy, to California for treatment for tuberculosis and Jessie stayed with her for some time. When she returned home, she never again went back to full-time newspaper work. Dorothy did recover and met her future husband, also a tuberculosis patient, there.

Fought for a library

Jessie not only reported and wrote about the news, sometimes she created it, though her name was not often mentioned. Yet, in one case, she did receive the credit she was due:

Such was the case with the opening of Port Angeles' Carnegie-sponsored library, which opened its doors on Jan. 6, 1919.

The city fathers tried to block her efforts, saying Port Angeles didn't yet need a Carnegie library, but she soldiered on.

She solicited the city's Reading Club for 100 of their best books. She also contacted the town's leading citizens for donations of books and financial donations. Another major factor in getting the library going was the Seattle Public Library's contribution of its discarded books.

Following a lengthy business process, the Carnegie Corporation eventually gave $12,500 toward the cost of the library. The city contributed $500 and the building was constructed.

The library was located almost directly across Lincoln Street from the *Evening News* building. It remained at that location until a new building was constructed at 2210 N. Peabody St. in 1998.

The new building is the main library of the North Olympic Library System. It is state-of-the-art and includes nearly 25,000 square feet with a collection of more than 151,000 volumes. It features spacious reading areas, a flexible use "living room" for special events, dedicated areas for teens and youth quiet study rooms, a conference room, the Raymond Carver Community Room, 32 public computers and an extensive history collection that includes microfilm of local newspapers.

All of E.B. Webster's out-of-print books are in the collection.

Today, visitors to Port Angeles can go to Jessie Webster Park on Eunice Street between Second and Fourth streets. The tree-lined park celebrates her effort to establish the city park system as well as her involvement with such groups as the Campfire

Visitors to Port Angeles can go to Jessie Webster Park on Eunice Street between Second and Fourth streets. The tree-lined park celebrates her effort to establish the city park system as well as her involvement with such groups as the Campfire Girls, which still has its clubhouse in that park. *(Bill Lindstrom photo)*

Girls, which still has its clubhouse in that park.

Following her husband's death in 1936, Jessie became president of the corporation until her own death on Feb. 11, 1940.

She died suddenly while visiting her daughter, Beth Webster, in Seattle.

Later in an *Evening News* article after her mother had died, Dorothy Webster Wenner told a reporter that her mother was "the backbone of the paper for a long time — at a time when women weren't doing those things. They even wanted her to be mayor."

G.M. Lauridsen and A.A. Smith's *Story of Port Angeles* was even more praiseworthy: "Endowed with native ability, tireless energy and an indomitable will, she was given the strength to win through."

The three Webster daughters all worked at the *Evening News* as teenagers. Beth graduated from high school in 1916 and from the University of Washington three years later. She taught high school in Shelton and Port Angeles for several years, then worked at Macy's in New York City from 1925-1928.

Mae also taught school for a time and joined Beth at Macy's for a short period. She met and married her husband, Lynn Duckering, in New York.

After Dorothy became ill and went to California for treatment, Beth returned to the newspaper and became society editor for several years.

She then moved to advertising and ran that department for several years. In addition, she wrote a weekly column.

After the death of her father in 1936 and her mother in 1940, (Jessie Elizabeth) "Beth" became president of the Webster Corp.

Like her mother, Beth was concerned with civic, cultural and church activities. Beth, who never married, worked for the betterment of Port Angeles. She died of a sudden stroke in 1948.

In her obituary, a tribute given by longtime *Evening News* staffer Billy Welsh, noted, in part: "The welfare of the underprivileged was paramount in Ms. Webster's life and she took a keen interest in the community's civic, cultural and charitable activities. ... For more than 20 years, every campaign for the relief of human suffering or for the betterment of social conditions carried on by the *Evening News*, was supported by Beth's purse and pen."

After their mother's death, Mae and Dorothy were named vice presidents. Their brother, Charles, who returned to the newspaper in 1934 as cashier and treasurer of the board, eventually would move up the ranks to editor and publisher.

Responsibility of running the newspaper rested solely in the hands of

Charles, Mae and Dorothy. Later power was shared with Charles' wife, Esther.

Esther, who had married Charles in 1929 in New York City, had a disdain for the women in his family, according to the *Olympic Leaders* book.

With Jessie gone, it became more obvious to those close to the family that she viewed Mae, Dorothy and Beth as antagonists. Esther never enjoyed the frequent family gatherings, but she attended them. Now, she felt freer to reject such invitations. In later years, this enmity would adversely affect some of Esther's decisions regarding the newspaper and the course of her life and that of others.

CHAPTER 3

Charles Webster

U nlike the rest of his family, Charles did not immediately become involved in his father's newspaper. He did have a paper route in grammar school, but it was his two older sisters who were more involved during the early days of the *Olympic-Leader* and *Evening News*.

Charles was born in Port Townsend on Jan. 1, 1903. His family moved to Port Angeles a year later.

When he was 11, Charles built his own radio receiving set from a diagram in *Popular Mechanics* magazine. He skipped at least one grade and entered Roosevelt High School in Port Angeles at the age of 11, graduating at 15.

His family considered Charles too young to attend college, so he trained as a ship's radio operator in Seattle and soon found a job on a ship going to Alaska.

He eventually entered college, or more correctly, three colleges. He attended Stanford University for a year, then Reed College in Portland, Ore., for two years and finally the University of Washington for one year.

During his college years, he worked as a radio room operator in summer and continued after college.

An intense and inquisitive young man with a love for the seas, Charles found jobs on passenger steamers and freighters that sailed to Alaska, South America, the South Pacific, the Far East, the British Isles, Germany and Scandinavia.

Adding to his adventures, Charles twice hitchhiked across the United States.

Charles was a voracious reader. His taste for literature was eclectic, adding great breadth to his knowledge. Family members said when he traveled, he packed more books than clothes.

In later years, his wife remembered that Charles agreed to attend a football game in New York City, only if he could bring along books to read.

On one summer trek into the Olympic Mountains with Chris Morgenrath, pioneer trailblazer and ranger, Charles trailed the other hikers because his backpack was laden with books.

In 1928, he went to work for Gulf Oil Co. in New York City in its credit and collection department. He later worked as an assistant manager of the Ford Motor Co.'s export division, in New York.

Later that year, he would be reacquainted with a young Portland, Ore., debutante, Esther Helen Barrows, whom he had met on a blind date when he was attending Reed College and she was an interior decorator for Meier and Frank's department store.

He took her to see John Barrymore on stage in "Hamlet."

"After 20 minutes of 'Hamlet,'" Esther said in an April 8, 1976, interview story by Virginia Keeting for the special 60ᵗʰ anniversary edition of *The Daily News*, "Charles fell fast asleep."

There was no second date, and she didn't see him again until a chance meeting many years later when she was in New York, working at Macy's, where she had become an assistant buyer in the interior decorating department and was attending art school.

It wasn't long before they were an item. On Sept. 23, 1929, they went on a cruise to Bermuda and, on the *HMS Bermuda*, were married.

A month later, the United States found itself in the middle of the Great Depression. Layoffs reduced the Ford staff and Charles was forced to work day and night to keep the company afloat.

Late in 1933, he and Esther visited his father in Port Angeles. E.B. was in failing health. Charles decided to move back home to join him on the *Evening News*.

This decision didn't sit well with Esther, who had been offered a position as an artist on *Harper's Bazaar* magazine. But in a few months, Esther decided to join her husband, who by then had not only started handling the *Evening News'* financial affairs but, was reporting for managing editor Bill Welsh and writing occasional editorials.

Charles knew that Esther was upset about leaving New York City for Port Angeles. He wanted to make her first impression of her new home a memorable one.

He told her to travel by train to Vancouver, B.C., then to take a ferry to Victoria and a ferry to Port Angeles. He wanted her to see the city for the first time with its majestic backdrop of the Olympic Mountains.

Esther's bad impression

Despite Charles' efforts, Esther got off to a bad start with her husband's friends by labeling Port Angeles a "cultural disaster."

The town certainly wasn't at its best. When Esther arrived, Port Angeles was suffering in the Depression. Buildings sat in disrepair with no money to renovate them. Downtown sidewalks, for the most part, were unpaved and many streets were still wooden planks. Many homes didn't have running water or flush toilets.

The *Olympic Leaders: The Life and Times of the Websters of Port Angeles* reveals a raft of incidents that added to Esther's unfavorable opinion of Port Angeles, and in turn the malevolence that relatives and townsfolk had for her.

Esther also wasn't much of a social person in those days. She was an opinionated and decidedly independent woman.

When her mother-in-law, Jessie, provided her with a list of acceptable clubs she should join, Esther bristled, telling her "Nobody's going to tell me what clubs to belong to," according to the *Olympic Leaders*.

Shortly after arriving, she was

Charles and Esther Webster arrived in Port Angeles in 1934. They continued to own the *Port Angeles Evening News* until Esther sold it in 1971 to Longview Publishing, ending 55 years under the Webster families. *(Courtesy of the North Olympic History Center)*

invited to a large formal tea. In those days, teas were important social events. Hats, gloves, high heels, your best dress, adorned with your finest jewelry, were expected, even required.

Esther wore white bobby socks and sandals and her favorite Scottish tam o'shanter. Her informal dress shocked the other women and left a negative impression that was long-lasting. She was regarded as rude and rebellious.

She never did establish a good relationship with Jessie nor with two of her sisters-in-law, Dorothy and Mae. Originally, she was aloof with Beth, but learned to respect her, working daily at the *Evening News*. She regarded her as a valuable associate.

Charles and Esther enjoyed visiting Beth at her home, not far from theirs, on Fifth Street. Beth, like Esther, was a member of the Soroptimist's Club.

Esther also had a close relationship with Charles' easy-going father, describing him to a friend as her "confidant." It was on trips with E.B. into the Olympics to explore the majesty of the mountains that she developed a life-long appreciation for the North Olympic Peninsula's mountains and beaches.

Charles sought to appease his wife's artistic endeavors, taking her to Seattle and San Francisco to art museums and theaters.

While Esther was happy to be outside Port Angeles' social circles, Charles rapidly was establishing himself as a civic stalwart and was all business — opposite, in many ways, from his father's laid-back style.

When he arrived at the *Evening News*, he became familiar with all phases of the newspaper by taking a job in every department.

Charles was an impressive-looking man — tall, broad-shouldered and trim. He was conservative in his dress and usually would wear a tweed sport coat with slacks.

Some said his demeanor was "intense and penetrating," commanding attention from those he was addressing.

He demanded that staff address him as Charles, never Charlie or Chuck. Some said he was rather stern with employees and unbending.

But those who knew him best said he was a friendly man who liked people and strived to know what made them tick.

After the death of his father on Jan. 7, 1936, Charles was elected treasurer of the Websters' publishing corporation and gradually moved up to managing editor and executive editor. In 1948, he was named president and publisher of the *Evening News.*

A year after his father's death, he purchased Olympic Stationers, which had opened two years earlier. It is still in business more than 80 years later. Webster sold it in 1958.

Drawing on his radio experience, Charles also saw an opportunity to provide the North Peninsula with something it did not have.

In 1937, The Evening News Press, the corporation's commercial printing division, applied to the Federal Communications Commission for a license to operate the area's first radio station. It took eight years before it was granted.

KONP finally went on the air on Feb. 3, 1945, and is still broadcasting today as the "Voice of the Peninsula."

In 1936, Charles and Esther purchased their first home, which delighted them, on the bluff at Caroline and Eunice streets, facing the Strait of Juan de Fuca.

Looking north all one saw were the water, the sky and the horizon. Charles and Esther could tell the time of the day by watching the arrival and departure of the ferries in the harbor.

It was here that Esther built her reputation as an artist of ability.

(More about this in a later chapter).

Like his father, Charles enjoyed forays into the Olympics, but the newspaper came first and was the center of Charles' life from the first day on the job in 1934 until his death in 1969. But the last half of those years took a cruel turn.

During the first 18 years, he was a force not only on the newspaper, but also in the community. He pursued getting the Olympic Mountains declared a national park. He was president of the Chamber of Commerce; he also lobbied as an advocate for local issues in Washington, D.C., and he operated the largest commercial printing plant on the North Peninsula.

Then in 1953, when he was 50, Charles suffered a debilitating stroke.

Two years later, he was stricken with another more paralyzing stroke. He tried to continue working, but it was difficult, and for the next 14 years, his role at the paper diminished.

Tribute to Charles

In a special section of the *Evening News* in 1969, then-editor Ned Thomas wrote an article, headlined "An editor 30 years ahead of his time."

In the few short years before illness overtook him in 1953, he established the economic base for the present Evening News *building and equipment. Beyond that, he dedicated his energy, leadership and the* Evening News *to initiating or accomplishing a number of lasting changes for the area.*

While no editor brings about improvements for his locale singlehandedly, not many revolutionary changes succeed without leadership or backing from a respected newspaper.

In his major battles, Charles, as he insisted everyone call him, had many helpers — national, state and local, voluntary and salaried. It is now apparent, he was 30 years ahead of his time in his militant struggle for local environmental improvement. In the often-bitter controversies, he didn't know the meaning of fear. He loathed writing but could do it when the need arose.

Thomas listed many major accomplishments:

1. Saving the Port Angeles watershed and magnificent old-growth timber across the face of Mount Angeles from being logged in World War II and including it in Olympic National Park in 1942;
2. Opening the way for professional management for School District 21 (in Port Angeles) and a modern building and scholastic program (1943-1945);
3. In 1943-1945, backing an enlightened and aggressive health department to raise the quality and sanitation of food products on the Olympic Peninsula;
4. Beginning the campaign in 1946 to obtain an interceptor sewer system and disposal facility in Port Angeles;
5. Dedicating the *Evening News* to clearing up wastes and working for clean water to improve fishing in the harbor and streams;
6. The establishment in 1938 and the promotion and development of Olympic National Park as a summer and winter attraction;
7. A similar interest and dedication to Olympic National Forest and harvesting of timber and reforestation methods there;

8. After Clallam County almost met with fiscal disaster in 1939, he became an authority on city, county and state finances to better protect the taxpayers' dollars;

9. In 1945, he built and operated radio station KONP and loaned his sizeable collection of classical recordings for programming. He also contributed the then-extensive wall space at KONP for the first regular painting exhibits from outside artists;

There were other accomplishments too:

- He established Olympic Stationers, the first large bookstore in the area in 1937;

- He published books that might not otherwise reach the public. Two of these became collector items: *The Roosevelt Elk*, by Fred William Graf, and *Birds of the Olympic Peninsula*, by E.A. Kitchen. These two and others often were printed first in series form in the *Evening News*;

Shortly before leaving in 1939 to work for the Zellerbach Corp., *Port Angeles Evening News* managing editor Billy Welsh, feet on his desk, is a picture of relaxation. *(Courtesy of the North Olympic History Center)*

- He also helped Ruby El Hult write *The Untamed Olympics*.

'Rarebitter' recalls shipwreck

In March 1939, William D. "Billy" Welsh, one of the family's two partners, resigned and sold his company stock to the Websters. For all but two war years, Welsh had been with the *Evening News* since its founding in 1916.

His front-page column, "Welsh Rarebits," written in a conversational style on a variety of topics, was hugely popular.

But Welsh and Charles didn't enjoy the same relationship that Billy did with Charles' father. When he was offered the position as director of public relations for Crown Zellerbach Corp., in San Francisco, he took it. The decision was a difficult one for Welsh, and for his readers, whose letters to the editor expressed their heart-felt opinions of this move. Welsh felt the same for his readers and wrote "Please miss me dreadfully as I will miss all of you."

Welsh's main beat for many years was the port and the vessels that arrived and left the harbor, many of them falling victim to the treacherous winds rounding Tatoosh Point. Among those stories were numerous shipwrecks, but one, in particular, was easy for Welsh to recall when asked to recap his most memorable story.

It was the 1921 wreck of the Chilean barge *Pirrie*, which was laden with lumber and being towed by the *Santa Rita* when it broke apart outside Cape Flattery and a few miles south of the mouth of the Quillayute River, killing 21 onboard; two did survive.

What makes it a great yarn, Welsh wrote, were "the events leading up to the wreck, the isolation of the locale, the lack of any communication from the stricken craft, the number of lost lives, and finally, the strategy and race of two newspapermen by shanks mare, rowboat, automobile and Lake Crescent ferry to file their story first for the waiting readership."

The Coast Guard tipped Billy to the wreck and he formulated a plan to get to the scene. He obtained an authority of marine travel and recruited a Filipino high schooler who spoke Spanish. They traveled by ferry, auto, boat and trekked on foot 4 miles through dense wilderness.

Climbing over surf-battered driftwood to reach Cape Johnson, near Mora, more than 60 miles from Port Angeles, the newsman was aghast at the sight.

"We found the greatest lumber yard I have ever seen, lumber floating in the small bay and piled in small broken pieces on the rocks and on the shore. Back from the high tide line, we found coast guardsmen preparing a funeral for the score of victims."

Welsh learned the Indians had rescued two survivors and were taking them to Quillayute. The race was on and when Welsh and company arrived there, they found the survivors spoke no English, but his foresight to acquire an interpreter proved providential in, what he called, "my best interview ever." The Seattle reporter he had seen earlier was nowhere in sight.

The survivors said the ship broke in two; the captain saved his wife and baby by locking them in the front half of the ship, but he stayed in the battered half and went down with his craft.

Welsh opted to go to Forks, the nearest city, to find a clear wire to send his story. That was a problem. First, he traveled on foot, then got a lift on a Quileute's motor boat.

At Forks, he obtained a typewriter and a clear wire to three metropolitan newspapers. The veteran reporter filed a story of more than 1,000 words and beat all the metro reporters with the breaking news.

Welsh also described his most dramatic story, recalling the day two Clallam Bay boys died in a house fire. He told of the tears flowing at the funeral in which the tiny homemade caskets were carried by the boys' daddy, who had sawn his pike-pole in two for handles.

While Welsh was best known for his journalistic expertise, he also played a significant role in the city's largest fundraising campaign in which he wrote as "Beacon Bill," In this column, he "blackmailed" civic leaders and others to donate to the needy at Christmas. That effort continues today, though it has had different monikers through the years. (Today, for nearly 30 years, it is called the Peninsula Home Fund.)

When he left the paper, a tribute to him cited his "spirit of compassion for the unfortunate, personified in 'Beacon Bill' that so caught the imagination of the people of the community that the life of Clallam County has been largely remolded according to the pattern laid out by the heart and eloquence of this man."

When he retired in 1955, he returned to live out his remaining days at his home at Lake Crescent.

Welsh died on Oct. 21, 1974, in Port Angeles. He was 84.

'Wandering Scribe' promoted

While the community missed Welsh's popular column, Charles did not. He didn't have to look far to find Welsh's replacement. He promoted Jack Henson to the role of managing editor.

Henson had been with the paper since 1922 and already had served in several capacities. He also traveled the peninsula for popular interview stories that went into his "Wandering Scribe" column.

Charles was not only editor and publisher of the largest (and only) daily newspaper on the North Olympic Peninsula but also, he had become a civic leader and took that leadership role to Washington, D.C., many times, advocating on behalf of issues that were important to the peninsula.

In April 1941, Charles celebrated the *Evening News'* 25th anniversary with a special 52-page "25 Years of Progress" edition, spotlighting local industry, education, agriculture and history.

A public open house was held, and to promote the peninsula, residents were encouraged to send copies of the edition to friends and relatives.

Jack Henson, known as the "Wandering Scribe," began working for E.B. Webster in 1906; he wrote his final column in 1964. *(Courtesy of the North Olympic History Center)*

Charles enjoyed traveling. His trips generally were lengthy as he abhorred flying and usually would go by train.

A trip in 1939 combined a visit to the World's Fair and a newspaper convention, both in New York City, with a trip to the nation's capital to make the rounds with government officials. In Washington, D.C., his schedule included sitting in on a Senate debate and attending a presidential press conference. He met with Interior Department officials about his most-pressing desire, the establishment of Olympic National Park.

Wherever he went, whatever he did, he was looking out for the Olympic Peninsula. He wrote in the *Evening News*:

I asked these young men what they were doing about better protection … for our northwestern pulp, lumber and shingle industries. In response, they loaded me down with reports on pulp production and reciprocal trade agreements with Canada.

They showed me cedar shingles which had been mailed from this state to congressmen at the capital. Each shingle was individually addressed and stamped and bore a message demanding protection for American production.

The legislators turned a few carloads of these shingles over to the tariff commission. There, they did find good use as backings in filing cabinets. Each time a tariff worker pulls a reciprocal correspondence file, a shingle pops up to remind him of far-western interests.

In 1942, Charles and Esther visited New York City once more, as well as wartime Washington, D.C.

Port Angeles was in the process of negotiating for a new shipyard. Congressman Henry M. "Scoop" Jackson arranged a meeting between Webster and Kemper Freeman, who owned a wood boatbuilding company, and was considering Port Angeles and another site on Puget Sound for a shipyard.

Two months after Webster returned, Olympic Shipbuilders in Port Angeles was awarded a contract to construct eight wooden barges. This resulted in "a year's steady work for about 500 men ... plus a market of more than twelve million feet of Olympic Peninsula fir timber," Webster wrote in a Page 1 article announcing the deal.

Freeman credited the "stories given me in Washington, D.C., by Congressman Jackson and Charles Webster" in convincing him to choose Port Angeles for his shipyard.

'Lady in the Lake'

One of the biggest stories of the late 1930s into the early 1940s was one which galvanized the Port Angeles community: Find the killer of Hallie Illingworth, a waitress at the Lake Crescent Tavern, who disappeared in December 1937. When her body finally was discovered floating in the lake on July 6, 1940, it was well-preserved.

The Port Angeles media dubbed the body "Lady in the Lake." It became one of the most macabre and legendary stories to surface (pun intended) at Lake Crescent.

Hallie recently had married Monty Illingworth, a beer truck driver, prior to her disappearance. Her co-workers at the tavern said she often came to work, showing bruises and was generally disconsolate. They lived on Third Street in Port Angeles.

Monty immediately became a suspect in his wife's disappearance, particularly after he filed for divorce and moved to Long Beach, Calif., with a female companion, Elinor Pearson.

It wasn't until Hollis Fultz, a special investigator with the prosecutor's office in Olympia, began looking at cold-case missing persons reports from the area that the case came together.

He obtained dental records from the dead woman's unique upper dental plate, which led him to South Dakota, where she had lived and had dental work done before moving to Port Angeles. The match was enough evidence for officers in Long Beach to take Illingworth and Pearson in for questioning.

The two had differing stories and Elinor wouldn't confirm she had married Illingworth. She said they received a postcard from Hallie from Alaska and later heard she had been killed in an auto accident.

Illingworth's story didn't match, and he was arrested in November 1941, charged with first-degree murder, alleging he strangled his wife on, or about Dec. 22, 1937, and dumped her body, wrapped in a rope-tied blanket, shortly thereafter.

He was extradited to Washington, where a lengthy trial was held. Jack Henson was there to report daily for the *Evening News* for all nine days of the trial.

The jurors were handed the case at 4 p.m. on March 5, 1942, ate dinner and returned a verdict by 7:35 that evening. Illingworth was convicted of second-degree murder and sentenced to 10 years in prison. He served nine years, was paroled and moved back to Long Beach, where he lived until he died in 1975.

The *Lady in the Lake* became the subject of a 40-page paperback by Northwest writer Mavis Amundson in 2011. Her husband is George Erb. Both wrote for a time for *The Daily News* in Port Angeles.

Charles vs. council, timber

Webster wasn't afraid to take on the Port Angeles City Council and the county. In 1948, the paper ran a well-researched series on the overspending in county government.

Charles also supported compulsory city garbage collection with a fee added to the residents' light and water bills. He said the need for a modern county health department was tantamount to public safety and to raise the quality and sanitation of food products. He undertook a campaign to upgrade the standards of the county's dairy industry.

In an editorial in the 1940s, he lightheartedly wrote "Can Port Angeles Afford to Have Street Signs?" He said it was annoying to newcomers and visitors to see the absence of street signs.

In an August 1941 editorial, he supported the then-new practice of sustained yield — replanting trees that had been cut and marketed. "Obviously, the future of this county and state demand that deforested lands which are suitable only for timber-growing shall be reforested immediately after the old trees are gone," he wrote.

He later opined that he deplored the practice of "shipping most of the county's most-valuable raw material — Douglas fir timber — to Upsound cities (Seattle-area and north) for manufacture into lumber, sash and doors, furniture, plywood, etc."

He continued:

... Lack of control to hold back Clallam County timber for local industry, which controls itself would have encouraged establishment of more industry here, has been this county's loss ... the forest service under existing law must sell to the highest bidder, thus preventing direct control over destination of the government timber. ...

From this community's standpoint, the small remainder of the Peninsula's once-great Douglas fir stands ought to be cut only as far as present and potential local industry will absorb.

In a July 24, 1941, editorial, Webster described the first large-scale reforestation project under private ownership in America — the Weyerhaeuser Co.'s Clemons Tree Farm to the south in Grays Harbor County.

Because nearly all logging of privately owned timber on the Douglas fir region has been conducted on the destructive "cut-and-get-out" principle, with no care for reforestation, the recently-launched forestry experiment by Weyerhaeuser on 130,000 acres of land is being watched with special interest.

The editorial was accompanied by pictures of the devastated "cut and run" clearcuts, which he said, "would be barren for years."

In the same editorial, Webster wrote, not too favorably, of the holdings of Crown Zellerbach in the northwest corner of Clallam County near Neah Bay.

These holdings are especially important to Port Angeles because they give permanent control of a continuous source of pulpwood for local industry. Lack of a tie-up between most of our timberland and local manufacturing has permitted this county's most valuable timber resource — the Douglas fir — to be stripped for the principle (sic) *benefit of upsound mills.*

On Dec. 10, 1941, three days after Pearl Harbor, the *Evening News* published a 28-page section on the grand opening of a new mill in Port Angeles, Peninsula Plywood.

Did his editorials make a difference with industry?

At the time, Crown was not replanting, but in just six months, the *Evening News* reported that a new tree farm was being established at Neah Bay, for the main permanent source of wood for Crown Z's paper mills at Port Angeles and Port Townsend.

Ten years later, the Merrill & Ring Tree Farm at Pyhst became the 11th certified industrial tree farm on the Peninsula.

In 1951, Webster published a 48-page special edition in the *Evening News,* including nine pages devoted to the "old ways and the new trends in raising and harvesting the Olympic Peninsula's biggest crop — timber."

Webster wasn't above taking shots at the U.S. Forest Service and the state Legislature.

Such was the case in an editorial in September 1951, after a forest fire nearly destroyed the town of Forks. Headlined "How We Prepared The Forest For Fire," the editorial lambasts the forest practices which had sent the fire racing through miles of logged-off land.

He sarcastically reminded readers of an editorial he had written nearly a decade earlier challenging the forest service and the state to change their forest practices:

Clear-cutting — leaving not a tree standing for mile after mile — leaving the land covered with waste wood which dried rapidly making wonderful fuel for flash fires ... leaving snags, which in a fire turn into our most efficient fire spreaders because of the sparks they shower ... leaving no seed trees, thereby delaying natural reforestation ... denuding the hillsides which encouraged erosion of the thin topsoil, which also delayed reforestation."

The editorial went on to say even the animals in the forest were managed poorly.

We even organized predatory shooters to kill off the animals which prey on mountain beaver who cut down the young trees which do manage to grow up between fires. … with our inexhaustible supply of virgin timber, we were heedless of future needs.

… Are we capable of learning from actually seeing these devastating results of our destructive forest practices on private and state-owned lands?

Throughout his newspaper career, and like his father before him, a concern for the future was a passion for Charles.

This was demonstrated during his 20-year campaign advocating openly and behind the scenes, for what was strongly opposed by many in Port Angeles — saving hundreds of acres of trees from timber company axes and creating Olympic National Park.

CHAPTER 4

Fight for Olympic National Park

We feel that from these memories you would call in the conflicting department heads and say to them: "Gentlemen, there is room on the Olympic Peninsula for both an adequate national park and a sustained forest yield for industry. Please stop bickering — and come to an early agreement on boundaries."

**Charles Webster, *Port Angeles Evening News*
in an editorial addressed to President Franklin D.
Roosevelt — 1937**

Olympic National Park — established in 1938 — was created later than most of the national parks in the United States.

The rainforests and glacier-jacketed peaks of the central Olympic Mountains were first proposed as a park in 1904, but timber and mining interests made sure the attempt went nowhere in Congress for years.

But by the 1930s, preservation of the country's natural resources had gained increased public support. New efforts for a park on the Olympic Peninsula now looked very promising — but there were angry disagreements about how much land to include.

Those supporting a small park included some Port Angeles business interests. They feared the timber-based economy of the peninsula would suffer if too much of the forest was included behind a park's boundaries.

They were supported by many of the state's timber companies, chambers of commerce, civic leaders and private citizens who argued about "locking up" public lands. Even the U.S. Forest Service did not want to surrender all the Olympics' marketable timber.

Among those working for the creation of a large park were New Deal conservatives in Washington, D.C., and many North Olympic Peninsula residents — including Charles Webster of the *Port Angeles Evening News*.

His support echoed the views of his father, E.B., the newspaper's co-founder, who had raised alarms about the environmental future of the peninsula at the turn of the century.

Charles Webster also used the *Evening News* to lobby successfully in the 1940s to add additional land to the park after its creation — including a creek that provided water to residents of Port Angeles and a peak that overlooks the city, his father's "Friendly Mountain."

In one instance, he won support by taking a government consultant on a horseback trek into the Olympics.

In addition, Webster tried to get an "ocean parkway" built — but on this issue he lost after finding himself opposed by his fellow conservationists who feared the highway would destroy the wild coastline portion of the park.

After a September 1937 visit to Port Angeles and a rainy tour through the peninsula's mountains, ocean and forests, President Franklin D. Roosevelt signed legislation creating Olympic National Park on June 29, 1938.

At 682,000 acres, it was one-third larger than originally proposed. Subsequent action by Roosevelt and his successor Harry Truman, and other acquisitions enlarged the park to what is today, 922,651 acres occupying the heart of the Olympic Peninsula and a strip along the Pacific Ocean.

In *Olympic Leaders: The Life and Times of the Websters of Port Angeles* by Helen Radke and Joan Ducceschi, the authors quote Chris Morgenroth, a peninsula pioneer and former forest ranger, saying:

It was the North Olympic Peninsula people who, after years of dedicated effort, staggering obstacles and reverses, and compromising their future economic benefits, should be given the most credit for the establishment of Olympic National Park.

And this local support couldn't have materialized without Charles

Webster and the *Evening News,* according to Radke and Ducceschi, (the wife of Frank Ducceschi, former publisher and editor of the *Peninsula Daily News,* successor to the *Evening News).*

Much of that local involvement was recorded — and instigated day by day on the front page of Webster's newspaper.

With the extensive coverage across three decades, the newspaper kept the park issue in the forefront of readers' minds and hearts.

In his "Welcome Mr. President" editorial that was published in the *Evening News,* the day Roosevelt visited Port Angeles, Webster wrote:

Tomorrow morning you will awaken in a delightful cottage at Lake Crescent, Mr. President —and from its front windows you will gain a vista of a lake we are all pleased to call "Our Lady of Moods." It is but one of the jewels of the Olympic mountain country of which a fair share should be spared and shared by people of future generations. Had you the time, it would have thrilled you to drive over one of these CCC roads you are responsible for. Drive until you reached the mile-high elevation of Hurricane Ridge, where carpets of flowers, gridirons of mountain peaks, shadowy parks and green forests form a fairy wonderland of delight.

We feel that from these memories you would call in the conflicting department heads and say to them: "Gentlemen, there is room on the Olympic Peninsula for both an adequate national park and a sustained forest yield for industry. Please stop bickering — and come to an early agreement on boundaries."

For we who live here, Mr. President, believe there is room for both. ... And now, Mr. President, thanks for coming to us.

Charles Webster's overlying passion during his days as publisher of the *Evening News* was the establishment of Olympic National Park. *(Courtesy of the North Olympic History Center)*

ONP, among most-visited

Today, Olympic National Park is routinely in the top 10 of most-visited national parks.

In 1976, it was designated by UNESCO as an International Biosphere Reserve, and in 1981, as a World Heritage Site. In 1988, Congress designated 95 percent of the park as Olympic Wilderness.

The Olympics rise from sea level to the majestic summit of Mount Olympus, at 7,980 feet. Rocky bluffs and sandy shores stretch along 73 miles of wilderness coastline and sea stacks that dot the waters offshore.

As wind currents sweep moist air inland from the Pacific, mist rises against the mountains, creating an incredible diversity of craggy mountain peaks, capped with 60 named glaciers (now shrinking because of climate change), vast green valleys and, on the western flank, a lush, old-growth rain forest.

It is home to black bear, Roosevelt elk, sea otters, cougars, bald eagles, salmon and steelhead — but no wolves or venomous snakes.

As a wilderness park, no road traverses ONP, but a dozen roads lead into it from U.S. Highway 101.

Parts of the park receive as much as 200 inches of rain a year, but just outside the northeastern edge, the community of Sequim and its famous "banana belt," receives an annual average of 17 inches, equivalent to the rainfall in many areas in Southern California.

Much of the central half of the North Peninsula enjoys the Olympics' rain shadow, too. Port Angeles to the west of Sequim gets about 25 inches, Port Townsend to the east gets about 20. The U.S. average is 39 inches.

Rainfall on the peninsula steadily increases as you go west from Port Angeles. On the West End of Clallam County, the town of Forks receives an average of 120 inches.

Wikipedia, the Internet encyclopedia, provides a good summary of the park's history before its official declaration as a national park:

Prior to the influx of European settlers, Olympic's human population consisted of Native Americans, whose use of the peninsula was thought to have consisted mainly of fishing and hunting.

When settlers began to appear, extractive industry in the Pacific Northwest was on the rise, particularly in regard to the harvesting of timber, which began heavily in the late 19th and early 20th centuries.

Public dissent against logging began to take hold in the 1920s, when people got their first glimpses of the clear-cut hillsides.

This period saw an explosion of people's interest in the outdoors; with the growing use of the automobile, people took to touring previously remote places like the Olympic Peninsula.

The formal record of a proposal for a new national park on the Olympic Peninsula begins with the expeditions of well-known figures Lieutenant Joseph O'Neil and Judge James Wickersham, during the 1890s.

These notables met in the Olympic wilderness while exploring, and subsequently combined their political efforts to have the area placed within some protected status.

On Feb. 22, 1897, President Grover Cleveland created the Olympic Forest Reserve, which became Olympic National Forest in 1907.

President Theodore Roosevelt created Mount Olympus National Monument in 1909, primarily to protect the subalpine calving grounds and summer range of the Roosevelt elk herds native to the Olympics.

Previously known as Olympic elk, they were being slaughtered by commercial hunters. The canine teeth of elk were prized for rings, necklaces and watch fobs. Some hunters took only the head or antlers and pulled out the teeth. After they were protected, the elk were renamed in honor of T.R.

Despite all this beauty and diversity, some in the National Park Service claimed it was "not of park-caliber," noting Washington already had a national park (Mount Rainier) and probably didn't need another one.

Those who disagreed found themselves opposed by many, who were against locking up as much as 1 billion board feet of timber.

Washington's Gov. Clarence Martin, in 1937, would only endorse part of the area for park preservation.

1933 crucial for park

The year 1933 was monumental for the eventual creation of Olympic National Park. There were several significant events that spurred the move to establish a national park on the peninsula. Among these were:

- The inauguration of Franklin Delano Roosevelt as president of the United States;
- A four-day open hunting season on Roosevelt elk resulted in the slaughtering of 240 elk, further galvanizing conservationists and indicating the Forest Service was unable to protect the elk herd.

This led to greater support for the creation of a national park on the peninsula;

- Roosevelt transferred management of national monuments from the Secretary of the Interior to the National Park Service;

- Two individuals soon would weigh in on the national park issue and have a major impact on the eventual creation of the park. They are Chris Morgenroth, a pioneer on peninsula settlements and a former forest ranger, and Congressman Monrad "Mon" Wallgren, an Everett man who would be a four-term state representative, a two-term U.S. Senator and then governor.

For E.B. Webster, Charles' father, the Olympics were a source of strength and solace as well as a majestic symbol of the peninsula.

His greatest pleasure was "taking the upward trail," scaling Mount Angeles, the three-peaked mountain that shadowed Port Angeles.

"When I want to forget business, to get rid of nerves, or insomnia, I hit the trail," he said. He loved to "hob-nob" with the elk, deer and bear of the Olympics. He was especially fond of the flowers and plants and even had a flower plant named after him, the *Senecio websteri*.

E.B. Webster, a pack on his back and walking stick in hand, loved to trek into his beloved Olympic Mountains to de-stress from the daily rigors of owning a newspaper. *(Courtesy of the North Olympic History Center)*

Preservation of the Olympics and condemnation of those who slaughtered its elk and deer for their horns and teeth (he called for the "rigorous prosecution of the unprincipled scamps" who did this) were the focus of many editorials E.B. wrote in the *Weekly Leader, Olympic-Leader,* the *Democrat-Leader* and finally the *Port Angeles Evening News.*

He was an early supporter of a national park.

"A national park in the Olympics, when it is opened by roads and trails so that it is comparatively easy of access, will not fear comparison with any other of the great national parks," E.B. wrote in 1905.

In *The Friendly Mountain*, his pet name for Mount Angeles, and in his three other books he never wavered as an advocate for his beloved Olympics.

E.B. was a serious climber, something he said he did to "get above the fog and drizzling rain that inundated" his city. In the book, he estimates that he made 176 trips to the summit of Mount Angeles and 220 trips to the timberline.

When Charles Webster arrived back in Port Angeles in 1934, there was a heated debate on the national park issue: Should there be a national park on the Olympic Peninsula and what areas would it include?

One flashpoint argued that the river valleys were the chief habitat of the Roosevelt elk and therefore essential in the "preservation of such a magnificent animal."

But little did Webster know that this issue would occupy the majority of the front pages of the *Evening News* for the next four years.

In December 1934, members of the Port Angeles Chamber of Commerce's Parks Committee, which had endorsed a national park resolution the previous month, trekked to see their local congressman, Mon Wallgren, to suggest the New Deal Democrat introduce legislation. Wallgren's office was across Puget Sound in Everett, 90 miles from Port Angeles.

Klahhane Club support

In an *Evening News* article later in December, the Klahhane Club backed the resolution for a park, noting that creation of a national park would bring much tourist traffic to Port Angeles and other Olympic Peninsula cities.

The newspaper noted the hiking club believed the "profits from tourists would more than offset any losses incurred by private interests who might be opposed to the establishment of the park."

Over the years, Forest Service rangers, local trekker Chris Morgenroth and others had suggested how much acreage and what areas to include in a national park. There were advocates for a large and a small park.

The chamber supported the small side that would leave more forest available for logging. It was interested in a "Mount Olympus National Park" that preferably encompassed around 300,000 acres, taking a later stand that it should not be more than 420,000 acres, a notion supported by O.A. Tomlinson, superintendent of Mount Rainier National Park, who addressed the chamber on Feb. 9, 1935.

But Wallgren's bill, introduced in March 1935, followed other suggestions and ballooned the park to 732,000 acres.

The chamber fired off a telegram to the congressman, protesting that the additional area included 10 billion feet of marketable timber which was "vital to continued operation of the local forest products industries."

Monrad "Mon" Wallgren, an Everett man, would be a four-term state representative, a two-term U.S. Senator and then governor. He was most instrumental in getting the Olympic National Park established. *(Courtesy of the North Olympic History Center)*

Nobody liked this bill, not even Wallgren, who defended his position in a sharply worded telegram to the chamber.

In his "Rarebit" column on the front page of the *Evening News* on April 10, 1935, the day after the chamber met, managing editor Billy Welsh sounded off to his readers, letting them know who was responsible for the new plan — and it wasn't the congressman.

"Representative Mon Wallgren's telegram to the Chamber of Commerce rather clarifies the atmosphere as to who is responsible for the bizarre boundaries suggested for the national park plan. It also causes wonderment here as to why the national park people speak one way in church and another way at home.

"Conferring with Port Angeles citizens regarding the boundaries, it was stated emphatically the park demanded straight lines that would not be

confusing. As outlined in the Wallgren bill the boundary lines resemble the course taken by goats that were drugged by eating coffee beans.

"The Western inclusion resembles an ice cream cone that had slopped over. The southern exposure resembles a sharp-toed riding boot of twenty years ago, and the Lake Crescent bit resembles a child's building blocks. As suggested in the bill, the boundaries are more than confusing. They are baffling and should be shrunk to the bare needs of a well-balanced park."

After being inundated by rebukes and new proposals, Wallgren finally called for a hearing in Washington, D.C., in April 1936, to discuss a new resolution. Charles Webster, his mother Jessie and his sister Beth (who was in D.C. on other business) attended the meeting.

Morgenroth, a peninsula pioneer and former Forest Service ranger, made an impassioned plea in support of a new proposal during the nine-day hearing before the House Committee on Public Lands. He testified that logging operations had "left a trail of devastation" on the Olympic Peninsula, and said he predicted the peninsula's infant pulp industry would outdistance logging in economic value and could be supported by sustainable trees.

The local congressional delegation was divided. Wallgren and Congressman Marion Zioncheck, whose district included Seattle, testified in favor. However, Wallgren announced during the proceedings that an amendment would be offered to eliminate a "heavy stand of fir and hemlock" from the western boundary.

An impressive array of individuals and legislators spoke in favor of a proposed new bill, including U.S. Secretary of the Interior Harold Ickes. The opposition's spokesman was Congressman Martin Smith of Hoquiam, who represented timber interests that included Forest Service officials.

Wallgren didn't submit a new bill immediately as memos and letters went back and forth between the warring factions, each seeking some compromise.

Ten months later, on Feb. 15, 1937, Wallgren introduced a new bill calling for a park of 648,000 acres, chopping only 84,000 acres from the original bill.

This didn't stop arguments pro and con about a national park from flaming anew — locally, statewide and in Congress — that Webster's *Evening News* covered closely.

Congress took no action as negotiations began in earnest.

Concessions paved way for bill

But unlike other bills over the previous 20 years to establish (and some to prohibit) a national park in the Olympics, this one stayed alive.

And, surprisingly, thanks to concessions on both sides, it paved the way for presidential involvement.

The state government was among the first agencies to pull back, due in part to Morgenroth's position being won over by Gov. Martin. They were persuaded that there would be a Park Service on the Olympic Peninsula and the proposed park would be a smaller than the initial Wallgren bill.

Preston Macy, custodian of the Mount Olympus National Monument, reported to Tomlinson on April 16, 1937, that Morgenroth had "won the governor over" to his side.

In *Administrative History of the Olympic National Park*, Guy Fringer points out the importance of this concession and the how that "agreement" opened the door to get President Roosevelt involved.

"The controversy over the proposed Mount Olympus National Park has reached a point, where, in our opinion, an indication of the National Administration's view should be announced," Tomlinson, an advocate of a large park in the Olympics, wrote in a letter to Roosevelt, on May 5, 1937.

The response to Tomlinson's request for a definitive statement by the Roosevelt administration and to the criticism of the second Wallgren bill by the national conservation organizations was President Roosevelt's visit to the Olympic Peninsula during the fall of 1937.

Tomlinson, a member of the State Planning Council's Olympic National Park Committee, probably knew he wasn't going to be disappointed by having Roosevelt enter the battle.

Inaugurated in 1933, one of the first moves the new president made was to pack his New Deal coalition with new breed conservationists.

Roosevelt was particularly concerned for the nation's timber, especially after watching that resource in his native New York decimated by lumber companies.

In his biography of FDR, Arthur Schlesinger Jr. wrote that Roosevelt "cared deeply about nature — about land, water and trees from his childhood onward."

After longstanding complaints that the Forest Service was too closely allied with timber companies and other commercial interests, President Roosevelt transferred all national monuments from the Forest Service to the Park Service shortly after taking office.

FDR tours Peninsula

It would be at the start of his Olympic Peninsula tour, in Port Angeles, that the president told a cheering crowd that there would be a national park. It was his first on-the-record commitment to the proposal.

On Sept. 30, 1937, the *Port Angeles Evening News* super-imposed a photo of President Franklin D. Roosevelt over Lake Crescent as the president arrived for a short visit, stayed at the lake lodge and continued around the Olympic loop. In January 1938, he signed the bill declaring Olympic National Park. *(Courtesy of the North Olympic History Center)*

Scores of people and dignitaries lined the streets of Port Angeles on Sept. 30, 1937, to welcome President Franklin D. Roosevelt to the peninsula. Automobiles head up Lincoln Street. The Port Angeles school band is on the right; The president is in the back seat of the second car; the courthouse is on the right, library and firehouse on the left. *(Courtesy of the North Olympic History Center)*

President Franklin D. Roosevelt greets the crowd after arriving in Port Angeles.
(Courtesy of the North Olympic History Center)

Indeed, it may have been a brief stop at the county courthouse, where more than 3,000 school children had gathered near a large sign reading "Please Mr. President, we children need your help. Give us our Olympic national park," that may have meant more to the president than any talks about the park in Washington, D.C.

The sign also may have inspired him to suggest a name change — Olympic National Park, instead of the proposed Mount Olympus National Park.

By the end of his two-day peninsula tour, after hearing all the pro and con arguments from state and federal officials, Roosevelt made it clear that he backed a large national park.

Nine months later he signed the legislation that created Olympic National Park.

The president flew into Seattle the morning of Thursday, Sept. 30, amid a steady downpour. His motorcade then drove north across the border to Vancouver, British Columbia.

There, the president boarded the destroyer *USS Phelps* and sped west in the Strait of Juan de Fuca to the B.C. capital of Victoria on Vancouver Island. Behind the *Phelps*, the *USS Porter* carried other members of the entourage and the press.

After a glad-handing visit in Victoria to bolster U.S.-Canada relations, Roosevelt and his entourage left for a 25-mile, 2½-hour trip across the strait to Port Angeles.

The visit to the Port Angeles was very much in doubt when the contingent reached Victoria due to the pelting storm. Secret Service personnel with the president had all but decided to cancel the rest of the trip.

But when the skies cleared, Wallgren, who was in Port Angeles, telephoned Marvin H. McIntyre, the president's secretary at Victoria.

The conversation was published in the next day's *Evening News*:

"You must come," Wallgren insisted. "These people must see the president, or he will miss a genuine treat and a great welcome, if you don't bring him over."

Officials reluctantly agreed that the president would spend at least a half-hour in Port Angeles, but the tour to Lake Crescent and around the peninsula was in doubt.

Crowds estimated from 8,000 to 10,000 waited many hours in intermittent rain to greet their president in Port Angeles.

He had been scheduled to arrive about 4 p.m., but it wasn't until 6 p.m. that they could hear the 21-gun presidential salute from the Coast Guard cutter *Samuel D. Ingham* as the *Phelps* rounded Ediz Hook.

More than 25 state patrol vehicles awaited the presidential entourage on the dock, along with a great yellow open car that carried the president.

Seated next to Roosevelt was his daughter, Anna Roosevelt Boettiger and her husband, John, who was the manager of the Seattle *Post-Intelligencer* newspaper at the time.

In the rear of the car with her parents were the grandchildren of the president, Eleanor and Curtis Dahl.

Behind that car rode members of the president's family, who accompanied him to the peninsula: His son James who also was special assistant to the president, and his wife, along with McIntryre, the president's secretary.

Senators and congressmen followed in the next cars.

The *Evening News* report of Friday, Oct. 1, captured the historic moment of the first president to set foot on the Olympic Peninsula:

As the motorcade pulled up to the front of the courthouse, the vehicles stopped, and the president rose to greet the children as cheers hushed, a blare of the trumpets and ruffle of drums from Boy Scout Troop 474 saluted the president.

The crowd stilled to a silent calm and the Roosevelt High School band, stationed on the courthouse steps, played the "Star-Spangled Banner." When the band finished, the courthouse clock tolled six o'clock.

President Roosevelt, head bared and face expressing calm dignity of a nation's leader honoring the national anthem, turned toward the school band. As he did, his eyes were directed on a large sign hung across the courthouse by friends of the national park movement. It read:

"Please Mr. President, we children need your help. Give us our Olympic national park."

The musical strains died away and Mayor Ralph E. Davis, who had ridden with the president from the Port dock, stepped to the side of the car, which was guarded on all sides by alert secret service men.

The mayor, speaking into a microphone placed at the scene by Port Angeles school officials, introduced the "president of the United States."

Mary Lou Hanify was a teenager in 1937, and like all students in Port Angeles, had the day off to see the president. She would recall later:

A hush fell upon the crowd when the president responded. This was the same magic voice that had charmed millions through numerous fireside chats.

"Mr. Mayor and my friends of Port Angeles," the president said, "That sign is the appealingest appeal I have ever seen in my travels. I am inclined to think it counts more to have the children want that park than all the rest of us put together.

"So, you boys and girls, I think you can count on my help in getting that national park, not only because we need it for us old people and you young people, but for a whole lot of young people who are going to come along in the next hundred years of America."

Roosevelt smiled and waved as the caravan moved along on its journey toward Lake Crescent.

After the president's short message of hope, a resounding cheer pierced the evening air. The president waved and beamed his trademark smile, shook hands with Mayor Davis and the motorcade was on its way 21 miles west to Lake Crescent.

The president and his group had dinner at Lake Crescent Tavern, now Lake Crescent Lodge.

The dinner menu featured food from many points on the peninsula: Olympic blackberry jam, Olympia oyster cocktail, Dungeness crab, prime ribs of Washington beef, Grays Harbor cranberry sherbet and Olympic blueberry pie or little wild blackberry pie. Dungeness crab cakes were offered as a late snack.

The group spent the night there, then had breakfast of Lake Crescent's famous Beardslee trout, caught by Willis Welsh, son of the *Evening News* managing editor, Sequim ham and Washington apple juice.

A late-night thunderstorm caused some concern, but it abated. A hastily called conference of presidential aides met, made a few phone calls to the lower end of the Olympic Peninsula and determined the presidential party would continue south.

President visits Forks

The caravan left for Lake Quinault, 100 miles to the south, the next morning, passing under a huge American flag as they drove away from Lake Crescent under rainy skies. There were orchestrated stops along the way that were covered by the *Evening News'* Billy Welsh and by Seattle newsmen and national wire-service reporters.

Roosevelt saw a reforestation project where Civilian Conservation Corps workers — Roosevelt created the CCC — had planted 2 million trees and a fire-fighting demonstration that included trains of pack horses loaded with equipment.

Fred Wilson, a young Forks logger in a red hickory shirt, raced up a 250-foot Douglas fir and, at about 195 feet, cut through a notch prepared earlier and brought down the top of the tree as the president watched.

The bashful Wilson walked over to the president's car and Roosevelt congratulated him.

As the entourage pulled into Forks, they were greeted with a large sign: "Forks Welcomes You, Mr. Roosevelt to Our Last Frontier."

The party halted at Cedar Creek for the president's first view of the Pacific as huge breakers crashed the shore.

Washington Gov. Martin and his son Frank joined the presidential party at the Lake Quinault Hotel (now Lake Quinault Lodge), where a salmon lunch was served.

The road south to Lake Quinault ran largely through untouched forests. However, as the sun started to emerge from the clouds when the caravan headed toward Hoquiam, the view was much different: miles of raw and ugly clearcuts.

Roosevelt turned to Congressman Martin Smith of Hoquiam and said: "I hope the son-of- a-bitch who logged that is roasting in hell."

That quote was recorded by Washington State historian and author Murray Morgan, at the time a young reporter for the *Hoquiam Washingtonian* and traveling with the president from Lake Quinault.

By mid-afternoon, the motorcade reached the Grays Harbor cities of Hoquiam and Aberdeen, where crowds of more than 50,000 lined the streets.

The motorcade also made stops in the communities of Montesano, Elma and McCleary, before finishing the loop to Olympia.

By the end of the tour, according to Tomlinson in a report to Park Service Director Arno Cammerer, the president "left no doubt in my mind that he favored a large national park desire to preserve typical stands of timber, particularly western hemlock."

Tomlinson quoted the president declaring: "The Olympic Peninsula will in the future be as popular as Yellowstone is now, and we must provide for the generations to come ... The western hemlock is a beautiful tree; and eastern people want to see it,"

Then, perhaps in response to the sign he saw at the Clallam County Courthouse, where the school children had gathered, the president also suggested, according to Tomlinson:

"Why not call it 'The Olympic National Park?' That would tie in with the Olympic Peninsula and mean something. Mount Olympus is too hard to say."

'Bet Your Shirt' on ONP

Tomlinson's report about Roosevelt's support for a large park was old news to anyone who had read the *Evening News*. The headline on the Oct. 1 story about the president's visit to Lake Crescent was "President Favors Creation of Olympic Park."

Under that, the sub-headline over Welsh's column read: "Bet Your Shirt On It, There'll be a Park."

Welsh wrote about the aftermath of a meeting that first night in which Roosevelt discussed the park proposal around his Lake Crescent cottage fireside with state and federal officials:

> ... *After three hours of wandering around in the charmed circle at Lake Crescent Tavern last night ... If you are in a wagering mood, bet your shirt, your marbles, your Ouija board and your father-in-law's store teeth that there will be a major national park in Clallam and Jefferson County within the year.*
>
> *The wager may sound frivolous, but what frivolity there is in the statement is only because the extreme joy this writer is showing that an American president is definitely for an adequate national park.*
>
> *What does he mean by an "adequate national park?"*
>
> *Simply this — that so far as boundaries are concerned, Congressman Wallgren is a piker.*
>
> *The president sat in a rain-drenched cottage at Lake Crescent last night after dinner and told national park and national forest advocates that he is for an even larger park than is contained within the boundaries of the Wallgren bill.*

> "... *If you are in a wagering mood, bet your shirt, your marbles, your Ouija board and your father-in-law's store teeth that there will be a major national park in Clallam and Jefferson County within the year.*"
>
> **Billy Welsh, managing editor of *Port Angeles Evening News***

During the next nine months, there were changes and compromises in the bill with both sides knowing the establishment of the park was near.

Roosevelt's visit forced the opponents of the national park and the various proponents of small-park options, to withhold public advocacy of those positions or risk being opposed to the president of the United States.

Tomlinson also noted in his report that the president's visit "has done more to convince the people of the state of Washington of the importance of establishing a large national park than all combined previous efforts.

"The president's public comment to support a large park also ended the criticism of the national conservation organization. And, it provided the Park Service with a justification for working toward attaining the largest possible park."

Roosevelt finally signed the legislation, sponsored by Wallgren, establishing a 682,000-acre Olympic National Park. It was June 29, 1938, and the *Evening News* front page headline screamed:

PRESIDENT SIGNS OLYMPIC PARK BILL

That headline, in 96-point, ran across the entire front page. Under it:

Roosevelt Declares Area
Interesting to Everyone For
Its Scenery, Forest Growth

Below that, still another headline

Logical Development
of Mount Olympus
National Monument,
Executive Declares in
Statement Today

The news story quoted the president:

I have taken the great pleasure in signing the act to establish the Olympic National Park in the state of Washington. … This is the logical development arising out of the establishment of the Mount Olympus National Monument during the administration of President Theodore Roosevelt, together with the added sections from the Olympic National Forest.

Roosevelt noted that the legislation authorized the president to enlarge the park in the future in consultation with the secretaries of interior and agriculture and the governor of Washington:

In the future, the New Olympic National Park may be extended in area by adding lands acquired by gift of purchase or additional lands from the Olympic National Forest.

The establishment of this new national park will be of interest to everybody in the country; its scenery and its remarkable tree growth are well worth saving and it is a worthy addition to the splendid national parks, which have already been created in many parts of the country.

But not everyone at the *Evening News* was happy.

Welsh had repeatedly cautioned in his columns that the park not be too large. And he was bothered that the president was authorized to add significant acreage to it.

He restated his feelings the day after Roosevelt signed the legislation. He was the master of ceremonies when Congressman Wallgren was honored at a huge victory party in Port Angeles as the "Father of Olympic National Park."

Welsh wrote his "Rarebit" column to Wallgren, saying in part:

Tonight, is your night. Make the most of it. But, won't you please use your influence to prevent expansion of the park boundaries? ... You have saved trees for generations to enjoy. You can save jobs so that hundreds may subsist. Thanks a million. And please be careful.

Welsh's views were counter to Webster's. They were likely at the root of dissention he had with his publisher that led him to leave the *Evening News* in 1939 to handle public relations for Crown Zellerbach Corp. in San Francisco.

One month after the park legislation was signed, Roosevelt consultant Irving Brant was assigned by Interior Secretary Ickes to conduct an on-site study and recommend what areas should be added.

Brant was a former newspaper editor and ardent conservationist who played a significant role in the enactment of the park bill.

He and Webster were long-time friends and held similar views for the park.

In his report and in his book *Adventures in Conservation with Franklin D. Roosevelt*, Brant quotes Webster and the *Evening News* on several points about Olympic National Park, referring to the *Evening News* as a "pro-park" newspaper.

Accompanying him on his tour of the park were Tomlinson, David Madsen, acting custodian of the park, and Preston Macy, acting director of the park.

Brant recommended 226,656 acres be added. The areas included what are today the jewels of ONP — Lake Crescent, the former Forest Service recreational area at Deer Park, Hurricane Ridge and Obstruction Point, and heavily timbered valleys of the Elwha, Bogachiel, Queets and Quinault rivers.

After arguments from others, including the Forest Service and Washington Gov. Martin, Roosevelt signed the proclamation on Jan. 3, 1940, adding 187,411 acres — and most of the areas recommended by Brant.

The added acres made ONP the third-largest national park in the nation.

Saving the Watershed

To be sure, not everybody was happy with the proclamation.

Those upset included the Port Angeles Chamber of Commerce — and Webster.

The chamber voiced disappointment in the inclusion of so much timber — but that was tempered with delight when it noted the new boundaries drew in Deer Park and Hurricane Ridge.

Webster was upset because the addition included only part of Mount Angeles, his father's "Friendly Mountain," and didn't include other areas near the city.

Webster repeatedly editorialized in the *Evening News*, complaining that the boundaries literally bisected Mount Angeles, which he called "the highest and grandest mountain on the north side of the Olympics."

The addition also omitted scenic Lake Angeles, the Heart of the Hills area, and importantly, the headwaters of Morse Creek, which supplied the city's residents with water.

"Destruction of the forest cover is considered especially harmful on the steep slopes characteristic of Morse Creek," Webster editorialized. "It seems especially illogical to leave this small isolated piece of land, under the forest service.

"Concerted pressure from organizations and officials in this community will go far towards getting this area transferred."

However, he found the chamber split on the issue. In an *Evening News* article on Oct. 8, 1940, he wrote that the chamber's National Park Committee and City Utilities Committee favored adding the Morse Creek watershed to the park.

But, the chamber's Forestry and Fish and Game Committees argued it would further restrict areas used for logging and hunting areas.

The *Olympic Leaders* book about the Webster family, has the backstory why Charles wanted Morse Creek placed within protection of Olympic National Park:

In the early 1940s, the water system for Port Angeles had no settling basin.

As a consequence, whenever rainfall or snow melt-off was heavy, the water faucets in homes emitted muddy water — sometimes almost as dark as strong coffee. It seemed obvious to most people that logging in the Morse Creek watershed would aggravate the situation.

Because the watershed was in the Olympic National Forest, the area could be logged at the discretion of the U.S. Forest Service.

Although a 1937 agreement between the city and the U.S. Department of Agriculture provided that the Forest Service would consult with the city before permitting logging there, the city's consent was not required.

Homemakers were vitally interested in a solution.

It was largely they who boiled tap water to protect the health of their families against waterborne diseases, who coped with washing dishes and clothes in dirty water, and who persuaded the kids to take baths in it. And guess who cleaned the tub afterwards.

No wonder the women's organizations of the city took a leading role in watershed protection.

In October 1940, Webster crafted a letter and sent it to President Roosevelt with copies going to other government officials.

Accompanying the letter was a colored map, emphasizing the critical areas for inclusion in the park.

The letter was signed by 11 business leaders and three county commissioners.

The letter requested transfer of the Morse Creek watershed and the east half of Mount Angeles to the park.

The letter also noted:

Mount Angeles, lying immediately in front of Hurricane Ridge, dominates the whole northern rim of the Olympics, of which it is the highest point. Located directly back of Port Angeles, its slopes offer the logical and most spectacular entrance to the national park.

Yet, the present park boundary cuts right through the middle of Mount Angeles, leaving out the entire main east ridge, including the beautiful alpine Lake Angeles and even the Heart of the Hills approach to both ends of the mountain.

We believe the whole of Mount Angeles, all being of prime recreational character, should all be administered as one unit, and not split up between two separate services: national parks and national forests as it is at present.

Under the Olympic National Park Act, the president still has authority to add 62,881 acres. The Morse Creek-Mount Angeles piece of the national forest now outside the park totals about 33 sections or 21,000 acres. We, therefore, request this area be included in the park.

Brant told Webster that he didn't include Morse Creek because he thought it was safe from logging because it was the city's source of water.

But Webster bombarded him with materials to emphasize that logging was indeed possible, unless it were protected between the park boundaries.

Horseback ride had impact

On Aug. 19, 1941, Webster invited Brant and his family to join him and Esther on a horseback ride to look at Lake Angeles and Morse Creek.

It made a big impact.

Brant told Webster it was the finest mountain trip he had ever taken, adding he had not realized the extent of the area's outstanding recreational advantages. He called the Mount Angeles area "breathtaking in both exertion and view."

When he returned home, he immediately wrote to Secretary Ickes, saying "as soon as possible, he should add 6,000 densely forested acres" of the Ennis Creek drainage to the park, leaving the rest of the Morse Creek watershed, which was less attractive to loggers, for future action. This would bring the mountain summit and Lake Angeles into the park.

Meanwhile, Wallgren had vacated his House seat to run for the Senate, and there was a fresh new face in the House: Henry "Scoop" Jackson.

Young Congressman Jackson soon discovered — in a three-hour town meeting on Aug. 21, 1941, at which Webster presided — that not all of Port Angeles favored an end to logging in the local area or adding more acreage to the national park.

Those speaking against logging were garden clubs, mountaineer groups, several women's groups, the sanitary inspector and city public works director. Members of the PTA and service groups signed a petition.

Among those in opposition were prominent attorney T.F. Trumbull, pioneer businessman Thomas Aldwell, chairman of the Port Angeles Chamber of Commerce; industrial groups; truck loggers; foresters and the Lumber and Sawmill Workers Union.

One week later, Webster had the issue on the front page again, occupying most of it with a 6-column photo of Mount Angeles. It was panorama taken from Heart of the Hills. A story pointed out the detailed boundaries as they existed and the boundaries Webster and those against logging were requesting.

An editorial in the same issue, entitled "Watershed Protection," leaves little doubt to the newspaper's opinion. Or rather, Webster's opinion, for there were those on the paper who held divergent views. It reads in part:

Caught between the needs of industry for raw material, vitally important in our local payroll and the needs of the community for adequate and pure water supply, what should one's attitude be towards logging in the city watershed?

... Usually, those who advocate logging the watershed preface their remarks by avowing that they would not favor anything harmful to the water supply: then, they declare logging (with emphasis on selective logging) under forest service supervision would not be harmful.

We have a great deal of confidence in the sincerity and good intentions of the forest service.

It is only that fact which in our opinion makes the logging argument worthy of much consideration.

For having seen the loggers' methods on private land in Morse Creek watershed in recent years, we haven't much confidence in the protestations of the operators themselves.

... In our opinion the risks of logging outweigh the other factors. We believe the watershed, left out of the presidential extension last year, is locally the most important area to have included in the park for permanent protection, and we hope Secretary of the Interior Ickes and our congressional delegation will recommend inclusion to provide permanent protection.

For the next year and half, arguments over the Morse Creek watershed issue dominated the *Evening News* front pages.

Webster probably was more aggressive on the Morse Creek issue than he was on the creation of Olympic National Park. Although newspapers strive to provide balanced coverage, there was little argument where he stood on protection of the creek's watershed.

On Jan. 9, 1942, an editorialized story on the front page, headlined: "How Your Water Supply Is Again Threatened by Logging Advocates," emphasized it was the lack of loggers that forced logging shipments to dry up.

Forest Supervisor Carl Neal said that wasn't the case, noting that "The lid was put on logging your watershed in Washington, D.C., and I am firmly of the opinion it won't be lifted without a war production board recommendation that watershed logs are necessary for the war effort."

The article served to ramp up both sides for a public hearing two days later.

About 200 people showed up for the hearing that was moved to the Naval Elks Lodge to accommodate the expected overflow crowd.

The meeting was scheduled to provide equal representation for the city commissioners to decide for or against logging on the watershed.

The Jan. 11, 1942, *Evening News* story, covering this public hearing was balanced. It also was one of only a few that did not carry Webster's byline.

The preponderance of opinion as expressed at the meeting was against any logging of the city watershed, and in favor of giving every aid to industries to obtain a log supply to insure continuous operation.

Their general attitude was expressed by several speakers who said, in effect,

"Let's forget about the watershed and all get behind an effort to release other logs immediately."

After the opening few paragraphs of summary (as quoted above) the two sides had the same amount of lines under the headlines "For Logging" and "Against Logging."

Thomas Aldwell
(Courtesy of the North Olympic History Center)

Port Angeles businessman Thomas Aldwell, a longtime advocate for watershed logging, wasn't content to just state his case. He took a shot across the bar at the *Evening News*:

"We have one newspaper here. From it we get one view of the problem, but not all of it which makes it difficult — although there may be some differences of opinion on that."

That likely rankled the publisher.

Among those testifying were angry women. Speaking for the Parent Teachers' Association, Mrs. Herbert McGee was the most vocal, noting that her group was against logging and advocated transferring the watershed to the national park for permanent protection.

"I want to tell you there is a large group of mothers who are getting pretty aggressive against these repeated attempts to log our watershed. ... It is the mothers who nurse the children through these intestinal problems which follow logging ... It is lots of fun to get into a fight, but we don't want to do it every year."

This hearing was the turning point in eventually getting the Morse Creek watershed added to the park.

Three days later, the *Evening News'* front-page article called the hearing "a most heartening experience," then asked the city commissioners to "step out in the lead" and urge President Roosevelt to place the entire city watershed inside the national park to assure its protection.

Park expansion bill

On May 29, 1943, Roosevelt signed the proclamation adding 20,600 acres to the park. The order secured the Morse Creek watershed and the slopes of Mount Angeles, enlarging the ONP to 866,011 acres.

In addition, the National Park Service announced plans to acquire about 42,000 acres of land along the Pacific Ocean and Queets River for future addition to ONP, including an oceanside highway.

In an editorial on June 7, 1943, that capped the Morse Creek fight, Charles thanked those he called "Indefatigable Organizers, dozens of individuals and organizations received fulsome praise, particularly Louise Taylor of the Garden Club and Congressman Jackson. The three-year campaign was a community effort."

There is no question that Webster's tireless coverage in the *Evening News* and the public sentiment he helped create, deserves a bulk of the credit.

Because of that effort and perseverance, the Morse Creek watershed and Mount Angeles were secure.

Webster also backed adding the ocean beaches to the park and, also supported building a portion of U.S. Highway 101 along the coast — "an ocean parkway with facilities — so visitors and residents could fully enjoy the rugged cobble- and log-strewn shoreline with its towering sea stacks."

Albeit, obtaining that coastal land the way the government proposed — forcing longtime settlers to sell their property — put Webster and the Roosevelt administration in opposite corners.

The *Olympic Leaders* book explains:

Ranchers who have pioneered their homes in the area object to being forced to sell their homesteads back to uncle Sam "for the benefit of a few tourists"

Anyone naturally must sympathize with a settler's feeling about parting with title to a place which he has carved out of the wilderness for himself and his family ... Even the most favorable "fair market value" offers scant consolation for the pioneer who does not want to move.

At one point, Webster sought a remedy for the settlers, writing to Secretary Ickes on their behalf, urging that they receive a lifetime lease on their property.

The plight of the West End settlers, protesting the "federal condemnation grab," made for sensational headlines and became fodder for many editorials in the *Evening News* against the government.

Webster's editorial on June 31, 1941, summarized his position.

(The ocean parkway's) potential value to this state, and particularly to the Olympic Peninsula, is great. The people and officials of Washington state and subdivisions ought to be shouting for the new parkway and urging onward its development, instead of resisting and ignoring it.

The federal government's not asking us to contribute a thing to the expense. They are even pouring out a million dollars into local owners' hands for land acquired. Recipients of this federal purchase money include county and state governments, as well as private owners.

… The people of Clallam county should cooperate every way possible. One way is to aid the transfer of county-owned land in the beach strip instead of resisting it … As part of a national parkway, that land will return dividends to this county, just as surely the industrial land which the county wisely provides at nominal cost to new industry.

Webster repeatedly chided the county to accept the government's offer and not resist, but the commissioners voted to resist the plan.

Truman slow to act

Roosevelt died on April 12, 1945. It would take a dozen years — and a new president, Harry Truman, and Congress

Ruby Beach, near Kalaloch, is one of the most-photographed beach locations in the Olympic National Park. Charles Webster bitterly fought for years for the strip of coastal highway to access it. *(Courtesy of the North Olympic History Center)*

— to resolve compensation and other issues surrounding the scenic coastal strips.

Getting that ocean strip of land added to the park was going to be an uphill battle, one that would be waged for the next six years. The biggest hang-up was the small amount of money the government was willing to pay homesteaders for taking their property. Some even went so far to call the government "crooked."

Lena Fletcher, a resident of the Hoh River Valley all her life and daughter of Dora and John Huelsdonk, the legendary "Iron Man of the Hoh," is a settler who was outspoken through the newspaper about the raw deal her family received from the government.

In her frequent *Evening News* "Stump Ranch" columns she wrote about life in the West End.

On Jan. 4, 1976, Fletcher wrote:

I think the first time I ever encountered bureaucratic crookedness was when the park service started to implement the reinstatement of the beach corridors of the Olympic National Park, which Congress had just deleted from the bill that our representative in Congress was sponsoring.

… The park service — as soon as the park bill was passed by Congress, went ahead and sent purchasing agents, appraisers, cruisers, surveyors, the whole bit, and selected the area it intended to acquire and tried to keep it all secret.

The whole process was so peculiar that everyone began to suspect a land fraud or something.

Nearing the end of his administration, Truman was not acting on the proposed land addition, and time was running out. He was to leave office on Jan. 20, 1953.

On Dec. 17, 1952, Webster decided to step up the pressure. He wrote a four-page letter to Truman and shorter ones to Sens. Jackson and Warren G. Magnuson, urging the president to act before he left office.

On Jan. 6, 1953, only days before he was to leave office, President Truman signed a proclamation that added 47,753 acres to the park. The expansion included the Queets River Corridor, a 50-mile strip along the Pacific Ocean and the western shore of Lake Ozette.

In addition, a 38-acre parcel in Port Angeles that businessman Aldwell had given to the federal government in 1944 in memory of his wife also was included. This was the land on which a park visitor center would be built.

But the coastal highway Webster had advocated was never built. Conservationists who supported a wild coastline portion of ONP won out over those in the Park Service who favored development.

Expansion of the park was only one of the projects Webster supported.

In the 1940s and early 1950s, he was actively involved in erecting a visitor center in Port Angeles for the national park; a lodge at Hurricane Ridge and a paved two-lane road from Port Angeles to the ridge.

On July 16, 1941, Webster wrote:

"If, and when, the park service constructs a first-grade road from Heart o' the Hills around the west side of Mount Angeles to Hurricane Ridge, it will be one of the most famous drives in the United States ... Such a road is needed in the Olympic National Park."

But World War II stopped anything new for the park.

After numerous prods by Webster and the *Evening News*, survey work for a road finally began in 1947, two years after the war ended.

The Ridge Road was built in several stages by different contractors. The first section, 4.4 miles from Heart o' the Hills to Lookout Rock, was opened to the public on Labor Day weekend in 1952.

Six years later, the next section — from Lookout Rock up the mountain through three bored-out tunnels, and from Hurricane Ridge down, 7 miles to the tunnels — was completed.

Work from the ridge began in 1955, its difficulty compounded since workers and equipment had to be transported by means of a steep, narrow road from the Elwha Valley.

The tortuous and dangerous section of the Mount Angeles Road from Port Angeles to Heart o' the Hills began in 1963 and wasn't completed until 1971.

When all the portions finally were completed, the road became the wonderful scenic drive that Webster had envisioned in numerous editorials in the 1940s.

Park Projects Complete Vision

Piece by piece, projects within the park were beginning to take shape. Congressman "Scoop" Jackson advocated the need for a lodge for the park when he spoke at the Olympic National Park dedication in June 1946.

Big Meadow at Hurricane Ridge was selected for the site. Construction began in 1951 and completed in 1953. The lodge was open, but not to visitors until that portion of the Ridge Road was completed in 1958. Until then access was via the Elwha Valley.

Today, Hurricane Ridge attracts growing numbers of hikers, snowshoers, cross-country skiers, snowboarders and other recreational enthusiasts. Hundreds of thousands of visitors annually make the 17-mile ride to the ridge's summit at 5,242 feet.

A new headquarters building for ONP was completed in August 1941, transitioning from a room at Rosemary Inn on Lake Crescent in 1934; a rental home in East Port Angeles in 1935, a leased warehouse building in 1937 to a makeshift office in the Post Office building in 1938.

This new building was a 36-acre parcel in a heavily-wooded site, that was the original homestead of pioneer William Bell, south of the city on Peabody Heights.

Webster described it in an editorial in the *Evening News* when it was dedicated.

The Olympic National Park headquarters is a showplace ... a great asset to the city ... the newly graveled Park Avenue was just the right address.

One more piece remained to complete all that Webster fought for within the new national park: the pioneer museum and visitor center.

The site for that complex was not in question. It would be constructed on the 36-acre parcel that Aldwell donated in 1944 in memory of his wife Ava. Aldwell also added $5,000, but funding was lacking until Clallam County Historical Society assumed sponsorship and conducted a fundraising goal of $30,000 in 1953.

Finally, in June 1953, the first shovel of dirt was turned. Members of the community donated time, labor and materials; the carpentry class at Port Angeles High School contributed volunteer hours.

Four years later, on Oct. 12, 1957, the Pioneer Memorial Museum, commemorating the pioneers of the North Olympic Peninsula, was dedicated.

Sadly, the two men whose visions led to Olympic National Park's important buildings were not around to see the projects completed.

Charles Webster wasn't even at his peak when most of the major work began.

He suffered a stroke in May 1953, then another in early 1955, and was never the same. He died on April 21, 1969.

Thomas Aldwell died in 1954 when work on the Pioneer Memorial Museum had just begun. He was honored at the dedication, and his life work was the first exhibit in the museum.

Today, when visitors look out across the Olympic Wilderness from Hurricane Ridge, they are viewing the "Dan J. Evans Wilderness."

The area, encompassing 95 percent of Olympic National Park, was renamed in honor of the 93-year-old former three-term Washington governor in a ceremony on Aug. 24, 2017.

Above, construction of the lodge at Hurricane Ridge began in 1951 and was completed in 1953. This photo was taken in the late 1950s, shortly after the Ridge Road was open to the public.

At right, Port Angeles businessman Thomas Aldwell poses with the plaque that shows he donated 38 acres in his wife Ava's memory in 1944, for construction of the Pioneer Memorial Museum, now the Olympic National Park visitor center at Hurricane Ridge Road. *(Courtesy of the North Olympic History Center)*

Below, The Olympic National Park visitor center on Hurricane Ridge Road in Port Angeles is open daily and offers information from park history to hiking and fishing to camping. *(Bill Lindstrom photo)*

CHAPTER 5

Esther Webster

Esther Barrows Webster, Charles' free-spirited wife, was to play important roles in the management of the *Port Angeles Evening News.*

Born Sept. 23, 1903, on a farm in Oregon's Willamette Valley, Esther told her new acquaintances on the North Olympic Peninsula that from an early age she wanted to be an artist.

In 1926, she drove cross-country in a Model T with two girlfriends to study art in New York. After marrying Charles in 1929, she continued to develop her talent as a painter while working as a textile designer in the early days of the Depression.

The Websters' home on Caroline Street had sweeping views of Port Angeles Harbor and the Strait of Juan de Fuca and, in the other direction, of the looming spires of the Olympic Mountains.

It was there that Esther — independent, even rebellious at times, not quick to make friends — cultivated her artistic passions that were to be recognized throughout the Northwest.

One of her oil paintings of the Rayonier mill in Port Angeles, *Mill with Smoke,* has been in the Seattle Art Museum's permanent collection since 1947.

Paintings such as *Lake Dawn, Heart o' the Hills, Old-Growth Forest, Salt Creek, Crescent Beach, Lake Sutherland, Mountain Landscape, Lake Aldwell, Autumn* and *Road to Mountains* attest to Esther's love of nature. These works of art and others of the Olympics captivated her mind and are expressed through her brush.

She won awards and had showings in Seattle, at the State Capitol Historical Museum in Olympia and in Tacoma. She was most proud

Charles and Esther Webster moved into this home at 1203 E. Lauridsen Blvd., in 1951. The home, designed by noted architect Paul Haydn Kirk, offered a sweeping panorama of the Strait of Juan de Fuca. From here, Esther began to flourish as an artist. In 1956, the home was featured in *Sunset Magazine*. Prior to her death in 1985, Esther began plans to turn the home into, what would eventually be, the Port Angeles Fine Arts Center. *(Courtesy of the North Olympic History Center)*

of a large exhibition of work at the State Capitol Historical Museum in Olympia in the 1950s.

The Websters — who had no children — lived in the Caroline Street home for 15 years until moving in 1951 to a hillside residence designed by innovative Northwest architect Paul Hayden Kirk. The home commanded dramatic city, water and mountain vistas.

The Websters generally were private folks in their home life. Occasionally, they would have family or friends over for dinner or socializing, so it was quite a shock to most in Port Angeles when *Sunset Magazine's* May 5, 1956, edition included a four-page pictorial of the Webster home for all the world to see.

After Esther's death in 1985, it later became the Port Angeles Fine Arts

Center, a facility that was dedicated in memory of her husband and father, nearly a half-century after E.B. Webster's death.

Duncan McKiernan, a noted sculptor, artist and Esther's friend and associate, became the first director of the arts center. He thinks she could have become the Georgia O'Keeffe of the Northwest.

"I have no doubt that she could have become a premier artist if she hadn't devoted so much time to newspaper publishing," McKiernan said in the *Olympic Leaders: The Life and Times of the Websters of Port Angeles* by Helen Radke and Joan Ducceschi, noting there is "a lot of action in Esther's work. She was flexible and willing to try different things."

By 1942, with the world at war and reporters from the *Evening News* among the recruits, Charles "rather brusquely directed his wife to report for work" in the newsroom, the *Olympic Leaders* book notes:

In telling the story later, Esther said she had been doubtful how much help she could be but thought she could at least answer the phone.

It was quickly apparent that she could and would do more than that.

Soon, she was trained as a reporter and was writing bylined stories.

Charles, Esther a good team

When KONP radio, owned by the *Evening News,* began operations in 1945, Esther's interest and duties expanded. She gravitated to the broadcast side and had a desk at the radio station.

She reported on air as Jean Earl, building a significant following as she interviewed civic leaders and local newsmakers.

She kept up on what was happening with the newspaper, rewriting press releases for the society pages. In later years she wrote articles about her travels and profiled local newsmakers.

Esther and Charles worked as a team in the 1940s and 1950s. Charles was in the lead position, but Esther's opinions were valued on most decisions.

In the late 1940s and early 1950s, Esther did a lot of traveling and wrote under the Jean Earl byline in the *Evening News.*

On one occasion, she took an extensive trip to Europe as a member of the Port Angeles Soroptimist Club to attend the 1948 International Soroptimist Club convention in London.

Earlier in the year, she was named Woman of the Year by the Port Angeles Business and Professional Women's Club.

Starting with the Aug. 1 edition, Esther filed 74 "Travel by Jean Earl" installments, running almost daily until she caught the train back home on Nov. 5.

The articles began with her train ride east to New York, then the trip aboard the *Queen Elizabeth* across the Atlantic.

She not only attended the convention, but spent an additional two weeks in London, then visited

Esther Webster maintained a desk at the *Port Angeles Evening News* in the early 1940s, then when KONP began operation in 1945, she conducted an interview program as Jean Earl and often wrote with that byline for the *Evening News*. *(Courtesy of the North Olympic History Center)*

Scotland, the Netherlands, Belgium, Switzerland, (including the Alps), Venice, Bologna, Naples, Rome, Paris and Chartres.

When she finally got to Paris and the Louvre, she didn't hold back the artist in her:

... Here are long-eared, enigmatic Egyptian cats of stone, long-eyed queens and their high-shouldered kings. Acres and acres of relics from the valley of the Nile.

But the rank and file visitors to the Louvre don't go to see the Egyptian exhibits. They are looking for Leonardo da Vinci's "Mona Lisa" and Whistler's "Mother."

Both canvasses are likely to be disappointing.

Mona Lisa is smaller than expected and seems crowded into her frame. Brown and greenish tones indicate layers of varnish.

The Whistler is of the same shadowy, visionary quality as the Mona Lisa. ... To see the Leonardo painting and the Whistler, one must pass a few hundred years of painting. ... The much-heralded 'Venetian glow' is a brownish mist, suggesting the sienna underpainting considered responsible. Of course, it could be lack of modern lighting, for these invaluable paintings have no artificial light, just the dirty skylights above.

Since she was writing for the women of Port Angeles as much as any other target audience, she described fashion and style in depth, some of which she called "hideous and frilly."

Beth Webster, the middle of three Webster sisters, was president of the corporation from 1941-1948. Employees called her the "balance wheel." *(Courtesy of the North Olympic History Center)*

When she returned home, Esther found Charles depressed and with health problems. He still was suffering from the unexpected death of his 49-year-old sister Jessie Elizabeth "Beth" Webster. She had died of a stroke in January.

Well-liked by the employees, Beth never married and managed the newspaper's business affairs as president of the corporation for her final eight years.

Co-workers said she "held it all together" and called her the newspaper's "balance wheel." Beth's style tempered Charles' often heavy-handed ways.

One veteran employee said the printers would do anything for her. "All she had to do was ask."

The stress of losing a sister and managing all the departments of the *Evening News* on his own for the first time aggravated Charles' high blood pressure. And his management style led to morale problems at the newspaper.

George Buck arrives

In 1951, a new employee joined the *Evening News* business office — George Buck, who would have a lasting repercussion with the staff from the time he signed on as the corporation's accountant.

Buck had never set foot in a newspaper office before Charles hired him. He was an attorney but had been working as a partner in a heating oil company in Seattle.

In May 1953, five months after turning 50, Charles suffered a serious stroke and was hospitalized in Seattle for more than a month.

Interestingly, the newspaper never acknowledged that Charles had a stroke.

Esther shrugged off questions and his friends thought Charles might be suffering from the flu.

In a business letter, written from the Seattle hospital in June 1953, he "described his painstaking struggle to walk, to relearn how to read and type," according to the *Olympic Leaders'* book.

Charles eventually returned to limited duty at the *Evening News*. By this time Buck had become familiar with all departments of the newspaper and Charles asked Buck to be his administrative assistant.

Buck was one who understood how difficult it was to overcome debilitating situations. While serving in the Army Signal Corps in World War II, he was stricken with polio in the Philippines. He was almost completely paralyzed and told he would never walk again.

But this was one determined young man. It took two years of concentrated effort at Madigan General Hospital and Fort Lewis near Tacoma before he relearned how to use his muscles and walk. He did have a noticeable limp, but that never slowed him down.

Charles sat in on budget sessions and meetings with staff, but his words were slurred and he tired easily. Soon it was Buck who was calling the shots for the *Evening News* and KONP.

Some staff members, including city editor Earl Clark, found Buck overbearing and impossible to work with.

"For me, this was not satisfactory," Clark said in the *Olympic Leaders*. He had been hired by Charles six years earlier. He left in 1954 and purchased the *Edmonds Tribune*, which he operated until his retirement in 1965.

He had a fondness for Port Angeles and returned to the peninsula, teaching journalism at Peninsula College for nine years. He also became active in the Community Players and Community Concerts Association.

Two new employees, hired in 1955, eventually would provide significant impact on the *Evening News*: Helene Phifer and Del Price.

Phifer was hired as auditor, and she became a friend and confidante as well as an employee for the Websters the rest of their lives.

Price was hired as an ad salesman and soon became the newspaper's top salesman.

But Price and Buck often were at loggerheads as Buck was called by others a "tight-fisted bean counter." Price labored hard and continued to build the advertising without much recognition from management.

He even was considered by the Webster sisters as a possible publisher.

Charles' health was fading, but nobody talked about the stroke he suffered. He made most of the staff meetings, but as employees said later, they tried to stay out of his way.

Price said the publisher had a habit of standing over a staff member and just watching, not saying anything. It was "odd," Price said, and unnerved people.

The big secret in the office was "what was wrong with Charles?" Price said in an interview for the *Olympic Leaders*.

The phrase used was "Before Charles became sick ... but we never knew what sick meant." Del's son, Scott, said that for his dad, "the reason for what was wrong was not as important as what the staff had to contend with. Morale at the paper was very low."

George Buck became sole owner and GM of radio station KONP in Port Angeles in 1969. *(KONP archive)*

Buck named GM

Charles' condition continued to deteriorate after a second stroke in 1955.

In 1957, Buck became general manager. He now had authority over the newspaper, KONP and Olympic Stationers, an office supply shop that was sold in 1959.

In making the announcement about Buck's promotion, Esther wrote in the *Evening News* that he was "cool under pressure and able to keep a tight hand on the reins in a business where almost anything can happen, and often does."

But the surviving Webster sisters, Mae and Dorothy, were no fans of Buck — and they never had gotten along well with Esther — and although neither sister took an active role in running the paper, both didn't like what was happening.

They talked with John Schweitzer, a former part-owner of the paper with their father who had stayed on as advertising director. They were thinking of asking Price to be publisher.

Owning 53 percent of the stock between them, the sisters could have fired Buck, demoted Charles and named Price publisher. But their conscience wouldn't allow it.

"We don't want our brother's blood on our hands," the sisters told Price, according to the interview in the *Olympic Leaders*. They were fearful that, for them to take over the paper and push Charles aside, it would kill him. They couldn't risk it.

Instead, Mae and Dorothy offered to sell their stock to Charles, or alternatively, to buy Charles' interest.

Charles and Esther opted to buy out the sisters, selling their house to Radio Pacific, Inc., the parent company of KONP, to come up with some of the money.

This was a difficult time for the paper, its management and staff. Both sellers and buyers obtained attorneys and negotiations began.

In an interview in 1994, two years before he died, Buck talked about this tumultuous time in the late 1950s.

"We had the resources to buy Mae and Dorothy's interest — in cash. We got that settled even though (the sisters) changed their minds about selling after negotiations were underway."

Agreement wasn't reached until September 1960, but the sale was not final until the Federal Communications Commission approved transfer of the radio station.

The purchase of all the outstanding stock of the newspaper and KONP by Charles Webster was announced in the *Evening News* on Jan. 13, 1961.

That article didn't mention Buck's name in the purchase. The paper's masthead at the time of the sale read: C.N. Webster, editor and publisher; Esther Webster, associate editor; George Buck, general manager.

Angry Price gets revenge

Six days later, on Jan. 19, 1961, Price debuted a competing newspaper, the weekly free distribution *Shopping News*. He later changed the name to the *Chronicle*.

He took with him Schweitzer, Lorraine Ross and a couple of issues later, Dave Partridge, from the *Evening News* — Price's competing newspaper.

The *Chronicle* endured for nearly 32 years, siphoning away valuable advertisers from the Websters.

Price's weekly spurred the *Evening News* to make some overdue improvements.

It hired a host of new staffers and debuted such features as "Dear Abby" and Sylvia Porter's financial column, "Your Money's Worth."

It most notably unveiled a new look in headlines and layout that new managing editor Ralph Langer said, "brought the newspaper's 1920's page layouts into modern times."

This was not only his first management role in newspapers, but when hired, Langer wasn't even involved in journalism. He was a young Army CIC (counter-intelligence) officer. But he had a journalism degree from the University of Michigan and had worked in several newsrooms. He was bright, creative and personable.

"About six months before my 'out' date (from the Army), I began sending resumes to newspapers," Langer recalled in an interview in 2015.

He replied to a blind ad in *Editor and Publisher* magazine that a newspaper in Washington state was seeking a managing editor.

"Subsequently, Buck sent me a half-dozen or so copies of the paper and asked me to critique them.

"I sent a fairly long and very detailed assessment of the 8-column page design, story content, photographs that included a lot of grip-n-grin images, poorly composed, ineffectively cropped and badly produced."

Buck hired him.

"My goal was to change the overall culture of working together, dumping the 8-column format, preaching that we needed few photographs of two to 20 people lined up," Langer said.

"Rather I wanted action shots of these people doing whatever it is they do."

Story content also was important to the new managing editor.

"I stressed that government actions or meetings needed to always consider 'How is this decision going to affect real people with their lives?'"

One of the first noteworthy accomplishments when Langer arrived was shepherding through production a massive, 12-section, 98-page special Centennial Edition, that was well under way by the time he arrived.

News editor Don Paxson, "Wandering Scribe" (Langer called him "Wonderful Scribe" in the interview) Jack Henson, who sat next to Ralph, and society editor Grace Charnell were the key proponents in getting this job done.

Scooter Chapman was in his first year of a dual role as sports editor for the paper and announcer with KONP. Langer said Jack Chapman, Scooter's brother, was a reporter and photographer.

Ralph Langer, pictured in 1964, was hired as managing editor for the _Port Angeles Evening News_ in 1962. Esther Webster wrote a glowing profile of Langer in 1964, but two years later, he had enough of Buck and left for Detroit. _(Port Angeles Evening News)_

The section, published on June 16, 1962, ushered in the city's week-long 100th birthday celebration. It was nearly twice as large as any special section the paper previously had produced.

While the story content was important to the _Evening News'_ staff and readers, a reprint of a telegram sent to Charles Webster, meant even more:

I am most pleased to learn from Senator Jackson that Port Angeles is observing its centennial this year. This is indeed a memorable event in the long life of your community. Port Angeles ranks as an important manufacturing and recreational center.

I wish your city many more years of continued success in these areas and in every other aspect of community life.

With the warmest best wishes
John F. Kennedy
President of the United States.

First offset paper in state

Langer's next project was to go with Buck and find a good offset machine to produce the newspaper and improve its production.

"We took a road trip to Oregon," Langer recalled, "and by 1963, purchased a state-of-the-art Goss press, becoming the first offset newspaper in Washington."

Buck continued his penny-pinching ways that had driven away Price, Clark and others.

"George was an absolute controller of expenses," Langer said. "He wrote notes that said only take a few paperclips at a time. One morning in the men's room, the paper-towel dispenser had been removed and a roll of newsprint was in its place.

"Drying one's face on newsprint is not efficient or morale building, but it was cheap. Staff feared the same change would be made in the stalls."

In 1963, the station manager at KONP had quit to become a salmon fishing guide.

"George asked me to become station manager, while he searched," said Langer.

"That involved putting out the afternoon paper before noon, going to the radio station, doing the noon news, calling on key advertising accounts, then covering the usual night meetings several times a week.

"Then I would return to the newspaper and develop film and make engravings for the next day's paper."

On top of running the radio station and being managing editor, Buck had made Langer the production manager at the newspaper. Buck put him on a bonus system in which he got paid extra if there were cost savings. This, too, fit Buck's parsimonious nature.

"When the first quarter was literally off the bonus chart, George moved the chart up and we started over," Langer recalled.

"That quarter was also off the chart and he moved it 100 percent higher again. I think he hated to write the checks, even though, if I made $10, the company made at least $100."

Obituary for 'Wandering Scribe'

May 5, 1964, was a particularly tough day for Langer, for the paper's staff and the community. The *Evening News* staff had to write an obituary for the "Wandering Scribe."

Jack Henson died at 80, 56 years after he first came to work for E.B. Webster on the *Olympic-Leader*. He had been with the *Evening News* since 1922.

Publisher Charles Webster, left, and managing editor Jack Henson look over an edition of the *Port Angeles Evening News*. Henson died at 80 on May 5, 1964, 56 years after going to work for E.B. Webster. He joined the *Evening News* in 1922 and wrote his final column from his hospital bed. *(Courtesy of the North Olympic History Center)*

"There will never be another like him. He belongs to the area and to the era. He was everyone's relative ... and we loved him," wrote Langer in one of several tributes to the longtime columnist.

Henson's final column was published on April 24, just 11 days before his death. He wrote it on a typewriter from his hospital room.

It was that indomitable spirit that he brought to the newsroom and to his columns. He began his "Wandering Scribe" column in 1929 and it rarely differed in style.

Some said he wrote in his dot-dot-dot style because he eschewed punctuation. It was the only punctuation his columns contained.

Here's an example of his style, written by the scribe to describe his style:

Its one purpose ... Has been to chronicle little things ... That go to make up life ... Perhaps give pleasure ... And never use malice ... A standing rule has been ...Only to say good things about folks ... And only to use names of folks Scribe likes ... And as he does not dislike anyone ... use of names has been very profuse ...

He often said he wrote columns in about 10 minutes during the noon hour when the rest of the staff was at lunch. His friend and longtime co-worker and editor Billy Welsh wrote a tribute after Henson died, saying his column grew in its influence over the years.

"In this column, there breathed a simplicity of writing and wealth of nuances that could only come from a man of tenderness, understanding and rich human experience. His column was an escape from grief, troubles, despair and boredom. Actually, it was a tonic."

Where was Esther while all of this was going on and what about Charles?

"While I was there," Langer remembers, "Esther was in and out of the newsroom and had no particular schedule that I was aware of. She did the profiles for the paper — and she enjoyed that. She would come in and drop them off."

Esther wrote a glowing profile of Langer on Nov. 22, 1964:

Quiet, soft spoken, a listener rather than a talker, Langer's youthful appearance is deceptive.

When on a story or managing the newsroom, his speed, efficiency and general know-how wins acceptance and then appreciation.

This is most apparent when pressured by both sides in a community controversy. Cool and calm, Langer draws the line down the middle and does not deviate.

As for Charles, he was basically a non-factor, Langer said.

"His illness, apparently, a form of dementia after his stroke, was severe. He would 'sort of freeze in place, perhaps staring at someone or into space.'

"He would occasionally come into the office in the morning and announce he was going to read galley proofs. I don't recall anything happening from them. He read them and then went home."

Langer said he would sometimes get odd "story tips" from Charles.

"Best example was a half-sheet note that he wrote saying on his way to the office, he had seen some boys playing a game in a field. They were wearing gloves that they called mitts. And they had wooden sticks that they called bats.

"I felt great sorrow at his condition. He seemed like a very nice man with principles, but now terribly diminished. And the more I learned about his history, of, among other things, advocating for the Olympic National Park, even naming his radio station KONP after it, and in the face of massive resistance, the sadder his situation was."

Charles, essentially retired, was listed as president. He became officially retired in November 1966. Esther became editor and publisher.

Ralph Langer in 2015. *(Courtesy of Ralph Langer)*

Meantime, Langer was becoming increasingly frustrated with Buck and his miserly demands.

Langer said he explored other job opportunities and by 1966, he had enough of Buck and his skinflint ways. He accepted a job as copy editor for the *Detroit Free Press*.

After Detroit, he was managing editor at Dayton, Ohio, and then editor of the Everett (Wash.) *Herald*.

In 1981, he became managing editor of the *Dallas Morning News*. He retired as its editor and executive vice president in 1999 and now writes novels while splitting his retirement time between homes in Texas and Montana.

Buck's adoption, marriage

During Langer's time at the *Evening News*, an odd rumor circulated that Buck had been adopted by Charles and Esther as the heir to their interest in the company.

"It was basically a weird-sounding rumor, but no one could find any documentation," Langer revealed.

It was true, according to research done by the authors of *Olympic Leaders*, it was done to ensure Buck didn't bolt to another job. Only 13 years younger than Charles and Esther, Buck became their son and legal heir in 1963.

"Buck said the Websters adopted him as part of a business agreement with regard to tax laws," Price wrote in his newspaper after Esther's death in 1985.

In a 1994 interview with *Olympic Leaders*, Buck told the authors he was "flabbergasted" by the Websters' wish to leave their stock in the corporation to him.

A confidante to the Websters said Charles was opposed to the adoption, but he was gravely ill. Scheduled for surgery, he acceded to Esther's wishes just before entering the hospital.

Esther almost immediately regretted the adoption, the confidante said. A few years later her relationship with Buck became worse.

In 1966, Buck went to California and married an artist, Peggy Fogliano, a move that didn't sit well with Esther. She and Charles both were invited to the wedding but did not attend.

Sandy Keys, who started work at KONP in the early 1960s and still is working there, knew Buck and Peggy well.

"He had a kind of thing for Esther, a romantic thing," Keys said, smiling. "When he went to California and married Peggy, Esther was unhappy."

Jim MacDonald, who was hired by Buck in 1975 as a program director and ad salesman for KONP, and in the next 21 years moved up to station co-owner, shared his view:

"Esther was kind of sweet on George. He told me that, but when Peggy and George started to hook up and then married, Esther kind of fell apart. (Buck) got the station, and that was the end of it."

This marriage, to whatever degree it was responsible, was the beginning of Buck's downfall at the paper, but there were other developments as well.

Despite what appeared to be major strides taken by Buck — improved circulation and increased revenue — Esther hired Russell McGrath, retired managing editor of the *Seattle Times* to study the newspaper's financial management, which she believed wasn't producing like it should.

After spending 10 days at the newspaper delving deep into the financial situation and unnerving department managers, McGrath concluded the paper wasn't being managed well and changes were needed if the goal was to make the newspaper more profitable.

Ned Thomas arrives

Esther, who was making all the operational decisions at this point, agreed. She reached across the state and brought in Edward Churchill "Ned" Thomas.

Hiring him as editor and associate publisher, Esther put Thomas in charge of all departments: news, advertising, circulation, composing, press room and the business office.

It was clear Buck's star had fallen.

Thomas, who arrived at the paper on Nov. 1, 1967, had just sold the *Columbia Basin Herald* in Moses Lake to Duane Hagadone of the John Scripps organization, after 21 years as co-owner and editor.

He was 60, not ready to retire and welcomed a new challenge.

After Thomas retired from newspapering in 1981, he wrote a short book of his memoires, entitled *My Reaction*. In it, he wrote about his first rocky days at the *Evening News*:

It was a learning experience. Instead of spending full time at the editorial helm as had been my responsibility at Moses Lake, I was in charge of all departments. ... the paper had been the first daily in the state to switch from letterpress and hot metal to the offset, cold-type system that was revolutionizing the newspaper industry.

I had no experience in this production system, and the Port Angeles installation, being one of the earliest, had made the switch on some rather primitive equipment.

There were four offset press units, each capable of printing four pages for a total of 16. Anything over 16 pages, which occurred regularly on Wednesday's and Sundays, meant two press runs. If we ran color other than black, it took one entire unit to do it, so with a 12-page press, it meant double runs.

Body type was punched on Justowriters, typewriter-like gadgets which produced a crude imitation of machine-set type and were so noisy the operators wore ear plugs.

*On top of all this, the entire business was housed in cut-up rented quarters.
It was a daily miracle to me when the paper got out.*

He had immediate clashes with Esther, and wrote not too kindly about
that situation in his book:

*While I had been my own boss at Moses Lake, at Port Angeles I was
beholden to a woman owner, who had no working experience on a newspaper
and, also had no respect for the chain of command. Orders flowed from home
to department heads responsible to me, without my knowledge.*

Thomas also had to deal with a deteriorating Charles Webster. After
his brother-in-law William Wenner died on Feb. 22, 1968, Charles failed
rapidly. He had been fond of Bill, his sister Dorothy's husband, and the
shock was too much for him.

Charles entered Angeles Convalescent Hospital in April, never to
return to the newspaper office or his home.

New home for *Evening News*

Thomas' first orders from Esther were to plan and supervise
construction of a new, modern building and to update the production
system, including a new press.

The new building was long overdue. The *Evening News* had been
published in the same building on Lincoln Street for more than 50 years.

Although scaled down from original plans, the new plant — at 305 W.
First St. — still cost $250,000 and officially opened on March 28, 1969,
with public tours.

After several enlargements, it is still the newspaper's home.

Thomas was proud of the new building and the breakthrough
technology the paper was installing. In an editorial on the open house
date, he wrote:

*It's a commitment to Port Angeles and the North Olympic Peninsula ...
a vote of confidence in the future.*

... The Evening News *was a pioneer in this change. Five and a half years
ago it became the first daily in the state to convert to the offset system of printing
and cold-metal method of production. It was a trying time, as the conversion
of people to new machines and new methods was painful.*

But, this is why the move into our new building has worked so smoothly.

We do have a new press and some other new pieces of equipment, but our people understand the process and had little difficulty in adapting to something bigger and better. And the production-flow design of the new plant has smoothed out their work immensely.

Now, the Evening News *has become the first daily in the Northwest to trade in a used offset press on a new one. The revolution has come that fast.*

Death of Charles

On April 20, 1969, three weeks after the open house for the new building, Charles died peacefully in Olympic Memorial Hospital. He was 66.

His body was cremated with no ceremonies.

Charles wanted no funeral, noting in a document he signed in 1948, that he thought such public display of grief caused added anguish for the mourners.

The *Evening News* acceded to his wishes and noted his passing in a short front-page story that reported his death, and in an editorial written two days later by news editor Don Paxson, titled "The Olympic Peninsula has lost a good friend."

Sadly, no one on the *Evening News* staff at the time knew Charles Webster when he was an effective editor and publisher. Paxson arrived at the paper in 1964.

He wrote about Charles' passion for establishing Olympic National Park. No doubt Esther helped him with the more introspective comments:

A hard driver, he drove himself even harder than those associated with him. He was an intense man, one who never allowed himself the frivolities of lesser humans. Everything he did, had to have a purpose. He was an incessant walker but not just for exercise, he walked to mix with people, to learn more about the flora and fauna which abounded his surroundings. He swam frequently in the community pool, again for exercise and to meet new people.

He had unusual powers of concentration which allowed him to pursue the subject at hand and to be oblivious to other things going on around him. It perhaps was this unrelenting pursuit of knowledge and perfection that led to his cerebral hemorrhage that caused his passing at the relatively early age of 66.

The editorial went on for several more paragraphs before the final sentences.

The staff of the Evening News *misses him, but there will be no pause to mark his passing, no closing of doors for a few hours in his memory. He wished it that way.*

Buck out, given KONP

About the time construction was underway on the new plant, the uneasy ties between the Websters (Esther, her sisters-in-law, Dorothy and Mae) and Buck were coming apart.

Buck was all but out the door, but not all the way out.

The *Olympic Leaders* book details this situation.

They needed Buck's resignation to nullify the inheritance, so the brain trust came up with a new agreement with him.

An agreed plan of reorganization was negotiated to divide up the company. Buck acquired the radio station in exchange for his four stock shares of the newspaper he owned.

The document stipulated that certain basic differences and disputes have arisen among (the three parties) which ... have seriously interrupted and interfered with the normal business of (the newspaper and the radio station) and which, if continued, would threaten the public esteem and good will heretofore enjoyed by both businesses and demoralize their staffs during a period of intense competition from other media in the area.

The reorganization was finalized on Jan. 3, 1969. The *Evening News* announced on Jan. 12 that Buck retained his posts as general manager and board secretary until the transfer was approved by the FCC in May.

The last day his name appeared in the *Evening News* masthead was May 7, 1969, still listed as general manager.

Keys recalls this period of uneasiness when Buck's days at the *Evening News* came to an end.

"There was a 'kerfuffle.' Esther was angry with him (for marrying Peggy) and disowned him. For penance, he was given KONP and dismissed as GM at the paper. My understanding is she said, 'Here is KONP, now get out of here.'"

Charles' will reflected the changed relationship with Buck, giving his "one adopted child" the sum of $1. Peninsula College journalism students would be the eventual beneficiaries of a trust fund of more than $500,000.

In the interview in 1994, Buck said little about his fall from power.

If he was indignant, he soon got over it, for Buck would remain owner or co-owner of KONP for the next 27 years until his death on May 4, 1996, at 79.

(More with Buck in the chapter on broadcasting).

Less than a month after the reorganization in 1969, tragedy struck the North Olympic Peninsula. Bill Fairchild, owner of Angeles Flying Service, was the pilot of his twin-engine Beechcraft air taxi on a routine flight to Seattle.

Not 1,000 feet away from the Clallam County Airport runway, the plane suddenly did a nose dive and crashed into the snowy Olympics, killing all 10 aboard.

The tragedy hit Esther particularly hard. She was good friends with the Fairchilds, and in 1961, wrote a profile for the *Evening News*: "No matter what the job, it's no barrier for Fairchild."

Ned Thomas wrote an editorial, titled "Our Day of Tragedy," on Feb. 6, 1969:

"Port Angeles walked softly and spoke in muted tones yesterday. It was a day of tragedy — the day 10 lives were snuffed out in an airplane crash.

News of plane crashes is fairly common this time of year. You read about one, hear about one, see television footage of one and it means little because it happened far away.

This one was different. It was our own air taxi service, and seven of the victims were local people, folks we all knew.

It was more unbelievable because of the fine safety record piled up by the small airline and its owner-manager Bill Fairchild. Never before, on a scheduled flight had an Angeles Flying Service plane gone down.

… And yesterday morning, it was Bill Fairchild in the cockpit with Bill Booze, his most experienced other flier. The eight passengers filled the twin-engine Beechcraft to capacity.

All were lost.

... People in Port Angeles could talk of little else yesterday. Even those who didn't know any of the victims were shaken up. It had hit too close to home."

Later in 1969, the airport, which was developed in 1934 and expanded through Roosevelt's Works Progress Administration, was renamed William R. Fairchild Airport. It has been owned by the Port of Port Angeles since 1951.

Meantime, this tragedy only added to the turmoil. The stress of Charles' death, losing her brother-in-law, the Buck situation, stress of running the paper and an eroding dislike for Thomas began to take a heavy toll on Esther's health.

She spent most of 1970 in and out of a hospital in Seattle and was transported each time by Helene Phifer.

Webster era ends

Her health eventually became stable and she returned to work at the *Evening News*. But her relations with Thomas didn't improve.

In April 1971, Thomas had enough and resigned. He and Esther did not part on the best of terms. Her final words to him were: "I am an intellectual and you're a socializer."

Murlin Spencer, who had been Associated Press bureau chief in Seattle, replaced Thomas. But he too, couldn't tolerate Esther's interference and he resigned after several months.

Esther didn't want to make another hire. She decided to sell.

Acting on advice Charles had given her many times, she called John McClelland Jr., the publisher of *The Daily News* in Longview to query if he was interested in buying. His family had owned the Longview paper since 1923 when John McClelland Sr. was owner and publisher.

It was the only call Esther would make regarding the sale of the paper. At least one local businessman was interested, but ultimately disappointed when he opened the *Evening News* on Aug. 16, 1971, to read "A local era passes."

It was Esther's final editorial and it ended the 55-year tenure of the Websters and the *Evening News*.

Esther was nearly 68 at the time of the sale. She remained with the newspaper for another five years under the sale agreement. She continued to be listed in the masthead as associate editor, though she had no authority.

She wrote occasional articles, mostly profiles as she had done in the past, though the paper she wrote for was no longer the *Evening News*.

McClelland almost immediately changed the name of the paper to *The Daily News*, the same as his Longview paper.

In the final chapter of Esther's life, she returned more to her painting, reading, gardening and travel.

In 1979, in an interview in *The Daily News* Esther noted that most of the paintings on exhibit at Port Angeles' Peninsula College, were of the Olympic Mountains and most were painted in the past three years.

I went up to the mountains nearly every clear day this summer," she told reporter Virginia Keeting.

It is the most satisfying thing I've ever done — the high clear air, scenery that carries you away, that magnificent frieze of the mountains.

She was diagnosed with breast cancer in 1979. Much as she did in her daily life, this independent woman decided to face the disease on her terms, without undergoing any definitive treatment.

Fine Arts Center

She figured she had about a year to live and immediately set out to explore how best to use her estate to its greatest advantage.

After talking to many people in her circle, she determined that the city was lacking a showcase for fine arts, crafts and their allied creative interests.

This set in motion plans to bequeath her Webster home, a plate-glass and timbered classic of modern Northwest architecture, and five wooded-acres to create the Port Angeles Fine Arts Center.

It took scores of meetings, discussions and numerous revisions before the center would be dedicated.

Prior to her death in 1985, Esther Webster made plans to turn the home she and Charles shared since 1951, into a Fine Arts Center. The building at 1203 E. Lauridsen Blvd., Port Angeles, was dedicated as an art center in 1986. *(Courtesy of the North Olympic History Center)*

Seeing her vision working its way toward reality may have had a positive effect on Esther's health, taking her beyond the one year she figured she had to live.

Esther was 81 when she died on Jan. 25, 1985. Final plans for the arts center and management were completed that December. Renovation of the home began almost immediately.

Grand opening ceremonies were held Nov. 22, 1986, with Frank Ducceschi, editor and publisher of *The Daily News*, master of ceremonies.

The center's gallery and the adjacent Webster's Woods, a "museum without walls," featuring more than 125 outdoor sculptures and quirky art works spread out along rustic trails, are free and open to the public year-round.

Less than a mile away is the Olympic National Park Visitor Center — and just beyond it are the Websters' beloved Olympic Mountains.

CHAPTER 6

A new era, a new name: The McClellands

On Aug. 17, 1971, the *Port Angeles Evening News* was published with someone other than a Webster in charge.

John McClelland Sr. and John McClelland Jr. were co-owners and McClelland Jr., 55, was the new publisher. The corporate owner was Longview Publishing Co. From here on, unless specified, McClelland refers to John McClelland Jr.

One day earlier, Esther Webster, the last surviving member of the newspaper's founding family, wrote her final editorial in the *Evening News*:

John McClelland Jr. became publisher when the Longview Publishing Co. purchased the *Port Angeles Evening News* in 1971. It marked the first time a Webster was not owner in 55 years. He changed the name to *The Daily News* almost immediately and ran the paper until selling it to Persis Corp. in 1984. *(Peninsula Daily News archive)*

It is with conflicting emotions that we announce the impending ownership transfer of the Port Angeles Evening News *from a family which has held it for so many years to new hands. Drastic change brings regret. At the same time, there is deep satisfaction that younger, progressive management will be taking over.*

Because of devotion to the community, and affection for those who live in it, we are happy the new owners will be Washingtonians, long-established and highly respected in newspaper circles throughout the state and nation.

We can recommend to you, without reservation, the McClelland family — John Senior and Junior. We have known them for a quarter of a century and have long admired the Longview Daily News *as a highly professional publication. We have been impressed by their devotion and dedication to their newspaper and their community.*

One can feel the pain that it caused Esther to let go of her "baby," from this editorial. She presents a better impression of what the industry meant to her, even if she didn't always exemplify what is best in a publisher.

Esther continued:

A newspaper is not just a building housing presses, type, cold metal and rolls of paper, which must be filled each day. It becomes a living thing because it reflects the life of the community — its moods and ambitions. It reports the good and the bad. It has potential for consolidating and strengthening or rupturing and weakening a whole area.

To borrow Winston Churchill's oft-reported phrase, 'blood, sweat and tears' actually have gone into the development of the Evening News. *It alone, among all the newspapers which were started in early days of Port Angeles, was able to survive the combination of depression, setbacks and intense competition.*

It is no easy thing to end an association which has been a part of one's daily life over a long span of time.

McClelland's editorial the next day focused on family ownership of newspapers versus corporate chains that were starting to gobble up small dailies nationwide:

"Some chain papers are well operated, but a great deal, we fear are not. A manager is hired and told to make money. If the profit and loss statement look good, it is considered a success, regardless of the quality of the news product itself.

The new publisher McClelland Jr. (he referred to himself in the third person) of the Evening News *is an active editor as well as publisher. In Longview, he writes a page 1 column or editorial comment five days a week. He insists that local news coverage be thorough and accurate.*

All of which is to say that the new owners know the responsibilities and obligation of newspaper ownership from experience and will insist on high standards of service to readers and advertisers in Port Angeles, as they do in Longview.

Furthermore, they confess to being motivated in their resolves to do a good job and earn acceptance … The obligations that go with newspaper ownership will not be neglected. Our hope is to win approval on the basis of performance that is satisfactory to the readers and advertisers of the whole region served by a newspaper with a long and honorable history."

Ned Thomas returns

One of the first actions by the new publisher — who planned to keep his home in Longview — was to hire an editor and associate publisher to direct the newspaper.

Ned Thomas arrived at the *Port Angeles Evening News* in 1967, resigned in April 1971 because he couldn't work with Esther Webster. He was rehired after the paper was sold to John McClelland Jr. in August 1971 and retired as publisher in May 1981. *(Courtesy of the North Olympic History Center/Port Angeles Evening News)*

He turned to a man he knew well and trusted — Ned Thomas, the same man who resigned four months earlier.

Thomas was only too glad to accept the position. He still lived in Port Angeles and had quit because he could no longer tolerate working for Esther Webster.

McClelland also changed the name of the paper to *The Daily News of Port Angeles.*

In making the announcement, McClelland wrote:

Ned Thomas is a man I have known for many years. Once we worked for the same company — the John Scripps organization. I have

129

great respect for his ability and believe that he can take up where he left off a few months ago, with no difficulty.

At the time of the purchase in Port Angeles, the McClelland family had owned the same newspaper for 48 years. They were exactly what Esther wanted — an established family to carry on the Webster traditions.

In addition to Port Angeles and the Longview *Daily News* (which McClelland Sr. had bought in 1923 when he was 39, after moving his family to Washington from Arkansas), the McClellands' Longview Publishing Co. owned several weeklies in the eastern suburbs of Seattle, including the Bellevue *American* (later the daily *Journal-American*) and Longview Cable Co., a major provider of TV services in the Longview-Kelso area.

Other than ownership and corporate decisions, McClelland Sr. was not involved with the Port Angeles paper.

The tall and ruggedly handsome McClelland Jr. was known as a man of impeccable integrity, with a distinguished record as a Navy gunnery officer in World War II.

He graduated from Stanford University in 1937 with a journalism degree. "I don't think there was a time in his life that he didn't want to be a journalist," said his son, John McClelland III (he dislikes the Roman numeral, but says it's needed for clarity, so he puts up with it). McClelland III, 72 when interviewed in 2017, still lives in Longview.

John Jr. married his high school sweetheart, Burdette Craig, in 1939, then returned to Longview to work as editor under his father.

Then, following the attack on Pearl Harbor on Dec. 7, 1941, he enlisted in the Naval Reserve and was assigned to officer training school.

Much of the history of his war years, John III writes in three articles for the Cowlitz County Historical Society, published in March and June 2014, and June 2015 in the *Cowlitz Historical Quarterly*.

His son said being in the war "changed him." He had seen action in the South Pacific at Iwo Jima, then Okinawa, where he came under kamikaze attacks. He toured Hiroshima after it had been destroyed by the atomic bomb.

At one time he served alongside Lt. j.g. Mark Hatfield, later governor, then senator in Oregon.

He returned to Longview by October 1945 and saw his son for the first time. John III was 6 ½ months old.

The war years deprived his dad of "the best years of his life and he was determined to make up for them," his son wrote.

McClelland Jr. returned to work immediately as editor, and two years later, wrested control of Longview Publishing Co., which until that time had been owned by the family of the original company and town founder, R.A. Long.

He was elected president of the prestigious Society of Professional Journalists in 1950. Five years later, he succeeded his father as publisher of *The Daily News*.

In 1971, just before purchasing the Port Angeles *Evening News*, the McClellands opened a new printing plant.

McClelland III said he never aspired to follow in his father's (or grandfather's) footsteps. He graduated from Lewis & Clark College in Portland, Ore., majoring in English. He married in 1969 and realized "writing was all I knew."

In 1972, he worked about a year for *The Daily News* at Port Angeles, then jumped at an opportunity to work for the Albany, Ore., *Democrat-Herald*. He later would work 13 years for *The Daily News* at Longview as a features writer, a job he enjoyed because "it gave me time to hone my skills and no daily deadlines."

John III said his father was a gentleman and a Renaissance Man — "never satisfied with the status quo, always looking ahead while exploring and learning beyond his vocation, a middle-of-the-road conservative, though he supported LBJ in 1964, and, if truth be told, I think he voted for Obama."

As a boss, McClelland III said, his dad "kept his distance, but inspired loyalty of his employees."

Frank Ducceschi was hired by Thomas to be managing editor in 1973. He was 29 at the time and grew to admire McClelland and Thomas.

"He was very news-oriented. He asked me what I wanted to do, and he let me run the news room. It was very encouraging," Ducceschi said in a 2015 interview.

"Ned was cut from the same cloth as John. No question. Both were intelligent and kept up with what was going on in the community. They were involved in the community. Ned wanted the paper to be good. He was supportive with what I thought needed to be done."

Ducceschi was later executive editor, then publisher under three owners: McClelland, Persis and Horvitz, spanning 25 years.

Ducceschi was working as news editor for Nixon Newspapers in Wabash, Ind., when he was hired by Thomas. A graduate of Arizona State University in 1967, Frank had married Joan, his college sweetheart, the year before.

He began his career as editor of a weekly in Sheridan, Ore., then was news editor at the Grants Pass, Ore., *Daily Courier.*

Ducceschi hired

"I flew out and interviewed with Ned Thomas and John McClelland Jr.," Ducceschi remembers. "We had dinner at Aggie's (restaurant in Port Angeles) and they offered me the job.

"On my first day at work, Ned introduced me to the staff as managing editor. Don Paxson had been managing editor, and I think Ned told him of my hire that day. Don was promoted to executive editor, but still answered to me. It could have been a difficult problem if Don hadn't been a gentleman."

Ducceschi outlined several changes that he implemented:

Frank Ducceschi in 1976
(Peninsula Daily News archive

- The newspaper's nameplate said *The Daily News* with a small display line under it that read "of Port Angeles." "I didn't think that was right. We were not just Port Angeles' newspaper, we had a mission to cover the entire county and Jefferson; we changed it to *The Daily News.*

- "We decided that in the newspaper we would refer to our coverage area as the North Olympic Peninsula, a phrase we did not coin, but one we certainly popularized.

- "We had a Women's Page run by Grace Charnell. I told her there wasn't going to be a Women's Page anymore. (Instead of being segregated as 'Women's News' her stories would be used throughout the paper); if she had a story of significance on the library or on the arts or something like that, we'd consider running it on Page 1."
- Improved news coverage from Olympia by sharing a correspondent that represented all Longview Publishing Co.-owned papers;
- *The Daily News* employees were able to participate in an Employee Stock Ownership Program (ESOP). All non-union employees were stockholders in the Longview company.

The pressroom at Port Angeles was unionized, but after seeing what a "positive thing the ESOP was, the pressroom union was decertified," Ducceschi recalled.

"That should give you a feeling for what it was like to work for the McClellands. Even the union members wanted to be part of it."

Other changes included an all-local new front page, a column on Page 1 highlighting inside stories and the addition of another opinion page, featuring local columnists Lena Fletcher of Forks, Patricia Campbell and Phyllis Miletch.

In 1976, the newspaper celebrated 60 years. Thomas, Ducceschi and Paxson engineered a 28-page special edition that featured articles about the Webster and McClelland families.

Northern Tier Oil controversy

One of the biggest stories for *The Daily News* began in 1976 when the Northern Tier Pipeline Co. announced it wanted to build an oil port at Port Angeles to transport Alaska crude across a 1,500-mile pipeline to Minnesota.

This sparked controversy, not only in Port Angeles, but throughout the state and nationally.

The $2.8 billion project hung on for seven years with the support of Ronald Reagan's White House, Puget Sound refineries, the state Oceanographic Committee and even Gov. Dan Evans. The governor pushed hard for an oil port "at or west of" Port Angeles.

It was opposed on the editorial pages of *The Daily News* and by community groups concerned about the impact on the environment and noted that an explosion or fire could place thousands of residents in harm's way.

An editorial by Thomas on Feb. 5, 1976, shortly after the project was announced, was headlined: "Thanks, but no thanks," and noted "There is no practical location west of Port Angeles for an oil port. We are talking only about Port Angeles harbor."

To be fair, Thomas cited the benefits of the project: Single largest construction project on the North Olympic Peninsula; permanent jobs for 75 to 100; additional tax revenue to the city, county, the port and school district, perhaps even eliminating the need for special school levies.

But the risks far outnumbered the benefits, Thomas wrote:

A major spill outside of Port Angeles could ... blacken the south shore of the Strait of Juan de Fuca;

A spill outside the harbor would be a disaster. Most of our economy is centered there — pulp and paper mills, lumber mills, overseas shipping facilities, the Coast Guard air station, the ferry service to Victoria. ... The tourist business, second only to wood products in importance on the Peninsula, could be ruined; the commercial fishing fleet would depart for good.

... So, what are we to do? It's up to us to convince the legislature, Gov. Evans and whoever else is necessary that we are united in opposition.

This issue caught the attention of *The New York Times*. On Jan. 2, 1980, it denounced the pipeline portion of the project in an editorial.

In the end, the decision to build a pipeline will have less to do with energy than with jobs and profits. But even if these political considerations were compelling, there is no strong reason to prefer the Northern Tier Route.

The response did trigger an avalanche of letters to the editor on both sides of the issue.

In its news pages, *The Daily News* did a thorough job of covering the Northern Tier, Ducceschi noted, singling out the balanced news stories done by reporter Lyn Watts.

Watts always interviewed supporters and opponents of the project. "There was nothing the people on the Peninsula didn't know about this issue."

On April 21, 1983, *The Daily News* story headlined: "Oil port foes claim victory in Northern Tier decision" noted that Gov. John Spellman had announced he was rejecting Northern Tier's application to build the pipeline.

Lyn Watts in 1976 *(Peninsula Daily News archive)*

Spellman said a pipeline capable of carrying nearly a million barrels of oil a day through an area with a history of earthquakes that could liquefy soils in seconds would be a "very real threat to Puget Sound, which in my mind is a national treasure."

Nobody was happier with the news than Norma Turner, wife of respected Port Angeles physician, Dr. Eugene Turner. She founded and promoted the grass-roots group No Oilport, Inc., of which she was president.

"Yeah, that's my bottom line," she said, grinning and glowing. "Now, the community can work together for a real future."

"A seven-year battle is over," said Port Angeles Mayor Dorothy Duncan. "It's taken a tremendous amount of our time, resources and energy. Now, we can move on to more positive things."

Not everybody was happy with the decision. "A lot of guys were just holding on, assuming things would get better in the future," said Scott Hopper, a Port Angeles developer, who founded the pro-oil group, "Stand Up."

The Northern Tier coverage won *The Daily News* a first-place award from the Pacific Northwest Newspaper Association.

Commissioners' recall

Northern Tier wasn't the only big story for the paper in 1976. On Feb. 26, 1976, Clallam County voters went to the polls and, for the first time in the county's history, voted to recall two county commissioners, while retaining a third after allegations of misconduct including illegal closed-door meetings and ethics violations.

Ousted were D.J. Caulkins and Bill Knapman. Voters elected to retain Frank Feeley.

Thomas wrote an editorial after the vote, pointing out the lessons learned from the recall:

- *You don't fire the county planning commission simply because you don't agree with its recommendations;*
- *You don't seek legal advice on official county business from outside and unnamed lawyers, bypassing the duly elected prosecuting attorney;*
- *You don't hire an architect to design a courthouse in an open-air impromptu meeting and without even knowing where you're going to build it;*
- *You don't openly criticize unpaid members of appointed boards and commissions, and you certainly don't give orders to agree with you or else.*

1979 was momentous for the North Olympic Peninsula. One disaster after another struck the area.

First, on Feb. 13, winds estimated at 120 mph struck the Hood Canal Bridge, sending the western draw-span and western pontoons into the water.

The Daily News provided extensive coverage of the disaster that cut off the Olympic Peninsula from the Kitsap Peninsula and the Puget Sound. Later, the newspaper wrote about the ferries necessary to carry cars and passengers across the canal and an attempt to add a toll to pay for the bridge's reconstruction.

Originally, officials

One of the most devastating events to hit the North Olympic Peninsula occurred on Feb. 13, 1979, when the area was struck with 120 mph-plus winds, sending the western portion of the Hood Canal bridge into the water. It paralyzed traffic into and out of the peninsula for nearly three years. *(Tom Thompson/Peninsula Daily News)*

expected the bridge to be repaired "sometime in 1980," but that didn't occur until late 1982.

Editorials in *The Daily News* and coverage of protests by angry peninsula residents helped abort the plans for a toll.

Boldt Decision divisive

Second, the U.S. Supreme Court in July upheld federal Judge George Boldt's historic 1974 ruling reaffirming the rights, under a treaty signed in 1855, of Washington's Indian tribes to fish in "usual and accustomed grounds and stations."

The Boldt Decision also allocated 50 percent of the annual catch to treaty tribes, which enraged other fishermen.

It was a split decision for those on the peninsula, and *The Daily News* covered it thoroughly. Commercial fishermen were disappointed, members of tribal councils were delighted, and the state Department of Fisheries said, "It's not as bad as we first thought."

McClelland, who rarely wrote an editorial, did so on July 10, 1979, citing "absence of clarity" as a flaw in the Boldt Decision:

It wasn't so much what the treaty's words, written in 1855, actually said, it's what today's judges imagine the treaty would have said, had it been written with more clarity, or if the writers had been able to foresee the future.

A third disaster struck when seemingly endless flooding and mudslides took a heavy toll from Dec. 13-23.

Hardest hit was the Dungeness area, 20 miles east of Port Angeles, where the Dungeness River overflowed its banks and threatened homes in the Dungeness Meadows, forcing homeowners to evacuate. Three homes fell into the swollen river.

Damage estimates reached $2.1 million.

John McClelland Jr. 1976
(Peninsula Daily News archive)

As the decade of the 1970s ended, Thomas wrote that Sequim had become one of the state's most attractive retirement spots.

By the 1990s, Sequim was on the annual "best places to retire" list and has seldom fallen off the list since.

On the West End, population estimates showed Forks was the fastest-growing Clallam County city, and at Neah Bay a new cultural center/museum opened.

In Port Angeles, Thomas wrote that the city had undergone changes, too:

"Ediz Hook, which was in danger of being breached, has been buttressed with armor rock. The school system has had a complete rebuild, and with it, a conversion from the junior high to middle-school system. And the chain stores have not discovered us, yet new shopping centers have emerged.

"Maybe we can catch our breath in the next decade. ..."

Mount St. Helens blows

Little did they know those events would pale in comparison to what was coming in 1980.

On Sunday morning, May 18, 1980, Mount St. Helens blew. The volcano's blast was felt in Port Angeles, 145 miles to the north.

In *My Reaction*, Thomas related his experiences:

... I had gotten up and was brushing my teeth when the first thud came. It felt like something pretty solid had hit the house. We looked out and could see nothing. I figured the Canadian Navy might be having gunnery practice.

When I walked out to the road to get the morning paper, another blast shook the house and rattled windows. It came from the direction of a nearby gun club, and I wondered if they were trying out a howitzer.

A telephone call from Frank Ducceschi, our managing editor, solved the mystery. Permission to charter a plane. Granted. Permission to go up four pages on Monday if stories and photographers could be produced in time. Granted.

The mountain's timing couldn't have been worse for newspapers, or better for television. There's no such thing as a Sunday afternoon newspaper. Our paper wouldn't get its first crack at the story until Monday afternoon, almost 30 hours after the eruption.

Ducceschi, in a 2015 interview, offered a blow-by-blow description involved in producing Monday afternoon's paper:

"I told Ned that we needed to get the color separations from Longview, which was very close to Mount St. Helens. We knew we wanted to get color photos in our paper. Bellevue wanted the negative plates too. Somebody had to go. I couldn't ask a reporter to fly into a volcano. So, I chartered a plane and a pilot to fly us to Longview to pick up the plates. The pilot's name was Mike Pancake. What a name for a pilot!

"We still had to fly to Bellevue, our sister paper, and give the *Journal-American* the color separations. There was a little airport there and we prepared to land, but there was a guy with a car and lights on the runway waving his hands to signal us that the runway was closed. We decided to fly to Boeing Field (in Seattle) and land.

"Someone from the *Journal-American* drove from Bellevue to pick up the color separations and then we flew back to Port Angeles."

Monday's paper featured full-color photos in a 4-page pullout. *The Daily News* later sold a 12-page special edition for $1.50 that Longview had produced. A cloud of ash, rocks and super-heated gas from the eruption killed 57 people. Ash fell as far away as Minnesota.

Accompanying stories on the blast in the next few days included one each by *The Daily News'* features writers Jim Guthrie and Sheridan Fahnestock.

Sheridan Fahnestock in 1976 *(Peninsula Daily News archive)*

Guthrie interviewed Archie and Thelma Helgeson from Port Angeles who had been camping at White Pass, only 20 miles from the blast zone. They were "ashed-in" until finally being able to drive out on Tuesday, two days after the eruption.

Both suffered from pulmonary problems, but as Thelma said, "Archie used his head and we stayed inside our camper most of the time." She said they spent time visiting with the 250 other campers who had to stay put.

"First, we heard the blast," said Archie, retired from ITT Rayonier and a PA resident

since 1928. "That's what we know now. It sounded like thunder, first one big clap, then some more. Then it started hailing. I reached my hand outside the window and got a handful of warm pebbles. Then I knew it was the mountain. They were too warm for hail."

Fahnestock took a different approach, meeting with Ron Crawford, a Peninsula College physics and physical science instructor, who had a special interest in Mount St. Helens. He calculated that the sound of the eruption took at least 12 minutes to reach the North Olympic Peninsula. The blast occurred at 8:32 a.m. and was first recorded in Port Angeles at 8:51, Crawford said.

In Port Angeles, some residents dashed up to Hurricane Ridge to see if the volcano or ash was visible from there. After hours of waiting, when the cloud cover slid off, they could see the ash plume as it headed east.

Meantime, *The Daily News* in Longview was in the process of producing more than 400 articles during the next month, a project that ultimately would earn it a Pulitzer Prize for comprehensive coverage. One of its photographers, Roger Werth, was specifically cited for his spectacular photos, one of which appeared on the cover of *Time* magazine.

Then, Mount St. Helens erupted a second time at 7:05 p.m. on Saturday, June 12, 1980.

Not a single staff member from *The Daily News* was on the Olympic Peninsula.

"The entire staff (and their spouses) were in Seattle at the annual Sigma Delta Chi meeting to collect awards for the paper's coverage of the collapse of the Hood Canal Bridge and, also the disastrous floods of December," Ducceschi said.

Ducceschi said the staff met early the next morning after he received word that the volcano had erupted.

"I called Bob Gaston, Longview's editor, to see if he needed any help and he said he could use another reporter, so I sent him Sheridan Fahnestock," recalled Ducceschi.

"It was scary for him to be so near the danger zone and with his wife here. But, it worked out for him. He participated in the paper's Pulitzer Prize coverage and was honored, like all of the Longview news staff."

The ash had barely settled when *The Daily News* produced a 92-page

Visitor's Guide in June. It included all the sites to visit and recreational opportunities in both Clallam and Jefferson counties.

Ducceschi becomes publisher

In July 1980, McClelland promoted Ducceschi, 37, to editor and associate publisher after eight years as managing editor. Thomas, who was 74, remained publisher. "I think John knew Thomas was ready to retire," theorized Ducceschi.

On May 15, 1981, Thomas announced his plan to retire, ending 14 years as the newspaper's chief executive. Ducceschi was the obvious choice to move up, but not everybody saw it that way.

John Brewer, Associated Press bureau chief in Seattle at the time, a long-time friend of Ducceschi and, who would be *PDN* publisher from 1998-2015, was present at the announcement. He recalls the drama surrounding it.

"The betting at the newspaper was between Erland 'Erl' Hansen and Frank (Ducceschi) with some thinking Erl would get it. I knew Frank for many years and I had enormous respect for him. I had no doubt he was going to be named the publisher."

When Thomas announced Ducceschi would be the next publisher, "Hansen was crest-fallen," Brewer said. Hansen later left the newspaper and became executive director of the Port Angeles Chamber of Commerce.

"We later became friends. He was a great bird-hunter and when he retired from the chamber in 2000, those of us who were on the chamber board went together and bought him a hunting dog. He was stunned."

In his retirement column, a portion appearing in *My Reaction*, Thomas wrote:

I enjoyed my time at The Daily News *under John McClelland. I did write some strong-worded editorials criticizing county commissioners and the state's efforts to foist off an oil port on the town (and an unfounded bridge toll), but that spark that goes with ownership was missing. We did grow in those 14 years, though. Circulation went from around 8,000 to 13,000 and the average number of pages rose from 10 to 24.*

The Daily News published a full-page tribute to Thomas on May 15, 1981.

Fahnestock, who was hired by Ducceschi in 1974, wrote:

… To a large extent, he (Thomas) is the architect of the newspaper since the late 1960s: building a new office and plant, a professional staff and a reputation for fearless reporting.

The date he chose for his retirement is his 74th birthday. However, the date of May 2, 1981, may have served better as the capper on an illustrious career. It was two weeks ago that fellow newsmen from throughout Western Washington bestowed on him the Sigma Delta Chi Distinguished Service Award for his life-long contribution to journalism."

Ducceschi and Paxson expressed the respect they had for their boss.

"He is a good person. Never, ever that I can recall, has he been critical of people in front of the staff," wrote Ducceschi. "He does not criticize people; even in discussions of a political nature; he is not disparaging of people; if he does really dislike anybody in the community, which I'm unaware of, he's kept it to himself."

Paxson noted: "It was under Ned, we began to get better pay. There was more an attitude of a working newspaper, and difference in the way news was handled."

Ned and his wife Toodie soon left for a spot where they often vacationed: Green Valley, Ariz. He enjoyed another 23 years in retirement there. In 1994, he published *My Reaction*, which included many of his writings from *The Daily News* and *Columbia Basin Herald*. He died at age 97, on July 5, 2004, and is inurned next to Toodie on a picturesque hillside overlooking Moses Lake.

Soon after Ducceschi was hired in 1973, he was given authority to strengthen his staff.

Today, long after retiring as publisher, he still sings praises of reporters, editors and executives he hired:

Dave Jacobsen, circulation director. "He's the best in that department. He was terrific in following through and had a great staff that liked to work for him. I never worried about him; he was never afraid to try new ideas, not hung up on contests, but stressed building circulation."

He was Brewer's circulation director for seven years.

"I found him to be honest and fair," said Brewer. "He was very creative with promotions. Dave was here during the time of highest circulation. That was 2005; it was 19,500, the highest it's ever been."

Jacobsen left Port Angeles in 2005 and moved to Everett, 30 miles north of Seattle, where he worked from home for Brainworks Software of Sayville, N.Y., as a specialist in newspaper circulation tracking systems.

Jan (Anderson) St. Laurent, news editor. "A news editor you want to have. Hired in 1974 as city editor, she recognized a news story immediately; bright, with ability to match the right reporter with the story that needed to be written; she was a good technical editor, very honest and thorough."

Sheridan Fahnestock and Jim Guthrie were hired when Ducceschi decided to add features columnists.

"Sheridan came from the East Coast and was a great writer. He had a background in history and politics and used it in his columns. He later became an editorial writer. I don't know how we got so lucky. He had worked with the *New York Post* and somehow got to Bend (Oregon). That's where we got him from."

Fahnestock retired in 1986.

"Jim was different, and we needed someone to write about the arts, and, also to write with humor. He did that, and he did it well. He was another writer with a lot of experience."

Guthrie wrote "Below Olympus," a weekly column until March 28, 2001, when he retired. In recent years he's directed numerous community theater productions in Port Angeles.

Kathy Wahto, business manager. "She was in the business office and I moved her from accounting to manager. She was smart and wanted to know all aspects of the paper, so she worked for two weeks as a reporter. She learned to respect that job."

Wahto left the news business and became director of Serenity House, an organization dedicated to finding shelter and food for the homeless and the poor.

Helene Phifer, accounting. "She could do anything, a tough cookie, who could be hard to deal with at times, but always supportive of the paper. Wahto was the 20th century version of Helene."

Phifer came to the *Evening News* in 1955 and served as controller until retiring in 1975. She then moved to Renton and died there on July 15, 2005, at 94.

Tom Thompson, chief photographer. "Tom started for us in 1974. He was at the AP, but not being used very well and was looking to move. We used photos much better after he got here. Tom also thought he would be a better photographer, if he could also be a reporter, so he took journalism classes at the college."

John Brewer was Thompson's boss the final nine years of his career.

"In addition to Tom being an outstanding photographer, he wasn't afraid of difficult community situations," said Brewer in a 2015 interview.

"I remember one time some members of the Quileute tribe came to see me. They were upset over some articles we wrote about illegal elk hunting. I wasn't available, so Thompson talked to them. They left

Tom Thompson, hired by Frank Ducceschi in 1974, was chief photographer for the *PDN* for 33 years, retiring in 2007. He died in 2012. *(Keith Thorpe/Peninsula Daily News)*

laughing, shook hands and were satisfied. "He had a great calming ability."

Tom retired in 2007 as chief photographer for *PDN* after 33 years and many award-winning photos.

He started a second career, establishing Clear Horizon, LLC, a general contracting company. Thompson, 64, suffered an aneurysm and died on Nov. 28, 2012. "Kindness and respect, a devoted family man, husband, father and grandfather" were the words echoed by family members about Tom, whose obituary in the *PDN* on Dec. 5, 2012, covered more than a half-page.

Keith Thorpe, now chief photographer. Thorpe was one of Ducceschi's last hires, starting at *The Daily News* on election night (November) in 1996. He was still snapping away in 2018.

In an interview in 2017, Thorpe said he found Port Angeles "a great place to live. Photography is a dying breed. The last two decades, the big change has been to the web. I now work with video and post photos online. It's been a learning curve."

Brewer said Thorpe is a great photographer. "We were lucky to have him and Tom (Thompson) for so long. Keith was really good on sports events, especially in low-light situations like Friday night football games. He is also an outstanding guy.

"Now, we only have him. Reporters often take their own pictures," Brewer related a year before retiring. "Some don't have the eye, but they do the best they can."

John Huston, advertising director. "I hired John in 1986 and he was here until 1998. He was very personable; he was a great team leader and directed a staff that worked hard and produced new accounts. When he left, he looked at his stock ownership balance and cashed it in."

After trying general contractor and other jobs, Huston went to work as ad director for the weekly *Sequim Gazette*. Now retired, he lives in Arizona and frequently visits Port Angeles.

Keith Mathis, production manager. "He wanted to be up to date with the latest equipment. Keith headed both production and composing departments. He was a great team leader and had help from the newspaper's IT manager Jay Cline, who was more into computers."

Virginia Keeting, reporter, photographer. "She took Grace Charnell's position after she left." She began writing a column under Esther Webster in 1956 and immediately won state Women's Press awards. In 1961, Esther Webster wrote an article about her, and in 1979, she wrote about Esther's art exhibit.

George Erb, reporter. "He was very solid and very bright, and it was noticeable in his writing. George really, really loved journalism. You could assign him a story and never worry. He needed very little editorial help. He was a terrific business writer."

George and his partner Mavis Amundson (another *Daily News* alum and author of several North Olympic Peninsula history books including *The Lady of the Lake, The Great Forks Fire and Sturdy Folk*) now live in Bellevue, across Lake Washington from Seattle.

After the *PDN*, he went to work for the *Puget Sound Business Journal* in Seattle, then became a journalism instructor at Western Washington University in Bellingham.

Erb also is a freelance writer, and in 2015, wrote a series of articles on the spotted owl controversy, published on the 25th anniversary of that historic event that changed the face of timber towns in the Northwest.

Campbell's history series

In 1974, Ducceschi asked local author and historian Patricia Campbell to write a special series — *History of the North Olympic Peninsula* — for the U.S. Bicentennial.

"I commissioned her to do that with the idea that each chapter would be like a book and would be published on Sundays throughout the year," Ducceschi said.

"But I told her we had to have the entire series written before we started running them. She wasn't too happy about that, but I told her: 'If you got hit by a truck or something, it needed to be done ahead of time. We can't start a series and stop in the middle.'"

The first installment "Indians Here for Centuries," appeared on Jan. 4, 1976, and kicked off the series, which ran, as designed each Sunday throughout the Bicentennial year.

"Sadly," Ducceschi said, "she got hit by a car and was killed (on Sept. 14, 1976) when she was crossing the street near the library. It was a terrible experience for all, but especially for me, personally. I had to not only live with the memory of my attempt at using humor to enforce a deadline, but since she had no relatives here, I had to identify her body." She was 74.

Phyllis Miletich wrote a "To Life" column for 25 years in Port Angeles. *(Peninsula Daily News archive)*

He also hired Phyllis Miletich to the column lineup. Phyllis and her husband, Fred, a seasonal Olympic National Park ranger, moved from Seattle to Port Angeles in 1976. They previously had spent summers at Lake Crescent, one of Olympic National Park's jewels, west of Port Angeles.

Her column was called "To Life" and featured witty comments on life situations.

One example appeared on Dec. 7, 1997:

"There ought to be a massive movement afoot to move Thanksgiving to June and leave Christmas where it is.

Why not? Not even a forensic scientist could prove that a bunch of frozen Pilgrims really sat down to turkey dinner on the exact last Thursday of November, so why not change it?"

Lena Fletcher, daughter of John Huelsdonk, the legendary "Iron Man of the Hoh," wrote columns about the West End of the peninsula. *(Peninsula Daily News archive)*

From Aug. 29, 1999:

"The truth is that diets are depressing because they take away just one more thing that you used to look forward to. Mealtimes become a routine of tolerable, dull, duty-food that you shove in with as much gusto as you feel while eating a horse blanket."

Miletich wrote for 25 years for the paper before retiring in 2001. She died on Sept. 16, 2003, at 79.

Another column addition was Lena Huelsdonk Fletcher, the first Caucasian child born in the wet, wild Hoh River Valley. She had written sporadically for the *Evening News* and the *Forks Forum*, offering a glimpse of life on Clallam County's West End.

She was 81 when hired as a columnist in 1975. In her "Stump Ranch" columns she often wrote about her father, John Huelsdonk, a legend known as "The Iron Man of the Hoh." She also took liberal shots at "ineffective government."

Lena wasn't the only member of her family to pick up the pen (or typewriter). Not nearly as prolific a writer as her sister, Elizabeth "Bettine" Huelsdonk Fletcher, at 82, turned author in 1979, writing about her legendary father in *The Iron Man of Hoh, the Man, not the Myth.*

Several other columnists — including a poet — made their way to the pages of *The Daily News* in Ducceschi's tenure.

"It was something I thought I would never do," said the publisher, "but we added Neva Whitfield's poetry column and it was very popular."

Ducceschi talked briefly about his relationship with Esther Webster, who held the nominal title of associate editor, when he was hired by Ned Thomas in 1973.

In the sales agreement with the McClellands she retained an affiliation with the newspaper for five years. She contributed feature articles.

147

"I didn't have much to do with her, but I would get calls almost daily from Esther. She talked on and on about something we did right or didn't do. I didn't know how to react," said Ducceschi. "I asked Ned what to do about it and he told me, 'Ignore it.'"

Intern's 'Summer to Remember'

The summer of 1981 was a memorable one for news, but even more so for a young intern at *The Daily News* from Western Washington University. Fred Obee received quick on-the-job training that would set him in good stead when he continued his career at the *Port Townsend Leader* in

Fred Obee was an intern for *The Daily News* in 1981 when he had a "summer to remember." *(Courtesy of Fred Obee)*

Scooter Chapman, shown in 1976, was *The Daily News* sports editor in 1981. *(Peninsula Daily News archive)*

1994. He worked 21 years for the *Leader* — the last 12 as general manager — before retiring in 2015.

It all begin in that "summer to remember" in Port Angeles. In less than three months, Obee wrote about a major spy caught, a murder trial after a killing at a bar and a salmon derby in which the winning fish was frozen, then disqualified.

Obee was the reporter on a Saturday night, Aug. 14, 1981, when he started hearing from law enforcement sources that Christopher Boyce, No. 1 on the FBI's Most-Wanted list, was apprehended in Port Angeles the night before.

"I started hearing that the marshals had arrested him at the Pit-Stop drive-in," Obee recalled as if it were yesterday. "But the marshals weren't saying diddly squat. I later found out that the FBI had been tracking him and his associate since Boyce had escaped from a prison at Lompoc, Calif., a year before.

Boyce had been serving a life sentence after being convicted of selling information to the Russians. When he was arrested in 1977, he had top-secret microfilm on him. He was sentenced to 40 years. He escaped in January 1980 and was believed to be on the North Olympic Peninsula for about three months.

Acting on a tip, Clallam County Sheriff's Office assisted federal marshals in apprehending Boyce, who was using the alias Sean Hennessey in Port Angeles.

Boyce, 27, was tried and convicted, sentenced to three years for his escape and 25 years for bank robbery, conspiracy and breaking federal gun laws.

His story later became the subject of Robert Lindsey's best-selling 1979 book *The Falcon and the Snowman: A True Story of Friendship and Espionage.*

The book was turned into a film by the same title, starring Timothy Hutton as Boyce and Sean Penn as Daulton Lee, an accomplice.

Over the next three days, the paper would publish nine stories on the case, three by Obee alone and three in which he shared the byline with Fahnestock.

The readers would learn that Boyce bought a fishing boat and had it moored at La Push, nearly 70 miles west of Port Angeles; he had taken flying lessons at the Port Angeles airport; he had been living a double life, using another alias, Anthony Lester.

"Exciting stuff for an intern," Obee said. "It was a national story. Everybody had it and it just dropped in my lap."

The second story involved a fatal shooting in a tavern in December 1980. The murder trial began in August 1981.

"It was the shooting at Goldie's Tavern by a rival motorcycle gang, the Ghost Riders," Obee said. "Walter Hatch was the lead reporter, but he was going on vacation, so the coverage of the trial's opening fell on my watch."

Recapping the tragedy, Obee said, "A guy walked into Goldie's in downtown Port Angeles and opened fire, killing a man. It was like a Wild West shootout."

Vernon Hultenschmidt, a former Port Angeles chapter president of the Ghost Riders, was shot and killed on Dec. 14 as he celebrated with other bikers the just-concluded "Toys for Tots" fundraiser.

Officers called it a "contract killing" and arrested two men from

Eastern Washington, Jeff Heath, 31, of East Wenatchee on the murder charge and also took into custody Kenneth Solomon, 25, of Nespalem, as a material witness.

Solomon, known as "Monkey," had been acquitted of murder in an earlier trial that Hatch had covered.

Obee was handed the story as the Heath trial began. After lengthy testimony by a several witnesses, Heath was acquitted. "It had too many holes," said one juror, noting that no witness could make a positive identification. Another juror said the "state's case was rambling and disjointed. It didn't add up."

Heath wasn't released. He remained in the Clallam County Jail, awaiting transfer to Chelan County to stand trial for killing a man at a party in Wenatchee in 1980. He was later convicted of first-degree murder.

Obee was busy almost simultaneously with a third blockbuster, the annual $50,000 Salmon Derby in which the winner received an 18-foot sport fishing boat, valued at $8,000.

His "nose for news" paid dividends while, on the morning visit to the fire department, he discovered a fishy story, almost too bizarre to be true.

"I heard one of the guys saying they didn't think the winning fish was fresh," Obee revealed. "I went to check it out and when I got there, a fish biologist was already there. Turns out the guy entered a frozen fish and that's a fraud, a felony."

Not only was the declared winner a fraud, but his wife and another man in the boat also turned in spurious fish. They were the top three weighed in.

Obee provided a fresh and eye-opening lead to the story, headlined: "Protest hits fish leaders" with a second deck: "Salmon Club members claim fish not fresh"

A week later the three perpetrators were arrested in Centralia and charged with fraud.

The derby celebrated its 71st year in 2018.

The Buccaneer

In 1983, a small — yet important — newspaper on the North Olympic Peninsula began to spread its wings.

The *Buccaneer*, the newspaper produced by communications students at Peninsula College in Port Angeles, had its first full-time advisor in its 22-year history.

"I was the first advisor who was full time on campus," said Robbie Mantooth in a 2018 interview. After serving as public information officer for the Port Angeles School District, she was offered the advisor position with the college's communications department, which included oversight of the student-produced college newspaper.

English instructor Marge Avalon was the *Buccaneer's* first advisor, according to Rick Ross, later the newspaper's advisor and in 2018 associate dean for athletics and student programs at Peninsula College. He also was a sports reporter for the fledgling Northwest Cable News under Dennis Bragg.

The paper was started in 1961, concurrent with the founding of the college. Avalon served as advisor until 1965.

Then, according to a listing Ross provided, followed: David Daheim (1965-1969); Jack Estes (1969-1970); Earl Clark, former managing editor at the *Port Angeles Evening News*, (1970-1979); Jervis "Jerry" Russell, also former *Evening News* editor (1979-1983); Mantooth (1983-1998); Ross (1998-2000) and Rich Riski, former *PDN* photographer, who started with Mantooth in 1993, then was with Ross for three years and in 2018 was in his 18th year as advisor.

It was under Mantooth that the paper began to flourish, garnering numerous (she counted more than 100) regional and national awards, not counting individual honors.

She said the students wanted to change the name to the *Peninsula Sun* and get away from the pirate theme (the college's mascot). It didn't last long — two issues. "The community and the some of the school's founders were irate," said Mantooth. "They wanted to keep the pirate theme." Two issues later the paper was back to the *Buccaneer* and it has remained that way.

Since Mantooth was PIO for the school district when hired, she was asked by then-college president Paul Cornaby if she would censor the students. "I said 'No, I will teach them.'"

The school was just starting to use computers, but the journalism department didn't have them. "I remember 80s by Tandy, but everybody called them 'Trash 80s.'" Prior to that, she said the procedure was for students to produce hand-written stories and the copy was taken to the *PDN*, where the ladies deciphered the writing and entered them into a computer.

She set up a structure for editors and those with experience to instruct the students who had little or no experience.

An important cog in the newspaper's history was the "Webster Trust," a $500,000 scholarship endowment set up by Esther Webster that stipulated the newspaper had to be first class and remain that way.

"Esther had some misgivings that the paper was first class, so she sat in on some of my classes," said Mantooth. "Her reservations were eliminated."

If the paper did not remain first class, then the scholarship would go to Reed College in Portland, Ore., where Esther's husband and former *Evening News* publisher Charles Webster attended.

"They would challenge us," revealed Mantooth. "I wanted to be sure the paper was first class, so I connected with the Washington Newspaper Publishers Association for their advice. Tom Koenninger (then publisher of the *Vancouver Columbian*, and at the time WNPA president) came up and spent a couple of days with us, attending classes and watching us produce the paper. He said we were indeed first class."

Mantooth said Dr. Cornaby tired of Reed's challenges and agreed to pay them from the scholarship money if they would never again challenge the *Buccaneer*. That ended Reed's attempt to get the scholarships.

She said one of her greatest joys was attending the national awards ceremonies for community colleges and seeing the *Buccaneer* earn trophies, but she wanted the students to live that reality as well.

"I started using some of the scholarship money for the students to attend those ceremonies. It meant so much to them," said Mantooth.

"I can't recall a year (during Mantooth's advisory) or since that the paper didn't earn major awards," said Ross.

Mantooth, 78, and working on her memoirs at the time of the interview, said she consistently saw that students were not aware of the large selection of jobs available in the communications industry, "so I started a class called Careers in Communications. It was very popular. After I stopped teaching, Ann Brewer (wife of *PDN* publisher John Brewer), took it over."

One measure of a newspaper's success is awards, another is the large list of students who went on to excel in the industry.

Among those early graduates was Kevin Jackson, who decided to pursue a job in sports communications through ESPN, then in its infancy. Now, nearly 40 years later, he is still with the largest sports communication business in the world, in charge of hiring.

Another of the early graduates to join ESPN was Lyle Crouse, who is now with the National Basketball Association's administration department.

A few more, but certainly not all, include Lynn Nowak, whose father was among the founders of Peninsula College. She went on to be an award-winning reporter with the *Port Townsend and Jefferson County Leader*; Mark Morey started as a reporter at the *PDN*, then moved on to more than 15 years with the *Yakima Herald-Republic*; Renee Treider became an editor at the *Omak Chronicle*; Laura Campbell became a writer for Costco's house organ; and Lee Reynolds is a graphic designer in Seattle.

Like most college newspapers when the students decide to push the envelope with what they printed, faculty and the community objected.

But Mantooth said it was part of the learning experience. "We adhered to the Poynter Institute's ethics policy," she said. When issues arose, "We would bounce the ideas off each other. We taught them to be responsible for what they wrote."

Upgrade for computers

Meanwhile, McClelland added a new front-end computer system to improve production at *The Daily News*. It involved building a new room for the computers. "I remember the core memory of the entire system was about 128K," Ducceschi recalled. "I have more than that on my (cell) phone." Don Paxson's last day was April 13, 1984. There would be no more droll-and-wisecracky "Captain Clallam," "Juan de Fuca Jr." or "On the Waterfront" columns. They were retired with him.

On the morning of his last day covering the county courthouse,

Superior Court Judge Gary Velie rapped the gavel and said, "We have a special occasion here today" and had Paxson hauled before him by the bailiff. The judge then read a proclamation and injunction:

"Know ye all men by these presents:

That Don Paxson has faithfully and dutifully reported the news of this *community for 30 years and one day while employed by* The Daily News. *While on the courthouse beat, he has been especially sensitive to the, sometimes conflicting requirements of full and prompt public notice of events and rights of the defendant to trial by jury that is unbiased by prior publicity.*

Don Paxson, *Port Angeles Evening News* **managing editor, executive editor and court reporter for 30 years, retired in 1994.** *(Peninsula Daily News archive, 1976)*

Virginia Keeting worked for more than 20 years for the Port Angeles papers. She wrote Paxson's obituary. *(Peninsula Daily News archive, 1976)*

"The court having considered Don's many years of employment, his lovely wife, Doty, his attainment of that age known as 'retirement' and all the fish to be caught, docks to be walked and coffee to be drunk, it is hereby ordered, adjudged and decreed that Don Paxson is hereby enjoined and prohibited from any further reporting of court proceedings and shall forthwith cease his use of paper and pencil in this court. He shall be allowed to fully enjoy his retirement and the many golden years ahead."

Done in open court, this day, April 13, 1984."

After retiring, fishing became Paxson's full-time job. But he found time to co-edit *Strait History*, a quarterly publication of the Clallam County Historical Society, of which he was a board member.

He suffered a fatal heart attack on Oct. 4, 1985.

Virginia Keeting, a reporter with *The Daily News*, wrote of Paxson in his obituary, calling him "Chief. Enduring patience is the way I think of him," said Keeting, who retired in 1976 after 20 years with the paper. "He would take a green beginner and make him into a writer."

In the same paper, Ducceschi's editorial "Community loses good man and good small-town journalist" paid tribute to his good friend and employee.

Paxson's death was too early. But those in the news profession who knew him could not be entirely surprised. The heart of his which gave out Thursday had been working overtime for years. Paxson put more heart into his work than any employer has a right to expect. He loved his profession and his community. That is what he worked for. He came to the office early and stayed late.

Tragedy and deaths

1985 was one of turmoil, tragedy and saying goodbye to longtime friends and employees.

It started on Jan. 27 with the death of Esther Webster. She died at home at 81, following a lengthy struggle with breast cancer.

Two weeks later, on Feb. 12, Lena Huelsdonk Fletcher died at Forks Community Hospital. She was 91.

On Nov. 5, 1985, former *Evening News* co-owner John Schweitzer died at 90. He spent more than a half-century with Olympic Peninsula newspapers before retiring in the mid-1970s.

And, there was one other obit to note. The death of the *Sequim Press*, which started publishing in 1911. Bob Jones purchased the newspaper in December 1984; in January, he wrote an editorial about big changes he had planned. On May 22, 1985, the *Press* published its final edition. One less newspaper competing for the advertisers' dollars.

Oil spill in the Harbor

On the afternoon of Dec. 21, 1985, the double-hulled, 126,226-ton tanker, *Arco Anchorage*, carrying 814,000 gallons of Alaskan crude oil, entered Port Angeles Harbor and struck rocks about 800 yards north of the former Rayonier pulp mill.

Oil began leaking through two long gashes in the ship and spread throughout the harbor in an almost clockwise direction — coating beaches, logs and wildlife. The slick eventually spread east and west for miles in the Strait of Juan de Fuca, to Dungeness Bay and Neah Bay.

The crew stemmed the leak about four hours later by transferring some of the oil to another tanker.

But the damage had been done. A total of 239,000 gallons of oil escaped, making it the eighth-largest spill in the state's history.

Thousands of birds lay lifeless, covered in oil. More than 4,000 waterfowl perished, an unknown number of harbor seals, shellfish, salmon and otters also died.

For several days, *The Daily News* staff produced up to five articles daily.

New laws on spill prevention and response have been enacted, making Washington one of the most prepared states in the nation.

*   *   *

In the spring of 1986, John McClelland Jr. suffered a stroke, which his son attributed to "tension after hiring an inept managing editor (for the Bellevue paper) who alienated the staff."

When McClelland recovered, he decided to sell all his properties, including the parent Longview Publishing Co.

In an interview with *The Daily News* on March 2, 1986, McClelland said the "decision to sell was made for estate reasons. At 70, it's time. Who wants to be working like that to their dying day?"

Most of the Longview Publishing Co., including *The Daily News* in Port Angeles, were sold to Persis Corp., owner of the Honolulu *Advertiser* and other real estate holdings. *The Daily News* in Longview remained in the McClelland family.

Throughout a career that spanned nearly 50 years, McClelland became the "most respected publisher in the state," said his longtime friend and colleague, Wilfred Woods, publisher of the *Wenatchee World*.

Ducceschi remembers a business conference he had in McClelland's office.

"It was before I was publisher, at a time when there was a newsprint shortage because the mills were on strike," Ducceschi said. "One of the young up-and-comers suggested we ask staffers to work four-day weeks, and we pay them 80 percent to keep profits up and still fill the reduced news space.

"There was a kind of a silence, while he waited for a pat on the head. Then McClelland said, 'We don't do that to our people.' He put people above the bottom lines."

After selling his stock, McClelland wasn't ready to retire. He wrote a book, *Wobbly War*, about the bloody, violent massacre in 1919 in Centralia in which six people were killed in a parade that celebrated the first anniversary of the World War I armistice.

The massacre resulted in many prison terms and an enduring bad blood between the American Legion, which sponsored the parade, and the IWWW (International Workers of the World).

"He wasn't a slave to work, but he had to have a project," said his son. In 1987, the same year he wrote *Wobbly War*, McClelland founded *Columbia: The Magazine of Northwest History*. He became president of the Washington State Historical Society, which presents the "John McClelland Jr. Award" each year for historical writing.

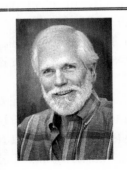

Thurston Twigg-Smith, president of Persis Corp., purchased the *The Daily News* in March 1986, changed the paper's name to *Peninsula Daily News* in March 1987 and sold the paper to the Horvitz Corp. in 1994. *(Peninsula Daily News archive)*

His death at 95, in an assisted living center in the Seattle suburb of Mercer Island, came on Oct. 30, 2010, just six hours before a scheduled memorial service for his wife, Burdette. They had been married 71 years before her death on Oct. 4, 2010.

"I'd say one of the biggest feathers in his cap was being elected to the advisory board of The Associated Press" in 1969-1972 and 1974-1982, said his son.

A new owner, a new name

After 55 years under the Websters and 15 with Longview, *The Daily News* was about to experience a major change — ownership under the Honolulu-based Persis Corp.

The sale became final on March 2, 1986. It

wasn't exactly a secret. Thurston Twigg-Smith, president of the corporation and publisher of the Honolulu *Advertiser*, visited the newsroom in November 1985 after he and McClelland had agreed in principle to the sale.

"Twigg-Smith declined to disclose the purchase price for the paper, but company records showed there were 1,133,525 shares of stock outstanding in the privately held company. At a sale price of $54.10 per share, the total value of the entire transaction would be about $61 million," according to reporter Kathleen Sharp of *The Daily News* in a news story on the sale.

"We didn't come in here with any preconceived notions as to changes," Twigg-Smith told the newsroom, noting that he was impressed with the paper, with Port Angeles and with the spirit and lifestyle of the area. "Both offer great opportunities and challenges," he said.

And he added: "We hope to improve the revenue picture and profitability, and expect, in the course of doing that, to continue good community relations."

Twigg-Smith founded Persis in 1967 in Honolulu, although it wasn't called that in the beginning. He named it Asa Corp. after his missionary forebear, Asa Thurston. It became Persis Corp in 1978.

He started his newspaper career at the Honolulu *Advertiser* in February 1946, but then he served in the military until 1954 when he became managing editor at the *Advertiser*.

In 1961, Twigg-Smith took control of the financially ailing paper with the help of outside investors. It became financially profitable. The *Advertiser* would have a succession of owners before it was bought in 2010 by Black Press Ltd., which also owned the Honolulu *Star-Bulletin*. Black merged two papers to form the Honolulu *Star-Advertiser*. (In 2011, Black bought the *Peninsula Daily News*.)

Twigg-Smith named Robert Weil, 35, as vice president and general manager, overseeing Port Angeles, the Bellevue *Journal- American*, the weekly Mercer Island *Reporter* and Cowlitz Cableview.

For the previous 4 ½ years, Weil had been publisher of *The Independent Journal* of Marin, Calif., a Gannett newspaper. Before that, he had been publisher of another Gannett newspaper, the *Valley News-Dispatch* in New Kensington, Pa.

Weil, whose strength was in advertising and marketing, said, "Our job is to find new ways to enhance your opportunities. We need to look hard at the marketing side ... to become more profitable to enable us to do more things down the road."

The new ownership made big changes.

Twigg-Smith announced the end of the Employee Stock Ownership Plan that McClelland had provided for all Longview Publishing Co. employees, including those at Port Angeles.

Staffers weren't sure what to make of that announcement and what would happen to their retirement.

Ducceschi said some of them made out quite well. "There was concern about this ownership, but when the sale was announced, their stock soared in multiples. Some employees made a whole lot of money. Some of them cashed in their stocks and left."

A year into the Persis ownership, Twigg-Smith decided it was time for a name change to reflect its huge 156-mile circulation area across the mountains, beaches and valleys of the Olympic Peninsula from the Hood Canal to La Push.

On March 22, 1987, the newspaper became the *Peninsula Daily News*. It was the third name for the paper that began life as the *Port Angeles Evening News* on April 10, 1916, and became *The Daily News* on Feb. 1, 1972.

In addition, the new *PDN* joined many other afternoon newspapers nationwide that had changed their delivery to mornings in the wake of the rise of television news and changing work patterns.

Subscribers who had received the *PDN* between 2 and 6 p.m. each day would now have it by 7 a.m.

In a note to readers, Ducceschi noted that when the *PDN* was founded as an afternoon newspaper in 1916 it did not compete with radio, TV or hectic after-school family schedules.

"And we're doing this because it will give us a better news cycle to cover news for you," he added. "For a nighttime meeting that ends at 10 p.m., the reporter will write the story, and we'll have it at your home, so you can learn about it the next morning."

The change was accompanied by a new design with more graphic elements and other changes to modernize the newspaper's look.

There also was an improved Sunday TV booklet, an enhanced daily

TV section and an earlier deadline to get the Wednesday paper to readers sooner. The newspaper also added correspondents to expand coverage on the West End and opened an office in Port Townsend to boost coverage in Jefferson County.

Local columnists were added and sports coverage was improved with the addition of popular *Los Angeles Times* columnist Jim Murray. The editorial page also was redesigned with space for more readers' letters, political cartoons and new columnist Ellen Goodman, a Pulitzer Prize-winning writer with the *Boston Globe*.

But those improvements cost money — and under Persis that meant there were constant pressures to improve revenue and find cost-savings.

"It was all about money," Ducceschi recalled.

"They thought the perfect newspaper was a Gannett newspaper (both Twigg-Smith and Weil had experience with that corporation). They told me to my face that they expected 20 to 25 percent profit. We were in the teens and I thought that was pretty good. It was a shock (when they said that)."

But, Ducceschi does allow that he learned more about the business side of being a publisher from the new owners.

"Robert Weil taught me all about the money end of the business — where it's at and how to make money. I hadn't seen my job like that. We wanted to have more advertising, more subscriptions, but only to the point that it supported the news.

"I was able to see ways to improve the bottom line. I learned if I can save them money, then they would leave me alone to run the newspaper for the benefit of the readers.

'It took a while, but I saw how I could run the newspaper to my satisfaction as well as theirs."

Timber issues

The 1980s ended with a new perspective about the timber industry, a key economic driver for the North Olympic Peninsula's economy. This was noted in a *PDN* story on Dec. 30, 1989:

The hard years brought major layoffs, bankruptcies, a scramble to cut costs through automation, and hotly debated state legislation, later rejected.

Soaring interest rates and a deep homebuilding recession finally receded and logging began a gradual recovery that recently quickened on the strength of a massive Asian appetite for wood and through more efficient logging and milling practices.

But, industry employment levels have yet to return to their 1980 high and debate rages over new problems. The federal shutdown of much old-growth timber to conserve the resource and save the spotted owl habitat; major export of non-federal timber to Asia creating hardship for domestic mills unable to compete for the expensive trees.

Another story that had a large impact on the peninsula came on July 22, 1991, when a Japanese fish-processing vessel *Tenyo Maru* and a Chinese freighter, *Tuo Hai*, collided about 25 miles northwest of Cape Flattery, the western tip of Clallam County.

The *Tenyo Maru* sank within 10 minutes, one crew member died and its fuel tanks, carrying 475,000 gallons of fuel oil, began leaking.

Oil washed ashore for several days along the coast, including Shi Shi Beach, Cape Flattery, the area between Tatoosh Island and Rialto Beach. Shorelines of the Makah Reservation and Olympic National Park were hardest hit.

An environmental online website: *www.sightline.org* reviewed all the oil spills in Puget Sound since 1965 for the nonprofit Sightline Institute lists this one among the worst. The website noted:

… Oil killed or injured *at least 4,300 seabirds, including federally threatened marbled murrelets, along with an unknown number of sea otters and harbor seals. The spill also did substantial damage to kelp beds where toxic concentrations of oil lingered for more than two weeks.*

In 1994, the Maruha Corporation, the owner and operator of the Tenyo Maru, agreed to pay $9 million in penalties and cleanup fees.

The oil spill wasn't the only event having an environmental impact on the peninsula.

It only got worse by mid-1990 when the spotted owl was listed as a threatened species. This curtailed timber-cutting and put many loggers out of work.

In June 2015, the 25th anniversary of spotted owl decision, the *PDN* published a revealing look at the chaos the elusive little bird caused.

The two-part series by former *Daily News* business writer George Erb headlined: "25th Anniversary of Spotted Owl Listing: Fewer owls, less timber industry," is printed, in part:

The elusive spotted owl, which decimated the peninsula's timber industry. *(Peninsula Daily News archive).*

The heated debate over whether to curtail the logging of old-growth forests to protect the northern spotted owl was at full throttle when the federal government declared the bird a threatened species June 22, 1990.

At the time, environmentalists worried that the federal plan would fall short of saving the spotted owl. Timber interests worried that a wave of environmental rules would gut the Olympic Peninsula's wood-products industry and devastate communities.

Twenty-five years later, the effects of the landmark decision can be seen in the reams of economic, industry and environmental data routinely gathered by state and federal governments. The outcomes are by turns expected, disheartening and surprising.

A quarter-century of state and federal data and studies show:

- *The number of spotted owls on the Olympic Peninsula declined an estimated 40 percent between 1992 and 2006.*
- *Between 1988 and 2013, annual timber harvests by all public and private owners in Clallam, Grays Harbor, Jefferson and Mason counties plunged 64 percent to 753 million board feet.*
- *Timber harvests on the Olympic Peninsula's federal lands plummeted 96 percent to 10.8 million board feet during the same period.*

In 1988, 13.2 percent of the region's commercial timber came from federal lands. By 2013, the figure was 1.4 percent.

- *Private timber harvests on the Olympic Peninsula plunged 61 percent to 598 million board feet during the same period. Over that time, timber companies on the Peninsula supplied between 69 percent and 92 percent of commercial logs.*

- *The number of wood-products mills in the Olympic Peninsula's four counties sank 71 percent to 32 mills between 1988 and 2012.*

Not all the blame can be placed on the spotted owl decision. Erb noted.

There were other reasons listed for the decline: a recession that clobbered the home-building sector; Asian markets tanked after 1990; skirmishes over forest management policies and timber sales.

In addition, environmentalists were challenging logging in public forests.

"They were relentless," said Port of Port Angeles Commissioner John Calhoun.

Horvitz tenure begins

After eight years of Persis, rumors of a new ownership began to surface. On Oct. 6, 1994, the *PDN's* front page confirmed the news:

"Ownership of newspaper changes," followed by: "Horvitz family pledges commitment to service and quality as it completes purchase of *Peninsula Daily News.*"

Peter Horvitz, president and chief executive officer of Horvitz Newspapers-LLC, based in Bellevue, made the announcement of the purchase jointly with Thurston Twigg-Smith.

"I'm delighted to take charge of this exciting group of family-owned newspapers and look forward to managing them with the same integrity and commitment to quality, customer service and community service that were trademarks of the Persis and Horvitz newspapers," Horvitz told the PDN.

Along with the announcement of the sale, Horvitz named PDN editor and publisher Frank Ducceschi an executive vice president of Northwest Media (Washington L.P.) and Horvitz Newspapers.

"During the months since the sale in principle was announced the local management team has come to know the vitality and commitment of Horvitz Newspapers," Ducceschi said. "The staff is eager to continue to expand and improve our service to the community."

No major changes are expected at the Peninsula Daily News. One change definitely not expected, Ducceschi said with a smile, is a name change. "The newspaper's name is very representative of its mission: to be the daily newspaper for every community on the North Olympic Peninsula."

The other Washington papers involved in the sale by Persis to Horvitz Newspapers are the Journal-American *in Bellevue,* The Valley Daily News *in Kent, and three weekly newspapers: the* Northshore Citizen *in Bothell, the* Mercer Island Reporter *and the* Snoqualmie Valley Reporter. *Also, included in the sale was* The Daily Times *in Maryville, Tenn.*

Terms of the sale were not disclosed, but industry estimates put the value in the $100 million range.

The sale marks a return to the newspaper ownership for the Harry R. Horvitz family of Cleveland, Ohio. The family owned newspapers in Ohio and New York for almost 60 years before selling them in 1987. Harry Horvitz, Peter's father, died in 1992.

At the same time, the sale marks the end of the Twigg-Smith family's 96-year association with the newspaper industry.

Horvitz, who moved to Bellevue to manage the newspaper group and serve as publisher of the Journal-American, *was named Publisher of the Year in 1990 by Gannett and was named "Newspaper Executive of the Year" in 1991 by the California Press Association.*

Peter Horvitz purchased the *PDN* in 1994 and owned it until selling to Sound Publishing Co. in 2011. *(Peninsula Daily News archive).*

In an email interview in 2017, Peter Horvitz shared some his family history.

"I was fortunate to grow up in a newspaper family. My grandfather, Samuel A. Horvitz, bought his first newspaper in Lorain, Ohio, in the 1930s. My father, Harry R. Horvitz, was president and publisher of Horvitz Newspapers which ultimately owned five newspapers in Ohio."

Peter began his newspaper career with a summer job at the *Journal* in Lorain; he earned his master's degree, worked for several of his family's papers in Ohio before leaving the family business in 1983 to work for Gannett papers.

His first job as publisher was in 1984 with the *Chillicothe* (Ohio) *Gazette*.

"I left Gannett in 1993, and with my family's support, decided to look for newspapers to acquire," Horvitz said.

That led to the purchase of the Persis newspapers in 1994, including the *Peninsula Daily News*.

Occasionally when a new owner comes on board, major management changes occur. This didn't happen with Horvitz.

"I was fortunate to inherit a good publisher (Frank Ducceschi) and a good controller (Kathy Wahto). They served our newspaper and the community well during their tenure," Horvitz said in 2017.

It was an immediate change in attitude, Ducceschi noted.

"When Peter bought the paper, employees were so happy to be out from under Persis. Peter was interested in producing the best newspaper possible. With Persis, it was all about money."

He said Horvitz gave him "relative freedom to run the newspaper," but they did differ on one big thing.

"Peter didn't think you could be a good publisher and a good editor. There were too many responsibilities as a publisher. If the publisher was more experienced in business, that could be true, but it works if your publisher is a former editor."

It might work, but it wasn't what Horvitz preferred. Looking back, he explained in 2017 how he felt about that situation in 1994.

"Frank was the editor and publisher of *PDN* when we bought the paper. I was okay with that since Frank had been a successful newsman, although I felt we needed a strong managing editor also. The publisher job requires great attention to business issues as well as editorial and community responsibilities."

While this wasn't a preferred situation, Horvitz said it worked because both Ducceschi and John Brewer after him, had a strong supporting cast.

"No one can run the business and the newsroom at the same time without significant help. Frank and John managed these responsibilities well with good managing editors. John was so passionate about his job and the *PDN* that he devoted an amazing number of hours each day to his work. This is one of the reasons why he was so successful."

Horvitz said, "I always had a very simple management style. I delegate responsibility but never abdicate it.

"The publisher is responsible for all aspects of his or her newspaper. Goals are set. Results are measured. Publishers are expected to make changes when necessary. I get involved when required."

Many changes for *PDN*

On the final day of 1995, an editorial summed up improvements to the *PDN* made after Horvitz bought the paper.

They included: new digital photographic technology; improved local weather forecast; *USA Weekend* added to the Sunday paper; six pastors as rotating columnists for Friday's Church page; a senior issues columnist; a comic "In The Bleachers;" a new feature "On the Road," to help cope with changing automotive technology; two pages of stocks and mutual fund reports; a Sequim office to handle news, advertising and circulation.

And inside the *PDN* building, the installation of a new computer system for the newsroom was nearly finished.

Ducceschi also was involved in a number of noteworthy community projects.

"I was surprised to find out that local social workers donated from their own paychecks to an in-office fund to provide help to those who needed immediate help and did not qualify for state aid on short notice."

To fill that need, the *Peninsula Daily News* started an annual end-of-year fund-raising campaign called the Peninsula Home Fund. The paper partnered with a local social service group to administer the funds it collected.

It built on the newspaper's long history of raising money for the unfortunate, which dated back to editor Billy Welsh's first charity drive campaigns as "Beacon Bill" in 1922.

To distribute the money effectively and screen applicants, the *Peninsula Daily News* partnered with Olympic Community Action Programs, the No. 1 emergency care agency on the North Olympic Peninsula.

The first Home Fund campaign was in 1989 and collected $4,811.53. "It helped 50 to 100 people," Ducceschi noted.

In 2016, the Home Fund raised $264,486 and helped 4,295 individuals and 1,144 households. In 2017, it again raised well over $200,000.

Ducceschi also helped the Clallam County Historical Society find a home for a museum in the old Carnegie Library next to the county courthouse.

Through newspaper sponsorships, he also played a key role in the start-up of the Juan de Fuca Festival of the Arts, the establishment of the Clallam County Community Service Awards, the creation of the city Resolve to Recycle program, the revival of a local literary magazine and in the success of the Begin With Books program.

He worked with the Clallam County Economic Development Council, the United Way and Port Angeles Symphonic. He also served as president of the Washington Associated Press News Executives.

Frank Ducceschi, who started at *The Daily News* in Port Angeles in 1973, served as publisher under three owners — McClelland, Persis and Horvitz — retiring in 1998. *(Courtesy of Frank Ducceschi, 2015)*

In mid-January of 1998, Ducceschi announced he was ending his career at the *PDN* after 25 years. He was 53 and had been publisher for 17 years. "It's a good time for me to make a change in my life," he said.

In an article on Jan. 31, 1998, under the headline "PDN leader off to greener pastures," the man, who had been through three ownership changes at Port Angeles, said one of his major achievements was overseeing a "first-class news team" in the 1970s when, as managing editor, he began a drive to increase the amount of local news in the paper including the creation of an "all local" news front page. The paper started focusing more on local news at the time.

"By the time we were done, we'd assembled all kinds of awards," Ducceschi said.

Horvitz said Ducceschi was an asset to the community. "Frank has certainly had a major impact on the newspaper and has also had a major impact on the quality of life of the residents of the Peninsula."

He also cited Joan Ducceschi's work on the new Port Angeles library and Frank's work in economic development.

It's one thing to be admired by those at your own newspaper, but another to be well thought of by your peers at other papers. Frank was such a man, according to John Hughes, at the time editor of *The Daily World* at Aberdeen, later publisher of that paper and now director of state history projects for the Secretary of State in Olympia.

Hughes, who formed a working partnership with the *PDN*, said the paper was first-rate and Ducceschi "strived to make it better. A big, personable guy who recruited talented reporters, Frank was a prodigy as a publisher, a principled, decisive newsman."

Brewer new publisher

Ducceschi had submitted his resignation letter to Horvitz the previous fall. A nationwide hunt began for his successor. On Jan. 13, 1998, a front-page news story not only announced his retirement but reported that John Brewer, 50, would be the new publisher.

"He is a person who loves newspapers, loves community journalism and really has a great interest and desire to be in this business," Horvitz told *PDN* reporter Mike Dawson.

From 1988 to 1997, Brewer had been president, chief executive officer and editor-in-chief of The New York Times Syndication Sales Corp.

He was in charge of *The New York Times* News Service, *The New York Times* features syndicate, including the newspaper company's first three websites in 1995, and New York Times Licensing and Permissions, which handled trademark and merchandise licensing for *The New York Times* newspaper.

Brewer enlisted such high-profile columnists as Mikhail Gorbachev, Bill Gates — yes, him — Martha Stewart, Ross Perot and Jimmy Carter for the *Times* syndicate.

The news service added 10 new contributing partner newspapers. Brewer also headed *The New York Times'* two-year Russian-language newspaper in Moscow after the fall of the Soviet Union.

Before joining the *Times*, he spent 19 years (1969-1988) with The Associated Press. He worked as an AP reporter and editor, became chief of the AP's bureaus in Seattle and Los Angeles, then worked as an executive in AP's headquarters in New York.

His first newspaper job was as reporter for his hometown weekly newspaper, the Upland (Calif.) *News* from 1965-1966, then *The Daily Report* in Ontario, Calif., 1966-1969.

Horvitz was well-acquainted with Brewer and shared the circumstances that first brought the two together:

"John was running The New York Times News Service in New York City at the time I was trying to purchase that service for *The Valley Daily News*. The *Journal American* had a contract for the NYT service, but *The Valley Daily News* did not. I wanted to combine copy editing for both papers, so I needed common news services, but the NYT would not sell us the NYT service for VDN because of exclusivity agreements with the Seattle papers. I was furious, and I called John to talk about it."

"When I was in New York we met to discuss it further. John told me that while he couldn't sell us the service immediately, he would work on it and see if he could find a way to change the exclusivity policy and sell us the service later. John was ultimately successful and we purchased the service."

"Frank had great respect for John and thought he would be a great candidate for publisher," Horvitz said in a 2017 interview.

"I called John to see if he had any interest in the position and when he said he would consider it, we worked to make it happen.

"John was married to Ann, another very accomplished journalist who had served as editor of the *Contra Costa Times* in the San Francisco Bay area during her impressive career, so we had the great benefit of both John and Ann in Port Angeles.

"Ann, who died from breast cancer in 2005, was beloved by the *PDN* staff and the community. Her passing was a tremendous loss."

Horvitz said he chose Brewer because of his integrity, business achievements and news career.

"No one could have achieved what he achieved without being an outstanding reporter, editor and news executive."

Brewer said, even today he still is asked why he would leave a high-profile position with the New York Times Syndicate Sales Group to be publisher at the *PDN*.

"It's complex and I had a successful operation," Brewer said in a 2018 interview.

He said he competed successfully against 350 other syndicates and news services within an intense, global market and built revenue by 30.9 percent during his presidency (to $16.140 million) and increased the profit margin by 7.7 percent to 35.3 percent ($5.697 million).

Then in January 1997, the job changed amid a complex reorganization when Syndication Sales and its revenues were merged into *The New York Times* newspaper, giving *Times* publisher Arthur Sulzberger Jr. and his team control of all print and electronic extensions of the newspaper.

"Times unifies content; Sulzberger gets responsibility for repurposing of Times information," was the headline on a story in *MediaWeek* magazine on Jan. 13, 1997, which Brewer said, "summarized it diplomatically."

The *MediaWeek* story noted that Syndication Sales was part of the *Times'* corporate Information Services Group, a division of The New York Co., "founded in 1993 by the former Times Co.

The magazine said the restructuring prompted several resignations, including James Cutie, president of the Information Services Group and a 16-year veteran of the company, and John Brewer, president and editor-in-chief of the Times Syndication Sales Corp.

The *Times* didn't let Brewer get very far. He was rehired immediately and spent the next six months as a paid consultant, integrating the syndicate and news service into the newspaper's operations.

In the *PDN* story announcing the new publisher, Brewer said his family fell in love with the North Olympic Peninsula during his six years as Seattle AP bureau chief. Brewer, his wife and two sons enjoy camping, hiking and steelhead fishing.

"I've always been impressed by the vigor of the area, and I think it is even more so now," Brewer said.

Ducceschi told the *PDN* that he has known Brewer for about 22 years. "During that time, his personal integrity, commitment to high standards and outstanding leadership have propelled him to the top of his profession.

"He is an exceptionally talented person. The *Peninsula Daily News* will benefit from his strength and experience."

Zoning the *PDN*

Under Brewer, the *PDN* soon had a new masthead incorporating the Olympic Mountains. And after Brewer reopened the newspaper's satellite news bureau in Port Townsend, which had been closed because of economic reasons, he began "zoning."

For the first time, the *PDN* published two customized daily newspapers — one zoned with local news and photos specifically tailored for readers in Clallam County, the other a zoned edition with specific news/photos for readers in Jefferson County.

"We zoned front page and two or three pages inside the first section," said Brewer in a 2018 interview. "It made us a better newspaper for audiences in two different counties. The zoning still continues today."

He also enlisted the *PDN* in the digital revolution and launched the *PDN's* website, *www.peninsuladailynews.com.*

"With our entry on the Web," Brewer told readers, "we will also be your primary news and advertising provider in the computer age."

It soon became the most popular website on the Olympic Peninsula.

In addition, the *PDN* in the fall of 2010 began offering readers Clallam and Jefferson "e-Editions."

Brewer said, "You could read, page by page, exact digital replicas of the two zoned *PDNs* on your computer, iPad or smartphone."

(The website and e-Editions were free to readers until April 2014, when they were put behind a paywall. Only *PDN* print subscribers with daily or Friday-Sunday home or office subscriptions) and "digital-only" subscribers had unlimited access to *www. peninsuladailynews.com.*)

John Brewer, who was named publisher of the *Peninsula Daily News* in 1998, spent three decades in journalism, retiring in October 2015, after 17 years as a local publisher. *(Bill Lindstrom photo, 2015)*

On top of the changes he made, Brewer had barely settled into the publisher's chair when a series of major stories broke, and they didn't stop until he retired 17 years later.

Here's a quick summary of his first three years in the publisher's chair:

Respected doctor accused of murder in a baby's death; pickets in parking lot during his first week as publisher because the doctor's name was used in the *PDN* story; an attending ER doctor in the baby's death was accused in the ax murder of his wife; the Makah tribe made its first whale kill in 70 years; a bear would terrorize Olympic National Park visitors; a suspected terrorist would be tackled on the streets of downtown Port Angeles; the first deputy in the county's history would be shot and killed and to top it all in the first trio of years — the events of Sept. 11, 2001.

An infant's death

Ducceschi's retirement became final on Friday, Jan. 30, 1998. At a party Saturday night for Frank, a reporter "told me the startling news that she was checking on rumors that a doctor – she didn't have a name then — had killed a baby," Brewer said in a 2015 interview.

On Sunday night an editor at the paper phoned Brewer, who was staying with the Ducceschis, and said the story was ready and the facts had been triple-checked.

"I asked him what the doctor's name was," recalled Brewer, "and he told me Gene Turner. I turned to Frank and asked him 'You ever heard of Gene Turner?' And I told him what the reporter said. Frank just about fell out of his chair."

Brewer learned from Ducceschi that Turner was the Marcus Welby of Port Angeles, a well-known and beloved pediatrician in the community with an unblemished record. He had delivered, and cared for, many of the town's children.

"We went to the office immediately," said Brewer "In the parking lot Norma Turner, the doctor's wife, was waiting. She knew what (facts) the paper had, and she wanted to be sure we didn't name the doctor.

"Frank talked to her for a while — they had known each other for years — and she went home. We used the name of the doctor."

On Tuesday, Feb. 2, 1998, the *PDN* headlined: "Baby's death investigated," followed by "PA doctor allegedly obstructed airway."

Christina Kelly was the lead reporter on the story:

Eugene Turner, a prominent physician who has practiced medicine for 37 years, is under investigation by police and a state medical quality board for allegedly facilitating the death of an infant.

Maryella Jansen, program manager for the state Department of Health, Medical Quality Assurance Commission, confirmed the investigation of Turner.

A news release issued Sunday by Port Angeles Police Chief Steve Ilk confirmed the law enforcement investigation but did not name the doctor.

The infant, Conor McInnerney, stopped breathing Jan. 12 while being breast-fed by his mother, Michelle. She and her husband, Martin, phoned 911, and the infant was taken to Olympic Memorial Hospital at 8 p.m.

The news release says the infant was treated by Turner and died at 9:55 p.m.

At approximately 10:15 p.m., the physician was called back to the hospital by emergency room staff because the child reportedly was exhibiting renewed life signs," the report states. "Treatment was resumed for approximately two hours before the infant was again pronounced dead."

On Jan. 20, a hospital employee contacted a Clallam County sheriff's deputy and reported circumstances surrounding the death of the infant may have been questionable, Ilk said.

The police chief confirmed his office used search warrants to obtain documents from the hospital, surrounding the infant's death. He said that he had not yet talked to Turner. But the doctor was alleged to have "facilitated the baby's death by manually obstructing the airway of the baby."

"The local radio station, KONP, and PNN, the local cable TV news channel, didn't name Turner as the subject of the investigation for more than a week, saying only that it was an "unidentified doctor," Brewer said.

"They believed it was OK to keep the public in the dark because Turner hadn't been charged with a crime.

"Many of Turner's supporters used this to say we were unfair and biased against the man they saw as a community icon.

"But this cover-up didn't work for us because of the seriousness of what had happened, and that state medical authorities had named Turner. In fact, the state always names the doctor if it finds enough evidence to warrant an investigation. It is considered to be in the public's best interest to know who and what is happening. If your doctor is under state investigation, wouldn't you want to know?"

On the next day, the paper had more stories, led by Kelly's doubtless difficult, but gripping interview with the infant's grandmother, Diane Anderson, a former licensed practical nurse, and a statement from Turner.

"Doctor did all he could" was the main headline, followed by a second deck: "Investigation: Turner says his actions were based on experience"

Looking weary, Dr. Eugene Turner said Tuesday that any actions he took, while treating an infant — who later died — were done based on his 27 years as a medical professional.

Turner, whose comments were limited due to the investigation, said briefly, "I know I did the right thing under the circumstances. There were mitigating circumstances."

Turner went on to say there was a snowstorm that limited ground travel and the hospital did not have an electroencephalograph to measure brain waves. He said the hospital is not equipped for neonatal emergencies nor does it have an infant ventilator.

The bulk of the story was from Anderson. She said Turner admitted to her that he "suffocated" the infant. She also said Martin McInnerney, the boy's father, did CPR on the infant before the emergency crew arrived.

"He wasn't without oxygen except for maybe two or three minutes. The baby had good color and did not turn blue at the time."

She said the doctor told the parents that the baby had suffered massive brain damage because of oxygen deprivation and was probably brain dead.

"I assumed when we were told this that they had taken an electroencephalograph and there were no brain waves," said Anderson, who questioned the use of a hand ventilator, instead of a respirator. She said she was told by hospital staff that they did not have one small enough.

"I opened the baby's eyes and saw that the eyes were fixed and dilated. That usually means no brain function."

She said the nurses wrapped the infant in a warm blanket and handed him to his father.

"We left the hospital in tremendous grief," Anderson said. "It wasn't until

two days later we were told that Turner was called back to the hospital because the baby had showed signs of life."

Anderson said the doctor had later called her and explained that his actions were because the infant had no viability. "From his lips to my ears, he said the baby was brain dead," Anderson said. "He then said he pinched his nose and placed his hand over the baby's mouth and suffocated him.

"He said he did everything in his power, and after about two hours, he decided enough is enough and let the baby go."

Meanwhile, reporter Mike Dawson had uncovered another story — the whistle-blower whose telephone call to a law enforcement officer suggesting he should look into the baby's death, had been disciplined.

He wrote in the *PDN*:

Hospital orderly Dan Heassler made the call because talk at the hospital was that the baby had been smothered. The deputy relayed the information to the police.

In return, the hospital suspended him and disciplined him without pay, but after Heassler obtained an attorney, the pay was reinstated, and he returned to work.

Heassler's attorney said he was punished for coming forward. "Essentially, he was disciplined for telling the police," Lane Wolfley said, speaking for his client.

The hospital had a different story, saying Heassler was disciplined for calling in sick the day after telling the officer when he wasn't sick. The orderly said he was distressed and didn't want to come to work.

Meanwhile, the community castigated their new publisher for using the doctor's name.

"I was under pressure from everyone," Brewer recalled. "They'd yell at me whenever I went out. He was only accused, they would say."

One afternoon when Brewer was at work, he looked out a window at the parking lot and couldn't believe what he saw: "There were picketers. They didn't like that we had named the doctor, but they carried protest signs that said, 'We love you Dr. Turner.' The story went on for months."

Six days after the first story, the *PDN's* executive editor Roger Morton wrote an editorial. It was headlined: "Name was important to story about physician."

He said the paper had been blasted for "yellow journalism, smearing a good doctor's name and doing anything to sell newspapers."

None of that is the true, the editorial noted. Morton explained that the usual policy was not to release names until an individual was charged with a crime or the results of an investigation were released.

"In Dr. Turner's case, we didn't have to debate the situation. It was very straightforward — his name was released to the news media by the state Medical Quality Assurance Commission. We were told they were investigating a local doctor. We called that agency to confirm the investigation and they provided the name.

"Port Angeles police are also investigating and released a statement without the doctor's name. That is usual police policy."

The editorial said, "We could have ignored the commission's report and not named the doctor, but then the paper would be accused of a cover-up, of protecting a prominent and influential local physician."

He said the fact the hospital found enough credence to report the facts to the state board also was critical.

"If someone walked in our door and made the statement, we certainly would not have used the name." He also pointed out that by just using the words *"a doctor is being investigated,"* would tar the entire hospital's physician staff with a broad brush.

"While it's fine to defend Dr. Turner, some people seem to be in a mood to shoot the messenger. But the Peninsula Daily News *has a responsibility to inform. We took that responsibility seriously in printing Dr. Turner's name, and we'll continue to take it seriously as the investigations continue."*

In the following weeks — after it was clear that both the police and state investigations were moving forward — letters to the editor from Turner's defenders were printed in the *PDN.*

One read:

"I have known Dr. Eugene Turner my entire life. Like many people who knew Dr. Turner, I was appalled by (your) allegation of facilitating the death of an infant. ... I am confident the truth will come out, but the damage has been done and I feel the Peninsula Daily News *is partly responsible."*

Another person wrote:

"I have watched the town's growth. Now I am watching its downfall. Have we become so bored with the unemployment issues in the town that we

are actually beginning to tear down the people who have made this community a place worth living in."

And one from a woman whose son Dr. Turner treated for leukemia for seven years.

"None of us were there in the hospital ER, but whatever he did, I would trust the man's judgment on anything. You must have faith in something."

Those in Port Angeles who were suspicious of Turner's treatment of the infant did not receive much public support.

A month after filing second-degree murder charges against Turner, Clallam County Prosecuting Attorney David Bruneau was voted out of office after 17 years of service.

In an article in the *Los Angeles Times*, Bruneau told a reporter, "We have no choice. ... Personally, I don't like God-playing. When someone starts making decisions about another person's life, that's the worst sort of overgrown arrogance."

Turner's supporters charged that the prosecutor was retaliating against the pediatrician because his wife, Norma, a community hero to many after the Northern Tier controversy, had organized the campaign of Bruneau's 1994 election opponent.

Heassler, the whistle-blower, who lost his job at the hospital, said he had coffee thrown at him, his car vandalized, and he had to shut down a video store he ran on the side, accusing the Turner supporters of orchestrating a boycott. He also said he couldn't sue because he couldn't find an attorney to represent him.

Brewer learned there had been a meeting of major *PDN* advertisers. Some wanted to punish the newspaper for its Turner coverage. A vote to launch an advertising boycott lost after auto dealer Howard "Mac" Ruddell spoke strongly in support of the *PDN*.

One of the ER doctors who was present when the infant was brought in was Bruce Rowan. In fact, he said he took the baby from the boy's parents and "found him unresponsive, cold and somewhat blue," according to the *PDN*.

A bizarre murder

A month after the infant's death, Dr. Rowan's wife was found bludgeoned to death with the blunt end of an ax and a baseball bat.

As Rowan was being questioned by officers, he left the room to tend to his 2-year-old daughter, Annika, went to the kitchen, grabbed a butcher knife and stabbed himself several times in the neck and chest. He stumbled back into the room and collapsed. He had emergency surgery to repair the wounds and recovered to stand trial. Ultimately, he confessed to his wife's murder.

Kelly's articles in the *PDN* revealed that Dr. Rowan told investigators that he had been terribly disturbed by baby Conor's death and began "hearing voices in his head that he was a horrible person."

On March 1, 1998, six weeks after the baby had died, Rowan and his wife Debra went to see the movie, "Titanic." He later claimed that a scene of a crew member shooting himself after shooting a passenger in the sinking ship's chaos showed him the "tremendous relief of being dead before you hit the ground."

Rowan said he was so disturbed that he couldn't sleep that night. He went outside and picked up an ax. "I just took it and swung it. I just hit her," he said later at his trial. "There was no reaction, no reaction at all."

Rowan cleaned blood from the bedroom walls, carpet and ceiling, then put his wife's body in their Subaru, propped a rock against the accelerator and sent the car hurtling into a tree to fake an accident.

Investigators weren't fooled. Clallam County Chief Criminal Deputy Fred DeFrang immediately noted Debra's injuries couldn't be caused by the accident.

He tried to explain the big rock on the accelerator of the crashed car. "Neighborhood dogs sometimes drop rocks into the car," he said. "One of the rocks might have caused the gas pedal to stick or obstructed the use of the brake."

After he left the room, entered the kitchen and stabbed himself, Rowan stumbled back into the living room. Asked why he had done that, he said: "I just don't want to say right now."

Deputies searched the shed on the property and found the ax and a bat, along with a garbage bag filled with blood and taped shut. Pillows, blood-stained men's clothing, Debra's bra and bedding also were found.

He was charged with murder and faced trial in October.

It was later learned a $500,000 insurance policy Rowan took out became effective on the day she died.

"One would have to be crazy, stupid or insane to kill your wife on the day the insurance policy took effect," Rowan's lawyer, eminent Seattle defense attorney David Allen, said during closing arguments at the murder trial. "And, we know Bruce Rowan is not stupid."

The jury agreed. Rowan was found not guilty — by reason of insanity and ordered to the psychiatric ward at Western State Hospital in Steilacoom.

Rowan was sent to a locked hospital ward for three years. In 2002, his attorney convinced the treatment staff to grant "conditional release," allowing him freedom for visits outside the facility in preparation for release into the community.

In 2005, a Clallam County Superior Court judge signed papers for his permanent release, much to the dismay of the Rowan family. Debra Rowan's parents had custody of Annika.

Rowan went to a half-way house in Seattle, then disappeared into the city.

Doctor censured ... Conor McInnerney

Meantime, the case against Dr. Turner also was moving forward. The legal and ethical drama of the issue had gotten the attention of national media. *The Los Angeles Times* and *The Washington Post* did a major takeout as did NBC's "Dateline."

The *PDN* reported that the state Medical Quality Assurance Commission absolved the hospital of any criminal wrongdoing.

The controversial second-degree murder charge filed by Bruneau against Turner was dismissed, but Turner still faced a hearing before the commission for alleged unprofessional conduct in the baby's death.

The panel allowed Turner to keep his medical license until his case was heard, but ordered another doctor be present any time he attempted a resuscitation.

Turner voluntarily surrendered his hospital privileges but continued to operate his Peninsula Children's Clinic.

On Feb. 1, 1999, the controversial second-degree murder charge filed by Bruneau against Turner was dismissed.

There was no evidence the baby's death was caused by "any criminal or even negligent act by any other human being," said the motion for dismissal, filed by Jim Townsend, a deputy prosecutor from Snohomish County who was assigned the case when it became an issue in the Clallam County prosecutor's race the previous fall.

The case was to have been heard by an outside judge as well, from neighboring Skagit County.

The *PDN* reported that the decision to drop the charges prompted a burst of cheers and applause from Turner's supporters in the crowded Clallam County courtroom. Turner could hardly speak through his tears.

The doctor always has believed "he did everything he could to save the life of Conor McInnerney on Jan. 12 of last year," said defense attorney Jeff Robinson.

"And he was right, and we think the decision today bears that out."

The McInnerneys were not in the courtroom.

On July 21, 1999, the medical commission ruled that "a doctor must not do what Dr. Turner did: place his hand over a gasping baby's mouth and nose, even if those breaths are only reflexes preceding death."

The only action it took was to censure Turner, now 63, for unprofessional conduct. He could continue practicing medicine without restrictions.

"We are elated," Turner said of the panel's decision, calling it "almost a total victory."

Turner eventually sold his practice and went to Africa to practice with the Peace Corps for several years. In recent years, he has been one of several volunteer physicians serving patients at VIMO (Volunteers in Medicine in the Olympics), a free clinic in Port Angeles.

Matthew Knopp, attorney for Martin and Michelle McInnerney, Conor's parents, told the *PDN* that his clients were pleased the commission agreed that what Turner did was not accepted medical practice. But they believed that the commission's action was too light.

They did not file any civil lawsuits against Turner or the hospital.

New York Times bestselling author Carlton Smith, formerly of the

Seattle Times, wrote a book on Turner and Rowan and their impact on Port Angeles and the *PDN, Bitter Medicine: Two Doctors, Two Deaths and a Small-Town's Search for Justice,* published in 2000.

Gottlieb, Wilson hired

During that first year, Brewer made two important, and long-lasting, hires.

In September 1998, Paul Gottlieb was hired as a senior reporter. In December, Rex Wilson was hired as executive news editor, and put in charge of the news operations. Gottlieb was still at the newspaper in 2018; Wilson retired almost three months before Brewer, on Aug. 1, 2015.

Paul Gottlieb *(Bill Lindstrom photo)*

"I like to write for a living. I tend to be fearless, and yes, sometimes I piss people off, but I write for the reader."

Gottlieb, 46 at his hiring, brought with him a bachelor's degree in English in 1977 and a master's in 1979, both from Rutgers University. In the 22 years since college, he had worked for nine weeklies and was hired from the weekly *Peninsula Gateway* in Gig Harbor.

"I like to write for a living," he said. "I tend to be fearless, and yes, sometimes I piss people off, but I write for the reader."

Covering government, he said probably was his favorite genre. "I like to ask the tough questions. If I am clear and accurate, I don't care (if some get upset). It's like you pour a lot of questions into a funnel and what comes out is the truth. I believe, if I am talking to a government official, they should know the answer. I don't take waffling for an answer."

Wilson agrees with Gottlieb's own assessment.

"He is a brilliant writer. He's a bulldog; he's a journalistic wolverine."

It is this characteristic that led Brewer and later Wilson, to assign new, young reporters to Paul for mentoring, something he still enjoys after nearly 20 years.

In addition to covering city government and writing investigative pieces, Gottlieb also served a tour as editor of *PDN*'s Commentary page.

Wilson had known Brewer since Rex was editing a small daily in Vista, Calif., and John was AP bureau chief in Los Angeles.

Prior to that, Wilson worked as a desk editor for the *Orange County Register* when it won a Pulitzer Prize for its Olympic Games coverage in 1984. "I learned to work with color there," Wilson said.

He later became editor at the *Times-Standard* in Eureka, Calif. "I heard John had become publisher at Port Angeles. I called him, and he told me to come on up. And the rest is history."

On Dec. 9, 1998, two days after Wilson began work at the *PDN*, the newspaper started a series, "Tribes of the Peninsula," an in-depth look at the five tribes that make the North Olympic Peninsula their home.

The series examined each tribe's treaty rights, hunting laws, family life, role of elders, social structure, economy and employment, government structure, future plans, historical and biographical information.

The timing was perfect. One of the tribes, the Makah, had received permission — from the U.S. government and international whaling authorities — to conduct its first whale hunt in more than 70 years. They would use a cedar canoe and hand-thrown harpoons.

Makah go whaling

Wilson, Gottlieb and the rest of the staff were deep into the Turner story in May 1999, when *PDN* reporters Mark Morey and Jesse Hamilton got word from the Makah Tribal Center in Neah Bay, the northernmost community in the continental U.S., that the tribal members finally had come close to harpooning a whale after months of on-and-off-attempts.

"I had to take a reporter off the Turner story and put him on the whaling story," Wilson remembered. "That was a big story."

Two attempts — on May 10 and May 16 — to kill a whale failed when harpoons, thrown by Theron Parker from the 35-foot black and red *Hummingbird* canoe, were tossed off by two gray whales.

The whale hunt had attracted angry protesters in boats and on land. Two anti-whalers from the Sea Defense Alliance had been arrested for investigation of first-degree assault after attempting to block the hunt. Later roadblocks were set up and anti-whale protesters were banned from entering Neah Bay.

Early on the morning of May 17, 1999, history was recorded when a 30-foot, 5-inch female juvenile gray whale was harpooned from the canoe, then finished off (as required by federal government monitors) with shots from a .50-caliber rifle fired from a motorized support boat.

"Such a sensation," screamed Arnie Hunter, who was in a support boat. Those words were bannered across the *PDN*, accompanied by several stories and pictures from *PDN* photographer Tom Thompson.

One of his photos, of two jubilant tribal members standing atop the whale in a triumphant pose after the whale was towed ashore, went to newspapers worldwide via The Associated Press.

The entire process took only eight minutes from the time Parker threw the harpoon until the animal was presumed dead.

"It was awesome," said a beaming Ben Johnson, tribal chairman, embracing Hunter and a dripping wet Parker on the beach.

"The Makah made history today," shouted Johnson through a megaphone to hundreds gathered on shore crowded around the beached beast.

Men from the tribe hauled the whale onto the beach, where it was butchered with blubber passed around to everyone.

Not everyone was as joyous. Reporter Mark Morey's sidebar story headlined: "Protesters close to tears in wake of whale slaughter" showed there was agony along with the ecstasy.

"This is a sad day because they killed one of my friends," said Alberta 'Binky' Thompson, a Makah tribal member, who was holding hands with her friend, Lisa Distefano, both near tears.

A *PDN* package of stories, photos and graphics told readers how the whale was harpooned. By this time, the *PDN* had formed a partnership with KOMO-TV in Seattle.

KOMO shared dramatic video stills of five sequential photos, from the harpoon being thrown to the whale being shot and eventually dying.

Meat cutters and grinders worked overtime for a couple of days, taking some of the whale to a rendering plant in preparation for a lavish ceremony and feast in the Neah Bay school gym.

PDN reporter Jesse Hamilton was there to record it, as were photographers Tom Thompson and Keith Thorpe. There were more than 1,000 guests. The readers had a front-row seat for this festive event.

Keith Thorpe, Photographer since 1996 for the PDN. *(Courtesy of Keith Thorpe)*

"It was my biggest story. I was one of the very few who took part in both Makah whaling stories (in 1999 and 2007). I flew out there. We chartered a plane from Rite Bros."

Veteran *PDN* photographer Keith Thorpe on Makah whaling.

The May 17 whale hunt "was my biggest story," said Thorpe of his nearly 25 years at the *PDN*. "I was one of the very few who took part in both Makah whaling stories (in 1999 and 2007). I flew out there. We chartered a plane from Rite Bros."

A 2000 hunt was not successful. Lawsuits from animal-rights advocates eventually reached the 9th Circuit Court of Appeals which put further authorized hunts on hold (although five whalers killed a whale without permission in 2007, an event the *PDN* also covered in depth.)

An exception to the Marine Mammal Protection Act must be granted before whaling can resume, and as of 2018, that still was under review.

In 2005, the Makah hung the 30-foot skeleton from the whale killed in 1999 in its cultural and research center in Neah Bay.

'Devil Bear'

Gottlieb had been at the *PDN* 11 months when the story of Olympic National Park's "Devil Bear" broke. The big black bear was raiding backpackers' tents, sending the campers fleeing and gobbling up their freeze-dried food and toothpaste.

"He had been causing so much havoc, but the Park Service couldn't catch him," said Gottlieb. "The story was so huge, they gave him a name, Devil Bear."

The headline of Gottlieb's story on Aug. 13, 1999, read: "Bear gets death sentence" Somehow, the bear escaped hunting parties, the noose and eventually disappeared (rumors were that it was killed by hunters when it strayed outside the park's boundaries).

But the pesky bear did prompt the Park Service to conduct a study of its rules, which eventually led to a list of regulations for campers in the backcountry, including securing food inside bear-proof containers.

The National Park website now has a list of acceptable bear canisters.

Terrorist tackled in downtown PA

The newspaper doesn't always get the story immediately; sometimes it takes several days.

Such was the case on Tuesday, Dec. 14, 1999. That night, this author was on the desk as the *PDN's* recently hired local news editor, working on Wednesday morning's edition. Two reporters, Mark Morey and Jesse Hamilton, were in the newsroom.

"We heard this scanner traffic and thought somebody had fled the (Victoria to Port Angeles *MV Coho*) ferry," said Morey, a reporter for the Yakima *Herald-Republic* when interviewed in 2017.

"We didn't realize how significant it was. A few days later we got a call from a reporter at the *Everett Herald*. They wanted to find out what we knew (about a suspected terrorist running through Port Angeles).

"At that point, we knew nothing, but I started pressing the authorities. We finally got the information put together for several stories on Sunday (Dec. 19)."

Morey learned from what happened. "A couple months later we heard scanner traffic about some guys bolting from the ferry and running toward town.

"This time I ran out the door; turns out it was a huge marijuana bust. They had come from Victoria with a great quantity of weed."

Meantime, the *PDN* had published a couple of short stories about a man being held for questioning after fleeing the *Coho* ferry on Dec. 14.

But authorities were close-mouthed about what had happened, giving out only bits and pieces of information.

"It wasn't until we read something in *The Seattle Times* about FBI sources saying that the man arrested in Port Angeles was a suspected terrorist," recalled Brewer.

"Turns out he was intending to drive to LAX (Los Angeles International Airport) and blow up the international terminal there, massacring holiday travelers on New Year's Eve, just before the turn of the 2000 millennium.

"At his trial in 2001, they called him the Millennium Bomber."

When the story finally came together, *PDN* readers learned that Ahmed Ressam, a 32-year-old Algerian national, boarded the ferry in Victoria for a trip across the strait.

Ressam was driving a rented luxury Chrysler and was the last man to leave the ferry when it docked in Port Angeles.

Customs Officer Diana Dean said Ressam appeared suspicious. "I asked him (to get out and) open the trunk."

Customs Officer Mike Chapman was checking a suitcase in the car when Ressam slipped out of Officer Mark Johnson's grasp, leaving his jacket in Johnson's hand and bolting from the ferry. He dashed across Railroad Street, up Laurel and down Front Street, in the downtown business district, with Chapman, Johnson and Officer C. Danny Clem in pursuit.

After a six-block sprint, Chapman tackled him when Ressam emerged from hiding under a pickup truck.

Morey reported in Sunday's *PDN* headlined "Terrorism's close call: How Port Angeles might have thwarted global bomb plot," revealing that Customs officials searched the trunk of Ressam's rented vehicle and found nitroglycerine, four possible timers and more than 100 pounds of urea — all ingredients that could be mixed into a recipe for destruction.

Morey also found eyewitnesses to the chase. "It's a scary thing, right here in our little town," said Dave Hendrickson, owner of the Retroville store on First and Lincoln streets, across the street from the Lincoln Theater.

"It was a surprise to me to find out what I saw," said Hendrickson, who noted he and his wife had just left the store and were headed home.

"He didn't look panicky at all ... if I was being chased by the cops, I would be hauling ass. He looked kind of resigned, if you will."

Jeff LaPierre-Shuck, owner of North Light Gallery, was just leaving a meeting on First Street when he came close to the suspect.

"Basically, he almost ran me over," the gallery owner said. "He looked back and the look he had on his face was almost like someone was chasing him."

Arla Holzschuh, the Downtown Association director, made the call to police dispatchers. By the time officers arrived, Ressam had tried to get into a car at the intersection of First and Lincoln, but the woman driver locked the car doors and sped away.

Chapman, Clem, Dean and Johnson received medals. Chapman also received an Exceptional Service Award for capturing the man,

Chapman later resigned from U.S. Customs and became a 16-year Clallam County commissioner. In 2016, he was elected to represent the North Olympic Peninsula as a Democratic state representative.

U.S. Customs inspectors, from left, Danny Clem, Diane Dean, Mark Johnson (at the microphone) and Mike Chapman were honored in Port Angeles when it was announced the four would receive the U.S. Treasury Department's Exceptional Service award in Washington, D.C., for capturing Algerian terrorism suspect Ahmed Ressam on Dec. 14, 1999. Ressam had bolted from the MV ferry Coho and was captured on the streets of Port Angeles. *(Peninsula Daily News archive)*

As for Ressam, he's serving a 37-year sentence at the SuperMax high-security prison in Colorado. He's scheduled for release in 2032.

"This (Ressam) story kind of went away for a while after his arrest and trial," Brewer said … "Until 9/11, when it was revealed that he was in terrorist-training classes with the Twin Towers bombers. He was supposed to be one of the first al-Qaida operatives to attack the United States.

"When all this came out, Ressam became news again, and we had reporters and TV trucks 24/7 in Port Angeles, filming downtown and the ferry dock and interviewing us about what we had reported. Even *National Geographic* came to see us."

Deputy killed

Clallam County Sheriff's Deputy Wally Davis had been called to the same East Ennis Street residence just east of the Port Angeles city limits many times in responses of reports of a disturbance or domestic dispute.

He knew the man who lived there. He knew he had a history of mental illness, but Davis always had been able to talk to him and calm him down.

Saturday, Aug. 5, 2000, was different. Davis, who wore a protective vest, responded about 1:30 p.m. to a report of a disturbance. But as he reached the steps of the house, Thomas Martin Roberts shot him in the head with a shotgun.

Neighbors heard the shots and called 9-1-1. When backup officers arrived, they found Davis dead on the porch and Roberts holed up inside. Negotiations continued before a SWAT team from Seattle arrived and rousted him from the house with tear gas and pepper gas canisters. Roberts emerged from a crawl space under the house and was arrested about 2 p.m. Sunday, Aug. 6.

During the following week, the *PDN* reported Roberts had been legally allowed to purchase guns and had a concealed- weapons permit — all OK, because he had never been involuntarily committed.

Roberts had court-ordered mental evaluations in 1996 and 1999. In both cases, he was released after 72 hours, medicated but not committed by a judge. Roberts' wife Sue filed a complaint stating he physically assaulted her, but the case was dismissed when Roberts agreed to participate in a domestic-violence counseling program. That Aug. 5 9-1-1 call was one of nine to that residence the sheriff had received over the past six years. All this was highlighted in a *PDN* story.

Lead reporter for this tragic story was Gary Jones, who ran the Sequim Bureau of the *PDN*.

Rex Wilson, the executive news editor, "was the straw boss," said Brewer. "It was his baby all the way and he did a superb job."

The coverage won the *PDN* the C.J. Blethen Award from the Pacific Northwest Newspaper Association for Distinguished Excellence in Breaking News Coverage for newspapers under 50,000 circulation.

The *PDN* published 51 articles, 39 photos and a Commentary page editorial or investigative column each day for six days.

"I first got a call on something going on down in the ravine behind Schuck's Auto Parts from our vacationing photographer, Tom Thompson, in the early afternoon that Saturday," recalled Wilson in a 2015 interview.

"I don't recall how Tom heard about it, but I suspect someone in the Sheriff's Office contacted him because of his deep contacts in his nearly 30 years with the *PDN*. He relayed it to me.

"We sent on-duty photog Keith Thorpe to the scene. Our Sequim editor, Gary Jones, was the Saturday reporter in our Port Angeles office that day. Gary shot over there, too.

"It was 'all-hands-on-deck' by evening as the situation progressed and we called in off-duty staff. Gary, who was a veteran newshound from, among other places, Olympia and the Los Angeles scene, parked his car in the Schuck's parking lot and spent the night.

"About 2:30 a.m., he was awakened in the back seat by the sound of boots thumping — a SWAT team from the Seattle area was marching down the road to the house in which Thomas Roberts was holed up.

The Sunday paper had gone to bed at midnight with the situation at a stalemate. "The off-duty staff, who were called in to work, pieced together a nice tribute for Sunday's paper that included a wonderful photo of Wally in a cowboy hat that Thorpe had taken a year or two before. The story also included what apparently happened that day to cause his point-blank shotgun death on the porch of Thomas Roberts' house."

Jones had the lead story with the bold 96-point (letters about 1 ½ inches tall) headline "Deputy shot, killed" across all six columns; with a second head: "SWAT team, agitated man standoff."

Davis, 48, was a popular deputy who left behind his wife,

Wally Davis, a Clallam County Sheriff's deputy, investigated a domestic violence complaint in east Port Angeles on Aug. 5, 2000. He was shot and killed. *(Keith Thorpe/ Peninsula Daily News)*

Lisa, pregnant with their fourth child, two adult children, Jeff and Joshua, and 15-year-old daughter, Jessica or "Jessie."

Jones covered Sheriff Joe Hawe's press conference, headlined: "Sheriff tearfully tells of friend's death" In that story, an extremely emotional one, Hawe stepped to the mic, but all he could get out was "Deputy Wallace Davis died at 1:39 p.m." as tears fell from his eyes.

Mark Morey wrote "Slain deputy also an author," combining that story with a profile on Davis that reporter Christina Kelly had done in 1997. Davis was not only an author of 10 books, mostly western or mystery, but also an accomplished cartoonist. Morey wrote that Davis was a religious man and his books "contained no sex or gratuitous violence."

The staff also dug into the history books and determined: "Deputy may be first area officer to die from gunshot (he was).

"After all these years, I still can't say enough about Gary Jones and his initiative in getting the story for us," Wilson said. Jones died in 2001 of kidney failure.

"Murder One Charge" screamed the headline across the paper on Tuesday morning. Roberts appeared in court and was charged with aggravated first-degree murder with the death penalty on the table.

Davis was honored in an emotional memorial service at Port Angeles Civic Field. There were many tributes.

The memorial included a procession of more than 1,200 vehicles — police cars and motorcycles — from throughout the Northwest; Gov. Gary Locke flew in to give the eulogy. Many others also spoke.

But, the most gripping tribute came from Davis' 15-year-old daughter, Jessie: (See box).

Keith Thorpe's long-lens photo of the procession led off the main edition, while Nick Haney's gripping photo of Sheriff Hawe presenting a folded U.S. flag to Davis' widow Lisa ran six columns across special edition inside that had almost 20 additional photos. Roberts, charged with aggravated first-degree murder, pleaded not guilty, by reason of insanity. A change of venue was ordered, and a jury of residents from neighboring Island County deliberated for just three hours before finding Roberts guilty of murder on Nov. 7, 2002. He was sentenced to life in prison without parole.

He died of natural causes behind bars on Jan. 24, 2013.

Gottlieb and reporter Jeremy Schwartz combined on the story of Roberts' death. Jessie, 15 when her father was killed, had married Dan Spicher of Port Angeles. She was expecting a child in July when informed of Roberts' death in January 2013.

"I'm actually a Christian. I forgave him a long time ago," she offered in a phone interview. "I guess there is a little closure, but it's OK; it is, and I'm really sorry for his family."

"I'll never forget"

I'll never forget how he made me laugh
Or the trouble I got into when I was bad.

I'll never forget the lectures on boys
That I should not play with them like I would toys
I'll never forget his beautiful smile
Or how he scared off my friends for a while.

I'll never forget how big his hands were
I'll never forget how his heart was so pure.

I'll never forget our discussion on evolution.
I'll never forget our discussion on pollution.

He'd pull out the scripture and read me verses
On Unicorns, Demons and Satanic curses.

He was a talented man, many books he wrote.
He built model trains and could carry a note.

I'll never forget the lullaby he sang when I was younger.
It was by the Beatles; it was called "Golden Slumbers."

I'll never forget the morning he died
I made him pancakes that were a mile wide.

His name was Wally Davis, need I say more?
He was a loved man and will be forever more."

Jessica "Jessie" Davis, 15,
Daughter of Wally Davis
Aug. 7, 2000

More tragedy

It seemed as if tragedies stalked the *Peninsula Daily News*, but this next one not only affected the newspaper, but the entire nation.

It was Tuesday morning, Sept. 11, 2001, forever referred to as 9/11.

Like others on the West Coast, *PDN* staffers were jolted when they woke that morning to the tragic news that two terrorist planes slammed into New York City's Twin Towers.

As the morning progressed, a third plane slammed into the Pentagon building in Washington, D.C., and a fourth plane crashed into a Pennsylvania field, killing all on board, after passengers and crew attempted to wrest control from the hijackers.

The entire U.S. was put on a heightened alert. Port Angeles, being a port city with a Coast Guard station and airfield, made for a natural story.

PDN reporters Luke Bogues and Stuart Elliott went to work. "We are on the second-highest state of alert," said Lt. Mark Hilgel with the U.S. Coast Guard station at Port Angeles. "All cutters have been deployed. Their primary role now is maritime security."

All helicopter flights off the base have been suspended and a sign at the entrance read, "Identification cards must be shown to enter" as National Guard troops stood ready.

Perhaps some locals had relatives who lived in New York City or maybe even worked in the Twin Towers? Reporters Phillip Watness and Roger Harnack pursued that possibility.

These two struck a bonanza with their story "Peninsula residents witness to havoc." Former Joyce resident Andy Duncan said

Rex Wilson was hired by John Brewer in December 1998 as executive editor and retired in August 2005.
(Bill Lindstrom photo)

"As we saw incredible photos coming over the wire from AP, John and I knew we had to share them with our readers,"

the images of New Yorkers running, screaming would stick with him forever.

A computer consultant living in Rutherford, N.J., Duncan worked less than a mile from the World Trade Center. He had been in a subway on the way to meet a client near the Center.

"When I came out of the subway, I saw billowing smoke all over the place. People were just freaking out and running around," Duncan said, adding it took nearly two hours to finally get a message out to let relatives know he was OK.

Other staff members were assigned to get more local reaction, a person-on-the-street story. Reporter Brenda Hanrahan wrote about a big blood drive in Sequim in which dozens donated.

In Port Angeles, reporter Brian Gawley wrote about the unthinkable on this day (or any day): A bomb scare forced closure of the high school, resulting in barriers at bridges. Officials took no chances; no bomb was found.

Commentary page editor Gottlieb immediately thought of the foiled Ahmed Ressam terrorist plot less than two years before. Ressam was captured by Chapman, who at this point, had become a Clallam County commissioner.

Gottlieb found him, patrolling the halls of county buildings looking for suspicious bags and taped cardboard boxes of unknown origin.

"We prevented a great tragedy (in December 1999), but the tragedy today is on a much larger scale," Chapman said, cautioning that "we must maintain at least a semblance of normalcy until we see a credible threat."

Meantime, The Associated Press staff in New York, where Brewer once worked, labored overtime to quickly supply news stories and photos of the tragedy and its ramifications around the world.

"As we saw incredible photos coming over the wire from AP, John and I knew we had to share them with our readers," said Wilson.

"We notified the production department that we would be running a special 8-page broadsheet section."

Copy editor Kerry Fox and Wilson held a planning meeting, then took four pages each and loaded them with photos in about two hours.

"I have always thought that the *PDN* was the only small newspaper in the nation to publish a separate special section on Sept. 12, and nobody's ever corrected me on that," praised Wilson.

"Even metros like *The Seattle Times* boosted pages within their existing front sections; ours was a separate broadsheet section."

At the direction of Brewer, the paper continued running special follow-up sections on 9/11 for the next three editions, with Fox and Wilson creating the sections.

Hanrahan produced an enterprise story talking to teachers and counselors, who were wrestling with how to explain the terrorist attacks to youngsters.

Friday's local story on the Commentary page, "Remembering another tragedy," was a retrospective piece by Emeline Cokelet on Pearl Harbor.

Three peninsula residents, survivors of Pearl Harbor, recalled that attack 60 years before and likened it to the Twin Towers bombing.

"The difference," said Earl Jones, 78, of Sequim. "It took two hours for the enemy to kill 1,900 at Pearl. On Tuesday, it only took five minutes to kill possibly a lot more than that."

Those interviewed were in total agreement with Jones that the "U.S. is getting a wake-up call right here, the same thing we got in Pearl, but this is four times worse."

The death toll continued to mount; more than 3,000 were killed in the Twin Towers attacks and the vicinity, including 343 firefighters and 60 police officers.

Tse-whit- zen

The Clallam County economy received a big boost in August 2003 when the state Department of Transportation began work on a "graving yard" — a massive onshore dry dock — along Port Angeles Harbor to build anchors and pontoons for the replacement of the eastern half of the Hood Canal bridge and future bridge projects.

Several hundred local jobs were projected over a 10-year period. It was front-page news in the *PDN*.

But shortly after construction began, the *PDN* had new revelations for Page 1: Workers had found human remains and artifacts. They had discovered the lost Klallam tribal village known as Tse-whit-zen, (pronounced ch-WHEET- son).

Tse-whit-zen was the largest ancient village unearthed in Washington and it became one of the most important archaeological finds in the United States. Parts of the site were at least 2,700 years old.

By the fall of 2004, more than 800 stones etched with sacred teachings, more than 100,000 other artifacts and 335 human remains were found there.

The discoveries — especially as state construction workers encountered more and more human remains, including many intact burials, which increased concerns by the local Lower Elwha Klallam tribe — ultimately resulted in the state halting construction in December 2004.

It cost taxpayers more than $100 million to move the Hood Canal bridge work to Tacoma and Seattle. The graving yard had an original price tag of $17 million.

It was a controversial decision for some in Port Angeles. They wanted the project to continue for the sake of almost 200 jobs at the site.

"We lost about 100 or more subscribers during the course of our coverage, usually with them complaining along the lines that we were pro-Indian," recalled Brewer.

"The cancellations often happened after we had the latest Tse-whit-zen news on Page 1. They got worse when discussions began about closing the site for good, and after the closure decision.

"There are many, many enlightened people in Port Angeles, but you also have some homeboys who saw things as 'You're the Indian, and I'm the white guy, and guess who counts?'"

One night in December 2004 after the shutdown, *Peninsula Daily News* production staff members found a box with the words "artifacts uncovered" and "Sasquatch" written on it outside the newspaper's Front Street warehouse. The box contained several large animal bones.

The discovery came after passersby shouted, "Have you found any of your ancestors' bones today?' at tribal workers doing archaeology work at Tse-whit-zen.

The *PDN* did two special sections evaluating what happened at Tse-whit-zen, and the events were chronicled with historical perspective in a book, *Breaking Ground: The Lower Elwha Klallam Tribe and the Unearthing of Tse-whit-zen Village*, published by a *Seattle Times* reporter, Lynda Mapes, in 2009.

Mapes' research on the book included extensive use of *PDN* articles, which combined with letters to the editor, totaled more than 1,000 entries in the newspaper's electronic news archives by January 2005.

She also interviewed Brewer, for three pages of quotes in *Breaking Ground* about Tse-whit-zen and relations between some city residents and the Lower Elwha.

Brewer said Mapes' book "was a very detailed evaluation of the whole picture. What happened is a very painful chapter of the North Olympic Peninsula's history, but it also left us with some important lessons."

Follow-up stories in the *PDN* reported that the city of Port Angeles, in compensation for jobs lost in the graving yard shutdown, received $7.5 million from the state for economic development, $500,000 to recruit and retain businesses and $480,000 to hire an archaeologist to monitor shoreline projects.

The Port of Port Angeles, which sold the property to the state for $2.9 million, also received $7.5 million and a shoreline slice of the site to link port properties on both sides of it.

The Lower Elwha received the central 11 acres of the site, a low-cost lease from the Department of Transportation on 6 acres where a museum may someday be built, plus $2.5 million to help build it.

As of 2018, the museum still lacks a design and the tribe needs more funding to begin construction. Some of the Tse-whit-zen artifacts are on display for the public at two tribal facilities at First and Peabody streets in Port Angeles.

Items include a delicate bone comb, crowned by an exquisite carving of cormorants hovering over a child; bone harpoon points and fishing hooks and spindle whorls carved from whale vertebrae, and much more.

On Sept. 14-15, 2008, tribal elders hooked up with Lower Elwha Klallam members in Victoria, B.C. for an elaborate two-day ceremony to "rebury our ancestors."

On Sept. 16, 2008, a front-page story in the *PDN* by reporter James Casey was headlined, "Ancestors' reburial brings closure to Lower Elwha Klallam tribal members." It read:

The ancestors have come back home.

In two days of painstaking earth moving, the intact remains and skeletal fragments that were disinterred from Tse-whit-zen have been reburied close to where they were unearthed.

The work ended late Tuesday morning with Indian Shaker Church prayers and Klallam songs, including one that, translated, said:

My heart aches for you.

You are so far away.

A large front-end loader dug clean fill dirt from a nearby pile, then slowly and carefully tipped it into the burial trench beside the handmade cedar boxes that held the remains.

Workmen shoveled the jet-black soil by hand over the boxes. Leveling the larger site also will be done manually.

"There will be no more machinery on top of them," said Tribal Council member Dennis Sullivan . . . "They're at peace. You can really feel it in the air, that peace and comfort," tribal chairwoman Frances Charles said.

Sequim This Week

On Sept. 13, 2006, a new publication on the North Olympic Peninsula appeared. The *PDN* debuted *Sequim This Week,* a competitor to the *Sequim Gazette,* owned by Sequim businessman Brown M. Maloney.

The free-distribution weekly was mailed to nearly 11,000 households in the 98382 Zip code. This includes Sequim, Blyn, Carlsborg, Dungeness and Diamond Point. It also was available on racks and counters at Sequim-area businesses and offices.

In addition to puzzles, a weekly "look-ahead" weather graphic and advice columnists, it had Sequim government news, Sequim School District news, Sequim business news, community event calendars, Sequim 9-1-1 police reports — and lots of advertising. *Sequim This Week* had its own news and advertising staffers.

Noting that the *PDN* published separate editions for Jefferson and Clallam counties, with news and photos tailored for readers in each county, "this is a weekly extension of our daily Clallam edition (to bring) more local news to our thousands and thousands of Sequim readers," Brewer wrote in a news story announcing the new publication.

"Sequim is the fastest-growing and, increasingly, the most complex area on the North Olympic Peninsula. We are bringing out this free weekly to better serve the residents of this area, and our advertisers."

It continued until November 2011, when it was closed after Sound Publishing bought both the *PDN* and the *Sequim Gazette*.

"Sound did not want two weeklies in the same market, and it felt the *Gazette* was a more important investment," recalled Brewer.

Steve Perry, the *Gazette's* general manager, soon went to work at the *PDN* as the advertising director.

Brewer later became publisher of not only the *PDN* but the *Gazette*. He was also named publisher by Sound of the weekly *Forks Forum* in Forks and a monthly real estate magazine, *Olympic Peninsula Homes-Land* plus those two publications' active websites, all of which were acquired with the *Gazette*.

U.S. Forest Service officer Kristine Fairbanks is shown with her K-9 dog Radar in a 2007 profile in the *Peninsula Daily News*. On Sept. 20, 2008, while checking on a van with no license plates, the Forks resident was shot and killed. *(Keith Thorpe, Peninsula Daily News)*

Forest officer killed

On Saturday, Sept. 20, 2008, a U.S. Forest Service officer was murdered in a whirlwind of tragedy that left three dead in just over eight hours.

Kristine Fairbanks, 51, was shot and killed while checking on a van with no license plates at the Dungeness Forks Campground.

Her killer, later identified as Shawn M. Roe, fled the scene and then murdered Richard Ziegler of Sequim and stole his pickup.

That evening he was confronted by two Clallam County deputies outside the Longhouse Market and Deli in Blyn and was killed in a shootout.

Fairbanks, her husband Brian and 15-year-old daughter Whitney lived in Forks. She had been with the Forest Service 22 years.

The tragedy interrupted what had been a quiet Saturday at the *Peninsula Daily News*. Reporters Jim Casey and Tom Callis scrambled to get as much information as possible for the Sunday paper.

Gottlieb went to work on a sidebar story recalling Wally Davis, the sheriff's deputy shot in the line of duty in 2000, along with a sidebar reprising the other officers on the North Olympic Peninsula who died while on duty.

Photographer Keith Thorpe pulled a file photo of Fairbanks from a story the *PDN* had published a year before. It showed the officer with her K-9 dog Radar. She had left the dog inside her vehicle when she went to check on the van.

Officers told reporter Paige Dickerson they believe Ziegler was working outside his fifth-wheel when he was shot. "I think he was in the wrong place at the wrong time," said Clallam County Sheriff Bill Benedict.

At a Sunday afternoon news conference, Benedict also revealed a cache of weapons found on Roe, whose last known address was Everett. Fairbanks' 9 mm service revolver was found in the suspect's hands, while Ziegler's rifle was in his truck. Roe had a history of domestic violence.

Casey went to work on a story about Fairbanks, her life and her work.

"This community has lost a wonderful person," said Nedra Reed, a friend of the family and mayor of Forks. "A wonderful peace officer, a wonderful wife, wonderful mother, wonderful friend."

Marcia Bingham, director of the Forks Chamber of Commerce, was a neighbor of Fairbanks, whose home was on the Bogachiel River, about 6 miles north of Forks. "They loved living on the river," Bingham said.

"Kris and her husband Brian attended all their daughter Whitney's games," said Bingham. Whitney, a sophomore, played junior varsity volleyball.

Casey scored another exclusive when he interviewed Roe's former mother-in-law and his ex-wife.

"Gunman's former mother-in-law says forest officer's sacrifice saved her family's lives," read the headline over the big bold "We lived in fear," a quote from Roe's ex-wife, Mary White.

"It is my firm belief that had Kris not called in his name that he would have ended up down here," said Mary's mother, Patti White, from her Shelton home. "And it's very likely we would have lost our lives.

"It's starting to sink in that we can stop looking over our shoulder."

About 3,000 people attended a memorial service at Civic Field. Gov. Christine Gregoire delivered the eulogy. Radar was there as well as 18 members of the Happy Tails 4-H club, which Fairbanks led.

The paper produced a special section, leading off with a *PDN* reprint of a 2002 profile on Fairbanks "Watching Over the Wilderness."

A black, rider-less horse was led onto the field, to symbolize a fallen officer. Then a cadre of uniformed officers escorted Fairbanks' husband and Whitney and their extended family slowly to the front of the field.

Fairbanks spent considerable time with the Forest Service in Alaska training K-9 dogs and their handlers. In May 2012, a patrol vessel for use by local law enforcement and the Forest Service was named in her honor: *PV Kristine Fairbanks.*

Fairbanks' daughter Whitney became a Port Angeles police officer. In 2018, she completed training with her K-9 partner Bogey.

'Twilight Fever'

By September 2010, "Twilight Fever" infected the North Olympic Peninsula.

Stephenie Meyer *(Lonnie Archibald photo)*

Stephenie Meyer's best-selling *Twilight* four-novel series of teen love, vampires and werewolves, captivated the Olympic Peninsula and other fans.

The books — *Twilight, New Moon, Eclipse and Breaking Dawn* — became top-grossing movies, with Forks and its surrounding moss-covered rainforests and moody beaches the epicenter of their plots.

In *Twilight,* the first book published in

2005, Meyer introduces Bella Swan, a 17-year-old, who moves to Forks to be with her police chief dad. She is torn between the love of Forks High School classmate Edward Cullen and best friend Jacob Black. Before long, she realizes Edward is a vampire and Jacob a werewolf.

Meyer did her first interview about *Twilight* with the *PDN*, and in 2012, the newspaper estimated that over seven years Forks had received 200,000 additional tourists thanks to the popularity of the series.

The town's population is just 3,500 and before the series started it typically received no more than a few hundred overnight visitors every year. The area's timber industry has been in decline since the 1990s; *Twilight* tourism helped keep motels and restaurants afloat.

The peak year was 2010, when 70,000 "Twi-hards" (as the fans are called) poured into Forks, according to Marcia Bingham, director of the town's chamber of commerce. Souvenir shops catered specifically to *Twilight* enthusiasts and tours took them around town.

Meyer told the *PDN* in the 2005 telephone interview from her home in Arizona that she had never visited rainy Forks when she picked the town as the setting for *Twilight*.

Instead, she chose it after an Internet search showed that it might be a good place for vampires to live since it receives relatively little sun and often has a thick layer of cloud cover.

The book initially was called *Forks* before Meyer and her agent settled on *Twilight*. The book series soon became five full-length feature films that have grossed more than $3.35 billion.

While Forks reaped most of the tourists, Port Angeles benefited from being where Edward and Bella had their first date and where she visited a bookstore.

The Port Angeles Chamber of Commerce jumped at the chance to host a three-day "Twilight Fest" on Sept. 13-15 in 2009. The dates were situated around Bella's fictional birthday.

The *PDN* reported in 2017 that *Twilight* tourism had waned in Port Angeles but was still strong in Forks, with more than 35,000 visitors expected that year, some of them from as far away as Japan and Australia.

Many "Twi-hards" come for the Forks chamber's annual "Forever Twilight" festival. We'll learn more about this phenomenon in the chapter on the Forks.

The dams are removed

After two decades of planning, the largest dam removal in U.S. history began on Sept. 17, 2011, on the Elwha River west of Port Angeles.

It was ushered in by a special Sunday section of the *PDN* with graphics, stories and photos which took weeks of planning by workaholic Wilson and Brewer and a collaboration across all corners of the newsroom.

Six months later, the Elwha Dam was gone, followed by the Glines Canyon Dam in 2014. Today, the Elwha River once again flows freely from its headwaters in the Olympic Mountains to the Strait of Juan de Fuca.

The ecosystem's restoration (including 70 miles of salmon spawning habitat) still is making news.

By March of 2018, the *PDN* had published 3,540 articles and photos about the $325 million dam removal and its aftermath.

The home page at www.peninsuladailynews.com played dozens of videos taken by *PDN* staffers and National Park Service photographers as the dams were deconstructed piece by piece and the two lakes behind them were drained.

Changes for the *PDN*

By 2010, the *PDN* had long abandoned a plan to publish on a seventh day, Saturday. It continued to print six days a week for morning delivery Sunday through Friday.

From the handful of people who produced the first issue of the *Port Angeles Evening News*, the newspaper's family of employees had grown to 75 full- and part-time staffers, plus more than 100 independent contractors who delivered the newspapers.

The *PDN* had just moved to using a lighter, locally made newsprint made by the Nippon Paper Industries USA Ltd. paper mill in Port Angeles, according to Brewer in a 2018 interview.

The paper mill recently had resumed newsprint production after a 25-year hiatus. Much of the new newsprint went to customers in China and India.

The 40-gram Forest Stewardship Council-certified paper was the result of the mill's years of expertise in making lightweight telephone book paper with less energy and with recycled fiber. It also was cheaper than standard newspaper newsprint.

But this change also was a reminder that the *PDN*, like other newspapers worldwide, remained tethered to expensive 20th- century industrial processes such as a printing press, tons of paper and delivery trucks.

Brewer said, like other newspapers, the *PDN* was being buffeted by the disruptive changes in society brought by the Internet and the digital revolution. News consumption was being fractured and fragmented.

Readership of print products was falling. The emergence of websites like Craigslist "gutted the lifeblood of newspapers' classified ads.

"Display advertising also had declined as one of the worst recessions in the nation's history ravaged retailers — plus fewer print subscribers and new digital media alternatives reduced newspapers' appeal to advertisers," Brewer explained.

By the fall of 2011, the *PDN* had a daily circulation of 15,030 and 16,300 on Sunday, down from its high of 18,700 daily and 19,500 Sunday in 2005. (In October 2017 daily and Sunday paid print circulation averaged 10,002.)

But what about the *PDN's* 12-year-old website, *www.peninsuladailynews. com*, which was far and away the dominant news and information website for the North Olympic Peninsula according to stats from Omniture, Quantcast and Google Analytics, all of which measured web traffic?

It logged a total of 8.66 million page-views in 2010. That was up from 6.47 million page-views in 2009. (The site was averaging more than 900,000 page views a month in 2017).

The website was a hit with readers, and this attracted new sources of digital revenue — though not as successful as hoped.

Horvitz sells to Sound Publishing

Horvitz and members of his family "began to realize that we might no longer be the best owner for *PDN* to succeed in the new media environment," he said in a 2017 interview.

"The most successful newspapers had been able to improve by taking advantage of economies, and we no longer could gain extra benefit from it (because he had sold his other newspapers in the Seattle-area and in Maryville, Tenn.)," wrote Horvitz.

"This drove me to seriously consider selling the *PDN* since it was the last newspaper we continued to own. I approached David Black and Black Press because of the huge presence they had throughout the Puget Sound region. I knew that they could take advantage of their economies where I could not."

The sale of the *PDN, Sequim This Week* and their related websites for an undisclosed amount was announced on Halloween, Oct. 31, 2011.

The buyer was Canadian-owned Black Press Ltd. (based in the Vancouver Island city of Victoria, across the Strait of Juan de Fuca from Port Angeles) through Black's U.S. subsidiary, Sound Publishing Inc.

Black published more than 170 newspapers, mostly weeklies, and other publications in Washington, British Columbia and Alberta, Canada, as well as the Honolulu *Star-Advertiser* in Hawaii and the *Akron* (Ohio) *Beacon-Journal* daily newspapers.

Its Sound Publishing division, then based in Poulsbo, 60 miles south of Port Angeles, is the largest community newspaper group in the Pacific Northwest. In 2011, it published 46 weekly papers. In 2013, Sound added the 46,000-circulation *Everett Herald* daily and free-distribution *Seattle Weekly* to the group.

Sound was the same company that had bought Horvitz's King County *Journal* newspapers — a daily (which became a weekly under Sound), two weeklies, a monthly magazine and nine semi- monthly community newspapers — in November 2006. (Horvitz' daily in Maryville, Tenn., was sold to Greeneville, Tenn.-based Jones Media Ltd. in 2010.)

The sale came 95 years after the *PDN* had been born as the *Port Angeles Evening News* and ended its 17 years with the Horvitz Newspapers LLC.

"I'm proud of what was accomplished during our years as owners," said

Horvitz. "The tribute really goes to the news employees and the entire staff of *PDN* since they made it happen day in and day out."

Speaking to a newsroom gathering on the day of the sale, Mark Warner, president of Black Press' Vancouver Island division, said the Canadian company "jumped at the opportunity to purchase the *PDN*.

"I love your local content. For a daily newspaper, it's very strong. Your circulation is very good."

Brewer told his newsroom that the sale "gives us a connection to more resources." He described Sound Publishing as "an excellent community newspaper company."

Starting with the Nov. 15 edition, the *PDN* would be printed at Sound Publishing's massive printing facility in Everett, north of Seattle. There would no longer be a need for production services or a pressroom at the *PDN*. This put 20 employees out of work.

Warner said the decision to close the print plant "was extremely difficult."

Brewer described the layoffs as "terrible (but) the economics here demand it. I know this. I'm very sad about it."

Wilson also expressed dismay at the decision. "It was a painful day," he recalled upon his retirement. "It was the worst day of my years here."

Warner added that closing the press was something many newspapers were doing, switching to a regional print operation.

> "It was a painful day. It was the worst day of my years here."
>
> Rex Wilson, PDN executive editor on closing the press

"The days of having presses in almost all newspaper offices like there used to be, unfortunately are disappearing. We do centralize that part of our businesses."

There also was more news that would be announced at the *PDN*.

Warner told the newsroom that Black Press/Sound Publishing also had purchased a longstanding rival to the *PDN*, Brown M. Maloney's 23-year-old Olympic View Publishing Co., which owned the weeklies, *Sequim Gazette* and *Forks Forum* and *Olympic Peninsula Homes-Land* and *Islander Homes-Land* real estate magazines.

Talks had begun with Maloney after Black began negotiating with

Horvitz. Horvitz didn't know Black was in sales talks with Maloney; Maloney wasn't told Black was working on buying the *PDN*.

Both Horvitz and Maloney learned of the separate negotiations only the day before their staffs were told of the sales on Oct. 31.

"Nobody knew what to say," Brewer recalled. "Almost 17 miles away, in Sequim, there was also stunned silence as Maloney told his staffers about both sales."

In a prepared statement, David Black, president of Black Press Ltd., said, "We have purchased other titles from Horvitz Newspapers in the past and look forward to adding the *Peninsula Daily News* and its related titles to our Sound group."

"As publishers of other titles in the area (neighboring Kitsap County), this acquisition is a natural extension of our marketplace."

In a 2017 telephone interview from his Victoria office, Black said the acquisition of the *PDN* and Olympic View Publishing "fit our cluster strategy."

He explained, "We found if you purchase a number of papers in an area, you can lower your cost.

"We can print them all on one press, have one bookkeeper, one ad director; it lowers the cost of operation and the cost to the advertiser."

David Black, chairman and founder of Black Press Ltd. of B.C., Canada. *(Courtesy of Black Press)*

Rick O'Connor, CEO and president of Black Press, detailed the cluster concept further in another 2017 telephone interview from his Surrey, B.C. office. He was involved throughout the sale process.

"With printing at one plant, it's far more efficient. Port Angeles was using their press only a few hours a day and did very little job work. It made sense to shut it down. Now we print the paper in a couple of hours.

"Advertising is another advantage (with this strategy), you have one person (Steve Perry) overseeing it, but it's profitable for the advertiser too. An advertiser, based in Port Angeles, for example, not only can see his ad in all Peninsula papers, but also in Kitsap

County (where there are weeklies owned by Sound), and if he wanted, even in Victoria. We've created a more efficient way of doing business."

Black said there was a downside to this consolidation strategy; it puts people out of work.

"We don't want to hurt people, but the truth is it's more efficient," he said. "If we had a good press man or crew, we usually tried to find a place for them, but the drawback is, they would have to move."

O'Connor said "We were absolutely thrilled to get the Peninsula papers, and yes, we have definitely met our goals we set when we acquired them. Going forward, I see us as a multi-media organization, including a digital platform."

Wilson, Brewer retire

The *PDN's* six-unit Goss color community press was dismantled and shipped to Canada.

Printing at Sound's Everett facility required the *PDN* to move back its deadlines from 11:30 p.m. to 6 p.m.

This meant that no longer could the *PDN* publish stories for the next morning about night events like Seattle Mariners' games and important city council meetings, Brewer explained. If police raided a drug house on Monday night, it couldn't be published in print until Wednesday morning.

Brewer was able to get a 9 p.m. deadline from Everett on election nights so at least the first ballot counts could be published.

Everett's management "bent over backward to be helpful when it could; it is a first-rate, very professional operation. But we were one of many papers being printed there. Our needs had to be balanced against those of others."

He said, the Internet helped — Mariner results and breaking-news stories and photos were posted promptly on *www.peninsuladailynews.com* — and most readers adjusted to the change. But more than 250 quit their print subscriptions in protest over the next year.

"We continued doing solid community coverage — accurate, in-depth, perceptive stories," recalled Brewer.

"But we lost our unique timeliness. People no longer could grab the *PDN* with their morning coffee and find out important news that happened the night before.

"Sound certainly wasn't trying to shortchange the *PDN* or our readers. The whole newspaper industry was making changes and cost-saving adjustments to stay in business."

In June 2015, Brewer discussed retiring with the president of Sound Publishing. So, there would be plenty of time to find a successor, it was agreed he would stay until October.

"I had my differences with Sound," he said in 2017.

"There had been some painful staff layoffs and other measures we had to do to keep costs in line. But the main reason was that I would be soon be 68. It was time."

Executive Editor Rex Wilson also was retiring.

A year younger than Brewer, Wilson had decided that Aug.1, 2015, would be his departure date. He and Olga, his Guatemala-born wife, had been planning for two years to move to Mexico. They now live in Guadalajara, where they operate a lingerie fitting and design business.

Wilson said in his farewell to the newsroom:

"Regardless of the platform, whether print, TV, radio or the Internet, we still need and will always need journalism — you know, the inverted-pyramid stuff that tells the story succinctly and accurately with ethics, passion, objectivity and concern for the truth.

"Continue to give a damn about the news, OK? I certainly will."

To replace Wilson, Brewer promoted Leah Leach, 62, the managing editor since 2006, to executive editor.

News editor Michael J. Foster, 34, who Brewer recruited from Massachusetts, was promoted to fill Leach's position as managing editor.

Wilson was in Mexico when he wrote the *PDN* story published on Aug. 23, 2015, announcing Brewer's retirement.

In it Brewer closed out his 17 years at the *PDN* — and five decades in journalism — by saying, "It's been a joyful, rewarding, challenging, fascinating and occasionally bumpy ride.

"There's never been a day when I didn't want to come to work. And there's certainly never been a dull moment news-wise."

The story about his retirement noted:

Brewer has overseen the newspaper's transition from a print-centered operation to one that also delivers content through the Web, social media sites including Facebook and the PDN's e-Edition, an electronic page-by-page replica of the newspaper's daily editions tailored for Clallam and Jefferson counties.

His career started with manual typewriters and rotary-dial telephones — and is ending with smartphones, Wi-Fi and the replacement of one daily printing deadline with the Internet's pulsing 24/7 news cycle.

Through it all, Brewer has been a hands-on writer, editor and administrator.

Since 2013, Brewer had been overseeing operations of two weekly newspapers on the North Olympic Peninsula, the *Sequim Gazette* and *Forks Forum*; the monthly *Olympic Homes-Land real estate* magazine; and those publications' active websites; he was retiring from those as well.

The story continued:

John Brewer *(Bill Lindstrom photo 2015)*

"There's never been a day when I didn't want to come to work. And there's certainly never been a dull moment news-wise."

The PDN's annual voter guides, the twice-weekly outdoors column, weekly golf column, Sunday "Eye on" columns about what government is doing, the PDN's weekly Peninsula Spotlight entertainment magazine, the weekly maritime column and several other mainstay features in the newspaper were conceived by Brewer and refined over the years.

"And we do more than just carry news and advertising," said Brewer.

"We are a major supporter of the Juan de Fuca Foundation for the Arts, co-founding its annual festival — plus we contribute to more than 25 other nonprofit organizations in both Jefferson and Clallam counties.

"We co-sponsor weekly outdoor concerts for the public every summer, and we conduct annual award programs saluting community heroes in Jefferson and Clallam.

"We set a record, $271,981, in 2014 for our Peninsula Home Fund, which gives a 'hand up, not a handout' to individuals, families, single moms, senior citizens and others from Port Townsend to Forks, and everywhere in between, who suddenly face an emergency situation and can't find help elsewhere."

Brewer is passionate about the Home Fund, which is managed for the PDN *by Olympic Community Action Programs, the Peninsula's No. 1 emergency-care organization.*

He oversees its operations personally — the PDN *does not deduct one penny for administration or overhead — and writes many of the stories about it during the Home Fund's annual community fundraising campaign from Thanksgiving to New Year's Eve.*

"This is the 27th year for the fund — and I have no doubt my successor will care about it as much as I have," Brewer said.

At his going-away party, he couldn't talk enough about the job he was leaving.

"There are a lot of people who think they have a great job. I might be prejudiced, but I've always thought I had the best job on the North Olympic Peninsula. I've been fortunate to have the front-row seat for almost 18 years on the Peninsula's history — and what a view!"

"You are only as good as the folks you work with. And in that, I've been incredibly blessed. I'll always be proud of the dozens and dozens of dedicated professionals at the *PDN, Sequim Gazette* and *Forks Forum* committed to our mission of being the Peninsula's definitive source of news and advertising."

Brewer also earned respect from John Hughes, the former editor and publisher of *The Daily World* in Aberdeen who today is writing books and publishing Web articles about Washington state history for the Legacy Project in the Secretary of State's Office in Olympia.

Hughes had known Brewer from his days as the AP bureau chief in Seattle.

"When John Brewer landed at Port Angeles as publisher of the *Peninsula Daily News,* a lot of people were surprised; he was unquestionably one of the top newsmen in America," said Hughes.

"On the other hand, it made sense. Brewer loved the Pacific Northwest and leaving the rat race probably extended his life by at least 30 years.

"His work as a reporter was marked by flair and painstaking attention to detail. He quickly became an insightful, decisive editor and an absolute whiz as a bureau chief — a job that in his day required diplomacy, salesmanship and an unfailing nose for news. He was thoughtful, witty and a good judge of people; he made a legion of friends; he was also intensely competitive and driven to 80-hour weeks."

Brewer continues to live in Port Angeles and is actively involved with the business community and volunteer organizations.

He was elected president of the Port Angeles Business Association in 2016. He also enjoys fly-fishing for steelhead and salmon, something he rarely had time for as a publisher.

Terry R. Ward, 43, former CEO of KPC Media Group Inc. in northeastern Indiana, took over from Brewer on Sept. 8, 2015.

Brewer worked with him for a month and introduced him to community leaders in Port Angeles, Sequim, Port Townsend and Forks before officially retiring on Oct. 9, 2015.

In addition to overseeing community newspapers and online publications, at KPC Ward launched a digital marketing division that helped small- to medium-sized businesses grow their revenues.

Before joining KPC in 2012, he was director of sales and digital for GateHouse Media's Community Newspaper Division, working with 142 publications in 11 states.

Reflecting Sound's consolidation philosophy, Ward also succeeded Brewer as publisher of the *Sequim Gazette* and *Forks Forum* and *Homes-Lands* magazine.

Later he was put in charge of all of Sound's weekly newspapers in neighboring Kitsap County — *Bainbridge Island Review, North Kitsap Herald, Port Orchard Independent, Kingston Community News, Bremerton Patriot, Central Kitsap Reporter* and the *Kitsap Military Times*.

In 2018 Ward was promoted to Vice President of Sound Publishing. This new responsibility includes all of the Sound newspapers in Clallam, Kitsap, Island and Grays Harbor counties. The Alaska division, acquired from GateHouse Media in April 2018, is also overseen by Ward.

With his additional responsibilities, Ward elected to settle in the Kitsap County community of Poulsbo rather than Port Angeles. He is on the North Olympic Peninsula on a regular basis, checking on the *PDN* and the other publications there.

Steve Perry, now general manager as well as advertising director, runs operations day to day.

100th birthday

For more than a century, on paper and electronically, the *PDN* has reflected the changing times — the growth, the successes, the disappointments, laughter and tears of the people who call the North Olympic Peninsula home.

A century after its start, the *Daily News* has separate mastheads for its Clallam and Jefferson County editions. Each masthead carries its own artwork and front page news articles are tailored to each county.

In April 2016, the newspaper celebrated its 100th birthday.

"As the media landscape continues to change in the digital age, the reach and influence the *PDN* still maintains on the Olympic Peninsula comes with a level of responsibility we don't take lightly," Ward told readers.

"Our readers have placed their trust in us for a century. We are dedicated to earning their trust as we move into the next 100 years."

The economics of the newspaper business remain difficult for the *PDN* and other newspapers.

By October 2017, the print *PDN* was smaller than it had been in 2011, with fewer news pages and print advertisers.

Daily and Sunday paid print circulation was down to just over 10,000 Monday through Thursday, 11,831 on Friday and 11,912 on Sunday. Following a national trend, the newsroom staff had been reduced by several staffers from what it was in 2011.

But *www.peninsuladailynews.com* and the e-Editions remained very popular and Internet advertising and digital-only subscriptions kicked up more revenue for the newspaper.

The website was logging more than 900,000-page views a month — with almost half of 213,900 unique users choosing to read the site on their mobile phones, according to AAM/CAC *Consolidated Media Report* (Third-quarter, 2017), which tracks print and web subscribers and users.

All print subscribers received free access to the website. Digital-only subscriptions totaled 684. (With a metered paywall in place, non-subscribers had to make do with free story summaries on the home page after they exhausted seeing 10 free stories.)

Almost 22,000 people followed the *PDN's* notices on Facebook.

A new age for newspapers had begun.

CHAPTER 7

The Chronicle: For 32 years an alternative Port Angeles voice

" Y ou can't fight the Websters."
        Del Price heard that admonition over and over again, so much so that it echoed in his ears. But those were fighting words for the disgruntled *Evening News* advertising manager.

Price joined the paper in 1955 in the advertising department, though his real interest was on the news side. He took the job to be near the woman he loved and hoped to marry, Polly Hayashi, whom he had met at the University of Washington. She recently had begun teaching in Sequim.

Hired in 1955 by the *Port Angeles Evening News*, Del Price rose from ad salesman to sales manager by 1961. But he left and started his own competing newspaper, the *Shopping News*, which later became the *Chronicle*. Price published that paper for 32 years. *(Courtesy of the North Olympic History Center)*

In short order, Price became the *Evening News'* top ad salesman, and then ad manager. The Webster sisters — Mae Duckering and Dorothy Wenner — eventually saw him as an aspiring publisher.

Their brother Charles had suffered a stroke in 1953 and a second one early in 1955. His wife Esther was gradually assuming a larger role at the paper. However, it was George Buck, who had been appointed general manager in 1957, who "ran the show."

The sisters never got along with Esther and the feeling was mutual. The best one could say is they tolerated each other.

"Buck and Price often battled over spending and news coverage. Buck, a skinflint and bean counter, demanded a tight budget and kept a lock on the purse strings. Price thought he wasn't being adequately compensated for being the top ad salesman, according to the *Olympic Leaders: The Life and Times of the Websters of Port Angeles* by Joan Ducceschi and Helen Radke.

Although he was working in advertising, Price also "had strong opinions about news coverage, which he was not hesitant about voicing to Buck — particularly when he felt the newspaper was not being fair."

Buck's reply, according to Price: "Who says we have to be fair?"

John Schweitzer started as a printer in 1916 for the *Port Angeles Evening News*, later became part-owner. He left to join Del Price's fledgling newspaper, the *Shopping News*, in 1961. *(Courtesy of the North Olympic History Center/ Port Angeles Evening News)*

It was likely after one of those head-butting sessions with Buck that Price began thinking about new options.

"Dad was bringing in record lineage and he felt he deserved a raise," Del's son, Scott Price, said during an interview in 2015. "He talked about going to Buck's office and said Buck would clasp his hands behind his head and lean back in his chair. He knew there was no chance. He better stop talking and just leave."

One of Price's staunchest allies and his best friend was John Schweitzer. He had worked for the Websters since 1911 when he was a printer's devil on their weekly newspaper prior to joining the *Evening News* in 1916. He also was a former partner of the *Evening News*.

Some believe it was at Schweitzer's urging that the sisters approached Price with a hypothetical question asking him if he would be interested in being publisher, since they owned 53 percent of the paper and could fire Buck.

However, the sisters couldn't go through with it. "We don't want our brother's blood on our hands," they told Price. They feared if they pushed their brother aside, it would kill him.

Instead, Mae and Dorothy decided to sell their stock to Charles and Esther. The agreement was made in September 1960, but the sale wasn't announced in the *Evening News* until Jan. 13, 1961.

By then, Price was out of work. He and Schweitzer had been called into the office just before Christmas and were fired by Buck.

The disgruntled ad man told the *Olympic Leaders'* authors that Charles was there for the firing, but Buck did the talking.

In a 1994 interview, Buck revealed that Schweitzer was let go at Charles' urging because the former partner was bad-mouthing the Websters. Price confirmed that Schweitzer indeed, was critical of management. That included Charles, Esther and Buck. Price said he was let go because he "argued too much and had a temper."

There were two qualities his father didn't care for: "Insincerity and phoniness," said Del's son, Scott. "If somebody was a phony, it set him off. He had a resentment toward wealthy people, who flaunted their wealth. He saw both traits in the Websters."

An alternative voice emerges

On Jan. 19, 1961, only six days after the transfer of ownership became final, a direct competitor to the *Evening News* debuted — the weekly free-distribution *Shopping News* (later changed to the *Chronicle*), published by Del Price.

An article in the *Evening News* on Dec. 23, 1960, announced that Price and Schweitzer were leaving the paper. It failed to mention they were fired.

"Dad said many of the advertisers were not happy with the *Evening News*," Scott recalls. "Dad knew them from working with them on the *News*" and he probably asked them hypothetically, 'if I start a new newspaper, would you advertise with me?'"

It takes time to establish a newspaper. No doubt, Price was actively arranging this from September through December. He expected the firing (word of his new paper likely had leaked to management) or he was going to resign.

Del Price was a risktaker, his son said, attributable to an early experience. "He had once passed on an opportunity to purchase some property for $1,500; a few years later, the property tripled in value. He learned from that. He was very independent. He took chances."

Schweitzer, who Del Price said was like a father to him, was in the start-up operation to help sell ads and aid in the paper's production process.

Lorraine Ross, a reporter with the *Evening News*, also made the move to handle the news side of the *Shopping News*. By the third issue, Dave Partridge, another of the daily's ad salesmen, joined the fledgling operation.

Later, Fred Raber and Clayton Fox joined the ranks. Then, came the woman Price once paid tribute to: "The most popular part of the *Chronicle* is our favorite writer, Elisabeth Zerbel. It was a lucky day for us when she agreed to write her column for the *Chronicle*."

Zerbel started writing when she lived in Beaver on the West End and called her column "This Week on Tobacco Road," then moved to Sequim and called it "Country Diary" in the *Press*.

Price also had other believers: Needing money to start the shoe-string operation, he borrowed $2,500 and got another $2,000 in credit from a Seattle-area printer.

In his farewell *Chronicle* column 31 years later on June 24, 1992, Price saluted the contributions of Jim Harvey at First Federal Savings and Loan Association, Port Angeles' local bank.

Another risktaker was one of the first to hop onboard, and that soon led to more *Evening News'* advertisers who would jump ship.

"When Cliff Swain opened Swain's General Store — in 1957, and it remains today as one of Port Angeles' most popular and successful stores — I did the grand opening ad for him," said Price in the milestone 25th anniversary issue of the *Chronicle* in 1986.

"Conventional wisdom around the coffee shops said he would never make it, being so far away from the downtown area. Those days the only full-page ads were from the big boys such as People's Store, but Cliff agreed to take a full-page opening ad, saying, 'we'll open with a big ad, and if the *$?*! stuff doesn't sell, we'll take another full-page ad and have a closing-out sale.' The rest, as they say, is history." Swains has been selling stuff ever since.

Scott Price said the paper eventually had "every grocery store (and other established businesses): West Dependable, McGlenn's Thriftway, Tradewell, Smitty's, People's, Penney's, Reidel's, Kaufman Miller and Howard's Ski Marina. And there were others."

> *"He was well-respected. People had a sense that he was the underdog and they appreciated it. They appreciated that this was the opportunity for another advertising option."*
>
> Scott Price, Del's son

Scott said the *Evening News* was running scared.

"They were damn afraid of the *Chronicle* pulling ads away," he said. "In fact, Erl Hansen, advertising manager, had a $500 bounty for anyone who could steal away any of Dad's largest accounts. Ironically, Erl and I became good friends when he led the Chamber."

Initially, the *Shopping News* was far from a good-looking newspaper. In fact, the first issues looked like a throwaway — only it wasn't. Ads were stacked high on both sides of the paper and there were a few full-page ads.

The news? What there was, was slotted into any nook and cranny Price could find. The type looked like it was composed on an early day Commodore or Atari computer. It resembled that from a manual typewriter.

In the 25th anniversary edition, Price talks about that first issue, calling it a "miracle. We didn't have much equipment; everything had to be done by hand, almost one letter at a time. The whole operation was a 24-hour day task."

He wrote that the *Chronicle* was well received by readers and advertisers and quickly became part of the community. Helping this was the fact that it was delivered free to every home in the city.

As is true with most papers, we have been praised and damned. We have never tried to win any popularity contests but have tried hard to be fair.

He also said the staff strived to make the readers feel the *Chronicle* was "their paper."

The first *Shopping News* office was on the first floor in the corner of the People's store, where Country Aire natural foods store is today.

"The Linotype was in our garage," Scott recalled.

"I remember there was hot lead everywhere. We later added a Friden Justowriter." That enabled the operator to set justified type on a perforated tape. It would be put through the Linotype and decoded into hot-metal type.

Price persevered and eventually his creation started to look like a real newspaper.

Two years into the operation — Feb. 7, 1963, Price changed the name of the now, 14-page weekly paper to *Shopping News/Clallam County Chronicle*; it included several full-page ads, and advertising occupied about 80 percent of the space in several issues.

On Sept. 19, 1963, the *Shopping News* became the *Chronicle*.

A full-page of classified ads was sold at 10 cents per word; gradually, photos, letters to the editor, local columns, obituaries, weddings, school news and meeting notices were added.

Price proudly displayed a front-page logo, boldly claiming his paper "reaches 10 out of 10 homes."

A few months later, on Sept. 19, 1963, it was renamed the *Chronicle*, which it remained until its last day, June 24, 1992.

Moving day

On Dec. 12, 1963, the entire *Chronicle* operation moved upstairs into the Morse Building at First and Laurel streets.

The move to the Morse was an adventure. Scott said his dad talked about it often.

"They had to move everything in the middle of the night because they couldn't close the print shop," Scott said. "They got dollies and pushed the equipment down the middle of First Street the one block to the new building. The cops came by and asked what they were doing. Dad told them and the cops helped them move."

Scott said his dad had many good friends. "He was well-respected.

People had a sense that he was the underdog and they appreciated it. They appreciated that this was the opportunity for another advertising option."

The paper was a notable accomplishment for the man, who was born in Portland on Oct. 31, 1929, just after the stock market crashed. His parents struggled through the Depression. The next year the family moved to Seattle, where he graduated from Roosevelt High School.

He went to the University of Washington until the Korean War interrupted his education. He joined the Army in 1952, training as an infantryman. Just as his unit was preparing to ship out, the peace talks began to take effect and his overseas deployment was cancelled.

Instead, he was sent to military journalism school on Long Island, N.Y., and spent the remainder of his Army time performing intelligence-related work. He was honorably discharged in 1954 and returned to the UW. He immediately found work with the *Evening News*.

One day in the university bookstore, he met Polly Matsuye Hayashi. A relationship ensued, then romance. They were married in 1956 and moved to Sequim, where Polly had begun teaching home economics at Sequim High School.

Polly had an interesting background that we learn from her obituary in the *Sequim Sun* (Feb. 21, 1991), another paper the Price family published.

She was born to Japanese parents in 1930 in the Eastern Washington town of Granger.

The attack on Pearl Harbor, Dec. 7, 1941, changed everybody's lives, including Polly, who was only 10. Her mother had died when she was 5, but Polly, her dad and three siblings were forced, by executive order from President Franklin D. Roosevelt, to leave their home and be interned.

Able to leave only with what they could carry, they were first confined to a horse stable at the Portland (Ore.) Livestock Yard.

Polly said she never forgot the stink and the hard, straw mattress, nor could she forget and never did understand why her own country was treating her like an enemy. Soon, they were transported in a sealed railroad car to Heart Mountain, Wyo., and housed in a tarpaper shack.

She would talk little about the "camps" as she called the internments but did say she "was vilified in her youth (after the family was released) by kids who said, 'Japs' were not welcome and threw rocks at her," Scott said.

Through all the adversity, the family persevered and all four children graduated from college.

The newspaper was a family operation, and even though Polly was raising four boys and two girls, she assisted in the operation when she could.

Scott graduated from Port Angeles High School in 1975. The next year he began working for his dad, while attending Peninsula College in Port Angeles.

"I drove the truck to get the papers printed," Scott said, adding this meant driving to the Kennydale-area in Renton south of Seattle.

"I drove the (page) negatives there, waited five or six hours and drove the printed papers back. It's what we called 'swamping,' getting the papers to the carriers and mailing others third-class."

He said his father wanted to get a second-class permit that would give him the prestige (and big bucks) to have legal notices printed in the paper, but "he didn't reach that."

In an article at the start of the fifth year, Del wrote:

In politics, as well as general news, the Chronicle *has not been, and will never be, the organ of any party or clique, but endeavors to be fair and honest in presenting the news.*

"They knew they would get a fair shake with Dad," said Scott. "He covered issues the daily would dance around. There was a mil; labor dispute — union versus owners. He'd go to the meetings and talk to both sides. If he found a situation he was passionate about, he was sympathetic and wrote about it. It kind of endeared him to folks."

One subject he was undeniably passionate about was the Northern Tier Pipeline. There was no mistaking which side he favored. It was summarized in an editorial when the pipeline demise finally was announced, Aug. 21, 1983:

The announcement that Trans Mountain Pipeline Company is dropping their proposed oil terminal west of Port Angeles is long overdue. In fact, it should have been made the day after the project was announced. … it was a pipe dream hatched in go-go-land and nurtured by pot-of-gold promises.

Interestingly, Del was on the same side on this issue as *The Daily News* – the *Evening News* had been renamed after its sale by Esther Webster in 1971. It also argued strongly against the pipeline on its editorial pages.

Scott said his dad would capitalize on any complaints that existed about the *Evening News* and fill that gap. One such example involved some of the local real estate agencies.

"They were really upset with the daily and came to us. Dad cooked up the *Realty Journal*, an 8-page paper initially, then four pages. I'll never forget Darrel Vincent, owner of Olympic Realty (now Windermere) saying when our paper came out, he had to put more people on staff to handle the calls."

Sports was another area in which the *Chronicle* found a need. "The daily wouldn't print photos of sports teams. We would, and people liked that."

That led to a new paper, *Sports Week*, which Price published in the "late 1970s for about four years. Fred Bird was the editor," Scott said.

Jim White, who had been sports editor at the *Evening News*, then worked with *The Jimmy Come Lately* in Sequim as news editor under two different publishers and freelanced with the *Sequim Press*, was a writer for the paper.

Dad also felt the logging industry was "under-reported and misrepresented. He gave them a new voice with *Olympic Logger*, a weekly, in 1979. I don't think it changed anybody's mind whether there were clearcuts or not, but it did rally the community of timber towns. They felt someone was on their side."

Steve Indelicato, who lived in Port Angeles, was the editor, with a small office in the timber town of Forks on the West End of Clallam County.

"There was a fierce loyalty," said Scott. "He immersed himself in the timber community as an independent from Port Angeles. He wanted to be one of them and was one who got the ball rolling for the timber museum in Forks. It galvanized the community, until the spotted owl issue came in 1990."

New voice for Sequim

In 1985, "Dad and Mom saw an opportunity for another voice in Sequim, and founded the *Sequim Sun. The (Jimmy Come Lately) Gazette* was healthy with ad revenue, but Dad felt there was a need for a fresh viewpoint in reporting, plus he had a good reputation there, which definitely contributed to its success."

The Price family published the *Sequim Sun* for seven years before selling it and the *Chronicle* to Brown M. Maloney in 1992.

Del Price *(Courtesy of the North Olympic History Center/ Port Angeles Evening News)*

Polly was intimately involved in founding the *Sun* and worked until she became too sick. Her obituary in the *Sun* notes that she was diagnosed with pancreatic cancer in 1989 and told she had six months to live. But, with the help of Dr. Robert Witham in Port Angeles and the staff at Virginia Mason Medical Center in Seattle, she rallied for two more years.

"Mom's death was a tremendous blow for everybody," said Scott. "It kind of took the wind out of Dad's sails. He was lost, and the business died shortly after that."

Del kept the business going for another 18 months before printing the final edition on June 24, 1992.

In that edition, he reflected on some highlights of his nearly 32 years publishing the paper. He relished being among the first to interview Booth Gardner when he became a candidate for governor; Gardner was elected and served from 1985-1993.

He wrote about weathering a million-dollar lawsuit against him by a man who wanted to start a plywood mill. The *Chronicle* printed that the man "dipped into the stock money and used it for personal lifestyle goodies." Prosecuting Attorney Nathan Richardson helped the man get convicted on fraud, he was sent "upriver" and the suit went away.

When a group of nurses complained about the dark parking lot at the hospital, "I wrote a story and exposed it, showing a picture of a nurse in available light. The problem got solved." Del said.

In the early days of the paper, Del said he reported striking mill workers at Crown Z and Rayonier.

"Those were volatile days," said Price, who got hassled by front-line picketers, but kept walking until he came upon the strike leaders, who knew him. "They announced loudly, 'Hey you guys, this is a reporter from the *Chronicle*. He's OK.' Suddenly, I was being treated like a friend, instead of an enemy."

Price signed off his final editorial by noting a resolution passed by the Port of Port Angeles.

It cited the *Chronicle* "for contributions to the community and efforts to educate, inform, promote and provide intelligent thought to the citizens of Clallam County."

• FREE! •

Final Issue Dedication

This final edition of the Sequim Sun is dedicated to Polly Matsuye Hayashi Price who was with us body and soul at the beginning and remains with us in spirit at the end.

— Del Price

June 25, 1992   *FOCUSING ON THE SEQUIM-DUNGENESS VALLEY*

The Price family started the **Sequim Sun** in 1985 and ran it until 1992.

Price wrote: "If we did all that, our mission was a success. We tried."

The final issue he dedicated to Polly Matsuye Hayashi Price, "who was with us body and soul at the beginning and remains with us in spirit at the end."

Polly never set foot in Japan, but after retiring from the newspaper business, "Dad became more intensely interested in Japanese culture and dove into the language, making several trips to Japan," said Scott. "He even worked in Japan as an English teacher for a time."

In July 2008, Del was diagnosed with CML, a form of leukemia. He continued treatments and died at home surrounded by his family on Sept. 7, 2009. He was 79.

His obituary in the *Peninsula Daily News* noted that Del was a voracious reader and had an extensive library. He also was an accomplished photographer for years and had a passion for sailboats.

He enjoyed cruising on his sailboat in local waters and participated in the annual "Swiftsure Classic," an international sailing event in the Strait of Juan de Fuca.

Del Price's *Chronicle* was the only newspaper that successfully held its own after daring to challenge the Websters.

And, it did so for 32 remarkable years.

PART II

Sequim

CHAPTER 8

Sequim: Papers on the Dungeness Prairie

M ost of the people living in Sequim today recall only two long-lasting newspapers in the city: The present *Gazette* (born as the *Sequim Shopper* and morphed into the *Jimmy Come Lately Gazette*)

Or the *Press*, the newspaper of their parents or grandparents, which existed from 1911-1985.

However, the *Press* was not the first paper in Sequim.

While it only existed for one year, the *Dungeness Beacon* was the city's first newspaper from 1892-1893 before the owner moved it to Port Angeles.

A few other papers had a brief fling: *Sequim Sun* was started as a weekly in 1985, sold in 1992, then folded. The *Olympic Review* operated from 1960-1961. In 2006, the *Peninsula Daily News* produced *Sequim This Week* as a free distribution for a few years.

Before we get into a discussion about the newspapers, let's examine a bit of history — or in Sequim's case — pre-history.

Mastodons in Sequim

Until 30 to 40 years ago, the first human inhabitants were believed to be members of the S'Klallam tribe with evidence that they fished the Dungeness River, the Strait of Juan de Fuca and Sequim Bay as early as 170 years ago and likely well before that.

The S'Klallams made their homes along the river and ventured inland in search of food. Tribal history indicates they were established in their townsites long before the first white man staked a claim in 1848.

That all changed in 1977 with the discovery of the Manis Mastodon, an archaeological find that would suggest there were humans in the South Sequim area as late as 11,000 and perhaps as early as 14,000 years before previous artifacts had suggested. That was a crucial discovery for historians, not only for Sequim, but the Olympic Peninsula.

Emanuel "Manny" and Clare Manis moved from California and bought a farm in South Sequim in 1975, in the shadow of the Olympic Mountains.

The couple intended to plant a vegetable garden, buy a few head of cattle and dig a permanent pond in the marshy part of their small farm to provide water for the animals and crops.

On Aug. 8, 1977, Manny was digging in a peat bog, where he intended to construct the pond, when his backhoe unearthed what he initially believed were old logs. But these findings were slightly curved, and they were larger than he was. He had a suspicion they might be an archaeological discovery, perhaps elephant tusks, or even from a mastodon or mammoth.

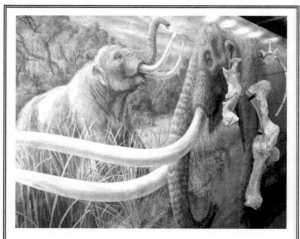

This massive mastodon display in the Sequim Museum and Arts Center shows where on the large mammal bones were recovered on the south Sequim property owned by Emmanuel "Manny" Manis in 1977. He was digging a pond when the bones were unearthed. The finding indicates human life existed as early as 11,000 years ago in Sequim. *(Bill Lindstrom photo)*

He immediately contacted Washington State University's Office of Archaeology and Historical Preservation. In short order, Dr. Carl Gustafson and others descended on the peninsula to examine the digs.

Indeed, it was an important find. The "logs" were tusks about 8-feet long, from a mastodon, believed to have inhabited the Olympic Peninsula 13,000 to 14,000 years ago.

Gustafson then made an exciting find with potentially major scientific implications — a rib fragment with a denser type of bone protruding from it.

The fragments were X-rayed with the conclusion that the wound produced by this foreign piece of bone was a "penetration fracture" that had healed for three to four months.

Gustafson detailed the findings in the book, *The Manis Mastodon Site: An Adventure in Prehistory,* he co-authored with Clare Manis, two years after her husband's discovery.

With Gustafson at the forefront, several grants from archaeological, geological, anthropological and other related scientific fields were obtained to fund the expensive venture. Some private donations also were received.

Sequim became a hotbed for national paleontologists, not just WSU archaeologists.

In an October 2011 issue of *Science,* titled "Pre-Clovis Mastodon Hunters Make a Point," author Lawrence Lawler wrote of the study conducted at Texas A&M University, "Scientists used DNA and radiocarbon dating to demonstrate that the point came from a mastodon bone shaped into a weapon by humans and used a startling 13,800 years ago. That's nearly 2,000 years before the Clovis culture, long considered to be the first culture in the New World. The find adds to the wave of recent compelling evidence demonstrating an earlier, pre-Clovis settling of the Americas."

These weren't the only discoveries around Sequim. Several other mastodon body parts, including tusks and teeth were found near the mastodon site. Numerous bison bones also were found. Some scientists suggest the bison might have been food for the much-larger mastodons and mammoth, some as tall as 12 feet.

In 2017, a giant molar, weighing more than 10 pounds was unearthed on the beach near Sequim.

The *Sequim Gazette's* (June 7, 2017) report of the finding by Sequim residents Lori Christie and Dean Flowers came as they were strolling the beach, several miles from the mastodon site, searching for petrified wood and rocks when they noticed the ancient tooth.

"When we looked down at it, Dean remarked it didn't look like other rocks," Christie told the newspaper. "The flat surface was showing and it had rocks around it."

In late May, the pair took the molar to the Burke Museum at the University of Washington that confirmed the object was a Columbian mammoth molar.

"Both of us were in shock," Christie told the *Gazette.* "There are artifacts here and fossils to be found, but it's not real common to find them."

Scientists estimated the molar was 19,000 to 20,000 years old and from a 35- to 40-year-old adult Columbian mammoth.

Christie said they would like to donate the molar to the Sequim Museum and Arts for others to see. Many of the Manis findings also are at the museum. Visitors can view a DVD, summarizing the mastodon findings. Tusks are preserved in a water tank, while larger bones are mounted on an elaborate mastodon display.

During the years of excavation, Clare and Emanuel Manis welcomed more than 50,000 visitors to the site. In 1978, when the site was added to the National Register of Historic Places, Sen. Henry M. "Scoop" Jackson made the announcement. In 2002, on the 25th anniversary of the discovery, Clare Manis donated the site to the National Archaeological Conservancy.

In November 2011, Shirley Manis, daughter of Emanuel and Clare Manis, authored the first and only children's picture book about the Manis Mastodon site, which includes the most recent research analysis to that date. Admission is free to the site, on Lester Way near Happy Valley Road in South Sequim. Visitors can obtain exact directions at the museum, 175 W. Cedar St., Sequim.

Early pioneers

Now, that we know a bit about pre-historic Sequim, let's turn to more modern history with help from Al Courtney's *Sequim Pioneer Family Histories*, Vol. 1 (1850-1947) and Volume II (1850-1966).

Although Spanish explorers likely were the first Europeans to set foot on the Olympic Peninsula, credit for naming Dungeness Valley goes to an Englishman. When Capt. George Vancouver sailed his ship *HMS Discovery* along the Strait of Juan de Fuca in 1792, he named a lowland property New Dungeness because it resembled the Dungeness area in his homeland.

In 1850, Congress passed the Donation Act, granting 640 acres of land free and clear in the Oregon Territory to all white or mixed-blood settlers, who arrived in the area before Dec. 1, 1855. The Oregon area also included Washington Territory.

The first man to stake a claim in Dungeness under the terms of the act was James B. Madison, who may have come as early as 1848. He claimed to have settled on his land on March 30, 1852. The first permanent settler was John William Donnell, also in 1852.

Another early settler was John Bell, who settled on the prairie, which is now downtown Sequim. His name has been applied to Bell Hill, Bell Street and Bell Creek, which meandered through his property.

There were many homesteads in the Dungeness Valley in the 1850s, but nothing was legal until the land was surveyed in the mid-1860s. By the time, settlers arrived, the Oregon Territory had been divided. Land north of the Columbia River became Washington Territory. It encompassed the entire North Olympic Peninsula. Jefferson County was created out of Thurston County in 1852 and Clallam County was created out of Jefferson County in 1854.

According to the 1857 Census, the Sequim-Dungeness area had 53 inhabitants with Dungeness the most populous and county seat. The Dungeness Lighthouse was first lit that year. In 1861, after the creation of the Homestead Act boosted the population, the Abernathy School was erected. Thornton Lane School followed in 1862 and existed until 1896.

After the first few years, the county seat was moved to the top of the bluff on land donated by Elliott and Margaret Cline, and the town of New Dungeness grew west along, what is now, Marine Drive and south on Clark Road.

There are many versions of how Sequim got its name. In one story, a post office was established on Aug. 12, 1879, at Seguim, a S'Klallam word meaning "quiet waters." But, when the charter was returned from

Washington, D.C., apparently someone couldn't discern the "g" from the "q" and copied Sequim. Thus, the name was changed in 1907.

Another story, revealed in the 1981 70th edition of the *Sequim Press*, calls it "the most logical explanation." The S'Klallam tribe, which subsisted on a steady diet of clams and salmon from the nearby waters, found the Dungeness and Sequim valleys abundant with an herb of the onion family. This herb "provided a steady alternative to the seafood. In the throaty Indian language, this onion was translated sskkwwmim or skwimming as we would say. It was later pronounced skwim and then given the English spelling of Sequim."

Until 1887, when the Puget Sound Cooperative Colony was established at Ennis Creek in east Port Angeles, New Dungeness (Also known as Old Town) was the largest town on the peninsula.

Former Sequim Museum director Katherine Vollenweider's book *Images of America: Sequim-Dungeness Valley*, notes that the 1887 Puget Sound Polk Directory lists the town with two hotels and two general stores, operated by Cyrus Clapp, also the postmaster, and E.H. McAlmond. It has a population of 75 and has regular shipments of livestock, grain and general farm produce to Puget Sound.

After the election of 1890, the Clallam County seat was moved from Dungeness (some accounts say it was hijacked) to Port Crescent, west of Port Angeles. This town was rapidly growing, and a developer predicted a railroad soon would be coming.

Despite the loss of political power, New Dungeness became one of the major sources of agricultural products for Port Townsend, Port Discovery, Port Gamble, Tacoma and Seattle.

As the bay began to silt and the channel around Dead Man Spit grew shallow, businesses moved out and toward the mouth of the river. There was talk of naming the growing community Groveland, but New Dungeness was well known; thus, the town of Dungeness came into existence in 1890.

Confusion reigned for a decade or two. Residents called New Dungeness "old town" and Dungeness "the new town." Eventually, all that remained of New Dungeness were a few homes and its main street, now Clark Street.

Charles Franklin (C.F.) Seal's Farmers' Mercantile, later Dungeness Trading Company, was the first and most important building. Later, the

The main street of Dungeness is viewed from the dock looking south toward the business district. The area was a prominent agricultural producer. *(Sequim Pioneer Family History, Vol. II)*

The Hotel Sinclair, Clallam County's first brick building in 1890, was at the southwest corner of Washington Street and Sequim Avenue. *(Sequim Pioneer Family Histories, Vol II)*

Sinclair Hotel, the first brick building in Clallam County, was erected. Other businesses, among the 20 listed in the Sanborn maps, included a blacksmith shop, mercantile store, saloon, grocery store, bowling alley, restaurant, drug store, post office, church and parsonage.

Later, Seal built himself a mansion, one of the more elegant homes in the county.

In an Oct. 21, 1960, *Sequim Press* article, Beth Seal Hart, daughter of the pioneering family, describes the estate as palatial, the showplace of Dungeness Gardens and the entire Olympic Peninsula. It was built in Old Town, but moved to New Dungeness and a kitchen was added:

Thanks in part to the Seal family, a bevy of dairies on the prairie, and logging to the south, the town of Dungeness boomed.

All it needed was a newspaper.

First newspaper

Three businessmen, R.C. Wilson, Col. R.H. Ballinger and G.K. Estes were about to remedy that. They teamed to establish the *Dungeness Beacon* on June 24, 1892. Ballinger was the lone man with newspaper production experience, but that was a bit star-crossed. Two years previous he and his son, Joe, came from Port Townsend and started the *Port Angeles Tribune*. But, the elder Ballinger got himself in a bit of a storm when he developed a dislike for T.J. Patterson, who ran the local weather bureau, and the colonel tried to oust him.

This didn't sit well with Patterson's backers and they hanged Ballinger in effigy. Ballinger lost interest in the paper after that.

Apparently when Wilson and Estes came knocking, his interest was reawakened. Wilson, an attorney involved in the receivership of the *Model Commonwealth's* liquidation in Port Angeles, was a stockholder with the *Port Angeles Democrat*, a competitor of Ballinger's *Tribune*.

Oddly, Estes, who doesn't appear on any early papers, was installed as the editor. Subscriptions were $1.50 for a year, 75 cents for six months and 5 cents per copy.

On July 1, 1892, the one-week old *Beacon* reported that the postmaster general had assigned Dungeness as the town's official postal delivery name. Vollenweider writes in *Images ...* that "both towns (New Dungeness and Dungeness) existed concurrently as businesses made the move from the late 1880s to early 1890s. A wharf existed at Old Town, and vessels with deeper draft used the services of S'Klallam canoes, scows and small boats while anchoring east of the spit."

A *Beacon* advertisement by H.J. Lipsett proclaimed a "great opportunity to obtain prime land through choices offered by Port Discovery Mill Co. More than 1,000 acres are available, 300 of it on cleared land."

The *Beacon* "provided world reports and stories of national interest. A smaller section was devoted to local news."

The newspaper was holding its own, but the owners decided it would do better in east Port Angeles. So, they moved the paper after less than six months.

Estes explained why he was moving in an editorial on Jan. 6, 1893, to help assuage the Dungeness subscribers.

We take this step believing that we will be able to get out a better newspaper for Clallam County than at Dungeness. A reporter at Dungeness will give the news from there each week. Because of arrangements made now we will be able to do better by the people of Sequim than formerly and will likewise give the news from Blyn and Bopa, so that our subscribers in the east end of the county need not complain. We hope to have correspondents from every neighborhood in the west end.

To the advertisers of the county, we will say that we believe the Beacon *will continue to go into every home east of Morse Creek, and that our agents will secure the subscriptions of new settlers as they come in. We shall make special efforts to extend our circulation in this city and to the west, through agents and numerous sample copies.*

The Beacon *is not a party paper, a trade paper, a boom paper, nor a story paper, but a newspaper. If you want the news, take the* Beacon.

The paper was politically orchestrated by Wilson, who was a candidate for state senator in the ensuing election. After the campaign, Estes sold his interest and the *Beacon* was absorbed by the *Tribune-Times* in 1901.

By this time, the Sequim-Discovery Bay area was booming with logging operations. In the *Port Angeles Evening News'* 1962 special section celebrating the 100th anniversary of Port Angeles, reporter Alice Cook writes that the first lumber mill was established by S.B. Mastick, who was attracted to the area from San Francisco. He built the Port Discovery Mill in 1858. Most of the logging in the 1860s and 1870s was done by the Port Discovery Company.

Robert (Bob) James Clark, a resident of Dungeness all his life, recalled those early days in his family's history. Clark, born in 1930, said in an interview in 2016, his great-great uncle William King engineered and installed the first machinery at the mill.

"He was a gifted machinist," said Clark, noting King received the first Land Patent granted in the state of Washington. "He was one of the first teachers in Dungeness. The school was in a log cabin about 100 yards south of present-day Anderson Road East."

King was a bachelor all his life, but his sister, Elsie Clark, came from Bay City, Mich., sailed down the Mississippi River, around Cape Horn, landing by Indian canoe on, what is now, Cline Spit. She brought two sons and a daughter with her, joining two other sons who already were employed at the mill.

Thus, began the propagation of the Clark, Cline and King families in Dungeness. Bob Clark's father, Thomas Stuart Clark, was the son of Elsie Clark. Thomas married Sarah Cline, the daughter of Elliott Cline (whose name when he arrived and founded New Dungeness was spelled Kline).

Clark writes of these folks and many others in the *Sequim Pioneers* Vol. II.

A trip down Sequim-Dungeness Way to Dungeness reveals many streets and areas named for the pioneers: Clark, Cline, Lotzgesell, Anderson, Cays, Abernathy, Mapes, Eberle and many more. Along the way, at Anderson and Towne roads, is the Dungeness Valley Schoolhouse, built in 1892.

Sequim's rain-shadow

Before the turn of the century, word of Sequim's climate was spread far and wide.

The rain-shadow effect makes living in the Sequim area pleasant with annual rainfall averaging 17 inches, while a few miles to the south, the Olympic Mountains average more than 100 inches in many areas.

As early as the 1870s, the Sequim-Dungeness valley area boomed with agricultural products.

The *Port Angeles Evening News* of 1962 reports "in 1872, oxen were considered a cash crop to farmers like Thomas L. Evans, who had a ready market at logging camps. He also found the camps ripe for his agricultural crops such as potatoes. U.A. Davis brought the first Jersey cattle to the Dungeness in 1875 by sailing sloop, then ashore by Indian canoe. His brother, Hall Davis, brought purebred Holstein cattle for his big farm near Jamestown, and is generally considered the "father of the Dungeness dairy industry."

Dungeness also held Clallam County's first fair on Oct. 5, 1892, an event called "Harvest Home." Three years later, the event moved to Port Angeles, where it remains.

Initially, settlers moved from one beach settlement to another via boats and canoes. A pier was the first structure built in a new development. Gradually, homesteaders moved inland, trails were cleared and narrow wagon roads constructed.

O'Brien, *Press* arrive

After the *Beacon* was moved, the East End was served by several Port Angeles-based papers and a few from Port Townsend, for the next 18 years until George O'Brien moved from Clallam Bay.

O'Brien, born in Dublin, Ireland, in 1865, was brought by his family to San Francisco when he was a youth. His father was a doctor and a druggist. In 1882, at the age of 17, George's family moved to Port Discovery, where the young O'Brien found employment at the Discovery Mill Co. as a timekeeper.

In school at San Francisco, O'Brien discovered he enjoyed reading and studying newspapers. He wanted to work on one, but in Port Townsend he found the publishers unwilling to take a young man without experience.

He would fix that, even though his interest was more into the business end of newspapers.

In 1885, he founded the weekly *Port Townsend Call* with Louis Flowers, but by Sept. 7, 1888, O'Brien had apparently sold his interest as the paper lists Flowers & Willoughby as owners and publishers.

In 1890, O'Brien moved to Clallam Bay and established the *Record*, which he published until 1907 when he took two years off to study law, then established the *Clallam Bay Press* in 1909.

George O'Brien established the *Sequim Press* on April 8, 1911. He sold it four years later to Angus and Vesta Hay. *(Washington State Archives)*

Two years later, he folded the *Press* there and moved to Sequim, where on April 8, 1911, O'Brien debuted the weekly *Press*, a paper that existed for 74 years until folding in 1985.

The first newspaper was one broadsheet, printed front and back. O'Brien proudly stated in the masthead: "A Republican Paper." The cost was $1.50 per year and the paper was published on Saturdays. It remained a broadsheet for about eight years, though quickly reformatted to four standard full pages.

O'Brien enlisted the services of George Hart, R.R. Cays and Charley Cays to build the paper's plant, located on about the third block on North Sequim Avenue. It featured pages devoted to world politics, fashion, innovations, inventions, agriculture, natural history, food, science, travel and serialized fiction. Type plates were stamped in steel and arrived by steamship, allowing residents access to current events. Local news, advertisements and public notices were covered by O'Brien, who by now, was not only an attorney, but also a notary public and land agent.

This first edition of the *Sequim Press* included three stories and a full 2-column ad from businessman C.F. Seal touting his 20 years of merchandising in Sequim. The stories included: "Democrats Organize

The first edition of the *Sequim Press* on April 8, 1911. The paper was published in Sequim for 74 years, and until 1974 was the only successful paper in the city. It was folded on May 22, 1985. *(Gazette file)*

House for Extra Session of Congress"; "Hanford Decides Favorably For Coal Claimants", and locally, "Democratic Caucus Outlines Sessions of Work."

In addition to the large Seal ad, two 3-column ads were purchased by Bugge Mercantile and Knight-Godfrey, a hardware store that also sold clothing, furnishings and shoes.

Bugge had at least three businesses: one at Sequim, where the post office was centered; one at Port Williams, which also had a post office and one at Port Washington. Port Williams was where the dock was located, and visitors disembarked from Puget Sound to access the peninsula.

The Bugge businesses touted many different cannery items, including "bring your beef or veal to us."

None of these stores listed addresses. Obviously, those in Sequim knew where they were located.

On Page 2, were stories from around the world: "Khartoum: Garden City of Africa," "China swept by Black Death," "Superstitions of Mothers Regarding Their Children. This was 1911 when newspapers were published with maybe one cut (or engraving), but Page 2 featured six engravings. Page 3 was for local news — all of it in brief form, plus 2 ½ columns of ads.

Pages 4-5 were for long features: "The Sheriff's Daughter," "Beautiful Gardens of Guatemala," "Pheasant: Friend of the Farmer," and "Corn Breeding in Water."

Page 6 featured several shorter editorials from O'Brien, plus a 3-column ad from Bugge Mercantile. Page 7 was full of ads, mostly national and primarily providing advice on health. The back page was a compendium of news around the nation, state and internationally.

O'Brien's editorial "A Word About the Press," set the tone for the paper and discussed the editor's vision for the paper and the opportunities for the city.

This newspaper is established at Sequim as a permanent business enterprise. It is printed in a building specially built as a home for the paper, and it expects to succeed on its merits as a newspaper.

We intend to give you your money's worth and we do not ask for your subscription unless you feel that you are getting what you paid for.

We want to publish a paper with about all of the local news of the east end of the county in it every week; with room in it also for letters from people discussing things that will benefit our communities here.

We desire a paper that will be useful, newsy and independent and we see no possible reason why any rightly conducted newspaper can fail to be a success in this locality.

On May 1, 1911, O'Brien's editorial tells his readers "Why Sequim Celebrates on May Day."

The people of Sequim now annually celebrate May Day with a picnic and general good old-fashioned gathering of friends and neighbors.

The reason for it is that the first of May is as important to this community as Thanksgiving Day or the 4th of July is to the state or the nation.

On the first day of May 1895, water from the Dungeness River was turned into a little ditch and it began flowing down into Sequim prairie, three and half miles away. The irrigation of the prairie started that day: a start that meant converting 5,000 acres of desert and barren land into fields of clover and fields of grain, into orchards and gardens; from a sullen waste spot of nature, neglected and desolate into a smiling land of beauty and abundance.

Lily Bell (Anian) Smith, 86, reads the *Sequim Press* in 1981 when the paper celebrated its 70th birthday. The granddaughter of Sequim homesteader John Bell, Lily was 16 and worked on that first *Press* paper as a typesetter in 1911. *(Sequim Gazette archive)*

And that celebration continues to this day, though it's no longer called "May Day Festival." In May 2018, Sequim celebrated the 123rd annual Irrigation Festival; it has grown into a major production, including a grand parade, fireworks, arts and crafts, vendors, farmers market, entertainment and carnival, among other venues.

The first irrigation system was built without one cent of public money. The Sequim Prairie Ditch Company exchanged stock for labor and material. When the job was finished, the company was debt-free.

O'Brien did his best to promote the town, as evidenced in an editorial he wrote in October 1911 titled "A Greater Clallam County," in which he refers to a meeting in Port Angeles in which an individual (Tom Richardson) took it upon himself to bring citizens together to promote the area.

It was high time someone took hold and started something moving.

Everybody complaining of dull times and not a soul doing anything to make times any better. ... We believe it is time for the people of this county to quit looking forward to railroads for help in making us prosperous and get in with this Tom Richardson Movement and build up a greater Clallam County ourselves.

We have the land here rich

The first *Sequim Press* building on the third block of North Sequim Avenue. *(Katherine Vollenweider, Sequim Museum)*

and abundant for new people to cultivate and improve and we believe that a greater county can only be had by getting more population on new ground; we need more homes on new soil, more cleared and cultivated farms, more gardens and orchards.

In 1981, the *Press* celebrated its 70th birthday with a 56-page section, edited by Mary Petroff. We'll visit this later in this chapter.

For now, a story on the history of the *Press* talks about two of the first employees, who were still alive in 1981.

The first *Press* employee was Lily Bell Smith, who was 86 when this special section was printed. She and the *Press* celebrated their birthday on the same day every year (April 11). "She finished the tenth grade at the age of 16 and began work as a typesetter at the *Press* in a small building located somewhere between the present (in 1981) St. Luke's Episcopal Church and Trinity United Methodist Church. It was between the second and third blocks on North Sequim Ave.

"She set type from the corner near the front with a side window giving her the best available view. No lights were used in the daytime. Mrs. Smith earned $2 per week at first, and two years later was making $5 a week.

"The paper was printed with a hand press by Mrs. Smith and 15-year-old Goodwin O'Brien, son of the owner by his first wife. Mrs. Smith ran a roll-over inker on a marble-topped table, then over the type. Goodwin placed a sheet of paper on the type and pulled down the hand press. The procedure was laborious and repeated for every sheet printed.

"It wasn't hard work," Smith said, "but we had to step lively to get the paper printed."

Smith was the granddaughter of John Bell, an early homesteader. Her aunt, Jane Bell, was the first white child born in Clallam County. In 1936, Lily Bell married Anian Smith. In 1974, she was honored as Grand Pioneer in the 79th annual Irrigation Festival. She died in 1992 at 97.

Sequim's first school was built in 1912 and had its first graduating class in 1915. Among those earning diplomas in that class was Goodwin O'Brien, who apparently worked for his father part-time before going to the new school.

Two years after the *Press* hit the streets, Sequim applied for city status. A "Notice of Election for Incorporation of the Town of Sequim" was posted in the *Press* on Oct. 14, 1913.

The voters easily approved the measure and Sequim became the second incorporated town in the county.

Angus & Vesta Hay take over

O'Brien owned and operated the *Press* until Nov. 1, 1915, when this notice appeared on the fourth page of the paper:

"Change of Ownership"

The undersigned has bought the Sequim Press *from Mr. George W. O'Brien, assuming control Nov. 1.*

The paper will speak for itself.

The editor and family extend most cordial greetings to the people of this district.

Respectfully,

Angus Hay.

Angus Hay sits in his *Sequim Press* office. He became the paper's second owner, taking over on Nov. 1, 1915, from George O'Brien. Angus suffered a stroke in 1921 and Vesta, his wife, essentially took over as publisher. Angus died in 1931; Vesta married Jack Yoakum in 1935 and, although retiring briefly twice, owned the paper until 1949. *(Sequim Pioneer Family Histories, 1850-1962, Vol. I)*

Below that, O'Brien's swan song:

"A word from editor O'Brien"

A change in ownership of the Sequim Press *was made November 1ˢᵗ by which Mr. Angus Hay of White Bluffs becomes the editor and owner of the paper.*

Mr. Hay is a newspaper man of many years' experience and is well equipped in every way to maintain a first-class local paper, and the people of this community can rest assured that Sequim will always have a good, strong weekly while he runs it.

In saying goodbye to the newspaper field here, the writer takes this occasion to thank the people of this progressive community for their hearty support at all times since the paper was started at Sequim in 1911, and to speak for his successor the same co-operation and good will that he has received since the establishment of the Press *here in April 1911.*

Thus, ended O'Brien's journalistic career. He remained in Sequim as a mover and shaker in the community. He was a lawyer, a city official and, in 1920 was elected to the state Legislature. He died on Oct. 21, 1926. He was survived by widow, Hazel, who at the time of his death, was principal of the Sequim grammar school, and his son, Goodwin of Seattle.

Angus Hay and his wife Vesta moved to Sequim to purchase the *Press*. Hay had founded the White Bluffs *Spokesman* near the present Hanford Nuclear Site in Benton County.

Readers of the *Press* were likely jolted by the look of the paper once Hay had become entrenched. O'Brien feasted on world news, which comprised the bulk of his front pages.

When Angus Hay took over the paper in 1915, he debuted a logo that retained the Old English style, but incorporated "The *Press* is for Sequim and the Great Sequim Country."

Not so with Hay. His front pages consisted of two sections of small ads down columns 1 and 2 and 5 and 6. Columns 3 and 4 were for local news. World news was tucked inside, if at all.

Across the top of the front page, across all six columns were the words: "The Press is for Sequim and the Great Sequim Country."

When the U.S. entered World War I on April 6, 1917, not a word was mentioned. A couple weeks later, the only mention was a single sentence:

Goodwin O'Brien, 19, Sequim, has enlisted with the U.S. Navy and will ship out to join the U.S. troops in World War I.

Hay evidently believed that by the time the *Press* was on the streets, world news was old, and the readers would somehow be aware. The *Port Angeles Evening News* was the other option for current world news. No doubt, some *Press* subscribers also took the *Evening News*.

One of the first purchases Hay made was a used Linotype machine to set type. Until 1916, all type was set by hand. Hay taught his wife to set type and she contributed daily to the operation, for which he would later be eternally grateful.

Hay also made the switch from a full broadsheet newspaper to a tabloid size, which it remained until its death.

The Hays had an efficient operation, but the management of the paper would take a turn when Angus Hay suffered a stroke in 1921. He recovered in part but was never the same.

Instead, he would instruct his wife on what not to do and she became the defacto owner/publisher. This strained arrangement existed for 10 years until Angus died in 1931.

Vesta became the official owner, publisher and editor. In addition to her newspaper duties, she sought commercial printing for added income.

Less than a year after Angus Hay's death, the *Press* seemed to be flourishing. Indeed, on Feb. 12, 1932, a short article was headlined "Press

Printing Plant Sets New High Record." Job work was an important revenue-producing side to printing the newspaper.

On March 24, 1922, the *Press* reported on the first bank robbery at the State Bank of Sequim. The robbers entered a window, drilled through an old-fashioned vault, went through 180 safe deposit boxes and strode away with $35,000. Authorities caught up with them at Quilcene, about 20 miles southeast of Sequim. One robber was killed, the other captured and all the money was recovered.

The paper made a big deal of it when The Dresden Theatre, now the *Gazette* building on the south side of Washington Street, opened its doors on Aug. 8, 1935. Its first feature was "The Hoosier Schoolmaster" starring Norman Foster and Gabby Hayes. With a seating capacity of 450 and features such as a modern oil- burning furnace, second-floor lounge room, box office and front doors made of mahogany, the Dresden was considered one of the finest talkie motion picture houses of its size in the Northwest.

Even the competition was praiseworthy of the job Vesta did. On the paper's 25th anniversary (1936), none other than managing editor Billy Welsh, the erstwhile "Rarebitter" for the *Port Angeles Evening News*, joined with the plaudits.

It is a pleasure to congratulate a contemporary on weathering the varying fortunes of a small community to arrive at its silver anniversary. The Sequim Press *is in its 25th year and looking more pert than ever from an advertising and news standpoint.*

… Mr. Hay worked for, and lived to see the Sequim valley fruitful and to see Sequim develop into one of the finest small towns on the Pacific coast. By dint of slaying "at the case," kicking the job press, and later running a linotype, Angus Hay made a success of the Sequim Press. *He belonged to the old-school. When he learned the facts, all the king's horses and all the king's men could not keep him from printing them.*

He was the original enemy of high taxation in his community, and he bitterly assailed the mounting costs of government. Yes, through it all, he had many fast friends, whom he cherished. When he gave his word, he kept it — and some day that epitaph might be written on his stone.

At his death, the duties of the Sequim Press *were taken over by his widow, Mrs. Vesta Hay. She has increased the advertising income, built up circulation and is giving her readers a great measure of news and editorial comment. Definitely, she has proved that a woman can successfully operate a newspaper in a small town. But it is hard job. If a newspaper doesn't express an editorial opinion, it is called "spineless." If it dares to express an opinion, it is "prejudiced." It simply isn't possible to please everybody.*

And so, in the very nature of things, it was just natural that competition developed for the Sequim Press *about two years ago. Then it was that Mrs. Hay proved her ability. In spite of the competition, she showed an increase in business, circulation and news.*

She worked hard, very wisely refrained from becoming embroiled in any dogfights with the competition and came out on top. The competition moved out one night. Her paper doesn't please everyone in the East End. But if any reader knows of a paper that pleases everybody, we'd like to hear of it. So, we congratulate the Sequim Press *on arriving at its 25ᵗʰ birthday, and with it, success in every year ahead.*

Vesta Hay was the big fish in the Sequim newspaper field, but a couple of others tried to usurp her monopoly, without success, as Welsh notes.

The first of these was the *Sequim Herald* published in July 1932 but folded less than a year later.

Several others, all based in Port Angeles, attempted to circulate in Sequim.

The first was the *Clallam County Journal*, established in December 1934 with Clarence L. Vaughn as editor. It was founded to support the rights of organized labor, but it survived only a year. The *Port Angeles Union Spokesman* came out July 3, 1936, with T.B. McCready as editor. It was succeeded by the *Independent*, neither of which lasted more than a year.

Angus Hay wrote hard-hitting editorials, often at odds with county officials, yet was friends with civic leaders, but generally stayed in the background. Unlike her husband, Vesta was front and center with the operation and was quoted repeatedly in the pages of the *Press*.

In her columns, she always referred to "Ye Editor" when speaking herself or sharing an opinion.

She enjoyed writing about her city:

Sequim has gained world famous status as the "Most suitable locality in the world for human habitation." With more recorded days of sunshine than elsewhere on the Pacific Coast, with an average yearly rainfall of less than 13 inches over a period of five years.

Incidentally, some of the original Press *subscribers are still on the mailing list.*

One is Mrs. Hazel B. O'Brien, widow of the man who established the Press *35 years ago.*

She has watched this paper change from the stage of Washington hand press, 7 x 11 Pearl job press and handset paper with a couple hundred subscribers, to a shop equipped with an Intertype Cottrell Babcock press, automatic Kluge feeding a 12x18 job press, and a well-equipped country weekly read by as many as thousands today as by hundreds 35 years ago.

And you haven't seen nothin' yet! If this community goes forward as by nature it has been endowed to do, the Press *will grow right along with it.*

Vesta & Jack Yoakum

On May 11, 1935, Vesta married Llewellyn John "Jack" Yoakum V, and while they were co-owners, it was Vesta who piloted the ship. Later, he is listed in the masthead as business manager.

From his obituary in the *Press* on Sept. 13, 1951, we learn more about Jack Yoakum than most of the community were aware. He was a businessman in Sequim, but never talked about his previous escapades.

Jack had no newspaper background whatsoever. He was born in Casper, Wyo., but when Jack was 6, his father was accidentally killed.

Coming from a long line of show people, his widowed mother, known as Madam Louise, took the youngster and both entered the theater and circus. They remained in that business until 1933.

He became famous in vaudeville, where he starred in the "Whirling Duo" and "Jack and his Girl Friends," touring Australia and New Zealand.

He was making his home in San Francisco, when he came to Sequim in November 1934 to visit the Hayes Evans family, and spent the rest of his life in what he deemed the "most beautiful place in the world."

Six months later, he and Vesta were married.

Vesta called her town "the Garden spot of the world." In 1938, she was asked to broadcast a 15-minute profile of Sequim and the *Press* on Seattle radio station KIRO's "Meet the Editor."

The transcription of this broadcast was printed in the paper in 1938 and reprinted in the *Press'* 70th anniversary edition in 1981.

Vesta touted the values of the town of only 800 residents with more than 5,000 in the greater area. She told of Sequim settlers, the strength of logging early on, then the dairy and agriculture industry. She talked about the climate, newly paved roads, modern businesses, housing developments, consolidated schools, churches and an expanded sewer system.

Perhaps most noteworthy, was the result of a two-year market research, conducted by the University of Washington in which "Sequim was found to be one of the two healthiest places in the world to live. The other is a little town in Essex County, England, but who wants to live in England," she deadpanned.

Vesta Hay Yoakum co-owned or owned the *Sequim Press* from 1915-1949. She died in 1964. *(Sequim Museum and Art Center collection)*

From that time on, Sequim became one of the most desirable towns for retirees.

Many areas change, but Sequim seemed to get better. On April 28, 2017, 79 years after that first survey, the burgeoning Clallam County town was named *USA Today's* No. 1 Most Desirable Northwestern Town in a readership poll.

Vesta and Jack operated the *Press* until 1943 when illness forced them to retire to their farm at Dungeness.

In her exit editorial, she said the U.S. entering World War II hastened their retirement. Her son, Gordon, was born just before the U.S. entered World War I, and now he would be going off to war. She decided life was too short and they wanted to grow vegetables on their farm for those less fortunate.

A.R. Horton was introduced as the operator of the *Press* on Feb. 26,

1943. He had an extensive background in newspapers for more than 25 years in Montana, then for the Denver *Post*, also as a compositor and commercial printer in Kansas City and St. Louis. In 1941, he came to the *Port Angeles Evening News* as a compositor but leaped at the opportunity to own a weekly paper.

His time at Sequim was short-lived and so was the Yoakums' retirement.

Two years later, on March 23, 1945, Jack and Vesta returned to the *Press*, buying out Horton. She explains their reason for returning in an editorial, citing an illness that compelled them to leave two years ago and that their son, Gordon was in the military. Now, they wanted to devote an entire news column to the service men.

Success of your local paper as a dispenser of local news, depends largely upon the friendly assistance of those interested in having a 'newsy' community paper. We need help.

In the past five years, we have had many opportunities to sell the Press *at a satisfactory price to all concerned. But there is a local man by the name of Gordon Hay, Printer 2/c USNR, now somewhere in the Central Pacific. ...*

To him, Sequim and the Press *represents that portion of America for which he fights. ... Although he knew the condition of his parents' health, he volunteered for service on January 10, 1942, asking that we 'hold the fort' until his return. That is why we are in Sequim today.*

On July 1, 1946, the Yoakums would attempt retirement again. This time, they sold to their son, Gordon, back from four years in the military, and Earl and Jeanette Allen. Earl had been associate editor and owner of the Kennewick *Courier-Reporter* for 18 months and a commercial printer in Tacoma before that.

The Yoakums purchased a 20-foot travel trailer and decided to see the USA, which they did for four months, visiting many states on their trip.

And, then on Feb. 28, 1947, they were back running the *Press* after buying controlling interest. They installed Gordon as publisher and continued to run the paper until selling it on June 1, 1949, to James and Betty Coble.

James & Betty Coble

On June 10, 1949, Vesta Yoakum wrote her final editorial:

"Farewell, but not Goodbye"

This is the hardest editorial ye editor ever wrote, for it probably will be the last. With this issue of the Press, *our family severs all connection with its ownership and management. On two previous occasions, we have tried to retire, only to re-enter again and take up active management. The third time should be a charm.*

... Looking backward to that time in 1915, when I first came to Sequim, it seems that my entire life has been spent in the print shop of this lovely little garden spot of the world. There have been ups and downs; joys and sorrows; and years of hard, grueling work; but with all the deep satisfaction of watching a sleepy little town develop into the thriving rural community it serves today. And the Press *has delighted throughout all those years in this growth, gladly assisting whenever possible.*

There have been disagreements, community squabbles and mistakes. But the Press *has ever stood for what it believed to be the right, never appeasing nor cow-towing to any little clique or self-interested group.*

Sequim is our home and will remain so. But we will engage in a business less-strenuous than that demanded by publication of a country weekly.

After selling the paper, Vesta and Jack built the Yoakum Apartments. Vesta turned to another genre of writing: poetry. She had several of her poems included in the *National Anthology of Verse.*

Jack Yoakum died in 1951 at the age of 49 from a heart ailment. Vesta lived until March 30, 1964, when she suffered a stroke and died later that night at Olympic Memorial Hospital. She was active in civic affairs and was a member of the Order of the Eastern Star, Sequim Rebekah Lodge 155, president of the Rhododendron Grandmother's Club in Gardiner, the VFW Auxiliary. She also belonged to bridge clubs and bowling teams.

The Cobles came to Sequim after publishing the *Thurston County Independent* in Tenino, Wash., for several years. Under Vesta's exit editorial, the Cobles wrote an introductory:

We, like many others, fell in love with Sequim at first sight. Admiring the beautiful scenery, pleasant climate and clean appearance, we have for some time hoped that we would one day have the opportunity to live in Sequim. Our opportunity finally came, and here we are.

Our main hope is that the people of Sequim will like us as well as we like them. We shall strive to merit your faith by giving you a good newspaper and we trust that the readers will bear with us until we attain that familiarity with the life of our town and area which is so necessary to the proper editing of a weekly paper.

The news columns of the Sequim Press *will be devoted to a complete and impartial coverage of events. The editorial policy will be politically independent and will ordinarily deal only with matters of local concern.*

... Sequim is a proud town. We want to maintain a newspaper of which it can be proud.

The masthead listed James Coble as the editor and publisher, his wife Betty the news editor and Hollis Fultz as associate editor.

Fultz was the brother-in-law of James. He wasn't known as a newspaperman, although he later would write books, including *Famous Northwest Manhunts.*

On Dec. 23, 1949, the *Press* unveiled one of the more unique front pages ever: The banner was "And Heaven and Nature Sing." The entire page included opening notes on a scrolled scale to five favorite Christmas carols. In the center, a brief description told how "Silent Night" was born.

When the Cobles bought the paper, Fultz was well known in the county as the federal prosecutor responsible for bringing Monty Illingworth to trial and subsequent conviction as the killer of his wife Hallie, known as the "Lady of the Lake," in reference to Crescent Lake. The story was later turned into a book by the same name and then a movie.

Midway through the four years the Cobles owned the paper, Fultz, who wrote a weekly column called "Just a Thought," was listed as a contributing reporter. Betty, who dealt with local news, was news editor.

However, when the Cobles sold the paper to Dorothy Haller on Feb. 26, 1953, and moved to Elma, Wash., where they purchased *The Chronicle,* Fultz went with them.

In their exit column, the Cobles note the history of the *Sequim Press,* pointing out that Dorothy Haller would be only the fifth publisher in the paper's 43 years.

It speaks well for the community and paper; for a newspaper can be no better than the community it serves. It must have the support of its subscribers and it must have the support of the advertisers in the area, if it is to be a readable periodical enjoyed by all.

It is with the usual regrets that the Cobles leave Sequim; you don't live with the people in a community for four years and publish their paper without forming definite attachments. It is only because we are going to a larger paper that we are leaving now. We have been told by many that we are leaving the sunshine for the rain. Be that as it may, a climatological report can not necessarily dictate the course of people's lives.

We are followed by an able successor. Dorothy Haller will serve her community well.

Dorothy Haller (Munkeby) owner

Haller was only 26 when she became owner of the paper, a gift from her father when she graduated from the University of Washington, according to Judy Reandeau Stipe, director of the Sequim Museum and Art Center, and was named Citizen of the Year for 2017 by the Sequim-Dungeness Valley Chamber of Commerce

While inexperienced in the print business, Dorothy knew Sequim.

She was the daughter of Julia and Albert Haller, her father being an early Sequim developer and conservationist. Albert Haller began working in the woods before he was a teen and, with Julia's support, gradually bought up land until he was the largest private landowner in Clallam County.

Stipe said Albert was known for his conservation policies. "He treated trees as a crop, when the logging was done, seedlings were planted." He distrusted banks. But, he told folks if they were turned down by banks to come to him. "For new employees down on their luck, he would set them up with credit accounts at the Carlsborg Store and Clallam Co-op for gas and groceries," Stipe said.

He had a lasting concern for his neighbors and county residents. When he died at 88 in 1992, he designated $8 million to the Albert Haller Foundation for charitable purposes, particularly the needs of children.

Dorothy was raised in railroad cars that were hauled from one logging operation to another when her father would move to the next business.

When Dorothy took over the *Sequim Press*, it also was publishing the *Olympic Farmer*. "Dorothy was a smart, formidable woman who was active in politics, social interests and economics in Sequim," said Stipe, who also worked for her, selling advertising, taking pictures, answering phones, writing weddings and school news.

"Known for her bat-wing glasses, high heels and strong opinions at city council and school board meetings, Dorothy was leader in Sequim for many years. She was instrumental in fundraising to purchase the land and get the Sequim Museum formed," Stipe noted.

On April 22, 1957, she married Terry Munkeby, a Port Angeles physician.

Dorothy Munkeby spelled out her editorial policy in the paper upon taking over the operation. This included a column for Sequim servicemen and women, coming events, greater coverage of local news in sports, club work, personals and community events.

She also emphasized deadlines, not only for advertising, but also for local news submissions. "All clubs, churches and lodges are invited to list their events in the coming events column and should include event, time, place and guest speaker, if any. Affairs which are for profit and fund-raising will be listed in coming events, if accompanied by a display ad."

One of the first things she did was move the *Press* office to 327 W. Washington St., on the main thoroughfare through Sequim. It remained there until the final issue in 1985.

Another innovation was to hire local Realtor Harrison "Bill" Tout to write a column for the *Press*. He wrote "The Press Box" for 25 years in Lincoln, Neb., before moving to Sequim. Tout wrote his column for the Sequim paper for another 25 years; his last column was printed in the final issue of the *Press* on May 15, 1985.

Tout, often an outspoken voice, wrote about every aspect of life in Sequim, rarely on sports, despite the column's title.

Sequim's prairies had been besieged by hunters trespassing on dairy farms. So, Tout encouraged the paper's office to print and sell "No Hunters" and "No Trespassing" signs, which then became the subject of his first column.

He was not above taking the other press to task. The late Jim Manders, former reporter and editor with the *Peninsula Daily News* at Port Angeles and the *Gazette* in Sequim, as well as the *Jimmy Come Lately* and the *Press*, wrote a tribute to Tout upon his death on July 5, 1989.

"He wrote with wit and stuck the needle in those in government who thought they could spend the public's money as if it did grow on trees. Tout was also interested in land-use issues of the day and was quick to chastise those who wanted to limit the rights of individual property owners."

After Dorothy and Terry Munkeby married, they lived in Port Angeles and she commuted four days a week to Sequim. She was active in civic activities, serving as the Clallam County Chamber's secretary-treasurer and was also co-chairman of the Irrigation Festival. She later became executive director of the county chamber, and still later served in that position for the state chambers of commerce. She died at 88 on Jan. 21, 2016.

Munkeby experimented with several different logo banners — all variations of SEQUIM PRESS — in different type faces from bold to light. Behind the printed logo was a cutout of the Olympic Mountains. One that didn't last long was **The Sequim Press**, which stretched in massive bold lettering across all six columns.

Briefly, a new paper surfaced in Sequim. In 1960-1961, the *Olympic Review* made a stab at competing against the *Press* but lasted only 14 months.

Harriet Fish, longtime Clallam County historian, noted in a July 30, 2014, *Gazette* article celebrating that paper's 40th birthday, a front-page *Olympic Review* story on Aug. 16, 1961, told of the grand opening of the $26 million Hood Canal Floating Bridge, touting it as "an engineering masterpiece, making the Olympic Peninsula part of the state," as one official said.

Owner and editor Genevieve Smith wrote the article and reported that Gov. Albert D. Rosellini cut the ribbon and cars lined up bumper-to-bumper for 3 miles to cross behind the governor's vehicle.

During the toll-free period from 12:30-6 p.m. that day, 5,916 vehicles cross; a total of 11,000 crossed on Saturday. The toll was $1.30 per vehicle and 30 cents per passenger. A 5-column aerial photograph, taken by

Harry Boersig, accompanied the article and showed a string of cars in both directions.

One of the reporters was Judy Reandeau Stipe, who was in high school at the time. "I was very grateful to Gennie for her mentoring. She was a lovely single mother, raising three sons and worked hard to make a living. She was the daughter of the pioneering Sprague family."

Stipe said some of her fondest memories of her days with the Review were when she accompanied Gennie's son Dan, who drove his Volkswagen with the completed page paste-ups to Shelton for printing; then packed the printed papers back to Sequim for delivery. "I was there to keep him awake," said Stipe.

Genevieve died in 1994, but her son, Ron Smith, a Sequim resident, remembers his mother worked as a proofreader for the *Evening News* in Port Angeles before starting the *Review*.

"When I was young, I went to the office with her and she showed me the Linotype machine. I was fascinated," said Smith. "I was about 13 when she started the *Review*. I didn't participate in it, except for doing chores around the office and later some pasting up of ads."

He said the office was on the south side of Washington, about a half-block from Sequim-Dungeness Way. Printing was done in Shelton. Smith said he didn't know why the paper ended after only 14 months. Stipe said she believed it was for financial reasons.

The editor's son emphasized that his mother wanted to do something to help the city. "She was very active and loved the Sequim community. She was involved in the Sequim Museum and the Chamber of Commerce."

After folding the *Review*, Genevieve Smith married John Jenkins, who would become owner of the *Sequim Press*.

Parade of *Press* owners

Munkeby owned the *Press* for six more years before selling to John Jenkins on March 7, 1963. Jenkins had owned a weekly in Brookings, Ore., for 20 years and prior to that three weeklies and daily newspapers in Southern California. He was a graduate of the University of Washington.

Jenkins only had the paper seven months — from March to October

1963, — but he did make a change in the paper's logo. Capitalizing on the area's huge dairy industry, on Sept. 19, 1963, the sun first appears. The sun wearing sunglasses logo is at the left of Sequim Press with the words "Heart of Sunshine Belt" over it; to the right of the paper's name is a milk cow, a barn and a silo; over it is in the inscription "Dairy Center of Olympic Peninsula." The Olympic Mountains are behind the Sequim Press.

One month later, on Oct. 31, he sold the paper to Myrna and Rob Brock, who had published several weeklies in the Kent area, south of Seattle.

Brock had big plans and the first was to ditch the busy logo, going only with a four-column name with the sun-glassed sun on the left. It remained until the paper's final day.

On the day he took over the paper, Brock wrote of his plans in a story headlined "Paper to be expanded – modernized."

Brock wanted to bring the *Press* into the modern age and highlighted changes in typography as one way to do it. He also instituted an editorial page, noting, "It is an obligation of a newspaper publisher

Harrison "Bill" Tout wrote his column "Press Box" for the *Sequim Press* for 25 years, surviving numerous ownership changes. *(Sequim Press)*

to speak out editorially for, or against, the issues which affect the citizens of the community."

He also said the page would be open for letters to the editor, which he hoped to expand.

His plans also included a sports page, a women's page and a classified ads page. He planned to retain Tout's "Press Box" column and "Brush Strokes" by John Pogany. Also retained were the Happy Valley News section and a coming events section.

The big change, however, would be in modernizing the print plant by bringing in a new press from California, which he said would be installed by the first of the year (January 1964).

"The new press is necessary," Brock said, "to allow better reproduction of pictures. A greatly expanded use of pictures is planned."

He also expanded the typefaces with modern fonts to allow a wider range, particularly for advertisers.

On March 22, 1965, the *Press* unveiled a 24-page Development section that was highlighted by a cover story on the $300,000 loan approved to co-owner Jess Taylor for construction of the 18-hole Sunland Golf and Country Club. An editorial cited the industrial and housing boom and the bottom half of the page was dedicated to the proposed 200-room convention hotel and marina. All of it is included the proposed $20 million complex.

That wasn't the only new development in the Sequim area in 1965. At Sequim Bay, Battelle Memorial Institute opened its Pacific Northwest Marine Science Laboratory, a division of the Department of Energy, which allows it to conduct research for both government and private clients.

While it wasn't that way initially, the facility "eventually would employ about 100 researchers and support staff, including internationally recognized experts in analytical chemistry, wetland and coastal ecology, ecotoxicology, marine biology, modeling and remote sensing. which allows it to conduct research for both government and private clients," the website www.pnnl.gov says.

This special section was a boon for the *Press*. In addition to the regular run of 3,500 printed papers, there was a record 15,000 overrun, making it the longest press run in the paper's 54-year history.

The Brocks also established a new publication, *The East End Advertiser,* a shopper which lasted until the Brocks sold the paper.

Rod and Myrna Brock operated the paper together only a couple of years when Myrna quit to raise their family.

Rod held the paper six years total until selling to Ken Geary, a 27-year-old Viet Nam veteran, on June 11, 1969.

Brock had formed the Olympic Publications Inc. in 1966 and was general manager. He said he planned to continue in the print business in Sequim.

Geary, an English major from Western Washington State College and Everett Community College, had only been out of the military two months when he purchased the paper from Olympic Publications.

He said, initially he "plans to operate the *Press* in much the same way as it has been," adding after he has become more familiar with its operations, he would likely make some selected improvements.

Geary retained Mary Lynch as news editor, at least for a couple years.

Geary wasn't the most popular owner the *Press* had. Far from it, yet he retained that lofty perch for 16 years.

The *Press* became known for its controversial stands on county politics. The look of the paper was dramatically different. For whatever reason, Geary resorted to the "not-so-journalistic" font of Courier, a face used by most typewriters. There were few photos and stories were of immense length.

The work that the previous editors had done to move the *Press* into a modern age was drastically undone under this administration.

The years of 1976 and 1977 were politically volatile for Geary and the *Press*. The paper took on one issue after another. And, the *Port Angeles Daily News* took shot after shot at the weekly.

In the elections in the mid-1970s, the *Press* faithfully endorsed Democratic candidates — except for county prosecutor Craig Ritchie. The paper ran an anti-Ritchie editorial series called "Ritchie's Ramblins'"

They gave an exceeding amount of coverage to the proposed "Dungeness County" faction, which sought to form a separate county in the North Sequim area, and who were outspoken during a recall, supporting those in office.

Occupying the front page, starting in 1976, was the question of the oil port for Port Angeles, known as the Northern Tier project. The group wanted to establish an oil port at Port Angeles and build a 1,500-mile pipeline to Minnesota to transport the crude. Geary editorialized on the benefits of having a "great influx of jobs, ignoring the dangers of such a project."

This was in direct opposition to *The Daily News* and resulted in a series of mudslinging editorials between the two publications, with the daily accusing Geary of "being in bed with Gov. Dixy Lee Ray," who strongly supported the proposal.

In September 1976, Dr. Werner Quast, a professor of political science at Peninsula College and vice chairman of the state Public Disclosure Commission, publicly attacked the *Sequim Press* in a letter on his official letterhead to the *Daily News*. This resulted in Quast being investigated, an issue that occupied the front page of the *Press* for weeks, if not months.

Quast's attack accuses the *Press* of attempting to "spearhead the anti-recall campaign on behalf of the east-end special interest groups, and of going far beyond the Canons of Journalism and the accepted standards of an independent newspaper."

In the *Press's* issue on Sept. 22, the controversy occupied the entire first two pages. The main headline streamed across six columns, two lines deep in 96-point bold type.

QUAST ATTACKS SEQUIM PRESS; GETS HIMSELF INVESTIGATED

That story was followed by the entire Quast letter and four columns of commentary by Geary (or Glen Wood, his associate publisher and co-owner).

In his commentary, Geary played hardball:

"Commissioner Quast's attempt to censor the *Sequim Press* is a threat to every newspaper, radio station and TV station in the state; for if he can censor one of them, he can censor all of them. He will find that ever since the times of Peter Zenger, there have been attempts to censor the press and all of them have failed."

The issue was debated in the competing papers for months with Geary calling for Quast's resignation, and the professor refusing to talk to the publisher.

Apparently, he did resign his position because a year later, he was sued on federal charges, again on abuse of his position. In that story, he is listed only as a former college professor.

On June 9, 1977, Geary was found guilty of "disturbing the Nov. 2 (1976) election."

Interestingly, we learn this not from the *Press*, but from Lorraine Berg, owner/publisher of the *Forks Forum*. She writes in her paper on that date:

He appeared in a non-jury trial before Judge ProTem Richard Headrick.

Geary was charged with talking too loud to election workers at three polling places in Sequim. He was fined $50 for each offense, a total of $150, *plus court costs and ordered to write an apology. ... The charges arose when Mr. Geary protested how election workers were handling the write-in vote for Frank Feeley," Berg wrote.*

Voters had crossed out Ron Richards' name, wrote in Frank Feeley's name and punched the card to vote for Feeley.

Geary warned the workers that these cards would be counted for Richards, not Feeley.

It was his loud protestations of this undisputed fact that led to charges of "interfering with an election" brought by Prosecutor Craig Ritchie.

The *Press* printed the verdict but buried it within the court reports.

It did include the following apology from Geary:

I am sorry if my actions upset anyone; certainly, I would not wish to dissuade anyone from voting. My intent was quite the contrary — I wanted everyone to be sure that his vote went where he intended it to go — without interference from those who were tampering with the voting system.

This all came on the heels of a contentious charge that went on for a couple of years. That was partially resolved in February 1976 when, after a recall petition, county voters elected to oust Bill Knapman and Commissioner D.J. Caulkins for ethics violations that initially surfaced three years before and continued until the recall. Feeley, mentioned above in the *Forum* article, was the only one of three county commissioners to survive the recall.

Geary's action did lead to improvements and greater attention to the polling procedures.

In the year-end, month-by-month review, the *Press* made no mention of Geary being found guilty of "disturbing the election" or even later in the year, if he remained "clean" through his six-month's probation.

A new paper is born

Meantime, in Quincy, Wash., in October 1973 irrepressible Shirley Larmore and her unassuming husband, Bob Larmore, were preparing to move to Sequim after selling radio station KPOR, the weekly *Quincy Shopper* and a downtown restaurant, Yankee Pedlar.

Shirley's plan was to move to the Olympic Peninsula for a slower-paced life for a while. She approached Geary, publisher of Sequim's lone paper, the *Press*, for a job as an ad salesperson. He turned her down.

That was the wrong thing to do to Shirley, who devised her own plan to get back at Geary.

She told them if they didn't hire her, she would start her own paper. And, she did. By January 1974, the *Sequim Shopper* was born, primarily as an ad-based weekly publication. Soon, a news section was added. On July 10, 1974, the *Shopper* became *The Jimmy Come Lately Gazette*, and subsequently in 1990, it became the *Sequim Gazette*, a paper which celebrated its 45th anniversary in 2018.

We'll revisit the *Jimmy* a bit later. Suffice it to say life in Sequim would become a bit more challenging for the *Press* and Geary.

While it was Shirley Larmore's intent to put the *Press* "Out of business," her daughter Troye Jarmuth revealed in a 2016 interview, it took her 11 more years to do it.

Somehow Geary and Wood would weather the challenge.

It wasn't all doom and gloom in 1976 and 1977.

In early 1976, John Wayne, the "Duke" from Hollywood and a frequent Sequim Bay visitor on his yacht *Wild Goose*, announced he would be donating 27 acres of property that he purchased from the state to build a 535-berth marina. It initially would be called Sequim Bay Boat Haven. Later, he added another four acres.

There was controversy, of course, over land use, water quality, construction noise and environmental impact. It wasn't until June 1977 that the Port of Port Angeles commissioners gave the approval to begin construction. It would be another two years before construction commenced.

Unfortunately, Wayne would not live long enough to see his vision of a large marina for Sequim fulfilled. He died on June 11, 1979. The marina was not completed until 1985; it was renamed for Wayne soon after the dedication.

The Manis Mastodon, which was discovered in August 1977, continued in numerous front-page stories with updates in the *Press* by WSU archaeologist Carl Gustafson almost weekly.

On Sept. 1, 1977, the *Press* unveiled a new journalistic-style font for its body copy, dramatically improving its looks. The next month, Jim

Manders was hired as sports editor and the paper had a dedicated sports page for the first time.

It also began coverage of recreational sports, perhaps because the associate publisher Wood and his wife, Laurel, won shooting contest prizes, although in some contests, every shooter won a prize.

In February 1979, the Hood Canal Bridge collapsed in a raging windstorm, and while the event occurred on a Tuesday morning, the *Press* did produce a story for its Wednesday edition. Its source also provided a closer estimate of two years for re-opening, while the daily, wrote "sometime in 1980." It was three years before it would re-open.

Dryke wins 'gold'

One of the big newsmakers in the 1980s in Sequim was Sgt. Matt Dryke, a six-time national skeet shooting champion. He qualified for the 1980 Olympics in Moscow, but that was the year the U.S. led a boycott of 65 countries, so Dryke could not participate.

"Competing in these Olympics will mean a lot to me," Dryke told the *Press* in a short story after he qualified for the 1984 Olympic Games in Los Angeles. "Of course, in 1980 I didn't get to compete, and I stayed in the service for the 1984 games. I've spent a lot of years training for this event and I want to win it, but a person never knows."

Dryke said going to the Olympics had been a goal he set for himself in 1976. He was a small arms instructor with the U.S. Army Marksmanship Unit at Fort Benning, Ga.

The son of Chuck Dryke of Sequim, said, "Mental preparation is 98 percent of the game and a person should have the physical aspect down before he enters the stage. I feel anyone can get to a certain stage, but to get to the top, a person has to have desire and really want to win. It's up to the individual and not just anybody can be top-notch."

Sequim and Port Angeles both held send-off parties for Dryke. The *Press* had to surrender the bulk of the coverage to *The Daily News* since the competition was Thursday through Saturday.

Dryke, who won the U.S. championship, entered the competition as the favorite — and he didn't disappoint.

Rick Ross of *The Daily News* was on hand for the pageantry.

With a crowd of over 4,000 flag-waving fans chanting "USA., USA., USA.," Sequim's Matt Dryke climbed to the top of the awards stand Saturday afternoon and received the gold medal in skeet shooting.

Dryke, 26, shot a perfect round of 50 Saturday morning to wind up the three-day competition with a 196 out of 200, tying an Olympic record. Dryke

Off the main road into Carrie Blake Park sits an enclosure with a bronze bust of Sequim's claim to Olympic fame. Native son <u>Matt Dryke</u> won a gold medal at the 1984 Olympic Games in Los Angeles. Dryke has bragging rights as an International Skeet Shooting Champion and world record holder. *(Bill Lindstrom photo)*

became the first American ever to win an Olympic medal in the sport of international skeet.

Dryke already holds the world championship and the world record as the only person (to that time) ever to shoot all 200 targets.

"If there are two factors in this victory, I would say one is experience and the other is knowing the range," Dryke said of his triumph. "Winning the world championship (in Los Angeles) built up my confidence and I wanted to show the Europeans that my world record was not a fluke."

Dryke said he never felt pressure but admitted to some nerves prior to Saturday's final round. "Butterflies? It was more like buzzards," he joked.

Then he went out and shot a perfect 25. "My confidence was pretty high after I shot my first round of 25," he admitted later. "Then I got a little hungry (for the gold) and I knew I would get the last 25."

The Army sergeant gave credit for his success to his family, dad Chuck" and sister Ellen, who watched from the stands.

He wasted little time in getting back to the peninsula, arriving at Fairchild International Airport in Port Angeles the next day to a crowd of more than 250 people. Sequim had planned a big parade but delayed at Dryke's request until he retired from the military a month later.

Dryke would later be a celebrity in Sequim's Irrigation Festival Parade and Derby Days parade in Port Angeles.

His gold medal? It was permanently given to the Sequim-Dungeness museum and is on display at the Sequim Museum and Arts today. An elaborate exhibit also is there.

Chuck Dryke established Sunnydale Shooting Grounds on Dryke Road in Sequim in 1955. He was an accomplished shooter but is better known as trainer of Matt and Ellen.

Ellen shot skeet and won the U.S. Women's Championship in 1985 with a record of 371 of 400 targets and made the World Championship teams for 1981-1982 and 1985-1987. She and Matt were the first brother/sister duo to represent the U.S. in the same World Championship (Caracas, Venezuela, 1982).

The *Press*: Beginning of the end

Around Christmas 1984, Ken Geary published his final *Press*, although nobody knew it until Jan. 9, 1985, when the new owner/publisher Bob Jones announced it in the paper.

There was no sign-off, no exit column, no editorial. Nothing.

The readers learned there was a change when they read the Jan. 9 issue. In a big bold bottom-of-Page 1-story, headlined:

Plans, goals, introductions and other miscellany
From the new management of the Sequim Press

In the opening paragraph, readers learn this is the third edition under new management. Jones introduces himself as a management consultant for five years in Federal Way, a former journalism professor and reporter and editor of a "variety of publications." He also offered that he "at one time worked for the CIA."

In the rest of the article, Jones spelled out his plans for the *Press*. "My goal is to produce a high-quality community newspaper. The first step has been taken by bringing Jim Jackson, Mary Petroff, Jan Conley and Helen McNemar back to the staff."

The second step, he said, would be to find quality correspondents to write specialized news for the *Press*. He said retaining feature writer Jim White was crucial.

When interviewed in 2017, 76-year-old, long-retired White chuckled when asked about this situation. "I was just a freelancer and they never paid me," remembered White, who added "I was just trying to help out Jim Jackson (advertising director)."

White, who had been a paid employee of the *Evening News*, the *Jimmy Come Lately*, the *Gazette* and Del Price's all-sports publication, *Sports Week*, did offer a humorous incident involving Geary's *Press* days.

"I was covering a Sequim football game (for the *Evening News*) and my wife was about to have our baby. A player for an Irish Catholic school ran the kickoff back 93 yards for a touchdown. They only printed rosters in the program for Sequim, not the visiting team, but I needed his name. I called the coach and told him I was in a hurry (because of the baby coming) and needed his name. 'What's a good Irish Catholic name?' he asked. 'Make one up.' So, that's what I did."

In the next issue of the *Press*, Geary picked up the story intact, including the fake name, and put his byline on it, White revealed. A few weeks later, Geary wanted White to cover a sports event for him. "I won't do it. You haven't paid me for the last story," White answered, then told Geary of the story with the fake name.

The third step Jones said was development of "a lively opinion page." He said it was important for *Press* staff members to keep their opinions out of stories. "If we have opinions, they belong on the opinion page as a personal column or editorial representing the position of the paper."

This statement was an obvious slap in the face to Geary, who believed nothing of the kind.

Retaining Tout's long-running column "The Press Box," and encouraging community support were other goals Jones outlined. "If we meet those goals, the *Press* will be around another 74 years."

Doable goals for sure, but apparently not for Jones. The *Press* would not last 74 years. On May 15, 1985, just 137 days after he purchased the paper, Jones rode off into the sunset.

That day was the final issue of the *Press*, one month and one week after marking its 74th birthday. There was no fanfare, no exit editorial, no regrets, no thanks for the memories. No new owner to introduce.

As the *Sequim Gazette's* longest-term owner/publisher Brown Maloney said, "It just went away."

White said he, like many others, did not know what happened to Jones. "I can tell you this. Jim Jackson was a hell of a worker. He did all the paste-up, ads and editorial content, then we stood around and waited for Jones to show up. We couldn't do anything with the pages until he saw them, and he was always late."

Perhaps, Jones tired of butting heads with the *Jimmy Come Lately*, now 11 years into its publication, or he might have heard of a new publication, the *Sequim Sun*, about to hit the streets.

Whatever the reason, the *Sequim Press* was no more, leaving the burgeoning city in the state's rain shadow with one paper.

Price's *Sequim Sun*

That situation didn't last long because quietly, Del Price was preparing to unveil a new publication. One month after the final issue of the *Press*, the *Sequim Sun* was born.

Price, a disgruntled ad manager, angrily left *The Daily News* in 1961 to establish *The Shopping News*, which soon became the *Chronicle*.

It was a family operation in Port Angeles, involving Del's wife, Polly, their daughter Tomi, son Scott and his wife, Shawn. Price also hired Mary Petroff, the *Press's* final news editor, and brought in Steve Indelicato to help run the operation. Price and Indelicato had begun the *Olympic Logger* on the peninsula's West End in 1979. Indelicato lived in Port Angeles but had an office in Forks. Now, he also would be spending time in Sequim with the new publication.

Doug McInnes, recognized as an authority on Sequim's history, was hired as a columnist.

Del's son Scott said, the biggest value with the *Sun* was the timing. The *Gazette* published on Wednesday and deadlined early Tuesday. The *Sun* published on Thursday and a reporter attended the city council meetings Tuesday evenings. "We got that report in the *Sun* and people liked that. The *Gazette* wouldn't have it for another week."

In its seven years, the *Sun* had three offices: first on Sequim Avenue, second in 1990 at Third Avenue and Washington Street, and third, the following year farther east on Washington Street. It was vacated in 1992 when the paper was sold.

With the children in school, Polly Price helped with bookkeeping and delivered tear sheets. "That kept advertisers happy," said Scott Price. "When they would see her, they knew it was truly a family newspaper. She always spread goodwill and was extremely well liked. She also served as Dad's sounding board on a lot of issues. She had an excellent memory for people, places and events."

Scott said his sister, Tomi, sold ads, helped in circulation and did a little composing. Scott and Shawn were involved in the production of the paper.

Polly was involved in founding the *Sun* and worked until she became too sick. Her obituary in the Feb. 21, 1991, *Sun* notes that she was diagnosed with pancreatic cancer in 1989 and doctors said she had six months to live. But, with the help of Dr. Robert Witham in Port Angeles and the staff at Virginia Mason Medical Center in Seattle, she rallied for two more years.

"Mom's death was a tremendous blow for everybody," said Scott. "It kind of took the wind out of Dad's sails. He was lost and the business died shortly after that."

Del Price kept the papers going for another 18 months before printing the final editions — the *Chronicle* on June 24, 1992, and the *Sun* the next day. By this time, the papers were suffering financially, and only a shadow of their previous years.

That left only one paper in Sequim. Brown M. Maloney, a 33-year-old journalist and businessman from a five-generation newspaper family, had purchased the *Jimmy Come Lately* in 1988. Then, in 1990, it was renamed the *Gazette*, shedding the *Jimmy* gradually over the first two years.

"Del came to me and told me he was selling the papers and asked if I wanted to buy them," revealed Maloney in a 2017 interview.

"He wanted $10,000 for each paper. I was in a quandary. They weren't worth anything and nobody was going to buy them. I was a friend of Del's; I worked for him (selling advertising) when I was at Peninsula College. I knew every day (at the *Gazette*) when we went out to sell advertising, I was taking money out of his pocket. We were competitors, but friendly. I knew nobody was going to buy the papers. They had been suffering financially. They weren't worth much at that point."

The *Chronicle* was a growing concern for the daily (*Port Angeles Evening News*) for the first decade, even into the second decade, but (in 1992) it was struggling.

The *Sequim Sun* was only 7 years old. "Del did a good job with it, out there trying to be a reporter and editor, going to council meetings, as well as selling advertising. Plus, Del was a really nice guy," Maloney said.

"If I bought them, I would retain the equipment, newspaper morgues and the name, but little else. I wrestled with it. Do I wish him well and send him on his way, or do I do a goodwill thing for the citizenry of the community and his family and buy the papers?"

Maloney's Olympic View Publishing bought the two papers, from Price's Chronicle Publishing Company and announced it to the public in the *Gazette's* June 17, 1992, edition.

Price sent a letter to his advertisers on June 10 announcing the sale.

"I'm real pleased for our company to be associated with a man such as Del Price, who has over 30 years (36 actually) of newspaper integrity on the Olympic Peninsula, and it's a compliment that he considered us when he decided to make a change," commented OVP Publisher Brown Maloney.

Maloney announced in that June 17 *Gazette* article, beginning July 1, 1992, the Chronicle Publishing Co. and Olympic View would jointly publish a weekly shopper, announced as the *Peninsula Weekly*.

This shopper, not really a newspaper, debuted, not as previously announced, but as *Countywide Classifieds*, which served the purpose, Maloney said, "to give Price's papers a market for the already-purchased classifieds. The name fit the publication — and our mission — perfectly."

The paper was made available in Sequim and Port Angeles as a free pickup, and in those days, shopper newspapers were in every grocery store, restaurant, motel and elsewhere.

Maloney felt the free publication made an impact, particularly in Port Angeles. "Intuitively, I felt the daily didn't like it one bit. They had owned the countywide market on classifieds, but that changed overnight. Yes, they stayed the 'big dog,' but make no mistake, it worked for us and probably cost them a few dollars."

It also made Maloney's Olympic View Publishing a countywide

publishing company. *Countywide Classifieds* lasted 10-12 years as a free publication.

In some ways, Del Price's legacy is still alive. Twenty-five years after Maloney purchased his papers in a goodwill gesture, the *Gazette* still retains "Countywide Classifieds" on its Classified page.

CHAPTER 9

Three names, one newspaper: The Shopper, the Jimmy, the Gazette

W hen Shirley Larmore and her husband Bob sold their weekly shopper, a radio station and restaurant in Quincy, Wash., and moved to Sequim, it wasn't her intent to own a newspaper. She wanted a job as an ad saleswoman.

From her oldest daughter, Troye Jarmuth, a Sequim resident, we learn the truth about the early days of the paper that eventually would become the *Gazette*.

"Mother went to the *Sequim Press*, owned by Glen Wood and Ken Geary," Jarmuth recalls. "She needed a job and told them they needed to hire her as a salesperson. She had sold ads for newspapers and radio stations she owned. But, they were old-school chauvinists and wouldn't hire her."

Troye said her mother gave the owners an ultimatum two weeks later. "If you don't hire me, I'll start my own publication and run you into the ground."

They probably laughed in Shirley's face, but the newsmen didn't know Shirley. This was a woman who had an independent spirit early on. In college in Missouri, she was expelled for starting a girls' football team; later, she took up bookkeeping simply to get a job and took night classes in accounting.

In Shirley's obituary in the Oct. 24, 2002, *Gazette*, then-publisher Sue Ellen Riesau describes the former owner:

Born out of her vision, determination and tireless energy to start new projects were a host of publications, a couple of radio stations, a restaurant and a general store.

But most important Shirley founded the Sequim Gazette. *Started as the* Sequim Shopper *in January 1974, Shirley and husband, Bob, quickly transformed this free-distribution paper into a news-based community newspaper,* The Jimmy Come Lately *on July 10, 1974.*

Shirley's intensity combined with her dynamic personality and endless energy made her good at whatever she undertook. Her reputation preceded her as a woman who was willing to say what she thought. She was a scrapper and a bubbling salesperson.

She started her career as an office manager/bookkeeper at KRIZ in Phoenix, Ariz. She met and married Bob, a draftsman and engineer, in 1959. Eleven years later, in 1968, they moved to Show Low, Ariz., to manage radio station KVSL, where she learned to sell advertising.

One year later, the Larmores moved to Quincy, Wash., buying KPOR radio and *The Quincy Shopper*. Bored with radio, 3 ½ years later, they started the Yankee Pedlar, a local eatery in downtown Quincy. Troye said her mother "loved to cook and aspired to own a restaurant."

In 1972, the Larmores went to Clallam Bay fishing and were close to buying a cannery on that visit. Her daughter added that later, on a visit to Port Townsend, "Mother wanted to buy the Manresa Castle. When she did something, she wanted it to be on a grand scale."

Shirley Larmore holds her dog Bear after retiring from the newspaper business. She started the *Jimmy Come Lately Gazette* as the *Sequim Shopper* in January 1974. She sold the paper to the Paulsons in 1978. *(Courtesy of Troye Jarmuth)*

Thus, when she landed in Sequim, her intent might have been to get a job as a salesperson, but she likely had loftier ambitions. It certainly turned out that way.

"My mother knew the economics of building a business," Troye said. "She was extremely intelligent, confident and spunky. When she set her mind to it, she did it."

Shirley approached the major players in the community for advertising and some big accounts jumped ship from *The Press* to *The Sequim Shopper*. Buz Edquist's ShopRite Food Center was one of the big accounts. Southwoods, like Swain's in Port Angeles, was another mainstay. It was located on Washington Street in the current A-1 Auto Parts store. The *Gazette* is across the street on the second floor.

At the time, *The Press'* management was dividing the city with its controversial stance on critical issues. Advertisers were hungry for another option.

"They gladly signed contracts," Jarmuth said. "Mother went to the bank and got a nice loan to get the paper started. It was mostly advertising, very little news in the beginning."

The Sequim Shopper debuted on Jan. 10, 1974, and six months later, buoyed by a news-based format and a successful advertising program, morphed into the *Jimmy Come Lately Gazette* on July 10, 1974. Its masthead proudly proclaimed, "A friendly newspaper in a friendly little town." A single copy was 15 cents.

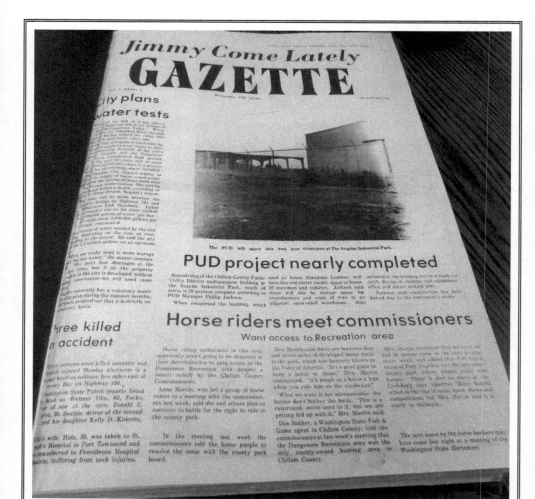

The first edition of the *Jimmy Come Lately Gazette* debuted on July 10, 1974. Shirley and Bob Larmore established the paper as the Sequim Shopper on Jan. 10, 1974. *(Gazette file)*

In late spring, Larmore conducted a contest to give the paper a new name. More than 60 submissions were received and the Larmores chose *Jimmy Come Lately Gazette*. "My parents wanted something that reflected the community, was catchy, yet different," Jarmuth said.

They couldn't have chosen a more unique name. Harriet Fish, a *Jimmy* columnist for a while as well as county historian, wrote of the name in an article, six months into the *Jimmy*.

In New England, where she grew up, a "Johnny Come Lately was a fellow traveler who followed you in time and floated on your coat-tail, in a manner of speaking."

When she arrived on the Olympic Peninsula, she purchased the Clallam County Historical Society's book *Jimmy Come Lately*, then drove up Jimmy Come Lately Road in Blyn, which follows the creek by the same name, asking longtime residents for their story of the origin.

"Apparently, by 1900, it was already a well-used term for the inn on the water by Blyn, where the creek enters the bay. Whenever someone new arrived, he was the newest Jimmy Come Lately."

Another story exists that there were three bachelors named Jimmy and the last one to arrive was given this durable title. Another version says that a squaw was asked where Jimmy was, and she answered, "Jimmy Come Lately," meaning he'll be right back.

Still another story is told that at the time Dungeness was a bustling port, an old Indian named Jimmy would fill his wagon with supplies for people living in the foothills. When the neighbors would meet each other, they would ask, "Has Jimmy come, lately?"

It's your choice, but as Fish says, "Each one of us is a Jimmy Come Lately to an earlier arrival, especially an almost 6-month-old newspaper — and transplants like me."

Jarmuth offered that her mother was the "chief of the operation and ran it like clockwork. My father was quieter and wasn't involved, except in art work and design work, some photography and production. He also transported the boards (paste-ups) to Winslow. My parents knew the folks who ran the print shop there and contracted with them for printing." Jarmuth said as a teenager, she was more into sports and girlfriends, but she did work in the darkroom and did some photography, which she developed as a strength. Later, she would help setting type first "on a big typewriter, open in front and I would take these plastic wheels out with all the fonts on them, type what I needed and process them."

When asked how it was growing up as children of parents, who owned a newspaper, Troye offered she enjoyed it, but "if you asked Janet (her sister), she would say it wasn't good. Janet was an amazing tennis player and Mom never made it to her matches."

The Larmores hired an experienced newsman, Jim White, as news editor. He was hired as a sports editor at the *Evening News* in Port Angeles in 1971, then was made news editor and county government reporter when Frank Ducceschi became publisher. "He wanted veteran Scooter Chapman to be sports editor and made me the news editor," White recalled in a 2017 interview.

White, a graduate of Skagit Valley College (where he met his wife Sandi) and Eastern Washington College, already had a variety of experience with the *Santa Maria Times* in California, the *Anacortes American* and *Greater Renton News* in the Northwest.

White remembers: "Shirley was a hell of a good business woman, hard competitor," and her husband, Bob, was "the best production man I ever worked with."

He said he especially enjoyed election nights. "We beat the hell out of the daily," he recalls. "We'd leave a spot for the election news and Shirley would call the final results into Bob, who was at Bainbridge (Winslow is on Bainbridge Island, where the paper was printed). We'd have it Wednesday morning and we'd beat the daily, which didn't print until the afternoon."

White worked for them for a couple of

Sequim resident Jim White talks in a 2017 interview about reporting for the **Evening News, the Sequim Press, the Jimmy Come Lately Gazette** and even a short-lived sports paper. *(Bill Lindstrom photo)*

"Shirley was a hell of a good business woman, hard competitor," and her husband, Bob, was "the best production man I ever worked with."

Reporter Jim White

years before leaving the business to freelance, work in landscaping and build fiberglass boats in Port Townsend, but he would be back.

Paulsons take over

In 1978, Shirley Larmore sold the *Jimmy* to Leonard and Linda Paulson. Shirley and Bob divorced, although they remained in each other's life as friends until the end, Troye said. "He was a good guy and they were good friends. They worked together, they just couldn't live together."

Shirley moved to Prince Edward Island and bought a little 100-year-old grocery store. Troye helped her refurbish it and the Glasgow General Store became a tourist attraction.

"I loved the store but couldn't stand the customers," Riesau would write of Shirley's comment on the store.

Thus, in 1981, she was off to Kingfield, Maine, where she bought a small weekly newspaper called *The Irregular*, and *Sugarloaf USA*, a magazine covering Maine's Sugarloaf Mountain ski scene.

The first thing she did, Troye noted, was to call Bob. "I just bought a newspaper and magazine and you are going to be the art director," Mom would tell him. And, off he'd go." She did same thing with the radio station she bought earlier, calling Bob and telling him he was going to be a DJ.

And just like that, Bob was back in her life — at least her business life.

While in Maine, Larmore sent the magazine to her good friend Ross Hamilton in Sequim, who eventually lured her back to the peninsula, where in 1986, she published *Peninsula Magazine*, on the same order as *Sugarloaf* or the highly successful *Arizona Highways*.

Peninsula Magazine was a slick, full-color coffee-table publication that earned the coveted "Ozzie Award" for design excellence and the 1988 "Georgie" award for media excellence, given by the state's tourism department.

Hamilton, a successful photographer on the peninsula, was chosen to shoot the cover, featuring a photo series, "Olympic Masterpieces." He had many cover photos for the magazine through the ensuing years.

The ever-modest Hamilton said he was honored by the selection, but didn't know if it was by choice or default. Jarmuth also was involved in the magazine's photography and helped with page design as art director.

"She always wanted to be busy. She had to have a project," is the way Troye describes her mother's ambitious spirit.

She operated the magazine until 1992 when she sold it to Scott Fivash, owner of *Washington CEO*. He changed the name, but the magazine was never the same and soon died.

Shirley Larmore's final publication would be *Peninsula Properties*, a local, color real estate publication she operated simultaneously with the magazine.

In 1993, Shirley retired and bought a quarter-acre farm, planting a big garden to aid in her cooking ability. Her obituary notes that "She went from publishing to processing and introduced her own line of fruit vinegars, salsa, roasted garlic oils and 'Awesome Dilly Beans' that she sold to QFC and Sunny Farms."

She died on Oct. 24, 2002, and as Riesau wrote, "Shirley Larmore never wasted a moment's breath."

Now, we'll back up to 1978 when Leonard and Linda Paulson came on the scene as new owners of the *Jimmy*.

They came to Sequim from Iowa, where Leonard and Linda married and melded two families together. Leonard was widowed with a son Rob and a daughter Mary. He was owner of three small weekly newspapers around Newell, Iowa.

Linda was divorced and raising two children, Denise and Nathan Hawkins. She was a nurse at a YMCA camp and a director of nursing at an area housing group. She also had been a school nurse when they decided to get married.

"Leonard was ready to leave Iowa," Linda revealed in a March 2017 interview. "We looked at newspapers on the West Coast of Washington and in Colorado. Our agent found the *Jimmy Come Lately* was advertising for someone to buy the paper and run it."

The Paulsons flew out, met with Shirley and Bob Larmore, and they liked the small town of Sequim and the small community newspaper, much like they had in Iowa, and the small school system. They were hooked.

"We struck a deal, went back home and sold the three newspapers we owned (including the printing press) and sold our two houses in a relatively short time. We waited until the kids were out of school for summer, then we packed four kids, two dogs and my folks, who helped drive, and headed to Washington. That was some caravan," Linda admitted.

Leonard jumped into running the newspaper immediately. "I theoretically helped get the family adjusted to the new environment. I really did nothing at the paper at this point. Maggie O'Hare was the star feature reporter and ran the show," Linda said.

A full page spread on the Paulsons ran on July 5, 1978, the first *Jimmy* under new ownership. It included a 5-column photo of the Paulsons and their four children: Robbie 14, Denise 15, Mary 13 and Nathan 12. Their two dogs, Dusty and Shadow, also were in the picture.

Leonard and Linda Paulson, shown in 1978, purchased the *Jimmy Come Lately Gazette* from Shirley Larmore that year. Leonard died in 1981 and Linda continued to own the paper until selling to Brown M. Maloney in 1988. *(Courtesy of Linda Paulson)*

The page also included photos and descriptions of all their personnel: Cindy Goebel (ad paste-up with the *Jimmy* for three years); Lucy Bird (receptionist, bookkeeping for 1 ½ years); Jim Manders (sports, photography and layout for three years); Maggie O'Hare (news editor, photographer for four years and author of 10 children's books); Florence Valdez (typesetter for four years); and Isla Yamamoto (ad sales for three years).

"We pledge to do our best to maintain the high standards of the Larmores during the time they started and built this newspaper," wrote Leonard Paulson. ... This is really your newspaper because without your readership our efforts are meaningless. We solicit your continued support and plan to prove our ability to keep it as time goes on."

The *Jimmy* was printed on Bainbridge Island and Linda helped get the paper ready for the press and "trucked it there in a Dodge van."

The paper was free, supported by advertising, with a circulation of nearly 8,000, building to 10,000 at its highest when the Paulsons had the paper.

"We had good support from auto dealers and grocery stores. They bought double-truck (2-page) ads and the paper was delivered by school kids all over on Wednesday mornings," Linda said. Rural addresses were delivered by the post office.

A key cog in the operation was Barb Adams. "I started in paste-up and later drove a truck all over the peninsula," she recalled. "We had paper drops from Bremerton to Quilcene and all along the canal."

Jim White was added as a news editor and reporter later. "We went to Moses Lake for an interview," remembers Jim's wife Sandi but added, "It was too hot. I didn't want live there."

Instead they came back to Sequim and "Leonard asked me to come and talk to him. I did and was hired for a couple of years. Leonard was a nice, easy-going guy, but then he died."

White said he retired from newspapers, except for freelancing, in the early 1980s and went to work for the Sequim Parks Department in landscaping. He retired from that after more than 20 years.

He says his journalistic career probably suffered a bit because "I like to speak my mind. If you don't want to know what I'm thinking about something, don't ask me."

He said that was something he learned early in his career. "If you do your job as a newspaper reporter, there are going to be some people who don't like you." He said he had no regrets with his career. "When I left, I closed the door behind me. I don't think about what happened or didn't happen."

Leonard Paulson dies

As owner, publisher and editor, Leonard was a "do-everything" kind of journalist. He also was sales manager and sold ads, helped in paste-up (as did all employees) and wrote a column: "Comments from the publisher ... L.A. Paulson."

> "She was my lifesaver; all the staff stepped up to the plate, but especially JoAnne. It was such a tight group, very social, like a family."
>
> **Linda Paulson, Jimmy owner after her husband Leonard died.**

Three years into the Paulsons' regime, tragedy struck when Leonard died of a massive heart attack at his home on July 1, 1981.

"I suddenly had a business and four kids to raise. I wasn't ready to run a newspaper. I didn't even know how to run a camera," Linda recalled.

"Linda. That poor woman. She was a nurse and suddenly a newspaper owner, publisher and mother of four kids," said JoAnne Booth, a young typesetter and later news editor for the *Jimmy*.

"She was my lifesaver," said Paulson. "All the staff stepped up to the plate, but especially JoAnne. It was such a tight group, very social, like a family."

Booth arrived on the scene with newspaper experience from Idaho Falls. She was hired about a month before Leonard died, quickly adapted and moved up the ladder. She began as a typesetter on the Compugraphic and did some paste-up. Soon after Leonard's death, the news editor left and Booth was promoted by Paulson to fill that role.

"She did so many things for me," Linda said. "I didn't need a publisher."

The obituary that appeared in the next *Jimmy*, July 29, 1981, "Thanks for the Memories," talked about the relationship the staff had with Leonard.

We all saw Leonard differently. Some of us got madder than hell at him. Some of us respected him. Some of us loved him to pieces. Some of us learned so much from him. Some of us quit on him. And some of us joined on because of him. Some of us had great adventures with him.

Leonard listened. No matter how trivial a suggestion or complaint from any of his staff, he gave it his courteous attention and consideration. With his keen enjoyment of even mundane things that most of us take for granted, he must have lived a very full life."

The Paulsons' good friend and pastor, the Rev. Bill Klink, officiated at the funeral in Sequim, then accompanied the body back to Iowa, where Leonard is buried next to his first wife and mother of his two children.

Linda Paulson said she stayed away from the office and mourned at home for a couple of weeks until Barb Adams paid her a visit. "You've got to come up here in the office," Adams said she told Linda.

She said she had to buy new clothes. "I felt I had to have a good image as a businesswoman and newspaper publisher." Then she got some instruction on Leonard's Nikon (camera) and started taking pictures.

"I kind of got in there and started learning what was going on. They were really great people," Paulson said of her staff.

She said her staff was a great help and let her grow slowly. Other papers stepped up to help. She credited Frank Ducceschi, managing editor at *The Daily News*; Frank Garred, publisher of the *Port Townsend Leader*, the paper's rival, *Sequim Press*; and Scott Price of *The Chronicle* in Port Angeles came and set type for the *Jimmy*.

The *Jimmy* hardly lost a beat and little-by-little, the nurse-turned-publisher learned her craft as best she could.

"The paper had a wonderful reputation within the community, a very positive one," Paulson said. "A lot of that was due to JoAnne because she built on the positive approach that we started. It was in stark contrast to the *Press*, which people perceived as negative. With the *Jimmy*, they now had an option."

In the mid-80s, Paulson bought all the staff new computers to stay up-to-date, and in some cases, ahead of the competition. "Everybody but me had one," she admitted. "I was afraid to use it."

That was one thing that stood out for Greg Booth, JoAnne's husband. "Linda did a very good job of providing support for her staff. It was an excellent little newspaper."

JoAnne Booth agreed with that. "Linda was very serious about her paper. We had a second-class mailing permit and that required 25 percent ratio for news to ads. She hired Judy Holder (Marie) as ad manager. She was very good, brought in a lot of new ads, a great salesperson and had great ideas for promotions. Wonderful things happened."

Booth said stressing the positive was so important to contrast with the approach by the *Jimmy's* rival.

"We always operated with integrity. I thought we did a good job dealing with people going through tough times. We were in the business of community news. We ran lots of pictures, covered meetings and talked about issues. We emphasized lots of people features: real stories about real people doing real work in the community."

'Let's Go Sequimming'

The paper published several strong special sections, most of which Booth engineered. During the interview, she displayed a few of these: "Fashion, Vacation," in 1987, a 24-page "Peninsula Woman" in 1986 and one for which she gave her husband credit, a 32-page visitor guide format called "Let's Go Sequimming."

"It's a good title because it also told people who didn't know, how to pronounce the town we live in," Greg Booth added.

The *Jimmy* might have been a typical weekly newspaper workplace, but it also was a family atmosphere for a group that knew how to have fun.

"There was a lot of talent on the staff," JoAnne Booth noted. "We had a bunch of young mothers, so we started a group, called Mom's Band. They included: Patty McManus (Huber), Laurel Gloor, Diane Christensen and myself. We played at charity events, for senior groups and nursing homes. We had fun,"

One year, the staff decided to enter a float in the annual Irrigation Festival parade. "Carla Stockwell, our graphic artist, designed a purple dragon with newspapers as sails. It was a big hit. We even went to the Rose Parade (in Portland, Ore.)," Booth said. "Some of us wanted to dance, so we took up dancing classes. It was such a family. I guess you'd call it serendipity, a coming together of talented people at the right time."

> "The paper became a mirror of the community. It reflected what the community was about."
>
> **JoAnne Booth, Jimmy news editor**

The Booths left the paper in April 1987 when Greg's job took him to

Tillamook, Ore. It gave JoAnne new opportunities as well. She went back to school and received her master's in journalism. Her thesis: "Journalists' Guide to Copyediting." She did know a thing or two about that.

Today, she and her husband are retired, splitting time between Vader, Wash., and Clatskanie, Ore.

Meantime, Linda Paulson and staff were building the *Jimmy's* circulation. "We emphasized school news. There never was much, so we worked on getting more of that into the paper," the publisher said.

When asked about a highlight of her career with the *Jimmy*, she didn't hesitate. "A connection with the community businesses, being a part of it. When we, as a business, started getting involved in the community, the people saw us as a community-oriented paper."

Booth also highlighted that as well. "The paper became a mirror of the community. It reflected what the community was about."

The staff also was developing stability with veteran journalists finding their way to Sequim.

Quinn, McCormicks arrive

Tim Quinn was an often-opinionated political cartoonist for the *Gazette* from 1984, and later in the *Peninsula Business Journal.* He established himself as a multi-faceted artist working in chain saw carvings, stained glass, painting and drawing. He died at 62 in 2009. *(Matthew Nash, Gazette photo).*

In 1984, Paulson hired Tim Quinn as an editorial cartoonist. He didn't have far to go to work. He had an apartment in the corner of the *Gazette* building.

Quinn, a Vietnam-era combat medic, was raised in Southern California. He earned a degree in graphic arts at Fullerton College, then became a valet at fashionable hotels. For six years, he worked as an art director in L.A., handling artwork for Hang Ten,

The final issue of the *Sequim Press* was published on May 22, 1985.

Hobie, Capitol Records and Kikkoman. He had his own stained-glass business in Huntington Beach.

When he arrived at the *Gazette*, he had been a professional cowboy, lifeguard, sheep shearer, camp counselor, ambulance driver, movie extra and an X-ray technician. More recently, he had been cartoonist for three peninsula newspapers.

Quinn's cartoons became a staple of the paper, initially the *Jimmy*, and later The *Gazette*. A signature Quinn cartoon addressed current events — sometimes political, sometimes opinionated and occasionally lampooning some erstwhile politician, civic leader, issue or situation.

The next year — 1985 — was a big year for the *Jimmy*, which rapidly was becoming a fixture in the minds of Sequim residents. It gave the readers, not only a news option, but also businesses an advertising option.

The struggling *Press* had been sold the previous December and the new owner, Bob Jones, who unleashed a host of innovative ideas in January, was unable to attain those. The *Press* closed its doors after printing its final edition on May 22, 1985.

That left the *Jimmy Come Lately* as the lone newspaper in Sequim. The goal that Shirley Larmore expressed when she started the *Sequim Shopper* in 1974, finally had been attained. She wanted to run the *Press* out of town. It took a while, but the longtime paper that had begun operation in 1911, was gone.

In 1986, Paulson reached out and hired an older and experienced journalist and his wife: George McCormick, as a reporter, and Kass, as classified ad salesperson.

By the time the McCormicks arrived in Sequim, he had nearly 30 years of newspaper experience, and as his retirement article in the *Forks Forum* in 2005 notes, "he burned down two newspapers."

Not exactly, but he was employed there when the offices burned, forcing him to move on. He began his career at the *Times Advocate* in Escondido, Calif., in the advertising department. Soon, he answered an ad for an editor for a weekly newspaper in Ridgecrest, Calif. That was the first office that burned.

He headed for the Pacific Northwest, where he met and married Kass in Spokane. The couple moved to Port Orchard, where George found work as an editor on the *Independent*, and that was the second newspaper office that burned.

George and Kass McCormick worked for the *Sequim Gazette* for 10 years, starting in 1986. His "By George" columns were a staple and the couple were entrenched in community activities. *(Courtesy of Hilary Steeby)*

Next came Sequim and finally stability in the workplace and in the community — and an end to the fires in newspaper offices.

George covered the school beat and wrote feature stories. Kass worked in telemarketing and covered the front desk before moving into classified ad sales. In the *Forum* article, she said she remembered the red, plaid carpeting, now long gone from the office.

"I never saw a word processor before I got here," George McCormick recalled, confessing even up until retirement, "I used the Columbus system: search for a key and land on it."

(We'll catch up later with the McCormicks, who became deeply entrenched in the Sequim community and eventually Forks).

In 1988, Linda Paulson began to think differently about her future with the *Jimmy*.

"All kinds of things were going to happen on the peninsula," said Paulson, noting especially, the deep recession that hit the area. "Because we were a free newspaper and totally dependent on advertising, I didn't feel I had what was needed to take on the daily. It was a very competitive time; I was struggling; I didn't feel I was adequate to do what was necessary (buy more expensive technology) to keep up with those things and keep the newspaper going."

She found a broker and the newspaper was up for sale.

Young Brown M. Maloney

Enter a young man from a five-generation family of newspaper owners: Brown McClatchy Maloney.

"Brown came and talked to me several times in early 1988," said Paulson. "One time he brought his uncle with him. Two very experienced newspaper people."

Also paying a visit to Paulson's office with an inquiry about possibly buying the paper was David Black, president of Canada-based Black Press, and its subsidiary, Sound Publishing, a news organization that was 1 year old and shopping for Washington state community newspapers.

Brown M. Maloney, 32, purchased the *Jimmy Come lately Gazette* in 1988 from Linda Paulson. Maloney owned the paper, which became the present-day *Sequim Gazette*, until selling to Sound Publishing Co. in 2011. *(Gazette file photo)*

"I did talk to Linda a few times," Black shared in a 2017 telephone interview from his Victoria, B.C. office. "But we weren't that close to a purchase."

Paulson added, "He was absolutely against a free newspaper."

Who was this other brash 32-year-old would-be purchaser?

First, he was no "Johnny Come Lately." Far from it. His family had been involved in newspapers since the 1850s.

His great-great-grandfather, James McClatchy, was a newspaperman who learned his craft under Horace Greeley at the fabled *New York Tribune.* McClatchy came west as part of the California Gold Rush in 1849. He never found gold, but he did land on what would become an information empire.

"He became editor of the *Sacramento Bee* on Feb. 3, 1857, and was editor when he passed in 1883," said Maloney. At the time, he owned half the newspaper. "His children ended up owning the entire newspaper. My father, J. Brown Maloney, was a fourth-generation owner and worked for the paper for 35 years.

"I grew up in the shadows of the *Bee*, starting there at age 16 in the summer, doing everything — pulling tear sheets (newspaper clips to show advertisers their ad), and working a lot in circulation and advertising; anything a 16-year-old could do."

His first introduction to the Olympic Peninsula came during his college years when he attended Peninsula College and lived with his aunt and uncle on their ranch on Deer Park Road in Port Angeles.

After college, he ended up working for the *Bee* family of newspapers. Between ages 22 and 32, Maloney worked for the *Sacramento Bee, Anchorage Daily News* and the *Fresno Bee.*

In addition to newspapers, the family also was involved in radio. "I didn't work in radio, but it was often the talk around the dinner table and I learned about the business," Maloney admitted. The family owned stations in Sacramento, Modesto, Fresno and Bakersfield in California, and Reno, Nev.

"When I was 31, I had the itch to work someplace other than the family business. It wasn't that I disliked working there. I didn't. It was that I didn't want to work for my family all my life. For me, I wanted to stick with something I was familiar with, and that was newspapers. I preferred to be in business for myself. Daily newspapers were prohibitively expensive, and dailies were not being bought by individuals. They were owned by corporations."

So, Maloney sought out weeklies, and with his college experience, zeroed in on two opportunities in Washington. Outside of California, this was one area he was familiar with.

The *Whidbey News Times*, owned by Wallie Funk and John Webber, and the *Jimmy Come Lately* in Sequim, owned by Linda Paulson.

"I was intimidated by Whidbey's $2.5 million price as too lofty, although it included property and they owned their own press. That was a prestige thing for weeklies," said Maloney. "It was a strong market, a good market, but I was scared of the price."

So, he turned to Sequim, a city and paper he had been familiar with in college.

"At that point, I was working with a broker named John Fournier, whose family in the '60s and '70s owned all the South King County newspapers. I think being a broker was a hobby for John. I don't think he took me seriously. I never heard back from him about Sequim."

Undaunted, Maloney revealed in a Jan. 14, 1998, *Gazette* column more about his adventures in buying the paper, essentially coming north on a whim.

"The itch to be in business for myself combined with too many phone conversations with a newspaper broker, got me going. I found myself heading north on I-5 in a U-Haul with no job, but a 'pretty good chance' this guy could find me a once-or-twice-a week newspaper in Western Washington."

After arriving on the Olympic Peninsula, Maloney still couldn't get a response from his agent. He had visited Sequim and was about to give up when he called his cousin, chairman of the McClatchy board, to share his angst.

"He told me to walk into Paulson's office and talk to her," Maloney said in a 2017 interview. "That's what I did. I walked in and asked her if the name Brown Maloney sounded familiar and she said 'no.' I asked her if the name John Fournier sounded familiar and she said 'yes.' I then got up and closed the door and I told her to call John and tell him a man named Maloney wants to buy your newspaper."

That's how Maloney became owner of the *Jimmy*, negotiating an acceptable price with Paulson and Fournier to complete the deal. He said the $560,000 price tag for the *Jimmy* was more palatable than the lofty price tag at Whidbey.

In the meantime, he heard that the *Whidbey News Times* had been sold — to David Black, the first of Sound Publishing's Puget Sound weeklies that has since become an empire.

Through 2018, Sound Publishing Inc. has become the largest community news publisher in Washington. The company's holdings include four dailies: *The Herald* in Everett, where all Sound papers are printed; the *Peninsula Daily News* in Port Angeles; the *Daily World* in Aberdeen and the *Tacoma Daily Index*, a government listings publication.

In Washington, their weekly newspapers by county number: 18 in King, three in Grays Harbor, one in Okanagan, eight on the Olympic and Kitsap peninsulas, three in San Juan, two in Snohomish and four on Whidbey.

It all started with the *Whidbey News Times*, which Maloney said just as easily could have been his first paper.

"If I had a little bit of confidence, I would have gotten Whidbey. If I had a lot of confidence, I would have bought Whidbey and Sequim both," Maloney admitted.

> "If I had a little bit of confidence, I would have gotten Whidbey. If I had a lot of confidence, I would have bought Whidbey and Sequim."
>
> Brown M. Maloney

But he was thrilled with the purchase of the *Jimmy Come Lately Gazette,* the first newspaper among several he would own. Brown, his first wife Lori and daughter Britney, moved to Sequim.

"I'm very excited about being able to be involved in this purchase," Maloney was quoted in the Sept. 1, 1988, issue of the *Jimmy*. "I'm impressed with the quality and integrity of the newspaper. I have no plans for major changes, other than improving a quality product."

A decade later in a 1998 *Gazette* column, Maloney revealed his thoughts on that big day in his life.

"So, 10 years ago I stood with Linda Paulson in front of 15 people when she announced she was selling her newspaper. At the time, I was 31 but looked more like 24 (I was later told). As I looked around the room, I was convinced the staff was ready to leave. Fortunately, they didn't. Well, OK, one did, editor John Teehan."

Paulson said she was "pleased to find a man of Brown's caliber to buy the paper. I'm looking forward to seeing the improvements he plans to make, and to begin a different life experience for myself."

Sharing her thoughts on the sale in a 2017 interview, Paulson said, "I think I was at the point that he wanted it more than I did. I think we made a positive impact. The people of Sequim felt the *Jimmy* was their paper. The *Gazette* was immersed in the town. I was too," she added, noting that she was the first female in the Sequim Sunrise Rotary Club.

Paulson said it had been her goal to return to school to pursue a different career. "I know I didn't want to go back into nursing. I moved to Corvallis, Ore., and got my degree in Health Care Administration in 1996."

She retired from Disability Services, a state agency in Oregon, in 2011, and now lives in Corvallis, though treks to Sequim frequently.

Olympic View Publishing begins

Taking baby steps rather than the giant leaps the deep-pocketed Black made, Maloney began to build his own little empire on the peninsula, forming Olympic View Publishing as the corporate owner.

Little-by-little, he established the *Peninsula Business Journal*, acquired *Homes-Land* magazine, the *Forks Forum*, the *Sequim Gazette* and created the broadcast corporation Radio Pacific, owners of radio stations KONP (News Talk), KSTI FM (Country Western) and a new station KZQM-FM (Rock Classic) in Sequim in 2018.

"My strength is on the business end," Maloney stressed. "I won't say I leave news alone, but I don't overly bother with news, unless it is necessary. I didn't want the news side to think I was their instructor or hanging over their shoulder."

Hiring experienced news employees was paramount to the newspaper's success. Jim Manders already was a known commodity, having worked at *The Daily News* when he attended Peninsula College from 1966-1968. Then, followed a four-year stint as sports reporter for the Lewiston, Idaho, *Tribune*. While there, he studied journalism and graphic arts at Washington State University.

His heart always had been with the Olympic Peninsula, so it was an easy call when he was offered a position in 1974 when Shirley Larmore expanded her *Shopper* to the *Jimmy Come Lately Gazette.*

During the late 1970s and early 1980s, Manders would work with the now-defunct *Sequim Press* and the *Jimmy.* Between newspaper jobs, he worked for NAPA Auto Parts and later as a bartender at Town Tavern.

In 1987, Linda Paulson rehired Manders as a reporter and photographer for the *Jimmy Come Lately Gazette.* He also served as Paulson's special assistant, particularly after Leonard died.

Immediately after Maloney bought the paper, John Teehan, the editor hired by Paulson, decided to return to Seattle. His resumé included such big-city newspapers as New York City, Boston and Seattle. He had been with the *Gazette* for 15 months and wrote his column "Strait Scoop" weekly. But, as he says in his sign-off, "the big city is calling."

That left the position open for Manders to move up.

"Jim applied for the position of editor and was promoted," said Maloney.

Jim Manders *(Courtesy of Hilary Steeby)*

"There is no question Jim was a newspaperman down to his very core. His local institutional knowledge is simply irreplaceable."

Brown Maloney

With his newspaper knowledge, background and familiarity with the peninsula, Manders was a natural for the position. "Jim loved this town and this newspaper and his dedication to both was huge," Maloney was quoted in Manders' obituary, written by then-publisher Sue Ellen Riesau in the *Gazette* on June 15, 2005. "There is no question Jim was a newspaperman down to his very core. His local institutional knowledge is simply irreplaceable."

Manders was editor at the *Gazette* for nearly 15 years until moving over to the *Peninsula Daily News* in 2002.

With Manders as editor and McCormick's "By George" column becoming a staple, Maloney and the *Gazette* had the nucleus of a strong newsroom.

"I don't know if we got along that well in my early years," Maloney admitted. "My youthfulness might have been off-putting. Maybe he (Manders) thought I was just a guy with money who bought the newspaper. Jim was territorial about the news. I don't think there was a lot of respect initially. But, I grew to appreciate his ability, his connectiveness to the community. He had a true relationship with city hall, the police department, the police chief. They respected him, respected that he was good at his job and they trusted Jim."

We will revisit Manders later, because he was the architect of an award-winning newsroom and responsible for molding the lives of young reporters for more than a decade.

The same day, Oct. 26, 1988, Manders was promoted, McCormick covered another important story. Battelle Marine Science Laboratory at Sequim Bay was having an open house. That was news, big news. The company that opened 23 years before had maintained a low image. That was changing and the city responded with more than 350 visitors.

"This was our attempt to change our image and let the community know what we are doing," said lab manager Dick Ecker in the *Gazette* story. "We have kept a low profile before and that's what we are trying to correct."

He said the biggest change was getting the community involved. "We employ local college and high school students, part-time for evenings, weekends and vacations."

He said Battelle, one of two marine science labs (the other is in Massachusetts) "is the largest nonprofit research facility in the U.S."

When Maloney bought the paper, he needed to register it under a corporate name and wanted to use the term Olympic Publishing, but a man in Port Ludlow had that name.

He registered the paper under Maloney Publishing, but said he didn't like that. He wrestled with finding another corporate name for weeks until he decided to hold a contest among the staff. "I told them we'd put all the suggestions in a hat. Everybody was welcome. I figured 30 people thinking about it was better than just one. I didn't even get back to my office from that staff meeting and it hit me: Olympic View Publishing. I felt bad involving the staff and them coming up with the new name myself." As a consolation, Maloney bought lunch for the staff.

No more 'Jimmy'

Three months later, the corporate name was changed. Gradually he also would change the name of the paper. "I wasn't overly keen on it," Maloney said of the *Jimmy Come Lately*. "To people outside the area, it didn't sound overly professional, and to others, they seemed to get the name wrong. It wasn't a geographical name of significance."

He said he wanted to "segue the name of the town into the newspaper name." So, he started gradually with a masthead that showed "**Sequim's**" in large bold letters on the left, smaller "Jimmy Come Lately," followed by large, bold "**Gazette**" on the right.

By April 4, 1990, the *Jimmy* was gone from the masthead — forever. This move didn't sit well with everyone and Maloney attempted to placate his readers in a column and a cartoon.

Longtime cartoonist Tim Quinn drew the perfect segue, showing a family reading the *Sequim Gazette*, revealing the new masthead. Above them the words "Has Anybody Seen The Jimmy?" It has become a signature of Quinn's storied career with the Sequim paper.

In his "Publisher's Corner," Maloney described the changes not only to the front-page masthead, but throughout the paper in a column headlined "Change in Gazette is from the inside out."

He explained how he could have made the change when he first bought the paper, but he wanted to bring

One of Tim Quinn's most popular political cartoons appeared on April 4, 1990. "Has anybody seen the Jimmy?" It was the first edition of the *Sequim Gazette* with the *Jimmy Come Lately* banished forever from its name. *(Gazette file)*

about change from the inside to the cover. Maloney said it was his decision, but he listened to the staff and the community for input before making the changes.

Among the alterations was the new logo, not just the name, but a design. The redesign committee settled on two logos. "One was very creative with good-looking artwork and a '90s look," said Maloney. "The other was simpler with a photo of our mountains across the top. We debated among ourselves and even singled out half a dozen community leaders and let them play a part in the decision-making process. ... After all, it's your newspaper, too."

He said both staff and community were virtually unanimous in their choice, saying the front page with art looked nice, but it could look nice on any paper. "The masthead we chose seemed to confirm that our area is special. As one person said, 'This just seems that it belongs on top of the paper that serves the Sequim Dungeness Valley.'"

The logo featured a panoramic photo of the Olympic Mountains in the background with *The Sequim Gazette* printed over it.

Along with the masthead, the changes included new column designs and headings; a better copy and photo layout.

"You will not find *Jimmy Come Lately* on the front page, but please know that we will still answer to that, proudly," Maloney said, recognizing that changing the name will take some time to get used to. "So, those of you that still wish to call us the 'Jimmy,' please continue to do so."

He concluded the column, "We hope you enjoy the new look of your newspaper. May it be as fresh as a sunny day in Sequim."

Peninsula Business Journal

When Maloney bought the paper in 1988, the wheels already were in motion to produce a business magazine. He said he admired the *Puget Sound Business Journal* in Seattle and one in Kitsap County.

"I wanted to start one on the Olympic Peninsula, covering Clallam and Jefferson counties," said Maloney. "I always appreciated those stories that profiled businesses, a new sign, what's going into that empty space and previewing new products. I felt the business pages were some of the more interesting parts of a newspaper."

First step in the project was to hire an editor.

"I saw an ad in the *Federal Way News* for a weekly in Sequim looking for a writer/editor with a business background," said Martha Ireland, living there at the time and working on a business trade journal. "That sounds like me, I said."

A montage of *Peninsula Business Journals*, which were published from 1989 for 10 years. *(Bill Lindstrom photo)*

An interview was set up and she was hired as the first editor and the lone writer in the beginning. The first issue of the *Peninsula Business Journal* hit the streets in August 1989. It was 28 pages and printed on high-quality (Electro Brite) paper.

"The paper owed its success to Martha," said Maloney. "She was out there. She made it happen. She was really hands-on. People would see her and know we had a product with value. That's what we tried to show the business community. This was a paper with value."

> *"The paper owed its success to Martha (Ireland). She was out there. She made it happen. She was really hands-on."*
>
> **Brown Maloney**

Each month had a different theme. "The first one was the price of gas on the peninsula; the second one on sign codes; and that is still going on," Ireland said in a 2017 interview.

"We started to build readership, but the greatest disappointment to me," she said with Maloney in the room, "was I didn't feel it was promoted that well. I would have liked to see the product with an ad campaign, what the *PBJ* was about, build curiosity."

Maloney nodded his head in agreement that the launch could have been better promoted.

Still, it received accolades from the community and a solid advertising base with merchants often getting the benefit of an ad in the *Gazette* and the *PBJ*.

When the timber industry crumbled, cottage industries started to spring up all over the peninsula. "That was another market we liked to cover. If somebody was making a special barbecue sauce in their garage, we wanted to know about it," Ireland said.

Ireland said a mainstay of the paper was cartoonist Tim Quinn, a regular with the *Gazette*. She did most of the writing, but also hired columnists such as Pat Neal for fishing and outdoors. Jenny Cooley was hired to help with ad sales, then would do layout and write some editorials.

"Jenny was kind of like a publisher," said Maloney. "She filled that role, so we gave her that title." She was also general manager for a couple of years before leaving in 1993.

In her final "Shop Talk" column in July 1995, Ireland announced she was leaving the *PBJ* and taking on a new challenge: Republican candidate for Clallam County commissioner, District 1.

Watching the county's way of doing business and observing issues facing us, I became convinced that I have no choice but to try to alter the freedom-devouring course we have been following.

Ireland won her race for the commission seat, ran for re-election and "I narrowly lost, for which I am eternally grateful," she admitted. She was offered a position as columnist by John Brewer, publisher of the *Peninsula Daily News*. She did that for "about 12 years until I took a couple week's off and decided I wanted to concentrate on writing western novels. It was my goal when I moved to the peninsula."

In 2016, Martha McKeeth Ireland authored *The Trail of the Snake*, Vol. I and followed immediately with Vol. II. Readers say, "It's a ride through hell as friends appear to be enemies and enemies appear to be friends."

At a time when many people are considering retirement, Ireland keeps her schedule busy. "I found I needed some structure, so I fill in one day at the Serenity House and now I am working three days a week writing grants and other things for the nonprofit that provides emergency shelter to the homeless."

Dick Landis, who had been with the *PBJ* for 10 months, was named editor. "We have been working together. We have completed a redesign that has been on the back burner for too long," Ireland wrote.

In the same edition, Landis introduced himself under a new column head: "Editor's Notebook." In it, he announced a new set of criteria for the *Peninsula Business Journal*, reprinted here in part:

Good newswriting requires more than just accuracy and clarity. We also need to be involved with and care about the people and businesses we write about. Honesty and fairness should never be abused to increase interest.

Landis wasn't there long and Jeff Chew, who joined the *Gazette* in 1996, was named editor. The publication began to decline in 1998, and the Olympic View Publishing's board, in its Oct. 13, 1999, meeting, voted unanimously to drop the print publication after the November issue, 10 years after it began.

The following April, the *PBJ* returned, this time to the OVP online site. "We will begin uploading comprehensive business news as it is filed by our contributing writers from Port Townsend, Sequim, Port Angeles, Forks and peninsula communities in between, much as we did with the print production," said Chew, the online editor.

In some ways, the online version was better than the print, which was published once a month. "We will upload business news as it breaks," Chew continued. The website was designed by Rob Chelgren, OVP's circulation manager, and accessed via hyperlink through all participating newspapers' websites.

Riesau, Roberts join team

When Maloney purchased the *Gazette*, he made two front-office hires who would each work for him for at least 20 years.

Sue Ellen Riesau and Hilary Roberts (Steeby).

Riesau, who moved from California in 1989 to be office manager, filled that role for four or five years. She was promoted to business manager, then general manager and in 2002, publisher. These roles were with the

Gazette, but she also served as GM and publisher of the *PBJ,* and when Maloney acquired the *Forks Forum* in 1990, she was also named publisher and oversaw that publication.

Riesau said "Forks was always there in the background. Everything we did in Sequim, we tried to duplicate in Forks."

Riesau was hired at the *Gazette* in March 1989, initially for ad sales, "but I told Brown I wasn't that good at sales; I was better at human resources and he made me office manager."

In 1990, when Maloney bought still another publication — *Homes-Land,* a real estate publication — he added that to Riesau's repertoire.

"Those were the days when real estate magazines were in every hotel, restaurant and at the chamber. When somebody came to town looking for a place to live, that's where they found it," Maloney said. He made an offer of $200,000 to the owner, Scott Hopper, and the magazine was soon his.

> *"When Brown said we were going to buy a real estate magazine, I was onboard. We were starting to build a nice, little empire."*
>
> **Sue Ellen Riesau**

Back then, the publication usually was 64 pages and some issues were up to 136 pages, depending on the time of year. It still is published, but with only 16-24 pages as Realtors are capitalizing more on digital marketing than print.

Olympic Peninsula Homes-Land magazine served Clallam, Jefferson and Mason counties. A sister publication, *Islander Homes-Land,* served Island and San Juan and counties.

Riesau graduated from UCSC in Santa Cruz, Calif., and held several positions in advertising and marketing before coming to Sequim.

"I had started a real estate magazine in San Luis Obispo County, so I had the background. When Brown said we were going to buy a pair of real estate magazines, I was onboard. We were starting to build a nice, little empire."

The other front-office hire of significance and lengthy duration was Hilary Roberts, then a 1989 Sequim High School senior.

"Jim Manders was my uncle, but I really didn't know him until I started at the paper," said Roberts. "He was my mom's brother, but they were seven years apart in age."

But Uncle Jim, the *Gazette* editor, hired his niece to be a typesetter. "I worked at a restaurant in town in the day and came in and set type on an old MacIntosh in the evenings. I also helped with paste-ups. They were all hand-done in those days, a lot of physical hands-on work."

She also did the tedious work of transcribing freelancers hand-written stories for Manders.

After Roberts had done that job for a little over a year, "Sue Ellen saw I had bookkeeping experience and she put me in that role, and I stayed for 20 years."

"She came in as a high school senior, but was a hard worker, very dependable. She more than earned her stripes," Maloney lauded. "Hilary has a fantastic memory with billing. Her knowledge of the customers and their paying experience was phenomenal. We'd just keep throwing things her way and she'd roll with them."

Manders had a tremendous effect on newcomers, helping mold them into good, young reporters and employees.

"He terrified me," Roberts said. "He was very hard on me, but he was hard on us all. He was very gruff, but he made his reporters into outstanding journalists. He was an excellent writer and wasn't afraid to go after the tough stories. He was fearless. I did learn to appreciate and respect him."

At his memorial, the testimonials said "he was an old-school journalist. He lived it, he breathed it," Roberts said. "He was also a very skilled photographer and won as many awards for his photos as for his writing."

She said he was "kind of like a father figure to the younger reporters and editors. Except for George McCormick, all the reporters were much younger than he was. Mike Dashiell (*Gazette* editor since 2010) is a perfect example."

When Riesau became general manager of the *Peninsula Business Journal* in 1994, Roberts moved into a comptroller's role with that publication. She fine-tuned her experience by attending Peninsula College at nights for five years.

Roberts often would help with the production of both papers, aiding in paste-ups when the staff was short-handed.

This was something that frustrated her when she left the *Gazette* in 2009 to work as a fiscal specialist for Clallam County Public Works, primarily doing bookkeeping for 70 employees in the roads and maintenance departments.

"I wanted to help out in the Treasurer's Office, but they wouldn't let me. I was not allowed to help these ladies, who were short-handed. I find that bizarre," said Roberts, who is now married and answers to Hilary Roberts Steeby.

But she wasn't ready to completely cut the ties with the *Gazette* until Nov. 1, 2011, when the paper was bought by Sound Publishing. "For the next two years, I did a lot of financial things, taxes, end-of-the-month reports, nuts and bolts things on nights and weekends."

With McCormick covering the school board, among other beats, and writing features, Kass helping on the front desk and with classified, and Manders keeping the city council and county commission in check, Maloney and Riesau had the makings of an award-winning newspaper that would make residents of Sequim forget about the papers that came before.

Albeit, there was more to a successful newspaper than beating a deadline and getting the paper on the streets.

"We had a revelation that, as a weekly newspaper, we had the opportunity to build the community and make the paper a central part of our daily life said Riesau. "We embraced the idea that we would not say 'no.' We would say 'yes' to as many things as we could. We would support the community in getting news releases published and not treat the community's needs as a pain in the rear. We wanted to treat the community's needs as our primary function."

Riesau said she started to get more involved in the community when the Sequim bypass opened in 1999 and then Sequim 2000 was formed to help rejuvenate downtown businesses.

"I realized the newspaper could be a big part of it," said Riesau, who added she also became involved with the United Way and the Lavender Festival.

In the early morning hours of March 25, 1993, one of the biggest crimes in Sequim's history would occur, a horrific double homicide, which the *Gazette* followed for more than two decades. Twenty-four years later, despite two court convictions and several appeals, Darold Stenson is still alive on death row in Walla Walla. So far, the cost to appeal and try this case has amassed $1.1 million, the most expensive in Clallam County history.

In 1994, Stenson, 40, was convicted in the double murder of his wife Denise, 29, and Frank Hoerner, 33, his business partner. They were both slain at Stenson's exotic bird farm on Kane Road near Sequim.

Stenson has maintained his innocence, claiming Hoerner shot Denise, then took his own life. Evidence by the prosecuting attorney showed that Hoerner was badly beaten, then shot and killed by Stenson.

He was sentenced to the death penalty and was a week away from lethal injection in 2008 when he was granted a stay.

In May 2012, the state Supreme Court, with an 8-1 vote, overturned the 1994 death penalty conviction and ordered a new trial. The High Court ruled that Stenson's rights were violated when new evidence emerged showing a photograph of a sheriff's detective wearing Stenson's blood-stained jeans. That photo originally was suppressed. In December 2013, he was convicted a second time of the two murders and sentenced to two consecutive life sentences.

Through the ensuing four years, there have been several court reviews and the last appeal on Feb. 22, 2017, that upheld Stenson's conviction. He likely will remain on death row.

More than 1,100 documents have been filed in Clallam County alone. In the most recent action, on May 5, 2017, Stenson's attorney asked the state Supreme Court to review his double-murder case.

Clallam County Prosecuting Attorney Mark Nichols said the decision would be made behind closed doors and likely occur within six months. "This is a very, very large case," he told *PDN* reporter Rob Ollikainen for the latest update.

Changes improve *Gazette*

In 1994, the *Gazette* underwent a series of cosmetic changes, all designed to improve the looks of the paper and to help the readers.

The changes were the result of meetings and brainstorming that began

In 1994, the *Sequim Gazette* banner was changed replacing the Olympic Mountains part of the flag with the Sequim Dungeness Lighthouse, drawn by Tim Quinn.

four months before the implementation on Nov. 2, Maloney explained in a column.

Most notably, the front-page logo was altered. "We've replaced the drawing of the Olympic Mountains with one of the Dungeness Lighthouse," a snappy drawing created by resident cartoonist Tim Quinn.

Page A-2 had a new name, "For Your Information," featuring an expanded weather box, list of public meetings, ferry schedules and coming events.

The editorial pages were moved to the back of the A section, bringing local news closer to the front. Business pages were expanded to four pages that preceded the editorial pages. An "Our Lives" page in the B section would record births, weddings, engagements and anniversaries. This page included a column, "Thanks a Million," written by multi-millionaire philanthropist Percy Ross, who gives money to the needy through this column. "Chalk Talk" and "School Notes" would head another B page.

"Snapshot" and "Bob Rogers" column have been moved to the B section from Page A-2. Marian Platt's "Kitchen Korner" featured cooking tips and hints as well as recipes. Other columns highlighted issue involving seniors, health, volunteers, gardening and home improvement.

Maloney made many changes, but emphasized in his "Publisher's Corner," the one thing that remains constant "is our promise to serve the people of this community in the best possible manner with comprehensive news and advertising to give you the information you want and need to have."

The McCormicks were not only fixtures on the paper but became entrenched in the community and were a popular couple. In a later retirement article on the McCormicks from the *Forks Forum* in 2005, *Gazette* editor Mary Powell wrote that Kass was "a Royalty mom, working with the queens and princesses of various festivals. She and George were Ditchwalkers, walking next to the Sequim float in parades.

"George and Kass were the honorary grand marshals for one of the Irrigation Festival parades. The Sequim Grange named George Citizen of the Year."

They also served on the boards for the New Dungeness Lighthouse Assn., the Museum and Arts Center, the Irrigation Festival and were members of the Sequim-Dungeness Kiwanis Club.

McCormicks head to Forks

Then came February 1996 when Maloney and Riesau had a meeting with George McCormick and presented him the opportunity to be the editor of the *Forks Forum*.

"I'll never forget what Brown told me on my way to Forks," McCormick recalled from his retirement story. "He told me I was getting older and I needed to take a job where I could relax."

That prompted a laugh as he looked back at the long hours he put in the editor's chair the past 10 years in Forks.

McCormick decided the time was ripe to make a change and meet a new community. So, the 68-year-old journalist, instead of moving into retirement, left Sequim, announcing the move in his final "By George" column on Feb. 21, 1996.

He called the move "Sweet sorrow." Sweet for the new opportunity and sorrow in leaving Sequim and the many friendships they acquired.

When it was time to leave Sequim, the town responded with their true feelings for the McCormicks.

"Half of the billboards in town wished us well," said McCormick in the article, his eyes tear-filled at the memory of leaving.

Jim Manders also had a hand when another newspaper debuted on the peninsula in October 1996.

Ever hear of the *Webster Tribune*? Probably not, unless you were a journalism student at Peninsula College. The paper was developed by David Hart, who came up with the idea as part of his internship in the journalism program at Western Washington University.

The students created the paper and wrote the content with the help of established pros — Manders, Todd Ortloff, KONP's station manager, and Robbie Mantooth, Peninsula College's journalism instructor and program coordinator. The paper trumpeted the school's

Jim Manders, *Gazette* editor, confers with Laura Campbell on a summer intern program for Peninsula College's Oct. 21, 1996, *Webster Tribune.* Campbell received Webster program stipends for internships in advertising and newswriting. *(Webster Tribune/Peninsula Daily News archive)*

Webster Scholarship program, established from more than $500,000 in funds by former *Port Angeles Evening News* owner/publisher Charles Webster.

In 1995-1996, Maloney struck a powerful chord for small weeklies like the *Gazette* and the *Forum* when he was elected president of the Washington Newspaper Publishers Association.

In 1996, a new festival began in Sequim that eventually would catapult the city into worldwide status. That year a handful of lavender farmers ventured to Sequim's downtown Open Aire Market (every Saturday from May through October on Cedar Street) to show the public what nature had produced. This was the first Lavender Festival, attended mainly by locals and their visiting friends. Ironically, it was the same year that the Irrigation Festival would celebrate its 100th anniversary.

The festival grew by leaps and bounds in rapid fashion. Eight farms in the beginning have ballooned to more than 30. Sequim now proudly proclaims itself "Lavender Capital of North America."

In 2002, Sequim resident and *Gazette* columnist Betty Oppenheimer, a seamstress by trade, wrote a book *Growing Lavender and Community on the*

Sequim Prairie, a how-to and history with more than 60 projects and recipes for using the fragrant herb. The 143-page book is available on Amazon.com.

Maloney sells 50 percent

In 1998, with a cluster of six publications — the *Sequim Gazette* (circulation 7,400), *Forks Forum* (circulation 4,600), *Peninsula Business Journal, Olympic Peninsula Homes-Land, Islander Homes-Land* and *Countywide Classifieds* — Maloney decided it was time to share the leadership role. The role in his family's newspaper company, the McClatchy Corp., was also expanding, necessitating more of his time.

He announced the change in the Feb. 21, 1998, *Gazette,* saying that he had opportunities to sell Olympic View Publishing, but "my personal belief is that a newspaper best serves its community when its ownership is right there and living in the community.

Maloney wrote:

To that end, I sought out the only privately owned and operated newspaper on the North Olympic Peninsula. That newspaper is the well-respected Port Townsend Leader. *It is co-published by Frank Garred and Scott Wilson. These gentlemen operate in a style similar to OVP and we're pleased to be given a chance to see this company remain local in ownership and control.*

So effective today, the Gazette *and OVP will have a new publisher. I am happy to introduce Frank Garred as that person. Among the community newspapers in the state, Frank is highly respected. He has published the* Leader *for 31 years and is past president of our state newspaper association WNPA (Washington Newspaper Publishers Association). In addition, Frank was president of the National Newspaper Association in 1990, one of (insert only) three publishers in our state to hold that position.*

Frank believes in community journalism. To have his talent and his commitment to this organization is a contribution to the communities we serve.

As for me, I plan to focus my attention on other business, not the least of which is a daily newspaper company my great-great-grandfather owned, which incidentally remains in our family today.

In the front-page article on the same day, he explained the partnership: it would be 50-50, with Maloney retaining half-ownership of Olympic

View Publishing and its publications and Garred and Wilson's Port Townsend Publishing sharing the other half. Wilson joined the *Leader* in 1989 as a partner with Garred and others. Wilson and Garred formed Port Townsend Publishing in the 1990s as a corporate owner of the *Leader*.

Maloney will continue as chairman of the OVP board, while Sue Ellen Riesau will remain the general manager.

Washington Newspaper, the publication for the WNPA, put this transaction into perspective in the lead in its February 1998 edition.

"Two of the strongest publishing presences on the Olympic Peninsula officially joined forces January 14 when *Port Townsend Leader* co-publishers Frank Garred and Scott Wilson took a 50-percent stake in the Sequim-based Olympic View Publishing."

In the *Gazette's* front-page article on the deal, Garred is quoted: "OVP is a strong company with solid publications and a record of service to the community. We look forward to strengthening them further and doing everything we can to better serve the readers and advertisers in Clallam County."

Maloney was equally pleased with the partnership. "In considering a change, I purposely sought them out because of their excellent reputation and commitment to community journalism."

Wilson said the transaction "was possible because of Brown's commitment to keeping his newspapers local and his trust that Frank and I would maintain Olympic View's independence. He bent over backwards to make this possible in the interests of his community."

Garred became known for his hard-hitting editorials, but the one he wrote in the Jan. 6, 1999, *Gazette* was heart-felt and inspiring.

Titled, "The real Gay Blade," it is an obituary tribute to one of journalism's most satirical, controversial, yet witty newspaper owners, Henry Gay. Since 1966, he owned the *Mason County Journal* in Shelton. From the opening issue of the *Jimmy Come Lately* in 1974, to last year when cancer got the best of him, his column "The Gay Blade," held its position on the editorial pages of the *Gazette*, often on facing pages with his political opposite, Adele Ferguson, casting a wary glance.

"Henry Gay was a man of passion. He was a cynic, satirist, realist. He personified the ethics of journalism: Objective, fair, thorough," wrote Garred.

"He was funny too."

Garred also reveals what few may have known. Gay was a business partner of Frank, along with Bruce Wilson (Scott's father) when he purchased the *Port Townsend Leader* in 1967.

In this editorial, Garred recalls the issue that perhaps defined Henry Gay. "Henry truly believed that his readers — his community — liked and respected a newspaper that tells them what is going on, everything that is going on.

"We remember vividly the editorial penned by Henry that won the national Golden Quill Award. It set out clearly the Shelton *Journal's* policy and beliefs relating to publishing in detail — naming names — the criminal trials in Mason County Superior Court. More specifically, it was an editorial dealing with the naming of rape victims in the court coverage, something over which the community was divided."

Gay's public nemesis was former Gov. Dixy Lee Ray, though they never met.

"Henry's editorials were the finest examples of clear, concise writing. He was a master of the language, of communication. His messages were dynamic, disturbing, challenging, always irritatingly thoughtful and direct. He would not compromise his principles.

> *"Henry Gay may be but a whisper in this passing life. His courage, his wit, his counsel were more than shouts in the wilderness of community journalism. He was the standard bearer. He will be missed."*
>
> **Frank Garred, Gazette co-owner, publisher**

"Henry Gay may be but a whisper in this passing life. His courage, his wit, his counsel were more than shouts in the wilderness of community journalism. He was the standard bearer. He will be missed."

On the same day, Garred wrote about an issue that had been percolating for more than 40 years in Sequim. The U.S. Highway 101 bypass was moving toward completion and he challenged the downtown businesses to get onboard with a new development group, Sequim 2000, a creation of the Sequim-Dungeness Chamber of Commerce.

"What downtown Sequim needs is a determined leadership, committed to reviving a business district that has for too long been forced to endure endless streams of traffic — noise and pollution, too — that has kept many townsfolk from negotiating and enjoying the unique ambience of our little town."

He encouraged residents and businesses alike to "Give Sequim 2000 the franchise independent of other groups. Let it collect and coordinate efforts to move forward with a downtown development plan worthy of this town.

"Most of all, this is a moment for Sequim's leaders to prove their mettle. ... Accept the refreshing challenge, or become a pallbearer to an economic wasteland. The choice is simple, the task daunting and rewarding."

Then came Wednesday, Aug. 18, 1999, the day the new Highway 101 bypass opened. The *Gazette* went all out for this grand event that would write a new chapter in the city's history.

The front page featured a 5-column photo by Manders showing an empty exit ramp from 101 at Sequim Avenue, a scene that soon would change. The cover story, written by reporters Robert Whale and Heather (the byline said Healther) Bloyer, jumped to a pair of facing pages, complete with bypass opening stories. Manders also wrote a first-person story as he meandered Washington Avenue easily just before the opening.

The 4.6-mile stretch starts just east of where the Dungeness River Bridge joins Highway 101 with the first off/on ramp at River Road, a mile east. The road travels east to just past Simdars Road, where it connects with 101 west of Keeler Road.

Civic leaders and legislators were on hand, as was Jerry Anguili, a member of the former U.S. 101 Citizen Involvement Committee.

"It has been a long time," Anguili told the *Gazette*. "The first comment I heard about the bypass dates to about 1955. It was another crackpot comment at that time. But, if you have gone down the middle of town in the last three to four days, it has become apparent that we are about 10 years overdue in getting it open."

Once the ribbon was cut by dignitaries, the road was opened in short phases. A parade of vintage autos was led by a 1907 REO (now on display at the Sequim Museum and Arts).

Garred wrote in an editorial:

It's kind of exciting. We'll get to talk to one another, we'll get to shop at

OUR stores; we may even get to jaywalk across Washington Street, once in a while without waiting indefinitely for traffic to subside.

Garred favored the notion that a change in attitude is necessary. He's onboard with one motelier, who said his business and other motel owners need to capitalize on events to build on, noting such recent events as the Lavender Festival, the annual Irrigation Festival and the October farm tours to name a few. "We need to become a destination recreation area, not just a quick-stop roadside attraction," he added.

Dashiell the intern

In April 2001, a bold young college student walked into Maloney's office in search of a job. "I needed an internship for my degree," related Michael Dashiell during an interview in 2015.

He was a senior and a student of Professor Pete Steffens at Western Washington University. The instructor was the son of Lincoln Steffens, a *New York Post* writer and one of the original "muckraking journalists."

Dashiell seemed molded in the image of the Steffens' clan as he climbed the *Gazette* ladder in rapid fashion, becoming the lead reporter in a couple of years, then sports editor and finally editor in 2010. Dashiell was still in that position in 2018.

But it wasn't that way in the beginning.

"It was awkward," he revealed in a 2017 interview. "I was interviewed by Frank (Garred), Sue Ellen (Riesau) and Jim Manders. I was starry-eyed and needed the internship, but Jim made it clear the job was full-time."

"Mike came to us as an intern from Western, but he looked like he was 12," smiled Riesau. "He had a presence about him. He was amiable. We put him on the city beat; it was brutal because there was so much going on in Sequim. It didn't seem to affect him. It wasn't long before he started moving up.

"He's a great writer. Throughout all the shuffling in management, he has consistently showed leadership. He is the rock in the newsroom. No matter what was going on in management, he stayed solid," Riesau added.

Dashiell was pretty green when he was hired and admitted the first three or four months were "like a classroom. It was an eye-opener. On my first day, Jim handed me a camera and said I was a photographer. I told him, 'no I am not.' My photos were terrible, but I got better.

"I learned so much in a short time from Jim Manders. He was like married to his job. He had a profound effect on me. Oddly, he left for the *PDN* in 2001, then after he got sick and we hired him back, and I was his boss."

Dashiell said all the editors taught him so much in their own way.

"Frank preached that it was our responsibility to show a good image of what we, the paper, are. "We can celebrate the good things, but learn from and fix the bad things we did."

> *"He's a great writer. Throughout all the shuffling in management, he has consistently shown leadership. He is the rock in the newsroom."*
>
> **Sue Ellen Riesau, *Gazette* GM**

Michael Dashiell hired as intern in 2001. *(Bill Lindstrom photo)*

"Jeff Chew had good experience, but he didn't write sports. I did, so they made me sports editor," Dashiell said of his first promotion in 2002.

Dan Ross was another of the young *Gazette* reporters who rose rapidly up the chain of command to become editor. Hired about eight months before Dashiell, he came from the *Gridley Herald*, a twice-weekly paper in Gridley, Calif., about 35 miles north of Sacramento.

His newspaper background started as a youth, spending nights in the composing room of the *L.A. Times*, where his father worked for about 17 years. Prior to coming to Sequim, a story he covered rose to national attention. Biggs, one of the cities in his circulation area, was the subject of the California Milk Advisory Board, which tried unsuccessfully to change its name to "Got Milk."

Sept. 11, 2001

Tuesday generally is a major production day, a very long day, getting in the last-minute news, final copyediting, proofing, and still in 2001, paste-up in preparation for driving the boards to the print shop. The day isn't over at that point as the driver must wait until the paper is printed, then truck the papers back to various distribution points.

All of that went out the door when Manders and his reporters walked into the office on Tuesday, Sept. 11, 2001.

"It was the toughest time I had as a reporter," said Dashiell, who had been a cub reporter for five months. "I walked in the door and saw the TV was on. It's never on, but it was this day. I saw two buildings on fire and I saw one building topple."

Manders arrived and called his troops together. "We know what the story is, now let's get out there and get to work," Dashiell remembers were the instructions from his boss.

Ross was the lead reporter for the biggest story of the year. Dashiell and Lucy Dukes were important contributors to the nearly 70-inch story that occupied three-quarters of the front page and several columns on two inside pages.

Meantime, Garred made a few phone calls and set up a couple of blood donation banks.

"I thought it was a great way to localize the event," Garred revealed in 2015 interview. "And Sequim could make a meaningful contribution."

The main headline captured Sequim's response to the tragedy. "Sequim rushes to help terrorism victims" with a second deck head "Blood bank overwhelmed as residents line up to donate."

A gripping photo by Ross showed a man lying on a gurney donating blood at St. Joseph's Catholic Church, which drew more than 50 donors by noon. Another blood bank was set up at the Knights of Columbus. By the time the *Gazette* went to press, nearly 100 had donated.

Dashiell said his assignment was to go to the grocery stores and post office. "I never saw the streets so desolate. People didn't want to talk about it. They were angry, a terrible, visceral anger. We rarely ran national news, but we had to this time."

Garred couldn't have been more pleased as a publisher. "The staff did a superb job of localizing this tragic event. Also, the next week. It was a buzz all over town. They didn't care about the choir program that night."

On Jan. 9, 2002, the *Gazette* went through another management shift when Garred announced his retirement after 41 years in journalism, the last four as publisher and co-owner of the *Gazette*.

Brown M. Maloney repurchased his share and Scott Wilson's share of Olympic View Publishing, and thus had become the sole owner of the *Gazette* again.

Garred went on to praise Maloney for his vision, vigor and vitality. "Brown has a passion unmatched in this business. He cares for his town and its people. He intends to serve it better than ever before. We're confident he will. The reward is a better community newspaper — and a better community."

Garred then discussed the personal commitment and responsibility he had tried to bring to the many newspapers he worked for or owned over the past four-plus decades.

"We must be honest with ourselves as well as with our readers. So often what some readers 'know' by rumor or innuendo, we must confirm with facts delivered in a fair and accurate report. That's what we have intended, and in most instances, we succeeded. It's not what we know that is so crucial here. It's what we can accurately confirm from reliable sources that provides readers with substantive accounts of actions and inactions that affect their lives. This is a public trust.

"We work on principle, not emotion. That's what we believe you have earned from us. That is what you must expect from those who follow."

In this same edition, Manders wrote an editorial "My good reason to vote 'yes'" on the Sequim School District's maintenance and operations levy.

It was his final editorial for the *Gazette* (until he returned in 2005). It wasn't announced in the *Gazette*, but by the end of January 2002, he had been hired as news editor for the *Peninsula Daily News*.

Gazette management, however, was aware of his move, for Jeff Chew was named interim editor the previous week. Chew, 49 at the time, had 24 year's newspaper experience in California, Texas and Washington. He was hired at the *Gazette* in 1996 after serving three years as copy chief for the *PDN*.

For Olympic View Publishing, the *Gazette's* parent company, Chew held various editorial and writing positions. As editor, he redesigned the *Peninsula Business Journal*. Also, he edited and designed the *Summit to Sea* visitors' guide that won an award in 2000 from the WNPA (WA Newspaper Publishers Association).

"Jeff Chew has a keen interest in Sequim and what is important to us," said Maloney, in making the promotion. "Add this to Jeff's ability to disseminate, edit and package news, and Sequim has a winning combination."

Five months later, Maloney removed the "interim" and made Chew the editor.

Maloney said Chew's roles, in addition to managing the news team and producing special sections, also will be to manage the newspaper's growing website, which is undergoing a remodel.

However, five months later, he left to become the county reporter for the *Peninsula Daily News*.

KONP added to empire

This announcement in the Jan. 9, 2002, *Gazette* not only included print media, but broadcast media.

Maloney's empire was about to expand even wider. Radio Pacific announced the sale of radio station KONP in Port Angeles to Olympic View Publishing and Brown M. Maloney.

Jim and Terry MacDonald had owned the

Todd Ortloff became a minority owner of KONP with Brown Maloney in 2002. *(KONP photo)*

"The opportunity was a good one for the station and it allows me to advance my career and continue to work at a community-oriented station."

station, which began operation in 1945, since 1983. They had worked at the station since the 1975.

Joining in the purchase as a minority partner is Todd Ortloff, 33, the station's operations manager for the past seven years. After the MacDonalds approached Maloney, he discussed it with Ortloff.

"The opportunity was a good one for the station and it allows me to advance my career and continue to work at a community-oriented station," Ortloff said.

The move to this genre is nothing new for Maloney. "I have radio roots and grew up around this medium too. There was plenty of radio discussion around the dinner table."

We'll leave this part of Maloney's empire and pick it up in full in the chapter on radio broadcasting.

Just a month after Chew was promoted to editor, the revolving publisher's chair took another spin.

On June 5, 2002, a front-page story announced Riesau would be the new publisher as Maloney was stepping down from that role.

"Sue Ellen is very plugged into both the businesses and the community. She is very capable, and I know she will do a great job," Maloney said of his newest promotion.

"Community journalism is the only kind of journalism I know," said Riesau. "Over the years, our association with the (WNPA) and other weekly newspapers in our region has taught me that we have a unique opportunity to serve the communities we live in. That's a responsibility I take to heart. I look forward to taking the lead in the growth and development of this company and participating in the vibrant future of Sequim."

In addition to her role with OVP, Riesau is an active volunteer in the Sequim area and with Clallam County. She is a founding member of the Community Foundation of the Sequim Dungeness Valley and has helped Sequim's Open Aire Market grow since its beginning in 1996. She also has been a board member for the United Way and was its president in 2007-2008.

Due to continuing responsibilities of the McClatchy organization and other business interests, Maloney said stepping down as publisher was still a difficult decision "Sue Ellen, though, helped make this decision much easier. She has the potential to be a superb publisher and maybe even the best this company has ever had."

In an interview in 2015, Garred also weighed in on the promotion of Riesau.

"Sue Ellen Riesau is a treasure. She is the one who kept the *Gazette* going. I have a lot of respect for Sue Ellen." He added that Riesau was not afraid to stand up to Maloney and tell him when she disagreed with him. "She made him toe the line."

Perry joins ad team

In addition to the promotion of Riesau, Maloney announced the hiring of Steve Perry, 43, as advertising director for OVP. He came from the *Peninsula Gateway*, an 11,400-circulation weekly, based in Gig Harbor, where he had been ad manager for three years. Prior to that, he worked 12 years for the Bremerton (Kitsap) *Sun*, and before that, seven years at the *Skagit Valley Herald* in Mount Vernon. He is a 1981 graduate from Washington State University, majoring in political science and minoring in communication.

Perry said he was "excited to be a part of the growing community of Sequim. I love community journalism and what it brings to both the readers and advertisers."

In a 2017 interview, Perry said, he had learned a little about Maloney because the *Gazette* was printed in Gig Harbor at the time, and because the *Gateway* was a McClatchy newspaper.

"I was interested in making a career change and our production manager Jim Easterly put a bug in Maloney's ear. I went to talk to him. That was about March 2002."

Maloney stressed Perry's passion for community journalism as well in the *Gazette* when the hiring was made.

"Steve Perry was hired by Brown Maloney in March 2002. In 2018 the personable and outgoing Perry was running daily operations for both the *PDN* and *Sequim Gazette*.

"Steve and I think alike in regard to service and quality. He comes from what might be the state's best community newspaper. Steve will be a great addition to our staff and an asset in meeting the needs of our customers."

Riesau also was excited about the hiring of Perry. "We knew we were hiring someone with experience to take us to the next level in sales. He's an integral part of who we are."

Within six years, Perry would be named General Manager of OVP, and when Sound Publishing purchased the properties, as well as the *PDN* (in 2011), Perry would be retained in that position with all Sound holdings on the Olympic Peninsula.

"As general manager, he has his hands on the community," said Riesau. "Although he lives on Bainbridge Island, he is invested here."

When Perry was promoted to general manager, it was in the heart of the Recession in 2008. Not only was he chief of operations for the *Gazette*, but the *Forks Forum* and *Homes-Land* real estate magazines.

The hit the *Gazette* took on *Homes-Land* was catastrophic. "We had been running 124 to 136 pages monthly, doing about a million dollars a year in that publication alone," Perry noted. "Suddenly, the Realtors weren't advertising (because of the slump in the housing market). By the end of the year, we were doing about one-third of that. To lose that much revenue in such a short time was hard to overcome."

Perry said that publication as well as the *Gazette* "went into survival mode for a few years. We had some staff reductions. I had conversations with Brown about staff cuts. I wanted more staff cuts, but we didn't act on it. We were sliding back in terms of profitability."

When Chew left in October 2002, Dan Ross was promoted on an interim status, but by Nov. 15, 2002, only 11 months after he arrived at Sequim, he was named editor.

"The support from all the *Gazette* employees is the reason I asked to be considered for the position of editor," Ross told Dashiell in the story announcing his promotion. He said one of his first targets as editor is "to help the *Gazette* strengthen its position as a voice for residents of the Sequim-Dungeness Valley.

"Expanding our coverage of community events is a major part of what I want to be able to accomplish," said Ross.

Dashiell recalled his early days when he was a cub and Ross was the lead reporter under Manders. "We had good chemistry," he said. "We hit a groove pretty much right away. We had a lot of personality and I learned a lot from all of them."

Early in January 2003, Riesau introduced the readers to more changes, including a weekly insert *American Profile*, a full-color national publication with a strong focus on hometown life

Riesau also unveiled a new design and the movement of pages to make the *Gazette* easier to read. A big change was moving the obituaries into the front section. Regular columnists Bev Hoffman and Doug MacInnes, garden and history columnists, respectively, will be part of a new "Lifestyle" section being added to "Strait Scenes," the newspaper's arts and entertainment section.

The news staff is expanding as well with the addition of Leif Nesheim to cover county issues and Lori Fonzi to write features.

The *Gazette* website, which was established in October, will be continually updated.

On Jan. 29, 2003, the paper's logo was altered again with a design that remains today. In the upper left corner, in stylized type, is the paper's website (www.sequimgazette.com). SEQUIM GAZETTE appears in a thin, crisp font about 96 points (1.3 inches). The city name and the paper name are separated with a photo of the Dungeness Lighthouse with the top of the light shadowed to appear lit. In the upper right corner is the date of publication. Under the folio are three small boxes, known in the industry as teaser boxes.

In March 2005, the editor's chair again became open when Ross announced he was leaving to become editor of the *Sooke News Mirror* in British Columbia, a Black Press publication. Sooke is a suburb of Victoria.

Riesau wrote a touching column, one in which you almost feel the tears falling. "Parting Ways for Now:"

She related that when she came to the publisher's desk, Ross was county reporter. Riesau conveyed she has a soft spot for people who can make her laugh, "but it wasn't until we had an opening for an editor, that I had the opportunity to know Dan in terms of his abilities to manage a group of wily reporters and astute copy editors and put out a great newspaper.

"Dan has proven not only to have the skills, the experience and the head for leading the pack, he helped me realign the way this company works together and interacts internally between the departments. His humor, coupled with his passion for this business, has been a huge part of our success. We are a strong team and Dan has been a key player in the forging of that team."

In the same column, she announced the *Gazette* would experiment with a dual-editor system, while the managers searched for a permanent editor. Sports editor Mike Dashiell and "Strait Scene" editor Leif Nesheim would share the role.

The community loses an icon

At 4 a.m. on Monday, June 13, 2005, the *Gazette's* world stopped turning, stalled in its tracks. Jim Manders, who started work at the *Jimmy* in 1974 and a couple of stints with the daily in Port Angeles, lost a vigorous battle with cancer. He was only 58.

Manders was diagnosed with squamous cell epiglottal cancer, a very aggressive form that metastasized throughout his lymph system and eventually his brain.

He had left the *Gazette*, returned to the *PDN* in 2002 and was back at the Sequim paper in 2004 to finish the fight.

Riesau's column in the next *Gazette* (June 15) gives some insight into his battle with the dread disease.

"Manders battled cancer with every cell in his body. 'Recovery is the only option,' he said soon after the diagnosis.

Manders battled cancer with the same grit and determination that was characteristic of him throughout his career in the newspaper business. His passion and love of reporting and photojournalism goes back many years and never waned. As recently as April, he wrote several editorials for the Gazette, *despite his inability to speak, or travel except to the doctor for treatment.*

... Manders had only two passions, outside of sports and newspapers: His 10-year-old son, Sam, and shuffleboard, a game he became interested in as a 21-year-old. He was so bound by the game that he had written magazine articles about it, and in 2004, he started his own zine, "Lagging 4s."

He was recently inducted into the Pacific Northwest Shuffleboard Hall of Fame. The induction ceremony is scheduled June 25 at the Whistling Oyster in Quilcene, where he played in many tournaments. His friends and family have decided to name that ceremony as a memorial to Manders."

Co-editor Mike Dashiell and other employees, past and present, wrote about this solemn occasion.

Dashiell was hired by Manders in 2001, and while the relationship was short, it was treasured. He found out not everybody was on Jim's side. Some were really peeved by him, but they respected him because they knew Jim "always had the community at heart. He cared so much for our senior citizens, our children, our businesses that he rarely backed off at the opportunity to challenge a school board, a city council, a county commissioner," Dashiell said.

"Like it or not, Jim was a true newspaperman. In nearly every sense of the word, he bled the ink that fills our newspapers every week. … He pledged not to give up just because cancer had ravaged much of his body in these final days. As shown by some of the editorials he penned for us a few months ago, the cancerous cells within had not thwarted his mind or his thoughts.

"Ironically, the cancer that finally took Jim from us, started in his throat and took most of his voice away. It could not take away the impact he made on me and the countless others, though."

Cathy Grimes, who was a freelancer when Manders hired her in 1994, weighed in from the *Walla Walla Union Bulletin*, where she was education reporter.

She regarded Manders as "a teacher, a mentor, a friend" her guest column headline would say.

"He worked us like dogs but worked himself with the same disregard of the clock. What he couldn't teach, he deferred to others.

"He also insisted we take risks and write hard-hitting news stories and explanatory articles as often as we wrote stories that would end up in scrapbooks or on refrigerator doors. His mantra was if there was news in our coverage area, we better know it and report it first."

From Sooke, B.C., recent editor Dan Ross, now editor of the *News Mirror* wrote:

I learned from Jim what community journalism was all about.

I learned from his passion for his work; I learned from his joy for his work; I learned from watching, from listening, from making mistakes and have him almost politely chastise me along the way; mostly, I learned I had a great friend in Jim.

My enjoyment of working for community newspapers — the chance to be editor for two years in Sequim and now here in Sooke — would never have developed, if not for the encouragement of that funny semi-round editor. I've tried to emulate his style, but so far the best I've been able to pull off is rounding in to a similar shape as Jim.

The Dashiell-Nesheim tandem continued for a few more weeks when

Mary Powell arrived from the *Columbia Basin Herald* in Moses Lake to assume the role.

In Powell's debut editorial she wrote, "I am honored to be managing editor of the *Gazette* and excited to serve our readers. I will continue to bring you the best community news I can."

Powell was editor from June 2005 through December 2008 and Riesau remembers her as a faithful writer of the weekly editorial during her tenure.

In her 3-plus years as an editor, Powell didn't miss a single week. Riesau added her editorials were timely and topical and always well-researched. No small feat for any editor.

"Although the *Gazette* continues to garner many newspaper excellence awards, in Mary's time as editor, the *Sequim Gazette* cumulatively earned more WNPA Better Newspaper Contest awards than ever in previous years and many were editorial awards," Riesau said.

Powell retired from the world of managing an editorial staff in December 2008 but continued to freelance, writing articles for the *Living on the Peninsula* magazine published by the *Gazette* until early in 2018 when she retired for good.

Three years later, Jim Casey, 61, who had been with the *PDN* since 2004, covering county government, the Olympic Medical Center and Native American tribes of the western sector of the peninsula, was named editor.

"Jim is a well-thought-of newspaperman, capable and respected across Clallam County," said Maloney. "He has earned this and the *Gazette* is fortunate to have him."

Casey said he looked forward to the challenge and sounded his respect for OVP and Maloney. "It speaks well of community papers, and the *Sequim Gazette* in particular, that OVP would fill this position. Larger newspapers — which don't enjoy the close contact with their readers — are cutting their staff in half."

Albeit, Casey's tenure was short-lived when he ran afoul of his readers and management in April 2010 with an editorial "that broke the rules," Riesau wrote in a damage-control column. In an editorial, Casey called the Tea Party movement "village idiots."

That's a no-no, Riesau emphasized. Casey's editorial "broke a cardinal rule we have here at the *Gazette*, which is 'do no harm.'"

"Using the words 'idiots' is name-calling, and for that I am truly sorry. There is no good reason and therefore no excuse I can use to explain it away."

Then Riesau sort of falls on her own sword. "I was not vigilant, and as a publisher I am as responsible as Casey for it being printed."

That alone could have had Casey fearing for his journalistic future, but when readers wrote in the Letters to the Editor column blasting the paper, some canceling their subscriptions, and accusing the *Gazette* of sharing Casey's belief, the situation became exacerbated. One reader took the right-leaning approach to tar the editor with the same brush without outright saying it.

"Since you are relatively new in your position, perhaps you don't realize that you come across as a pseudo-intellectual preaching to the unwashed masses."

No doubt, the publisher or other members of the management at the *Gazette* wished they could have said it so well.

In the same edition, the *Gazette* reported about a new feature of its website, a comments section added to the end of every printed story.

Casey was out the door by early May.

Dashiell, the editor

Again, the search for an editor didn't involve much time. The man who had been groomed to eventually step up was ready for the challenge.

"It gives me great pleasure to offer the editorship of the *Sequim Gazette* to Mike Dashiell," Maloney announced to the staff on Oct. 7, 2010. "Mike has consistently proven himself to be a dedicated and committed member of the *Gazette* staff. He has thrown himself into most every area of local news and Mike is ready to lead what may be the best news staff I have had during my ownership of the *Gazette*."

Dashiell, 24, came to the *Gazette* in April 2001, as an intern; after graduating from Western; he became a reporter, and was promoted to sports editor in 2003; twice he served as interim editor or co-editor.

"I appreciate the opportunity to help lead this organization," said Dashiell.

"This is an exciting time for journalists, with the growth of the web, social media and other advances in technology."

Perhaps with a nod back to the problem that beset the previous editor, he added, "We need to be vigilant as ever in our reporting. Hopefully, we at the *Gazette* can continue to bring quality community journalism to our readers."

Riesau also weighed in on the appointment in a column the same day as the promotion was announced.

"Mike has seen his share of challenges, professionally and personally, and in his quiet way, he has met them with the kind of grit and determination a publisher usually only hopes to get from an editor. Mike earned this opportunity to

Mike Dashiell was 24 when he started as an intern with the *Gazette* in 2001. In 2010, he was named editor and, at 42, was still in that position in 2018. *(Bill Lindstrom photo)*

be editor of the *Sequim Gazette*. Nine years later, I couldn't be happier he chose the *Gazette* to begin his journalistic career."

In an interview in 2016, Riesau expressed delight, but shock that Dashiell is still the editor at the *Gazette*. "I am surprised he's still there," she said, adding, the usual pattern for weekly editors — good ones — is to pay their dues and move on to a daily in four or five years.

In the same 2010 column, Riesau lauded her staff for their recent accomplishment, adding to its string of successes:

"… Huge congratulations to my entire staff. You did it again! For the fifth time in the past six years the *Sequim Gazette* was awarded First Place General Excellence from our statewide newspaper association, the WNPA. I recently celebrated 21 years with Olympic View Publishing and remember well watching other newspapers win this award, and how it built my resolve to one day have the *Gazette* be No. 1."

Dashiell remembers those early days after being named editor during a 2017 interview. "In a space of two or three months, we had two double homicides. I sent out a young reporter, Amanda Winters. She didn't tell me until later when she was out there, they sent in the SWAT patrol where the shooter was held up," the editor said. "We had a talk about being careful."

Dashiell, who had his share of hard-hitting breaking news stories over the years, said he prefers to write personal stories, and sometimes it requires a reporter or editor to sit on the story a while before publishing it. He cited one example from 2014:

"Nick Barrett was a young kid with Down syndrome. He was a tough subject to interview. Nick had never competed in sports before but decided to go out for wrestling. That was a story in itself, but I opted not to write the story right away. I let the season progress and the story got better."

In December, Barrett appeared in a jamboree for the junior varsity against a wrestler from Olympic High. "Dominic Battaglia let Barrett pin him. Later that month, he was in his first varsity match against North Kitsap, which didn't have a wrestler at 285 pounds. I waited, and the story got better."

It finally ran on Feb. 7, 2014, and Dashiell won first place in the WNPA for it.

"You don't always have to write the story immediately," he emphasized.

He noted that the best-selling book *Boys in the Boat* "could have been my book. I interviewed (Sequim resident) Joe Rantz before the book came out. Rantz was one member of the U.W. crew team that defied odds and Hitler's rebukes to win Gold in the 1936 Olympic Games in Berlin. Daniel James Brown captured this story for a No. 1 best seller in 2013.

"Stories that resonate the most with me are people stories, those who have overcome great odds. I get to live vicariously through my subjects."

He said he recalled one time he had to run downtown and interview a guy in a banana suit. "Another time, I was assigned to write about a city promotion for elk nuggets. I was shocked it was a story, shocked I got to write it and shocked they ran it." No word if it ever won an award.

He also learned reporters are not immune from tragedy. "I remember we had a reporter who lived in an apartment across the street. While she was at work, the apartment caught fire. She wrote a story on her home going up in flames, a first-person account about watching it happen." One big upside — she had renter's insurance.

Being editor sometimes limits Dashiell's writing opportunities with the other responsibilities taking up his time.

"I love writing and that's something I don't get to do that often as an editor. Managing is about solving other people's problems. On a weekly (newspaper), people come to know you and say they look forward to your stories. What other job can you do that?"

Gazette sold to Sound Publishing

In 1995-1996 Brown M. Maloney, publisher of the *Gazette* and the *Forks Forum* and the *Peninsula Business Journal* was elected president of the Washington Newspaper Publishers Association. In 2011, he sold the paper to Sound Publishing Co. (Gazette file)

Monday, Oct. 31, 2011, was changing day for the *Gazette* and for Brown Maloney. That morning, in a staff meeting, he announced to his employees that he had sold the paper and its sister publication, the *Forks Forum,* to Sound Publishing. That came on the same day, Sound announced it had purchased the *Peninsula Daily News* in Port Angeles.

The transaction was so covert that neither side knew of the other's sale, until it was announced that Monday, revealed Maloney and Perry as well as the broker, Dave Gauger, a longtime friend of Maloney and a board member of the OVP.

In an accompanying column to the breaking news story in the *Gazette's* Nov. 2, 2011, issue, Maloney writes his final column:

Today, represents the first day in 23 years I have not owned this newspaper. Many of you have read in this same issue that Sound Publishing will be the next caretaker of the Sequim Gazette *and the* Forks Forum.

I took on this role in 1988, thinking I would do this for three, five or maybe seven years as I took a break from working at a family business. My first introduction to the harshness of the business was my editor quitting the very next day. So much for instilling confidence in my new staff.

Maloney went on to remind readers when he bought the *Jimmy Come Lately* he thought of it as a small "cutesy tabloid newspaper in a cutesy town. Now, it has shed the *Jimmy* and is the award-winning *Sequim Gazette*, a broadsheet packed with news and advertising filling 28 to 32 pages or more."

Like the newspaper, the town also had grown from a one-stoplight town to one with seven lights, a bypass that gives downtown a new identity and hundreds of thousands of additional shopping opportunities.

Maloney continued:

Sequim residents care about civic life. They read. They think. They tell the Gazette *when we're wrong, and occasionally when we are right.*

"The community believes in the power of local journalism. The Gazette's *reader percentage is high, and thankfully, the advertisers believe in us too.*

Maloney went on to thank his staff for all they did for the paper. "They have worked tirelessly as news reporters, account reps, production designers and newspaper carriers. To all of you, I appreciate your efforts more than you know."

In a 2017 interview, Brown candidly revealed he received $3.1 million from Sound Publishing for all his publications: *Sequim Gazette, Forks Forum, Olympic Peninsula Homes-Land, Islander Homes-Land and Countywide Classifieds*. However, he cautioned, in the 23 years he owned the papers, "I easily put that much into them."

Sound Publishing became only the fourth owner for the *Gazette*, preceded

> *"They have worked tirelessly as news reporters, account reps, production designers and newspaper carriers. To all of you, I appreciate your efforts more than you know."*
>
> **Brown M. Maloney praising staff after sale to Sound Publishing**

by its founders, Shirley and Bob Larmore, then Leonard and Linda Paulson and finally Brown M. Maloney.

Unaffected by the deal was Port Angeles radio station KONP, which was to remain owned by Maloney.

Most people have no idea what might go into the sale of a newspaper, so with the help of Dave Gauger, owner of Gauger Media Service, Inc., in Raymond, Wash., we'll try to shed some light.

When an owner contacts Gauger about potentially selling his or her property, the first step is to complete a lengthy Question and Answer form with information essential to determining if selling is the best option. Additionally, that information helps identify prospective buyers, best time to sell, and where to find the best buyer prospects.

The process begins with an appraisal, which contains a barrage of information, including a detailed summary of major advertisers on contract, including beginning date, terms, total inches and rate; media kit and promotional material with a list of special sections; and detailed circulation figures for each publication involved in the contemplated sale. And finally, relative mechanical information (where the publications are printed and what services are included) is summarized.

Gauger said, "Annual gross revenue from the company's income statements used to be the primary barometer determining the company's value and marketability. All that changed after the recession of 2008-2009." Gauger explains that now the primary factor for determining value of newspapers is cash flow; although, gross revenue is not unimportant.

He said cash flow is determined using the EBITA formula: (**E**arnings **B**efore **I**nterest, **T**axes (income), **D**epreciation, **A**mortization). EBITA, together with add-backs equals adjusted cash flow. Add-backs include all discretionary, extraordinary and non-recurring expenses that could be eliminated if running lean and mean.

A comprehensive company profile is created. It includes confidential information such as corporate shareholders, officers, board of directors, detailed financial reports spanning at least three consecutive years, and debt obligations. Interestingly, Gauger points out the company's management of accounts receivable can impact its value. New owners do not like to enter the market as "bad guys" by breaking with past policies of loose management of accounts receivable.

Further, a detailed room-by-room inventory of tangible personal property is tabulated. This includes office furniture, computers, printers — even the breakroom microwave and refrigerator.

"We also look closely at human resources," said Gauger. "How does the staff relate to each other, to management, to the community. Is there a strong interaction?" He adds, "All the new technological advances notwithstanding, newspaper publishing remains primarily a people-driven business." Personnel management often is critical to a newspaper's bottom line so, Gauger pulls together details relating to staff, including date of hire, summary of duties, pay and benefits.

When all the data is compiled and collated, Gauger Media Service, which proudly proclaims "Where Integrity and Results Go Hand In Hand," prepares an analysis that typically includes a detailed profile of the city and county with demographics and photos. In addition to the market profile, there is a profile of all newspapers and ancillary publications to be included in the transaction. Also included are photos of machinery (press) involved, if the paper prints its own product.

The Information Memorandum often contains as many as 50 to 60 detailed electronic pages to be sent to prospective buyers. Gauger said the Information Memorandum for Maloney was an inch thick.

In order to protect his seller clients, Gauger requires all prospective buyers to sign a Non-Disclosure Agreement, which severely limits use of the shared information.

Then a negotiation process begins with corporate attorneys involved. "I am the bad cop," says Gauger, who lives in Raymond.

Gauger said negotiations can drag on, and even get a bit testy, but he didn't find that in Maloney's case, or others on the peninsula.

"With publishers like Brown in Sequim, Scott Wilson and Frank Garred at Port Townsend and the Mullens at Shelton, you have a unique group of great weekly publishers, fine gentlemen all," he said.

He said working with weeklies is among his pleasures.

"Publishers operating their family owned weeklies are more likely to take editorial risks, if convinced it will serve their communities. With large corporate ownership, this commitment to community often is missing. I so enjoy the people I represent. They apply ethical standards you don't find in other businesses."

When Maloney announced the sale to the *Gazette* staff he said, "It is with mixed emotions that I reflect upon selling my company, but there is a sense of pride in what my staff has achieved over the past two decades.

"I am pleased to see Olympic View Publishing pass into the hands of Sound Publishing, who are as passionate about newspapers and as committed to community journalism as I have been since 1988."

Maloney added that he had been considering selling Olympic View Publishing for some time but was looking for a buyer who would be a "good steward for the company publications."

Under Olympic View Properties, Maloney continues to own the block on which the *Gazette* is located. In addition, in 2013, he took ownership of a foreclosed 180-unit community development in East Sequim, above John Wayne Marina, called Cedar Ridge. He still lives in Sequim and is the managing partner of Cedar Ridge. As of mid-2018, it is 60 percent sold.

Regarding his ownership of the *Gazette*, "It was never about making money," Maloney admitted in 2017. "I wanted to have a career, aside from my family, working for myself in a community I loved. It turned into a nice quality of life."

Maloney also has been active in collecting vintage automobiles, something that started in 1956 when his parents bought him a '56 T-Bird and he has added to it since then. In addition to collecting cars, he shows them and also does concourse judging in shows.

At the same time, he wants to spend more time working with the McClatchy Company, of which he is a fifth-generation owner. Along with being a McClatchy board member, Maloney is a board member of the *Seattle Times*, of which the McClatchy organization owns 49.5 percent.

Following the first interview for this book in 2016, Maloney shared a series of letters with David Black, dating to 1995, considering a possible sale. But, in the final correspondence in 1998, Maloney told Black to forget it, that they were "too far apart."

Today, Sound, a division of Black Press Ltd. of Victoria, B.C., owns 46 newspapers with a combined circulation of nearly 700,000. Black Press owns more than 160 newspapers and 17 printing facilities (including Everett where the *Gazette*, the *Forks Forum* and the *PDN* are printed).

David Black, corporate CEO, said he was thrilled with the purchase of the *Gazette*.

"We have been publishing community newspapers for 22 years in Washington state and see this as an opportunity to expand our operations to the North Olympic Peninsula which is a good geographical fit with our other newspapers and website titles. The *Gazette* is one of the best newspapers in the state in terms of quality. We are proud to be the new stewards of the business," Black said.

Riesau was retained as publisher, Dashiell would continue as editor and Perry as advertising manager.

Riesau's column, headlined "New owners, same *Gazette*," on this day of ownership change emphasized exactly that:

As you see changes in the newspaper, have no fear; there will be little tweaks here and there to improve page design and layout; the classifieds might look a lot different; there will be a lot more of them, for one thing. But the quality of the writing and reporting and the excellence of advertising and overall graphic design will not change.

In fact, this newspaper and all our special products, will not change, and that is a good thing. For we know, if we become complacent, we will fall behind.

Dashiell shared the column space with Riesau and pointed out a few changes that will occur, and some that already have been implemented.

He called attention to a slightly smaller print edition to conform to Everett's printing press and a switch from two front sections to a single large one.

On our website, we have gone to a story comment process that requires a Facebook account. Hopefully, that will quell the small cadre of online readers, who like to make personal attacks.

Expect a few more changes coming down the perennial pike but understand these primarily will be how you get the news, not what you get. We still aim to bring you the relevant and timely news via print and web to celebrate who we are as a community.

Nine months later, Riesau decided a life-change was in order, telling her readers on July 11, 2012, she was retiring in an exit column "It's not goodbye, but until we meet again."

She talks about leaving California for Sequim 23 years ago, saying "Quality of life was the central thing on our minds and just about everyone else's who came to Sequim during the 1990s.

"I wanted to find a place to live with like-minded folks who valued their community and its environment and who cared enough to preserve those things which, when you walked out on the front porch, made you feel like you were living in the backyard of a park."

Neither Sue Ellen nor her husband had jobs, "I'll be darned if I didn't find a job and one that would sustain me and my family through 23 years of what has been a pretty good ride!"

She noted that with Maloney's stewardship, the *Gazette* became "one of the top three community weeklies in the state." The staff has earned General Excellence Awards first place seven of the past eight years.

Riesau praised her first owner Maloney for giving her a job and believing in her. I think Sound Publishing will continue to strengthen while retooling an industry that some predicted wouldn't make it into the millennium. We showed them."

To fill Riesau's post, Debi Lahmeyer was promoted from the advertising department to interim general manager. Exactly one year later, the management of the *Gazette, Peninsula Daily News* and *Forks Forum* was reorganized, combining the advertising, production and circulation staffs at all three papers. All news staffs will continue to operate separately.

John Brewer, who became publisher at the *PDN* in 1998, assumed the role of group publisher for all three newspaper operations as well as their websites.

Perry admitted in a 2017 interview, "That first year (under Sound, but with papers operating independently) was awkward. I was asked to run the advertising departments at the *PDN* and the *Gazette*. Though the Sequim paper was still being run independently, I was competing against the sales staff I had just left. About a year later, Sound brought the three papers together, so sales departments at the *Gazette* and at the *PDN* would be selling ads for both papers.

"Looking back, it was probably the wrong decision. It was very awkward," Perry said. "The *PDN* was the first daily in Washington that Sound owned. It was a different kind of animal they wrestled with. During that first year, we actually reported to someone in Canada, then it changed."

He said there are pluses and minuses between family owned papers and corporate operations. "When the opportunity came to work for a family owned paper in 2002, there was a certain romance to it," he revealed, adding that he had worked only for corporate-owned papers until then.

"I had known about Sound for quite a while, and when I heard they had bought the *Gazette* and *PDN*, I admittedly was skeptical. But, through the years, getting to know Black Press, I learned this was a really good thing," Perry said.

He pointed out that on small weeklies there are no good health insurance plans and no 401k. Through Sound, there are both, plus a counseling service and other benefits. He also pointed out the benefit of shared resources, which weren't available under Maloney.

Perry said the *Gazette* and *PDN* share their reporters as well. "Since we are owned by the same company, it didn't make sense to have a reporter from each paper covering the same event." He said, there still is an individuality to the stories. "The *Gazette* stories are still Sequim-centric. It's not our paper, it's their paper. Our readers are who we report to."

One month after Riesau retired, she received the ultimate honor from WNPA, the Miles Turnbull Master Editor/Publisher Award, given annually to honor an active editor or publisher who has worked hard and unselfishly and made a significant contribution to his or her newspaper community and state, as well as the WNPA. She was one of only two women at that time, in the history of the WNPA, to be awarded the honor.

"What truly matters is someone who values their community," said Bill Will, executive director of the WNPA. Will also pointed out Riesau's contribution to the WNPA as an active board member.

"She pitched in and worked hard with the WNPA, just like she does with the Lavender Festival and other community events in Sequim. She's the kind of person you want to have working with you."

It was a banner night for the *Gazette* when reporter Matthew Nash was named the state's "Feature Writer of the Year," a high honor because in this category, the *Gazette* competed against larger papers. The Better Newspaper Contest judges, who were from New York papers, said Nash's "eclectic range of topics offers readers a look at the humanity and courage of a wide variety of local people."

The article on Oct. 10, 2012, also included a first-place award for every *Gazette* reporter/editor. Editor/Sports Editor Mike Dashiell won for best sports page design and best editorial; reporter Amanda Winters won a first and second; reporter Mark Couhig a first and second. In addition, special sections editor Patricia Morrison Coate and designer Cathy Clark combined to win first for *Living on the Peninsula*, a magazine section that featured Olympic Peninsula photographers.

The paper's design and advertising staff also captured six honors. First-and-second places were won by Mandy Kay Harris and Debi Lahmeyer for Most Original Ad Idea: "Success — Make It to Your Mountaintop."

Perhaps the most unusual award went to Couhig in the category: News of the Weird for his feature "The Compleat Geoducker," a first-person account of his geoducking experience in Sequim Bay, which the judges said, "was well-written, funny and pretty darn weird."

Two years later, in October 2015 another big change affected the *Gazette*. Brewer announced his retirement after 18 years as publisher of the *PDN*, and since 2013, publisher of all three newspapers.

Terry Ward was named to replace him.

When asked about how change affected the *Gazette* since 2011 when Sound purchased the paper, Dashiell deadpanned "the one thing that stays the same is change."

He said there have been some personnel changes and cuts, but noted the biggest struggle is the paper's "edge toward more digital. Trying to juggle print, video and social media is time-consuming. We try to keep it unique, but also combine forces to get the most out of the personnel we have."

He said big papers, such as the *Seattle Times*, just move people around or hire new personnel to handle it. "With a small weekly, we have to take our staff and tell them we are going to take some hours from what you are already doing and apply it to the new job."

Such is the life on a weekly.

And, that's one thing that never changes.

PART III

Port Townsend

CHAPTER 10

The Key City

The peninsula's first paper; the *Leader*, the North Olympic Peninsula's longest-continuously operating paper

"In entering the field of journalism at Port Townsend, the Morning Leader *does not come with a flourish of trumpets and the broad declaration that its mission is to fill a long felt-want. We come to stay."*

A bold statement, indeed, by W.L. Jones on the front page of the initial *Morning Leader*, Oct. 2, 1889.

Nine newspapers prior to the *Leader* operated in Port Townsend and failed, or would soon fail, but Jones knew of which he spoke.

While it has undergone many name changes, the Key City's primary newspaper after it was founded, always has been the *Leader*. The current rendition, *Port Townsend and Jefferson County Leader*, marked its 129th anniversary in 2018, the longest-continually operating newspaper on the North Olympic Peninsula, or as the early *Leader* called it the "Lower Sound."

Jones founded the paper as a daily and weekly publication, then about 1908, it reverted to weekly-only, then semi-weekly in 1928 and to weekly in 1932, a format it uses today.

From 1889-1906, there were as many as ten different owners/publishers. The remaining 111 years its ownership has been remarkably stable. From 1906-1967, first Winslow McCurdy, then his son, Richard, were involved in the ownership for 61 years. In 1967, Frank Garred bought the paper in association with Bruce Wilson and Henry Gay.

In 1989, Scott Wilson became a partner with his wife, Jennifer. After Garred left in 1998 to become part-owner with Scott Wilson and Brown M. Maloney of Olympic View Publishing and publisher of the *Sequim Gazette*, the Wilsons gradually moved toward sole ownership, which occurred in 2002. The Mullen brothers, Lloyd and Louis Mullen, purchased the paper from the Wilsons in 2016.

Occasionally — not very often — a researcher in the archives of vintage newspapers (such as this author) comes upon a nugget that makes the job that much easier.

That was the case with Joan Ducceschi and Helen Radke's book *Olympic Leaders* in the Port Angeles chapter. It became my bible. The same can be said for Tom Camfield's book *Port Townsend: An Illustrated History of Shanghaiing, Shipwrecks, Soiled Doves and Sundry Souls.*

Camfield worked for the *Leader* for 44 ½ years before retiring in 1988. For much of those four decades he collected and catalogued information about Port Townsend, particularly the city's newspapers. I came across Camfield and his book *after* I had already spent countless hours corralling print-outs of early newspapers.

Camfield had already done that. So thorough is his media research and knowledge in his chapter "Newspapering," that he even includes one publication that survived for but one issue. He points out a couple of instances where errors were made in other reputable sources and corrected those with documented data.

When I cite Camfield's book as an attributed source, I'll use Camfield writes, or according to Camfield. If the reader wants to read a thorough account of newspapers in Port Townsend, this is it But, don't short-change yourself. This book is a delightfully, entertaining account of the town's history, its leaders, its businesses, buildings, maritime history — and many warts, particularly the bawdy days of prostitution and numerous shanghais.

While it wasn't the first newspaper to circulate in the city, the *Port Townsend Register* is the first documented, organized newspaper on a regular basis, first going to press on Dec. 23, 1859.

Two newspapers, published in Olympia, were known to have been dropped off in small bundles at the steamer dock as early as the 1850s.

The *Columbian*, which began publication in 1854, and the *Pioneer and Democrat*, beginning in 1856, were among the papers seen in the Key City.

Steamers didn't make regular stops at Port Townsend yet, so residents couldn't depend on getting news via the Olympia papers. Gold was discovered in Alaska in 1849 and ships often would bring prospectors from California or Portland north, stopping overnight. In 1858, an even closer gold rush brought panners and miners north and onto the Fraser River Valley in B.C.

The area, encompassing the current Jefferson County was originally part of Vancouver County, named in 1845 for George Vancouver. In 1849 Lewis County was created out of the Oregon Provisional Territory and included land all the way to Sitka, Alaska.

In 1852, Thurston County was created, and almost immediately, Jefferson County was carved out of Thurston; the next year, Washington Territory was formed, thus Port Townsend officially ceased to be part of Oregon. In 1854, Clallam County was established from the northwest portion of the Washington Territory.

We'll examine Jefferson County and Port Townsend's history a bit later. For now, it's important to note that 189 people were counted in Port Townsend in the 1853 census.

Register first paper

A few more folks were there when Travers Daniels and Dr. Sam McCurdy printed the city's first regular newspaper, *The Port Townsend Register.*

As Camfield relates, "This was an ambitious undertaking." McCurdy (no relation to Winslow and Richard), had the deep pockets and Daniels the savvy to produce the editorial content. James G. Swan assisted with the first issue and remained a part-time reporter.

Swan was an important figure already and would become a legend in the city before his death in 1900. He arrived on the Olympic Peninsula early in 1859 after serving in Olympia as secretary to Territorial governor Isaac Stevens, who had negotiated the Point No Point Treaty with the state's tribes in 1855.

In his book, *The Northwest Coast*, Swan writes that the *Register* published the first "Extra" in local newspaper history after the steamship *Columbian* arrived with news that the vessel *Northerner,* carrying supplies for the military garrison at Fort Townsend and more than $5,000 in goods for local business, had wrecked at Cape Mendocino.

Daniels only published eight or nine issues of the paper, but it continued to log 18 editions before expiring. C.H. Hill was chief compositor and he would make his way through several newspapers in the city. In 1859-1861 he was hand-setting type, letter-by-letter for each issue for the *Register* and later the *North-West.*

"The *Register's* troubles began when just two months after the initial issue, Daniels sold out and embarked for the East Coast. McCurdy's interest apparently also ended at that point as the paper quickly came out the first week of March (1859) with William T. Whitacre as owner and editor," Camfield writes.

James G. Swan, noted author and entrepreneur, worked on Port Townsend's first newspaper, **The Register,** in 1860. *(Tom Camfield)/ Port Townsend: An Illustrated History of Shanghaiing, Shipwrecks, Soiled Doves and Sundry Souls)*

Daniels published a strange valedictory, saying he regretted to end his stay as owner/manager, but "duty compels me to leave." He then added it was not due to a family emergency, but he missed "the friends of his youth in Baltimore."

Whitacre greeted his new readers with an equally strange salutatory:

"The Register *will be democratic in its true and Catholic sense, believing that all governmental powers exist in and emanate from the people, we shall jealously guard their rights, and vigorously oppose all attempts to exercise any powers not derived from their voluntary authority. The great landing principles of the democratic faith, as understood and exercised by its expounders for three-quarters of a century, will constitute our political platform."*

Who knows what that political platform might constitute.

It didn't matter much as Whitacre wasn't around long; he caught typhoid fever and died on Aug. 31, 1860.

The *Register*, which abandoned the Port Townsend part of its name, was "resurrected the following Nov. 15, under the ownership of M.H. Frost and Dr. P.M. O'Brien with Henry Sutton as editor. It was published until Sept. 18, 1861, when it bowed out of competition," Camfield writes.

Sutton was a controversial lightning rod. Two days after he began his editorship, the steamship *Oregon* arrived from San Francisco, bringing with it news of Abraham Lincoln's election as president. Sutton, a staunch Democrat, refused to believe a Republican could be elected president.

In his book, Swan writes "the Republicans burnt a bar barrel in honor of the supposed victory. Sutton looked askance at the celebration. Our exchange papers above us on the Sound and beyond, in Portland, have been handsomely hoaxed by the election returns, purporting to be received from the eastern states via Sacramento."

The amused editor of the Portland *Oregonian* responded concerning Sutton's incredulity: "The *Register* can't possibly believe that Mr. Lincoln is elected."

Swan ended his association with the newspaper at the beginning of 1861 because of Sutton's erratic behavior and violent nature. The paper folded for good in September 1861 after Sutton attacked a man in Billy Bowen's barbershop and fled to avoid arrest.

Thus, began the history of newspapering in Jefferson County and Port Townsend.

Most likely started to counter the Democratic *Register*, the first Republican paper in the Washington Territory was the *North-West*, hitting the streets on July 5, 1860, seven months after the *Register*.

The Rev. John Fox Damon and E.S. Dyer are listed as co-founders, and at some point, Enoch S. Fowler became a partner, or at least, held a financial interest. When Fowler pulled out, the paper folded, about three years after its first issue.

"Damon combined the inspiration of righteousness, the vision of a pioneer and the flair of a poet with the resourcefulness necessitated by his time and place in history," Camfield writes.

The masthead of the Territory's first Republican newspaper stated, "Be Just and Fear Not."

Indeed, his third issue leads off with a lengthy poem: "Press, the Home Journal: The Music of Nature," by Thomas Ripley. Damon supported

Abraham Lincoln's preservation of the Union in the Civil War and editorialized at length on the pressing need for a local cemetery.

After the *Register* went under, Hill moved to the *North-West* as compositor. When Damon left for Seattle 11 months later, the paper expired.

(We'll catch up with Fowler and the building named for him a bit later).

On Oct. 28, 1860, the *Northern Light* made its one and only appearance.

Camfield uncovered the following:

"It was struck off by Sutton while he and Hill were cleaning up the printing plant in preparation for the re-birth of the *Register*. Swan, in his diary, said it was 'done in mirthful mood and designed solely for local amusement.' The editor of the *Port Townsend Leader*, with a copy of the *Northern Light* in hand in August 1925, erroneously proclaimed it to be the 'first newspaper ever printed in Port Townsend — but did give a thorough account of its content, which dealt largely with shipping."

No papers for five years

An issue of the weekly edition of the Puget Sound Argus, 1878

The *Puget Sound Weekly Argus* was founded in 1871 by Al Pettygrove, brother of the city co-founder F.W. Pettygrove. It operated until 1889, including one year as a daily. This issue is from Jan. 11, 1878. *(Tom Camfield)/Port Townsend: An Illustrated History of Shanghaiing, Shipwrecks, Soiled Doves and Sundry Souls)*

Apparently, there was a five-year dearth when no newspaper was published in Port Townsend.

Next up was *The Message*, a weekly established by Al Pettygrove on May 6, 1867. It was later purchased by Fowler, who installed Henry Sutton as editor. Sometime after July 1868, Pettygrove sold the paper, perhaps to Sutton.

Divesting himself of the *Message*, Pettygrove founded the *Puget Sound Argus* in July 1871. A year later, the *Message* was merged with the *Argus*. It was purchased by C.W. Philbrick in 1874 and sold to Allen Weir in 1877. It began as *The Weekly Argus*, then became a semi-weekly from Feb. 20, 1873, to Aug. 10, 1873. A daily edition was added from May 19, 1882, to May 23, 1883, when it returned to a weekly until its final issue in December 1889.

While known primarily as the *Weekly Argus*, the full title on the masthead was *Puget Sound Weekly Argus* from January 1876 to December 1889.

Camfield cites James G. McCurdy's book *By Juan de Fuca's Strait*, on the demise of the *Argus*. "The *Argus* was published until its plant, including all files of early issues, burned to the ground sometime early in 1890." But, Camfield continues, the *Port Townsend Leader*, established in October 1889, states on Jan. 23, 1890:

"We understand that the Argus has suspended publication, owing to this city being too small a field for three dailies. No paper was issued

Allen Weir, owner/ publisher of the *Puget Sound Weekly Argus*, later became Washington state's first Secretary of State. *(Washington State Archives)*

from that office yesterday, and it is generally understood the paper has closed down." Camfield asserts that McCurdy "appears to be in error; perhaps the plant burned down sometime after the newspaper had suspended operation.

No issue of the *Argus* has been uncovered since December 1889.

Weir editor, then wore many hats

In his closing valedictory Philbrick praises the new owner of the *Argus*.

"Mr. Allen Weir, who will immediately assume the control of the establishment, is

345

a gentleman of well-known ability, as his editorial career, in connection with the *Olympia Courier*, has abundantly demonstrated."

Weir had the advantage of a new telegraph service in Port Townsend as noted by a string of cablegrams appearing in the first issue he published.

He owned the *Argus* for 12 years, longer than any publisher, and was at the helm the longest of any newspaper owner in Port Townsend until 1906.

Weir shares his background and experience in, what he calls the "Exeunt," or his exit column when he sold it to William F. Newell on Feb. 7, 1889.

"In the spring of 1877, fresh from college, I began business life by the purchase of the Puget Sound Weekly Argus *and job printing office from Mr. C.W. Philbrick. The paper was at that time, a small patent-inside weekly. Entering upon the duties of editor, business manager, printer, office boy, solicitor, etc., I have grown up with the business and with the town.*

"In June 1882, I began publishing a daily edition — a small, experimental thing at first — under circumstances that led every newspaper publisher in the Territory to expect failure to result from the effort. Neither edition of the paper, however, has ever missed an issue and the Daily has grown; it is a handsome, seven-column paper, all home-print, of course, a credit to the city, and a powerful factor moving forward every material interest of the public. ... It is and has been the best newspaper town in Washington Territory, in proportion to its size."

Weir said he would regret leaving journalism, but will remain in Port Townsend, welcoming rest.

This only scratches the surface of one of the more interesting and successful businessmen in Port Townsend history. The book, *Washington, West of the Cascades*, published in 1917, tells us much more.

Weir was born in California, but his family migrated to Clallam County when he was a youth. His father settled in the Dungeness Valley (near Sequim), cleared property for farming, built a road, constructed a plow and the first wagon in the area.

Allen didn't inherit his dad's mechanical and woodworking expertise but did exhibit his work ethic.

When he was 19, he started a business by renting land on his father's farm, then cultivated it for crops and raised hogs. He then spent two years driving ox teams for logging camps.

He enrolled at Olympia Union Academy and while there, worked for the *Territorial Printer*, then after graduation, became editor of the *Olympia Daily Recorder (later Courier)*, a weekly for a short period.

He desired to own a newspaper, so he moved to Port Townsend and, at age 33, purchased the *Weekly Argus*, which also did commercial job-printing. Three months after he became owner, he married a Canadian, Ellen Davis. She assisted him on the paper.

While in Port Townsend, he filled the office of Justice of the Peace, and was chairman of the Chamber of Commerce.

"He was well-suited for leadership by reason of his keen mind and his natural oratorical powers, which had been developed while he was a member of a literary society in school," his unnamed biographer writes for the Washington State archives. "He became a pronounced advocate of the temperance cause, and in this, as in every other public question, he studied every phase of the problem and his utterances were based on thorough knowledge."

When Weir sold the *Argus*, he was drafted by the Jefferson County Democratic committee, representing Clallam, Jefferson and San Juan counties, to attend the State Constitutional Convention in Olympia.

He declined; he was a staunch Republican.

So, the GOP drafted him, seeing great political leadership in him. Allen Weir, former newspaper publisher and editor, became Washington state's first Secretary of State, serving one term.

This ambitious man had other goals in mind.

After retiring from the high office, he longed to be a lawyer, studied for the bar, a degree that, in those days, was conferred by the U.S. Supreme Court. Weir became the first member of the Washington state bar in 1892. He practiced alone, specializing in land issues, particularly tideland regulation.

He was appointed to the Board of Regents for the University of Washington and served six years as board president. He also was elected to the Territorial Council of 1888-1889.

Weir practiced law until September 1913, when ill health forced his retirement. He suffered a paralyzing stroke in January 1915, and he never recovered. He was badly injured in an auto accident in Port Townsend in which the driver, state Senator David S. Troy, was killed in August 1916. Weir died on Oct. 31, 1916.

The new *Argus* owner, William Newell, had big shoes to fill and came out with both barrels blazing.

He holds back no words in telling the readers that the paper will be Republican, not only that, but "Men aspiring to office, which in my judgment they are unqualified and incompetent for, will receive my strongest denunciation."

Newell's reign would be short-lived, however, as the paper ceased publication (or the office burned) in December 1889.

The Leader was two months old when the *Argus* ended; we'll look at a handful of other publications that attempted to find a footing in the Key City.

Camfield's book describes them, and a few more papers than the State Library has on file.

The Cyclop: A daily paper that debuted in October 1871, published by Julius Dickens, a young Swede, who had been associated with the *Message*. McCurdy wrote that the *Cyclop* had a brief existence, and that Dickens, after helping establish the *Puget Sound Express* in Steilacoom, died in 1876.

The Democratic Press published weekly at least during the period of Aug. 31, 1877, to Jan. 13, 1881. Founded by Dr. H.C. Ellison and M.L. Blanchard, it was taken over by Frank Myers in 1879.

Port Townsend Star was established in 1882 by F.M. Walch.

Port of Entry Times appeared in 1884 with R.R. Parkinson and Hugh Gleen as publishers.

Port Townsend Call, founded in 1885 by George W. O'Brien and Louis R. Flowers, originally was a weekly. An available issue of Sept. 7, 1888, is identified as *The Daily Call*, published by Flowers and Willoughby. It was published as a daily and weekly sometime in 1887, returned to weekly only in 1910, continuing publication until 1914. From February 1898 to February 1902, it was called *Townsend Call*. Its location, according to Camfield, "is believed to be at the corner of Taylor and Washington streets."

In September 1886, a disastrous fire "all but destroyed Block 6 of the waterfront," Camfield writes. "Despite a stiff wind, the firefighters contained the fire to Block 6. A teacher, Miss Annie Van Bokkelen, rendered a great service by ringing the school bell as soon as she was alerted to the fire, although she didn't have her key. Instead she entered the building by placing a plank against the building and gallantly climbing up to raise a window sash."

John Cary "Jack" Pringle was the lessee/publisher or editor for several years.

In a 2015 interview, Camfield said he believes it was Emma Pringle (Jack's wife) who taught him typing at Port Townsend High School in the late 1940s.

Pringle's youth was spent working in the silver mines in Nevada, where his father was a superintendent.

Camfield writes, that Jack "possessed literary talents of a very high order and soon gravitated to the newspaper offices of the city. He was a member of a little coterie of young men of exceptional talents who contributed most of the leaven in the way of special human-interest stories which made their way into the columns of local newspapers during the hard days following the busting of the real estate bubble in the early nineties."

Pringle was associated not only with the *Call*, but also the *Morning Leader*, as well as local correspondent for other leading Northwest newspapers and news-gathering organizations.

About 1909, he left the industry and went to work for the federal government in the immigration and customs department.

Issues of the *Call* in 1903 list M.F. Satterlee & Sons as publishers, and a May 1, 1909, issue shows F.A. Willoughby as manager. This may have been the same man, who would later hold interest in the *Leader*, and operate a commercial printing business at the same time.

Working for the *Call* for about four years as printer was Robert "Bobby" Greenwood. Camfield's history notes that he opened R.F. Greenwood Co. Printers, which he ran for 52 years until his death in March 1941. His shop was sold to F.A. Willoughby.

Backing up a few years to Aug. 21, 1883, when Allen Weir owned the *Argus*, a young man, W.L. Jones, came to the paper after a few years with the Hillsboro, Ore., *Independent*. Weir must have seen immediate potential in Jones for he sold him half-interest in the *Argus*, which only three months previous had been a daily, but was now a weekly.

Weir's column introducing Jones noted that the job had become too large and demanded too much time for one person.

"By this new arrangement, the financial backing of the Argus *will be increased a couple of thousand dollars. Mr. Jones is a young man of steady habits, excellent abilities and experience in the newspaper business. His valuable personal efforts, with the increased money capital, will make the paper infinitely stronger in every way than it has been heretofore."*

Capt. Enoch S. Fowler built the stately stone structure in 1874. It became the home of the *Leader* in 1916 and still is today. In this photo from ca 1934, managing editor Richard McCurdy, left, and publisher Ray Scott stand outside the Fowler Building. *(Port Townsend Leader archives)*

Jones worked for Weir for three years before an illness forced him to resign in 1886. He would return to Hillsboro, where he regained his health and served on the city council.

The *Leader* is born

It would be three more years before Jones would be back in journalism with a new goal — to purchase a newspaper in Port Townsend. There were two weeklies in the city at the time: the *Townsend Call* and the *Weekly Argus.*

His friend and former partner, Weir, had left the *Argus* in February to run for Secretary of State, and W.F. Newell now owned it, but apparently didn't want to sell. The *Call*, owned by the redoubtable Jack Pringle, was not for sale.

So, if Jones wanted to own a newspaper, he would have to start a new one. Brimming with confidence, he returned to Port Townsend, now a burgeoning waterfront city with more than 6,000 residents. A recovered Jones exhibited renewed energy, health and finances.

The first issue of the *Morning Leader* in Port Townsend debuted on Oct. 2, 1889.
(Port Townsend Leader archives)

Owing perhaps to the good rapport he had with the city's businesses when he worked with Weir, Jones had little trouble rounding up advertisers, who would support the fledgling operation.

So, from a small shop on Water Street on Oct. 2, 1889, editor and proprietor Jones launched the *Morning Leader*. Little did he know that leap of faith would result in the same paper existing for more than a century. In 2018, the *Leader* celebrated 129 years as the Key City's newspaper.

The ambitious Jones founded the paper as both a daily, promising a weekly "in a few days." He met that promise and it existed as both a daily and weekly until March 1904, when it reverted to weekly-only. Two other sources say it was 1908, but the Washington State Library has weekly papers on microfilm from 1904.

Jones was adamant that Port Townsend could support three newspapers. He wrote in his initial column:

We cannot join with hackneyed writers in the sweeping declaration that there is no room for three papers in the coming empire city of the great Pacific Northwest. We admit, without argument, that two good papers may benefit a town in a greater degree than three poor, sickly, orphaned publications. But there should be no helpless journals here.

The present population, large number of business houses, manufacturing establishments and ocean commerce of Port Townsend ought, and should give, a respectable support to three papers, provided that they are conducted in the interest of present active and worthy conditions and labor for the rapid development of our many resources and the peopling of this city and the large areas of agriculture, horticultural, mineral and grazing lands directly tributary to it.

He wrote that there were 5,000 printed copies of the first paper, an 8-page edition that included a complete summary of buildings erected during the past summer, a valuable shipping compilation, customhouse statistics, manufacturing industries of the city and the bay, business write-ups, descriptive articles regarding the rich country tributary to Port Townsend, the outpost and lime works of the San Juan archipelago.

Two big stories on Page 1 were about the Yukon Gold Strike and many ships stopped at Port Townsend on the way to Alaska, bringing with them miners and their supplies; it also brought the bad news that many miners were dying of scurvy; a second story told of the resources of Admiralty Inlet and Island County; and a third was an apology for late election returns "owing to a breakdown in the wireless."

The rest of the page was a smattering of ads; Page 2 featured nearly three columns on the Roche Harbor lime works, a short story on the sawmill at Port Discovery Bay, and three columns of ads the length of the paper, the largest of these from the Port Townsend Foundry and First National Bank; Page 3 had a story on the vast resources and industries in and around the city. This story included nine decks of headlines leading into the story, the main being "One Million Dollars Invested in Industries." The right three columns were all ads, the largest for Whittlesey and Fenimore customs and insurance brokers, and Corrigan, the tailor.

Page 4 was devoted to editorials; Page 5 featured Port Townsend's building boom, listing all recent building permits; Page 6 included three large ads, each occupying one-third of the page: Nolton and Adams Hardware on top, then Sisley and Bell, real estate loans and investment brokers, and at the bottom, Smith, Ellis and Co. new clothing and famous corsets; Page 7 featured a lengthy story about a new naval yard in town as well as a full 3-column ad from Ward, Harper and Hill real estate brokers.

On Page 8, Jones introduces the *Leader* readers to his city editor, J.W. Lysons, in a very brief item leading off the page that includes several personals, arrests and three columns of small ads.

"Mr. Lysons is a young man of considerable ability as a local and descriptive writer and the publisher of the Morning Leader *recommends him to the citizens of Port Townsend as worthy of your respect and confidence. Tell him all you know and don't blush at the expectation. Your aid is necessary to the success of the local department."*

Jones is most proud of the equipment he has acquired for his new paper and writes about it on the editorial page.

All our machinery, type and office equipment are new and of the best manufacture. We have put in steam power, a fine Hoe cylinder press with all the latest improvements and attachments, two first-class Gordon job presses, paper cutters and a complete line of job, news and advertising type, embracing all the latest faces, from the justly renowned houses of the East, including the Mackellar, Smith and Jordan Co., and Johnson's foundries.

Without boasting, we claim our office cost thousands of dollars more than any other office in Port Townsend and is unequaled by any printing establishment north of Seattle."

… We shall not be narrowed down by no factions, isms or dogmas and reserve to this journal the right to laud that which is right and good and condemn that which is wrong and hurtful to moral, social and commercial developments. We have secured all the telegraphic news available at the office at the present time and will increase the service as facilities and encouragement are offered.

In a separate editorial, Jones wrote briefly on the possibility of a railroad to the Quimper Peninsula.

"In Port Townsend, may be found a few doubting Thomases upon the question of early railway communication, if any at all. … The pessimist is among us and we must bear with him the burdens of a pleasant thought or kind word until the cars roll inland, laden with ripe grains and all matured products of Oregon, Montana, Idaho and Eastern Washington.

"The railroad will be built and speedily too. In conversation with a prominent railroad official a few weeks ago, the editor of the Morning Leader *was informed that the road would be completed from Portland to this place within two years, and that the Oregon Railway and Navigation company would unite with the Union Pacific system in giving that railway a seaport at Port Townsend."*

Starting in April 1890 and continuing through September of that year, a full-page ad from the Oregon Improvement Company ran daily in the *Leader*. The ad, backed by Union Pacific, touted the land available in Port Townsend, saying more than 100 lots were sold the first day. It also noted that "more than 1,500 jobs were available in Port Townsend with the construction of the railroad."

The ad called Port Townsend "the most prosperous city in Washington. Never have people felt so much confidence in the greatness of Port Townsend."

These ads fueled a city whose residents watched railroads completed all around them, albeit on the other side of Puget Sound. Port Townsend was the only city on the North Olympic Peninsula that did not grow up as a result of sawmills being constructed. There were a few, namely at Port Discovery and Port Ludlow, but they were small compared to other areas.

We'll digress a bit to talk about the desperate, but failed attempt to bring a railroad to Port Townsend.

Railroad: Nothing but talk

In 1853, Isaac Stevens, the territory's first governor, surveyed a northern route for a transcontinental rail line and recommended to Congress that somewhere in Jefferson County should be the site of the railroad's western terminus. Nothing would come of it, but the idea did become a civic obsession in Port Townsend.

A few years later, in the city's first newspaper, the *Register*, editor Travers Daniels wrote of a future when "ships from the Indian Ocean, from Canton and Calcutta cross the Pacific and deposit their rich freight at the terminus of the great highway of the nations of the civilized world on Puget Sound."

According to the website: *history.org/porttownsendrailroad.com* in August 1887, a group of five prominent men of the town, joined by two San Franciscans, filed incorporation papers for "The Port Townsend Southern Railroad Company" (Articles of Incorporation). The corporate articles gave an expansive definition of its intended purposes, but what the people of the town wanted desperately was a railroad:

To be built, purchased, constructed or maintained to commence from a point at the Bay of Port Townsend, in Jefferson County, Territory of Washington, and run thence southward, or in a southerly direction, through the Counties of Jefferson, Mason, Chehalis, Thurston, Lewis, Cowlitz and Clark to a point in said territory on the Columbia River.

After nearly two more years with no takers from the established railroads, a civic effort raised funds to lay a planned 6 miles of track heading south.

"On March 23, 1889, almost every living soul in Port Townsend gathered two miles out of town near the homestead of Albert Briggs to watch the work get started. ... When the men wearily put down their tools, the Port Townsend Southern had but a single mile of track, and it ended in no useful place."

If nothing else, the residents had determination, even spunk. They gathered more than $100,000 to fund a drive to lure a major rail line with a contract to have a railroad built within two years. Giants of the industry descended on the city to get in on the ground floor.

Among them, writes historian Murray Morgan in a 1951 pamphlet, *James G. Swan, Promoter,* were Gen. Grenville M. Dodge, fabled chief engineer of the Union Pacific Railroad, and Elijah Smith, who headed both the Oregon Railway & Navigation Company and the Oregon Improvement Company (OIC).

Despite a deal being struck, the OIC failed to deliver, the track reached only to Quilcene, about 27 miles south of Port Townsend by early 1891.

It would get no farther south.

The OIC, the Oregon Railway & Navigation Company, and the Union Pacific were all in severe financial difficulty. OIC filed for bankruptcy less than three years later amid the financial Panic of 1893.

In his pamphlet, Morgan cited one of Port Townsend's most-noted citizens had given up hope.

Upon learning of the collapse, James Swan, a tireless Port Townsend booster and former agent of the Northern Pacific Railroad, sent a despondent telegram:

Ship captain Enoch S. Fowler arrived in the Puget Sound in 1849, even before Port Townsend's founders. *(Tom Camfield)/ Port Townsend: An Illustrated History of Shanghaiing, Shipwrecks, Soiled Doves and Sundry Souls)*

"The jig is up. Reliable word reached me that Portland court today appointed a receiver for OIC. This kills all hope that road will be extended, Swan wrote."

Founding of Port Townsend

One man who wouldn't let the economic slump stop him was Capt. Enoch S. Fowler. He settled in San Francisco and made several trips to Puget Sound. In 1849, he was in the Pacific and, as mate aboard the brig *George Emery*, saw the forested coastline of what would become Port Townsend in 1851. His passengers that day were Alfred Plummer and Charles Bachelder, who would help found Port Townsend. Fowler settled in the new town in 1852. But his duties as skipper of ships between the Northwest and San Francisco kept him busy until 1857 when he settled in town for good.

He married and retired from the sea in 1857, we learn from "A Centennial Salute: The evolution of a community newspaper: The Leader," in an Oct. 3, 1989, special edition honoring the 100th anniversary of the newspaper.

He continued in the mercantile business, buying and selling ships while making loans to the city's residents. In 1859 (the article says 1959), he built the city's first dock and two years later donated two lots near Lawrence and Tyler streets for the city's first school. He also owned more than 300 acres near Point Wilson, offering it to the University of Washington for $500, but was refused, "a figure too much for the regents."

Fowler later sold the acreage to the U.S. Government for $3,000, which held it in trust until deciding to locate a military base, Fort Worden, on the site.

In 1868, he built a prominent home that was recently restored at Polk and Jefferson streets, uptown.

Fowler Building

Fowler was a man of many interests. In 1867, he purchased the *Message*, a newspaper that survived for three years.

Fowler also saw a need for a large stone building in downtown. He paid $3,100 for the land on Adams Street.

"The stone used for the face of the building was quarried at Scow Bay (on Indian Island). The front was fine-cut ashlar, the sides and back, rubble walls. When completed, it stood as the lone stone structure among the frail-looking wood structures that occupied most the downtown area."

When it opened in 1874, it was the first two-story stone structure in the Washington Territory. The building was constructed by Morgan Carkeek, a mason who would later erect the Dexter Horton Union Bank, one of the rare downtown buildings to survive the Great Seattle Fire of 1889. The bank eventually became Bank of Seattle and later SeaFirst Bank.

In its early days, the 2,870 square-foot Fowler Building was home for four years to a retail business. It also was rented out for lectures, dances and balls. For two years, it was the Masonic Temple. In 1880, Fowler sold "Stone Wall," which he called the building, to the county for $4,000 to be used as the Jefferson County courthouse. It served until 1892 when the county government moved the courthouse into a new facility on Jefferson Street.

That new courthouse was built at a cost of $125,000, featuring Romanesque style architecture with Baroque frescoes. A clock tower rises 143 feet.

In 1888, the S'Klallam chief Chetzemoka died on Indian Island. For three days, his body lay in state in the lobby of the Fowler Building so the pioneers could pay their respects.

The Fowler Building was described in the *Leader's* May 4, 1951, edition celebrating the 100th anniversary of Port Townsend:

The building "became a seaman's brothel, described in early accounts as an establishment for the advancement, spiritually and socially, of sailors … who seek a resting place while sojourning in Port Townsend. In other words, a high-grade flophouse."

In 1912, it became the private dwelling of August Phillip, a pioneer cigar manufacturer, who leased the space.

The pungent aroma of cigar tobacco was replaced in 1916 by newsprint (though the tobacco odor probably never left) as the *Leader* and its stogie-chomping management moved in.

That year, Winslow McCurdy bought the building, the *Leader* took up residence and never left. The Fowler Building is one of the oldest surviving two-story stone buildings in Washington State

In 2016, the *Leader* celebrated its centennial in the same building, though ivy, initially planted in 1918, gradually has overtaken the structure. In the 1980s, some of the ivy was cut back to allow for building restoration, but the fast-growing vines are once again shrouding the structure.

The Fowler Building, at 226 Adams St., was one of the original city buildings listed on the National Register of Historic Places. It has undergone numerous interior changes over the decades.

The *Leader* was still in its initial building on Water Street when Washington officially became a state. One month and 11 days after the first *Leader* hit the streets, President Benjamin Harrison signed the proclamation declaring the Territory of Washington to be a state.

On Nov. 18, 1889, the *Leader* describes the historic event:

The last formal act of the equipment of Washington in the panoply of statehood was consummated when the officers of the new government were inaugurated with great ceremony and with a display of military and civic magnificence that had never been excelled in the pretty city of Olympia.

The buildings were gorgeously decorated, the streets crowded with spectators, visiting and resident, and the exercises were altogether conducted in a very successful manner.

That's how the *Leader* described Washington's christening ceremonies, but the reality was much different as told in a story in the *Leader's* centennial edition about the Olympia celebration.

It seems that particular Monday morning was normal for November in the Pacific Northwest, that is to say, it was chilly, murky with strong threat of rain. Main Street, (there is no Main St. in Olympia today), magnificently decorated with bunting and flags, emblems and evergreens for the grand parade, was lined three-deep with spectators; it was also three inches deep with mud.

At about 10 a.m. just before the procession was to begin, the parade route was changed from Main to Adams Street, three blocks east.

However, the crowd unfortunately wasn't told of the change, and their exodus to the correct route was confusing. But they got there, trudging through the mud, the *Leader* account noted.

Most of the parade was military; it also included the Pioneer Association, which number about 600 members, but only 49 made the trek from the Key City. These hardy souls marched bravely through the muck the entire parade route.

Among them were James G. Swan, W.L. Jones, Albert Briggs, Ben Pettygrove and wife, Capt. H.L. Tibbals and wife, and Frank Hastings and wife.

Adding insult to injury, the pioneers registered their disappointment in the opening speeches, which addressed the early homesteaders who crossed the mountains in wagons, but ignored those who came by water, which amounted to about 75 percent of the state's residents.

The speeches called attention to Capt. Robert Gray and Capt. George Vancouver, both who came via water, noting that Gray, whose ship (*Columbia Rediviva*) "gave the name to Oregon's mighty river and whose prior discovery gave to the U.S. the very state of Washington, did not come here by ox team."

Lysons saves *Leader*

However, Jones had to give up the paper due to his ill health. In the May 18, 1890, *Leader*, he cites his health problems, which plagued him several years earlier when he was with the *Argus*. "The management of this paper has been placed in the hands of J.W. Clarke, who had editorial experienced for a period of ten years, five of which were spent in Southern California."

Clarke retained J.W. Lysons as city editor and noted that it would not change policy in that it would be "thoroughly Republican, because believing that the promulgation and practice of the Republican principles are most conducive to a sound and successful government.

"… Whatever concerns the growth and advancement of our city and its varied interests shall be of foremost importance in all departments of the paper."

With the Dec. 11 issue, Lysons and Albert Searl became new editors and managers. Lysons would be the manager of the paper and Searl would handle the local news as city editor.

The managers formed a new corporation as well, changing the Port Townsend Publishing Co. to Key City Publishing.

Camfield notes that Searl's name was dropped from masthead at the end of March, and on July 23, 1891, founder W.L. Jones was back as editor-manager, having recovered from his illness.

Lysons retired just after Jones returned for the same reason, returning to work on the Northwest News Bureau of which he and Searl owned a controlling interest and acted as Port Townsend's correspondent for other newspapers.

In January 1892, W.B. Dennis became editor and manager, and on April 3, he changed the paper's name to *Townsend Daily Leader*, dropping "Port" and "Morning" because they were "useless handles," and inserted Townsend because "we want to advertise the name of our great city in all that we do."

While the city housing and building industries suffered in the first Great Recession of 1893, the *Leader* fought through it and survived, owing to the hard-sell of Lysons when a concerted letter-writing campaign by Dennis to pursue, and often threaten, advertisers to pay their bills, had failed.

Lysons discovered that Dennis had put the *Leader* further in debt than he figured. But the determined editor won favor with its creditors, and his plea not to foreclose on the paper paid dividends. He was able to buy enough time to keep the paper functioning and paid off the creditors in an agreed time.

The *Leader* was so close to folding; it not only survived, it thrived.

A concerted advertising campaign touted the circulation of the *Leader*, noting that a sworn circulation for Jefferson, Clallam and San Juan counties showed 1,280 for the daily and 1,670 for the weekly with a subscription price for the weekly of $2 a year in advance. The campaign cited that this was the best advertising value of any paper on the peninsula.

From 1894 on, the paper's financial health improved, albeit, gradually.

Camfield wrote that Lysons "likely suffered an attack of nervous prostration while Clarke was still at the helm." Somehow his health remained strong through the recession years. Lysons continued with the paper until 1905 when he moved to Seattle to practice law.

On April 9, 1895, under Lysons, the paper returned to its original name, *The Morning Leader*. The owner wrote an editorial, saying it wasn't a change in name, but only in style. "We will always be the *Leader*." He began a series of daily ads touting the *Morning Leader* (in big type) "as the most reputable and reliable newspaper in Port Townsend. It prints the news and all of it, and gets up in a terse and interesting style, without any attempt at sensationalism or blackguarding. It is the City Official Paper, and its aim is to make the utterances as reliable and trustworthy as those by city officials."

Along with the promotional ad, was a description of the paper's new technology, the Thorne Typesetting Machine, complete with a picture of the unit. Until then, all type was set by hand, a laborious task.

The Morning Leader was setting type mechanically, right along with such publishing giants as the *New York Evening Post*.

A parade of owners continued for *The Leader*, including Dennis and W.A. Halteman, L.F. Shaw, Theodore Beuhn and W.L. Jessup in 1903.

In 1906, Jessup was ready to move on to Bremerton, where he would establish that city's *Sun* newspaper, which has had several names, but today is known as the *Kitsap Sun*.

Jessup sold the paper to Winslow McCurdy, a native of Port Townsend, who lost his father at age 14, but grew up in the office of the *Leader* as a "printer's devil."

This was the beginning of 61 years of ownership by the McCurdy family.

Parade of newspapers

We will return to Winslow and the *Leader* momentarily, but a few other newspapers emerged in Port Townsend following *The Leader* and prior to McCurdy.

Camfield's book and the Washington State Library's microfilm are the sources.

Founded nine months after the *Leader*, the **Key City Monitor** began weekly publication on June 13, 1890. Local estate agents Miller and Burkett were the publishers, but the 4-column tabloid folded by mid-August that year.

The City of Landes appeared on Aug. 15, 1890, as a full-column advertisement for local banker Henry Landes, touting his real estate investment near Seabeck on Hood Canal.

The *Evening Incident* was described in the *Leader* of July 3, 1891, as "that journalistic freak which is three parts Democratic ass and one-part Republican calf." Camfield adds, "It's possible that the *Evening Incident* was a sarcastic pseudonym utilized by the *Leader* writer, referring to the *Call*, which had been in business six years and was the *Leader's* chief competitor."

Next came the ventures of Milton F. Satterlee — the *Key City Graphic*, 1892-1893; *The Herald*, founded in 1893, and the *Port Townsend Daily Democrat*, June 1894 to at least March 19, 1895, or for which date an available issue lists M.F. Satterlee & Sons as publishers with W.A. Wilcox as city editor.

The *Leader* reported on Oct. 7, 1898, a *Swedish-language* newspaper "is a new candidate for journalistic honors soon to be launched in Port Townsend and will be conducted in the interests of the Swedish citizen residents. ... the *Leader* bespeaks for it a hearty support." No record of it ever being published exists.

Little is known of the *Key City Mirror*. A copy in Camfield's library, dated July 27, 1901, is identified as Vol. 1, No. 5. A bit ahead of its time, it utilized color (red) in a number of advertisements. M.F. Satterlee was identified as managing agent.

The *Jefferson County Journal* is listed as having published in 1906.

The *Weekly Record*, a small tabloid, was still another of the many publications given birth by the prolific Satterlee. It began the first week in December 1906, as an available copy dated Jan. 28, 1907, is identified as Vol. 1, No. 8.

The *Jefferson County Herald*, while not flourishing financially, was an outspoken weekly published for most of a decade, beginning in the late 1940s. Camfield knows this because he moonlighted there as a printer in 1950, while working for the *Leader*. The founder was Roderick Dhu Weir, a Canadian and not likely related to the *Argus'* Allen Weir. His sons, Jim and Tom, assisted him in the *Herald*, which later evolved into the *Port Townsend Tradesman* as late as 1965.

Other Jefferson County newspapers of earlier years included (with dates verified) in Quilcene: *Megaphone* (1909-1918), *Olympic Mining*

Record (1897) and ***Quilcene Queen*** (1891-1893); in the Tri-City area: the ***Irondale News*** (1911), established by Winslow McCurdy in conjunction with the *Leader*.

An interesting item about the *Megaphone* is that one issue notes it was published weekly by Satterlee. Its flag boasted: "Circulation Less Than a Million and A Half Weekly."

The weekly ***Hood Canal News*** was printed in the *Leader* shop for a time in the late 1950s and early 1960s. No files are available, though it began publication as a tabloid and had a short life.

None of those papers could hold a candle to the *Leader*. Few existed longer than a couple years at most.

CHAPTER 11

The McCurdy generation

There was no question, journalistically, Port Townsend and Jefferson County in the 20th century belonged to the McCurdys: Winslow McCurdy, 1908-1926; his son, Richard "Dick" McCurdy, 1936-1967.

A Port Townsend native, Win was born on Oct. 10, 1877, and lost his father, William A. McCurdy, when he was only 14. From Win's obituary in the *Leader* on July 20, 1928, we learn glowing, inspiring information written about this giant of a man, who spent all but four years of his life in the Key City.

William was a cousin of Francis W. Pettygrove, one of the founders of Port Townsend, and came to the young city in 1857 from Boston. In Tom Camfield's history book *Port Townsend: An Illustrated History of Shanghaiing, Shipwrecks, Soiled Doves and Sundry Souls,* he tells us he was "originally a ship-joiner, he became a builder of homes and business houses in the area. During the Civil War, however, he worked for several years at Mare Island Naval Yard in California. He returned to Puget Sound and shipbuilding, at Seabeck, Tacoma and Port Ludlow."

In 1868, he married Joanna Ebinger at Portland, Ore. They returned to Port Townsend and began construction trade in the area. In addition to Winslow, William and Joanna were parents of Frank and James G. McCurdy, later a banker and author. William died in 1891.

James' son, Horace Winslow McCurdy, is the name most known in Port Townsend. *HistoryLink.org/McCurdy, H.W.,* relates he was a shipbuilder and constructed bridges. A supporter of maritime research and maritime collections, his firm, Puget Sound Dredging, constructed the Lake Washington Floating Bridge (1940) and the Hood Canal Bridge (1961), renamed William A. Bugge Bridge for the state's director of transportation and a Port Townsend native.

In 1978, the McCurdy estate established the Northwest Maritime Center on McCurdy Point in Port Townsend. In 2004, the foundation donated $150,000 to establish the H.W. McCurdy Maritime Resource Library.

The family is unrelated to Dr. Sam McCurdy, who constructed business buildings still standing in downtown Port Townsend.

Winslow lived with friends and didn't attend high school. He was only 15 when he began working for the *Leader* founder, W.L. Jones during the boom days of the city.

In his obituary:

Owners might change, but Win McCurdy remained steadily with the paper, advancing in the intricacies of his trade, and gaining experience, varied and valuable. He learned his trade in the old school, and no change in printing and composing methods came with which he did not keep pace.

When he was 21, Win and his brother, Frank, tried gold-mining in Alaska.

Win was temporarily a miner, but ever a printer, and enthused about the invention of the Mergenthaler type-setting machine and what it meant to the printing world. He returned to Port Townsend with the intention to purchase a paper, but he had other notions to tend to first.

He immediately traveled to San Francisco to take a course in the innovative typesetting system, not only learning how to use the machine, but mastering its construction and possibilities for a newspaper he now wanted to buy.

When his study was completed, he returned to Port Townsend in 1906 and immediately began work on the *Leader*, finding the city and paper in the throes of a depression and sinking rapidly.

It was ripe for a new owner and W.L. Jessup jumped at the chance to sell and move to a larger city — Bremerton — to start a new paper.

Winslow, O'Rear buy *Leader*

Winslow McCurdy teamed with Newton W. O'Rear, who had owned the *Leader* in 1893, to assist with the purchase. In 1908, McCurdy would buy out O'Rear and become sole owner.

Acquiring the "Merg," typesetter, he almost singlehandedly produced the paper. He wrote copy, practically all of it on the new machine. He not only attended meetings, wrote stories, set type and ran the press, he attended to the business affairs of the paper.

For the next 12 years it was essentially a one-man operation by a tremendously talented individual that kept the *Leader* going — make it two *Leaders*, for he published both a daily and weekly until 1922.

The writer of his obituary, most likely the paper's manager and longtime friend Ray Scott, knew his subject well describing in detail the indefatigable spirit of this man.

The capacity of work contained in him was unquestionably remarkable; few men have found it possible to maintain steadily the tremendous work schedule he followed for many years, and his ability to produce single-handed, a daily newspaper, six days of each week of each year, year after year.

In his "A Brief Historical Sketch of Port Townsend," William D. "Billy" Welsh, the "Rarebitter" news editor for the *Port Angeles Evening News*, later director of public relations for Crown Zellerbach paper company, describes McCurdy, as a man he cherished and knew well.

Win would interview captains of incoming sailing ships, meet passenger steamers, check up on things at the city hall, chin with the deputy collector of customs, then make a round of the business houses. Then, when night settled down, he would spread these notes before him on the Linotype copy board and set his story on the keyboard. By early morning, the Port Townsend Leader *would be ready for the postman and Win would be home and in bed. We number him with our true friends and one of the most interesting newspaper men of his time.*

On July 9, 1908, Winslow married Jennie Iffland. They had four children: Richard, Jean, Winslow Jr. and Barbara.

Winslow McCurdy was ever a booster of his city, and in 1909, he supported the prospective advent of the Olympic Peninsula's branch of the Chicago, Milwaukee and St. Paul railroad line, predicting a bright outcome for Port Townsend.

In the "Saga of Port Townsend," published in the *Leader* in 1951, a special 98-page section celebrating the city's 100th birthday, Scott, then-publisher, called on Welsh again, citing Win's editorial "Boost Port Townsend!" on Jan. 6, 1909.

For a year, the Leader *has been persistently hammering on the theory that there should be a sentiment to help one another and if carried out in letter and spirit, the boosting of our Key City will bring even greater prosperity than now prevails.*

Let's exhibit our products in the Alaska-Yukon-Pacific Exposition and tell the world what we have here.

The spirit was willing, but the flesh weak; the railroad never made it.

In "Saga ...," Welsh continued to praise McCurdy for his "editorials of deep understanding and reports of excellent journalistic quality far beyond the usual in contemporary newspapers that gave credit where due, and criticism, always constructive, where deserved."

After the first decade of the 20th century when it appeared Port Townsend had weathered the storm of the Recession of the last decade, McCurdy went to bat for the forest industry, touting new developments by the Mats Bay Logging Company.

When the timber industry tanked after the first decade, he capitalized on the steel excitement at Irondale, southeast of Port Townsend, and established the *Irondale News* in 1911. It was during the time that this small village was excited to become a steel-manufacturing center. The fury didn't last long, and when that industry collapsed, so did the *News*.

Leader moves into Fowler Building in 1916

In 1916, McCurdy purchased the Fowler Building and immediately moved the *Leader* operation into that stone structure. In 2018, the *Leader* marked 102 years in the same building.

Prior to moving into the Fowler, the *Leader* was located off Water Street, moving to the Terry Building on Washington, then the Jones

Crouten Building, back to Water Street, and then the second floor of the Tibbals Building.

Aside from his life in newspapers, McCurdy also developed a keen interest in politics. From his obituary (and his editorials) we learn he was an "unswerving Republican, and in time, came to exert considerable influence in political circles, extending far beyond the confines of Jefferson County."

He served on state committees and his opinions often were sought by leaders of his party. He was a "good judge of men and possessed the ability to frequently foresee conditions which were not, at times, widely realized by others."

He loved the outdoors, especially the saltwater, and became one of the peninsula's first power-boat owners. He encouraged yachting and cruising.

His sports prowess also was noted in his obituary:

Athletics always appealed (to him) with more than ordinary power. He played baseball and football in his early days, and it is not unreasonable to say that no other man of this part of the state had more to do with the encouragement of honest athletic competition than did Win McCurdy. He was a "clean sportsman;" he would rather see his boys win than lose, but to him an honest defeat was nothing more than an urge for better endeavors in the next game.

Postmaster McCurdy

In early 1922, McCurdy's career went in another direction when the Warren G. Harding administration appointed him postmaster of Port Townsend, a position he sought and occupied until he died in 1928. He took the position seriously and "filled it with efficiency, courtesy and confidence," the obituary writer notes.

To accept this appointment, McCurdy had to relinquish sole ownership in the *Leader*. Wrestling with this decision, which he apparently didn't agree with, he decided he had the able men ready to take the reins of the newspaper.

On March 22, 1922, he announced he would be retiring from active participation in the Leader Company, though he would still own the property. Through a lease, McCurdy assigned F.A. Willoughby, a printer with the *Leader* from its early days, to be manager of the company and in complete charge; he also said E. Morris Starrett would be city editor, the man in charge of local news.

Camfield's history notes that Willoughby became an apprentice printer at the *Leader* in the 1890s, later established his own job-printing business, which he conducted from 1896-1920. He operated in conjunction with the *Leader* from 1906-1922. Starrett, known as Morrie to his friends, had been a reporter for the *Leader,* then when Win McCurdy was appointed postmaster, he became city editor and held stock in the company's lease. During this period, he was believed to have worked as a "stringer" for The Associated Press.

His work with the AP, and likely the *Leader,* ended when he "wrote a piece about a baby being abandoned in the muzzle of one of the coastal defense canons at Fort Worden. Someone, it seems, took a look at the smaller-than-baby bore of the weapon in question — and ratted on Morrie," Camfield wrote.

The *Leader* historian notes that "there was a good measure of pestiferous gadfly in the nature of E. Morris Starrett." But, Camfield also says while many stories of Morrie are mostly mean-spirited, he found them humorous, in retrospect.

When his journalism career abruptly ended, Starrett went into the insurance and real estate business and became a longtime member of the Chamber of Commerce, active in Democratic politics. In the 1930s, he was appointed by the Franklin D. Roosevelt administration, postmaster of Port Townsend, succeeding Win McCurdy.

Willoughby, Scott take over

In 1927, Willoughby made his first *Leader* change, switching the makeup of the paper from a time-honored 7-column format to a 6-column format, which kept the paper in line with progressive small-city community papers in the state.

On the editorial page of the *Leader* on Jan. 28, 1927, Winslow McCurdy wrote his final opinion piece:

Effective Feb. 1, a change will take place in the ownership and management of the Leader. *All the property of this paper, of which I have been the sole owner for more than twenty years, will be transferred to The Leader Company, a newly formed corporation, whose members are W.M. McCurdy, F.A. Willoughby and Raymond O. Scott.*

The reorganization is deemed advisable in meeting the changing conditions of a developing field.

He went on to introduce management newcomer Scott to the readers as the man who will assume the business and editorial management of the *Leader,* adding that Willoughby would be in charge of the commercial print department, soon to be established.

Scott may have been new to the management team, but not new to the *Leader* or the city. A Port Townsend native, he first became involved in newspapers as a carrier for the *Daily Call,* then learned the fundamentals of printing, serving his apprenticeship in the *Leader* office on the Linotype machine under McCurdy years ago. He left the city in 1912 and worked four years as a typesetter at the *Morning Astorian* in Astoria, Ore., where he married Inga Thanem.

Four years later, he pursued a business opportunity at the *Anchorage Times* as a printer, then became a major stockholder in the paper and later business manager. After eleven years there, he sold his interest in in the paper in 1927 and returned to Washington, working briefly for the *Longview News,* before returning to Port Townsend, fresh to move into management of the *Leader.*

Win McCurdy wrote of Scott:

With ample practical experience in the newspaper game, from washing rollers to heading the activities of a live newspaper, Mr. Scott combines a realization that hard and incessant work is the price which one must pay for success in this business. Knowing him as I have for many years, I feel certain, under his management, the Leader *will expand and grow more than ever before.*

Less than six months later, the *Leader's* beloved owner/publisher Winslow McCurdy died from blood poisoning on Saturday, July 14, 1928. He was taken to St. John's hospital five days previous. He was 50 years old.

His front-page obituary in the *Leader* noted that he had acquired erysipelas, a blood disease that had apparently followed a bruise he sustained while picking blackberries.

Camfield tells us that Winslow had been "batching" at the time with his oldest son, Win, Jr., while his wife and other children were visiting out of town. It was a simple scratch that Winslow incurred. "He ignored the minor infection until it was too late."

As testament to his stature in the community, "all businesses closed during the funeral, and from the rural districts old friends gathered with those of the city to pay their last tribute."

The obituary in the *Leader* continued:

In his chosen field, Win McCurdy became one of the well-known editors of this part of the country. "He wrote with skill and conciseness. ... he was fearless and fair; he naturally created both friends and ill-wishers, but the former outnumbered greatly the latter. ... As a man, a citizen and a friend, Win McCurdy stood high in the community in which nearly his entire life had been spent, and his 'going away' has created a vacancy which is widely looked upon with sadness and regret.

One writer to the paper, Leo Zeil, a manager of what would become the Crown Zellerbach paper mill, said, "He was a good citizen, a good neighbor, a good friend, and he was not given to forgetting his friends."

In another tribute, one writer, signed "Just Me," talks about Winslow the man, who left a legacy for today's youth.

Few have done more for Port Townsend's headway than Mr. McCurdy; and few have done more to better our morals than he. ... No figure was better known on the football field than he, always pulling for Port Townsend; ... speaking for the younger folk, so, he was our friend.

Winslow's widow, Jennie, retained his stock, along with Willoughby and Scott.

Crown Z arrives

Oct. 6, 1928, was a big day in Port Townsend when the new Crown Zellerbach kraft paper mill, then known as the National Paper Products Co., started operation.

It probably was the one single industry that lifted the Key City out of an economic depression that had existed since 1890. The railroad was expected to provide the buoy, but that dream sank, as well as a predicted land boom in 1889-1890. When the panic of 1893 hit the nation, many people bolted Port Townsend, abandoning businesses and homes.

The website *historylink.org* notes the city's population dwindled from 7,000 inhabitants to a mere 2,000. In 1913, the city suffered another blow when the U.S. Customs Office was moved from Port Townsend to Seattle.

The city languished until 1927 when David Zellerbach, a man with a vision and president of the Zellerbach Corporation's National Paper Products Co. in San Francisco, made a visit to the Key City. He recognized the potential for Port Townsend and announced plans to build the mill at Glen Cove, the site of the homestead of Albert Briggs, one of the city's early settlers.

The mill would produce kraft paper, a heavy, unbleached product used to make grocery bags, multi-walled bags for heavier products such as cement, fertilizer and feed, and cardboard containers and boxes.

Zellerbach announced earlier in the year that he had his eye on two sites on the Olympic Peninsula: Port Townsend and Aberdeen. The citizens of Port Townsend fought hard to secure the site, and almost lost it because of an antiquated water system.

Bolstered by repeated editorials from McCurdy and others in the *Leader,* the city's voters approved issuing $800,000 in municipal bonds to provide the necessary funds to build a dam and pipeline capable of bringing 14 million gallons of fresh water per day from the Big Quilcene River, more than 30 miles away.

The Zellerbach Corporation agreed to pay $200,000 in advance royalties and $10,000 per year to lease the water system from the city for 30 years. This allowed the city to decrease the bond issue to $600,000, a savings of $12,000 in annual interest.

Construction began in September 1927, water began flowing from the water supply on Oct. 5, 1928, and the mill began operation the next day when the first digester was started and the first of the mill's two paper machines went into operation.

With the sudden increase in jobs, Port Townsend became a boomtown. Zellerbach spent more than $2.5 million on construction of the mill's first unit; more than $3 million on the second unit and employed more than 600 workers.

According to the U. S. Census report, Port Townsend's population boomed between 1920 and 1930 from 6,557 to 8,346.

In April 1928, when construction on the new mill was well underway, Zellerbach, already one of the largest companies on the West Coast, acquired Crown Willamette Paper Co. in Camas, Wash., and the ensuing merger created the Crown Zellerbach Corp. The new mill would be the Port Townsend Mill Division of Crown Zellerbach Corp.

Despite the Great Depression hitting a few weeks after the mill began operation, it did not shut down at any time. In fact, the mill's employee numbers rose from 275 at start-up to 375 in 1933. In 1935, a bag factory was added, along with jobs for an additional 40 employees. Further expansion in the 1940s swelled the employee total to 630 by 1949 and to 820 by 1955.

In 2015, Port Townsend Paper Corp. was purchased by Crown Paper Group, which immediately pumped $30 million into improvement projects and another $30 million in maintenance projects. While it is far from the 820-employee base in the 1950s, the mill with nearly 300 workers, is still the largest private industry employer in Jefferson County.

In a Feb. 22, 2017, article in the *Leader*, editor Allison Arthur wrote about two big changes for the mill.

"In 2017, we plan to invest an additional $25 million in capital and maintenance upgrades and improvements," said Steve Klinger, Crown Paper Group CEO. "In addition, we are evaluating multiple potential major upgrades for the next several years. We are committed to continually improving this mill and building its long-term value."

Two of the projects that the mill owners say put the aging paper plant in good position for the future include the completion of the Boiler Maximum Achievable Controlled Technology compliance project and the conversion to using compressed natural gas.

Klinger added, "Over the last two years, we have been moving toward container board."

Leader publisher Ray Scott sits at the Linotype machine in this file photo from the 1950s. Behind him, from left, are printers Fred Willoughby and Claude Mitton and managing editor Dick McCurdy. *(Leader archives)*

Leader experiment

On Dec. 1, 1928, the newspaper managers unveiled an experiment. They would begin publication of the *Leader* twice a week, adding a Monday edition to the customary Thursday publication.

This coincided with the acquisition of a new Linotype machine to replace the one that had been in operation for 25 years. "The new equipment represents an outlay of approximately $5,500 and will give Port Townsend one of the best equipped newspaper plants to be found in a city this size in the state," the publishers wrote.

The experiment lasted until June 27, 1932, when the Monday edition was scuttled. From then on, it has been published primarily on Wednesday or Thursday.

When Monday publications ceased, a change in newspaper delivery was announced, switching from the customary carrier delivery to mail for all subscriptions. The publishers announced the change was due to "lack of revenue to support the Monday issue, but emphasized no loss of local news." Subscription rates, which had been raised to $2.50 a year for the semi-weekly papers, dropped to $2.

Dick McCurdy moves up

Meantime, waiting in the wings was Richard McCurdy, known to all as Dick. The second son of Winslow had grown up under his father's wings and was being groomed for the newspaper business at an early age.

From his obituary in the Nov. 4, 1987, *Leader*, Peter Simpson, a former *Leader* employee and active Port Townsend civic leader, describes Dick's ancestors.

His paternal grandfather, William Augustus McCurdy, Jr. emigrated to Port Townsend from New Brunswick, Canada, in 1857, where he was greeted by his cousin, Francis W. Pettygrove, one of the city's founders.

His maternal grandfather, John Iffland, was a native of Germany, who arrived in Port Townsend in the late 1870s or early 1880s; he became the manager of the Central Hotel, the city's major hostelry for many years.

In an October 1989 *Leader*, celebrating the paper's Centennial, reporter Deborah Daline wrote an article headlined, "Leader spirit crafted by Editor-Publisher Dick McCurdy," that his earliest childhood memories were looking through the window of the Tibbals Building (where the paper was published in those days) and seeing someone running the Linotype machine.

There was a man working for the Leader *in those days by the name of Charlie Meyer, who had two daughters who were frolicking around with some Fort Worden soldiers. Meyer wrote quite a strong editorial in the paper directed at what he called '$17-a-month lovers' (that's what Fort Worden privates were pulling in at that time). The next night a volley of bricks blasted through the Tibbals building window, doing quite a bit of damage to the Linotype machine.*

Daline writes that Dick was about 6 when his dad bought the Fowler building and moved the *Leader* equipment into it. He remembers asking how his father managed to move all the heavy machinery to which Winslow replied: "By the strength of my strong right arm."

When he was in the fourth grade, Dick became a delivery boy. During his high school days, he worked as a janitor in the mailing room, rolling and stamping papers. That is, when he wasn't playing sports. He was a three-year letterman and was on the 1927 champion Port Townsend basketball team. Win Jr. also was on the team, regarded as one of the best Redskin teams ever.

He continued to work at the paper during vacations while attending the University of Washington, where he majored in communications and worked as a sports editor of the *Daily*.

After graduation, he wanted to learn all he could about operating a newspaper. To learn the printing process, he apprenticed as a Linotype operation at the *Leader*, then spent two years traveling around the Northwest putting on circulation campaigns for weeklies and dailies.

In the summer of 1934, he traveled to Havre, Mont., where on July 2, he married Eleanor Clack, a Montana country girl, whom he had met at the University of Washington.

In 1936, all his preparation paid off when he accepted a position as city editor under Ray Scott. He held that job until the outbreak of World War II when he enlisted in the U.S. Army. In 1943, Corporal McCurdy was selected for Officers Candidate School at Fort Benning, Ga. He was commissioned as second lieutenant.

In November 1944, while serving on the front line in Germany, he was seriously wounded in action when a bullet pierced his lung and shoulder. He spent 13 months recuperating in England before retiring as a captain due to the disability.

He returned to Port Townsend in 1946 and was named editor of the *Leader*.

Leader reorganization

On May 1, 1946, The Leader Company announced a reorganization with Winslow's widow, Jennie McCurdy, selling her stock in the company as well as F.A. Willoughby, who retired after nearly 20 years as a stockholder and part-owner. Neither had been active in the operation in recent years.

The new management consisted of Richard McCurdy, Claude Mitton

From left, Ray Scott, Claude Mitton and Dick McCurdy stand outside the *Leader* **building in the 1940s.** *(Leader archives)*

and Dan Hill. Ray Scott, manager and president of the corporation since 1928, continues as president-manager and will be joined on the board of directors by McCurdy as treasurer, Mitton as vice president and Hill as secretary. Plans call for the addition of an employee to the typographical department.

Under the reorganization, McCurdy, news editor-reporter since 1936, save for three years he was in the military service, takes full charge of the editorial and advertising department. Mitton, with the firm since 1929, continues as shop foreman and will be adding a full-time assistant when available. Hill, a full-time employee since May 1944, except for eight months in the Army, will continue as a part-time Linotype operator and general office assistant.

Willoughby, who had been in ill health, fully retired. Thus, ended his role with *The Leader* that began in 1906, escalated to lessee-manager in 1921, and seven years later to stockholder and member of the board of directors. Lamentably, Willoughby died one month after the reorganization.

Jennie McCurdy was never active in the daily business but served as corporation secretary and majority stockholder after her husband died in 1928. Mrs. McCurdy suffered from a heart ailment for several years and died after a pair of paralyzing strokes on Aug. 21, 1947.

When she married Winslow, she was a Port Townsend High School teacher; a world traveler, visiting Germany on several occasions, and later, after her husband died, took trips to China, the Philippine Islands and Japan.

Scott had been in the management of the *Leader* since 1927, and ably assisted Dick McCurdy in the operation until he suffered a heart attack at a local basketball game, in December 1949, forcing him to retire. But, he retained a 51-percent interest in the paper until selling out to McCurdy in April 1955.

Scott also was an astute businessman, a director of the First American National Bank, a trustee and deacon at the First Presbyterian Church and a charter member and past-president of the local Chamber of Commerce.

As Camfield writes, sardonically:

"Despite a lifetime of efficiency in harness, Raymond Olney Scott exhibited a lack of concern for deadlines when he died on a Thursday after the weekly *Leader* had already hit the streets."

It would be a week later, Dec. 29, 1955, before the paper would print his obituary.

Because of his long membership and great interest in the Presbyterian Church, a memorial fund was established in his name.

Mitton, who began with the *Leader* in 1929 and before that apprenticed with early day printer Bobbie Greenwood, was one of the last of the old-school printers. His career would "span from the days of handset type

Claude Mitton works on the type deck. He was a master printer for the *Leader* from 1929-1975. He also was a minority stockholder in the company. *(Port Townsend Leader archives)*

and hand-fed presses to modern clean-hand methodry and high-speed mechanization," his obituary in December 1977, notes. Ill health forced his retirement in 1975.

The writer touts Mitton's expertise and ethical acumen in the print shop. "During most of the subsequent half-century he was a standard-bearer of the 60-hour work week, and when the job demanded, a 70- or 80-hour week. It became a matter of a customer's need or pride in his own craftmanship."

In 1949, Hill left the business and Scott retired; in 1955, McCurdy bought out Scott and became a majority owner with Mitton holding minor shares.

In November 1946, Jefferson County became the proud owner of an airfield, known by some as "Jefferson County International Cow Pasture," writes Peter Simpson in *City of Dreams: A Guide to Port Townsend*. Simpson, who later would become assistant editor at the *Leader*, also wrote that the airport is known "by others as the shortest international airport in the country, and by others as the issue that won't die."

Regardless of the controversy, the airport was designated as one of 49 point-of-entry airports in the United States, meaning customs service is available 24 hours a day.

Today, amid endless debates primarily due to its proximity to residential areas, the Jefferson County Airport, 4 miles south of Port Townsend, serves the county year-round.

Republican 'to the core'

Meantime, McCurdy labored to produce a newspaper for the Key City for another two decades after the reorganization.

McCurdy, a "Republican to the core," often editorialized about the area's natural resources. One example was his opinion piece on Feb. 17, 1955, on the 50th anniversary of the U.S. Forest Service.

A government agency of which Americans can be proud, and of which means much to the Jefferson County area, is celebrating its fiftieth birthday this month.

It was fifty years ago that Theodore Roosevelt and Gifford Pinchot organized an agency to preserve what was left of the fast-diminishing American forests.

We in Jefferson County have since had the opportunity to see what careful management of our national forest land can mean. Most of the Olympic National Forest is within the county's confines.

Not only has the forest been administered and protected in systematic and commendable manner, but this area has, in addition, received millions of dollars in benefits — both in payroll to forest service employees and to logging operations on the national forest, and in funds returned to the county for exclusive purpose of maintaining and improving roads and schools.

Two months later, on March 10, 1955, McCurdy's editorial praised the volunteer effort that helped erect a new church building.

Two years ago, members of Grace Lutheran Church decided they must have a new place of worship, better Sunday School quarters and facilities for their meetings and social events.

They were able to raise less than half of the funds needed and decided the only way they could get the amount of building they wanted was to build it themselves.

Services Sunday will mark a new high point in Lutheranism in Port Townsend. The dedication rites will be a truly heart-warming event for the hard-working congregation, of which the community can be proud.

The Lutherans will dedicate the handsome new church built entirely with volunteer labor in a method well known to our forefathers, but now vanishing from the American scene.

The project has been unique in that not one dime was paid for the jobsite labor on a building which has a value of over $35,000, including the property. Thousands of hours of purely voluntary work by non-professional builders went into the project. Not only does Port Townsend have a new House of God, but it also has a monument to the hard-working, co-operative spirit of a wholesome segment of its population."

In the *Leader's* 100th anniversary section (1989), reporter Daline writes that McCurdy remembered the days when the paper was printed on a 4-page flatbed press. When power went out and stayed off for days, it presented problems, but McCurdy had the solution.

Recruit some big husky roustabouts from the street to turn the flywheel of the press by hand.

In another improvisation, Daline writes:

One day in the mid-1950s the main gear of the press snapped. Dick, being very conscious of the fact that the Leader *never missed an issue in its history, called Western Gear Works in Seattle at closing time. The manager of the business said Port Townsend would have to wait a week.*

McCurdy pleaded, saying not one issue had been missed since Oct. 1, 1889. Finally, the manager relented, promising to put on a night shift, McCurdy

*rented a pickup truck and one of his employees, Jack Mullen, took the broken
gear into Seattle and waited until a new one was made.*

*The whole staff had been alerted to be available by 5 a.m. when Jack
returned from Seattle with the new gear, McCurdy recalled. "The paper was
out on time, thereby keeping its record perfect.*

The staff in the 1950s was small and dedicated. At times, there were
only two people in front, the office manager and Dick, who handled all the
news and advertising. He did everything except keep the books, and when
the office manager needed a vacation, he did that, too. It was common for
McCurdy to work 100-hour weeks.

The *Leader* had three full-time employees in back: plant supervisor
Claude Mitton, a linotype operator and an apprentice. The *Leader* did
a lot of job work in those days, printing for Crown Zellerbach, a bank,
the telephone book and some out-of-state firms. On those occasions,
additional help was hired.

In the 1950s, the *Leader* would hire two men, Tom Camfield and Peter
Simpson, who also would catapult their journalistic skills into authorship
as historians of Port Townsend.

Camfield authored *Port Townsend: An Illustrated History of Shanghaiing,
Shipwrecks, Soiled Doves and Sundry Souls*, in 2000 and followed that with
his second volume of city history, *Port Townsend, the City That Whiskey
Built*, in 2002.

Simpson wrote *City of Dreams: A Guide to Port Townsend*, in 1986 and
co-authored *Days That Are Gone* with James Hermanson in 1979. He also
wrote *Victorian Port Townsend*, a 46-page pictorial in 1961.

First century celebration

On May 17, 1951, the *Leader* produced a 44-page special section
celebrating Port Townsend's 100th anniversary. McCurdy had a lot of
help for this effort. He recruited one of the top reporters to ever grace the
peninsula, William D. "Billy" Welsh, for years a reporter, then managing
editor and later even co-owner of the *Port Angeles Evening News*. In 1939,
he left the newspaper to work in public relations for Crown Zellerbach in
San Francisco.

With Crown owning a mill in Port Townsend, McCurdy had direct access to Welsh, even though his office was in San Francisco. No doubt, he told Welsh to write everything he could about the founding of Port Townsend. The article, "Saga of Port Townsend," spanned 20 standard-size newspaper pages and left no stones unturned. In addition, the section was resplendent with dozens of historical photos of early days in the city.

Before getting into a bit of Welsh's reporting, the *Leader*'s front page also pointed out to its readers that the Key City's Centennial celebration was the second for folks who were in the city in 1892.

That was the centennial marking the day when Capt. George Vancouver first discovered the area, where Port Townsend would be settled 59 years later. He named the site after the Marquis Townshend in England.

McCurdy writes from the *Leader* of that day:

For on May 12, 1892, there was prominently reported on the front page of The Port Townsend Leader *a masterly written record of that event by this newspaper's editor of 59 years ago, W.H. Dennis. It was called, similarly, the Centennial Celebration, 1792-1892, and gay indeed was the throng of visitors who came from all points of the Puget Sound to be the guests of folks of that day who called our Key City home.*

They joined to pay tribute and commemorate the discovery by Captain George Vancouver of this site he named Port Townsend and his subsequent exploration and naming of Puget Sound as well as many, many other prominent landmarks.

Welsh exhibited a bit of literary prose in his introductory lead.

This is the saga of Port Townsend. It is a history of the town and its people. But more than that, it is a case record. To the inquiring mind the tale of this city symbolizes an American epic. ... It delineates the spirit that founded, settled and advanced America. Values of independence, courage, hope and strength are found in abundance as this saga unfolds. These were the resources that settled and welded the United States. They are the culture and heritage that have been given to us. If we apply them with a touch of the old spirit in Port Townsend and in America, there will be no need for the garb of dissatisfaction and disillusionment. New frontiers will open, and pioneering will not vanish.

Welsh writes of Juan de Fuca, a Greek mariner in the service of the

Viceroy of Mexico, commissioned in 1592 to explore the west coast of the New World, discovered by Christopher Columbus a century before.

When de Fuca sailed through the strait later named for him and saw people clad in skins, he determined the land was fruitful and rich in gold, silver, pearls and other valuables. He was convinced he had discovered the fabled Straits of Anian, the connecting link between the Pacific and Atlantic oceans.

Explorers who followed him essentially discredited de Fuca and proclaimed his voyage was a myth.

However, another Englishman, Capt. John Meares, who entered the strait in 1788, was convinced it was de Fuca's waterway and named the great sound for the explorer Peter Puget.

It would be more than 50 years after Capt. Vancouver's discovery before Port Townsend would have its first white settlers, though Indians had previously inhabited the area.

Welsh colorfully describes the fire that burned within Alfred A. Plummer, an unemployed harness-maker from Boston, 3,000 miles from his eventual destination.

Through a circuitous route, Plummer found his way to Texas, then joined the Army as quartermaster to obtain free passage to Mazatlán, Mexico. From there, he sailed to San Francisco and on to Port Townsend.

As he sailed toward the Olympic Peninsula, he pointed to his friend onboard, Charles Batchelder, and said that harbor is "one of the finest on the coast; it would make an excellent townsite."

The "Saga of Port Townsend" reveals on April 24, 1851, Plummer and Batchelder in a borrowed canoe, arrived on shore to an unceremonious greeting from the Klallam and Chimakum tribes that inhabited the district that, as Welsh describes, were "fickle in their disposition — friendly and childlike and suspicious and sullen in turn. They spoke 'Chinook jargon,' an Indian-English form of expression introduced to them by traders of the Hudson Bay Company."

The Plummer-Batchelder cabin was built in 1851 by Alfred Plummer. It was the first structure erected in the city. *(Leader archives)*

Two of Port Townsend's founders: Alfred J. Plummer, right, filed the first land claim in Port Townsend in 1851, then built the first house, known as the Plummer-Batchelder cabin. Francis Pettygrove, left, built the First American National Bank in 1960. *(Tom Camfield)/Port Townsend: An Illustrated History of Shanghaiing, Shipwrecks, Soiled Doves and Sundry Souls)*

The archives of the Land Office at Olympia revealed that only Plummer's land stake was filed on April 24, 1851, six months before the founding of Seattle. It is recognized as the founding of Port Townsend by Plummer. Batchelder staked a claim but didn't complete the filing.

Plummer and Batchelder, with assistance from Francis Pettygrove and Loren Hastings, immediately erected a two-room log cabin with a cedar roof and a flooring of rough planks. It was located at the corner of Water and Tyler streets.

Because the cabin is known as the Plummer House, he is recognized as the founder of Port Townsend. But most sources indicate all four — Batchelder, Hastings, Pettygrove and Plummer — share the honor.

The Plummer House existed until Hastings' widow Lucinda partnered with another local businessman to erect the James and Hastings building there in 1889. That building still stands today, as does the Hastings Estate Building, less than a block away, built the same year and entirely funded by Lucinda Hastings.

This was the beginning of Port Townsend as a city. Things progressed rapidly from that point. By May of 1852, the city's population included three families and 15 bachelors; later that year, 144 blocks were platted for the city and applied for at the newly constructed post office; a small sawmill was built at Port Ludlow, milling about 3,000 board feet daily; Glen Cove was homesteaded by Albert Briggs, who would become the first customs collector.

That same year, the settlement of Dungeness began at Whiskey Flats. In December 1852, Jefferson County was carved out of Thurston County in the division of the Oregon Territory. In March 1853, Washington Territory was created, including Washington, northern Idaho and western Montana; Olympia was made the capital with Isaac Stevens named governor.

In 1854, the first customs office was established at Point Hudson, with a short interval in Port Angeles, it lasted until 1913. In Simpson's book, *Victorian Port Townsend*, he notes that the customshouse was the "center of raging controversy during those 59 years. One squabble was so violent that it took the action of President Lincoln to settle it.

"Years later, President Cleveland commented that the district had caused more discord and annoyance than all other districts combined."

Because shipping activity was so great, agents and consuls of Great Britain, France, Norway, Sweden, Chile, Germany and Hawaii were located at Port Townsend.

How important was the maritime industry to the city?

The Nov. 3, 1889, issue of the *Port Townsend Argus*, one of the city's earliest newspapers, reports "Shipping grew to such proportions that the Key City was second only to New York City in the United States."

South of the city, in Chimacum, dairy farms were established; other farms specialized in vegetables and other agriculture.

Returning to "Saga ...," Welsh writes that Hastings also was instrumental in erecting the first school in Port Townsend on property he purchased. In 1854, he also brought in John Hall from Portland, Ore., to become the first school teacher. The first school, a log cabin near Hastings Pond, was moved a couple of times and eventually burned down in 1855. Capt. H.L. Tibbals donated property at the corner of Franklin and Harrison streets to replace the one that burned.

After a series of male instructors, Miss Sarah Cheney of Seattle, who had been the instructor at the new University of Washington, was recruited to teach Port Townsend youngsters.

Capt. Enoch Fowler arrived in town in 1854 and later donated two lots to build a more permanent school on Lawrence Street in 1874.

When gold was discovered in the Fraser River Valley in 1858, it brought thousands of newcomers to the city. Many stayed even after the strike bottomed out.

One of those who arrived from San Francisco was H.B. Mastick, who then trekked out to Port Discovery and established the area's first sawmill. It employed about 300 workers, many living in Port Townsend. They had no way to get to work until Mastick and his crew blasted a tortuous road from the Key City. That road was not straightened until the Olympic Highway was completed in 1931.

The area's first general mercantile was the "Kentucky Store," established in 1858. Built by D.C.H. Rothschild, it carried everything from "needles to anchors." Soon after, Solomon Katz and Sigmund Waterman opened a store at Water and Adams streets.

The next year, the city's first newspaper, the *Port Townsend Register*, was established by Travers Daniel and Dr. Samuel McCurdy.

That year, 1859, two legislative motions failed: a proposal to move the capital of the Washington Territory from Olympia to Vancouver and an attempt to build the state's penitentiary at Port Townsend.

In 1858, Charles Eisenbeis and family arrived, and he established the Cracker Bakery along Water Street in Port Townsend. He added a saloon, a flour shop, then in consort with J.F. Blumberg, became the city's first promoter. More saloons, rooming houses (brothels) and a restaurant were added. His buildings — some taken down and rebuilt — would later become the Eisenbeis Block.

Eisenbeis, the city's first industrial real estate agent, was elected Port Townsend's first mayor in 1860. Francis Pettygrove, one of the city's celebrated founders, established the First American National Bank in the Eisenbeis Block. The builder, however, ran out of funds before he could complete the structure and the third and fourth floors were not completed until later.

Charles Eisenbeis, Port Townsend's first building entrepreneur, erected the Manresa Castle in 1875. *(Tom Camfield)/Port Townsend: An Illustrated History of Shanghaiing, Shipwrecks, Soiled Doves and Sundry Souls)*

Presidential visits

In September 1880, President Rutherford B. Hayes made the first presidential visit to the peninsula, though years later (1937) media and civic leaders claimed it was Franklin D. Roosevelt who first set foot on the peninsula when he visited Port Angeles and Lake Crescent.

"When President Hayes stepped from a steamer at Port Townsend he found the entire population at tidewater to greet him. Dressed in their best bibs and tuckers, school children abandoned their studies for the day and joined their mothers and fathers at the wharf," Welsh reports.

The noise was deafening with cheers for the nation's leader. People were jammed in so deep that the trombone player in the school band had trouble playing "Hail to the Chief." The crowd was ecstatic when Hayes stepped onto the scroll-embroidered porch of the Central Hotel and told how glad he was to be in Port Townsend.

Four years later, Sen. Benjamin Harrison, Republican from Indiana, would visit Port Townsend. Four years after that, in 1888, he would be elected the 23rd president of the United States.

The decade of the 1880s would end the lives of three of Port Townsend's pioneers — Loren Hastings, 1881 at 67; Alfred Plummer, 1883 at 61; and Francis Pettygrove in 1887 at 75.

They had landed on a lonely beach but built a prospering community.

Peter Simpson wrote about a "City of Dreams;" Tom Camfield "The City that Whiskey Built." Who was right? Perhaps both.

Settled on the heels of the Gold Rush, there were hopes that Port Townsend would thrive as the largest port on the West Coast, a gateway to the Northwest. It was a "City of Dreams" to be sure, but reality made it more like the "City of Nightmares." The gold boom fizzled quickly, the promise of a railroad connecting Port Townsend with Portland never materialized, the Civil War and a subsequent recession in 1893, sent the entire nation into a tailspin.

Meantime, Anne Kazel-Wilcox, for the travel website: *TravelSquire. com*, aptly describes what became reality.

Transient sailors, soldiers and miners converged in saloons along the wharfs; contraband was plentiful; parlors of ill repute even more so. It was sin at sea level. Take that seagoing lore in the town, add in Victorian architecture at every turn, update it with a plethora of art, music and boating festivals, and Port Townsend becomes a modern-day city of dreams for getaways on the Olympic Peninsula.

Noted author visits

One of the transients was 21-year-old John Griffith "Jack" London, who on July 28, 1897, booked passage from San Francisco bound for Canada's Klondike region, along with gold stampeders.

City of Dreams recalls the legend that also is posted at the Jefferson County Historical Museum, of the-then unknown Jack London, who disembarked at Port Townsend and was delayed there overnight. What transpired that night is a story of legends, though not clearly documented, the story persists that he spent one night in the basement jail of the Port Townsend City Hall.

His year in the Yukon provided him with experiences on which he built a career of fame, later writing the classic *The Son of the Wolf, White Fang* and three years later, his best-seller *Call of the Wild*, among the 11 books he penned.

From *City of Dreams*, Simpson writes:

Certainly, there were diversions on Water Street that could lead a careless man into trouble with the law, but with his half-sister's elderly and ailing husband as his partner, it's questionable that he chose to pursue such pleasures.

More likely, they took a cheap hotel or slept on the beach and simply waited out the twenty-four hours. In later years, London was quoted as saying, 'I never realized a cent up there (in the Klondike). Still, I have been managing to pen out a living ever since on the strength of the trip.' Much could be said for Port Townsend about the benefit it gained from his overnight stay.

Camfield's account is similar, though not as detailed. He did note that no documentation has been found as to why he ended up in jail, allowing it to "youthful boisterousness." He does, however, document that London was in Port Townsend. Camfield published a photo of London aboard the schooner *Emilie* with the courthouse clearly visible in the background. He could have stopped in the city on the way back from the Klondike the next year.

However, a bit more research into his biography uncovers more enlightening information.

Todayinhistory.org relates:

"Hollywood always portrayed him as a defenseless, threadbare youngster when he arrived in the Yukon. Not so, he was an oyster pirate, an accomplished seaman, a socialist sympathizer and a hard drinker."

In 1893, as a 17-year-old who dropped out of school, London joined a march of unemployed workers and was jailed for vagrancy for a month. After that, he decided to earn his high school equivalent certificate and then attended U.C. Berkeley for a year, dropping out to search for gold in the Klondike.

Another interesting note is that he wouldn't make the journey until his brother-in-law James Shepherd grubstaked the voyage by mortgaging his home. But he would only do that if he could accompany Jack. London relented, even though Shepherd was of poor health.

It was more likely, too, that London stopped at Port Townsend on his return trip as the pair sailed north aboard the bark *Umatilla*, but the photo of London at the museum clearly shows him aboard the *Emilie*. Adding credence to that notion is that Shepherd didn't make the return trip with London, instead a couple of months into the Yukon in search of gold, his health failed, and he booked an early passage home.

That would leave the rowdy, hard-drinking 22-year-old London free to cavort when the ship landed at Port Townsend. A life of drunkenness accompanied him throughout his years as an author. He died of liver failure at age 40 in 1916.

While young Jack may have disdained the pursuit of pleasure on that trip, the bawdy life was rampant in Port Townsend, much like most port cities, where sailors or loggers cavorted.

Uptown society in Port Townsend's early years had a saying that "sin flourishes at sea level." Those who dwelled on the hill, shopped on the hill, established their schools and churches on the bluff in what Simpson calls "the rarified air of assumed purity, away from the soiled quarters of the other element downtown."

At the height of the maritime years (later 1890s and into the 1910s), saloons outnumbered all other types of businesses in Port Townsend. Initially, the sailors' bordellos, staffed primarily by half-breeds and white women, were located at Port Hudson. Captains and mates had their own brothels (mostly white women) up against the hill identified as "female boardings."

Simpson writes of one account in which an old sailor reminisced about his life as a young man in port:

In the evenings, we went down to Water Street and visited the bars. We sit for a while in the honky-tonk and order a few beers. Now and then a half-breed woman would come out on the platform and try to sing, and we would clap and jeer. On the sides of the big room were chicken coops, the management called 'boxes.' Painted old whores sat in these boxes, trying to get the sailors to sit with them. After the honky-tonk, we would visit the whorehouses and finish off the evening in the gin mills.

Victorian homes

Despite the recessive economy, the city's pioneers and their kin built lavish Victorian mansions. The first of big homes, though not the largest, was erected by D.C.H. Rothschild in 1868. He had established the Kentucky Store mercantile shop a decade earlier.

In 1875, successful gold miner and sea merchant Henry Morgan bought property (now known as Morgan Hill) and constructed his Victorian-era house on Tyler Street.

Eisenbeis, the city's first mayor, built a magnificent mansion for his wife Kate on what would become known as "Castle Hill." The 30-room structure with 12-inch thick walls, was patterned after the Prussian castles in Eisenbeis' homeland. The bricks he used were made in his brick and kiln factory at Point Wilson.

According to a report in the *Leader* in 1897, their son Charles Jr. "was despondent and shot himself in the head in the building." Some claim the ghost of this man haunts what would become Manresa Castle. Eisenbeis died in 1902, his wife remarried and moved out. The home was empty for about 20 years.

In 1925, a Seattle attorney rebuilt the edifice, which afforded a beautiful view overlooking the town and the harbor, to provide a vacation resort for visiting nuns.

That didn't last and two years later, Jesuit priests bought it as a training college. They renamed it "Manresa Castle" combining the hometown of the Jesuit order founder Ignatius Loyola in Spain and the previous castle. They operated it until 1968 when it was renovated into a hotel. It has had several owners in the past half-century.

Eisenbeis also erected a huge hotel on the bluff in 1890 and Joe Saunders added a magnificent mansion in 1891.

While it was an immense structure, it wasn't the tallest on the hill. In 1890, the four-story wooden St. John Hospital was built with a view even Eisenbeis coveted. He did have a hand in the building, however. He and Joe Kuhn donated the land to the Sisters of Charity of Providence for the city's first hospital. Kuhn and Eisenbeis owned every strip of land on the hill.

Its location was praised in the *Morning Leader* for its view of Port Townsend Bay, stating that the view from the upper stories "is one of rare beauty, inspiring in the hearts of the afflicted a feeling of peace and quiet."

The hospital, with its three towers, is prominent in early photos of the hill. Cost of the building was approximately $50,000.

Linnea Patrick, former Port Townsend librarian, writes a column "Back When" for the *Peninsula Daily News*. On Feb. 17, 2017, her column featured the hospital.

The Sisters of Charity of Providence sent two nuns, Sister Mary Conrad and Sister Mary of Nazareth, to Port Townsend on June 30, 1890, with the intention of starting a hospital for this already flourishing city. They initially rented a two-room house and began treating patients and soliciting donations. Many citizens seemed happy to contribute because there was no other general hospital in Port Townsend at that time.

Sister Mary Conrad later said, "There were big donations and little gifts. Someone gave a cow; others sent vegetables and fruit. Donations came from as far away as Chimacum and Whidbey Island."

The Sisters immediately began to plan a hospital building, and once they had the site selected, they were provided with a plan by Mother Joseph.

The hospital opened with 43 patients and was expanded to 130 beds in 1929 with a brick wing at a cost $90,000. In 1942, a fire destroyed the fourth floor, but quick response saved the other floors and no injuries occurred. The fourth floor was rebuilt, and it served for another 20 years when the 1890 wood structure was razed, and a new brick building was constructed. It opened in 1965 and 10 years later, it became a county hospital. In 2016, the Jefferson Healthcare facility was added.

Another of the Victorian homes was built by George Starrett for his wife, Ann, in 1889. He was a prolific developer and noted in several sources that he "built about a house a week. I had more than 350 built," he told the *Leader.*

In 1889, Lucinda Hastings, widow of Loren Hastings and believed to be the first woman in Port Townsend, built a huge house on Cass Street. The Hastings home, built for $45,000, was reportedly "the most elegant in the city."

Other early era pioneer homes still standing include those built by Frank Bartlett (1883) at a cost of $10,000, Albert Bash (1890) and James B. Hogg (1891).

Uptown, business sprang up in clusters: The Taylor Block (1886), the Mount Baker Block (1889), and Bishop Block (1898), established when a British sailor became stranded in port, then stayed in the city.

Then there is the fabled Palace Hotel, built by Capt. Henry Tibbals in 1889. This building has a checkered past. After its early days as the premier downtown hotel, it became known in the 1920-1930s as "Palace of Sweets," referring to the "cribs" or brothels that occupied the upper floors.

Many of these Victorian homes, renovated and remodeled in recent years, are available for tours, which have been conducted since 1963. When the tours are available, the *Leader* provides details and photos for visitors.

Fort Worden erected

After the recession of 1896 and subsequent years, Port Townsend experienced a boon to its population when Fort Worden was among three fortifications erected by order of Congress. President James Polk had directed the forts be built on the Pacific Coast 52 years before. It wasn't until 1896 that construction would begin on Fort Worden, Fort Casey and Fort Flagler for the protection of Puget Sound. These forts also are known as the "Triangle of Fire."

On Aug. 16, 1973, the day Fort Worden State Park was dedicated, the *Leader* published a 24-page historical section on the fort. Reporter V.J. Gregory wrote the bulk of that section on the history of the fortification.

Fort Worden was named in the memory of Rear Admiral John Lorimer Worden, the commander of the Monitor in its historic battle with the ironclad Merrimac. On March 9, 1862, he was wounded and temporarily blinded. From 1869-1874, he would be Superintendent of the Naval Academy, then from 1875-1877, he was Commander of the U.S.'s European Squadron. He would not see the fort, named in his honor. He died in 1897, one year after construction began. He was 71.

Activity began at Point Wilson, where Fort Worden is located, in 1883 when the Wilson Lighthouse was built. Episcopalian pastor the Rev. John B. Alexander erected Alexander's Castle, utilizing bricks from Eisenbeis' brick and kiln factory, near the lighthouse.

Fort Worden officially was declared an Army post in 1902 and on May 2, the steamer *Majestic* arrived from Seattle with 87 enlisted men. The next year, 23 buildings, including barracks, were constructed. In 1904, Harbor Defense of Puget Sound was transferred from Fort Flagler to Fort Worden. During World War I, another six buildings were constructed. In 1921, a balloon hangar was added.

Worden remained an Army installation until 1953 when it was decommissioned. Five years later, it was re-opened as a juvenile diagnostic and treatment center. In 1965, Fort Worden was acquired as a state park; in 1973, Centrum was founded as a nonprofit arts and education organization and the Puget Sound Coast Artillery Museum was opened.

In 1981, the Marine Science Center was dedicated; a year later the Commanding Officers Headquarters Museum opened; in 2002, Fort Worden celebrated its centennial, and today, along with camping facilities, folks can stay in a few of the barracks' buildings.

We'll revisit this facility later in this chapter.

Tom Camfield arrives

Camfield began his career with the *Leader* in 1944, when, as a sophomore at Port Townsend High School, he was hired as a "printer's devil" intern under Claude Mitton. "I quickly learned a lot from Claude and jammed a lot of work into my limited hours," said Camfield in a 2015 interview and on his personal blog, "The Newspaper Years."

His "newspaper career" started much earlier when he was a carrier boy for the *Seattle Star* and later the *Seattle Times*. When he started at the *Leader*, he said he worked 4-6 p.m. weekdays, 9-noon on Saturdays, and sometimes on print days, which were Wednesday.

He said those were the days of "old-style, type-high composition, hand-set type (letter by letter) and hand-fed presses. As many as three of us hand-fed various-sized sheets into a clanking old machine that folded the newspaper after it was printed."

He said 12 pages were the norm, but occasionally there were 16 pages, which required stuffing two 8-page folded sections by hand.

Much of the work Camfield did in the days as a printer and pressman required a bit of danger. "When I crawled into its interior to oil that big old press, I first had to remember to remove and set aside the handle with which it was started."

Among the work he did was to cast advertising illustrations out of hot, lead-based metal, then trim them on a metal saw and finish them with a router. "All of which explains why I had to go before the Superior Court judge with my mother and obtain a work permit at age 15."

Camfield said "Our publisher was Raymond Olney Scott. He was a Port Townsend native — a short, balding, cigar-smoking man who whistled quite a bit (but couldn't stand it from others)."

He said pay in those days was about 40 cents an hour and noted "Pay throughout my 44-plus years, was consistently poor, so whatever the rewards, they were not material."

News editor for Scott was Dick McCurdy, who was called into the Army while Camfield was a printer. Camfield remained at the *Leader* during his high school years but left in summer months following his sophomore and junior years to work at the Zellerbach mill, getting 90 cents an hour initially, and later $1.10, more than double his *Leader* pay.

Camfield worked closely with Scott, McCurdy and Mitton, but not the fourth partner, Dan Hill, who was supposed to be selling ads. "As I recall it, young Dan took to spending more time at the bar in the Legion Club than in the shops of potential advertisers and was cut adrift by the others. He later bought the newspaper in Raymond, Wash., and had a successful career there."

Camfield graduated high school in 1947, studied journalism at Washington State College for two years, then returned to the Olympic Peninsula to work as a truck driver at Fort Worden and as a clerk at Safeway, when he was hired back to the newspaper.

He returned to the *Leader* and worked 12 to 13-hour days in late 1949 and 1950, alongside Mitton. He also did some moonlighting at the *Jefferson County Journal*, a weekly that he said needed printing help. McCurdy's sister Barbara was recruited to run the Linotype and do some front-office work until Vern Sampson joined the team, Camfield added.

On Jan. 15, 1951, Camfield enlisted in the Army and was assigned to a topographic engineering battalion. He was stationed in San Francisco, and on Feb. 15, 1952, married Jean Westall. In 2018, the couple celebrated 66 years of marriage.

He was discharged from the Army in January 1953, at the Presidio of San Francisco, then completed his final years of college at U.C. Berkeley, while Jean worked at a medical center in nearby Alameda. He earned his degree in September 1954 and was immediately recruited by McCurdy to return to the *Leader*, working on the news desk as McCurdy's only assistant. He also sold some advertising and worked on the press on print days.

Camfield was given a "few minutes instruction on an old Speed Graphic camera, with 4 x 5 film, two sheets to a holder, and told to cover the town's first Applebox Derby (patterned after the unaffiliated Soapbox Derby) on Lawrence Street. I shot much of the day with the lens cap on but discovered the problem in time to get some pictures for the paper."

'Modest' McCurdy

While Camfield was gone, the publisher Ray Scott died and McCurdy "gobbled up most of the stock and promised to distribute it among the employees. We waited and waited," said Camfield. "It never happened."

Dick McCurdy is shown during a dinner celebrating an event at the Crown Zellerbach paper mill. He likely took a tour of the mill before dinner. *(Leader archives}*

Although his stature in the community loomed large with his position and many commission seats he held, McCurdy was a modest man.

In 1956, when he was named "Man of the Year" by the Port Townsend Chamber of Commerce, the resulting story in the *Leader*, which he likely wrote, mentioned him only once. The remainder of the 2-column piece was devoted to William A. Bugge, a Jefferson County native, who the chamber also honored that night as "Man of the Year" for his part in the planning and development of the Hood Canal Bridge.

The bridge officially is called "William A. Bugge Bridge after the man who was the state's director of transportation and highways during the planning and construction. He was director when the bridge opened. The *Leader* story in August 1961, noted that the bridge was steeped in controversy.

The *Port Angeles Evening News* reported in its Aug. 17, 1961, issue under the headline "Extinguished (sic) gathering totals 5,000." A caravan of 60 cars from Port Townsend and Port Angeles trekked to the bridge. In separate vehicles, the high school bands from Port Angeles, Port Townsend, Chimacum and North Kitsap played during the ceremonies. The paper reported one family, which crossed the bridge in their car, all wore life preservers.

Camfield had his eye on buying a newspaper, if not the *Leader*, then another. But he dismissed the idea of acquiring a dying paper in Eastern Washington, and debunked Dorothy Munkeby's "horrendous" price tag of $40,000 to buy the *Sequim Press*.

Instead, Camfield, married with one child, left for California in 1958. He purchased a small weekly, *The Record*, at Greenville, which he operated virtually as a one-person staff for a couple of years.

In his blog, he states that "those years in California were perhaps my best journalistic years," though they didn't involve much honing of his writing skills.

In 1960, Camfield returned to the *Leader*, this time earning $600 a month, compared with the $100 a week he had earned when he left the paper two years previous.

"Dick McCurdy had some personal problems and he and his wife were preparing a sojourn which lasted a couple of years to the island of Mallorca in the Mediterranean. He lured me from California with promises to sell me the paper, and I returned in September of 1960 to become managing editor," recalled Camfield in a 2015 interview.

Before leaving, McCurdy also promoted Jerry Simpson to assist Camfield in the news department. Simpson first appeared on the masthead as assistant editor to McCurdy in March 1960, but he had been with the *Leader* since December 1959. Camfield returned from California and appears on Oct. 13, 1960, as managing editor with Simpson as assistant.

Prior to leaving, McCurdy purchased a new Ludlow Typographic machine to improve its production.

McCurdy explained the process for *Leader* readers.

The system uses molds, known as matrices or mats, which are hand-set into a special composing stick. The device casts bars, or slugs of type, out of metal primarily consisting of lead. These slugs are used for printing, and then are melted down and recycled on the spot. The true worth of the Ludlow lies in the fact that the printer always has fresh, clean type to print from, and never has to worry about running out of fonts.

In addition to making new type-faces available for use in Leader advertising, news and job printing, it also will allow the casting of line of type in larger sizes, eliminating hand assembly of type still required by the limitation of Linotypes.

He introduced the readers to the new equipment with a full-page explanation and a series of photos with second-generation printer Terry Mitton, son of Claude, doing the honors.

McCurdy gone 19 months

McCurdy left in December, leaving the paper's management to Camfield as editor and Simpson as his assistant the entire time he was gone.

Camfield said Simpson "was heavy into the arts but did have some newspaper experience with the *Shoreline Reporter* in East Seattle from September 1958 to when he joined the *Leader.*

"So, we were a 'Tom and Jerry' duo. I continued to get in my shop time on Wednesdays, making up the pages. In those days, Jerry was very close to the arts community," Camfield recalled in his blog.

He also held out a slim hope that he might one day become a stockholder after McCurdy sold him an interest in the paper — for $1 — so he could more easily sign important documents without delay while the owner was in Europe.

The *Leader's* Centennial edition in 1989 addressed McCurdy's problems a bit differently:

By the early 1960s, Dick was beginning to feel the effects of those long hours. He had an ulcer, high blood pressure, not to mention the punctured lung from the war. He was sick, so Camfield and Simpson took over the paper for two years.

Dick McCurdy, Jr., 69, a Bainbridge Island resident when interviewed in 2017, shared still another reason for the family traveling to the island off Spain.

"Dad suffered from hypertension and a severe war injury to his shoulder. Since my sister (Catherine) was attending the University of Madrid, he decided we all needed a break. I have very fond memories of Mallorca," he continued. "My wife, Mary (Dietz), and I honeymooned there at the hotel where I used to sneak in as a 12-year-old to go swimming." They were married on Aug. 20, 1988, just 10 months after Dick Sr. died.

Dick Jr. did allow that "all families have problems and ours was no different. Mom (Eleanor) was a country girl from Montana, but she went to the University of Washington and liked the lights of the big city. Adjusting to life in Port Townsend was hard for her."

Dick Jr. was 12 and Catherine was 20 when they spent 19 months in the Mediterranean on Spain's largest Balearic Island. Dick said his dad still had his hand on the *Leader*, managing "in absentia."

Camfield said that was true. "I vividly recall that while he was over there, he wrote and strongly suggested that I desist in my editorial criticism of the local port commission manager Julien Oen. But return he did, and as before, I and the rest of the staff waited, and waited and waited for him to retire and sell us the newspaper."

Dick Jr. said his father was a normal dad who took care and pride in his family, but "he was a hard-worker and gone long hours. I looked forward to weekends. Sunday was family time."

He fondly remembers when he was 3, the Christmas card his dad designed for the family. "I was lined up to kick the football and he was holding it. He was a big sports fan."

The publisher/dad was a huge football fan and Husky season-ticket holder. "I played football at Port Townsend High School and Dad attended all the games. He would cover a lot of the games, but he was a fan and went when he didn't have to work," Dick Jr. said.

So, did Dick Jr. aspire to be a journalist? "Not at all. I wanted to be a sailor, a seaman. When he was ready to retire, he asked if I was interested in following in his footsteps. I told him rather solemnly, 'No, I am not.' He respected that. I knew the long hours he worked, and I didn't want that. I told him I wanted to be a seaman."

After earning a bachelor's degree in engineering and a master's in wood chemistry, Dick Jr. took a few years to build a boat, then became a pilot and escorted ships from Port Angeles. He had that job for 25 years before retiring in 2014.

He said as a teenager, he would carry his dad's camera bag with film and flash bulbs, and occasionally sweep the office floor for "gum balls." But that was the extent of his involvement with the *Leader*.

He has two older sisters: Catherine Chatalas, was 78 in 2018, and Betsy Lee turned 81 that year. Catherine has two children and Betsy has three. They live in Seattle.

Dick Sr. and family returned to the *Leader* in July 1962, delighting Camfield, who still held out hope he would sell him and other staff members stock in the paper.

Career-change for Simpson

Simpson stuck around until May of 1963 when he left to work a few years with the *Port Angeles Evening News*.

His son, David, a Seattle-area resident, said his dad left journalism in July of 1966 when he became director of the Community Action Council for Clallam and Jefferson counties. In June 1968, he moved to Virginia to manage a Head Start program, then in 1973, he decided to change his first name to Peter.

"He simply didn't like the name Jerry," Dave Simpson said. "His given name was John. His father's name was John, so to eliminate confusion, he was called Jerry. I think he just got tired of it and decided to change it."

In November 1978, Peter Simpson returned to Port Townsend to direct the housing program for the Community Action Council. In 1981, he became CAC director for the second time and then president of the Jefferson County Historical Society. The next year, he joined the Washington Historical Society and served as that board's president from 1988-1994. In 1999, the Port Townsend Film Festival was founded and in 2002 Simpson served as president of the board. He died on April 16, 2009, of cardiac arrest. He was 74.

The obituary, written by *Leader* reporter Kathy Meyer, praises Simpson's love for the arts. He was in the midst of planning the film festival's 10th annual celebration.

Peter shared his love and passion for the cinema as a vital contributor to the intricacies behind the film festival's silver screens.

Peter's unbridled enthusiasm for film never dimmed in the almost 10 years I came to the festival, which is amazing considering the wear and tear that film festivals can do to people," said Seattle film critic Robert Horton. "The PTFF always seems like a collective enterprise ... but Peter was unmistakably the solid center of the whole thing.

Camfield fondly recalls that Election Days were fun times in the *Leader* office. He said they would work the usual day hours on Tuesday and get everything ready for printing, take a break for dinner and return to the office.

"We ran the elections out of our office. We would stay up for 36 hours and worked all night on Tuesday. We wanted to get the late results in the paper on Wednesday. The last results would always be from the remote areas, usually Queets. The auditor, Helen Eads, would come down and hang out at the office until we got the results. We arranged to get them as soon as possible, but it was 4:30 and sometimes 6 in the morning. We'd take a break for breakfast and then get the results in the paper."

He said they didn't get any overtime pay, just the pride of getting the results in the *Leader* for the reader. The office was crowded with many people arriving to see the results.

I was also a stringer and got about $10 for calling the results to the Associated Press."

Camfield wrote about the town "That Whiskey Built," and experienced first-hand whereof he had written.

He remembers being assigned to cover the ongoing battle between the area's sports and commercial fishermen and writes in his personal blog, "The Newspaper Years:"

A fleet of purse seiner boats was scooping up a salmon run off Whidbey Island near the entrance to Admiralty Inlet. McCurdy made hurried arrangements for me to fly over and photograph the scene — as a passenger in Scotty Macfarlane's private plane. It was my first time ever aloft in any aircraft. I had to lean out the flimsy windowless side door and shoot with my bulky old-fashioned camera. I tried to get Scotty to fly low over the boats, but he feared getting shot at. Back at his one-man office (he managed Olympic

Gas Co.), we had a little scotch he kept in his desk, which was the attraction for stopping there occasionally during my weekly advertising calls.

On another occasion, Camfield writes about making weekly stops at the law offices of County Prosecutor William Daly in the Mount Baker Block. "For any reason, one, often as not, had to accompany him to the nearby Elks Club bar for his hourly pick-me-up. Printer Claude Mitton's wife Winnie worked at Bob Burnett's jewelry on Taylor Street in the back of the premises. Getting a haircut at Cal's barbershop on Taylor Street would generally involve stepping into the curtained alcove for a snort."

McCurdy's tales

In the Centennial edition in 1989, the writer Deborah Daline recalls an earlier interview with McCurdy in which he listed a few of his highlights.

One cites the day he was held hostage by the military.

It all started on a relaxed Sunday afternoon when Dick got a call about the collision of two military planes over Dabob. He leaped into his car, wife and young son along for a ride, drove to the scene and made his way through the crowd that had already collected. He went into the woods with his camera and came upon the plane wreckage. McCurdy quickly snapped some photographs.

On his way out, a State Trooper collared him and took him to the military personnel. There, he was relieved of his camera and his film and put into custody.

Later he found out there were some secret rockets on the downed plane that might have been revealed in his photos. McCurdy was not released until Air Force officers arrived from McChord Air Force Base near Tacoma, but he was allowed a telephone call.

He placed it to the Associated Press in Seattle, to whom he related the story. The wires sung that afternoon about the military infringing on the freedom of the press of a small weekly newspaper.

McCurdy received an Award of the Month from the AP for his work on another plane crash.

A small plane carrying a Seattle family went down on a ridge just south of Chimacum. The wreckage was spotted by a search plane, which directed ground searchers and McCurdy to the site. The plane had been upside down for three days, but the mother and daughter were still alive. McCurdy photographed the two being pulled from the wreck after authorities used crowbars to pull the metal apart. The father and son had died.

McCurdy was at the scene of many tragedies, in part due to Bill Haigh, a good friend who also was a State Trooper. When Haigh heard of a wreck or tragedy, one of his first moves was to radio the Patrol's Port Angeles office with instructions to call McCurdy.

One of McCurdy's favorite stories was the night Aldrich's Store was robbed. It was a scene right out of the Keystone Cops. Daline describes this incident in the 1989 Centennial edition.

The local police had been alerted by authorities in Seattle that some robbers were coming to Port Townsend to knock off a store. They knew because the Seattle police had bugged the hotel room, where one of the suspects discussed the caper. The police had the license numbers of the car and they were spotted near Discovery Bay. The robbers cruised on into Port Townsend.

The local police lost them in a crowd of football fans as they arrived at the time the game was over. Not knowing what to do next, the police decided to stake out several stores, including Aldrich's at Lawrence and Tyler streets.

P.T. Police Chief George Willestoft and his number one deputy, Tom Edington, got up on the mezzanine floor inside Aldrich's. The safe wasn't up there, but it was a good place to watch the whole store. Roy Dale, another policeman, was across the street."

They didn't have to wait long before they heard noises coming from the basement. The robbers headed straight for the stairs to the mezzanine. "Willestoft hollered for them to halt and the burglars fired, hitting a beam right over the policemen's heads. Then one of the burglars ran out the back and the other ran through the store, with Willestoft firing at him, shots hitting the floor and the refrigerator's tin pan.

The moving target let out a wild scream and dived through a 3/8-inch glass door to be met by a barrage of bullets from Dale from across the street. The terrified man managed to make his way through town and hid in a ditch overnight, then hitch-hiked back to Seattle, where he was arrested.

The other burglar, who sneaked out the back, was caught by a neighborhood dog that kept him cornered in the bushes right behind Aldrich's until the police came.

The whole town heard about the 3 a.m. robbery and came to see the commotion. What did the store manager do?

Ben Aldrich, never one to lose a business opportunity, got down there on the double, unlocked the cash register and sold Coke and candy bars," said a snickering McCurdy.

Camfield and others continued to labor long hours, holding out faint hope McCurdy might sell them stock in the paper.

That never happened.

CHAPTER 12

The next half-century:
Garreds, Wilsons, Mullens

R eaders of the *Leader* no doubt expected McCurdy to make a change. Perhaps that decision was in motion before he left for Europe. He had been a prolific editorial writer, albeit generally quite short. The opinion pages usually published two and sometimes three McCurdy editorials with each issue. The paper also, without fail, printed a masthead, including the owner/publisher; managing editor, assistant editor and business manager.

After returning from Europe, a random, but extensive sampling of papers indicated he wrote nary an editorial over a five-year period. He also failed to include the masthead in any edition over those same five years (from 1962-1967).

When McCurdy resumed his publisher's role, Camfield said he also asked for the return of the $1 interest he held. While Camfield said he still hoped he would be offered a financial interest in the paper, this gesture cemented the deal: No paper ownership for Camfield.

Five years after returning from Mallorca, McCurdy completed a transaction to sell the paper to three out-of-town businessmen — Frank Garred, Bruce Wilson and Henry Gay.

When the sale was announced in the *Leader* on Sept. 7, 1967, it marked the end of a 61-year reign by the McCurdy family.

Following his father, Winslow as owner, Richard McCurdy purchased a minority interest in the paper in 1946, then became majority stock holder and publisher in 1955 when he purchased the 16 percent owned by Claude Mitton.

Mitton, who had been with the firm since graduating from high school in 1931, continued as shop foreman under the new ownership. His son Terry, who came onboard in the late 1950s before McCurdy left for Europe, assisted his father. Terry remained with the *Leader* into the 1990s. Claude Mitton died in 1977.

Garred (et al) era begins

Frank Garred was only 31 when he became co-owner of the *Leader* with Bruce Wilson and Henry Gay in 1967. *(Courtesy of Frank Garred)*

Garred arrived in August and spent one month with McCurdy in transition. "He (Dick) stayed until Sept. 1, the day the sale took effect," said Garred in a 2015 interview. "When he left, he had nothing more to do with *Leader*."

In addition to the publishing, commercial printing and office supplies business, the sale included The Leader Co.'s pioneer building at 226 Adams St. The paper, established in 1889, moved into the Fowler Building in 1916 and has been there ever since.

According to the transaction, "Garred will be the resident publisher and president of the corporation. Wilson is publisher of the *Omak Chronicle*, which he and his wife, Merilynn, own and Bruce published from 1956-1980; he will be secretary. Wilson previously had published the *Ritzville Journal-Times* from 1947-1956. Gay is owner/publisher of the *Shelton-Mason County Journal*.

Wilson and Gay are silent partners, stockholders and members of the board, but not involved in the newspaper's weekly operation, Garred noted.

"We started negotiating with Dick about 1965. He was ready to sell and be done with it," Garred said. "I contacted Dave Averill, a friend of mine, at Poulsbo (now the *North Kitsap Herald*). We were interested, but kind of let the thing float until mid-1966 and Dick called us again."

By then, Garred said Averill was buying the paper at Bainbridge Island and backed out. Averill did put Garred and his wife Pat in touch with Gay and Wilson.

"I asked my mom for financial help. She mortgaged her house to get $10,000 for my share of the down payment," Garred said, adding that Wilson and Gay contributed the remainder to equal half of the down payment McCurdy wanted.

"We agreed to give Dick half by Sept. 7 and the remainder by Jan. 1, 1968." Garred said, since they were acquiring the building, in a bit of creative financing, they mortgaged the building to obtain the rest of the money and made annual installments to McCurdy over the next 10 years. "We never missed a payment," he said.

Garred and Wilson formed a new corporation, Port Townsend Publishing Inc., the entity that purchased from McCurdy's Leader Co.

Garred, 31, graduated from the University of Washington in 1958 with a journalism degree and a minor in business. He and Pat were married on Aug. 2, 1958, and celebrated 60 years of marriage in 2018. They have two children.

Commissioned as a 2nd Lieutenant upon graduation, Garred served two years active duty as an infantry officer in the Army, including 13 months in Korea, before completing his obligation in December 1960. He left the Army as a captain in 1973, after 13 years in the active and inactive Reserves.

Garred landed his first newspaper job as a reporter from 1960-1962 at the *Daily World* in Aberdeen, then was editor of the *Suburban Times* in Tacoma from 1962-1967 when he purchased the *Leader*.

McCurdy left the *Leader* with a reporter (Camfield), printers Claude Mitton, and his son, Terry, a bookkeeper (Laverne Horton) and Florence Judy, who punched the tape for the Linotype.

Claude Mitton was a master-printer, who ran the *Leader's* commercial job printing, which constituted a large share of the company's profits.

Garred said his first hire was his neighbor Betty Grewell in 1967. She worked at the *Leader* in various book-keeping and front-office capacities, both full-time and part-time. In 2018, she still was working there more than a half-century later.

On Sept. 7, 1967, a week after he took over the *Leader*, Garred's editorial introduced the readers to some of his policies in an opinion piece, titled "Tenor of the Leader."

"A newspaper contains ... the printed account of a moment in history — cold and impersonal at times. The community newspaper reflects the community it represents; it doesn't make the news, it just prints it.

This is not all a newspaper should be. We believe a newspaper should challenge its readers. It should print the cold facts without comment in its news columns, but it should also strive to excite the reader in its editorial columns. Here lies the distinction.

Under the new Leader *management, you will continue to read complete and comprehensive coverage of community events, objectively and accurately reported. You will also discover what we hope are thought-provoking editorials and columns, searching in depth for reasoning behind the news.*

Our readers are not expected to always agree with the Leader *point of view. What we are trying to stimulate is a community dialogue — a place where community citizens can exchange views.*

To this end, we welcome and invite letters to the editor, debating Leader *editorial opinions, discussing community issues, or just sounding off."*

Leader goes offset

The anticipated production change McCurdy feared was in process within two months of the new ownership.

"By Thanksgiving, we were creating our newspaper for offset rather than letterpress printing. The difference: We made single-page proofs from our metal-cast type proofs and screened paper photo prints," Garred explained.

"Then pages were driven to Shelton, where they were printed on what is called an offset press. The page images were transferred from aluminum plates to fast-paced rolls of newsprint, formed together into sections, cut and folded in a single run.

"The process replaced a system where pages were printed on the

Leader's flatbed reciprocal press, a lengthy manual process. The printed sheets were gathered, folded and trimmed in a second machine-manual process on equipment destined for the recycle bin, Garred continued detailing the innovation.

"Three years later, the *Leader* trashed its heavy metal equipment, shut down its metal-making pots, cleared away the production area steeped in lead-based history, and installed carpeting over the

Tom Camfield and Claude Mitton work on newspaper production in the composing department. *(Courtesy of Tom Camfield)*

old wood floor, along with the first photo-based cold-type machine. A darkroom for photo processing and page-making occupied a corner of the production area formerly shared with the huge newspaper printing press.

"A new age of newspaper production was now planted at the *Leader's* historic Fowler Building."

The production transmission might have been good for the *Leader*, but it was the eventual undoing of production foreman Claude Mitton, who gave the paper nearly a half-century of his experience. The new process, plus ill health, forced his retirement in 1975. Mitton died in 1977.

The *Leader* was not the first paper in the state to print using the offset method, but it became one of the most recognized community papers, winning awards annually from the Washington Newspaper Publishers Association.

Garred said when he took over, "some 300 people were getting the paper free. "When we purged our subscriber list, our paid circulation was 3,313. In a county of about 11,000, that wasn't a bad start. We added reporters and built the advertising. By the 1990s, circulation was over 9,000 and the county had grown to 20,000.

"The thing that was exciting was that people couldn't wait to get their paper. I'd go to the restaurant on publication days, Wednesdays, and people would be reading it, there, and at the barbershop and the library. We even had anxious readers lined up at our front door, ready to drop 10 cents for their *Leader*."

In the beginning, the paper would be eight pages, sometimes 10 and sometimes 12. "I'd drive the pages to Shelton and wait for them to be printed and processed for mailing, then drop them off at Brinnon, Quilcene, Chimacum, Discovery Bay and Port Hadlock, Nordland, Port Ludlow and be back to Port Townsend by 6 a.m."

The early-morning hours often presented hazards, such as the one in the late 1960s. Today, Garred can laugh about it, but not then.

"I had a '60 Chevy Impala that I used to bring the papers back from Shelton. That is, until I ran into a herd of cows on fog-shrouded Center Valley Road. I was damn lucky to escape injury. Even the cow I hit survived. She was pregnant, and belonged to a county commissioner, B.G. Brown. The papers did get delivered, though I bet there were a few shards of glass mixed among them. I needed a new car after that."

Civic activities

Meantime, McCurdy accelerated his civic involvement. He had been president and trustee of the Chamber of Commerce; chairman of the county Red Cross; vice president of the United Good Neighbors, crusade chairman for the county Cancer Society, board member of the First American National Bank, and when it was bought by Seattle-First National Bank, he became a member of that institution's advisory board.

In the early 1960s, he was active in a fund drive to build a new hospital; he pursued legislation to build the Hood Canal Bridge, which was completed in 1961.

He worked on several Rhododendron Festival committees since he was with the *Leader* and enjoyed being master of ceremonies for the crowning of the queen each year.

The festival, which celebrated its 82nd annual event in 2018, was started in 1936. A year before, local businessman Clive Buttermere convinced the Hearst Metrotone News organization to come to the city and film the rhododendrons in bloom. As a prelude, the city held a queen contest, so a group of young women could be photographed among the flowers. Myrtle Olsen was voted the first Rhody queen and was photographed by Hearst for short subjects released to theaters through the U.S.

The American Legion captured the spirit of the 1935 events and decided to sponsor the celebration of beauty of the rhodies in an annual event. In 1936, the first Rhododendron Festival, including a one-day parade was held.

The chamber took over the festival in the 1950s, expanding it to a week-long celebration, always the third weekend in May. Many different events were added such as a golf tournament, baseball tournament, cow-chip throwing, bed race, trike race, beard-growing contest, keg toss, pet parade, kiddies parade and many more.

When the chamber decided to step away from the festival operations, there was a struggle to find volunteers to organize and run the event. Garred said an uptown barber, Fred Lester, joined him and they formed a partnership to "restore the festival with a new corps of supporters. The independence of the new order of volunteers has sustained it since."

By the 1980s, the festival became a nonprofit corporation; Royalty rode on floats and participated in other festivals as a way of promoting Port Townsend's event. The Royalty received expenses for this as well as scholarships.

McCurdy was actively involved in promoting the arts while he was publisher of the paper and for many years after that. He was a board member of the Port Townsend Festival Theater and the Summer School of the Arts, a program that was established in the early 1960s.

Mary Johnson, a city council member, was responsible for promoting the arts festivals in Port Townsend. McCurdy once wrote in the *Leader*, describing her as "the prime mover in cultural, community development, and restoration activities. When she was not restoring old buildings, running a gallery, founding and running an arts school, or raising funds to support these projects, she was concerned with the city's future growth; a charter member and the first secretary of the Washington State Arts commission, author of children's book, published when she was 78; a poet, an artist, a farmer and cattlewoman, a puppeteer, a wife and mother of four children, a hostess, and an all-around community spark plug."

Former *Leader* employer Peter Simpson would write about Johnson in *City of Dreams: A Guide to Port Townsend:*

Mary became director of the first Summer School of Arts in 1961, supported and partially funded by McCurdy. The year before, she became acquainted with a young man who brought arts skills and knowledge to the city. Tom Wilson was the perfect foil for Johnson. She and her husband, Harry, bought and remodeled both the Bartlett Home and the Clapp Building on Water Street, their art gallery and store and two stylish Victorian mansions in the city.

In founding the arts school, she said its purposes were to "provide the best possible instruction in the arts; to provide absorbing goals for greater understanding of the arts; to explore the relationship of the arts to each other for creative accomplishment; to provide direct involvement in the arts for people of all ages; and to broaden interest in the arts in Port Townsend and the Olympic Peninsula."

Centrum established

Simpson, heavily involved in the art community, was well-acquainted with another pillar of that medium, Joe Wheeler.

The nucleus of the Summer Arts Program was melded into Centrum by 1973. Joe Wheeler worked closely with Washington State Arts Commission, the Office of the Superintendent of Public Instruction and the Parks Commission to establish Centrum at Fort Worden.

Wheeler became the founder and the executive director of Centrum for 23 years until he died in 2009. Under his direction, the program became one of the nation's pioneers in presenting week-long workshops and concerts at Fort Worden for many different art forms, including jazz, acoustic blues, chamber music and traditional folk-art programs such as "Fiddle Tunes," one of the nation's largest festivals for traditional music, Simpson wrote.

"It was about participation in the arts. Centrum was to be a program where people did not come simply to see performances: the major focus was to be that people would come and be involved in the arts; to live here and get their hands in it," ptleader.com would note in Wheeler's obituary on Nov. 2, 2009.

A few years after opening, Centrum added nationally known lecturers to its program and established Copper Canyon Press for the promotion of poetry, a language it says, "is vital and living."

Concerts are now held in the 300-seat Army Theater (now Joe Wheeler Theater) and a World War I-era dirigible hangar was renovated into a 1,200-seat concert hall, named McCurdy Pavilion, honoring the involvement of the former *Leader* publisher, Richard McCurdy. Pat Simpson, wife of Peter, also was actively involved with Centrum.

Camfield on city council

Fifteen years into his *Leader* employment, Camfield decided to make a change in his life.

"Driven by principles and the incompetence of one particular city council member, I exacerbated the plight that was my work load in 1969 and entered politics," Camfield revealed.

He was elected to the council and served for 10 years.

"It was difficult for me to stand up and speak publicly for part of the first year," he said. "But after that, I found that the rest of the council generally followed my lead on various matters."

At one point, he even was elected mayor pro-tem. From his blog, he writes that those 10 years were "one of the most difficult periods of my life. I pretty much burned up the decade of my 40s during the subsequent 10 years on the council."

Camfield served during the mayoral

> *"The earlier years were the worst, as I had to cover the meeting while sitting as a council member. Taking notes was tough, but writing the story was even more difficult."*
>
> **Tom Camfield, *Leader* reporter**

terms of Frank Smith and Joe Steve, and apparently, they were satisfied with the job he did. The public also must have agreed, for the only one to question the possible conflict of interest was the reporter himself.

"It wasn't the most ethical situation," Camfield said, "but Garred told me to cover it, anyway. I don't think he wanted to cover those meetings because they would often last well into the night, and sometimes I wouldn't get out of there until 2 or 2:30 in the morning.

"The earlier years were the worst, as I had to cover the meeting while sitting as a council member. Taking notes was tough, but writing the story was even more difficult. I maintained a measure of objectivity in my reporting by downplaying my role and making a point of quoting every other official and audience member, who participated in any particular session."

Camfield said it was a stressful time because "during my tenure, the council adopted zoning, building and fire codes, built the first sewer treatment plant, installed gas meters, turned to contract waste disposal, combined the offices of clerk and treasurer and created Pope Park," among other accomplishments.

Camfield said, until Garred eventually hired another reporter and intern, he would cover the council, the county and city hall as well as selling outside advertising, doing photography for all departments, handling sports coverage, doing ad makeup, and on press days, even page makeup.

Garred said when he took over, Earnest Phegley, the police chief, would help. "He was a photography nut and would come in late at night and develop film for us. He would even take police calls in the darkroom."

In 1973, Garred added the Compugraphic Photo Typesetter, a large computer that would expand the fonts and type used for text. A second Compugraphic was installed for larger display type.

At the same time, Western Washington University in Bellingham was trying to re-establish its journalism program. "We hooked up with them to hire an intern," Garred said. "I think Western was the first (Washington) college to require an internship for a journalism degree."

Garred cleared out the upstairs and created an apartment for the interns.

About 1975, Garred said he hired his first ad manager, Dan Huntingford, son of longtime county commissioner George Huntingford.

Reporter/photographer Tom Camfield, shown in the 1970s, started at the *Leader* in 1944 and retired in 1988. In the 1960s, he was managing editor for a time. *(Courtesy of Tom Camfield)*

"He had just graduated from Washington State University and came to me," said Garred. "I didn't have anything at the time, so I told him I'd consider it."

Garred did hire the young graduate. "I came up with a salary commission job. He was terrific and developed great ads," Garred remembered in a 2015 interview.

"We developed contracts, but also emphasized that we wanted to give advertisers we recruit the same treatment as those who had contracts."

The *Leader* suddenly began to grow — from 12 pages to 28, then 32 pages, then up to 44 and 48 pages. "Dan was so good at creating ad campaigns and getting contract ads. We also built the classified ad section," the publisher said.

Advertising dilemma

With a downturn in the economy, Safeway decided to pull its ads from the *Leader* in December 1979 and print its own circular. That was a huge jolt for a community newspaper. The grocer was running four full-page ads weekly, so what did Garred do?

"We weathered the storm. We concentrated on cultivating small ads for our local businesses, developing campaigns rather than relying on just occasional ads with instant focus. I hired a second sales ad rep, Craig Dennis, who came out of Stanford. He told me 'Here's what I want to do. I want to work here for five years, and then I'm moving on.'"

Dennis was there five years, then he bought the *Chinook Observer* on the Long Beach Peninsula.

Huntingford stayed with the *Leader* until the early 1990s, then he bought a printing business in Port Townsend.

There was a rough period for Huntingford when Garred elected not to endorse his father for county commissioner. "George had asked me to be his campaign manager," said Garred. "I told him I couldn't do it. We figured it was time for someone else."

When the Garreds moved to Port Townsend, they had two young children, a first-grade son and a daughter in pre-school. "I'd get home about 11; it wasn't much of a home life. But in the 1980s, Pat became more involved and ran our classified and legal advertising department, along with guiding our circulation program," Frank said.

He added, when his children became older, preparing the paper for mailing became a family event, joining the *Leader* staff. "Often the kids would help, but as night emerged with morning, they found comfort napping on the mail sacks in a corner as the parents toiled."

Weathering the storms

In his 35 years with the *Leader*, Garred said there were more than a few bumps in the road.

He talks about a few of them:

- "An employee in our production department adjusted an ad for a client and no one checked it out. It was a very strong error on our part. We talked to the advertiser and agreed to provide twice, if not more space to let the community know what his business was about. I kept that employee and she apologized profusely to the advertiser. She and the advertiser responded positively because the community respected the paper. I made a dangerous decision to keep that person when she disgraced our business, but it paid off."
- Most newspapers are hit occasionally with libel suits, but in the *Leader's* situation, a case in the early 1980s went on and on before the paper finally came out the winner, most likely because of its affiliation with the National Newspaper Association, whose insurance would fund the case.

"We paid the $2,500 deductible, but insurance paid almost a quarter of a million dollars in pre-trial expenses," said Garred.

In this case, the paper published a quote, attributed to a deputy, that the reporter didn't check out. "We printed that the deputy said this defendant in a child molestation case had a prior conviction. It turns out he didn't," said Garred.

Ironically, six years later, the guy was convicted of the same offense in Kitsap County. "These things happen, and you hope you learn from them. You look at the errors and become so sensitive that you are afraid of doing anything. But we didn't approach it that way. When the trial was over, we printed everything on the case."

- Another landmark case opened the closed doors of public agencies dealing with salary issues.

Garred said the case involved the Jefferson County Commissioners, who met late one afternoon and closed the session to the public and the press, announcing they were going to discuss personnel salaries, which is permitted.

"Instead, they discussed salaries for their budget, not personnel issues. They talked about the amount of money that would be allotted for various positions. We sued the county and when it came to trial, Judge Tyler C. Moffett came to me and said, 'It's stupid to go on with this. You know I'm going to rule against you.' I said, 'Probably, but let's go on with it.'"

Garred believed getting it to an appellate court, a more regional effect would be in play. "Once it got to Appeals (Court), that meant it involved Clallam, Grays Harbor, Kitsap and other west and southwest counties.

The District Court of Appeals upheld Moffett's decision. "Then, the state newspaper associations took up the battle, lobbying the state Legislature to clearly define the limits local governments had in public meetings. The Legislature acted. Salary discussions were open to the public," Garred said.

The decision was based on precedent from the Public Disclosure Act adopted by the voters in 1972 and the Open Public Meetings Act in 1971.

Garred apparently reveled in holding the Jefferson County Commissioners' feet to the fire. When they went astray, the publisher was there to take them to task as he did with other Jefferson County and local public boards, commissions, councils and committees.

One such example was in the *Leader* on July 26, 1973, the same year he was elected president of the Chamber of Commerce. "That was quite a deal for this 36-year-old 'kid' to be head of these old-line chamber guys," Garred marveled. It also was the year Garred served the Washington Newspaper Publishers Association as president, the youngest to that point in WNPA history

In the editorial, titled "Wake up, Commissioners," in this issue, the county panel apparently tried to get away with a clandestine meeting in which an important decision was made.

They should have known better than and try and pull one over on Garred.

"Our Jefferson County Commissioners appear to meet each Monday to solve the county's problems.

Two even meet clandestinely to plot their political maneuverings and apparently to set their course for future commission action — such as hiring of a professional planner. We haven't seen, nor heard discussion at regular commission meetings on any criteria for the addition of a planner, or a job description.

Yet, commissioners A.M. O'Meara and B.G. Brown introduced their "favorite" candidate to the planning commission last week.

Where is the commission decision to establish a full-time planning post? If any exists, it was made at one of those "Thursday" lunches or study sessions O'Meara and Brown have been holding behind the scenes.

Also emerging is more and more speculation on the development of a 'multi-service center' for Jefferson County. We attended one such 'think' session on the subject, called by the Clallam-Jefferson County Community Action Council. But the subject has been rather prominent by its absence from general county commission discussion — except, again, behind the scenes.

Later, in the same issue, the publisher attacks the "service center playfield," saying, in that location, it would "detract from the open, attractive view the courthouse presents."

On another issue, he accuses the panel of being naïve to the problems that a proposed Trident development would present, calling attention to its negative impact on schools, basic utilities and services, such as sewer.

Our county commissioners should be taking the lead in discovering answers to these questions, and to confirm or reject some of the speculation going on ... It's about time our county commissioners quit their gamesmanship and behind-the-scenes manipulation. And, it's about time the commissioners WAKE UP

> *"So-called secret meetings are easy to deny, hard to prove. It is a minor thing as done in Jefferson County. Misappropriation of funds is a potentially disastrous thing."*
>
> **Frank Garred, Leader**
> **publisher**

and discover that those Monday meetings are something more than a time and place to take a nap.

On Aug. 22, 1974, Garred noted that it is the *"Leader's* duty to point out irregularities in the administration of a public office, calling attention to the secret meetings the commissioners continue to have.

"So-called secret meetings are easy to deny, hard to prove. It is a minor thing as done in Jefferson County. Misappropriation of funds is a potentially disastrous thing."

Such was the issue in this editorial.

That the five percent cost-of-living raise for the county employees has been surrounded by irregularities is a fact.

The raise was paid without an authorizing resolution, which is a misappropriation of funds. Verbal authorization was given to pay the raise before the commissioners' regular public meeting in a fashion purposely designed to go undetected by members of the public who were present.

After several paragraphs, he declares the action:

… Was not an accident, but a foolish judgment by the auditor to allow the commissioners to disregard the established money-handling procedures. It was a mistake by the treasurer to accept the faulty warrants that were made out without going through the proper procedures.

Spending money is a serious business. Spending tax money is an even more serious business. One mistake has been made. Rather than forgive and forget, let us forgive and remember. There is no room for a second mistake of this kind.

Wooden Boat Festival

In 1977, Port Townsend was crawling with boats — commercial and recreational fishing boats, small motor boats, speed boats, an occasional tri-master, and lots of wooden craft.

That's when Sam Connor and Mary Kearn, with help from Tim Snyder and Gail Glassen, took what sounded like a wild idea and ran with it, establishing the first Wooden Boat Festival. Today, that event is one of many reasons visitors flock to the Key City. Held the second week in September, it has expanded to include educational programs, boat-building, lectures, a chandlery, maritime library and boat shop.

In 1981, capitalizing on the popularity of the boat festival, the Northwest School of Wooden Boat Building was established by Robert Prothero, Libby Palmer and Henry Yeaton, at the Boat Haven in Port Townsend.

It has been at several sites over its 36-year history, locating at Port Hadlock in 2004, where at the turn of the 20th century, wooden schooners were built to transport lumber to California. The land for this school was donated by Capt. John and Evelyn Westrem. In 1988, Jeff Hammond became chief instructor, a position he has held for more than 30 years. In 1991, the school began an associate degree program.

Garred pointed out that the Port Townsend Publishing Co. managed a book-publishing venture, Quimper Press, from the mid-1970s through the mid-1990s. "That unit published several historical books including *Keepers at the Gate*, by local historian V.J. Gregory, encapsulating the history of Fort Worden; *Marrowstone*, a history by island residents Karen Russell and Jeanne Bean; *Port Townsend: Years That Are Gone* by Peter Simpson and James Hermanson, and reprinted the historical novel *Dub of South Burlap* by Quilcene *Megaphone* Publisher-Editor Brandon Satterlee.

Jim Whittaker

In 1983, Port Townsend was back on the map once again when Jim Whittaker and his second wife, Dianne Roberts, purchased property in the city.

Twenty years prior, on May 1, 1963, Whittaker became the first American to summit the 29,029-foot Mount Everest. Only Whittaker and Sherpa Nawang Gombu, among the 20 who began the expedition, reached the summit. They were out of oxygen and suffered from frostbite, but persevered until Whittaker planted the United States flag at the summit.

Gombu was the nephew of Tenzing Norgay, the Sherpa who accompanied Edmund Hillary, a British mountaineer, who was the first to summit Everest in 1953.

Whittaker had retired as CEO and president of Recreation Equipment Inc. (REI), where he began work as a salesman when he was 25. He and Roberts, who was his photographer for *National Geographic*, in 1978, would be the first Americans to reach K-2's 28,250-foot summit.

After retiring from REI, Whittaker built his Port Townsend dream home, a 6,000-square-foot edifice, he called "Log Mahal." They sold the home in 1996, bought a 53-foot steel-hulled ketch named *Impossible* and sailed 20,000 miles around the world, the website historylink.org notes.

They returned to Port Townsend, and even after double-knee replacement surgery, Whittaker was skiing in 1981. He also was an active public speaker stressing that "life is an adventure and nature is the best teacher. My thirst is to get people out. I tell them there should be no child left inside."

In 2018, Whittaker, 89, and Roberts, 20 years younger, still make their home in the Key City.

Paper's name change

On Oct. 14, 1987, Garred made a change to the paper's name, something he said people from the south end of the county had vehemently been suggesting for months.

In the previous issue, a letter to the editor headline "South County Residents Feel Slighted By Coverage," highlighted several times that the Quilcene writer felt the *Leader* "slighted" the south county, including the fair and sports activities with only minimal coverage.

The writer, charged with the responsibility of submitting photos, articles and suggestions to the *Leader*, said she "came under fire" because of the coverage.

Whether this letter was the tipping point or not doesn't matter, but the very next issue, the paper became forever named the *Port Townsend Jefferson County Leader*, the first change in the paper's name since 1934.

South County coverage improved and areas such as Brinnon and Quilcene were no longer "treated like a stepchild," as the letter writer called it.

Tribute to 'Mr. Port Townsend'

Nov. 4, 1987, was a somber day in Port Townsend. Retired publisher Richard McCurdy died after a month-long illness.

Nearly 300 people gathered at the First United Presbyterian Church to honor the man, who had been editor, publisher and owner of the *Leader* for 31 years until selling the paper to Garred 20 years before his death.

Peter Simpson, who was briefly assistant editor of the *Leader*, was charged with writing the obituary as a contributing writer. Tributes flowed for the 76-year-old Port Townsend native, who was memorialized in the same church where his father, Winslow McCurdy, was eulogized nearly 60 years before.

"How do you get to know a person? I don't really know. Maybe 40 years does it. We're all very complex; we're all different types of people. Dick was one the most complex people I've ever known," said long-time school superintendent Gael Stuart, who had been friends with McCurdy for more than 40 years.

In 1956, McCurdy was named "Man of the Year" by the chamber and in 1960, Stuart was accorded the same honor.

"He was loyal, but skeptical; loving, but critical; stable, but changeable; proud, but modest; serious, but humorous; hard-working, but he enjoyed life and he loved recess."

Stuart then shared a humorous event that occurred in their long relationship.

"Dick was proud of the fact that he had what he thought was the perfect garden in town." He was proud of the many zinnias that he gave to various activities and to visitors on the Victorian homes tours.

'You know Gael, you realize that you can tell a lot about a man by the looks of his garden, how he keeps his garden,' and then he handed me a dandelion out of mine."

Stuart said Dick was proud of the McCurdy family as he pointed out the relatives seated in the front pews of the church.

Among them was a cousin, Horace W. McCurdy, who became a prominent Seattle industrialist, shipbuilder, maritime promoter and bridge-builder. Nine years before he was honored when the Northwest Maritime Center in Port Townsend was named for him

Joe Wheeler, director of Centrum Foundation, of which Dick was a charter board member and one of its early presidents, turned to a foreign language to describe his friend.

"The French have an expression, *la joie de vivre*, which means the joy of living. I can think of no one who exemplified the joy of life more than Dick McCurdy.

"… The breadth of his activities within our community earned him a title I was to hear often — 'Mr. Port Townsend.'"

In summarizing the life of Dick McCurdy, the Rev. Raymond Smith told the congregation "Sometimes a person becomes so much a part of the personality of the community and the town becomes a part of him, that it's difficult to tell which is which.

"And when he dies, a part of the town dies too."

Garred, who didn't know McCurdy as a newspaperman, wrote a "Salute to a Favorite Son," in which he highlighted Dick's war years and his later activities.

It would be the first time McCurdy's war wounds would be detailed to the *Leader* readers. To many, how he escaped death was a revelation. He had talked about being wounded in the lung and shoulder, injuries that sidelined him for 13 months in England, but no details; no comments about how he cheated death.

Richard McCurdy went to war in 1942.

After rolling around the countryside from one Army camp to another, he finally made the big show on the battlefields of Northern France and Germany.

This isn't going to be an obituary. Dick survived, but not without battle scars.

As Weapons Platoon leader with a forward rifle company, Dick felt the sting of death. In the pre-dawn grayness one morning his unit was sent to capture and occupy a little lump of Germany countryside. But the Germans had other ideas.

In a hail of mortar fire and automatic bullets, the unit was slashed to pieces. Dick fell wounded.

As the struggle subsided, the German counter-attackers began probing around the carnage. A leather-tipped toe prodded young Lieutenant McCurdy. 'Kaput,' the voice said.

But Richard McCurdy was not dead. After the enemy left, he crawled some 600 yards to friendly lines and safety. Thus ended, for him at least, the epic liberation of Europe.

… Dick's battle scars failed to slow the dedicated pace he set for himself in community affairs.

Port Townsend has reaped the harvest of his ideas and leadership over the years.

Camfield retires

Meantime, Camfield, the lone editor from the McCurdy regime, makes no bones about the run-ins he had with the new owner. His blog and some writings in his books indicate there was no love lost. Yet, he must have done an acceptable, even credible job; he lasted 21 more years under Garred, covering the city council and serving on the council for 10 years. He retired one week before Christmas in 1988.

He said once he returned to the paper in 1960, his disappointment in not being sold stock in the paper was apparent.

"I was pretty much stifled for the next 28 years, doing two men's work and getting half-man's pay. I resigned as an aging whipping boy with no retirement late in 1988."

Camfield, then 60, said his retirement decision was hastened after his father died of a heart attack. "I considered the growing stress of my job and my own mortality."

He has since published two history books on Port Townsend and several others on family genealogy. His books and James McCurdy's *By Juan de Fuca Strait*, are considered by many the definitive sources for the city's history, particularly the newspaper history.

Camfield might have felt restrained, but his work "Influenced a future journalist," as indicated by a letter to the editor on Sept. 27, 1989.

"Tom Camfield has retired? I knew there was something different about the Leader. *He is missed.*

Tom Camfield was the Leader *of my youth. When I played high school sports, he was there taking pictures and making sure that as many names as possible got into the story. When I was in Vietnam, he kept me informed of all the local happenings in Port Townsend. And, for the 20 years that I've lived near the "other" Washington, he has provided a chronicle of all that was good or not good in Jefferson County.*

I do not know Tom Camfield well and he may not remember me at all. But I do know that his bylines ... whether above news stories, under photos or on occasional commentaries, were influential on my selection of a career. His writing made it clear that working on a newspaper was an important occupation.

So, I became a writer, a reporter and then managing editor of a community newspaper. It was everything I ever thought it would be — and more. Still later, I chose to go into public information, but the influence of Tom Camfield was still there. I suspect that we share a mistress — a love affair with the language. But I also suspect that I am not the only one whom he has influenced.

Thank you, Tom Camfield. I will still read the Leader, *but with a bit less enthusiasm. You are missed. Enjoy your retirement.*

John Bertak
Acting Deputy Director Public Affairs
United States Department of Education
Washington, D.C.

Author's note: That letter to the editor was not submitted by Camfield; my research uncovered it.

Meantime, Tom's wife, Jean, continued her civic involvement with Port Townsend. In November 1989, she was elected to the city council for a third term. She served 11 years in all. She also served on the Planning Commission, alcohol advisory board, Chamber of Commerce, Victorian Homes Tours, school scholarship committees and was registrar for Peninsula College's Port Townsend branch.

Camfield, 86, in the 2015 interview, and his wife Jean reside in Port Townsend.

Pat Sullivan hired

A few months after Camfield's departure, Garred hired a young man with nearly eight years' experience in community journalism to fill the void.

Patrick Sullivan began work as the *Leader's* news editor on March 20, 1989, eventually rising to managing editor status. On March 21, 2017, he left the *Leader* and print journalism 28 years after he was hired.

When interviewed for this book in 2017, he was director of communications for Joe D'Amico's Security Services Northwest, a multi-dimensional security company in Jefferson County.

It almost didn't happen for him in Port Townsend. "I had a job offer at Toppenish (in Eastern Washington). I was in the back shop (composing room) and saw an ad for a job in Port Townsend. I called and talked with

Frank Garred. He said he was leaving for Hawaii and wasn't sure when he was going to decide. I told him, if he didn't make a decision before he left for Hawaii, I was going to work at Toppenish."

The rest is history.

Sullivan graduated from the University of Montana's journalism school in 1981 and landed a job at the *Ritzville-Adams County Journal* as editor. In a bit of irony, the *Journal* was one of the papers that Bruce Wilson had owned prior to partnering with Garred. Wilson's son Scott eventually would become Sullivan's boss at the *Leader*.

Sullivan left the *Journal* in 1987 and went to work at Thompson Falls, Minn., but one year was enough in the frigid Midwest and he headed west, landing at Toppenish, where he saw the ad for the *Leader*.

Three times in his career he had been on the cutting edge of progressive technology. "At Thompson Falls, at Ritzville and at the *Leader*, I helped dismantle Linotypes. In all three places, I was there when they got rid of Linotypes and I helped close them down," Sullivan said in the 2017 interview.

"I've seen journalism come from the raw dark room and hot lead to Compugraphic to computers."

It was a couple of months later when the *Leader* joined the modern age, launching a total computer process.

"We got all Apple equipment with a Mac-based (MacIntosh) program," said Garred. "We had about four Mac-Pluses and upgraded to MacSE as a server and printer. We had the whole building wired for Intranet working. We still did cut and paste because those machines were not paginators."

Scott, Jennifer Wilson join team

After 22 years at the helm, Garred decided he wanted a junior partner, who, in addition to holding a financial interest also would be one he could train to eventually take over the business.

He found the perfect man to fill that role when he hired Scott Wilson, the son of his partners, Bruce and Merilynn Wilson.

"We joined Frank as *very* junior partners, with a handful of stock in Port Townsend Publishing," said Scott, referring to his wife, Jennifer, as co-partner.

"We spent the next 11 or 12 years purchasing stock whenever we could afford it, buying from Frank's silent partners, who were my parents and Henry Gay. Thanks to Frank's commitment to an independent *Leader*, we slowly bought into the company.

"It was the only way someone without a lot of resources could do something like that."

Scott was born into a newspaper family on April 30, 1955, in Ritzville, Wash., where his parents owned the *Journal-Times*.

The family moved to Omak the following year, where Bruce and Merilynn owned the *Chronicle* from 1957-1980. Bruce was the editor and publisher; his wife was an unpaid assistant and wrote a popular weekly column, "A Word from Home."

By the time he was 7, Scott was involved in the newspaper business, working in the folding and bundling department and sweeping up Linotype shavings.

Meantime, Bruce began a second career when he was elected state senator, representing the entire northeast corner of the state (Okanogan, Ferry, Stevens and Pend Orielle counties) in 1968. He would serve three terms.

Merilynn was active in the Campfire Girls, the library board and was a member of the Wenatchee Valley College Board of Trustees. Together, they helped found the Okanogan County Historical Society in 1963, later spearheaded the construction of its museum, where there is a Wilson Historical Research Center. In 1971, Bruce wrote a definitive history of Okanogan County, while Merilynn worked on the committee to rebuild the Omak Library.

In 1974, Scott enrolled in the University of Washington's School of Communications, majoring in journalism. Following his junior year, he had his first hands-on role with a community newspaper.

It was a no-brainer where he ended up — interning at the *Leader*, where his father still had a financial interest. He would work under Frank Garred in 1977, then return to the U.W., where he was the editor of *The Daily*, and completed his degree in 1978.

In October 2017, when he was inducted into the U.W. Department of Communications Alumni Hall of Fame, (the same honor accorded to Garred in 2007), he spoke fondly of those days when Watergate was prominent, and he was thrust immediately into the fray.

"There was a driving energy on campus, a great deal of political activity; many people at the time were ready to topple governments and challenge the administration.

"As student journalists, none of us were backing away from the controversy, but it was really important to me that *The Daily* be respectful in how we operated. We had a good relationship with university leaders because I didn't want *The Daily* to be used as juvenile 'gotcha' toy. However, I take pride in the fact that media was, and still is, a true check to power."

Scott Wilson sits at his publisher's desk during a 2015 interview. He became co-owner of the *Leader* with Frank Garred in 1989. In 1998, when Garred retired from the *Leader*, Scott and his wife, Jennifer, became co-owners. They sold to the Mullens in 2016. *(Bill Lindstrom photo)*

After receiving his BA, Wilson would work the next 11 years in the industry before getting the opportunity to own stock in a newspaper.

And, what an eclectic resumé he would bring with him to Port Townsend. By the time he and Jennifer would get to the Key City for good, he would have done it all in the industry, including a freelance stint in Nicaragua.

- 1978-1980: *Whidbey News-Times*, county reporter;
- 1980-1983: *Everett Herald*, labor and business reporter;
- 1983: Freelance reporting in Nicaragua, covering the Sandinista revolution and the "Contra" counter-revolution;
- 1984-1987: Pursuing and achieving master's degree at the U.W. School of Communications.
- 1987-1989: *Tacoma News Tribune*, primarily as Olympia Bureau Chief.

Then his life came full circle when Garred came calling for him and Jennifer to join the *Leader*.

Weekly route the best path

While he had a couple of short stints with a daily newspaper, his heart was with community journalism.

"I think every journalist should start here," Wilson said referring to the weekly route. "Working for a community paper means that you will be thrown into the process right away. You'll experience total immersion in the field because you'll be assigned two to three beats, work closely with senior staff and write for multiple platforms. The challenge is that because you are truly up close and personal with members of the community, you damn well better do good journalism."

When asked how he arrived at the *Leader*, Wilson offered, "We kind of found each other. Frank was looking for a junior partner to be sure the paper remained independent, and Jennifer and I were looking for an independent paper. We came to Port Townsend and talked to Frank. He put together a plan that worked for us both."

Garred said he had plans for Wilson to take over from the time he was hired. "We agreed on a plan that Scott would be the editor for five years upstairs (in the Fowler Building) and then we'd switch places. I'd be the editor and he would move downstairs to the publisher's chair."

Eventually, Jennifer also would become an integral part of the working machine.

"When we arrived (1989), I had a 2-year-old daughter, so I did some copy editing," Jennifer said in a 2017 interview. "I worked maybe 20 hours a week, then two years later, I was pregnant with twins. I proofed pages and did some work in the front office. I called it 'Plan Z,' basically I filled in where needed."

Meantime, Garred began formulating a strong newsroom. "We picked up George Leinonen, extraordinary photographer. He was doing drywall when we got him."

He became well-known for his weekly photo-pages, which would highlight everything from business to maritime to human-interest features.

Another hire was Lynn Nowak, whose father was among those credited with the founding of Peninsula College in Port Angeles.

"She became in a family way when she worked here," said Garred. "After the birth, Pat would take care of the baby upstairs while managing our circulation program. In fact, we had a number of women employees, who were pregnant. Insurance wasn't much in those days, but we kept them on staff and provided day care."

Sullivan also talked about that aspect. "Jennifer and my wife Marilou were both pregnant at the same time. In fact, several of our employees had babies at the same time. We were like a family and we grew together as a newspaper family."

Nowak, who worked at the paper until the early 2000s, wrote a column called "From the Observation Deck," covering many aspects of the peninsula in a conversational tone.

Later, the column would be picked up by Sullivan and retained until he left in 2017.

Garred noted a couple of other hires:

"One was a waitress, but she had a terrific mind and was interested in writing. Robin Biffle, a refugee from the LaFonda Café, became an excellent reporter. Later, she became a Port Townsend cop and is now a minister in Montana."

He cited a freelancer from the woods of Quilcene. "She was one of the real hippies in town, but what a great mind and she tapped into personalities," said Garred. "She worked three years part-time and three years full-time, then went back to school and became, in my mind, one of the finest teachers at the high school — Gina McMather. She taught drama history and would take students on world trips to live the history they were learning."

Integrity is No. 1

Editorially, and on the news side, the *Leader* became "very aggressive," Garred emphasized. "Once we called the mayor 'the biggest drug dealer in Jefferson County. He worked for the liquor control board and managed the local liquor store.

"Our editorial integrity comes first, even if we piss off 9,000 people. We are going to examine it carefully."

He said the paper also became strong on political endorsements, something that had not been done before, and in fact, it hadn't been done by many papers. "Sometimes, the candidates even thanked us," he said, "the ones we didn't endorse."

In 1991, Scott Wilson would suffer a personal loss when his father Bruce died from emphysema on June 16 in Omak. He had been appointed to the state's Public Disclosure Commission in 1987 by Gov. Booth Gardner, but resigned in 1990 because of health concerns.

Merilynn not only retained her husband's share in the *Leader*, but she would move from Omak to the Olympic Peninsula to be near her son and his family. She immediately began serving on the Port Townsend Publishing board of directors.

In the Key City, she was involved in her grandchildren's school and sports activities, a member of the Quimper Unitarian Universalist Fellowship and a volunteer for civic projects. She was a constant supporter of the arts, especially local painters and musicians and live theater, even until her death at 90 in 2013.

Frank Garred became co-owner of the *Leader* in 1967 and retired from that paper in 1998. *(Courtesy of Frank Garred)*

"Our editorial integrity comes first, even if we piss off 9,000 people. We are going to examine it carefully."

Frank Garred, *Leader* publisher

Realtors pull ads

"When we arrived, the real estate market was booming," said Wilson. "My wife and I could not find a rental anywhere. We had to go 15 miles out of town. Prices were through the roof, which was also why there was so much real estate development."

Apparently, the Realtors were unhappy with the *Leader's* coverage of their group.

"The Realtors as a group pulled out of the *Leader*," said Wilson. "There were a lot of development issues, political contention too, but we prided ourselves in being committed to the community. Frank and I discussed it and we stayed the course.

"Some thought we were over-aggressive in our stance, but I felt our coverage was fair. We held to our guns, and in about three months, they all came back."

Obee returns to Peninsula

In 1994, Garred would make another key hire when Fred Obee came to work.

He had a "summer to remember" in 1981 when he interned at the *Daily News* in Port Angeles following his junior year at Western Washington University.

That internship is detailed in the Port Angeles chapter in this book. It included the trial of a shooter at Goldie's tavern; a fraudulent salmon derby in which the announced winner used a frozen fish, and the capture of Christopher Boyce, the most-wanted man on the FBI's list.

Obee returned to Western to earn his journalism degree in 1982, then landed at the Whidbey Island *News-Times*, where he was a reporter for a couple of years, under the redoubtable Wallie Funk, then became editor.

In the dozen years at Whidbey, Obee would have several big stories, but the biggest by far was in December 1984. "Neo-Nazi Robert Mathews burned to death in a hail of gunfire," Obee recalled in a 2015 interview. He and a photographer had to conduct a covert operation to eventually get the story and award-winning photos.

Obee said it didn't take him long to decide he was in the right business. "From the moment I stepped into it, the job was exciting. I just wanted to write. It fit like a glove."

He already had experienced enough "big" stories to last a lifetime; that was just the beginning for Obee.

He enjoyed working under Garred. "Frank had a great approach to journalism, so completely dedicated to it — in every way. Every Tuesday, he'd call downstairs and say, 'I'm adding pages.' He didn't care about the ad lineage, if we had copy to fill it, he'd add pages.

"I remember there were times when we had page after page with no ads and I asked Frank if we were doing OK financially. He sighed, and said there weren't many ads that week, but with a half-smile, he said, I guess we'll have to live on quarters from the news-rack sales.'"

However, the *Leader's* circulation income was strong and advertising revenue was growing. Its financial posture was reasonably secure and strong, Garred emphasized.

Obee nominated for Pulitzer

In April 1995, Obee's "nose for news" would thrust him into the middle of an embroiling story that would eventually end in a landmark decision by Gov. Gary Locke and result in a Pulitzer Prize nomination for the reporter.

Details from the *Leader's* article in January 1998 and the Associated Press story in April 1998 summarized this three-year nightmare.

A country boy from Chimacum had endured years of torment and abuse by his classmates at the rural high school in Jefferson County. On a spring day in 1995, 19-year-old Brian Cade Sperry was in class when a female classmate who was icing a leg injury threw the bag of ice at Sperry's head as the class was breaking up. She ran from the room and he chased her, dragging her to the ground. Other boys chased after Sperry and caught up with him at his locker.

There, Sperry feared for his life as a student assaulted him at his locker, grabbing him and pinning his arms at his side.

Dozens of students surrounded the two boys.

"Kill him, hurt him," the crowd shouted; he feared the worst; somehow in the struggle, he managed to reach into his locker and pulled out a wooden mallet-like club he made from a 2-by-4 in shop class. Nails were partially driven into one end to make it look "neat," he would later say.

He swung the club several times over his shoulder at his assailant's head and then at his shins. He broke free and escaped, only to be arrested later and charged with assault.

A Jefferson County Superior Court jury convicted Sperry on two counts of assault stemming from that April 1995 fight and sentenced him to 15 months in prison because the club was deemed a deadly weapon.

John Raymond, Sperry's defense attorney, argued with Brian's parents, Ed and Debora, to accept a plea bargain, but Brian didn't want to. He wanted it to go to court. Raymond said the lengthy prison term for a schoolyard brawl that went wrong was because of the plea rejection.

Debora Sperry said, "He will be the innocent victim of a felony charge the rest of his life because he tried, but failed, to defend himself."

The Sperrys sought an appeal, claiming their son's appointed attorney was "inadequate." Brian didn't testify, and the only person Raymond called to dispute the version of the attack was Brian, himself. The appeal was denied but chewed up two years and the Sperry's bank account in the process.

"Brian didn't have any money to hire a real attorney," Debora told Obee. "We got what we paid for. A public pretender."

During the two years while awaiting the appeal ruling, Brian attended a technical school in Arizona and became a certified heating, ventilation and conditioning technician. At the time he was taken into custody, he was employed full-time in Seattle. He had no further offenses.

Obee wasn't covering the courts when the assault happened and was unaware of the case until the appeal's court decision was handed down, and Sperry was sentenced to prison.

"I was doing my routine courthouse reporting, and somebody said he was convicted and was going to prison," recalled Obee in a 2015 interview.

"The courthouse was in shock. The buzz was that nobody was in favor of the prison term. Everybody said he shouldn't be going to prison."

In an interview with Eric Scigliano of the *Weekly* (in Seattle) in Jan. 20, 2014, Obee talks about the importance of having the open records, which he says were "crucial" to completing the story. "I had to get those trial transcripts, the whole court file," he said.

"We filed to get a copy of the reports that were sealed by a judge. They contained a pre-sentence report and some frank testimony from teachers about the abuse Sperry suffered at the hands of other students. There was a smoking gun."

The result was a sweeping, riveting, nearly four full pages in the Jan. 14, 1998, *Leader*, while Sperry was at McNeil Island Penitentiary.

A total of 202 inches of copy told the reader everything that transpired in this story, including a 157-inch main story, chronicling the events that began when the shy country boy moved with his family to Chimacum, where he endured nearly four years of torment and abuse from his schoolmates."

From the transcripts, Obee learned that leading up to the assault, Brian had been the victim of several harassments, including obscene messages left on his phone; one girl rubbed "goo" all over him (it was hair gel), then hair-sprayed his face and threw a bag of ice at his head; more than $1,000 in damage was done to his car and he reported having a stick broken over his back in shop class.

When the school was apprised of the events, Brian was told to "just stay away" from his tormenters. Nothing was done. A criminal complaint was filed against the students in the car-damaging case, then "inexplicably" was dropped by the county sheriff's office.

Obee's insightful analog attempts to answer the questions: "Why was such a long prison term imposed for a boy, now a man, with no police record before or after the incident? Why wasn't a more effective case for self-defense presented? Why didn't the police or school officials act when Brian pleaded for help to stop the vicious harassment he suffered?

"There are no clear answers to these questions. In virtually every case, procedures were followed, options were offered and the letter of the law prevailed. The only problem, according his parents, friends and teachers, was a boy who doesn't belong in prison, was sent there."

The situation divided the city. More than 3,000 petitions were signed and a "Free Brian" committee was established. They raised money for a new attorney, asking that the case be forwarded to the state clemency board.

Others bristled at the implied criticism of the Chimacum School

District and local authorities for not acting to stop the harassment directed at Sperry

Leader co-publisher Scott Wilson staunchly defended his paper's handling of the case with a series of editorials, starting the week after the massive missal appeared. Obee continued with breaking stories as they occurred.

Jan. 21, 1998: A "Pardon Brian" editorial summarized this situation and called for clemency. "What can you do?" Wilson asks. "Plenty." And he listed phone numbers for the clemency board, Gov. Gary Locke and all legislators. The board was scheduled to meet March 13. In that meeting, the board voted in favor of clemency and forwarded the recommendation to Locke.

"I know it's up to the governor and he could overturn it, but I don't think he will," Debora Sperry told Obee.

The Sperrys waited patiently in Chimacum for the answer from the governor.

On Thursday, April 9, 1998, the phone rang as an anxious Debora Sperry sat in front of her computer, praying.

"I think the governor himself calling me this morning said it all," she told Obee. "He said to me, 'Happy Mother's Day early.'"

Locke told her "After reviewing all the facts and the available information on the case, it is clear that justice is best served by granting a conditional pardon. It is also important that Mr. Sperry took responsibility for his actions and had no prior history of violent or criminal activity."

In his pardon statement, the governor noted that Sperry, now 22, acknowledged he should not have allowed himself to be goaded into striking out, but the punishment didn't fit the crime.

The Sperry case marked the fourth pardon Locke issued, "but the first for someone still in prison," Hunter George wrote for The Associated Press on April 10.

The Sperry case ended when Brian returned to his job in the Seattle area.

But the story rode on and it eventually led to Obee being nominated for the Pulitzer Prize. He didn't win, but the story got serious attention from the Pulitzer judges and ended up in the top two dozen stories that were submitted. What an honor. That is the aspiration and ultimate goal for most reporters.

School teacher raped

Garred recalled another landmark story when the paper stepped up its coverage of the courts. "It was a rape case with the victim wanting to be identified. She was a school teacher, who chaperoned a bus trip to go skiing. Later, a boy broke into her house, pistol-whipped her, raped her and left her for dead. She knew the suspect: one of the boys on the ski trip.

"I interviewed her afterward and she demanded to be part of the process. She didn't want to be isolated. The guy was convicted," said Garred.

A big proponent for naming rape victims was Henry Gay, one of Garred's silent partners and owner/publisher of the *Shelton-Mason County Journal*.

"He would say he was naming the complaining witness and defended that by saying the *Journal* would always name witnesses in every other instance," Wilson explained. "Henry and his son, Charlie Gay, would say that a complaining witness is not a 'victim' until there has been a conviction."

"Henry and I didn't necessarily agree on the outcome," said Garred. "But we totally agreed on the rationale that led to the outcome. A rape victim is not a victim to be ashamed of or victimized by exposure but becomes a part of the legal process. Rape is an assault and shouldn't be any different from someone who pokes you in the eye. But society has made it such. The cases are public and should be."

Entering digital age

In 1995, Wilson began attending leading edge conferences on the direction newspapers were heading — toward the Internet and the digital age. "I was in a race with the *Seattle P-I* to be the first," Wilson shared in 2017. "The reason I got into it was I recognized the web would change the media, but I also saw that most publisher peers treated it as a terrible threat, responding by either dissing it, ignoring it or fighting it. Instead, the *Leader* would master it and be an early adapter."

The *Leader* won the race and became the first newspaper on the North Olympic Peninsula to have the paper available in digital format; and the *Leader OnLine* was the "first independently created electronic community newspaper in Washington," Wilson told his readers on Aug. 2, 1995, when it was launched, beating the *Post-Intelligencer* by a couple of months.

Those with Internet access would find the same stories that appeared in the print version, plus updates as they occurred. Community events, government meetings and classified ads also were included with retail advertising scheduled to follow.

Readers could send letters to the editor, messages to reporters, ad reps and classified operators through electronic mail.

"It takes our local news and makes it instantly available to residents," Wilson added.

Leader publisher Scott Wilson led the paper into the digital age in 1995 *(Bill Lindstrom photo)*

"It takes our local news and makes it instantly available to residents,"

Scott Wilson, *Leader* publisher

"The launch was made possible by drawing on the talents of some very smart professionals who lived in Port Townsend," Wilson said in a 2017 interview, adding that Steve Schumacher, "a genius-level programmer, was talked into coming in and developed programming that automated the upload of our news content onto a web platform.

"This was so effective that he and I set up a subsidiary called Community News Online, and went off to sell the automation software to other newspaper companies; we were far ahead of the game."

Wilson said if he had focused on that aspect, it could have been a "gigantic business, but I wasn't smart enough to relegate my job as *Leader* publisher to the lower shelf; my ambition remained to be publisher of the *Leader*."

He also cited professional designing help from Carrie and Jon Muellner of Winds Eye Design, who recently had moved to Port Townsend. "They created our independent full-news website with its early customization and feedback features."

Alaska-bound

In April 1996, Wilson would set a *Leader* record that still stands. On Thursday, April 18, of that year, Scott met commercial fisherman Dennis Montgomery at the dock to board his 49-foot troller *Ellie IV*, heavily laden with 10 tons of equipment to build a fishing resort in Gull Cove, Alaska.

"I went with Dennis just to help him drive his old troller to Alaska but wound up keeping a journal and turned it into what has to be the longest article in the history of Olympic Peninsula journalism," Wilson shared in 2017. "But, if you own a newspaper, why not go for it, from time to time."

The novella in the June 12, 1996, *Leader* spanned five full pages, 210 inches of copy and 17 pictures, most of them taken by Wilson with a few submitted by Montgomery.

This was the longest article, but only by a few inches. The Sperry summary was 202 inches with only five photos, but that included two sidebars.

Wilson's journal details much of the fabulous scenery they came across, the numerous islands, straits, inlets, fjords and mountain ranges in the distance. He even took a turn as skipper. "*Ellie* rode the 7-foot rollers with all the assurance of a tractor," Wilson said.

All along the journey, Dennis would expound on reasons why he was leaving commercial fishing in the past and embarking on a new journey. When they passed, what Wilson said, "looked like a house being towed on a boat," Dennis explained that it was a warehouse for a salmon fish farm.

"Almost every troller in Alaska is considering getting out of the business because of that," Montgomery explained. He also said unreasonable fish quotas had destroyed his livelihood and that of every commercial fisherman.

Leaving Ketchikan, the *Ellie* ran into 25-knot southeasterlies and Wilson was surprised when Montgomery said they were heading to the open ocean.

"My experience is with power-boats and I was instructed to head toward shore in storms," Wilson said. "But, it's different with fishing boats." Dennis explained "on the high seas, you are not only the skipper and navigator, but the mechanic, the engineer, the boat-builder and plumber; you want to have time to fix something that a storm might break before getting thrashed onshore."

When they arrived at Gull Cove, there was little celebration as Dennis had to build three cabins, a floating dock, a generator house and two yurts before the first of June when his wife Peggy already had signed up the first customers.

Already at Gull Cove was the resort of Paul Johnson; a lodge, floating dock and three cabins.

But, Dennis and Peggy's South Passage Outfitters on the unspoiled wilderness, would be different. It would have no guides to do all the work, bait the hook, help land the fish. No, it would be for the experienced anglers. Visitors would be furnished a cabin, a skiff or kayak, first-aid kit, fishing gear and given sound advice on where to go.

Wilson, who also wrote the brochure for the Montgomerys, said he summarized the brochure this way: "If the bears don't get you, the treacherous tides will." Dennis said, "It might scare some people away, but this is the kind of place a guide might want to come to, if they are not guiding."

"And you can't beat the price," said Wilson. "For about $1,000 a week, South Passage Outfitters comes at about half the price of other resorts in the area."

Wilsons take over

In the late 1990s, Garred and Wilson formed Olympic Peninsula Communications LLC, a legal and operational decision that came into play on Feb. 18, 1998, when OPC would purchase 50 percent of the *Sequim Gazette* and Garred would become publisher of that paper.

Garred and Wilson would share ownership with Brown M. Maloney's Olympic View Publishing, owner of the *Gazette*, a business journal and a couple of real estate magazines.

This decision by Garred left the operation of the *Leader* in Wilson's hands, although Garred did continue as a board member and advisor with Port Townsend Publishing Co., the *Leader's* parent.

After 31 years as publisher/editor of the *Leader*, that ended for Garred on Feb. 18.

Ownership of the *Leader* was a bit more complicated. Garred retained a share of the ownership for a few more years. Wilson explains: "We were never wealthy people, but instead we worked over the long term to generate the funds needed for the buyout. In 2001, we completed the purchase of stock from Frank's silent partners (Scott's parents and Henry Gay initially). That triggered our purchase of Frank's shares via a seller-financed note in early 2002. So, at that point, we became sole owners."

While he was with the *Leader*, Garred was involved with a number of civic groups and activities. He led the effort to re-establish a United Way program for Jefferson County when the organization lost board members and leadership in the 1970s; Garred served two years as its board president.

He also served more than 30 years as an original and ongoing board member of the Port Townsend Marathon Association, the operational arm for the annual Rhody Run in conjunction with the Rhododendron Festival.

He remained active post-retirement with government transparency groups and college journalism programs.

In addition, he was an original executive director serving four years with the Washington Coalition for Open Government, a statewide organization advocating for government transparency, and a governor-appointee to the state Sunshine Committee where he served six years.

In 2001, Wilson also shared in history when he was named president of the Washington Newspaper Publishers Association, an honor that his father, Bruce, was accorded in 1957 when he owned and published the *Omak Chronicle*.

That year also a major tragedy struck the entire nation on Sept. 11 when four terrorist-guided planes disrupted American lives from coast-to-coast.

Wilson was getting the *Leader* ready for press when the tragedy unfolded on Tuesday morning. After a quick staff meeting to triage, reporters were dispatched to the ferry terminal, the airport, the port, city hall, retail stores, local eateries and taverns.

By late afternoon, the front page and two inside pages were constructed and the *Leader* was ready for the printer.

Under a banner headline, "Terrorist attacks felt on peninsula," Barney Burke's story captured the patriotism in the town. Jack Carney bought a handful of flags, one for his car, the rest to give away. "It's a good time to celebrate our freedom," he said.

Others talked somberly and questioned "Why? How could this happen?" *Leader* columnist, T.A. Gillory, 71, an Army veteran, said, "Unlike Pearl Harbor, I haven't seen anger. I've seen disbelief; the anger will come tomorrow."

Under the same banner, Wilson corralled several locals who had loved ones in the terrorist zones. Thankfully, all relatives of those interviewed were safe.

In town, the Port Townsend Rotary Club was led in prayer by the club vice president. "If there was ever a time to say, 'God Bless America,' this is it," he said.

Shorter stories told readers that the airport was closed and planes were grounded; the ferries were open to cars only, no foot traffic; locations for donating blood were identified; emergency numbers were listed and reporter Jan Huck wrote that the tragedy would cause a major ripple among the financial markets.

Meantime, Wilson crafted an editorial "A People Respond," calling for "all of us to come together as a People, as one."

His concluding remarks are powerful:

"As a People we're ready to do whatever it takes to seek out the remaining plotters and bring them to justice. It should be swift, but sure.

As a People, we must be sure. This is not the time to lash out at suspects because of their race, their religious beliefs, their position on the burning issues of international affairs. In the past, in our haste for retribution, this country has made mistakes that today, as a People, we should ensure are not made again. These mistakes have included hitting the wrong target, or painting all persons of certain background or beliefs with a wide brush of condemnation.

Measure twice. Cut once.

But, cut we should. And then be better prepared for what the future brings.

Part of that future must be our own work in progress: Continue the work of trying to create the best, most capable, most just, most equitable nation on earth, in our time, in our own way."

When the *Leader* hit the streets on Wednesday morning, the reader had a newspaper, crafted primarily in a few hours to present localized stories and up-to-date news of the tragedies.

Obee leaves, returns as GM

Obee was no longer at the *Leader* and was not part of the team in 2001.

Fred Obee, shown in 2018, began his *Leader* career as a reporter in 1994, left in 2001 and returned as general manager in 2003. He retired in 2015. *(Courtesy of Fred Obee)*

He had desired to be part of the management team, but "Scott told me there was nothing available at the time," he shared in a 2015 interview. "In 2000, I had the opportunity to be managing editor at the *Daily Triplicate* in Crescent City, Calif., so I took it. It was a five-day daily and I loved it. But, my wife, Mary, couldn't find a job there. It was in the heart of the redwoods on the coast."

Obee edited the *Triplicate* until 2003 when he got a call from Wilson saying he needed a general manager. "I came back as GM and wrote some editorials, a few features and established *Living on the Peninsula*, a magazine we started in partnership with the *Sequim Gazette*."

Obee said his duties as GM included creating budgets, overseeing them, running circulation campaigns and acquiring new software for computers.

"The website was pretty rickety when I returned. I had some tech savvy and we launched a new one."

Meantime, Patrick Sullivan was churning out copy and running the newsroom as an effective managing editor. "I had a chance to buy the Ritzville paper, but I was only 25 and not interested," Sullivan offered. When the purchase of the *Gazette* came about, he said he had a call from the broker, Dave Gauger, "but I wasn't interested."

He said he didn't get in the business to get rich. "You're in it for the passion; I enjoyed it, but wondered, financially if it was the right choice," he shared not long after ending his *Leader* tenure in 2017.

One of his jobs with the *Leader* was to oversee the intern program with Northwest colleges. "I am continually impressed with the quality of journalism students who come here to be writers. When I started, journalism was fueled by that breakout deal — the Watergate era. I am encouraged that people don't give up the ghost. It's harder to make a living today, but they stick with it."

Sullivan said by the time students finish an internship with the *Leader*, they are well-rounded and know if this business is what they want or if they should pursue another direction."

Another of Sullivan's assignments was to direct the "Better Newspaper Contest," in which he and others would judge newspapers from New York, Texas, Oklahoma and all over. He worked with the contest for more than 20 years of the 28 he was with the *Leader*.

"It's how we recognize individuals, teams of people as a whole for the quality of work we do in, with and for our communities," Sullivan said. He added that he continues to be impressed how the *Leader* is "so much better than papers in other states."

When asked for his favorite stories, Sullivan pointed out one "that made a difference."

He had taken a picture of a little guy in Chimacum. "His name was Short and all he wanted to do was play football. He wasn't very good, but he made the team in his senior year and I took his picture for the paper. It wasn't artistic; it wasn't an award-winner, but by gosh, it meant the world to that family."

Sullivan said that during his tenure when he covered some sports, the *Leader* was not treating the South County schools equally. "I made it a point to spread our coverage to Chimacum and Quilcene, not just for boys, but also to include the girls' sports."

Meantime, Wilson, now sole owner of the paper, continued to trumpet his support for the little guys.

> *"Community journalists may be casting a smaller net, but they have the potential to make a big difference."*
>
> **Scott Wilson,**
> ***Leader* publisher**

"Good journalism has a deep and rapid impact on a community," Wilson would say when he was inducted into the University of Washington Communications Alumni Hall of Fame in October 2017.

"In Washington state, there are about 120 community newspapers, all of which are closely read and have a greater influence on what happens locally than any of the larger publications. Moreover, when a local story appears in a regional, state or national publication, chances are that its point of origin was the local weekly.

"Community journalists may be casting a smaller net, but they have the potential to make a big difference." Wilson also pointed out in a 2015 interview, when he was a youth and his parents published newspapers, "There were about 90 weeklies and every single one of them were family owned. Today, there are only about 10 that are independent."

During his tenure, Wilson was one of the founding members and later president of the Washington Coalition for Open Government. He also was president of the Washington Newspaper Publishers Association in 2005 and longtime chair of its foundation and scholarship program for college journalists.

His peers awarded him the Miles Turnbull Master Editor/Publisher Award, the highest honor for community journalism. Garred also won the honor and so would Fred Obee — a monumental accomplishment for a community newspaper.

"Scott was a strong advocate for a higher education presence in the county. He approached the state Legislature and secured a $100,000 commitment toward that goal," said Garred. This led to development of a comprehensive college-level homesite at Fort Worden.

"He also helped guide the community's first successful Public

Development Authority to secure management of Fort Worden's tourist facilities, a partnership between the PDA, City of Port Townsend and State Parks Commission," Garred added.

Strong editorials

Some say newspaper publishers shouldn't rock the boat; others say rattle the cages and don't let up.

"As a community journalist, I try not to make enemies," Wilson said. "But you have to be willing to go after the bad actors when you need to. Often the press is the last chance a community has to address its problems. Sometimes you just hang in there and see it through."

Wilson wasn't afraid to tackle any subject, and in a series of editorials in 2006 even took on the U.S. Navy. In one, Wilson editorialized that the Navy was not "being a good neighbor," chastising the service and its new local commander for refusing to hold a public forum to discuss the problems that offloading submarines at the Indian Island munitions depot would bring about.

That decision was "unfortunate and unnecessary," Wilson said, explaining the openness that ensued under a previous commander.

Townsend Bay Marine formed in 1999 to take over the bankrupt Admiralty Marine. It grew from 15 to 70 employees and paying wages were increased from $12 an hour to $20. Yet when it sought permission from the Port of Port Townsend to expand the 4,000-square-foot facility, it was denied.

Wilson went to bat for the proposed expansion:

This is exactly the kind of company this county wants. It uses the high skills of the local workforce to make high-quality, value-added boats and components that bring into this county millions of dollars.

The owners are local, and they are involved in the community. This is the kind of company that other ports, when casting about for new tenants, salute.

It took a while, but the expansion ultimately was approved when, in 2015, Port Townsend Shipwrights Co-op purchased the business and signed a 17-year lease with the port, expanding to 40,000 square feet.

It was 2006 again when Wilson came out with both barrels blazing.

The chamber was holding a forum to discuss the proposed draft Comprehensive Plan, but it turned into a litany of complaints against the city and the chamber.

Wilson, however, pointed out an even bigger problem: "The 800-pound gorilla in the room." He said even the best plan can't counter the fact that "somewhere near $75 million to $100 million is headed by locals to out-of-county retailers and left there.

"If even a fraction of the out-of-county business was welcomed back home, it would make a huge difference to local business with the ripple effect on new jobs, better wages, stronger tax base and healthier communities. That's not to mention the consumer benefits of shopping locally."

That year, 2006, was a banner one for the *Leader* in the WNPA Better Newspaper Contest. It garnered a Port Townsend record 28 awards (to that date), including 10 for first places in news, sports, editorials, advertising, special sections and production. The paper was awarded a second for General Excellence from the judges, who were from New York.

"It reflects on the high level of talent and commitment that we have here, because most the newspapers in this competition are owned by daily newspapers and chains," praised Wilson.

"We remain an independent, locally owned community newspaper staffed by highly skilled people who care."

The judges lauded the *Leader* for a paper "that has it all: Community news, people, local government, business, police, sports, issues, leisure, health. It's just what a great hometown newspaper should be."

Jennifer Wilson filled various roles at the *Leader* while raising their family. She came to work full-time in 2013. *(Bill Lindstrom photo)*

"I came back to work full-time in 2013; "I started the Leader Reader Project to build readership. I also organized the Leader's 125th anniversary party in 2014."

Jennifer Wilson, *Leader* co-owner

In 2010, under the category of "Why the Hell Not?" Wilson organized a serialized novella with 10 local authors (all but him were published). The series ran on successive weeks in the *Leader*. "I wrote the first chapter, then passed it on to the next author. Each writer had only one guideline: You must leave the next writer in some kind of trouble. After we published in serial form, we did a reprint with the whole thing in one section. It was a ton of fun and the community loved it."

Jennifer's role expands

As the Wilson children began to exit the local school district for higher education, Jennifer Wilson took on more responsibility with the paper. She also found another way to make a difference in the community and won a position on the school board in 2009. She was re-elected in 2013 and ran unopposed in 2017.

"I came back to work full-time in 2013," she said in a 2017 interview. "I started the *Leader* Reader Project to build readership. I also organized the *Leader's* 125th anniversary party in 2014. That was big celebration. We had about 350 people in our parking lot."

She said one of the highlights was taking portraits of readers with a label showing how long they had been a *Leader* reader. "One had been a reader since 1947," she said.

The celebration also marked the Fowler Building's 140th year, the 98th as home of the *Leader*. It also was the 25th anniversary of the Wilsons joining the *Leader* family.

Having lost his father in 1991, Scott Wilson's mother Merilynn Wilson died on June 29, 2013, at 90. She had suffered congestive heart failure for several years.

In June 2015, Obee wrote his last column for the *Leader*, announcing his retirement after 18 years with the paper and more than 40 years in the industry.

"The job newspapers do in communities like ours is indispensable. We connect governments with the governed and businesses with customers. We build communities every day by making connections between people who need services and folks who provide them. We leave behind the record of our times, written by the people who observed events firsthand. I consume a lot of digital media, and it is a great thing, but I'm glad we have a paper copy that can be bound in a book and saved for generations. It's hard to improve on that technology for reliability and staying power," Obee wrote.

He continued, "Newspapers do the hard work of democracy. Someone has to press for answers, look for connections and question assumptions. For all our history up to this very day, newspapers have shouldered the biggest share of that job, and I am proud to have been a part of that."

Obee also was immersed in the community — he was president of the Jefferson County Chamber of Commerce, a member of the East Jefferson Rotary Club and executive director of the Washington Newspaper Publishers Association.

That October, he became the third *Leader* manager to receive the Miles Turnbull Award.

Outgoing WNPA president Kevin Graves was the key presenter at the ceremony, asserting that "Obee has ink in his blood, which is why he is editing *The Washington Newspaper* (house publication for the WNPA).

"So, if you ever wonder what makes a well-rounded newspaperman or if you wonder whether what you do is important, or whether community newspapers matter, take a look at the career of Fred Obee and know that you can, and probably do make a difference."

Once Obee retired, Wilson had to find a new general manager. All he had to do was roll over and see the answer. His wife, Jennifer.

When she came on full-time in 2013, Jennifer was associate publisher, then when Obee left, she became general manager.

"I never wrote any editorials," she deadpanned. "I left that up to Scott. I did work in human relations and coordinated political advertising. Prior to that, it fell to the salesperson to handle political ads."

As Wilson neared his 60th birthday and 40th year in the business, he began to think about retirement.

"We called a broker, Dave Gauger," said Wilson. "He's very close to the industry. He told us, 'get your books in order.' We wanted an independent owner, close to the community."

"We started thinking about it, and it happened rather quickly, almost instantly," Jennifer added. We had two or three parties interested; that was surprising to us."

The Mullen era

One of those was the Mullen family, who owned the *Shelton-Mason County Journal.* Tom Mullen had bought it from Henry Gay's adult children: Charlie, Julie and Steve Gay, who became owners upon their father's death.

"We were familiar with them and began talking," Scott said. "We came to an agreement that was in all of our best interests."

"Scott sent an email to have a staff meeting, and I knew he was going to sell," admitted Sullivan, the paper's managing editor.

Indeed, that was the case. The sale was effective on Sept.10, 2016, and announced in the *Leader* on Sept. 14.

Tom Mullen's sons, Lloyd, 28, and J. Louis Mullen, 31, were announced as co-owners.

The sale marked the end of the Wilson era. Scott and Jennifer had been with the *Leader* since 1989, as Scott points out, that makes the average ownership of the *Leader's* recent owners about 30 years. "As media all around us go a more corporate route, this is a special thing that will now be carried forward by Lloyd Mullen."

In bowing out, Wilson couldn't say enough about his staff of 24 (full and

Lloyd Mullen was 28 when he became co-owner of the *Port Townsend and Jefferson County Leader* with his brother J. Louis Mullen in 2016. Lloyd is the current publisher. *(Bill Lindstrom photo)*

"I've known Scott for a few years and had the opportunity to come to Port Townsend multiple times. It's a phenomenal newspaper. I'm grateful to be here."

Lloyd Mullen, Leader publisher

part-time), he said is the best in the state. "They set a very high bar for themselves and each other, and reach it almost always," he said.

He pointed out when he retired, four employees had been there longer, or as long, as he and Jennifer: Betty Grewell since 1968; Chris Hawley, since 1986; Patrick Sullivan, since 1989; and Marian Roh, since late 1989.

"We have been truly honored to spend most of our working lives with this group of people," Wilson added.

Lloyd Mullen, at 28, became the youngest publisher in the *Leader's* history, edging Garred, who was 31 when he took command.

"I've known Scott for a few years and had the opportunity to come to Port Townsend multiple times," Lloyd said. "It's a phenomenal newspaper. I'm grateful to be here."

In welcoming Mullen to the helm, Wilson said, "We sustain the independent local ownership that has been so important to us and the community the *Leader* serves. ... He's the new publisher Jennifer and I were hoping for."

The Mullen duo grew up in the newspaper business, learning every aspect of it. Their parents, Tom and Ann, own and operate community newspapers in Montana, Wyoming, Idaho and at Shelton.

"We'll continue in the Wilsons' standard of excellence," Lloyd Mullen said. "My family has been committed to the betterment of the communities we live in. We've always found the best way to do that is to give voice to the community."

Mullen came to the *Leader* after three years at Shelton, the largest newspaper in the Mullen empire. Louis, the first of the Mullen brothers to venture out on his own, is co-owner, but continues to own and operate two Wyoming papers: *Green River Star* and *Thermopolis Independent Record*.

The oldest Mullen son, Jesse, is now publisher of the Colville (Wash.) *Statesman-Examiner.*

Lloyd Mullen's road to the Key City was a circuitous one, precipitated in part by his father's moves to a variety of publications.

His journalism career took him to Iowa in 1994-1995, then to Newcastle, Wyo., near Custer. In 2010, his dad offered him a job at the *Silver State Post* in Deer Lodge, Mont. It was one of two Montana papers Tom Mullen owned.

Lloyd said his role was split, "50 percent editorial, 50 percent advertising. I was a general reporter and wrote a lot of features. The biggest story was the 100-year flood."

By this time, Lloyd was getting serious with his girlfriend, Karen, who was in Phoenix, Ariz., and did not want to move to Montana.

When Lloyd was offered a job at Phoenix University in Arizona, he jumped at the opportunity, even though it wasn't in journalism. Lloyd didn't like the heat in Phoenix but did propose to Karen and they were married in 2012.

In August 2013, Dad came calling again and Lloyd arrived at Shelton, eager to get back into journalism. When he started with the *Journal*, he lived on a houseboat at Alderbrook in Union and commuted to Shelton.

"I was working under (publisher) Tom Hyde. "Editorially, he was very good, and I learned so much from him, particularly his photography. I did about 50 percent advertising and 50 editorial."

Two years later, Hyde left, and Lloyd's job became 90 percent advertising. He was named advertising manager, then promoted to general manager in May 2016.

'Sweat equity'

He was only GM for four months when he and Louis purchased the *Leader*.

"It's been sweat equity," Lloyd admitted in an October 2017 interview, one year into his tenure. "I got in just because I'm a Mullen. In a couple of years, I will be vested."

He admitted the first year "has been extremely challenging." When asked what he learned in the first 12 months, he deadpanned. "I learned I knew nothing. I went in overly confident because of how Shelton worked. Dad had it working like a well-oiled machine. I didn't have to do much."

He said he wasn't putting down the *Leader* or its previous owners. It was more his style is much different from Scott Wilson.

"Marian (Roh), one of our graphic designers, said it best," Lloyd admitted. "The Wilsons make soup this way and the Mullens make it that way, and we try to combine the recipes."

He said the first three months were "like trying to climb an avalanche.

I couldn't just come and say, 'we are going to do it my way.' It's a gradual give and take between the two. Let's try to find a common way to put out the best newspaper possible. We are still working on that."

One of the biggest changes came with personnel. Wilson had a staff of about 24 (including part-time), but as Lloyd explained, "he owned the paper and could have as big a staff as he wanted. I have a monthly base payment to make for the next 10 years. For our debt-service, the paper was over-staffed."

Sullivan hit the nail on the head when he admitted after he had retired in March 2017, "I told Scott at that meeting when he told us of the sale, that I expected about half the staff would be gone within six months."

Mullen said his staff today (in 2017) was about 15, including four in the newsroom, led by managing editor Allison Arthur, who has been with the paper since 2006.

Arthur left in 2018 and was replaced by Kelli Ameling.

"I wouldn't say they were seven over," emphasized Lloyd. "He had what he could afford. I have what I can afford. I tried to make the cuts one from each department; some were due to retirements and some attrition. But, I've been growing the newspaper each month I've been here."

He said the biggest change aside from staff, has been Scott vs. Lloyd. "Scott was editorial, the voice of the newspaper. I am on the business side. I heavily rely on (the editor) for that voice that was Scott Wilson. Moving here into a position that he held for 27 years, it's big shoes to fill."

He said he was most proud of the circulation drive the department held in April 2017. We got about 600 new subscribers, and we are roughly at the same circulation (7,000) as when Scott had it."

Mullen made a cosmetic change to the *Leader* operation in 2017, moving the newsroom office from upstairs to the ground level, something Wilson wanted to do, but never did.

Lloyd has two residences: an apartment on the second floor of the Fowler Building and a home in West Olympia, where his wife, Karen, is a dietitian with the Department of Health, and is in a graduate program at The Evergreen State College with a year to go. Sometimes, he is in Olympia on weekends and other times, Karen is in Port Townsend.

Wilson started the *Leader Online*, and while Lloyd recognizes the website as an integral part of the paper, "it's a secondary product. I use the web to tease to the newspaper. It's important, but not our bread-and-butter."

He did say, when there was breaking news important to the *Leader* readers, he would update the website with crucial information. "If it's important enough, we'll put it online," Mullen said, noting two days previous, the Hood Canal was going to be closed for a repair. "We put that on the website."

Mullen said much of his success within the community he owes to Scott Wilson. "He has had my back. When I came here, he took me door to door. He took me to a chamber meeting and I got a standing ovation, not because of who I am, but because of Scott and Jennifer."

He said he has since acquired an honorary seat with United Good Neighbors and attends the noon Rotary group at Fort Worden.

One year into retirement, Wilson is complimentary of Mullen. "Lloyd is very capable. We were healthily staffed. We knew there were going to be some changes. I think as time goes on, the bumps will be fewer and the transition will be smooth.

"I told him my door is open, and if he needs some help, let me know."

Jennifer added, "I think the town has been willing to accept the transition."

Six months into the new ownership, Sullivan decided the time was ripe for a change in his life. That was March 21, 1987, one day and 28 years after he began.

"I knew it was time. The family atmosphere we once had was gone. I feel blessed here," he said in a 2017 interview at Discovery Point, where Joe D'Amico's Security Services Northwest is located.

"It's less stress and more money. I have deadlines, but not the same. It's a welcome relief, and personally, in terms of stress and health, it's a good thing," Sullivan said.

He described the company as "a multi-dimensional security company. We do dispatching, call center, public and private alarm installation and monitoring." He said, "The marijuana industry in Washington is a big business, and we provide security for companies like Fred Meyer as well as maritime security."

Meantime, the Wilsons have had time to visit their daughter Hana, 30, who is a marketing and merchandising specialist for a company in

France. The twins, 26, are also successful in business: Sophie is a paralegal in Portland and Walker is a middle school history teacher in the Bronx.

That trip to New York also might include a visit with Scott's one-year-older brother Duff who is a celebrated journalist, working with Reuters' global investigative team. Previously, he had been a finalist three times for a Pulitzer and is the only two-time winner of Harvard University's Goldsmith Prize for Investigative Reporting.

Duff, a 1976 graduate of Western Washington University, earned a master's degree from Columbia University in 1982. As an investigative reporter for the *Seattle P-I*, Wilson broke stories on Gary Little, a King County Superior Court judge who committed suicide after sex abuse allegations. He also broke the story of sex abuse against then-Sen. Brock Adams.

Because of those investigations, Wilson authored *Fateful Harvest: The True Story of a Small Town, a Global Industry and a Toxic Secret*, a Harper-Collins publication, which won "Book of the Year" from a group of national investigative reporters in 2001.

Betty Grewell, known on the *Port Townsend and Jefferson County Leader* as "Office Mom," started at the newspaper in 1968, and in 2018 celebrated 50 years with the paper. *(Allison Arthur/ Port Townsend and Jefferson County Leader)*

The *Seattle Times* lured him away from the *P-I*, then in 2004, he was hired as a sports investigator by the *New York Times*. He was cast into the steroid scandal involving many major league baseball players, then covered the pharmaceuticals and tobacco industries for the *Times*. He joined Reuters in 2012 and he is adjunct professor at Columbia.

When he was inducted into the University of Washington's Communications Department's Alumni Hall of Fame in 2017, Scott Wilson was asked what he wants today's journalism students to know.

"I want them to know that good, fearless, independent journalism is more important than ever. I want young, morally strong people to enter this profession, and I expect and trust the UW to produce them," he said, then after a pause, "that gives me more hope than anything else I can think of."

'Office mom' for half-century

On May 9, 2018, the *Leader's* then-editor Allison Arthur wrote a glowing profile of Betty Grewell, celebrating her 50 years with the paper. She was Frank Garred's first hire when he became publisher in 1968. Grewell, 78, has served under three publishers and witnessed the paper evolve from hot metal and Linotypes to cold metal and computers.

Her second publisher Scott Wilson called her "office mom" for the duties she did in the office, handling payroll, billing, sending out subscription notices and even selling office supplies when the *Leader* was in that business. She was always friendly, upbeat, kind, generous and had a smile that never faded, Wilson added.

"I doubt there are (many) others who have dedicated so much to the success of Port Townsend's small-business community," said Garred. "She was professional, loyal, competent and exacting, knew details and history that no one else knew, and was a joy to work with. I depended on her," said Wilson.

Why has Grewell worked so long? "It's been interesting. I just like it. I like the people I work with. It's always been fun to come to work and it still is," she told Arthur.

PART IV

Forks

CHAPTER 13

Forks: From the Forum to 'Twilight'

N estled in the northwest corner of Washington state, the city of Forks sits within the Quileute Indian land on a West End prairie with its 3.65 square miles and 3,532 inhabitants.

Surrounded by Olympic National Park and forestland, a tropical rainforest and the Pacific Ocean, Forks was founded in 1911. It is one of three incorporated cities in Clallam County, though incorporation didn't come until Aug. 28, 1945.

The *Forks Forum*, established in 1931, is the most-western newspaper in the contiguous United States, but it was not the first newspaper to be established on the Olympic Peninsula's West End, nor the first claiming to be the "most-western."

It wasn't even the first newspaper published in Forks or the vicinity.

The distinction of first on the West End (west of Lake Crescent) belongs to the *Beaver Leader*, established about May 21, 1889. The founder is not known, but the date of its first paper can be determined from the first existing edition, Vol. 5, No. 39 from Feb. 8, 1895. Its last known edition was in 1897.

For a while there were two papers in the West End. George O'Brien from Port Townsend started the *Clallam Bay Record* in 1890 and operated it until 1909, then retired briefly and established the *Clallam Bay Press* the same year at West Clallam, changed to Sekiu in 1917. He ran that paper for two years before leaving to start the *Sequim Press*, which operated from 1911-1985.

The first newspaper in Forks was the *Quillayute News* in 1901-1903, but it wasn't much of a paper.

From 1911-1931, there were no known newspapers on the West End until the *Forum* was established. However, the *Port Angeles Evening News*, established in 1916, did circulate there, though papers arriving by stage, canoe or kayak were delivered as much as a week later and contained stale news.

We'll get back to the newspapers later, but let's step back in history to see how the West End municipalities and hamlets came about, and how they survived one disaster after another, yet bounced back stronger.

The Quileute Indians once occupied lands throughout the interior, including the area now known as Forks. Their territory stretched north from La Push at the mouth of the Quillayute River (the tribe and river spellings differ) to adjoin Ozette and Makah lands, then east to the headwaters of the Sol Duc (early spelling of Soleduck abandoned) and Hoh rivers, and south to the Quinault River.

James G. Swan, an early West End pioneer, lived among the Quileutes and wrote a book, *The Indians of Cape Flattery*. *(Tom Camfield/Port Townsend: An Illustrated History of Shanghaiing, Shipwrecks, Soiled Doves and Sundry Souls)*

According to Olympic Peninsula historian and explorer, James G. Swan, in his book, *The Indians of Cape Flattery*, the Quileutes "believed they were wronged by the 1855 and 1856 treaties that ceded their territory, not realizing they had signed away their traditional lands. A reservation was eventually created around the village of La Push in 1889," the same year Washington became a state.

Forks sits 12 miles inland from La Push on a prairie one mile wide and three miles long. Tribal members regularly burned the prairie to regenerate young fern fronds eaten by elk, which the Indians hunted. Forks originally was called Indian Prairie.

"Two names for Forks Prairie were in the Quileute language — the only surviving language of its kind — both mean 'prairie upstream.' The open area is bounded by the Bogachiel River (muddy water) to the south and the Calawah (in the middle) River to the north.

"Except for the Forks Prairie and Quillayute Prairie 10 miles northwest, settlers were greeted by towering forests of Sitka spruce, Douglas fir, hemlock and cedar," Swan wrote.

Eli Peterson, Ole Nelson and Peter Fisher were trappers living on the prairie when Luther and Esther Ford arrived by way of La Push with their family in 1878, staking claim to a 160-acre homestead a mile east of Fork's present-day town center. The Fords were the first white family to settle on the prairie.

A post office was established in 1884 in Nelson's cabin, but the name Ford's Prairie was already taken by another Washington settlement, so, Forks Prairie was chosen. "Prairie" was dropped soon after and Forks became the name of the city that lies between the forks of the Calawah and Bogachiel rivers and near the Sol Duc.

One of the first buildings erected at any townsite was a post office. In a 1953 special edition dedicated to the 100th anniversary of Washington as a state, the *Port Angeles Evening News* included a summary of the early post offices. The newspaper listed post offices and their established date: Neah Bay 1850s, Ozette 1870, Sekiu 1870, though originally called West Clallam; today's Clallam Bay was called East Clallam 1909, Tatoosh Island 1890s, Forks 1899, La Push 1909, Beaver 1903, Mora 1904.

A crude wagon road was hacked out from Forks to Clallam Bay, roughly 28 miles through heavy timberland. There was a dock at Clallam Bay, where homesteaders could connect with a steamer. However, the ships didn't regularly stop, and the wait for a connection could often take weeks or months.

The trail south wasn't much better, although early settlers in the 1890s were known to pack supplies on their backs. Legendary among them was John Huelsdonk, the "Iron Man of the Hoh."

In the late 1890s, a foot trail was developed from the prairie to Lake Crescent, where a canoe could be hired to make the crossing. A ferry was later established, but it wasn't until 1927 before a single-car wide road was opened, and in 1931 before a continuous roadway opened as the Olympic Loop Highway.

President Grover Cleveland didn't win many friends among West-End settlers, provoking the ire of residents and logging companies, when in 1897, he designated nearly 2.2 million acres of the Olympic Peninsula as forest reserve, placing it off-limits to individual claims.

William O. Douglas writes at length about this problem in the chapter, "The Last Frontier in a Dark Forest: Forks, Washington," in *A Vanishing America: The Life and Times of a Small Town:*

Reductions in 1900 and 1901, and then partial restoration in 1907, trimmed the Olympic Forest Reserve by 623,000 acres — only about a third of the area, but containing some three-quarters of all timber by volume. The remaining reserve would become Olympic National Park (established as a monument in 1909, then the ONP in 1938), ringed by the Olympic National Forest.

The country suffered through a recession in 1907 that slowed timber development and further isolated Forks. When World War I broke out, an amazing thing happened to the timber industry. The war prompted an urgent demand for the Sitka spruce to build airplanes.

Growth came slowly to Forks, though it was the center of commerce for settlers from the Hoh to the Quillayute Prairie. The town that was first platted in 1912 on the Whittier homestead, was little more than a block of buildings set among a few homesteads and looming forests until after the early 1920s.

Blowdown and fires

If there is one word that describes Forks, it is resilient. So often it has been knocked down, only to come back stronger.

On Jan. 29, 1921, a 120-mile-per-hour hurricane raged through the West End and flattened nearly 20 percent of the forest surrounding Forks. Residents recall the air "full of flying limbs, a hurricane roaring overhead." The road from Forks to Lake Crescent was a tangle of downed trees, some 300 in the first mile.

Then, on Jan. 9, 1925, a fire burned most of the east side of Main

Street, including the Forks Hotel, the Odd Fellows building, two pool halls (the fire was believed to have started in one of them) and the general store.

A U. S. Naval Auxiliary Air Station was built on Quillayute Prairie in 1944 and servicemen and their families briefly swelled Forks' population. Nearly 2,500 sailors were on duty during the war. The airfield, now home to a National Weather Service weather station, was deeded to the City of Forks in 1999. A fire destroyed the old control tower in 2007.

On Sept. 21, 1951, the Great Forks Fire almost claimed the town. It began east of Forks and raged almost 18 miles toward the town in eight hours. Many residents evacuated or joined the fire-line with bulldozers. The inferno spared the city, stopping about 2.5 miles north of downtown, but 23 homes and nine cabins in the north end were destroyed.

Merrill & Ring, ITT Rayonier and Bloedel Donovan operated large sawmills, while small woodlot owners engaged in secondary wood processing such as cedar shingles for roofing and siding. Forks proudly laid claim to "Logging Capital of the World."

Forks Shingle Mill, near the Hoh River, operated from 1934 to the 1960s when it burned down. Another major Forks' employer was the Rosmond Brothers Sawmill, that opened in the 1940s and grew through two ownership changes until the 1980s. Then there were the "gypos" or independent contract loggers, who became popular after World War II when logging camps became less prevalent.

Forks — and the entire Olympic Peninsula — in the late 1980s and 1990s became forever changed when the spotted owl was declared a threatened species. Logging was curtailed in owl habitat — old-growth forests.

Timber harvest fell dramatically on public lands, which many smaller companies and independent loggers relied on. The allowable cut in Olympic National Forest plummeted from 250 million board feet a year in the 1980s to 10 million board feet after the owl's listing, and by 1994, 2.4 million acres of Washington's forests were closed to logging. This was followed by protections for the threatened marbled murrelet in 1992 and the endangered Pacific salmon and steelhead beginning in 1999.

The demographics of the town shifted dramatically, according to the Census Report of 2000. The Hispanic population rose to 15.5, and by 2007, had risen to 20 percent. A Latino store (Tienda Latino) opened in

1992. Mexicans were the dominant Hispanic group, but Salvadorans and Guatemalans followed.

Sideline timber industries in the 1980s suddenly became major producers: Cedar-bolt cutting from downed logs and greenery harvest for the florist market boomed. Picking work was seasonal but generated a quarter of a billion dollars a year by 2006.

And, that year too, another phenomenon struck the area: "Twilight-a mania."

Who would have thought that a four-book series about vampires would be the impetus, giving life to a dying town?

Twilight author Stephenie Meyer made her first visit to Forks in 2006 to read her book to the townspeople. It sparked "Stephenie Meyer Day," first a one-day, then later a three-day celebration on Sept. 13, the fictional birthday of Bella Swan around whom the four-book series is crafted. Many of the books' scenes are set in Forks and surrounding areas such as La Push and Port Angeles.

We'll visit this incredibly fascinating phenomenon later.

Through all the fires, blow-downs, hurricane-force winds, timber set-asides, recessions and economic slumps, Forks has survived.

The *Beaver Leader* building at Sappho, ca. 1890. William Sparks and his wife Betty ran the business and were later joined by Peter Sparks, William's brother. *(Bert Kellogg Collection of the North Olympic Library System)*

The *Port Crescent Leader* office and store are shown ca. 1890-1891. B. John Baker and William R. Hoole started the newspaper in 1890 as the *Star*. It later became the *Leader*. *(Bert Kellogg Collection of the North Olympic Library System)*.

It's population today — 3,783— is a little more than it was in 1990.

Nedra Reed, former *Forks Forum* news editor and later two-time mayor of the city, said in a 2017 interview: "The major employers today come from two prisons (Clallam Bay and Olympic Corrections Center) and the school district. There are still logging jobs, but greatly reduced."

Beaver Leader

With the background discussed, let's return to the newspapers of the West End.

The first *Beaver Leader* arrived in 1889, but a year later, two elected officials from Port Angeles, auditor B. John Baker and deputy auditor William R. Hoole, took over the paper after they sold the *Port Angeles Herald*. A year later, these two would move a bit north to establish the *Port Crescent Star*, which would merge into the *Port Crescent Leader* the next year.

William H. Sparks, a brother-in-law to Hoole, owned the paper with his wife Betty as clerk/reporter in the earliest existing *Leader* (Feb. 8, 1895).

A photo caption of the *Leader* building from the Bert Kellogg collection in the North Olympic Library System, indicates the structure was at Sappho in 1890. If it was at Sappho (and oldtimers say it was), then that was later, and that photo caption is incorrect.

Here is an excerpt from the 1895 *Leader* that disputes that notion.

There has been a feeling among the ranchers of the Quillayute valley for some time past that a town should be established somewhere in the interior so as to afford better accommodations to the settlers; to collect the business of the valley as much as possible at some certain point; encourage capital to come in and work for the up-building of the entire valley. This will be the object of the promoters of the new town to be established two miles northeast of Beaver and which will be christened "Sapho."

If the *Leader* was headquartered at Sappho, it was after 1895.

Two years later, on June 4, 1897, the paper is owned by the Sparks brothers, William and Peter, with a large ad from A. Sparks, owner of a town grocery, and father of Bill and Pete.

The front page of this edition proclaims: "Gold discovered at

Bogachiel Hill; assayed to $10 to the ton." Another long story featured Cuba, headlined "MC'S CUBAN POLICY." So, who is MC? It's President William McKinley, of course, but you'd have to read several paragraphs into the story to know that.

More than 60 years later we learn more about the *Leader* from a July 1, 1966, edition of the *Port Angeles Evening News*, which produced an eight-page special section "A Salute to the West End: Celebrating the 55th birthday of the founding of Forks."

The primary person interviewed is 92-year-old Guy Lesure, who resided at Sappho at the time, though he also spent time at Beaver.

Lesure, a timber-cruiser by trade, is highly complimentary of the *Leader*, calling it "a well-edited newspaper that survived for a number of years."

He also confirms that the paper was edited by the Sparks brothers, adding that "Pete was crippled, but in body only. His writing was incisive and marinated with sarcasm. His surname was fitting. His trip-hammer mind struck sparks from the anvil of public opinion. The readers didn't necessarily agree with his writings, but they awaited each edition with anticipation. If not apprehension."

The Sparks boys did well, Lesure said, adding they built their own *Leader* publication office. They also set up their father in his grocery business, adjacent to the printing office. When they abandoned the newspaper business, Bill went to work for the postal service, which had been expanded to Clallam Bay and Mora.

Lesure doesn't say when the *Leader* was abandoned, but its last known issue is June 4, 1897, though it likely existed after the turn of the century for a brief period. It wasn't the primary West-End paper in its later years.

That was George O'Brien's *Clallam Bay Record*, which he established in May 1891 and published until 1909. Lesure also thought a great deal of this man, particularly his financial savvy.

"A man of considerable acumen, landed in Forks with a small printing plant and big ideas (though that city had not yet been established). He had himself appointed land commissioner for whose moderate services timber-claim applicants forced $5 upon him, while homesteaders anted up $3.50. In addition, he received $10 from each for a series of required legal ads, which he

PUBLISHED FARTHEST WEST OF ANY NEWSPAPER IN THE UNION.

THE QUILEUTE CHIEFTAIN

LA PUSH, WASHINGTON, WEDNESDAY, FEBRUARY 2, 1910.   NO. 11.

NEWS OF INTEREST TO EVERY AMERICAN

It didn't last long, but the flag for the *Quileute Chieftain* in 1910, proclaims "The farthest west of any newspaper in the Union." Later, the *Forks Forum* touted the same: "Farthest west newspaper in the contiguous United States."

type-set but once. News was limited to two or three line-items between legal notices."

Lesure maintains that after two years "prove-up ads had slowed to a trickle. Editor Willis shook the moistened dust of Forks from his boots and strode over the horizon with $40,000 in legal tender on his person."

The well-heeled O'Brien weathered the loss and published the *Record* until 1909, then established the *Clallam Bay Press*. He ran that paper for a couple of years before heading to Sequim to start that city's *Press*.

Starting about Sept. 22, 1901, the Quillayute News was printed in Forks with W.H. Willis as editor. The only existing paper available is from May 22, 1902, which is Vol. 1, No. 32. It's not known how long that paper was published, but an issue in November 1903 has surfaced; the paper printed all the legal notices, primarily announcing upcoming or pending timber sales. Willis later went to work for O'Brien.

The University of Washington Library confirms at least two other West-End papers. One was the *Quileute Independent*, the first volume, edited by W.H. Hudson, appeared on Dec. 17, 1908, printed by Indian Printers at La Push. It was still operating a year later. A large ad is the only visible copy, but the three-column notice invites everyone to see the La Push football team.

Most of the news in the existing papers pertained to the Shaker religion and its gatherings, along with other information about the Indians of the area.

It's not known how long the *News* existed, but it likely morphed into the *Quileute Chieftain* as the existing copies show Hudson, also proprietor of the La Push Hotel, as the editor on Jan. 26, 1910. Not only is he the editor, but a large ad touts: "Let me paint your pictures; I can also teach you how to take good pictures."

Each of the three existing issues appears to have a different emphasis. The third edition of the *Chieftain* touted the importance of a good education:

The school education is a great and useful part of the needed life training of every boy and girl. No one has yet been put on record as having too much of this sort of equipment for their lifework, whatever that may be. But when we come to think of it, the school education is only a part, even though it is a large and important part, of our whole, all-around education.

Great Blowdown

As mentioned earlier, disasters seemed to befall the Forks area through the years.

One such timber tragedy was on Jan. 29, 1921. Since there were no West End papers at the time, it took two erstwhile reporters years later to produce two stories that detailed this hurricane-force disaster: Gilbert Pilcher in 1936 and Jack Henson 30 years later.

The man who did most of the news writing for Mae Wenham, owner-manager of the *Forum* in the mid-30s, was Pilcher. Among his stories was an interview with W.F. Taylor, a Mora resident who was an eyewitness to the Great Blowdown 15 years before.

A Tennesseean, Taylor came to the peninsula in 1898 and bought the store at Mora, and for many years, sold supplies and food products to residents along the Quillayute, Bogachiel and Calawah rivers. Later, when gasoline boats came into prominence, he built a large scow and sold gas to commercial fishermen.

Taylor has a clear and vivid recollection of that Jan. 29 day, writes Pilcher in the Oct. 22, 1936, *Forum.*

Mr. Taylor and his son were engaged in building a shed across the road from the store. Almost mid-afternoon, the atmosphere grew very heavy and a strange darkness fell over all. From the ocean sprang a cold wind. The wind and the darkness compelled the men to discontinue their work.

Taylor and his son returned to the store, built a fire in the stove and awaited the impending storm.

It became pitch black, rain fell in torrents and the wind was very strong. Sudden gusts bellied in the back of the store and water entered through cracks between the boards as if thrown in by buckets.

The men said they could hear the sheds behind the store being torn apart, but they dare not leave their shelter. By night time, the winds diminished, and they went outside to inspect the damage.

When daylight came, they couldn't believe what they saw. There was desolation everywhere. The beautiful green hills were destroyed. As far as the eye could see, the hills were stripped bare. Some of the trees were 250 feet tall. They were all on the ground. The entire forest was a mass of twisted and torn wreckage; the rivers in the valleys choked; the destruction was complete.

Taylor said the storm started in the "Aberdeen-area and traveled northward at a great pace, striking almost without warning. The hurricane force spun its way toward Cape Flattery, across the Juan de Fuca Strait, on to Victoria and across to Vancouver."

Guy Lesure's memory was equally as vivid in his 1966 interview. He had been a timber cruiser for a Lacey company at the time of the Great Wind Storm.

At 3:30, the hurricane struck with awesome force. The wind shrieked, debris flew through the air, mighty trees snapped like dry macaroni. At the Sappho store it took the weight of five men to keep the door from slamming open.

Lesure recalls a miracle on that devastating day. It involved a mail carrier, Bill Klahn, who "alarmed by the mounting intensity of the storm, parked his Model T Ford under an eight-foot thick fir tree and sprinted for the Calawah River bridge. A minute later, he saw a huge tree topple and smash directly on his truck." Klahn was fine, the truck was not.

Lesure said, "in one mile, I counted 742 trees across the road. A half-mile swath where the gale hit the strongest was completely denuded."

Patricia Campbell, a feature columnist for *The Daily News* in Port Angeles, wrote about the Big Blowdown in Chapters 46 and 47 of *A History of the North Olympic Peninsula*. This book was the result of a 52-week series that ran in *The Daily News*, starting on Jan. 5, 1976. Publisher Frank Ducceschi insisted Campbell complete the series before it was published.

Campbell did that, then tragically was killed when hit by a car on Sept. 13, 1976. The next year the paper published the book.

She noted that the North Head weather station recorded winds of 132 mph before the anemometer broke. Guesses varied from 150 to 160 mph as the storm raged north from the mouth of the Columbia.

Campbell also related a little-known battle for prize timberland and the basically abandoned Spruce railroad, which was generally unused after World War I ended.

This contract dispute involved Bloedel Donovan, a logging company based in Whatcom County. Bloedel wanted the timber but didn't want to pay $1 million sought for the railroad.

"In the fall of 1920, Bloedel Donovan's Seattle office began negotiations for the 12,000 acres of timber, owned by the Clallam Land Corporation, based in Grand Rapids, Mich. The price to acquire the land was a "cool $2.5 million, which isn't exactly the kind of purchase accomplished by counting out silver dollars and saying, 'Wrap it up,'" Campbell wrote.

By Jan. 28, 1921, a signed contract for the sale reached the broker's office in Michigan. That was a Friday, and unbeknownst to anyone in the east, a good share of the timber involved in the sale was lying in a tangled jumble after the Jan. 29, 1921, Blowdown.

"The companies wisely decided to settle out of court and allow logging to start before the timber became worthless. A half-million dollars was dropped from the purchase price.

"This proved to be a pretty fair guess, for 80 percent of the Douglas fir was taken out, though with much greater difficulty than if it had been felled in an ordinary way. The spruce and hemlock, being less durable, decayed in the woods," Campbell wrote.

Thus, Bloedel Donovan's unusual contrivance accounted for its first appearance on the peninsula. The company would operate its logging business until the mid-1940s when ITT Rayonier bought much of its timberland (that hadn't been gobbled up when the Olympic National Park was established).

The *Evening News* reported "it was the greatest disaster to ever hit the West End in recordable history," and this report came 15 years after the Great Fire. This 1976 story was 41 years after an inferno on January

9, 1925, burned most of the east side of Main Street, including the Forks Hotel, the Odd Fellows Building, two pool halls and a general store.

Forks had barely recovered from the Big Blowdown when a devastating fire struck at midnight on Jan. 9, 1925. The *Port Angeles Evening News* covered the story with a six-column, banner headline the next day: "Fire destroys Forks Business Block."

The story noted that six buildings on the east side of the street were destroyed.

The fire started at Kirby's pool hall and spread from a chimney fire that destroyed that building, then burned to the ground the Forks Hotel, where occupants escaped only half-clad, Krogh's pool hall, Groffman's general store, the Odd Fellows Hall and an adjacent pool room.

"A call was sent for the State Forestry pumper at Tyee, and that apparatus, when it arrived, succeeded in saving the rest of the buildings downtown."

The buildings that burned comprised the bulk of the downtown business district: One of two hotels, George Groffman's store, the largest in town, and the large auditorium at the Odd Fellows Hall.

None of the buildings on the west side of the block were burned.

Billy Welsh of the *Evening News* penned the following editorial: "Forks to Rise from the Ashes:"

The citizens of Port Angeles and the Port Angeles Evening News extend their sympathy to the people of the city of Forks who were burned out in the disastrous fire of last Friday night, and offer everything it is in their power to give help out in this calamity.

From all we can hear the fire sufferers have stood their loss nobly and will rebuild on the site of the burned buildings. We may hope to see a new Forks, rising Phoenix-like from the ashes of the old.

Having sufficiently recovered and rebuilt from the fire, the city of Forks sought incorporation from the Clallam County Commission on July 3, 1930, less than two weeks before the *Forum* would debut. However, that petition, signed by 70 of the town's 400 inhabitants, was denied. Forks would become the county's third incorporated city, but not until 1945.

Arndt launches *Forum*

This portrait of Benjamin Arndt is on display at the Timber Museum in Forks. Arndt was the first editor/ publisher for the *Forum's* first edition on July 16, 1931. *(Forks Forum archive)*

After 20 years without a newspaper on the West End, Benjamin A. Arndt established the *Forks Forum* on July 16, 1931. The earliest available *Forum* for many years was April 26, 1934, Vol. 3, No. 42, listing E.J. Beard as owner/publisher.

But in mid-2018, a donation of papers to the *Forum* archives included the first edition confirming Arndt as the editor/ publisher.

The papers came from Karyn (James) Markin of Snohomish, Wash., northeast of Seattle. Her grandfather J.E.L. James saved the papers and even wrote on top of the first edition not to destroy it. After her grandfather died, Markin found the papers in a box.

A portrait of Arndt hangs in the Timber Museum in Forks.

Arndt operated the *Forum* for about three years when he became a delegate to the state convention and sold the paper to E.J. Beard in 1934.

Little is known about Arndt or Beard, but one thing was clear in the *Forums* available, unlike the papers two decades earlier, Beard advocated local news first — and plenty of it. The April 1934 issue, for example, shows 22 front-page stories — all of them local and 12 of them above the fold. Forget design; there was none, unless you call one story starting across each of the seven columns and no 2-column headlines, design.

Beard also liked to take on local issues in a Page 2 editorial column and wasn't shy about rocking the boat. Interestingly, two editorials in 1934-1935 strike home today, much as they would have when written.

In one, with the advent of the spring season, he called for all residents to participate in a beach clean-up. In another, he opines on the dangers of drinking and driving just months after the 21st Amendment to the Constitution was passed on Dec. 5. 1933, repealing Prohibition.

The first issue of the *Forks Forum*, July 16, 1931, was recently donated to the newspaper. *(Forum archives)*

On Jan. 22, 1935, a great storm struck Forks and the vicinity, flooding many homes. Billy Welsh, the "Rare-bitter" from the *Evening News*, along with his wife, visited the area for a first-hand report. Beard paid him to submit a report for the *Forum*. Here are some excerpts, written in Welsh's humanely descriptive style. Take a deep breath:

The mighty Quillayute — Old Man River of the North Olympic Peninsula, carrying on its flooded crest thousands of giant uprooted fir stumps, logs and other forest debris — snatched at the lives of pioneer families on the La Push delta during a great storm Monday and Tuesday, and was cheated only by superb seamanship of coast guard surfmen from the La Push station, and of Indian canoeists, who launched small craft into the current and took families from rooftops and second-story windows.

Fought back from draining into the Pacific Ocean by high tides, heavy surf and onshore winds and carrying rain and snow waters from a dozen valleys, the Quillayute surged over its banks with a mighty roar Monday afternoon in a few hours' time trapped six pioneer families and a number of coast guard families.

Other rescues were delayed when a surfboat capsized in the Bogachiel River on the way to La Push. Johnny Hermanson, who had a farm at La Push, was believed to have drowned, but he came limping into shelter Tuesday night after spending the night in the loft of a neighbor's barn.

Perhaps an indication that the *Forum* was struggling, came in August 1935, when a full-page ad announced in huge, bold letters: "Printing," then in slightly smaller lettering: for Letterheads, Office Forms, Placards, Hand Bills, etc. Call the *Forum*.

On Dec. 15, 1935, the *Forks Forum* had a new owner, Mae Wenham, who recently had taken over from E.J. Beard.

It took a bit of digging to come up with the dates Wenham owned the paper. Two weeks after she sold to Jim and Mamie Astel, Wenham writes on Feb. 15, 1940, a one-paragraph "Goodbye and Good luck" buried under the masthead on Page 4.

"This is presumably the last issue by the present publisher.

"It has been five years, lacking two months since we (she and her daughter) took over publication of the Forum, *and an interesting five years it has been. We have enjoyed our association with the people of the West End and wish them individually and collectively the best of luck."*

Astels take over *Forum*

With that one paragraph, we can presume Wenham sold the paper to Jim Astel on Feb. 1, 1940.

Interestingly, the Astels are announced as the new publishers two weeks hence. Jim Astel wrote an introductory "Howdy" column on Feb. 8. However, Wenham is listed in the masthead as editor-manager in the Feb. 15 edition. It sounds as if the sale might have been pending.

The rest of the *Forum* ownership is much clearer.

The Astel family owned the paper until Marion Astel (Jim's second wife) died on Oct. 22, 1966, just 18 months after her husband died. Ownership of the paper is a bit suspect after Marion Astel's death. Fran Etchison is listed as managing editor through Nov. 17, 1968, when Gordon and Betty Otos, who owned Forks Broadcasting Company, bought the paper. They owned it until selling to Lorraine and Hartley Berg on Sept.

4, 1975. Lorraine then sold to Brown M. Maloney in 1990, and Maloney sold to Sound Publishing Company in 2011.

But, let's return to the Astels' tenure. This was an interesting time, to be sure. James Astel and Mamie Wright married July 1, 1937, and came to Forks in late January 1940, after working for the *Oak Harbor News*, where she operated a Linotype machine and he worked in production.

The Astels' beginning in Forks was a bit star-crossed. En route from their home at Oak Harbor on Whidbey Island, Jim Astel came down with pneumonia near Mount Vernon and their arrival was delayed several days.

"Both are, we believe, zealous and progressive, and they will no doubt give Forks a good, live newspaper," wrote Mae Wenham in announcing the sale of the paper. "We believe that they will be a good asset to the community, and that Forks and the West End will cooperate with them for the mutual good."

By the next edition, Feb. 8, 1940, the Astels were at work in Forks. Jim wrote a brief front-page article, headlined "Howdy."

He said they were glad to be in Forks, having visited the city about two months before, finding folks friendly and full of enthusiasm.

We want to take an active part in community affairs and help you, the readers, in any way we can.

A weekly newspaper is judged by the amount of good, live local news it carries in its columns. We want to develop just that type of paper, but in order to do that, close cooperation is needed between the editor and his readers. So, if you have any news items, stories or anything else of interest, we would appreciate it if you would either call in or bring it to us personally.

If you have a desire to express yourself editorially, use our 'Open Forum' column.

In the next edition, Feb. 15, 1940, the front page contained 24 stories, every one of them local. Inside was the five-column ad, taking up all but one column of this page. It read simply:

"This space available for a businessman who appreciates the value of advertising in a live medium."

On Oct. 17, 1940, Astel unveiled a new paper, *Northwest News Weekly*, an 8-page tabloid, which, in the introductory column he says, "will appear periodically." It lasted two weeks.

Interestingly, Mamie was listed in the masthead as editor/advertising manager from the time of the purchase until Nov. 22, 1945, when the couple divorced.

Jim ran the paper by himself for the next nine years until he hired Janice Rickman to be editor/advertising manager from Nov. 11, 1954, until April 1955.

In August 1954, Astel married Marion White of Seattle in a unique ceremony we will discuss a bit later.

After the divorce, Mamie moved back to Oak Harbor and married and divorced at least two other times. She died in 1985 at Oak Harbor.

Adhering to his concept of local news first, Astel even stuck to that premise in the Dec. 11, 1941, edition, the publication that followed the bombing of Pearl Harbor.

No mention of the bombing or the fact that the U.S. was now at war, instead the lead story was headlined "Proper Use of Blackout Suggestions will allow Usual Trade and Recreation."

Due to military importance of the entire peninsula, the following recommendations have been made by defense authorities to insure the safety of our communities.

"From now until further notice, blackouts will commence at 12:30 at night and continue until daylight. Follow the times given over the official radio station, KIRO, Seattle unless otherwise advised.

A year before Pearl Harbor, a Naval Air Station was established on the remote Quillayute Prairie, about 10 miles west of Forks.

We learn much about how the war affected Forks and the western Olympic Peninsula from a book written in 2014 by longtime Forks resident, journalist and photographer Lonnie Archibald. In the book, the author interviews Forks-area residents about their experiences during the war.

His book, *Here, on the Homefront: World War II in Clallam County,* reports that the air station at Quillayute was regarded as the most difficult and challenging outpost the Navy operated.

"Grummer Torpedo bombers and Hellcats were flown to carriers off the straits or from there to the airport at Quillayute," Archibald writes. There was a 6,000-foot runway and two at 5,000 feet. Gravel had to be trucked from Rialto to create cement for the runways. Trucks tore up the crude road.

"Daring pilots would buzz the Quillayute Union High School as the

Forks school was known then, but if they were caught, they were punished and shipped out." Adria Furhman, with the West End Historical Society said it was about the late 1940s or early 1950s, that the school was renamed Forks High School. It was originally called union because it encompassed students from Forks, Quillayute, Beaver and Shuwah.

Many of those at the air station lived in the Forks area. It was 13 miles to the air strip and "if you missed the Liberty bus, you had a long walk."

Ten days after Pearl Harbor was bombed, the school at Quillayute Prairie burned to the ground. Students were then bused into Forks.

Some of those interviewed by Archibald recall when blimps from the Tillamook station in Oregon were blown down during a heavy storm at Quillayute.

On the prairie, the Navy developed a 6-page newspaper, *Quillayute Quill*, which carried news of the servicemen, announcements, some sports news and other local items.

At Ruby Beach and Forks, there was a heavy military presence. Road blocks were set up on all roads that had bridges and drivers had to show their IDs. A Coast Guard station also was established at La Push. "For some time, the roads were full of Army vehicles and skies busy with airplanes," Archibald was told.

The many mills in the area no longer produced wood for housing and building projects; virtually all the wood milled was used for war products, such as PT boats and airplanes. The spruce in the area was highly sought because it was lighter and made for faster planes that fly under radar detection.

In the *Forum*, Jim Astel left any war news to the daily at Port Angeles.

This also was the case with the devastating fire that threatened the town on Sept. 20, 1951. That was a Thursday and the *Forum* for that week was already on the streets.

In the *Port Angeles Evening News*, the Forks fire was the biggest story. "Raging Forest Fire near Forks; Residents Fleeing," read the main headline over the story. A boxed "Bulletin" carried the latest news:

State Patrol Sgt. Cliff Aden ordered complete evacuation of the town of Forks at 2:30 this afternoon. At that time, the sound trucks were warning residents they had twenty minutes to get past the fire, which had reached the Olympic highway on the north side of town. Residents can still get out south of town toward Aberdeen. Firefighting equipment has been called in from the edges of town and firefighters have given up trying to save it."

The main story spelled bad news for the small town, but not nearly as bad as the Seattle *Post-Intelligencer's* report:

"Fire Destroys Forks; 1,100 men, women, children flee town" read the two-line, six-column banner headline across the *P-I*, one day after the blaze erupted.

The *Evening News*, however, provided the more accurate report, sending not only its city editor Earl Clark to Forks, but also its owner/publisher, Charles Webster, and later Jack Henson.

Clark wrote the main stories and recapped the news for Olympic Peninsula residents, reporting that the blaze erupted about 3 a.m., at Camp Creek, about 18 miles northeast of Forks and traveled at a speed faster than 1 mile per hour, fanned by a northeast wind.

Shortly after noon today, a fast-moving forest fire reached the northern limits of the town of Forks. Some of the residents had left and others we're told are alerted to leave at a moment's notice.

It soon reached the North Fork of the Calawah River, threatening road-making machinery at the Osterburg Company, building a road for Peninsula Plywood. All machinery, but a power shovel was removed.

Mr. and Mrs. Ray Cooper were evacuated from their home on the Calawah Valley, but lost their home, barn and cattle.

The next-day's story in the *Evening News* was a bit rosier:

"Forks safe; fire hits 25,000 acres," read the headline across two columns of the front page.

"The town of Forks is safe today after losing 23 houses, nine cabins, four garages, a mill, a ranch house and three barns in a raging forest fire."

By Friday morning, the wind had subsided, a heavy fog fell on the coast and the fire burned out a few miles south of Forks, skirting the north end of town.

Clark wrote a gripping story: "Smoke Makes Nightmarish Scene in Battle to Save Forks."

The sky has been so dark with smoke that no one can tell when daytime ended, and night began.

Fire ashes rained down from the sky in a ceaseless flow, filling eyes, hair, ears and mouths, and coating everything with a fine powdering cover. There were only three kinds of sounds — the roar and crackle of flames eating into town, the scream of fire trucks careening through empty streets and urgent shouts of men's voices.

"I never saw anything so pitiful in my life," one fireman said after encountering more than 50 cars of those fleeing the city. "It was like those pictures of refugees fleeing some town in a war zone."

Within an hour of the 2 p.m. evacuation order, more than 1,120 people living in town, were, at least for the time being, homeless, Clark wrote.

The homes that were saved were due to residents and firefighters who soaked the roofs with water prior to leaving.

By 6 o'clock last night, firemen were confident they had it licked unless the wind reversed itself and swung back across town. "About 2 o'clock this afternoon, I wouldn't have given you two bits for the whole town of Forks," said Oscar Herd, acting chief of the volunteer Forks Fire department. "Then, every time I looked up, there was a new red fire truck coming into town."

Webster used the power of his pen to rake the Forest Service and the state over the coals for failing to provide for sustainable yield in the forests.

Headlined "How We Prepared The Forest for Fire" was directly under a photo taken 10 years previous, showing the dense forest in the Calawah-Soleduck region.

With a note of sarcasm, he writes that the runaway fire in the area illustrated how well the system works under the just the right weather conditions.

"Here's how we did it:

First, we clear-cut the old forest, leaving not a living tree standing for mile after mile. After logging, it left the land with waste wood.

Lacking shade trees, this dead wood dried rapidly, making wonderful fuel for flash fires during our hot, dry summers.

By leaving no seed trees. We delayed natural reforestation. This gave the waste wood more time to dry without shade and more years of exposure to repeated fires which destroyed young growth and sometimes ruined invaluable topsoil."

With Forest Ranger Sanford Floe by his side, Webster said he walked through the burned-out area.

Yesterday, Floe watched helplessly while the enemy he feared most — fire driven by a dry northeast wind — raced past his station for 20 miles down the Soleduck-Calawah country in the most destructive of the many fires he has seen in his 23 years as a Snider ranger.

One week later, the *Forum* had its first story on the fire. This was not due to negligence, but timing. The fire was first reported at 3:15 a.m. Thursday, one day after the paper was on the streets.

Trying to get new information is the goal of weekly newspapers and the *Forum* was able to do that.

The main headline read "Forks Returning to Normal Self After Devastating Forest Fire."

Another story revealed that by Monday morning, gypos, other loggers and crews were at work cleaning up the burned debris. *Forum* publisher Jim Astel, was named chairman of the finance committee to solicit funds to aid in the salvage operation.

Quad-marriage

One of the most interesting, fascinating — and heartfelt — stories in Olympic Peninsula journalism occurred in Seattle on Aug. 14, 1954.

On that date in Seattle, Superior Court Judge Malcolm Douglas officiated a quadruple marriage in which four Seattle natives — all sisters — were married in the judge's chambers.

Three of the eight involved in the ceremony were Forks

Four happy bridegrooms put wedding rings on the fingers of their respective brides during the quadruple wedding ceremony of four Seattle sisters on Aug. 14, 1954, with Superior Court Judge Malcolm Douglas. From left, James D. Astel, owner/publisher of the *Forks Forum*, and Marion White; Carmelita Coffman and Herbert Del Monico of San Francisco, Calif.; Fred J. Wettrick and Dolores Lopez of Seattle; Emily Baarstad and Walter Roberge, mayor of Forks. *(Forks Forum/ Seattle Post-Intelligencer archive)*

residents and one was a former resident. Included in the festivities were James Astel and Marion White — yes, the same man, who had bought the *Forum* 14 years prior, with his then-wife, Mamie.

This ceremony was covered by the Seattle media, the *Forks Forum*, local television stations and even a motion-picture photographer.

The front page of the Society section of the *Seattle Times* on Sunday, Aug. 15, 1954, recapped the event with a headline: "Love Conquers Eight as 4 Seattle Sisters are Wed in One Rite."

A four-column photo showed the four couples in their wedding attire.

"There wasn't any music yesterday when four lovely Seattle sisters were married to four smiling men in a swift, single ceremony.

The flashing eyes of the brides were dark and liquid, hearts were young and gay, the scene was bright and happy.

The younger set could have learned a lot about love from the octet of romancers — even if the newlyweds all had been married before, then left single again through death or divorce.

Four of the newlyweds were grandparents, and between them have a dozen grandchildren.

Mrs. Marion White of Seattle, who started the whole chain-marriage idea, wore aqua lace as she said, 'I do' in the matter of James D. Astel, Clallam County newspaper publisher."

Marion's sister, Emily Baarstad, proprietor of Farwest Motel in Forks, tied the knot with Walter Roberge, Forks' mayor and Clallam County commissioner (holding both offices concurrently).

Another of Marion's sisters, Delores Lopez, proprietor of Fashion Modes Millinery in Seattle, married Seattle attorney Fred Westrick, and the final sibling, Carmelita Coffman of San Francisco became the bride of Herbert Del Monico of San Francisco.

The wedding party, which hosted a lavish reception at the Arctic Club in Seattle, was interviewed on television on Monday night and a newsreel feature was released later that week to accompany motion pictures of the day.

The *Times'* reporter captured an interesting dialogue, which was published.

"Are you the parents of the brides?" inquired George B. Astel, assistant professor in the University of Washington's School of Communications and brother of Jim Astel.

"Yes," said Mrs. John C. Fryer, a daughter of Mrs. White and Ronald Baarstad. They spoke without thinking, and simultaneously.

"No," corrected Mrs. Fryer. "My husband is baby-sitting for the grandchildren's grandmothers while they are getting married. We are the children of two brides."

Astel no doubt felt a bit sheepish after having his own wedding scooped by a metro, but the *Forum* did recap the day's and week's events in a bit more detail on Aug. 18.

He shared a conversation that his wife had with the judge:

"This is the first time I've ever done that, and I'll bet it's the last," Mrs. *Astel revealed, adding the ceremony went off beautifully. "But, never again will I get married with three sisters. It's too difficult to get them all together."*

Mayor Roberge also revealed a difficult moment, the only one of the weekend, he said. The four couples all stayed Saturday night at the Mayflower Hotel on the same floor. "The only cloud in the sky was the several futile hours Walter Roberge spent trying to awaken his sleeping bride, who had retired early and had the only key to the room. The entire wedding party joined in the attempt to arouse her. But the new Mrs. Roberge is definitely a sound sleeper.

"After Walt had paced up and down the hallway for four or five hours, he finally was let into the room by the sympathetic hotel clerk," the article noted.

The Astels returned to Forks, where Jim continued as publisher. Marion didn't appear (in the masthead right away). Janice Rickman was editor and ad manager until June 9, 1955. Marion was editor and ad manager for the next 10 years. In mid-1964, Jim was stricken with cancer.

On April 1, 1965, he wrote an impassioned editorial, not only about his disease, but a hope he perhaps clung to as research progressed on the insidious malady — and a likely glimpse into the terminal diagnosis of his disease. It was a plea for donations to the American Cancer Society.

How soon can we expect a cure for cancer?

It is a disease of tremendous complexity, yet research gains already made have led some scientists to predict that we will see the problem solved within our lifetime."

At present, there is no preventive or cure for leukemia, but the lives of patients are being prolonged with new combinations of drugs, and many scientists believe that cures will be found for this type of cancer sooner than for any other cancer."

There isn't. Keep this in mind this month when you are asked to donate during the American Cancer Society's April fundraiser. Your dollars can help.

Within three weeks, Jim Astel died. The dread disease took his life on April 23, 1965, after a nine-month battle with lung cancer. He was 53.

In his obituary, we learn he was named Forks fire chief, serving from 1944-1948, then became an honorary member of the department. The obit also identifies his only marriage came on Aug. 14, 1954, to Marion White, though we know he was married before to Mamie.

Marion Astel took over ownership of the paper and immediately hired an assistant, Fran Etchison, to help her with reporting. Marion wrote a front-page flowery column called "About This — That and Those ...," which was nothing more than a gossip column.

Fran also wrote a front-page column, called "Raindrops," which also wasn't much more than a gossip column.

That's what the *Forum* was reduced to when Marion suddenly died on Oct. 25, 1966, just 18 months after her husband. It marked the only time in Olympic Peninsula journalism that husband and wife owners/editors both died while owning the paper.

The obituary shares a little light on her life prior to coming to Forks. She attended Cleveland High School in Seattle, then sang and danced on the Pantages circuit.

Marion Bonnilla was born in Hawaii in 1914, had only a high school education and was a milliner by trade, certainly not a journalist, and definitely not a publisher. She married Herbert White in the 1940s. They lived in Berkeley, Calif., for a time. After divorcing, she moved back to Seattle until marrying Astel.

The Astels' 26-year ownership was the longest of any *Forum* owners, but it dwarfed in comparison to the Websters' 55-year tenure in Port Angeles and the McCurdy family's 61-year reign in Port Townsend.

From October 1966 until Nov. 9, 1967, Etchison was listed as managing editor. She recruited several correspondents and expanded coverage with news columns dedicated to Beaver, Sappho, La Push, Mora and Clallam County.

At this time, no publisher or owner was listed, but a printer, Roy Black Jr., a Quileute, was included in the masthead.

On Nov. 16, 1967, Earlene Anderson was listed as the managing editor and Etchison dropped out of the picture.

Otos new owners

That month, a new owner/publisher emerged when Gordon and Betty Otos, who owned the Forks Broadcasting Co., and radio station KVAC, purchased the paper, which they started one month earlier.

The *Forum's* office and production plant was in a building across from the Chevron Station, said David Otos, Gordon's son, but was soon moved into the same building where the radio station is located today, at 260 Cedar Ave.

A few months later, Otos hired Forks resident Nedra Reed as news and copy editor.

Reed had been working as the West End reporter for the *Port Angeles Evening News* under society editor Grace Charnell.

Gordon Otos and his wife Betty owned the *Forum* from 1968-1975. *(Forum archive).*

"I was covering a wedding or something," Reed remembered in a 2017 interview. "I sent in my story on the local bus. I got a call back from Grace and she told me, 'Nedra, punch is ladled, not poured.' I made it a point to learn the terms."

A few months later, Reed said Gordon Otos approached her and asked if she wanted to work for the *Forum*, adding it would be part-time.

"They wanted me to sell ads. Maryann Bullock was an all-around ad sales person and Gordon sold ads too," Reed said. "I couldn't sell ice cream on a hot day."

She started covering city council and school board meetings. "I was news and copy editor (under Ralph Hilt) and helped out with lay-out and pasting up pages. I did everything, even emptied wastebaskets. News and copy editor? That was a misnomer. And, it was a full-time job."

Reed said after Hilt left, Otos promoted her to editor with a salary boost to $500 a month. "It wasn't big, but good. I was going through the files one day and saw that Ralph had been paid $800. I asked Gordon about that, and he said Ralph was the head of a household. It was so indicative of how women were treated. Maybe, I helped make it easier for other non-traditional jobs for women coming up in the future."

She said she can remember one big error she made that a lot of people got a big laugh over, but not the Latter-Day-Saints.

"I was writing about a fundraiser that the LDS church was holding, but the letters got transposed and it came out LSD. The phone rang off the hook," she said chuckling.

"Gordon's first love was radio," said Reed. "He was a smart man, but the paper was a necessary evil to pay the bills."

Gordon's oldest son, Randy, 67, of Ketchikan, Alaska, said "Dad's first love was the radio, but Mom's was the paper." In fact, all three Otos boys, Randy, David and Cliff, helped on the paper.

"When the *Forum* came up for sale it seemed like a good fit, so he picked it up," Randy noted in a 2018 email. "I would type out the stories and headlines on a Linotype machine and then Dad would cut them out and paste them with beeswax to a board."

Randy drove the prepared pages to Port Angeles for printing, then after a while, he left town, and David took over. David also would help pasting up pages. Younger brother Cliff stamped addresses on the paper and his sister Debi mowed the lawn," David said.

"Gordon worked hard for the community," Reed added. "He left me alone and let me do my job."

That situation existed until March 1971, when the economy was in a downturn and Reed was laid off. Betty Otos took over as news editor at that point.

"By 1971, I was out of newspapers. I enjoyed it, but it wasn't what I was cut out for. It was hard to write stories that were sad. I liked writing editorials. I had more latitude. I definitely learned to work with a diverse people, and I learned to be more assertive. I didn't enjoy having to work until 2 in the morning to get the paper ready to print and wait until it was printed and bring them back."

Nedra's husband, Phillip, worked for the Olympic Corrections Center at Forks (Clearwater), but the facility closed, and he was transferred to Vancouver. Nedra ran a sheltered workshop for handicapped adults, finding them jobs in the workplace, until 1976 when OCC re-opened and the couple returned to Forks.

She worked as an accountant and business manager for the prison, then when Clallam Bay Prison opened in 1985, she managed that facility.

She retired the first time in 1998, then, acting on her husband's suggestion, she ran for Forks City Council in 1999 and won, then was elected mayor of Forks in 2001, a position she held until 2009.

With a couple of exceptions, the Otos' tenure was uneventful, but those were critical moves.

The first came in 1967 when Hilt was still the editor and spotted an exhibit of photos by a young shutterbug at Olympic Pharmacy. He liked what he saw and thought the photographer would be a good addition for the *Forum*.

Thanks to Hilt, the *Forum* and that photog, Lonnie Archibald, celebrated a half-century relationship in January 2018.

"I began taking pictures when I was a senior in high school," said Archibald in a 2017 interview. When he started taking photos for the *Forum*, it also led to some writing. "I had to write captions. I did a little sports and outdoor columns (called 'Outdoor Lore'), clamming, hiking and fishing.

"About a year after that, Scooter Chapman (sports editor for the *Evening News*) called me and asked if I'd take photos for his paper. That opened the door for me. Scooter officiated basketball games and when he came out (to Forks), he'd bring a roll of film with him. I'd shoot it and he'd take it back," added Archibald, who turned 75 in December 2017.

Other times, Archibald said he would put the exposed film in the *Evening News'* paper box and the carrier would take it to Port Angeles.

There was an instant change in the look to the *Forum*. Where it previously had small, and frankly uninteresting photos, with Archibald's expertise, the front page now featured a striking large action photo of local sports.

By August 1973, Otos also ditched the Courier type for more conventional news type font. But the new type was very small. There were more stories, but who could read them? Letters to the editor issued complaint after complaint. In time, Otos switched to a larger font size.

The other major developments during the Otos' ownership were in 1971 when he bought the *Peninsula Herald*, then on June 12, 1975, when he merged the *Forum* and *Peninsula Herald* of Port Angeles.

In the announcement in the *Forum*, he said he did this for two reasons: "(1) to cut down on publication expense and (2) to give *Forum* advertisers coverage in the Clallam Bay/Sekiu area, and the Clallam Bay advertisers the advantage of the Forks market."

Otos said the move had been anticipated for some time and the graduation issue was the "opportune time" to begin publication.

The owner said the new publication "will have good solid coverage of the west end of both Clallam and Jefferson counties, from Joyce to Amanda Park."

The *Peninsula Herald* began in 1946 in Port Angeles by three local businessmen, with emphasis in the West Olympic market along the strait. A year later they sold it to Arthur and Ruby Poolton, who published it until 1970 when they sold the paper to Russell and Jean Fulcher of Olympia, who sold to Otos. The *Herald* was associated with *Forum* until 1995 when the name was dropped.

By September 1975, Otos decided to seek other opportunities in Battle Ground, Wash. His wife and kids already had moved, and he already had sold Forks Broadcasting Co. and radio station KVAC to his employee, Buddy Howard.

All that remained for him to move, was to sell the *Forum*.

The Bergs take over

Meantime, Lorraine Berg was busy as an accountant in her husband Hartley's shake mill. But, she had a problem with the *Forum*.

"I was a mother and I felt the paper wasn't doing a good job reporting on babies and weddings," said Lorraine (Jacobson) in a 2015 interview. "That got me going."

She didn't have much experience in journalism, but she had a good instructor in *Evening News* city editor Earl Clark at Peninsula College, and another good professor in Jack Estes, who taught mass media.

With that background, the Bergs purchased the paper from Otos in 1975 with Lorraine serving as editor and Hartley as publisher.

Lorraine Jacobson talks about her life as owner/publisher of the *Forks Forum* in a 2015 interview at her home in Forks. Lorraine and her husband Hartley Berg bought the newspaper in 1975 and she sold it to Brown M. Maloney in 1990. *(Bill Lindstrom photo)*

Lorraine was born in Port Townsend but had been in Forks since she was 14. Basically home-grown, she is the only owner and one of two editors to be raised in Forks.

In Betty Otos' story announcing the owner, she wrote that Lorraine "doesn't want to take sides on political issues. We'll try to cover both sides of all issues. We'll also try to point out some areas in the communities served by the *Forum-Herald* that need attention."

She added that much attention will be given to "building public support of the paper. Local coverage of activities, happenings and events in all areas of the circulation of the paper will be the goal."

It was a learning experience for the young couple to be sure.

Two years into their ownership, she shares some of the challenges with her readers in the weekly "Country Editor" column when the *Forum* moved into a new office in the Assembly of God (now Nazarene Church). It was a tongue-in-cheek column.

"I keep asking myself, 'How did I get into this mess,'" she wrote.

"After two years, it's hard to fix blame, but there are several suspects. Take the former publisher Gordon Otos, who sits in Vancouver smiling as he reads this, and his wife (and former editor) Betty, who left this note:

"The 't' & 'g' do not work on the typewriter. Call weather reporter on Monday. Tuesday bring a large bottle of aspirin."

"Then, there is our publisher, Hartley Berg, who put up the money and helps out when it gets rough down here. Without him, we wouldn't have a paper. We'll get him for that."

This column served to tell the readers that the *Forum* was moving.

"On July 1, when you see trucks go down Main Street with paper flying and odd machines, and weird, dazed people singing, 'Get Me to the Church on Time,' it's not the 4th of July parade early.

"It's just moving to the church."

Lorraine revealed that she eventually learned how to repair computers when she junked the old IBM Selectric with the unworkable letters.

"You have to do that on a small weekly in a remote area. You can't rely on waiting for someone from Seattle or even Port Angeles."

Three years into managing the paper, she was hit with a personal issue when she and Hartley divorced, and suddenly she needed a publisher.

"When you are a publisher in a small town, you live your life in a bubble. I was always being confronted by people when we went out to dinner. It was difficult, and he didn't like it," revealed Lorraine Berg.

Two years later, a new name emerged in the masthead as owner/editor of the paper — Lorraine Maris. In 1980, she married John Maris, who owned a print shop in town. "We didn't print there, but on Bainbridge Island. That's all they did, print papers."

She hired several individuals who stayed with the paper for many years. She cited Prue Miller as office manager and Traci Kettel. "What a little termite Traci was. She was kind of a traffic controller for us. She did everything. She was only 18 or 19 when she started, but she didn't take any static from anybody."

She also hired Dave McCorkhill as assistant publisher, rationalizing that she could handle the job of publisher and editor and save some money.

But Lorraine seemed to be a star-crossed owner for she lost her mate, John Maris, who died of a heart attack while on a hike with friends.

In June 1978, Maris undertook a major project — producing a 52-page visitor's guide that was inserted in the 14-page *Forum*, along with a shopper — and did it almost singlehandedly.

She accomplished the task, although the paper was a bit late. In the next issue, she explains why.

With 52 pages of a magazine, a new camera, and a tired crew, were just a little late last Wednesday — about four hours.

The Cent Saver was late to Olympic Graphic Arts.

Then the 14-page paper was plagued by last-minute ads and we had to add two pages.

By the time, Dave (McCorkhill) got to Sequim, he discovered several pages had been left in Forks. Howard grabbed the pages and met Dave at Lake Crescent.

The printers had trouble in Bainbridge Island — everyone was printing magazines.

At 7:30 a.m., after working all night, Dave jumped in the truck to haul the papers home. The truck was dead.

A few repairs got it on the road, and sleepy Dave wove along toward Forks. The State Patrol stopped him.

Learning he wasn't drunk or doped, the Stater let him go, but first he checked the registration license and discovered the license had expired.

Finally, about noon on Thursday, Dave rolled in with his load.

Meanwhile, Prue, the bookkeeper, kept answering the four lines with about 600 callers wanted to know if their subscription had been cancelled because the paper wasn't there.

Such were the travails of a weekly newspaper owner.

One of the staples of the *Forum* at this time was a weekly column written by Lena Fletcher, daughter of John Huelsdonk, known on the West End as the "Iron Man of the Hoh."

Her columns, which also appeared in the *Evening News* at Port Angeles, were insightful, witty and educational about life on the Hoh and Forks prairie when she was young.

Writing under the column title "Stump Ranch," she pens a humorous column in June 1975, about her adventures with grocery shopping for the first time in almost two years after being an "innocent bystander when a fight erupted, and I got dumped into a pile of rocks, thereby crushing a hip."

On July 8, 1893, she was the first white child born in the wet and wild Hoh River valley. In 1979, at age 84, she was honored as the Grand Marshal of the annual Forks Old-Fashioned Fourth of July parade. In the *Forum* of June 28 that year, she wrote a sweeping column describing life growing up in the Hoh valley.

She never left the Hoh River valley until she was a teenager, then went to the University of Washington, where she majored in chemistry. She returned home and taught school for many years.

She addressed her column style in an earlier *Forum* interview. "I just try to have good sense. Some of what I write is history; some of it expressing my opinion; and some of it is for when something looks very wrong. You know every citizen is supposed to protest."

Fletcher was fond of taking on bureaucrats when she thought they were wrong. She was outspoken when it came to the government "stealing" land from the pioneers, including her family, for Olympic National Park without adequate mitigation.

Fletcher died Feb. 25, 1985, at the age 91, and had written columns for the two papers until illness overtook here late in 1984.

Lorraine Maris would never be mistaken for a shrinking violet. When she disagreed with someone or something that was being done, she wasn't afraid to write about it.

"Are our priorities out of line in local education?" she asks in an editorial questioning angry parents who were up in arms at the school board meeting when told that the state had cut $42,000 from the Forks sports budget. Parents would have to raise the money to get the sports program reinstated.

But there was no anger when the board voted to spend $487 to replace 20-year-old text books for the school's vocational program.

After putting both issues into perspective, she concludes saying that one might think she is anti-sports, but she says she is not. "I'm just reminding parents what the real purpose of the school is."

But, the next week she is in the forefront for a fundraising project that the school's Extra-Curricular Committee had started, needing to raise $42,000 within the next month for sports to be funded at Forks High School.

When small communities get hit with adversity, that's when the

The Bogachiel River bridge collapse on Dec. 20, 1979, was one of the most devastating events to occur on the West End. *Forks Forum* publisher Lorraine Berg covered the story only to discover her friend Russell Barker was killed when the bridge fell into the river. *(Forum archives)*

parents, residents and business leaders jump into action. Forks was no exception. Thanks to a $15,000 combo donation from three sawmills, the project raised $49,000 and sports continued to be a staple of extra-curricular activities at the school.

Bogachiel Bridge collapse toughest story

The toughest story Maris had to cover in the 15 years she owned the paper? She didn't have to think long.

"The Bogachiel River bridge collapse on Dec. 20, 1979. I remember it well," she said tears forming in her eyes. "One of my best friends, Russ Barker, was killed. I was down there getting the story and I saw the body covered, but when I saw an arm sticking out, I knew who it was. It's tough to find out your best friend had been killed, but I had a job to do and I did it."

The front page of the *Forum* carried a 5-column photo of the bridge collapse by Lonnie Archilbald, along with Lorraine's difficult story.

Dead is Russell Barker, 44, of Forks, who was killed instantly when his state sanding truck plunged off the end of the broken bridge, striking the other side of the river bank. Barker was on his midnight sanding and road patrol when the 5:30 a.m. accident occurred.

The river levels had raised quickly during the night after more than 10 inches of rain fell in 24 hours, according to Jerry King, Forks weather observer.

Five persons were rescued immediately after the state vehicle crash when the car in which they were riding plunged over the same abutment and landed forty feet below on the remains of the fallen bridge ramp. They were taken to Forks Hospital for treatment."

One other driver, Pat Yarr, saw the bridge collapse and veered left to avoid tumbling into the water.

The collapse of the bridge, erected in 1925 on what is now U.S. Highway 101, was built when there was no Olympic Loop road. Nobody could have foreseen the traffic it would carry 55 years later. The mishap disrupted all north- and south-bound traffic for weeks until a Bailey Bridge was installed temporarily. A crude detour through forest woods also was established.

In 1995, a Senate resolution renamed the rebuilt structure, "The Russell Barker Memorial Bridge."

The economy changed so harshly in the early 1980s and Lorraine was forced to cut costs.

"Going to tabloid was one way to do that," she said. "We also started giving the paper to everybody in the Forks area, a total market coverage." She said the advertisers liked the wider market for their products and they supported the paper with their ads. "People in town expect a paper; they needed the paper and the advertisers needed it. I watched so many friends go out of business. I was determined I wasn't going to let that happen to me."

Clallam County's economy got a major boost in February 1985 when the Department of Corrections' Clallam Bay Corrections facility opened. The $56 million project would bring jobs to more than 200.

In addition to the main paper, Maris helped produce an 8-page section on steelhead on Nov. 16, 1988.

She unveiled a new design for the paper to make it look more professional, building on the lively action photos, primarily from Archibald. She recruited more correspondents to bolster the coverage on the west end of the peninsula.

But, she took it one step further. "I was in the Soroptimist Club; several of us owned businesses and we wanted to start an Economic Development Council, so we did. We had our first meeting at Sekiu and it built from there."

The economy started to bounce back early in the 1980s, but it didn't last, and prospects were harrowing by the decade's end.

Plunging logging levels were anticipated by a 1988 consultant's report commissioned by the Port of Port Angeles. The Columbia Consulting Group estimated that the North Olympic Peninsula's timber supplies could plummet 50 percent in 10 years.

The consultant was so wrong, very wrong.

The most-hated acronym of all was SOHA, spewing out of loggers' mouths preceded by every expletive in their vocabulary. The Spotted Owl Habitat Area impacted all of Clallam County with more than 2.4 million acres of national forests already set aside for owl habitat, even though only 40 pairs of the nocturnal fowls were located.

By Feb. 1, 1989, Lorraine Maris' front-page perspective story spelled the bad news, far worse than any consultant's prognosis.

"According to Dick Carlson, interim District Ranger at Soleduck Ranger District, the proposed cut for fiscal 1989 has been reduced from 78 million board feet to 36.2 million board feet."

Maris wrote that the "owl may be small, elusive and few in numbers, but its impact is great. In the entire Olympic National Forest, which surrounds the ONP (Olympic National Park) like a doughnut, 126,000 acres of old-growth have been set aside as habitat in 42 SOHAs of 3,000 acres each."

Estimates revealed between 1,500 and 2,000 people in Forks, Queets, Neah Bay, Port Angeles, Beaver and Sequim will lose their jobs; a number of timber sales already have been canceled due to the owl; to this date, 17 mills in the two-county area already have been affected and some have closed due to timber supply.

Clallam County Commissioner Larry Gaydeski uttered the most ominous prognosis of all.

"The impact on Clallam County if the logging shuts down to protect the spotted owl, is similar to what would happen to King County, if Boeing was suddenly shutdown. It would affect the entire state, but the Olympic Peninsula would bear the brunt."

For several months, Maris wrote weekly editorials and the *Forum* was filled with letters to the editor.

Most asked the same question: Why? Some took matters into their own hands and went on hunts to kill the owl. The problem with that is that it added to the mess they already had. The fewer the owls, the larger the setasides.

Then, on April 19, 1989, Maris wrote an editorial that echoed the thoughts of virtually everyone on the peninsula:

I'm sick of the Spotted Owl.

I'm sick of writing about it. I know you all are sick of reading about it,

It will soon be over, and I'll have something new to write about. U.S. District Court Judge Thomas Zilly is scheduled to rule on the endangered status of the notorious owl about May 1.

> *"The impact on Clallam County if the logging shuts down to protect the spotted owl, is similar to what would happen to King County, if Boeing was suddenly shutdown."*
>
> **Larry Gaydeski, Clallam County Commissioner**

The ruling didn't come until June 1990 when the spotted owl was declared a threatened species; logging was halted on almost all old-growth timber areas; and the areas set-aside for protection of the owl was increased exorbitantly.

It was a death knell for the logging industry.

William Dietrich noted in his 1992 book, The Final Forest: Big Trees, Forks and the Pacific Northwest, which most authorities believe to be the definitive look at both sides of the owl situation, "It was not the trees themselves that finally brought this conflict to a political boil. It was, of all things, a bird, so rare that few in the Pacific Northwest have even seen one, and so conveniently trusting in responding to human calls, that it made it possible for scientists to count and quantify its decline. The Northern Spotted Owl came to symbolize the struggle between conquering nature and worshipping it."

Lorraine Maris' editorial after Zilly's announcement, hit the nail on the head. "We have to make the changes," the headline noted.

"Things have got to change. We cannot keep running an economy like this, with no stability and no assurance of tomorrow, for the biggest single industry and employer in the area."

Those who made changes in their mills to log second-growth and move toward other woods products, survived. Those who didn't were mothballed in a short time.

Meantime, not all the news was about the spotted owl.

A series of four meetings were held in Forks, Seattle, Port Angeles and Aberdeen with the result that a proposal was submitted to have the coastline off the Olympic Peninsula declared a marine sanctuary by Congress.

Congressman Mike Lowry and Sen. Brock Adams submitted the bill, noting the sanctuary would include south to the Copalis Wildlife Refuge near Ocean Shores, west to the outer Continental Shelf and north to Tatoosh Island.

Maris' front-page story noted that the "Sanctuary rules can be used to stop or limit oil, gas and mineral exploration and development, the subjects most speakers addressed at the Forks' meeting."

> *"Things have got to change. We cannot keep running an economy like this, with no stability and no assurance of tomorrow, for the biggest single industry and employer in the area."*
>
> **Lorraine Maris, *Forum* publisher**

An EIS (Environmental Impact Statement) hearing and comment period, then a 45-day waiting timeline, was required. It stretched beyond that.

Finally, in 1994, the resolution was adopted.

Maris said, in a 2015 interview, that the most-challenging aspect of the job was "covering an area as big as Vermont — from Neah Bay to Clearwater and Queets, five or six communities, and four tribes — Makah, Queets, Quileute and Hoh. The hours we had to work were challenging, but when I think about it, yeah, I might do it again, but I'd do it differently or better."

Late in 1989, she began to search for a buyer and eventually found one in Brown M. Maloney, who only two years previous purchased the *Jimmy Come Lately Gazette* at Sequim.

"I didn't want to sell, but I suffered from lupus and it was getting worse," she said. It was better in 2015, though her step was slower and she often walked with a cane.

Maloney new owner

Maloney revealed that he purchased the *Forum* for $160,000 on Jan. 1, 1990, quite possibly a handsome price during a period of economic decline, that was sure to become even more challenging as the effects of the spotted owl continued to plague the peninsula.

Meantime, Maris, 74 in 2018, went to work in the real estate industry before marrying her long-time neighbor, Peter Jacobson, in 2008 when they eloped to Bullhead City, Ariz., where the couple had split residences with Forks. He died in 2014.

When Maloney purchased the paper, oversight of the *Forum* fell to Jennie Cooley, then to whomever was general manager at the *Gazette*. For a few months, it was Cooley, next Sue Ellen Riesau and later Frank Garred.

"What we were doing at the *Gazette*, we tried to duplicate at the *Forum*," said Riesau, who spent 23 years working for Maloney.

The paper had a news editor, who generated most of the copy. Rob Rochon was first in line for about a year until he returned to school at Washington State.

On July 3, 1991, Bill Buley was editor for nearly two years; Mike Henneke served an interim role for a few months; then Don Gronning, who had been at Sandpoint, Idaho, working for Buley, the editor of the *Bonner County Daily Bee*. "Bill was always telling me how great Forks was," admitted Gronning in an editorial when he accepted the position at Forks on Jan. 12, 1994.

In June 1994, the *Forum* produced a 94-page pony tab (half-tabloid size), "Who's Who on the West End." This magazine-sized section profiled every mover and shaker from Neah Bay to Clearwater and Queets. It was an insightful look, providing the readership with all the information they needed for whatever task was at hand.

Gronning held the job until February 1996.

Buley was editor through much of the storm caused by the spotted owl. It is without argument that no editor was more actively involved in a short tenure as Buley. He attended rally after rally, protest after protest, hearings from Port Angeles to Tacoma, and finally the Timber Summit in Portland.

Gradually, the tenor of the climate among the timber community changed from 1991-1994. First, there was anger, even rage, then fear, then protests to effect change, then the realization that change would have to come from within; little help was offered from government.

On July 8, 1992, an issue that had boiled for several months, festered. Larry Mason, a Forks-area resident, former mill owner at Beaver, and executive director of the Washington Commercial Forest Action Committee, argued that loggers should be allowed to cut and market the thousands of acres of blowdown timber. When he couldn't get a satisfactory answer from the U.S. Forest Service, which said its hands were tied by bureaucracy, he took matters into his own hands.

Buley was there with 15 to 20 loggers who illegally cut salvageable timber on restricted habitat land about 2.5 miles off Burnt Memorial Road. A front-page story and 3-column photo by Buley recorded it all.

Following two days of peaceful protests, Mason and 36 other loggers were arrested, charged with cutting five acres of timber on land prohibited by the government.

Within a week, the group, calling themselves the "Coal Creek 21," had set up a defense fund to aid in financing their cause. Mason, who knew there would be legal ramifications, vowed, "We are going to fight these charges. We are fighting to save our way of life."

Mason wrote a letter to the editor in the July 22 *Forum*, saying just that. It was an editorial spelling out his concerns as "The Coal Creek 21 Fight to Save Way of Life."

In the July 29 *Forum*, Buley sounded the trumpet for the "Coal Creek 21" group in an editorial "Dissident Loggers Deserve Our Support."

In September 1992 Mason and 20 others entered innocent pleas in federal court.

In a Feb. 10, 1993, Buley's story sounded the knell. "It's over; the pleas result in 90-day suspended sentences for those who entered guilty pleas. Seven entered guilty pleas; six were found guilty and given 90-day suspended sentence, plus 90 days' probation. The seventh, a disabled logger, was found not guilty.

Despite the nearly $50,000 in attorney fees and court costs, the "fight was worth it," Mason said.

Meantime, the wheels were spinning in Washington, D.C., as legislators implored President Bill Clinton to set up a timber summit. Mason made a trip to the Capitol in late 1992, urging the president to set a date for the summit.

Showing strength in solidarity, more than 200 attended a rally in Forks in mid-January 1993.

"It was like taking a roll call of victims, living in a timber-town, four years under siege," wrote Buley.

But the loggers wanted Clinton to be the host for the summit, not Vice President Al Gore, who was no friend of the logger.

As unemployment in Clallam County rose to 10.3 percent, mill after mill was preparing to shut down. Logging companies said the owl numbers were skewed. Some said they had never seen a spotted owl.

Yet, this heretofore unknown creature was proving to be far from helpless.

Timber summit

Mason made another trip to Washington, D.C., in late February and announced that the summit would be held in Portland, Ore., in April or May with President Clinton and Vice President Gore in attendance.

Once again, Buley was there to give a balanced report for the *Forum*. He was in the same room, on Friday, April 2, 1993, with Clinton, Gore and key Cabinet members, who listened for six hours to the passionate pleas of the logging industry representatives and those on the opposite side, including the Sierra Club and a few logging companies, who sought balance in the decision.

Mason said it was the "greatest moment of my life" when he faced the nation's leaders on center stage for about five minutes, sharing "what I felt and what this situation has done to my community."

The Forks activist refuted the notion that some made that the unemployment figures in the timber industry would have declined anyway. "I can tell you, Mr. President, that is not so. We in Forks just want to roll up our sleeves and go to work."

"Transition takes time," Mason added, to the argument from some that said loggers need to make some changes. "You don't make those changes overnight when your timber supply is disrupted by a court injunction. You can't make those changes overnight when your American dream has become a nightmare."

In summary, Mason urged the president to read the letters he brought from Forks Middle School students who told of the impact to their town and the gridlock in the federal forests.

"It's a tragedy of great consequence. It's a tragedy that breaks my heart to tell you about. It's a tragedy we have to deal with," Mason concluded.

The forest executive told Buley he was satisfied with the summit. "I think he's going to do the right thing," Mason said.

"It's too late for us," said Hoquiam Mayor Phyllis Shrauger, noting that the ITT Rayonier mill recently had shut down, leaving 600 jobless. When Mike Espy, Secretary of Agriculture, suggested Hoquiam needed to diversify its market, Shrauger replied: "All we have to market is an empty log truck and a rusty old spar."

> *"It's a tragedy of great consequence. It's a tragedy that breaks my heart to tell you about. It's a tragedy we have to deal with."*
>
> **Larry Mason, Timber Summit member from Forks**

Timber executives and business leaders shared the podium with those on the opposite side.

Bill Arthur, director of the Sierra Club's Northwest office in Seattle, said, "We're at the edge of the Pacific Coast. The timber frontier is over."

With that, Clinton issued instructions for his Cabinet to come up with a solution to break the deadlock within 60 days.

On July 7, 1993, the Clinton Plan decision was announced. A crowd gathered at a Forks coffee shop, along with Mason, and a Seattle TV crew ready to record his reaction.

The *Forum* was represented, of course, but it wasn't Buley. He left three weeks prior to accept a position as editor of the *Bonner County Daily Bee* in Sandpoint Idaho. No one could blame him for jumping at this opportunity. As editor, he would have five other reporters working for him.

Mike Henneke was named interim editor and he was immediately tossed into the fray.

There was no question what Mason thought of the announcement that was couched as a compromise by the Clinton Administration officials between environmentalists and timber communities. It was far from a compromise, or at least Mason didn't view it that way.

"You liar," shouted Mason at the TV. He had been optimistic after the Timber Summit two months before that the Clinton plan would give unemployed loggers hope, "not the phony crap like we heard this morning," Mason added.

"There's no hope at all in that plan," he added when interviewed later on TV. "We may fight outside the system," he proclaimed, but didn't elaborate.

"We're not going to play by the rules anymore," echoed the sentiment of Barbara Mossman, spokesman for the American Loggers Solidarity, a separate grassroots organization.

Two months later, on Sept. 23, the pain became exacerbated when the Environmental Protection Agency announced that marbled murrelet, a nesting bird that required old-growth habitat, would be added to the list of threatened species.

That was enough for Dean Hurn. He announced he has two months of product left and then he is shuttering the Hoh River Mill, putting about 100 workers on the unemployed list.

By the start of 1994, the *Forum* had a new editor in Don Gronning, sent to the peninsula by his boss Buley in Idaho.

Some positive signs also started to appear in an around Forks. At a time when mills were closing, Portac, which operated a mill at Beaver, announced it would open a facility at the Forks Industrial Park. The company would spend $4 million for a lumber-drying building on that site.

Portac signed a 9-year contract that was expected to bring 40 jobs, paying $9 to $15 an hour.

'By George'

With a handful of editors using the *Forum's* revolving door in the first five years of the new ownership, Maloney and Olympic View Publishing, the corporation he created in 1991 to oversee all his publications, decided it was time to find some stability.

Oddly, he found that with a man, who at age 68, wasn't yet ready for the rocking chair. George McCormick would be at the *Forum* as editor for nine more years when he retired at age 77.

George McCormick's "By George" columns were a staple of the *Forum* for nine years. He later wrote a book *By Gones By George*, a compilation of his columns. *(Courtesy of Lora Malakoff)*

"I'll never forget what Brown told me on my way out to Forks," McCormick shared in his retirement story. "He told me I was getting older and I needed to take a job where I could relax."

Having worked in Sequim for 10 years, Maloney was quite high on the McCormick pair — and with good reason.

George and his wife, Kass, (they were a tandem; she worked in classified ad sales) came to Forks. Previously he had spent more than 30 years at various newspapers in California, then Port Orchard, Wash.

In his introductory column in the *Forum*, McCormick talked about getting involved in the community, something they had done swimmingly well in Sequim.

The move was made easier by the help we received from old friends and new," McCormick wrote. *"And, Forks has lived up to its reputation for being a friendly town.*

It appears that Forks is a more closely knit community than Sequim, but shares some common problems, particularly not being taken seriously by the powers that be in Port Angeles.

I believe the role of a community newspaper is to reflect the interests of its community and to be supportive — in as much as possible — of the community. That doesn't mean to be blind to its shortcomings, but it does mean to be realistic in championing its causes and, perhaps, in helping guide its future.

In 1998, Maloney stepped down as publisher and installed Frank Garred in his place. Maloney had sold 50 percent of his stock in Olympic View Publishing to Garred and Scott Wilson, co-owners of the *Port Townsend Leader*. Garred would come to Sequim as publisher of the *Gazette* and would manage the operation at Forks from his Sequim office for about four years before he retired.

As he did for 10 years in Sequim, McCormick continued writing his "By George" column in the *Forum* for nearly another decade. Many of his columns took shots at what he called "ineffective bureaucracy," but his cherished columns were those that probed the personal side of his subject.

Archibald's first photo in 1968

In 2004, he wrote about the Olympic Peninsula's most-loved photographer, Lonnie Archibald.

In that column, we learn Lonnie was born in 1942 in Carlsborg near Sequim and his mother, Vay Archibald, wrote about the city for the *Sequim Press*. His father moved the family to Forks in 1957 and started the Chevron station there. After graduating from Forks High School in 1961, he earned a degree from Peninsula College, then attended Edison Tech in Seattle, where he took business administrative and automotive courses.

Lonnie Archibald started taking photos for the *Forum* in 1968 and marked a half-century as a published shutterbug in 2018. During a 2017 interview at his property at Lake Pleasant, he talked about his experiences with the *Forum* and the *Evening News/Peninsula Daily News*. (Bill Lindstrom photo)

Archibald returned to Forks and worked for a time at his father's station, then for Peninsula Telephone and Telegraph in 1969, retiring from there after 30 years (it was Century-Tel by that time).

He revealed he took his first photograph for the *Forum* in 1968 and branched out to Port Angeles the next year. Later The Associated Press wanted to use his photos.

In 1999, Archibald wrote his first of four books, *There Was a Day: Stories of Pioneers*. "We did about 38 interviews and I had videos," Archibald said, adding he took information from the tapes and videos and wrote the book. "I hope this book helps preserve the local history, so many people are gone now."

When interviewed by Mark Morey for a *Peninsula Daily News* article in 1999, he said, "I hope it's something for the pioneer families and it's something for new generations — an opportunity for them to learn more about their heritage."

In a 2017 interview, Archibald said he had been involved with Little League in Forks for about 22 years. "I coached, umpired, was commissioner and officiated football even before the kids played."

He spent four years — 1980-1983 — on the Quillayute School District Board. "Four years was enough," he said. "Seems like we spent most of our time talking about sex education."

Archibald said he enjoys taking sports pictures, but not baseball. "It's too slow," he said. "I love taking pictures of kids — not portraits. I want them to be doing something. Fishing Derbies, Play Days, fairs — they're my favorites."

He's an editor's dream.

He also admitted "loving to cover fires. I have a scanner and it's on at night. If there's a fire, I'll be there," Archibald said.

That has resulted in a couple of award-winning photos, including the September 2010 amazing shot of the fire that destroyed the Old Olympic Theater. He was awarded first place for News Photo of the Year by the Washington Newspaper Publishers Association. In that category, he was competing against larger newspapers.

"The lighting is what sold that," admitted Archibald. It was a combination of red lights from the fire trucks, blue from the police and flashing yellow at the stoplight."

Another award-winner was the fire at the Odd Fellows building that had been there since 1920s. He also recalled the Sappho Café. "That was a hot one," he said.

Archibald didn't have any problem recalling the most emotional photo he took. "It was a local boy (Jason Hanson) killed in Iraq. I was covering for the *Daily News*. They wanted pictures of the family. I didn't do that. I knew the family; it was an invasion of their privacy; too emotional."

Hanson, 21, who had enlisted in 2005, was killed in August 2006 when a nearby explosion caused a building to collapse, killing him and two others. "I took pictures of his boots and some of the speakers. It was tough for me. I knew him."

Archibald adapted rather well to the digital age. In fact, he loves it.

"There was a little learning curve for settings, but before digital, I often carried two cameras, one for inside, one for outside. Now, I just adjust the setting. State tournaments are a breeze, too. I can shoot for different papers, go back to my hotel and send the file." He said he doesn't miss having to soup his own film in chemicals as he did before digital.

> *"Taking pictures of old logging camps, the old Shaker Church at La Push, the old Moritz place on the Hoh and the old school at Barlow's, that type of stuff. It got me interested in history and that got me interested in the old-timers."*
>
> **Lonnie Archibald,**
> *Forum* **photographer**

An oddity occurred on his first day shooting digitally. He went to take a picture of a transit bus that overturned at Snider. "Before digital, I'd put my film on that bus and they would take it to Port Angeles. My first digital photo was of the bus that used to take my film to PA."

While he is in demand mostly for sports, he says his real passion is taking pictures of ruins, but most of them are all gone, he admitted.

"Taking pictures of old logging camps, the old Shaker Church at La Push, the old Moritz place on the Hoh and the old school at Barlow's, that type of stuff. It got me interested in history and that got me interested in the old-timers."

But something ranks far above photography in Lonnie's life. It's his two grandchildren, Scott, a 2018 Forks graduate and Madelyn, a junior that year.

Lonnie and Marjorie Archibald have been married 55 years and have two children: Lynn, nicknamed "Oly" is employed by the Olympic Corrections and Brad works for the Clallam County Highway Department.

He said his kids and grandkids make good use of nine boats — rowboats, kayaks, fishing boats, sail boats, salt-water boats — he has at his Lake Pleasant property, and at home on the Sol Duc River.

The Clallam County Historical Society presented him with the Heritage Award in June 2001 "for being a key player in the preservation of the oral history of the West End." In July 2004, he was named Grand Marshal for the annual Forks Fourth of July Parade. "I think I've seen every parade since 1957," he said.

In 2014, Archibald wrote *Here on the Homefront*, followed in 2016 by *Old Trucks and Gear Jammers*, then a somewhat sequel, *Keep on Truckin'*.

In 2017, Archilbald was accorded still another honor when the Forks Chamber of Commerce named him "Citizen of the Year," acknowledging his 50 years of local photos and book contributions.

Is Archibald, 76 in 2018, about ready to retire? Not hardly. "Even if I am in a wheelchair, I can still take pictures," he said grinning, while his arms showed the motion of wheeling a chair.

In 2002, Garred retired after 41 years in journalism and Maloney returned for six months as publisher of the *Gazette* and the *Forum*. In June 2002, Maloney stepped down and Sue Ellen Riesau assumed command, directing the *Forum* from her Sequim office. She said in a later interview that she had a hand in the *Forum's* management for most of the 23 years she worked with Maloney.

> *"Our desire is to provide you with the best possible newspaper committed to the best in community journalism for the West End,"*
>
> **Sue Ellen Riesau,**
> ***Forum, Gazette* GM**

With the economy trending downward in a downward spiral, in August 2004, the *Forum* took on a new look, shaving five inches off its page length to make it a tabloid.

Riesau identified other changes to the *Forum* in an editorial.

"The front page has a new look, with a new flag featuring our ubiquitous Roosevelt elk. An index will make it easier to know what is inside."

The *Forks Forum* banner features trees — the area's most valuable natural resource.

She said the news pages were being rearranged for better organization with community news following news pages, grouped with public notices. Business news is in the second section, followed by schools, sports, editorial and opinion and classified. All include new headings with more space between columns.

"Our desire is to provide you with the best possible newspaper committed to the best in community journalism for the West End," said Riesau.

In a separate editorial (on the same page), she wrote that a "great deal of engineering and planning went into the new design and package. We knew we needed to identify the icons that would best represent the West End. Once we agreed on, and chose the Roosevelt elk and salmon, we were on our way to creating a pleasing and functional layout."

She also praised the *Forum* staff. "My heartfelt thanks to George (McCormick), Traci (Kettel), Mamie (Morales) and Janeen (Howell). They are the ones who have invested themselves in this paper's redesign and worked closely with the Sequim staff to make it happen."

McCormick retires

When November 2005 rolled around, McCormick decided to retire, ending nearly 50 years in journalism.

"It's Time to Go" was his final "By George" column on November 16. *Sequim Gazette* editor Mary Powell wrote a lengthy retirement story, covering all the bases from when McCormick started at the *Times-Advocate* in Escondido, Calif., in the mid-1960s.

"George and Kass are people who involve themselves in the community," said Maloney. "If there was a bazaar or community breakfast, there they were, flipping pancakes.

Forks Mayor Nedra Reed agrees. "George came into this community and became a part of it very soon. He has been there when times have been good and bad."

In his closing column, he wrote:

Change is the only constant in the universe, and it is now time to make a major change in our life and at the Forum.

To put it briefly, I have retired and am no longer editor of the Forum.

He went on to list the things he will miss, citing working at the *Forum*, being in contact with you (the reader) on a weekly (and sometimes daily) basis, writing an almost weekly column, being in the know, stress and pressure of editing and writing and photographing for a weekly newspaper.

He said neither he nor Kass would have trouble adjusting to retirement. But Latté was another matter. His little dog was his constant companion for many years, named because "she looked like the foam on a latté," McCormick said. "She's used to my being gone, so she and her 'mother' can have quality time together. I will miss her welcoming me home at lunch or each evening."

The McCormicks continued to make their home in Forks until George died on Sept. 1, 2009, at their home. He couldn't completely retire from journalism. At the time of his death, he was Northwest regional editor of *The Seniors Sunset Times* and a Realtor at Lundsford & Associates in Forks.

Lora Malakoff, publisher of the monthly *Seniors Sunset Times*, calls George and Kass "My most-dearest friends. We became very close." Malakoff worked for *The Daily World* in Aberdeen in 2005, then the *Pacific County Press* in 2006, before starting the *Times* in 2006. She and the *Times* celebrated a dozen years in 2018.

McCormick, who had retired in November 2005, "started working for me right after my first issue came out, and Kass was my ad rep.," recalled Malakoff. She used to answer the phone 'This is Mamma Kass, the skinny one who can't sing.' She was such a delight."

Malakoff said, the McCormicks were "The most influential people in my life ... the *Seniors Sunset Times* is what it is because George took me under his wing and taught this ad girl what I needed to know about the bones of a good publication and how to make it a good part of the community. He was my friend, my mentor, and I still miss that man."

In its 12-year-history, the *Times* has been an invaluable source of information and entertainment for the senior citizens in Clallam, Jefferson and Grays Harbor counties. A similar publication also is in Thurston County. The *Sunset Times* includes columns of interest to the community it serves, as well as a calendar of events, feature articles profiling active seniors, health issues, classified ads and strong ad support.

But Malakoff's relationship with the McCormicks went far beyond the professional level. "George officiated at my wedding in 2009, shortly before he passed away," Malakoff added.

"We all know in the industry, newsprint will not make you financially sound, and George and Kass were struggling, so much that Kass could not find the funds to collect his remains, so I paid for his internment and funeral and tried to help Kass out," Malakoff shared. "My kids called them 'Grampa George and Grandma Kass.'"

He authored one book, *By Gones by George*, a collection of his columns, which Malakoff published in 2007 and printed chapter by chapter from September 2006 to June 2008. The foreward to the book was written by Brown M. Maloney, his publisher and boss for 18 years. In it, we learn how George became interested in writing:

"As far back as he can remember, George always wanted to be a writer," Maloney writes. "Perhaps because as a child he remembered his grandfather writing longhand a biography of President Warren G. Harding and writing daily in his diary."

McCormick wrote his first novel at age 16, his second in the 1930s, but neither were worth publishing. George was a history aficionado, perhaps garnering that interest when he was in Germany and Switzerland, "learning a strong dose of history in the making" during the late war years as an Army brat.

After Germany, during his high school years, he returned to the states and graduated from Missouri Military Academy, then attended Ohio University in Athens, Ohio.

"George says that some of his proudest achievements were the awards that he won during his newspaper career from the Washington State Newspaper Publishers Association." Some were for his "By George" columns, but he also won for his photography and earned community service awards while an editor for the *Forum*.

He even earned a national award in the "Zen Pet Contest" for the One Spirit Book Club. The photo was of his beloved Latté, prancing happily. It was accompanied by a quote from the *Dhammapada*, with the words of the Buddha ... "And there is no joy like the joy of freedom."

George and Kass married in 1976, and "have worked together so much that people sometimes have difficulty separating them in their minds," wrote Maloney, also noting that "at the *Gazette* and at the *Forum*, George surrounded himself with history buffs in the communities and spent countless hours at the museums in each town.

"The greater Forks area is lucky to have both he and Kass as residents," Maloney summarized.

At the time of his death, a second book, a 30-year project about his spirituality, was in production. The working title was *A Course in Parallels*, alternately titled *A Lesson in Miracles*. "He left it in my hands before he passed, and I've been shopping around to find a publisher and get funds to publish it," Malakoff added.

Seven months after George died, Katherine Mae "Kass" McCormick died at Forks Hospital.

After McCormick retired, Denise Dunne Devaney was named interim editor for a couple of months, but the *Forum* was basically managed and produced by the *Gazette* staff until the end of December 2006 when Allen "Dusty" Routh was hired.

Routh had been regional editor for *Fishing and Hunting News* and had written two books about fishing, occasionally writing columns for the *Gazette* and the *Peninsula Daily News*.

When asked why he would want to move to Forks, his short answer was "Why not?"

Management was delighted they had the man who could fill the big shoes left by McCormick's retirement.

But Routh's tenure was short-lived. He had been on the job a scant two weeks and attended a Forks High School basketball game on Jan. 11, 2007, when he experienced chest pains. He drove himself to the hospital, where he died about 9 p.m.

In a front-page *Forum* story, written by Mary Powell, and accompanied by a 3-column photo of Routh holding a huge steelhead, she wrote:

One would like to think if there is a heaven, Dusty Routh is there, fishing pole in hand, waiting to snag the big one. … Ask anyone who worked with, was a friend, or simply knew his name, what Dusty's favorite pastime was and the answer was unanimous: fishing and hunting. A close second was writing.

Forum publisher Riesau took his death hard, as did the Forks community.

Over the three-month period that I interviewed people and got to know Dusty, I was certain he would be an asset to our team and do a great job, and the best part was that he was an outdoorsman and had a passion for the West End. Dusty's death was a huge loss to this paper and the Forks community.

Chris Cook, 'Twilight' arrive

It took two months, but on March 21, Riesau (insert and Maloney) found the paper's next editor.

"Chris Cook has a wealth of experience in newspapers, desktop publishing, feature writing as well as marketing and tourism promotion," said Riesau in a column introducing the new editor.

Cook graduated from the University of Hawaii and spent 25 years living and working in the Hawaiian Islands before moving to Idaho.

"My wife was a skier and wanted to get back to the mountains," said Cook of his move as editor at *The Garden Island* in Kauai, Hawaii, in 2005. "She left ahead of me and went to Vail and other mountains." He said they eventually "rebuilt an old house outside of Coeur 'd Alene" and spent two winters there. He was working in pre-press for the *Coeur 'd Alene Press*, but was ready to get out of the Rockies.

"My wife helped me and noticed an ad for an opening at the *Forks Forum*," Cook said. "I never heard of Forks, but I googled 'Forks Washington surfing' and discovered a surfing community I had never heard about prior."

He didn't just enjoy surfing, he lived it. In his college years at the University of Hawaii, he lived on the North Shore, home of the Bonzai Pipeline, one of the world's premier surfing locations. He wrote surfing articles for the student newspaper, then through the 1970s, "was an early surfing arrival to the island of Bali in Indonesia, and went on extended surfing trips to Australia, New Zealand and the Basque coast of France."

When he visited for an interview with Maloney and Riesau, then drove to Forks and La Push, he was sold. He later said the town reminded him of his grandfather's town, where he operated a dairy in Idaho.

Little did Cook know when he arrived in the spring of 2007, that a worldwide phenomenon was about to strike the little town of Forks. A four-book teen vampire series would put Forks on the map in a big way.

"Twilight was already percolating when I arrived," said Cook in a 2017 email interview from his home in Hawaii. "I think the town first heard about the book when a City of Forks employee picked up a copy while visiting in New York City."

The first book in Stephenie Meyer's four-book series, *Twilight*, was published in 2005, and the following year she visited Forks, giving a reading and signing books for "Twi-Hards," as fans of the fabled teen books are called.

The fever had already begun. Mayor Nedra Reed declared July 20, 2006, "Stephenie Meyer Day," the day she would arrive and read to fans at Tillicum Park. It was a dark and stormy day. Meyer loved it. "It's quite an honor to have a nationally known novel set in your hometown," said Reed.

Two years later, it was easy for the *Forum's* advertising department to sell and produce an 8-page tabloid — all on Meyer.

It wasn't until a 2008 interview headlined: 'Vampire Tourism Breathes New Life Into Small Town," that the Arizona woman, a Mormon mom of three, revealed she had written the first book without ever having been to the gritty town on the edge of the Olympic Mountains.

In 2003, she took up writing full time. She had a dream, and in three months, transformed that into *Twilight*, that sold 29 million copies in its first year. She followed with three more and more than 100 million sold. Then a five-movie series was produced, based on those four books. Through 2017, those movies had grossed more than $392 million.

She said she chose Forks because "it was the rainiest city in the United States, (212 rainy days a year when she did her research), yet when she arrived there, it was bright sunshine, which she said disappointed her.

The rest of the storyline she manufactured in her mind, yet it was astonishing how much of it fit perfectly, she revealed in the interview. "It was eerily similar to my imaginings," she said. "Walking down Main Street, shopping at Thriftway (now Forks Outfitters), driving up the side streets until we found a house that could have been Charlie's, then finding a beat-up, once-red, early-fifties Chevy truck parked across the road.

"The word surreal gets overused a lot, but this really was like walking around inside of a dream."

In the book, she introduces the world to Bella Swan, a 17-year-old, who moves to Forks, and is torn between the love of Forks High School classmate Edward Cullen and best friend Jacob Black. Before long, she realizes something isn't right when she discovers Edward is a vampire and Jacob, a werewolf. Meyer's fans

Marcia Yanish, left, and Pura Carlson, right, both of Forks, receive autographs from *Twilight* author Stephenie Meyer during this *Twilight* celebration at the Forks Visitors center in 2013. "Twi-Hards" invade Forks each September for a three-day festival that includes bus tours to sites that are "Twilight-Centric." *(Lonnie Archibald photo)*

were hooked, even dividing themselves between the "Edward Team" and the "Jacob Team." As she wrote the series, releasing the books annually, visitors started flocking to Forks and the city welcomed them with open arms.

As the pages kept coming, the series' cult-like following increased. Before long, fans started showing up in Forks, looking to see if that magic would spark when imagination collided with reality. What they found was a one-stoplight town(it was erected in December 1974), where a foot of rain falls each month. A place where success is measured in sweat and four-wheel drive trucks.

But Forks was quick to embrace the frenzied fans.

"I was there when it happened," said Lorraine (Maris) Jacobson, former owner of the *Forum*, explaining how the first tour evolved.

"I was in Edna Leppell's flower shop when some folks came in and asked when the next tour bus was leaving. Edna didn't flinch. She told them 'just a minute,' went out and cleaned out her van that had flowers in it and returned. 'Right away,' she told them, charged them $1 and they were off."

Now there are big buses, even uniforms. "It's great. It gave the people here something to focus on."

Marcia Bingham, the Chamber of Commerce executive director in 2008, deserves much of the credit for capitalizing on the phenomenon that has brought a great influx of tourists to Forks since the first Twilight Festival in 2008, the largest being a gathering of 70,000 in 2010, when the first of the five-sequel movie series, starring Kristen Stewart as Bella and Robert Pattison as Edward, was released.

Bingham told the *Seattle Weekly* in a 2010 article Forks has become a "vampirical Holy Grail," where visitors hope to get a glimpse of where Bella Swan lived.

In 10 years (from 2000-2010), tourism has "increased 600 percent. We've probably had more than 100 people a day," says Bingham, who has eagerly watched as van after van of giddy readers — mostly female — pull up in front of the town's visitors center.

Michael Gurling, chamber office manager, capitalized on the opportunity to start his own "Twilight Tours," enlisting a few locals to pick out sites mentioned in the book. They identified the Swan house, a field where the vampires played baseball, the police station, where Bella's father Charlie works, the hospital, where Edward's father is a doctor. A beaten-up red truck that belonged to the Swans. And, of course, the high school where they attended.

The frenzy widened to Port Angeles too, identifying the book store (likely Port Book and News, though it could have been Odyssey), where Bella and friends visited, Gottschalks, where they went shopping and Bella Italia, where Bella and Edward had their first date.

Other areas were soon enveloped, such as La Push, a beach environment depicted in the books, Lake Ozette, Ruby Beach and the Hoh Rainforest.

Cook said, as editor, he got hooked into the frenzy in a big way. "It was a hoot. I helped out in dreaming up activities to attract the 'Twi-Hards'.

Marcia Bingham got a committee together and we held the first Twilight Festival in mid-September on Bella's fictitious birthday."

He said he was transfixed by the "amazing, can-do attitude of folks on the West End of the peninsula, creating a low-key Twilight Disneyland at little or no cost."

Cook noted that the Miller Tree Inn Bed and Breakfast became the Cullen House, a school teacher's house became Bella's home. A "Doctor Cullen reserved parking space was put up at Forks Hospital, the chamber put out a map with the stops on it like a Hollywood star tour."

The tumultuous fervor was worldwide. "At times, being the editor with the 'Twilight' vampire overlay, was surreal. I wonder how many community newspaper editors have given a report about thousands of vampire fans flocking to their town on the global BBC (British Broadcasting Company) radio network? Or been interviewed within one week for feature stories published by *Der Speigel* in Germany, the *L.A. Times* and the *Wall Street Journal*?" Cook asked, rhetorically.

He said one of his highlights during the height of the mania was when he "wrangled a couple dozen invitations for Forks High students to attend the premiere of one of the 'Twilight' films in Seattle. The theater was filled with fans who won promo tickets and journalists, so they would get the full effect. DJs on the stage announced the Forks High kids are here. The students made their entrance through a side door wearing varsity jackets and school sweatshirts to an ovation from the fans that shook the house, a moment I am sure they will never forget."

What began as a one-day fun fest has expanded to a three-day annual festival around Bella's fictional birthday, not only in Forks, but also in Port Angeles. It's actually a full week of activities, something for every Twi-Hard. In the center of town, Forever Twilight is a store that had specialized in Native American memorabilia, but now sells shirts, sweaters, cups, DVDs and books — all "Twilight"-centric.

The chamber's website has a separate link called "Forever Twilight," providing everything you wanted to know about the phenomena and links to the festival activities.

Forest officer killed

The entire peninsula was shocked in September 2008, when U.S. Forest Officer and Forks resident, Kris Fairbanks, was shot and killed while investigating a van with no license plates. This story is well documented in the Port Angeles chapter. But the *Forum* played a huge part as well. This was the community that knew her best.

"This community has lost a wonderful person," Nedra Reed, a friend of the family and mayor of Forks, told the *Peninsula Daily News*. "A wonderful peace officer, a wonderful wife, wonderful mother, wonderful friend."

Bingham, director of the Forks Chamber of Commerce, was a neighbor of Fairbanks, whose home was on the Sol Duc River, about 6 miles north of Forks. "They loved living on the river," Bingham said. She and the Archibalds were neighbors.

"Kris and her husband, Brian, attended all their daughter Whitney's games," said Bingham. Whitney, a sophomore played junior varsity volleyball.

In addition to the news coverage in the *Forum*, Cook wrote a column: "Mourning following tragic death of Kris Fairbanks cuts across community," writing that she was a friend of the *Forum* and always there to help:

Kris was a friendly, but firm, loving law-abiding woman, who took on a big job. Any call from the Forks Forum *for help on a story or for information was always met promptly and often in person. We knew Kris was someone we could depend on, be it in our office, or in the national forest, which was her domain of responsibility.*

We knew Kris too, as a loving mother and a dog-lover, roles she often mixed in her connections with the Forks 4-H dog club, known as 'Happy Tails.' The club was recently pictured in a Forks Forum *article, showing happy children who knew what they were doing with dogs. Her trusty lab, Radar, was with her when she was shot.*

Kris' legacy will live on with these kids, and in her daughter, Whitney, who has grown up as part of the 'Happy Tails,' and as the daughter of a mother who knew the forest well.

Cook also was the editor when a pair of tragic accidents struck Forks

in 2010: A helicopter crash
at La Push and a fire that
destroyed the Olympic
Theater.

"Lonnie Archibald was the star of the theater fire," Cook said. "He was on call 24/7 and was there in the middle of the night. He got an incredible color photo of the firefighters battling the blaze. He won an award and I was in Everett that night to accept it for him."

On the helicopter crash, three people were killed when the H-60 craft, often used in rescue efforts by the Coast Guard, struck a powerline that connected to the electrical grids on La Push. Two others on the copter were later rescued.

Cook said the *Peninsula Daily News* did the breaking news of the event that happened on mid-morning Wednesday, July 7, after the *Forum* had been printed.

"We focused more on the impact on folks at La Push and the memorial service." Years later, Cook went out in a surf boat in large waves to photograph the dropping of a memorial wreath. "They knew I surfed and we surfed in the biggest wave of my life into the mouth of the Quillayute River." That photo appeared in *Living on the Peninsula* magazine, published by the *Sequim Gazette,* and won a WNPA award.

On Nov. 15, 2011, the *Forum* had a new publisher when it was announced that the paper, the *PDN,* Sequim *Gazette,* the *Peninsula Business Journal* and a couple of real estate magazines were purchased by Sound Publishing Co., ending Maloney's 21 years as *Forum* owner.

Sound, the first corporate owner of the paper, would be only the seventh owner in the *Forum's* 81-year history. Sound's parent company was Victoria, B.C.-based Black Press.

While Cook had many memorable events during his tenure at the *Forum,* he pointed to a spirited community effort to modernize Forks High School as the endeavor that "left the biggest impression on me." A bond issue passed, a cutting-edge wood-waste boiler was installed to heat the formerly chilly classrooms, and the core of the aging high school was torn down and replaced with a 21st-century facility, Cook said.

One group which provided funding help was "Twilighters for Forks," based locally, but spread throughout the nation. They helped raise funds for the new school.

When the modernized school opened in 2012, Cook said, "Diane Reaume, the superintendent of the Quillayute Valley School District, told me I played a key role in gaining support for the project and seeing it through."

Cook, who had written two books on the history of Kauai and Hawaii, left the *Forum* in the spring of 2013 to return to Hawaii and finish his book on the Obookiah family in Hawaii, chronicling the rise of literacy in the early 1800s in Hawaii. That family, while Hawaiian, had a big influence in New England, which is the essence of his book.

"I am currently working on a photo color version of my non-fiction narrative genre book *The Providential Life and Heritage of Henry Obookiah*, Cook said. He is targeting the book to be finished by the 200th anniversary of the Hawaii mission arrival in 2020.

Cook and Buley have quite a distinction. Both were editors of the *Forum*, the "farthest west newspaper in the contiguous United States," and they both were editors of *The Garden Island* in Kauai, which Cook said he believed was the "farthest west newspaper in the world." Cook was there before coming to Idaho, then Forks, and Buley is currently editor at Kauai.

After Cook left, two editors — Mark Couhig and Joe Smilie — filled in temporarily.

But management, specifically *PDN* publisher John Brewer, who had *Forum* oversight, had his eye on someone else.

For the past seven years, Christi Baron, a Forks native, had written the West End Neighbor column.

"I was at Forkestra (Forks Community Orchestra) practice one night when Chiggers (Stokes) said he didn't want to write the column anymore and I said I would do it," Baron related in a 2017 interview. Stokes, a former Olympic National Park ranger, had written the column for seven years, but retired to his home on the Bogachiel River.

"He didn't want to do it anymore," said Baron. "I had worked in real estate and was working at city hall when Brewer offered me the part-time job. They were looking for someone who knew the West End and could write."

Baron said, after seven years of writing the column, "John called me and offered me the job as editor of the *Forum*, but it was only part-time with no benefits. I told him that it wouldn't work. But, it was killing me. I really wanted that job," she revealed.

"So, I called Brewer again and discovered that they had now made it full time with benefits and were setting up interviews." She was offered the job and didn't hesitate. "I'll take it," she said.

Christi Baron is hard at work as the editor of the *Forks Forum* in 2017. A native of Forks, Baron became editor in November 2013 and was there in 2018. *(Bill Lindstrom photo)*

Baron became the editor in November 2013, and she was still in the position in 2018.

"I wanted the paper to get that 'Forksy-feel' back that had been missing," she said. "I have that because I was born here, I was raised here, and I live here. I trained with Joe Smilie in Sequim for a couple of months, then they left me on my own. He was a little crazy, in a good way, but he taught me everything I know; I will always be grateful."

Baron and her husband, Howard, celebrated 41 years of marriage in 2018. They have no children, but three dogs, two cats, chickens and ducks keep them busy at their North Forks home.

Baron said she had a brief association with the paper when she was in high school. "My boyfriend at the time was the son of Gordon Otos, the owner of the paper. David and I would help out, doing some paste-up. We did it because it was fun."

She admitted that the job has been a huge challenge. "I know everybody, but that's good and bad. I had to put someone's name in the paper for a crime and his wife called and begged me not to do it. I told her, if it was my own brother, I'd have to do it."

Baron said one of her biggest mistakes in her tenure thus far came during probationary court proceedings. "I couldn't read the prosecutor's figures. It looked like he had written 9 days (for the sentence), but it was 0 days. The guy called me and complained. It was nice to know criminals read the paper too," she quipped.

Baron admitted Archibald has been a life-saver. "I couldn't do this job without Lonnie. He may be getting older, but he is at all the sporting events, accidents and other events; all I have to do is ask him. One time there was an accident on my road, and he lives off Sol Duc (miles away). I drove down to the accident and he was already there."

She takes exception with those who say Twilight is dead, and there are some, although the furor isn't as electric as it was six or eight years ago.

"They need to come here in the summer and in September when we have "Stephenie Meyer Day" (now called "Forever Twilight in Forks") and the week-long festival is held," Baron said. "People play along with the tourists and do the best for them. The other day a busload of people from China were here doing a TV segment. They still come from all over."

But the one thing the editor says that disturbs a lot of residents is "People in Forks don't want the city to be known as the 'Twilight Capital of the World,' they still want to be known as the 'Logging Capital of the World.'"

She does like where the *Forum* office is located, in a building that Brown M. Maloney bought shortly after purchasing the paper in 1990.

"It's right next to a drug and alcohol counseling service. If this job drives me to drink, I don't have far to go for help."

PART V

Broadcasting

CHAPTER 14

Voices from the peninsula: KONP, PNN, others

The year was 1945; the nation was mired in the depths of World War II and the government had ordered rationing of food, clothing, coffee, gas, fuel oil and tires.

However, on the Olympic Peninsula there was reason for smiling.

It was Feb. 3, 1945, and the reason for the exuberance was the first broadcast from Port Angeles radio station KONP, at 6:30 a.m. When the station at 1450 AM began its broadcast with the national anthem it launched the first radio station on the North Olympic Peninsula.

That station is still in business and marked its 73rd year in 2018 and has had only four ownership entities.

It was founded by Charles Webster's Evening News Press, the commercial arm of the *Port Angeles Evening News.* In 1969, George Buck became sole owner, established a new corporation called Radio Pacific, and occupied that position until Jim and Terry MacDonald became co-owners with Buck in 1983. When Buck died in 1996, the MacDonalds became sole owners.

In 2002, Brown M. Maloney, publisher of the *Sequim Gazette,* purchased KONP radio from the MacDonalds. He brought young Todd Ortloff along as a minority owner. The Maloney-Ortloff tandem operates the station today.

Getting KONP on the air in 1945 didn't come about easily or quickly. The steps toward establishing the station started in 1937 when Webster, publisher of the *Evening News*, first petitioned the Federal Communication Commission for a radio license.

Webster's vision of a radio station first surfaced when, as an 11-year-old, he built a ham radio set from a diagram he saw in *Popular Mechanics* magazine. Unlike the rest of his siblings, Charles did not have the ambition to be in the newspaper industry. He did have a paper route, but that's the extent of his involvement with the paper until much later.

His parents, E.B. and Jessie Webster, likewise didn't see Charles involved in the industry, even after he graduated from high school at age 15. They considered him too young for college and enrolled Charles in trade school in Seattle to be trained as a ship's radio-room operator. Later, he found employment on a steamer headed for Alaska.

Eventually, he attended college and graduated from the University of Washington, the third of the higher learning institutions he attended. Following college, he secured jobs on sailing vessels as a radio-room operator with a vision of managing his own station.

After several jobs in New York City with Gulf Oil Co. and Ford Motor Co., he marred Esther Barrows in 1929. In 1934, he decided to leave Esther in New York to pursue her art career, while he joined his father at the *Evening News* in Port Angeles.

In 1936, the elder Webster died and Charles' role at the paper increased.

The following year, with a well-planned format, he began the steps necessary to establish a radio station. Among the documents he presented to the FCC in Washington, D.C., in December 1937, was a list of 75 prospective advertisers and 45 organizations, that had indicated they would contribute.

Detailed in the *Olympic Leaders* book, Charles testified that the station would "benefit local industries, including agriculture and logging. He also had plans to broadcast the annual Salmon Derby and music of Port Angeles community orchestra."

The call letters for the station were locally significant, though in part federally regulated. The FCC had deemed that every station east of the Mississippi River would start with a W, while west of the river all stations would start with a K.

Charles, like his father before him, envisioned an Olympic National Park eventually would be established, thus the rest of the station letters

ONP, was an easy pick for him, reflecting pride he had in the area. While the moniker suggests otherwise, the park never has been associated with the radio station, other than the call letters.

Numerous delays plagued approval of the license, then an outright halt to license applications occurred when World War II broke out in September 1939. Meantime, three other groups filed applications for a license to operate a station on the peninsula.

Local officials and Webster made a plea in 1942 that a local radio station would aid civilian defense.

In 1943, Port Angeles banker Benjamin Phillips and Carl Fisher of Portland, Ore., under the name of Olympic Broadcasting Co., became the fifth group to file an application for a license.

Seven years until permit approval

Finally, in June 1944 the FCC granted approval to the Evening News Press. The ownership consisted of Charles N. Webster, his sisters, Beth Webster, Mae Duckering and Dorothy Wenner, and John Schweitzer. When application was first made in 1937, Jessie Webster and William Welsh were included. Jessie died in 1940; Welsh resigned and moved to San Francisco to work for Crown Zellerbach in 1939.

There was still much work to do before the first broadcast. A building had to be acquired as war regulations prevented any further construction.

The owners acquired the former Little Brick Tavern at 313 W. First St., but much renovation was needed. It was no longer a tavern, but a second-hand store when Webster bought it. The tavern had moved one block.

In 1995, when the station marked its 50th anniversary, Sandy Keys, who began working there in the 1960s, wrote in the station's newsletter about those early days when he interviewed Port Angeles resident Harry Bong.

Bong said he became involved in the renovation of the building for KONP. "Marvin Young recruited his teenage crew for Saturday work parties to clean up the mess, so contractors could start remodeling," he said.

"The unfinished west front portion of the building (which became the sales department) was used as a meeting room for *Evening News* carriers for a while, even after the station started broadcasting," Bong recalled. "Later it became Esther Webster's art gallery,"

Bong continued to say that in the fall of 1947, the janitor for the paper and KONP quit, and "I, as an ambitious high school senior, got the job on an interim basis. This involved opening KONP at 6 a.m. to sweep out, empty wastebaskets, dust the grand piano and whatever else was needed."

Bong also was responsible for firing up the huge, manually fed coal furnace, which heated the building, so it would be warm when Bill Taber, the morning announcer, went on air at 6:45 a.m.

When the old tavern building was acquired, it was perched on piers and stilts with a false front and peaked roof. One half of the building was converted into a studio and offices.

The rest of the building had to wait until after the war was over to get a face-lift. A sign was fashioned out of wood strips, painted in forest green and placed on the building that was painted white for the Olympic snow-capped mountains.

In the same anniversary newsletter, Terry MacDonald, then co-owner with her husband Jim and George Buck, wrote "Our roots are in water heaters and Douglas fir."

She noted "quite literally KONP's first antenna was a 180-foot Douglas fir pole, trucked in by Sam Antenon. It arrived at the station's first location on a salt water tidal flat the first week of December 1944. The ground system for the antenna was created in part from old water heaters, collected

A microphone and an early Thomas radio are among the archives at the KONP building. *(Bill Lindstrom photo/KONP)*

from J.R. McDonald (no relation to then-station manager, James R. MacDonald), who had been the city's garbage collector."

McDonald still possessed many discarded heaters, and "two hours after KONP head engineer J.P. Ernst expressed the need, McDonald arrived in an old truck. An amazed Ernst had all the water heaters and sundry other pieces of metal that he needed."

Terry continued, "when the tide was out, Ernst and his ground system helper, Harry McNutt, laid 25 tanks in the sand, end-on-end. Later 120 copper wires were welded to these water heaters, which were radiating out from the base of the antenna. The ground system used to be visible every time the tide went out."

The antenna could be seen through the station's rear window, with the messenger cable running from the tuning box at the base of the antenna to the transmitter in the control room.

The station used the original Douglas fir antenna until the mid-1960s, when a metal lattice was constructed and used until 2013. It was dismantled the next year and the station began using the antenna on Melody Lane, formerly used by KAPY, KKNW and KIKN.

The station broadcast from the original site until moving into a newer building, 721 E. First St., in 2008.

Because of the station's wooden structure, a no-smoking order was invoked by the city's fire chief.

Finally, the station was ready for its trial broadcast. The station's personnel included H.J. McAllister, manager; J.P. Ernst, chief engineer; Mildred Ernst, salesman-announcer; Stanley Parker, operator-announcer and Violet Munro, office secretary.

A detailed report in the *Evening News* of Feb. 2, 1945, noted that, after equipment tests, "the station received reports of good reception throughout Port Angeles, and strong reception as far as Neah Bay, Sequim and even a report from Albuquerque, N.M."

First KONP broadcast

All systems were go for an elaborate opening day, commencing at 6:30 a.m. with the *Star-Spangled Banner*, followed immediately by Bill Taber's popular "Hotcakes and Coffee," a program where listeners called in song requests; for much of its 70 years, it was hosted by Scooter Chapman. Requests on opening day inundated the telephone lines from regions ranging from Neah Bay, Tacoma and Victoria.

One special request, the *Evening News* reported, came from a man at a Canadian lookout, who signaled by blinker light 18 miles across the strait to a U.S. Coast Guard station, which relayed the message to KONP by telephone.

A special dedicatory ceremony started at 6:30 p.m. on that historic Saturday, Feb. 3, 1945.

A half-page ad in the newspaper detailed the station's broadcast celebratory log for the evening program:

Keys would write about the exciting climax to the first day's broadcasting 50 years later.

"The Music of the Blue Danube Orchestra, originated live, on location, at the Blue Danube Dance Hall, an enormous wooden structure, located where McDonald's fast-food restaurant is today. Nobody then had a clue that there would eventually be a McDonald's on that location, or even then had a clue what a McDonald's restaurant was.

"Yet, often people who were planning on dancing at the Blue Danube, would say 'We're going to McDonald's tonight, and drive or walk right to today's location. It wasn't the Twilight Zone. The Blue Danube was built by Clyde McDonald, and it was McDonald who coaxed

KONP's first-day broadcast

6:30-6:45 Piano and chatter, featuring Al Smith, CJVI, Victoria;

6:45-6:55 Variety music

6:55-7:00 Salute to KONP from Washington State College president Dr. William Compton;

7:00-8:00 Lou Michael and His Melody Swingsters from KONP studio, with accordion solos by Elaine Crist, Port Angeles high school student;

8:00-8:15 Salute to KONP from Commander D.O. Reed, of Port Angeles Coast Guard station;

8:15-8:30 Salute to KONP by Lt. Commander Dobbins, executive officer, Quillayute Naval Air Station;

8:30-9:00 Port Angeles Concert Orchestra, broadcasting remote from the Elks Building;

9:00-9:15 First regularly scheduled quarter-hour broadcast from United Press International;

9:15-10:00 Studio variety program, featuring Charlie Smith and the Harmonaires, versatile orchestra from Forks with banjo by Roy Horton and western song by Warren Strasser;

10:00-10:30 Salute to KONP from University of Washington;

dancers from all over Western Washington, proclaiming it was the finest dance floor in the Northwest."

There were no commercials that first day. Keys would note in the newsletter, "Except for the aftermath of the Kennedy assassination, it hasn't happened since. That's how it was on that first day — commercial-free."

It was a long-standing tradition for new stations to air without commercials. Advertising started on the second day. On the 50th anniversary, Keys saluted the first advertiser — "the most popular restaurant in Port Angeles, Goneis (pronounced Go-knees) on Front Street."

Longtime resident Pete Capos remembers the restaurant was "built immediately after the ashes of the Port Angeles Opera House cooled down in 1923. It was part of the new Olympus Hotel, located at the former Seafirst parking lot near Front and Laurel," Keys would write.

"Five decades later, there would be another fire at the same location, and the former Goneis Café was ashes and rubble. But, by then, it had been purchased by Lloyd Snodgrass, and at the time of the explosion, it was called Haguewood's."

The dedicatory weekend continued Sunday with transcribed broadcasts from other Northwest stations, a special concert by the First Methodist Church choir and other religious programs.

Commencing Sunday, the station began broadcasting all day and evening, starting at 6:30 a.m. weekdays and 9 a.m. Sundays.

Transmitting with 250 watts of power on the 1450 kilocycles, KONP was a resounding success that had Charles Webster and his siblings beaming with pride, greeting a select group of invitees to the small confines of the station. The public was asked to wait until the following week to visit the station.

After the initial weekend, the station continued to bring local talent into the station's programming.

Listeners recollections

In the 50th anniversary newsletter, Keys asked listeners for their recollections of the early days. He was inundated with responses.

Betty Porsch Schumacher of Port Angeles remembered songs by the

Andrews Sisters, particularly "Rum and Coca Cola," the calypso hit for the girls in 1945. She also recalls the letters to Santa with KONP announcers Keith Patterson and Jim Fritz.

"Our daughter, Jeanne, was about four and wrote her letter to Santa, to be read. We listened every night," said Schumacher, "and when it came on, I never saw such an excited girl."

Others recalled "Amateur Night" when the high school band was asked to perform in the station's studio.

Judith Lindberg of Port Angeles recalled Florence Johnson, "The Story Lady," noting that she wrote a poem called "1949," in which "I paid tribute to her. Johnson died on March 26, 1993, at the age of 94."

Lindberg also remembered the Roosevelt Rhythms from Roosevelt High School.

On June 15, 1946, KONP broadcast its first remote program from the dedication ceremony of the establishment of Olympic National Park at Rosemary Inn at Lake Crescent.

Not long after KONP began broadcasting in 1945, Esther Webster began live programs as Jean Earl. *(Courtesy of the North Olympic History Center)*

Jean Earl at the mic

Not long after the station began operation, Esther Webster gave up her reporting desk at the *Evening News* for the microphone at KONP. She reported on air as Jean Earl, using the interview process to build a significant following. Most of the day was spent at the station, rather than at the *Evening News*, but she kept up on what was happening with the newspaper and continued to write articles.

She began her radio career with a women's feature program called "Women's Club of the Air," in which she read United Press wire news edited for the female audience. She would bring a wide array of local personalities to the KONP microphones. As Jean Earl, she also would moderate roundtable discussions on current topics of interest.

When the station celebrated its seventh anniversary in 1952, the Jean Earl show was rated the most popular KONP program by listeners who responded.

An indication of how much Esther enjoyed her job at the radio station is her oil painting, titled *Radio KONP*, in 1947. The *Olympic Leaders* describes the work as "strongly cubistic, the abstract is a kaleidoscope of impressions that signify the purview of radio, using a montage of visual forms, including text. Waves in the painting represent both radio waves and the waves of the strait."

This painting by Esther Webster in 1947 indicates how important radio was in her life. The cubistic art of her station KONP represents a montage of radio equipment. *(Courtesy of KONP)*

From Aug. 1 to Nov. 5, 1948, she filed 74 installments, called "Travels with Jean Earl," while on an extensive trip to Europe with the Port Angeles Soroptimists. Her reports not only appeared in the *Evening News*, but also were read periodically on the radio.

Scooter starts with a broom

In 1951, a teenager started hanging around the station, so chief engineer Fred Fields gave him a job, sweeping floors and spinning a few discs.

In 2018, that teen now, 84-year-old Howard Chapman, marked 67 years working for KONP. Never heard of him? Sure, you have. Except nobody called him by his first name. He was known as Scooter "since he was a baby," he admitted, without detailing the derivation of the name.

Scooter Chapman sits behind the mic after an interview in 2015 not long after a fall at home hospitalized him. He has been with KONP 67 years. *(Bill Lindstrom photo)*

He was a junior at Roosevelt High School, keeping stats and spotting at Roughrider football games. He gained a knowledge of sports by listening to Leo Lassen broadcast Seattle Rainier baseball games.

"I was excited to be around the station," he said in an interview in 2015. "I did whatever they wanted me to do. I never knew what I was going to end up with."

After graduating high school in 1952, he attended the University of Washington for three quarters before he ran out of funds.

He returned to Port Angeles and did some odd jobs, yet, found time to hang around the station. Scooter admitted later that the station manager liked that "because they didn't have to pay me."

In 1954, he married his wife Loretta. In August 2017 they celebrated 63 years of marriage. The Chapmans have four boys, 12 grandchildren and eight great-grandchildren.

A two-year stint in the Army as a radio broadcast specialist (1957-1959) paved way for his journalistic career in communications.

"It was life-changing," Chapman added in 2015. "I loved radio, but Loretta and I wanted to start a family and decided to return to Port Angeles. I never left here."

Soon after arriving back in Port Angeles, he began work with the *Evening News* as sports editor and at KONP as sports director. A one-year military service stint in 1961 interrupted his career. He returned for good and, after working more than 30 years of a dual job, he left the newspaper business in 1988 and began full-time with the radio station, doing sales, sports announcing and the "Morning Show."

"I get up about 4:30 and get to the station by 5 or so," Chapman said. "It takes about an hour to prep, then I'm on the air from 6-9. When I get off at 9, the rest of the day is mine."

He said during football season, he tries to arrive at the high school about 4:30 and get information from the coach for that week's game. "I believe in face-to-face talking. I don't believe in calling up the coach. Through the years, I have earned their trust."

As much as his morning talk show or his golden announcing voice have become KONP staples, so too has his sports column, "Spotlight on Sports," in the *PDN* and later, the *Sequim Gazette*.

"I try to keep my writing and broadcasting positive," he admitted. "I pattern my writing after Royal Brougham (the late, longtime Seattle *Post-Intelligencer* sports columnist). He was the best."

His career began quietly, but more than five decades later, Scooter is known as the "Golden Voice" of Port Angeles athletics. He told Mark Schubert of the *Peninsula Daily News* in 2011, that he estimated he had called more than 500 football games and more than 1,500 basketball games.

That same article announced Chapman would be inducted into the Washington

Scooter Chapman relaxes in his office chair at KONP during an interview in 2011. That story in the *Peninsula Daily News* would announce that Chapman would be inducted in the Washington Interscholastic Athletic Association Hall of Fame for his career in radio, newspaper and sports officiating. *(Peninsula Daily News archive)*

Interscholastic Activities Association (WIAA) Hall of Fame, not only for his announcing of games on radio, but also his newspaper and sports officiating careers. For more than 30 years, he was the assigning secretary for the Peninsula Umpires Association.

"It's humbling," said Chapman, modestly. "There's not many broadcasters, writers or umpires in the Hall of Fame. He said that event was the highlight of his career, but he also received the "Silver Helmet Award," given annually by the state's football coaches.

Among his greatest thrills in broadcasting basketball games, Chapman lists three big events: The 1966 Roughrider boys finishing second in Class AA; the 1970 Peninsula College men winning the conference title and the 1988 Rider girls finishing second in Class AA.

"They should give this guy the key to the city of Port Angeles for what he has done for student athletes in this community," former PA boys' player and head coach Lee Sinnes told the *PDN* for the 2011 article.

Todd Ortloff *(Courtesy of KONP)*

> *"He's an icon and embodies everything that broadcasting is about. He's engaged in the community. Scooter gets it."*

From 1961-2011, he said he only missed four football games. Three came after triple-bypass surgeries in 2005. He was back broadcasting by basketball season.

"He's an icon and embodies everything that broadcasting is about," said station manager Todd Ortloff. "He's engaged in the community. Scooter gets it. He is amazing (at his age), the energy and drive he has. That's a unique commodity. He is literally the lifeblood of community journalism."

Scooter suffered a bit of a bump in the road in 2015 when he fell from his porch at home, tearing the quad muscles and meniscus in both legs. After six hours in the E.R., he was placed in a half-body cast for 86 days, recuperating at Crestwood Convalescent Center.

The timing of the accident was fortunate as he recuperated outside the football season.

Scooter admitted Todd told him he had used up his vacation and sick pay, so by July 28, he left Crestwood, Todd picked him up, and with a use of a walker, Scooter was back on the job. "When he got hurt, he was so committed. His main goal was to get back in that chair as soon as possible," Ortloff said.

Scooter Chapman talks to his fans who gathered on Sept. 29, 2017, when the Scooter Chapman Press Box was unveiled at Civic Field in Port Angeles. Chapman, 84, started working at radio station KONP in 1951 and in 2018 is still calling sports events. He estimates he broadcast more than 2,000 games in his 67 years. *(Keith Thorpe/Peninsula Daily News)*

"My first goal was to get out of the convalescent center and to announce the Sonny Sixkiller Golf Tournament on July 24, and I did that."

Chapman said a lot of people helped him, singling out the Lions Club, whose members built a railing and ramp for him at the house.

When last interviewed in March 2018, Scooter's gait was a bit slower, but he is still the same Scooter.

As a testament to his value to the community, he was accorded another tribute on Sept. 29, 2017, when the press box at Port Angeles High School's Civic Field officially was named "Scooter Chapman Press Box." A plaque hangs in the working area.

"Scooter, you've been the voice of the community for many, many years. You've shared your talent and passion for the community's youth. It's a unique and very special opportunity to thank you on behalf of the city and the fans here," said Port Angeles Mayor Pat Downie in a *PDN* dedication story.

"It's not often you get an honor like this when you're still alive and kicking," Chapman said. "It's been a fun ride and it's not over yet," added the man, who figured he has announced more than 2,000 games.

"He has always given his life to sports in this area, especially Port Angeles," his wife, Loretta, told the *PDN*. "Even though he could retire, he just really enjoys the work that he does. That's all he knows."

Chapman has another reason for continuing his career. "The kids keep me young. I don't feel my age."

Scooter still was sweeping floors when one of the most important remote broadcasts occurred on Jan. 15, 1952, the day a helicopter crashed into the Olympic Mountains, about 17 miles south of Dungeness, killing three; five were rescued.

On the front lawn of Olympic Memorial Hospital was James Fritz, KONP announcer, who was snapping up interviews with the survivors to relay to the radio listeners. Inside the hospital, station manager Keith Patterson had obtained an interview with the pilot.

About 2 p.m., the station began broadcasting by a remote line. At the same time, he related that an ambulance was going up Palo Alto Road to get three survivors left there by the helicopter. When the aircraft landed on the hospital lawn, he had more on-the-spot news.

Later that evening (about 6 p.m.), a crew from KING-TV in Seattle arrived, but KONP and the *Evening News* already had beaten the metro boys to the punch.

Sandy Keys at the fair

In 1962, at the Clallam County Fair, a young man out of college wandered into the KONP booth and was asked by Evelyn Tinkham if he heard the station's new announcer.

"Yeah, I did, and he murdered the pronunciation of Pysht and Sappho," the young man replied, referring to the small towns west of Port Angeles.

"Well, if you can do better, come on down to the station Monday and we'll give you an audition," Tinkham replied.

Sandy Keys did, and he passed. Thus, began a career that continues today, 56 years later.

It wasn't a smooth beginning, the "Sandman" would note more than 30 years later in the 50th anniversary newsletter, sharing that a relative said he wouldn't last 30 days.

"I shouldn't have. I was very bad," he admitted. "There were times in the first 30 days I wanted to throw in the towel. There was the incredible mess I made of engineering my first remote broadcast from the control room. I was all by myself. Not a soul in the building," he continued,

Longtime announcer Sandy Keys relaxes during an interview in 2015 at his Port Angeles home. Keys started at KONP in 1962 and was still there in a more limited role in 2018. *(Bill Lindstrom photo)*

describing that first experience, engineering the Port Angeles High School basketball game from the state tournament.

"Everyone was listening. I read the wrong commercials, mis-named teams, tried to cover my mistakes and only talked myself into corners of no return."

He survived that slow beginning and started engineering "Tink's Talks," then doing remotes from the dedication of the William Shore Pool and graduation ceremonies.

"It must have been hilarious," he said, "a just-out-of-college kid trying to sound like Walter Cronkite. Maybe that's why my first station manager Bob (you're paid to play them, not to like them) Eubanks never gave me suggestions, face-to-face, but left copious notes in the mailbox."

Interestingly, Keys admits, "I was never told I was hired and I never told them I accepted the damn job. In a business dedicated to communication, there isn't much communication. But, I got a paycheck. I think $5 or $6 an hour. In the beginning, it was just on Sunday, and it expanded from there."

He also noted that through the years, he has worn several hats — all while moonlighting at KONP.

There's the radio announcer, the college teacher, travel representative and tour organizer, car collector, gentleman farmer (because he didn't have to shovel manure), leaded-stained glass window builder, architect, the museum board trustee, the Clallam County Blood board member, Port Angeles High School history teacher and vice principal.

The ones he enjoys the most? "Car collecting and organizing and escorting tours to Russia, Greece, Turkey and Rio de Janeiro." While teaching high school contemporary issues, he has taken students to Russia more than 25 times. His house overlooking the strait reflects that culture with numerous pieces of Russian art, sculpture, tapestries, furniture, and the dining-room ceiling is a painting from a cathedral near Moscow. From the outside, his house is unmistakable with towering gold cupolas rising from the roof, all of which Keys designed.

Sandy, who turned 81 in May 2018, said through the years, "I have never really felt I was bossed. They just left me alone and let me do my job." He said he would do a Monday broadcast, "which was usually a bunch of whacky things that were a roundup of weekend activities." To this day, he still does Weekend Roundup on Mondays as well as spot announcing throughout the week.

Keys noted that, even though Esther Webster did her Jean Earl columns before she came to the station, "she never had a position there."

By the time, Sandy arrived, Charles Webster had suffered two debilitating strokes, yet still made occasional trips to the newspaper, which was located next to the radio station.

"We called him the cookie man," Keys said. "He'd leave the newspaper office and come by the station (next door). He'd purloin cookies from the station. He was a pretty quiet man, but very nice."

In a bit of irony, one of Keys' students in high school was Todd Ortloff. "Now, he's my boss. We've come full circle."

Sandy recalls those early days when budgets were limited. "Rudy Swanberg used Scotch tape to repair things. He showed me how to fix a lot of stuff around the station. He was one of the most-beloved men at the station."

He also remembered Fred Fields, chief engineer, who used to feed Elmer, the seagull. "He became like a pet. The station was built on stilts on the tide flats and seagulls were rampant. One day, Fred coaxed the seagull onto the porch and he just kept coming back," Keys recalls.

Keys also had fond memories of station manager, Ron Bayton. "We called him the 'coin man,' because he walked around flipping a coin in the air. He was one of the good ole guys. He'd walk around, slap you on the back and tell a few jokes. You don't get that from anybody anymore."

Sandy recalls one of the earlier remote broadcasts he was involved in. "It was a Bob Eubanks' idea. They had opened up a swimming pool at the new Chinook Motel in the 1950s, and he wanted to try something new. We built a platform and extended the broadcast box out across the water."

Keys said most of the time he was his own boss and worked alone. There were a couple of big stories that broke on his watch. "One was the big gas explosion in the '70s (Sept. 30, 1971). I heard it and went up there right away. The Olympus Hotel and Haguewood's restaurant blew up. I did on-the-spot coverage with that."

Another time, he recalled a house explosion on Lincoln. "I got there before the fire department. It was dangerous, but I went inside. I was there to give coverage. I got to talk to the residents before the fire chief threw me out."

Since Keys was a car collector, his Silver Cloud Rolls Royce has seen its share of personalities. "I did an interview with Sheb Wooley and gave him a ride to the Clallam County Fair," the radio broadcaster said of his connection with the man who sang "Flying Purple People Eater" to fame.

George Buck given KONP

Just before Keys came onboard at KONP, a change in leadership was announced when Buck was made general manager of the station in 1957. He held the same position at the *Evening News* and with the other entity, owned by the Websters, Olympic Stationers.

Buck, who passed the bar to become an attorney following graduation from the University of Washington, came to the *Evening News* in 1951 and served as auditor with the paper for two years. In 1953, shortly after Charles Webster suffered the first of two debilitating strokes, Buck was made administrative assistant to the publisher, which gave him oversight not only for the paper, but also the radio station and Olympic Stationers. In 1957, Buck was appointed general manager of all the properties.

Charles suffered his second stroke in 1955 and was not the same after that. He loaned the station some of his sizeable collection of classical records. Despite his interest in radio, he never had a part in the day-to-day operation.

Buck was the man in charge and made most of the decisions regarding all three properties. In 1961, Esther wrote a glowing profile of Buck for the *Evening News*.

Indeed, George had been the architect of progress for the corporation. He guided the paper through transition to cold type and offset; he made positive program changes for the radio station, including broadcasting city council meetings; helped inaugurate the first annual Home Show, sponsored jointly by the *Evening News*, KONP and Chamber of Commerce.

Buck served as program director for the chamber, was director of the Port Angeles Downtown Association and president of the Community Concerts Association.

Some say Buck was "sweet on Esther and her with him," but all that changed in 1966 when Buck went to California and surprisingly returned married to Peggy Fogliano.

George Buck was owner or co-owner of Radio Pacific, which operated KONP, from 1969 until his death in 1996. He is pictured here in celebration of the station's 40th anniversary in 1985. *(Peninsula Daily News archive).*

That appeared to be the beginning of Buck's fall from grace with the Websters, who apparently had adopted George as their son in 1963. Esther hired Ned Thomas in 1967, and in a short time, he usurped all of Buck's powers with the paper. A year later, as Charles Webster was bedridden, Esther, likely with power of attorney, changed Charles' will, assigning $1 to Buck, essentially revoking his adoption, the *Olympic Leaders'* authors wrote.

Charles died in March 1969, just two months after Esther divested

Buck of any association with the newspaper by exchanging his four shares of the *Evening News* for sole ownership of KONP and Radio Pacific, its new corporation.

In the *Olympic Leaders* book, Buck is quoted in a 1994 interview that Esther told Thomas "I was totally unable to manage the paper." To which Buck replied, "This graveled me after 15 years of managing completely on my own."

If Buck had any problem with that arrangement, he didn't let it overtake him. He would remain sole owner until 1982 when Jim and Terry McDonald started acquiring ownership, and in 1983 became co-owners with George. Buck was still majority owner when he died on May 4, 1996.

Keys recalls those days — fondly in some ways and with warts in others — when management style changed from Buck as general manager to Buck as sole owner.

"George was a thrifty man, but very conscientious. He wanted to keep an eye on his staff, so he arranged his office, so he could see everyone's desk; he strived to have the most economical operation. He was sort of like an Ebenezer Scrooge," Keys noted, referring to the miserly curmudgeon banker in Charles Dickens' *A Christmas Carol*.

But Sandy also added that Buck was "very, very bright. He had polio as a young man, but he licked it. He had a slight limp, but I remember him as a quiet, patient, very gentlemanly man."

Buck, born in New York in 1916, but a Seattleite four years later, graduated from the University of Washington, then joined the ROTC in 1941. In 1945, he was stationed in Manila, the Philippines, when he contracted polio.

Rather than spend a life confined to a wheelchair, Buck fought to overcome the disability.

Buck's a battler

In the KONP newsletter at the time of his death, station co-owner Terry MacDonald wrote about Buck's battle with the dreaded disease.

"He was determined to overcome any obstacle that characterized his approach to any problems that came his way; he devoted two tortuous years to re-educating his muscles to do their job. He had to learn to sit up, to dress himself and to use a knife and fork all over again. He also had to learn how to walk."

As the radio business began to change, "George made sure that KONP stayed up with the times, especially when it came to the technical aspects of the business," MacDonald continued.

One year after Buck became sole owner, KONP was featured on the front page of the Dec. 12, 1970, *Billboard* magazine. The headline: "KONP goes to Cassette," as one of the first stations in the country to begin using cassettes for broadcasting.

MacDonald said the station used cassettes "until the early 1990s when computers became the new wave of broadcasting. Again, KONP was one of the first in the nation to convert to computerized digital audio."

In KONP's 50th anniversary newsletter, Keys writes of Buck's desire to stay ahead of the game.

"… At a time when others were doing nothing more intellectually challenging than walking grandkids, Buck became completely computer literate.

"When pressed, he would stop to reminisce about days gone by. One such occasion," Keys wrote about Buck's recollections of a particular station manager. "He recalled with a smile Keith Patterson, one of the station's more colorful managers, who in the 1950s would read the funny papers to young listeners on Sunday morning. At Christmas, Patterson played Santa Claus on air, and at locations around Port Angeles."

Ironically, in 1969, the same year he exchanged newspaper shares for the radio station ownership, he was chosen the North Olympic Chamber of Commerce "Man of the Year."

"George challenged us all to disagree with him, never holding it against us for doing so, but cheerleading us to prove our position and win," wrote Terry MacDonald. "I don't think anything made him happier than when we did just that. Good work is seldom an accident; it's done by people who care. That personified George Buck."

Paul, Shirley Bragg arrive

Paul Bragg, 82, and his wife, Shirley, 79, were hired by George Buck in 1969 and enjoyed 45 years with KONP, retiring in 2014. Sadly, Paul died in 2018. Among their most popular programs were *Memories in Music* and *Dock Time*. *(Peninsula Daily News archive)*

The year, 1969, also was when Buck hired Paul and Shirley Bragg, who came from KSOP in Salt Lake City, where Paul was station manager. He began broadcasting in Montana in 1955 and Shirley joined him two years later.

That KONP relationship would last 45 years until the Braggs retired in September 2014 and moved to the Tri-Cities in Eastern Washington to live their son, Paul Jr. Combined, they had 116 years in radio broadcasting; When they signed off on Sept. 27, 2014, Paul was 82 and Shirley 79. Sadly, Paul died in July 2018 at 86.

They were known for many regular programs, but probably most noted was "Memories in Music," which lasted from 2003-2014.

When they first arrived, Shirley did some producing, while Paul hosted two shows: "Dock Time" in which he interviewed folks coming off the *MV Coho* ferry; and "Bragg About Washington," a travel show, which eventually led to a series of pamphlets.

In a *Sequim Gazette* Business section celebrating KONP's 70th anniversary on Feb. 11, 2015, station co-owner Todd Ortloff talked to reporter Patricia Morrison Coate about the way programming has changed through the years.

"In the old days, there were programs like remotes from Bernie's Restaurant and Lounge, and over the organist, listeners would hear banter back and forth between the customers," Ortloff said.

He noted in the article that the format "was all over the place: chatter programs, kitchen chatter, interviews with visitors coming off the ferry and always the music of the day. A lot of kitschy things."

The music that was spun also went through a drastic transition. "In the 1940s, was the Big Band/Swing era, and in the 1950s-1960s, KONP played the Top 40s." Ortloff added a popular program with the younger set was "Tunes for Teens," that local high school students helped produce.

MacDonalds arrive

As KONP began to grow and its listener-base in the mid-1970s widened, Buck saw the need to make changes. He found the help he needed in Omak in Eastern Washington. Jim and Terry MacDonald moved to Port Angeles in 1975 with Jim serving as program director and ad salesman. Jim was 28 and Terry 24 when they came to the Olympic Peninsula. They were married in 1971.

Jim had experience as evening announcer at KAAR in Yakima, a country music station. He moved to KOMW in Omak for three years as program and sports director.

Terry had experience in real estate, retail and direct sales. At KOMW, she was doing copywriting and production. Jim was program director.

Terry and Jim MacDonald became co-owners with George Buck of Radio Pacific in 1983. When Buck died, the MacDonalds became sole owners until selling to Brown M. Maloney in 2002. They are shown here in 1985 when the station celebrated its 40th birthday. *(Peninsula Daily News archive).*

But she didn't come onboard at KONP right away. "George didn't want a husband and wife working together at the station," she said, "but eventually Jim convinced him it would work."

Terry joined the team in 1982 in sales and quickly moved up to sales manager.

"George and I were a lot alike," admitted Terry. "He wanted everyone to leave a clean desk, so we would cram everything in a box and shove it under the desk. It used to drive us crazy."

Jim said he respected George Buck. "We learned a lot from him. He was kind of like a father to us. He taught us a lot about the business. Yes, he was frugal in a lot of ways, but not when it came to new technology. We were one of the first to go to cassettes and one of the first to go digital. We were a model for others."

By 1987, the station was ready to advance to the next level — moving from a 250-watt station to 1,000 watts. "The FCC granted Class 4 stations a blanket increase to 1,000 watts, except KONP and a station in Minnesota," Jim said in a 1997 *Peninsula Business Journal* article, written by Bonne Smith. "We didn't get the blanket increase because of our international treaty with Canada."

Jim MacDonald met with Congressman Al Swift, a former broadcaster from Bellingham (Port Angeles was in the same district) and "he went to work to rewrite the treaty language," Jim shared in a 2015 interview. "Within six months, both stations had their increased wattage."

He said the real power came from two engineers in Seattle, Ben Dawson and Jim Hatfield, two of the premier engineers in the nation. "George had a good relationship with them. We were fortunate they took us under their wing. They were known all over the world and we were small potatoes."

The increased wattage enabled the station to reach into Sequim during daylight hours, but the bigger stations in Seattle still drowned out KONP at night.

That same year, the station switched from Mutual Broadcasting to ABC, enabling it to add Paul Harvey, the quintessential talk show broadcaster/ newscaster to the lineup. "He was huge in those days," said Terry.

In a 2015 interview, Jim MacDonald beamed when he started to talk about the early 1990s when the station went from cassettes to digital programming.

"It was the cat's meow," he said. "Word got around that we had that system and others came here to see how it worked."

Again, it came down to Buck spending the bucks. "We told him we needed three computers just for commercials, not music," Jim said. "We needed three 25-megabyte hard drives and each one cost $2,500. He wrote out a check for $7,500. It's funny. I now have more memory than that on my phone," he chuckled.

"It was a matter of progression for us. We got all our equipment from a station in Mountlake Terrace that went off the air. That includes the transmitter. We didn't have a backup, so we used that one for the main transmitter and the old one for backup. Up to then, when it went down, we were off the air."

> "It was the cat's meow. Word got around that we had that system and others came here to see how it worked."
>
> **Jim MacDonald,**
> **KONP co-owner**

Terry shared that KONP was more than just a radio station on First Street. "It was the pulse of the community. George wanted it that way, and he wanted us to be involved in the community. He paid our service club dues and our lunches."

Terry said it wasn't just about doing remote broadcasts; they did a share of those, some which they sponsored: Clallam County Fair, Port Angeles Salmon Derby, the Home Show, Food-a-thon, Pepsi Club Kiddies' Matinee, Turkey Shoot, Easter Egg Hunt, graduations, local grand openings, local elections and local sports events.

It was more than that. Terry, as a member of Soroptimists International, worked with the Port of Port Angeles on the Valley Creek Estuary project, which converted the log pond on West Front Street at Marine Drive back to its natural water habitat.

Jim was in Rotary and Kiwanis and Scooter (Chapman) was a longtime member of the Lions Club.

"George kept tight tabs on the money, but he really turned running the business over to us," said Jim. "His attitude was 'I am here if you need me,' but he let us run it."

Jim MacDonald didn't have to think long when asked to cite the biggest story in his tenure.

"The sinking of the Hood Canal Bridge," he said of the tragic event on Feb. 13, 1979. "I was on the air and I got this caller, who said her sister told her the bridge just sank. Well, I couldn't go on the air with just that, so we set out to confirm it. It didn't take long. That was a big story, and it remained a big story after the bridge was completed. Some people wanted the tolls taken off. They were still collecting tolls and the bridge was paid for."

Terry pointed to the establishing of the KONP Home Show in 1983 as another big story. "It was in the old Roosevelt School gym. It was a huge event, but the gym had not been remodeled and the floor buckled. There were a lot of difficulties and the bathrooms didn't work."

Still, it was a hit with 45 businesses in the first event. It doubled the next year and built from there, eventually moving to the Port Angeles High School gym and now has a new name: Clallam County Home and Lifestyle Show.

"It has been a huge thing for the station and the community," Terry added. The event in 2017 drew more than 30,000 people to view 180 booths in (insert what is now) the largest two-day marketing event on the North Olympic Peninsula.

> "It has been a huge thing for the station and the community."
>
> **Terry MacDonald, KONP co-owner on the first KONP Home Show in 1983.**

On May 4, 1996, KONP lost its fearless leader, owner and general manager. George Buck succumbed to liver cancer, a malady that had plagued him for more than a year.

"He loved the station, and was down there until the end," his son, Richard, of Bellevue, told the *Peninsula Daily News* in his obituary. "He was determined and said, 'never give up, never give up.'"

Emergency service

Small-town radio stations also can prove invaluable in providing information to the community in emergency situations. Such as it was with the MacDonalds in a December 1996 snowstorm that crippled the peninsula.

"We were communicating with the State Patrol and Clallam County emergency services in matching people who offered assistance to callers needing help," Jim MacDonald recalled in a 1997 *Peninsula Business Journal* article, adding that he and Terry knew the time had come when their federal mandate to serve the community meant more than covering local news and broadcasting public service announcements.

"People were calling us. Little old ladies were genuinely panicked. ... It was operation central," Terry said.

"Radio at its best," added her husband, noting that people would call in and offer to shovel driveways to those in need.

As a result, a new emergency warning system for the Olympic Peninsula was developed with Clallam County and the state. He said in a 2015 interview that, with the addition of computers, in small radio stations there are times when the office wasn't manned. In the case of an emergency, nobody would be there to notify the public. Radio often received messages to broadcast from the president, state and local officials.

Jim was named chairman of the Olympic Peninsula Operational Area. "The new system required every primary full-time, full-wattage station in the nation to be wired with new equipment that connects to Clallam County emergency services. When there is an emergency, it activates all the EAS boxes for Clallam County. The box cuts the station's audio and the county emergency services will have control of the station. When the emergency is over, the radio station resumes regular broadcasting."

Meantime, a young man was being groomed to move into the business. Todd Ortloff had been in Sandy Keys' contemporary issues class at Port Angeles High School, then served two years on the Peninsula College (1986-1988) *Buccaneer*, doing everything from reporting to managing editor. He interned summers at KAPY and KONP while going to Peninsula College on a Charles Webster Scholarship.

Ortloff continued his education at Washington State University, graduating in 1991 with a degree in communications and earned the Edward R. Murrow Award for the School of Communication. While at WSU, he interned at KAPP-TV in Yakima.

After college, he returned to the Olympic Peninsula and married Kim Zook. "She wanted to go to law school," Ortloff said, "so we moved to Portland and I ran a news operation for a cable TV for a few years. Jim

(MacDonald) called me and said he needed an operations manager, so we returned here in 1995."

KAPY: Competition for the airwaves

Beginning in 1961 and continuing until 1997, two AM radio stations served the Port Angeles area, though KONP always remained the big fish in that pond.

On May 4, 1960, John Mowbray purchased property from Frank and Jeanette Christman, according to information supplied by Jim MacDonald. The transaction included a 40-foot easement for a road and utilities at 1 Melody Lane, southeast of Port Angeles, outside the city limits.

Mowbray created Port Angeles Radio, Inc., an FCC requirement to operate the station and build a transmitting tower. The corporation was granted a license to operate a Class 4, two-tower directional array at 1,000 watts for daytime only.

KAPY officially went on the air on June 16, 1961, at 1290 on the AM dial. This information was confirmed by a citation from *Broadcasting Yearbook,* accessed through a Calgary, Canada, blog: *RadioWest.ca.* The Port Angeles Polk Directory of businesses also lists Mowbray the owner and president in 1961.

Port Angeles Radio possibly named the site Melody Lane because of its musical format, but in reality, it was County Road 3468. The location was noted on a document application, submitted by a later owner Charles Herring in 1973, asking for an easement road to purchase a strip of land along the BPA power line property for the antenna anchor.

"KAPY was licensed as a daytime-only station," noted Todd Ortloff, current technical operations and programming director for KONP. "It was allowed to

Have a KAPY Day On 1290 Radio

This sticker was prominent on the bumpers of loyal KAPY listeners. *(Courtesy of KONP)*

broadcast from one half-hour before sunrise to one half-hour after sunset each day. This was a classification of AM stations the FCC created to allow more local stations on the dial."

Removing the signals at night, eliminated interference with larger stations to take advantage of the nighttime "skywaves" to reach regional and national audiences, Ortloff added. "This meant in the winter, KAPY's broadcast (Have a KAPY day, a bumper sticker proclaimed) was limited to 10 hours a day."

The *Port Angeles Evening News*, still under the Webster family ownership, failed to congratulate or even acknowledge the second radio voice. The newspaper published the KONP broadcasting schedule daily.

Some speculated that the newspaper's general manager George Buck, who also held the same position with KONP, was not that well liked. He was known as a penny-pincher and wasn't beyond ostracizing those who might be his competition. KAPY fell in that area as the two stations would be battling for the advertiser's dollar.

Whatever the reason, Mowbray felt the time was ripe for a new voice over the airwaves.

Mowbray operated the station for a few years before selling to John Thatcher and Janet Forsberg. According to the Polk Directory of Port Angeles, Herring became the owner in 1967, and followed all mention of KAPY with the slogan: "The Quality Sound of the Olympic Peninsula. Later he would add: "Where You Always Have a KAPY Day."

MacDonald considered KAPY as a competitor for the daytime airwave and for the advertising dollar, adding "we were friendly rivals with Herring and with Tom and Shirley (Newcomb)."

Sandy Keys, who started working at KONP about the time KAPY began, said he really didn't have much to do with the other station. He did recall one situation that was upsetting at the time. It was at a Port Angeles High School graduation and KONP was doing a live broadcast. A KAPY announcer put his microphone next to Sandy's. "I would say, 'you are listening to KONP radio 1450,' and then I'd have to say, 'you are listening to KAPY radio 1290.' I felt odd saying their name."

Herring operated the station until 1975 when Tom Newcomb rode into town. Newcomb, a resident of Great Falls, Mont., apparently had inside information that the Northern Tier Oil Pipeline was being proposed, along a 1,500-mile stretch from Minnesota through Montana, ending at a new oil port at Port Angeles.

The pipeline, which was proposed in 1976, was mired in controversy for eight years; it never materialized and its proponents gave up the fight in 1983.

But Newcomb and his wife, Shirley, bought the station from Herring in 1975 and operated it for more than 20 years. "He offered a mix of music and news programming, but the station struggled to compete with the more established KONP," said Ortloff.

In 1997, Newcomb sold the station to Q-Media, whose principal partners were John Stephens and Steve McCormick from Texas. This tandem changed the call letters to KKNW and moved the operation to uptown Port Angeles. The new location featured a small coffee shop where visitors could watch the DJs work through a window, Ortloff added.

They ran the station for a year, but on the eve of the station's one-year lease renewal for the "Studio Café" space, the staff was promptly fired, and the company deserted Port Angeles in the dark of the night

"It was strange. You just don't do that with a radio station. You've got the FCC and others to deal with," said MacDonald. "They spent a lot of money, had new equipment and built a new station."

It also resulted in the station being off the air from July 31 to mid-November 1997. "That put 11 people out of work," said MacDonald.

The previous year, longtime KONP co-owner and general manager George Buck died and the MacDonalds became full owners.

They saw the second station as an opportunity to expand their operation and offer another listening option for Port Angeles residents.

Q-Media's contract for the purchase of the broadcast license was in default and reverted back to the Newcombs

Jim and Terry MacDonald bought the station (KKNW), which had a Classic Hits format, from Newcomb. "It would be a little

This sticker was favorite of KIKN Country Music fans. *(Courtesy of KONP)*

crowded, Jim said, "but we plan to operate both stations out of the same building, for now," he told the *PDN*.

The MacDonalds wanted to change the call letters to KIKN and install a kickin' country-western format, but needed permission from a station in South Dakota, which also operated with those call letters on the FM dial.

Country-western music was popular on the peninsula. The station featured Hot Country Hits, Country Store, a classified ad program and the "Dog Gone News," a pet lost and found service. "This gave us the opportunity to offer a different format," Terry said.

Maloney ownership

By the summer of 2001, the MacDonalds were contemplating selling the station with one stipulation. "We wanted local owners," said Jim. "That was important to us," Terry added.

Almost providential, there happened to be a local man who was interested in getting into radio station ownership: Brown McClatchy Maloney, owner of the *Sequim Gazette* and Olympic View Publishing.

"I think they were ready to push the 'off button,' so they contacted me, and I am glad they did," admitted Maloney.

"They had a great radio market. It was almost ideal, basically all by yourself; the Pacific Ocean to the west, the Strait to the north, the Olympic Mountains to the south and Sequim and Port Townsend to the east."

While Maloney's businesses centered around newspapers and magazines on the Olympic Peninsula, he grew up in a radio-centered family. The McClatchy family owned radio stations in Sacramento, Modesto, Fresno and Bakersfield in central California, along with Central Valley newspapers in those cities.

"Growing up, I never worked in radio, but radio was a part of our family business; it was discussed at the dinner table. As such, I didn't feel at all a stranger when the opportunity arose to acquire KONP in Port Angeles. Taking on KONP was not only appealing, but it made sense because we (Olympic View Publishing) are an Olympic Peninsula media company," he shared in a 2017 interview.

Brown McClatchy Maloney purchased Radio Pacific and KONP in 2002 with Todd Ortloff as a minority co-owner. *(Courtesy of KONP)*

"Growing up, I never worked in radio, but radio was part of our family business. As such, I didn't feel at all a stranger when the opportunity arose to acquire KONP in Port Angeles."

Brown Maloney, KONP co-owner

Todd Ortloff *(Courtesy of KONP)*

Maloney said he knew he wouldn't be at the station daily, so the natural station manager for him would be Ortloff, who had been well-groomed by the MacDonalds.

"I told Todd I was considering buying it, but I was direct with him. I told him 'I think you should buy 10 percent of the station,'" Maloney said.

Ortloff wasn't in position to buy 10 percent, so Maloney offered him 5 percent and told him "we will work out a portion of time and pay, getting you eventually to 10 percent."

Todd said Maloney needed somebody to run the station and he was happy with the deal. "We closed on it by the end of the year and had a dedication on Valentine's Day."

At the same time, but in separate arrangements, KIKN also was sold to Caron Broadcasting, Inc., of Camarillo, Calif., a subsidiary of Salem Communications Holding Corp. of Salem, N.C. That sale silenced country music and put KIKN in direct competition with KONP for the talk-show audience.

KIKN featured conservative talk radio programs during afternoon and evening hours, such as Oliver North, the Iran-Contra figure during the Reagan Administration, and Michael Reagan, the president's son. The broadcast was simulcast from Seattle's KKOL-AM 1300.

KONP AM 1450 aired conservative talk-show icon Rush Limbaugh on weekday mornings.

"I was pleased to have Todd along," Maloney said. "He is an asset to the business and Port Angeles community and this was an important part of my decision," he said in a 2017 interview, reviewing the history of the sale.

Maloney told the *Peninsula Daily News* in a Feb. 26, 2002, article that he and Ortloff didn't plan on changing the format, and would emphasize local coverage as did their predecessors, Webster, Buck and the MacDonalds.

"I am happy that the format is local-focused," Maloney said. "It really fits with me since I have such a strong passion for the community."

Maloney and Ortloff have owned KONP and Radio Pacific for 16 years and continued to make changes as progress and technology demands. In 2008, they installed a digital transmitter giving the station a high-tech boost.

Ortloff told the *PDN's* Luke Bogues the transmitter would allow Radio Pacific to offer multiple broadcasts and clearer reception. "We're planning now for something that's probably going to take place in five to 10 years," he said. "It's going to level the playing field for us with CD-quality audio."

That year (2008) was also when the station moved its broadcasting operation 10 blocks east to 721 E. First St. in a building that Maloney owned. The station had been at 313 W. First St. since its 1945 founding by *Evening News* publisher Charles Webster. "It was about time for a move," Maloney said.

The old building is now the Port Angeles Baby Store.

The new building became officially the Olympic View Building when a 10-foot, 350-pound KONP sign was installed in October 2008. It is now known as the KONP Building.

Maloney called the sign a "neon throwback from the 1950s." He said it was designed by Rob Campbell of Miller Signs in Carlsborg.

"They wanted something that would stand out and this kind of vintage look isn't used all that often," Campbell told the *PDN* in October 2010.

The red-and-yellow-sign spelling out the station call letters also fits with the station's architecture.

KSTI FM established

In 2015, KONP found itself in competition — albeit briefly. In a lengthy bidding process, Maloney and Ortloff were seeking to obtain another FM station for the peninsula under an FCC auction process. About 160 bidders were in it at the beginning before it was whittled down to just two: Radio Pacific (KONP's corporate affiliate) and Mark Jones, who owned Owensville Communications in Vicksburg, Miss.

"It got pretty expensive and I finally told Todd to let him have it," said Maloney.

Jones, who owned two radio stations in Vicksburg, said he spent "a couple of years listening to the wonderful job the people at KONP were doing. I've had assistance from great people locally who have helped us build this station," he said, lauding Sue Roberds with the City of Port Angeles and Jonathan Shotwell, who owns the land where the KSTI antenna is located.

> "We struck a deal for far less than the original bidding war. It had all the infrastructure, even a tower. It was about as turnkey as you could get."
>
> **Todd Ortloff on acquiring KSTI**

Jones chose the call letters (KSTI) because of the proximity to the Juan de Fuca Strait.

"They built the studio right across the street from us (734 E. First St.), put up a tower and even joined the chamber," said Ortloff. "When I met him, I was surprised to see he had a companion with him. Jones was blind, and needed a helper, a nice guy, an old-school radio man."

Maloney said he thought Jones was "like a guy pushing a boulder uphill. Indeed, he was an out-of-towner, having the disadvantage of being blind and trying to start a radio station. It could not have been easy."

Apparently, it was not easy. Jones never went on air with KSTI.

"He came to us and said he wanted to sell," Ortloff said of the conversation in April or May. "We were thinking we just might get another shot at this station."

Just that quickly, they agreed on a price. "We struck a deal for less than the original bidding war," said Ortloff. "It had all the infrastructure, even a tower. It was about as turnkey as you could get."

Maloney was just as pleased that Jones "first offered us the opportunity to purchase the FM station."

KSTI first went on air on July 15, 2015, at 102.1 FM with Classic Hits from the Top 40 from the 1960s-1980s.

"Radio Pacific and KONP are well-positioned for this opportunity. We are fortunate to have the professional capacity to take KSTI into its launch and onto a successful future," Ortloff said in a station newsletter. "It's also exciting we will have the chance to offer Port Angeles some additional diversity in local radio."

Maloney also announced with the purchase agreement that Ortloff's title would change from station manager to general manager, overseeing both stations.

2018 a year for change

Three years after KSTI went on air, Maloney and Ortloff had an opportunity Radio Pacific to a third station as well as expand (delete their empire to a third station and change the format for KSTI.

First, Radio Pacific won the FCC auction, granting a broadcast license for a new station in Sequim.

This station became full licensed through the FCC in the spring of 2018 and was launched as KZQM FM on June 4. Ortloff said the 6,000-watt station at 104.9 is the "highest-powered FM station on the North Olympia Peninsula."

The KZQM transmitter is "essentially a camouflaged fir tree on Brigadoon Avenue, 3 miles north of Sequim. It's a multi-user tree," Ortloff said, noting a fire district also will use it as well as another FM frequency of KONP.

The format for KZQM is Classic Hits from the 1960s through 1980s.

At that time and to avoid a music overlap, Ortloff said, KSTI, which launched in 2015 as Classic Hits, switched to an all-Country music station.

"We are trying to diversify, so we don't compete against ourselves," he said. This also expands the advertising base to three markets. "We sell ads as a cluster. All stations in the Seattle-area are doing that."

While the FM stations are music-based, KONP's format has remained constant. "We're not changing from a news/talk station," said Ortloff. "We cut out the music in about 1998. We had one show, "Memories in Music," hosted by Paul Bragg for a while. We are strictly the spoken word: We have a few old-time radio shows on Sunday night, but our drive times are local news and talk shows the rest of the day." A bit later in summer 2018, KONP in Port Angeles expanded its range, adding an FM frequency to the Sequim tower.

"Our listeners in Sequim are able to get us on 1450 and also at 101.3 FM," said Ortloff, explaining the signal sometimes gets lost about Carlsborg. "This will enable that market to pick us up all day long."

Sue Ellen Riesau started working for Brown M. Maloney in 1989 and spent 23 years with his publications. Today, she is in charge of business operations for Maloney's Radio Pacific broadcasting stations. *(Courtesy of Sue Ellen Riesau)*

In addition to initiating KZQM in Sequim, Maloney and Ortloff launched a new website: *myclallamcounty.com* where all Radio-Pacific information can be accessed on one site.

The expansion to a three-station system and expanded market demanded a change in management.

The new face on the block is Sue Ellen Riesau, who had been employed by Maloney for 23 years, primarily as GM and publisher at the *Sequim Gazette* and other Olympic View properties. She had been working for Maloney in his other businesses when he lured her to KONP.

"We really co-manage," she explained. "I handle technical operations and programming," said Ortloff. Sue Ellen now manages the business operations."

One thing is clear with small-town

radio stations. Change is inevitable; you either change for the better or get swept aside. KONP and Radio Pacific are changing and appear ready for the challenges ahead.

Peninsula News Network (PNN): Local access cable television

The man primarily associated with local access television in Port Angeles was Dennis Bragg, who operated through Northland Cable News at 725 E. First St. from late 1992-2007.

Jack Chapman was the man who was the catalyst for an eventual TV station. He operated Chapman's Antenna Service in the 1950s, according to his son, Mike, of Joyce. In 1960, he started Port Angeles Tele-cable, which provided remote broadcasts for local events and interviews. He had that business until selling to Northland in 1988. "It wasn't a station, only a cable operation," Mike Chapman clarified. "He started the ball rolling."

Telecasting began through Northland, which organized in the Port Angeles area in December 1992, according to an ad in the *Peninsula Daily News*. Dan Withers was regional manager and Rose Wilhelm office manager. Bragg was news director and Rick Ross reported on sports.

Ross had been a staff member of *The Daily News* in Port Angeles from 1977-1991, then joined Bragg for about four years.

Bragg, born in Montana, to Paul and Shirley Bragg, was raised in a radio family.

"My father was in radio, so we lived all over, just like 'WKRP in Cincinnati'; town to town, up and down the dial," Bragg related in a June 15, 2007, *PDN* story when he left the Olympic Peninsula and returned to Montana.

The Braggs moved to Port Angeles in 1969; Dennis' first radio job was in 1974 with KVAC in Forks, then moved to the now-defunct KAPY in Port Angeles in 1977.

He described his job as a "utility infielder, doing a little bit of everything, including covering city council meetings and writing them up for broadcast at 2 a.m.

Bragg identified two big stories in his 33 years of broadcasting on the

North Olympic Peninsula: the sinking of the western half of the Hood Canal Bridge in 1979 and Makah whaling kill in May 1999.

In 1984, Bragg lost a bid to be a Clallam County commissioner, falling in a close race to then-Port Angeles Mayor Dorothy Duncan.

His toughest story to cover, he told the *PDN*, was the killing of Clallam County Deputy Wally Davis in 2000.

"I was one of the first ones on the scene; it was a difficult watershed kind of moment. I knew so many of those involved."

The next year — August 2001 — Bragg initiated local access television through Pacific News Network (PNN). For the next six years, the station would broadcast local sports, news and community events.

John Brewer, now-retired *PDN* publisher, recalls, "We used to sponsor a lot of their forums." Executive editor Rex Wilson, Commentary page editor Paul Gottlieb and Bragg conducted candidate forum and debates at election time.

Gradually the business started to change: According to a *PDN* story on July 11, 2003, Northland Cable was sold to Kirkland-based Wave Broadband, which "brought the offer of high-speed, two-way cable broadband Internet access to Northland customers.

Wave said it was negotiating with Bragg and his wife, LaRee. "We have offered to pay quite a high amount of revenue that we obtain from subscribers to PNN," Angela Higham, marketing director with Wave, told the *PDN* reporter Jeff Chew.

But Bragg expressed concern that PNN would be charged an access fee under Northland's franchises in Port Angeles and Sequim.

"There is no way we will be able to continue if we have to pay a fee — not in this market," said Bragg.

PNN's staff operated a separate company out of its own studios but had programming access through Channel 3.

The relationship with Wave didn't last long. Wave ceased operation in Port Angeles in June 2007.

On June 15, 2007, Bragg told *PDN* reporters Brian Gawley and Jim Casey he was pulling the plug and moving to Montana, where he would be news director with KPAX-TV, covering most of Western Montana.

'Lack of cable support' blamed

He blamed his departure on a "lack of cable support and a hardscrabble advertising market."

Bragg said no direct financial support from Wave Broadband and its predecessor Northland forced his decision, along with the inability to crack the "big-box" advertising market.

"With more national chain stores that don't spend money on local advertising and an increasing amount of festivals competing for limited dollars," Bragg said, "it simply becomes too difficult to bring television to a market the size of Clallam County."

Bragg told the *PDN* he was "wistful" when talking about the future of small-market news operations.

"The Peninsula is pretty small for a television market, and we found ourselves somewhere between nonprofit community access and small over-the-air television.

"There just isn't a lot of growth potential there, especially with the changing landscape in cable television."

Bragg, who turned 60 in 2018, is still with KPAX-TV in Missoula, Mont.

Several companies have been involved in TV broadcasting in Port Angeles since 2007 — Princeton Server Group, Telvue Virtual TV Network and Broadstripe, and for a short time, PTTV, out of Port Townsend, and currently Wave but none had the success of Bragg and PNN.

CHAPTER 15

Voices from the peninsula: KSQM FM, Sequim

Sequim resident Dennis "Rick" Perry, a retired commander in the U.S. Navy, had a vision to establish a radio station in his city, 20 miles east of Port Angeles.

Perry's plan for KSQM FM 91.5 was two-fold, said Jeff Bankston, current program director for the station, in a 2017 interview. "He saw a need for an emergency broadcasting service for Sequim and he also envisioned a station with live, local broadcasting."

After four years of planning, and more than a little adversity, KSQM was founded as a full-power, non-commercial education radio service of Sequim Community Broadcasting, a nonprofit corporation, registered as a charitable organization.

The little station, with only 700 watts, first went on the air on Dec. 7, 2008, a somber date when the nation remembered the Japanese bombing of Pearl Harbor, but that day in Sequim also was a time of rejoicing.

The station was incorporated in 2004 with Perry and two others involved, but they dropped out and left Perry to finance and plan for the entire operation.

A lesser man might have given up the dream. But not Rick Perry. He was resolved to get the project done.

"It became a family affair," said Bankston, adding that Perry's daughter Lisa played a big role and handled media relations. Rick's wife Darleen and his mother Judy were also involved. Bob Sampson was chief engineer and presided over the advisory board, along with his wife Cathy.

Sampson was the station's IT guy and technology guru, working countless hours with computers and the tower.

"Who ever heard of starting a radio station without capital investment?" Bankston asked rhetorically. "We had the cart in front of the horse, but we did it."

Rick Perry was founder of KSQM, which first went on the air on Dec. 7, 2008. *(Courtesy of Rick Perry)*

Perry leased a building in a strip mall at 577 W. Washington St., on property owned by Robert and Edith Rittenhouse. It would serve as the station offices and broadcasting rooms. A site for the tower still had to be located.

"Rick decided to attach it to his house," said Bankston, adding the first tower was 700 watts.

Perry immediately put together a board to help with preparations. One of the early members was Lynda Perry (no relation to Rick).

"I came on before the building permits were approved," said Lynda, now the president of the board.

Bankston also was an early board member, though he initially applied to be a helper when Rick put out an appeal for volunteers. Bankston's wife Tama followed soon after. "We were only married about six months," said Tama. "I figured if I wanted to see my husband again I better volunteer."

Now, she is director of office administration and volunteer coordinator and her husband is director of development and a board member.

The operation initially might have been Rick Perry and family, but it soon ballooned into much more than that.

"In the first year we had more than 600 people — individuals and businesses — offer their support respond to the call to volunteer," Bankston said. Tama added, "Now, at any given time KSQM can count on more than 100 active volunteers."

All-volunteer radio

Bankston said this station is unique. "What separates us from every other community radio station, is the radio side is all-volunteer. We have more than 25 announcers, and about 90 percent have never been in front of a mic before."

In 2017, 27 volunteers qualified for the Presidential Service Award through the RSVP (Retired Senior Volunteer Program). "They had to serve at least 100 volunteer hours to qualify," said Tama. "Many of them served at least 400."

While Rick Perry's premise was still the same — provide the community with emergency information — the station still needed a music format.

With a volunteer base that included a police chief, county sheriff, former mayor, educators, retired military officers, nurses, mothers, business leaders and housewives and even an actress, among others, the foundation was set. However, only four or five had previous broadcasting experience.

Those who didn't were given an instructional lesson by Perry.

Another board member, Albert Friess, a former mayor of Corning, N.Y., explained how he became involved.

"I was raised with the radio and I remember listening to 'Make Believe Ballroom' show on WNEW in New York. 'Set your clock by Martin Block ... It's Ten o'clock.'

"We had no TV; radio was what it was about. We were entertained by it. It's why I listen today, why I am involved. Music makes our lives so much better."

Jeff Bankston, an early KSQM board member, later became program director at the all-volunteer station. *(Bill Lindstrom photo)*

"What separates us from every other community radio station, is the radio side is all-volunteer. We have more than 25 announcers, and about 90 percent have never been in front of a mic before."

Jeff Bankston, KSQM program director

Music is what Rick Perry discovered the people of Sequim wanted. In a *Sequim Gazette* article on the station's one-year anniversary, he revealed he took an informal survey prior to opening the station. "I asked the people of Sequim what they wanted to hear most. They said music from the '40s to the '60s."

That was the format Perry established for the live programs, which run from 7 a.m.- 9 p.m. daily on the 24-hour station. He would call it the "Great American Songbook."

After four years of bureaucratic, regulatory and financial challenges, the station was ready to broadcast, less than a year after its building permit was approved.

'Classy' Bob Massey

Bob Massey and Pepper Fisher provided the professional voices and helped train the KSQM announcers in the early days, the station's portfolio noted. They were joined early on by Kent Welborn and Dick Goodman, both former professional radio broadcasters.

Massey wasn't just a veteran broadcaster. He was a legend.

"Classy" Bob Massey was the first voice listeners heard when KSQM went on the air. Massey hadn't been broadcasting since 1992 when he and wife Margaret retired and moved to Sequim.

This was only a blip in the 83-year-old Massey's career that started in 1945

When KSQM first went on the air on Dec. 7, 2008, the first voice listeners heard on the all-volunteer radio station was "Classy" Bob Massey. The 83-year-old began broadcasting in 1945 for the U.S. Army. On his 90th birthday, March 9, 2015, the City of Sequim honored him as "The Oldest Broadcaster. Massey died on July 26, 2015. *(Sequim Gazette archive)*

when he was in the U.S. Army and broadcast for the U.S. Armed Forces Radio to soldiers in Germany. He was a member of Gen. George S. Patton's Third Army.

After the war, he moved to Palm Beach, Fla., worked for several small stations in Southern Florida before moving to Alaska in 1963. He was on the air on Good Friday, March 27, 1964, when a 9.2 earthquake devastated Anchorage. He learned about the role of the radio as an emergency service information source from that event.

He moved to Yakima in 1970, working for KIT radio, then finished his career at KBRD in Tacoma, moving into a life of retirement in Sequim.

So, he thought.

After his wife died in 2006, Massey felt the call of radio again.

Then a chance meeting with Rick Perry in a doctor's office re-ignited his broadcasting spirit. He had previously read about the call for volunteers for the radio station in the *Gazette*.

"He volunteered as a helper," Perry told the *Gazette* in a March 2015 article in which Massey was presented a special honor by the Washington state Senate, a resolution, sponsored by 24th District Sen. James Hargrove. Sequim Mayor Candace Pratt also honored Massey.

He was more than a helper. On that first day, Massey was on the mic for eight hours, Bankston said.

He was quite possibly the oldest radio announcer still on the air, supported by this statement:

"There are no known active broadcasters older than Massey currently on the air in the U.S.," said Bruce DuMont, founder and the president of the Museum of Broadcast Communications at Radio Hall of Fame in Chicago.

On his 90th birthday, March 9, 2015, Massey was honored by the City of Sequim as the "Oldest Broadcaster." The *Gazette* featured a large photo of Massey surrounded by 11 of his relatives, many who had arrived from the East Coast.

Of course, lunch with the relatives was on hold until he finished his usual morning broadcast "The Classy Bob Massey Show," featuring a trip down memory lane with the Best Music Ever Made, a hallmark of his program.

Nothing, not even a birthday party, supersedes his radio broadcast. That's the kind of professional he was.

"He remains the foundation, the very heart and soul of this phenomenal community radio," praised Bankston, in the *Gazette*.

"What an honor," Massey said, "Radio gets in your blood. So many stations have gone talk. There is a place in the world for a station like ours; it fills a niche; it's great to have a station like this in Sequim."

Massey said the technology had changed drastically from the early days when he spun 45s and LPs, but he adjusted well.

"My goal for my listeners is to brighten their day, to make theirs go a little easier."

Massey was honored with a big newspaper spread, family gathering and other accolades on his birthday, March 9; the Senate resolution was passed on May 27; in June, Bob became ill and, sadly, died on July 26, 2015.

"He was always professional and brought a lot of experience, Lynda Perry said in the July 29 obituary in the *Gazette*. "Our community radio would not be in existence without his tireless work, professionalism and devotion."

While Massey's morning program could vary, it centered around Big Band, swing and traditional jazz music. Among Massey's favorites were the Dorseys, Glenn Miller, George Gershwin and Vaughn Monroe.

That was only one aspect of the programming.

"We say music tends to inspire artists of all kinds," said George Dooley, another board member and announcer for "Dr. D's Roots of Rock."

He said the program plays many varieties of music. "We are probably more identified by what we don't play — rap, hard rock, and metal."

Jim Hindes, another board member, said, "Each announcer selects his (or her) favorites." For example, he said his wife Linda produces "Linda's Latin Quarter."

Friess chimed in with a statement that summarizes KSQM's music programming.

"My degree of music favorites is like wine. There is no such thing as bad wine, only varying degrees of 'good.'"

Linda Hindes said she kind of focuses on the 1950s and 1960s, but also picks up a few hits from the 1940s and 1970s.

"My program goes back to the '40s," said Dooley. "That's when good music developed."

Emergency service

It's not all music, however. Ed Evans is the news director and provides the weather forecasts, ferry and road reports. Chuck Bolland comments on sports.

The station wasn't on the air a year yet when it had to put its emergency program into operation.

"There was a bomb threat and we coordinated with the state patrol and Clallam County sheriff," said Bankston. "We had to alert people that a street was closed. We tried to get important information out. In an emergency, people are scared until they know what is going on. That's the job of the radio — provide critically important and accurate information. It calms them down when they know what's happening."

Bankston said the station connects with all departments of transportation, including the airport and ferry.

Tama Bankston shows some of the station's large collection of vinyl records. She is KSQM's volunteer coordinator. *(Bill Lindstrom photo)*

"We are a key information source," added Lynda Perry. "When power is out, or a bridge is closed, a road is blocked, we are that source. People often call us and tell us first, then we contact PUD."

Rick Perry, like Massey, experienced the importance of radio in emergencies.

He was in San Diego (Calif.) in the Navy when an airliner crashed. "He was working for the Air Force radio and realized that a simple radio transmission could get life-saving information out," Bankston said.

Some of the announcers came by their position by accident, such as Dorothy Zapata, who said she saw an ad for volunteers and figured she could do clerical work. "Then they approached me about going on air," Zapata told the *Gazette* for a story on the station's first anniversary.

Now, she hosts a program called "Dorothy's Doo-Wop Drive-in."

Pepper Fisher was an announcer and DJ for KUBE in Seattle before retiring in Sequim. Along with Rick Perry, he was responsible for training those without experience.

He told the *Gazette* that he volunteered because he believes community radio is valuable. In his first year as DJ at KSQM, he said he reported and gave updates on two different Amber Alerts.

Some civic leaders became involved, such as Police Chief Bob Spinks. "Whatever we do is a reflection of what the community wants to hear. When I used to go to the grocery store, I was stopped about police business by people, but now it's all about music," Spinks told the *Gazette* on the station's first anniversary.

The station also struck gold when another volunteer, Shelley Taylor Morgan, walked into the office.

She had been an actress on "General Hospital" and "Hunter" on TV, and as Barbro in the movie, "Sword & The Sorcerer," the radio station's website: www.ksqmfm.com notes. In the 1990s. E: Entertainment Television became her home when she hosted "Pure Soap," a live talk show.

"For the longest time, I thought, why don't radio stations play (movie) soundtracks? So, I created a radio program where I can share with listeners my love of 'the music that makes the movies.' That's Audio Cinema," Morgan said.

A sampling of the other announcers includes Evans, a veteran of 32 years broadcasting, including KIRO and KOMO-TV in Seattle, among other stations; "Wild Bill" Hegerty, who says "on my watch, you will hear Big Band music, marches, popular music from the 1920s through the '60s, Viennese waltzes, jazz, folk and Hollywood productions"; veteran broadcaster Dick Goodman, who says tune in to Muffin Mondays, Waffle Wednesdays and Fritter Fridays from 9 a.m.-noon. "Don't forget the maple syrup."

A full lineup of programming and announcers can be found on the website.

It takes a lot of money to run a radio station, even a nonprofit one. Bankston said he was overwhelmed by the generous folks who responded for pleas for donations. "The first year we got $43,000 from about 600 donors, but we need $55,000 to $60,000 a year for rent, insurance, utilities, equipment and paying music royalties," he noted.

John Wayne tower dedication

By 2010, the station was progressing well enough that Perry decided to take it to the next level.

"We needed to expand our wattage and our coverage base," Bankston said. "We wanted 2,400 watts."

To do that, a new tower was needed and once again the call for donors helped bring that about.

Sequim Community Broadcasting found suitable land and leased it from the state Department of Natural Resources. No longer would the tower need to be attached to Perry's house. Instead, the 155-foot tower would be atop a 435-foot ridge off Blue Mountain Road.

It took three years to complete the process, including raising the $325,000 for the construction and acquisition of the tower and transmitters.

The additional wattage would expand the station's range to Victoria, B.C., along the I-5 corridor, even to Bellingham.

Legendary actor John Wayne was a frequent visitor to Sequim and was well-known to the community. The marina at Sequim Bay was named for him, and after he died in 1979, a foundation was formed by the Wayne Estate.

Bankston said that "John Wayne's granddaughter, Anita LaCava Swift, once told him 'if my grandfather was alive today, this radio station would be his favorite.'"

KSQM was thrilled to be given the opportunity to name the tower after the actor.

Swift came from Newport Beach, Calif., pinch-hitting for Ethan Wayne, her uncle and the actor's son, who was ill at the time.

The John Wayne Memorial Transmission Facility was dedicated on Nov. 8, 2013, as TV character Gumby threw the switch activating the tower and expanding the station's wattage from 700 to 2,400. Swift cut the ribbon and spoke at the dedication.

Once again it was a community effort. Thirty station supporters donated $1,000 each. First Federal gave the station $50,000 in underwriting funds to help pay for the tower; The M.J. Murdock Charitable Trust of Vancouver, Wash., made an initial grant of $50,000 and followed up with matching funds of $30,000, which helped KSQM bring in over $110,000 toward construction of the new tower.

As the switch was thrown, a commemorative John Wayne plaque was unveiled; the station began by broadcasting John Wayne's eloquent soliloquy, "America, Why I Love Her."

At a later reception at the station, Swift said, "That was a beautiful touch."

Bankston said the station's special programming has been very popular.

"Precious Memories" is a week-long opportunity for the community to come on air and record music that was memorable in their lives. "Precious can be a double-edged sword," he explained. "It could be a song evoking a special memory in a couple's life, or it could be a song saying goodbye to Uncle Louie."

Dooley said "Voices of Veterans" asks the listener what their favorite memory was. "We have a lot of veterans in the community. This gives the community the opportunity to memorialize a veteran."

Bankston said the station has expanded the Veterans Day schedule. "It's not just the one day, it's a whole week every November and we honor each service for a day; invite people to share anecdotes and songs important to them. On Veterans Day, we honor all services."

Again, Friess shared a simplistic thought.

"One of the most unique things we do at the station is that we are humanistic. From the beginning, we were a not-for-profit 501(c)3. We have no payroll. We are all volunteers from top to bottom. All the contributions

we receive are for KSQM broadcasting expenses, not management/
executives.

"We are a positive double-edged sword; we serve the community, and
we create opportunities for members of the community, many retired,
some looking for ways to serve their friends and neighbors. Typically,
being in the number of all aspects of the finished product of broadcasting
beautiful music, it's a win-win for all!"

Voice of America

KSQM was the first radio station in Sequim, but there were plans for
one as early as 1952.

According to the *Sequim Pioneer Family Histories, Vol. 2, 1850-1962,*
the Washington State Department of Fish and Wildlife announced in
January 1952 it wanted about 1,200 acres in the Sequim-Dungeness Valley
for Voice of America (VOA) — a "super broadcasting station which would
take the story of democracy behind the Iron Curtain."

The area would extend from McDonnell Creek east toward Dungeness
Spit (Holgerson Road) and from Woodcock/Cameron Road north to the
bluff.

By Jan. 24, the state F&W said it had options on 884 acres from 10
owners.

The elaborate project, featuring 200 antennas, each 300-feet-tall, was
endorsed by both Port Angeles and Sequim Chambers of Commerce,
though Sequim was miffed because national publicity listed the location
as "near Port Angeles, instead of Sequim," the book explained.

First step was the removal of all man-made structures from the newly
acquired acreage, meaning the uprooting of several long-time families for
which mitigation would be made. A Seattle construction company leveled
all the homes and other structures and cleared the land, including wooded
property to produce a flat area near the present Kitchen-Dick Road.

"A year later all construction was halted," according to the book, "when
an engineer testifying before the McCarthy Congressional Committee
charged that millions of dollars were being spent at sites where broadcasts
would be ineffective."

Work remained halted and the project came to an end. The problem remained what to do with the land. Clallam County commissioners asked the state to build a new road east of the project to replace the vacated county road.

Eventually, all construction and electrical equipment was removed. Rumors circulated that the Air Force might take the land for a military base, or that the state F&W would use the entire area as a game reserve. "Liquidation costs to the federal government totaled more than $4.5 million," the book noted.

The land eventually was returned for agricultural use and added to the county's tax rolls. Property ownership was a lingering question. Four of the previous owners said they didn't want their former property back. Others paid and re-acquired their original land, minus the topsoil. Some held it for investment, deciding not to use it for agriculture.

Clallam County acquired a parcel above the bluff for a county park and named the road into the park Voice of America Road.

A radio station for Sequim in the 1950s wasn't that close to a reality, nor would it have been for local use.

It took another 56 years for that to become a reality.

CHAPTER 16

Voices from the Peninsula: KVAC, Forks

It wasn't a desire to start a radio station that brought Gordon Otos to the North Olympic Peninsula. It was fishing.

He had been to Forks (and the peninsula) many times on fishing trips while working at KTAC radio in Tacoma, wrote Christi Baron, current *Forks Forum* editor, for an article on "Small-Town Radio Stations," she crafted as a reporter for the *Peninsula Daily News* in 2010.

In 1966, Otos likely decided he would make no more long-distance drives to catch fish. Instead, he would establish a radio station, move to Forks and do all the fishing he wanted to in his backyard.

He hooked up with a friend, Bruce Elliott, an instructor in radio and TV broadcasting at Washington State University, and they filed the necessary applications — with the FAA for the 200-foot tower and FCC — for the call letters, KVAC.

In October 1967, the station, operating with 500 watts daytime power and 250 watts at night, was launched with a frequency of 1450 kilohertz.

The station broadcast Monday through Saturday from 5:30 a.m.-11 p.m., and from 8 a.m.-10 p.m. on Sundays with a varied musical lineup.

Otos was a career broadcaster, growing up in Vancouver, Wash., attending Clark College there, before enrolling in broadcasting school in Los Angeles. After graduation, he worked in radio stations at The Dalles, Ore., and Tacoma.

Gordon Otos, his wife Betty, three sons — Randy, David and Cliff — and daughter Debi, all moved to Forks.

"Prior to moving to Forks, Dad spent a lot of time working for George Campbell, pouring concrete for septic tanks," said David Otos, of Vancouver.

That connection worked favorably when Gordon was looking for property to locate the station. David said Campbell sold his dad the land.

"My Uncle Eldon came down from Fairbanks, Alaska, and together with my Grandma Ruth, shot the stumps and cleared the land," noted Randy Otos, 66, of Ketchikan, Alaska.

The Otos boys remember the day a grand opening was held for the radio station.

"There was a carnival in town during the grand opening. The ringmaster was an ex-TV personality by the name of Sky King. His black and white TV show consisted of Sky and his niece Penny flying around the Southwest fighting crime and helping people," noted Randy in a 2018 email.

Gordon Otos moved to Forks in 1966 and established Forks Broadcasting Co. to operate KVAC, the first radio station on the West End of the North Olympic Peninsula. *(Forks Forum archive)*

"Sky was my hero and brother Dave's, too," Randy wrote. "Dad hired Sky King to come to the grand opening and run the American flag up the tower. Half-way up, the flag snagged on the first set of guy wires. As Sky was looking up the tower fighting the flag, his large cowboy hat fell off and got stepped on, pretty much smashing it flat. The whole scene was accompanied by language unbecoming the idol of two youngsters. The flag was untangled and went to the top without further incidence."

It was an ominous start but the first radio station in Forks was underway.

At the age of 16, Randy had a radio/telephone license. "I worked the rock and roll show, called 'Teen Beat,' from 6-10 each night, except Sunday," he noted.

David said his only involvement with the radio station also was the

"Teen Beat" when Randy wasn't available. He also helped his dad pick out music when Randy couldn't.

"Mom acted as news editor and typed the radio ads," Randy said.

He also remembered a colorful DJ, who went by the name of "Big Burly" Rob Anderson. "He was anything but; he had a heart condition that stunted his growth. His life's dream was to be a radio personality; he smoked to lower his voice," Randy shared. "He died on the air; was found sprawled across one of the turntables."

The radio station was only one month old when Gordon and Betty Otos heard that the *Forks Forum* was for sale, so they bought it, and a few months later, moved the paper into the radio station building.

All three boys worked at the paper; Betty became news editor after a time.

David said his mother preferred working at the paper to the radio; she often would head to La Push "and look for jasper at the beach when it got stressful. It was her favorite time." The family had lived at La Push for a while.

Meantime, Gordon was involved with civic organizations and even ran for Clallam County commissioner in 1970 and 1974, both unsuccessful. He was president of the Forks Chamber of Commerce, president of the West End Democratic Club and a member of the Lions and Elks.

From 1968-1970, he chaired the Forks Old Fashioned 4th of July Festival.

Gordon had "a beautiful singing voice and performed at weddings, funerals and graduations. He also is responsible for starting the Quillayute Valley Scholarship Auction, which is now in its 54th year, raising money for high school students. In 1967, he held a live impromptu on-air auction and raised $2,400. Last year, (2018), the auction raised $142,000," Baron added.

Betty and David Otos believe Elliott was only involved a couple of years with the station.

In 1975, the station went up for sale and it was purchased by Buddy Howard; the newspaper was sold to Lorraine and Hartley Berg.

The Otos family moved to Battle Ground, Wash., where Gordon worked at several jobs, including *Loggers World* magazine. He died in

March 1996 at 68. Betty, 86, lives in Vancouver, and "is going strong," according to David.

In 1978, Howard pushed KVAC to the next level, adding FM to its services, operating at 103.9 megahertz. Howard told the *Forum* "the next step will be approval of building permits for the transmitter and studio in the present building. An FM tower will be placed on Ellis Mountain," about 20 miles northwest of Forks.

The addition of the station will allow two formats.

Howard also noted that he has put the station up for sale.

KVAC 'on Ice'

In December 1979, the transaction was complete, as noted by the *Forum's* Jan. 7, 1980, story, headlined: "KVAC on Ice."

The station was sold to Don and Eola Ice, who vowed to improve the news coverage, while leaving the musical menu untouched.

The station played country and western music from 5:30 a.m.-noon, easy listening from noon-6 p.m. and moderate rock from 6-10 p.m. Ice said country and western was his favorite.

Top priority, Ice told the *Forum*, is to "finish work on the station's new production room, so they could write and record commercials during broadcasting hours, instead of having to do it in the main studio after they are off air."

Born and raised in Ohio, Ice moved to the West Coast in 1970. KVAC is the first station the couple has owned, although he has managed several.

He got into radio quite by accident after 18 years managing a finance company. He was in Everett when a friend bought a radio station. Ice promoted it so well, he was hired as an ad salesman. When the company purchased three stations in Alaska, he went north to manage them.

These included 50,000-watt KYAK and the FM rock station KOOT in Anchorage. He also decided it was time to put a ring on Eola's finger. The couple had known each other for years, but the Washington-Alaska phone bills were getting out of hand.

They were married in 1978 but have children in the Seattle area from previous marriages.

Ice, a former Marine and a licensed commercial pilot, became an immediate productive member of the community.

In the 16 years he owned the station, he probably was best known as the "Voice of the Spartans," broadcasting the high school football and basketball games as well as other sports.

He also served two terms on the Forks City Council, one with the Planning Commission, and broadcast the annual Quillayute Valley Scholarship Auctions.

He also ran unsuccessfully twice for Washington State governor and once for mayor of Forks.

Ice told the *Forum*, in his retirement story, written by editor Don Gronning on Dec. 27, 1995, "When we first came, we broadcast every (football and basketball) game. We said that was too much, but we still did thirty-some games, four nights a week."

His first broadcast partner was Rich Franks, Forks Athletic Director, then later high school teacher Scott Seaman.

Ice shared one story of trying to broadcast a game in small towns.

Arriving at the football stadium, he discovered he couldn't hook up electronically. He had a slight acquaintance with people who owned a house that overlooked the field.

> *"We broadcast from a phone in their bedroom," Ice said. "It looked right down onto the field and Spartan fans heard the game that night."*
>
> **Don Ice, KVAC owner**

"We broadcast from a phone in their bedroom," Ice said. "It looked right down onto the field and Spartan fans heard the game that night."

In the retirement story, Ice said he and his wife have enjoyed their time in Forks, noting that when he arrived, he planned to stay indefinitely. "I never planned on retirement," but failing eyesight and diabetes took their toll.

"We tried to give back to the community because it has been so good to us," he said, bowing out.

Don Ice died in 2002.

Al Monroe purchased the business and operated the station until 2003 when he died.

"The station was sold to an investment company based in Dallas, Texas," Baron wrote in her small-town radio article.

Lamb gives station hope

"Then in December 2010 the music literally died when the station tower took a direct hit by lightning." The station was off the air for more than a month before another company purchased the crippled station and kept it going until selling to Mark Lamb in August 2013.

This was the first radio ownership for Lamb, who introduced new call letters: KBDB 96.7 FM and KFKB 1490 AM.

"The Ices controlled the tower and studio and leased to other operators," Lamb explained the convoluted status of the station and tower in a 2018 email.

"My company, Forks Broadcasting Inc., bought the licenses from former operators and the property from the Ices. We subdivided the property to separate the non-radio parcels but were unable to sell them and create an economic model for the business at the overpriced property," Lamb said.

He said re-engineering a plan first developed by Don Ice to relocate the KBDB-FM signal to Ellis Mountain resulted in an "upgraded signal, while delivering additional digital program channels on the same signal."

When he bought the station in 2013, Lamb related to Baron that he had been interested in radio since his high school days in Westport, Conn. He said his mission was to bring the AM station back to life with a local morning news program, weather and community information. He also said the station would host Spartan football and baseball games, and the Seattle Mariners baseball games.

An open house was attended by about 80 people. Lamb said he wanted to provide radio that will make the difference and have a station that connects more with the area than the station has in the past.

In 2016, the station went through an FM upgrade that "moved the majority of our revenue generation on the mountain; we were unable to negotiate an economic deal with the Ices for the 260 Cedar property."

In August 2017, the old station reverted to Eola Ice when no deal could be reached.

Lamb said his only option was to turn the AM off and abandon the facility as "the expense we believe had ruined operations through several owners."

Lamb said the studio and offices are now operating at 51 N. Spartan Ave., which once housed the Forks City Hall. "KBDB has effectively radiated power of 18,000 watts, three times what we packed at 260 Cedar."

He said the facility is more efficient. "Our new rent and utilities are 30 percent of what Ice paid. Nobody's made money at 260 Cedar in 50 years except the Ices, in my estimation.

"We first became cash-flow positive after abandoning their facilities. We received a substantial rebate from PUD with our mountain signal upgrade"

The former KVAC AM is now KFKB-AM and silent. "We are considering resurrecting the signal at a new tower facility we may build in 2018," Lamb continued, adding that the "grandfathered use of the Ices' tower lapsed on the anniversary of going out of service; the structure at 260 Cedar is of scrap value only."

Lamb said that property was offered for sale in January 2018.

CHAPTER 17

Voices from the Peninsula: KPTZ, PTTV Port Townsend

E stablishing a small-town radio station requires a lot of early planning, a strong volunteer base, patience, and, according to KPTZ co-founder Colin Foden, a bit of luck.

"We had a lot of luck, to be honest," said Foden. "Each time we needed someone to volunteer, they walked through the door."

He cited the situation with chief engineer Bill Putney. "We were just talking about how we needed an experienced engineer to get us going," Foden said, "and Bill walked in the door."

Putney became the station's first chief engineer and he is still there today as KPTZ celebrated seven years in operation in 2018.

It all began in 2007 when Sherry Jones and Colin Foden connected. Jones, a local attorney and producer of public access cable station PTTV, saw a notice that the Federal Communications Commission was accepting bids for non-commercial educational radio licenses.

"Sherry ran into me at Swain's (now Quimper Mercantile) and asked me if I like radio," Foden said in a 2018 interview. "I love radio," I told her. "She asked me if I'd like to help build a radio station. I told her 'Sure, how difficult can that be?'"

Jones formed a nonprofit organization, called "Radio Port Townsend," to operate the station.

"Radio is uniquely relevant media because it's everywhere, it's low-tech and it's free," Jones told Barney Burke of the *Port Townsend Leader* for a story on Sept. 5, 2007.

To launch the station, Jones said she was looking for level-headed, visionary and enthusiastic people.

"Instead she settled for us," Foden told the *Leader*, referring to himself, Collin Brown and Ann Katzenbach, who formed the corporation's first board.

They filed the necessary paperwork, agreed on the call letters, and about a year later they were granted the license to construct a station with a three-year window to be in operation at 91.9 frequency on the FM dial.

In June 2009, the organization received a federal 501-C nonprofit tax status, opening the door for fundraising and grant applications.

Word spread rapidly that Port Townsend soon would have its own radio station after two attempts had failed at the turn of the century.

"We put the call out for volunteers," said Larry Stein, the station's first program director, and is still in that role today.

Stein splits time between Seattle and Port Townsend, but he was the perfect man for the job, having been the founding producer of "To The Point," (formerly "Which Way LA") on KCRW Santa Monica, L.A.'s major NPR (National Public Radio) station. In Seattle he produced literary and arts programming for KUOW. Before radio he produced educational and documentary films on TV.

"Our format is going to be a very eclectic mix," Stein told the *Leader* on Oct. 21, 2009, adding the station would offer interviews and talk, music, news, documentary and literary programs.

The station received a $150,000 grant from the federal government and raised $50,000 from local donations to fund most of the initial equipment.

Foden explained that the station was founded on a four-leg premise, similar to a foot stool. "We wanted it to be:

- Independent, financially as well as programmatically;
- Local, to build the community around the station; it's all volunteer, people participating because of their love for radio;
- Eclectic, open to many different ideas and styles of music;
- Breaking news and news-magazine program."

Jones, the board's first president, summarized it for the *Leader* story: *We don't want to be a transmitter station for a national radio chain; it's about local news, information and culture; it's about supporting local artists, local issues, local interest.*

If you think about public radio, most of what they offer is the same nationwide or pertains mainly to urban areas; it's easy to get excited about all the unique programming possibilities in Port Townsend.

"There's so much going on in the community. Content is not a problem," Brown told the *Leader* in 2007.

After receiving the nonprofit status and grants in 2009, the next year was one of big changes for the yet-to-be-heard station. After three years steering the project, Jones stepped down and Foden was elected president. In 2010, Stein joined the board as did Putney.

That spring, a five-year agreement was reached for space at the Mountain View campus on Blaine Street. The 750-square-foot portable classroom was converted into the station studio with two rooms for broadcasting and one for production.

In October 2010, a 10-year lease was signed for locating a tower, antenna and transmitter, a 190-foot structure on Jacob Miller Road, about a mile from the station.

One problem with the transmitter, Foden explained, is "the signal stretches out," he said, spreading his arms like wings to indicate the signal is like flanks. "We can reach Sequim, Port Hadlock, even Whidbey Island, but not downtown on Water Street."

> *"I was fortunate to be the first person who said, 'You are listening to KPTZ 91.9 FM,'" Foden said. There were not too many times in my life that I could be a part of a spectacular success. This was one of them."*
>
> **Colin Foden, KPTZ co-founder**

Weather problems caused a delay in the tower construction and the station was able to get an extension on the federal grant. In April 2011, the tower was constructed.

Scott Wilson, then publisher of the *Leader*, wrote a congratulatory editorial on May 11, 2011, citing the start-up efforts of the four founders, the countless hours of volunteer effort and a celebration that night for the community at the Northwest Maritime Center. It's a fundraiser with a $25 asking donation, Wilson noted.

Finally, on the air

The station went on the air for the first time on May 14, 2011, at 8 a.m. with 2,000 watts of power.

"I was fortunate to be the first person who said, 'You are listening to KPTZ 91.9 FM,'" Foden said. There were not too many times in my life that I could be a part of a spectacular success. This was one of them.

"We decided to use the metaphor for launching of a boat. The launch party that night was even more phenomenal when more than 500 people showed up.

"Our engineer Bill Putney did an amazing job, and is still doing it, although he is now a port commissioner," said Foden, who was born near Manchester, England, and spent a few years in New Zealand and Southern California before moving to Port Townsend in 1992.

"I grew up listening to the BBC and I loved radio," said Foden, who had no background in the industry. "I had a career in information technology and worked for a lot of non-profits. My background is what qualified me for this job and gave me the confidence."

Foden also spent seven years as a systems and operations director for Centrum. "We are tied into Centrum. They have outstanding performers come through there; some come to the station for interviews and to play. We help them sell tickets."

He said he was amazed at the wealth of talent in Port Townsend, though only a few of the volunteer announcers had experience in radio.

People who were involved were "aficionados of the genre they enjoyed," said Foden. "They are familiar with many different types of music — blues, jazz, pop, world music. Barely anything we don't cover."

"We had people bringing us their tapes, vinyls from their collection. These are people who love music, not only love it, but enjoy talking about it," Stein said.

Most of the DJs add to their programs with background of the music, the artist and history. "They know all there is to know about their genre and share it with the audience," said Stein. He picked up on that and started his own show "Bring Your Records." Stein said he enjoys playing other people's favorite records. "Once in a while I get to play mine."

Another of the music-based announcers to step up early was Tim

Quackenbush, who Stein said, came from KVMR, a music station in the Sacramento Valley. He had been a prison guard and has a program called "Discovery Road," named after a popular street in Port Townsend.

One of the more extensive programs is "Tossed Salad," a four-hour program of music variety and interviews by Phil Andrus, formerly of KRAB in Seattle.

The lineup of talent is rather lengthy (and can be viewed at *kptz.org*), but a couple more include "Stringband Theory," with Dave Long, a former Boeing engineer; "Midlife Crisis Dance Party," with Ray Serebrin, a former Jefferson County Library director, who Stein said, has a background with KRAB in Seattle and "writes a funny, spacey monologue"; former *Leader* reporter Burke has a blues program and Putney's nostalgic "Old Time Radio" looks at the Golden Age of radio.

Stein also noted that the station has several talented female announcers. He cited Susan Bublitz, whose "Plugged-in Planet," features a mix of music from all over. "Music you can dance to," he added.

Two other female announcers include Lizz P., whose "Musical Chairs" program is geared toward the youth, and Ruby Fitch, popular in Port Townsend restaurants, also caters to the younger set with pop music and cowboy songs with "Beach Rubble."

It's not all about music, however. Chris Wilson has a show called "Booklover's Café," conducting interviews with local authors or discussing a recent book release, such as the March 2018 show with Port Townsend's Leif Whittaker, talking about his book *My Old Man and the Mountain*, a memoire of his father Jim Whittaker's ascent as the first American to climb Mount Everest.

Foden, who stepped down in 2017 as board president, produces a monthly opera show. "Opera is 400 years old," said Foden. "I may play anything from the early days to the modern." But the show also is educational, he says. "This is a complex show. Whatever nation, whatever language, I try to focus on that, tell the story and give history."

He said his program, "Live From the Met," is centered around the opera season (August to May) and the programs featured by the Rose Theatre in Port Townsend. "Whatever they are doing, is what my show focuses on."

Ambrose board president, GM

The board's new president and station general manager, Robert Ambrose, became a volunteer when he moved from Alaska in 2015. He moved in with "Rhythm Connection," a program focusing on African music, that weaves in Caribbean, Latin American and other world music."

Ambrose, 62, said he gained his interest in African genre when a friend gave him a tape of the music when he was living in the San Francisco Bay area. He moved to Talkeetna, Alaska, in 1993, just as KTNA was established. He later became music director for the station, then a board member and general manager.

While there, he became the African music columnist for *The Beat Magazine*. Now, he is sharing his knowledge with KPTZ listeners.

"Robert knows more about that genre than anyone I know," said Stein. "He brings a lot of influence from 20 years in Alaska. We are lucky to have him."

Ambrose said one of the things he looked for in moving from Alaska was a city that had a good community radio station.

In 2013, the station began to develop a role with the Jefferson County emergency services. "We are an authorized partner with them," said Foden. "We have a team ready to embed at their facility (in Port Hadlock). They can contact us for assistance to get information on the air, or if they need help, we can send people out there. All of our emergency team staff members are trained and have to pass a course (in emergency preparedness)," Foden said.

The station has not yet had an emergency where it had to embed anybody, but there have been major storms and a burst water main situation in which the station had to relay critical information to the listeners. Foden said the station helps get information out in the event of a flooded street, road closure or bad accident.

The fourth leg of the stool is one the station is working to improve: Breaking news coverage and other local news.

"We don't have room for a full-time news reporter," Foden said. Steve Evans is the news director, but his focus is on "Compass," a weekly program that centers around one theme.

Vision for the future

The next few years will be interesting for KPTZ. It must find a new location for its tower and transmitter, and a new studio site.

"The board has been struggling for a couple of years to find a permanent building," said Ambrose, who is spearheading the station's move in that direction.

The future has a rosy outlook. A new tower location and a building site are getting close, he said in a March 2018 interview.

"In December (2017), we signed a Memorandum of Understanding to be part of the Maker's Square complex at Fort Worden," said Ambrose.

The lease expires on their tower location in 2020 and the Port Townsend School District, which owns the Mountain View complex, is making changes. It is planning to demolish the portable building that houses the radio studio and turn the site into handicapped parking. The police station also is moving out of the complex.

The new site for the 190-foot tower is on Artillery Hill at Fort Worden with no bluff interference, enabling the signal to reach in the downtown sector.

"The good thing is the Army had a radio station out there with a transmitter," said Ambrose.

Ambrose estimated cost for the tower and renovating the building for broadcasting and production will be $500,000 to $600,000. "We are looking at fundraising and researching grants. We have an agreement with the county for emergency service; some funding will come from that, and we know there is funding through the arts community."

> *"It's all about good programming. We have real shows, by real people who love music and the community."*
>
> **Larry Stein, KPTZ program director**

He said the board also will be looking for local donors. He figured the staff likely will have to raise about $100,000 and the rest will come from grants.

"We have built into our plans to have a news reporter we can pay, so we can improve local news broadcasting."

No matter where the station is located, Foden, Stein and Ambrose agree: How KPTZ delivers its programs needs to change.

"We have to be more interactive," said Foden. "We already have the listeners, but we have to keep them. Some autos are eliminating radios from cars. Every show is streamed now, and we have built a Podcast library (allowing listeners to hear their favorite program when they want it)."

Stein said, "It's all about good programming. We have real shows, by real people who love music and the community."

PTTV Public access cable

Creating a cable television station in Port Townsend was the result of six folks who got together for a brainstorming session.

Gary Lemons said "it was in the early 1990s" when he, videographer and later Port Townsend Mayor Mark Welch, Robert and Jeanette Force, Peter Badame and Dan Harpole met to discuss establishing what later became PTTV.

Lemons and Welch supplied the equipment and technical expertise, while Summit Cable offered the channel. They went live with election coverage and this became the seed that later grew into a full-fledged PEG Station (Public, Education and Government). The city used the franchise agreement money to fund the overhead and purchase the necessary equipment. The school district donated space in the Gael Stuart Building across from the high school.

"We spent the first year" remodeling the old administrative offices into a professional studio complex, said Lemons.

"I was a contractor when I was hired as station manager and designed and built the light grid, the editing suites, a live studio, and post production rooms that were separated from the walk-in office."

Lemons' background was as a videographer and technician. Tom Moffat — co-manager at the beginning — had extensive audio experience. Lemons and Moffat were the only paid staff. A committed and increasingly skilled group of volunteers formed around them.

> *"We couldn't have done it without those dedicated volunteers."*
>
> **Gary Lemons, PTTV co-founder**

"We couldn't have done it without those dedicated volunteers," Lemons said.

To satisfy the government aspect of the franchise agreement, the station covered council meetings and conducted interviews with council members as well as documenting ongoing City of Port Townsend projects such as the building of the new fire station, the new annex at city hall and reconstruction of the Bell Tower.

The election in 1997 was the station's first live programming.

Covering school events was important for the educational aspect. The station ran live feeds for high school football and boys' and girls' basketball.

The station was tied into the high school's computer classrooms. "Students worked with us and received Running Start credit," Lemons said.

Live at the festivals

Among the highlights for Lemons were live shows from the Wooden Boat Festival, the Rhody parade and festival, and Centrum, where visiting musicians and performers were interviewed on TV in advance of their show.

"There is a saying in the art world, called 'sculpture moment.' That's what this experience was like," said Lemons. "The idea is a sculpture is not limited to rigid forms and materials, but it's an actual interaction that creates a sculpture event in time."

He explained that the theory fit for those who volunteered at the station.

"We had a group of complete strangers who came in and learned to support each other as camera operators, script consultants, editors, field technicians, lighting and sound assistants. They all learned at the same time how to lean on each other and pick up necessary skills to make professional productions."

Other programs the station included were spirituality, yoga, tai chi and public opinion.

It was this last aspect — public opinion — that eventually became the station's undoing.

"We had a lot of strange shows," said Lemons, pointing out, among them: Andy Lee, who said he was a grandson of martial arts actor Bruce Lee (he wasn't); a man who called himself "Emperor Turtle," who claimed he could communicate with other worlds; and a show called "Sex Puppets," which pushed the envelope for that subject.

"It was all legal, according to our attorney," said Lemons, who was station manager. "It was my job to allow public opinion and freedom of speech" for those who had programs. "We did not allow censorship as long as everything was legal and not libelous."

Station was a model

He said the station had become "a model for how small-town TV can operate with an all-volunteer base. People came from all over to see how we did it."

Lemons said city officials became "very intolerant of shows that criticized city government. We got subtle requests to tone it down."

Then in 2005, Lemons was fired by the city manager in concert with the city clerk. Lemons took the issue to Mayor Jeff Massey, who said "they couldn't do that."

About 90 people showed at the next city council meeting to protest the city's interference with the station and the firing of Lemons. "They were allowed three minutes each to talk. It was a long meeting. The council voted to override the city manager, and even gave me a raise," Lemons said.

From that point, "There was a lot more discord leveled at the council; there was a lot of micro-managing and budget requests that were ignored or delayed," Lemons said.

Finally, after working seven days a week, the stressful situation became too much, and Lemons submitted his resignation.

"We had as many as 25 to 30 shows," he said. "As soon as I left, the city cut programming almost overnight to five or six programs." He said most of the public opinion shows were cut, adding robotic cameras covered live events.

"I have a huge gratitude for the volunteers. It was electric the way they came together," said Lemons, who was 70 in 2018, and released his seventh book of poetry, *Hunger Sutras*, the third in the *Snake Quartet* series.

"I've had lots of jobs, but the one at PTTV was the best of them," said Lemons, adding "It's a shame that today it's just a shadow of what we had."

BIBLIOGRAPHY

Aldwell, Thomas. *Conquering the Last Frontier*, 1950.

Amundson, Mavis. *Sturdy Folk*, 1994.

Amundson, Mavis. *Lady in the Lake*, 2011.

Archibald, Lonnie. *There Was a Day: Stories of the Pioneers*, 1999.

Archibald, Lonnie. *Here on the Homefront: World War II in Clallam County*, 2014.

Archibald, Lonnie. *Old Trucks and Gear Jammers*, 2016.

Archibald, Lonnie. *Keep on Truckin'*, 2017.

Bloedel Donovan Co. abstract, 1927.

Brant, Irving. *Adventures in Conservation with Franklin D. Roosevelt*, 1940.

Camfield, Tom. *Port Townsend: An Illustrated History of Shanghaiing, Shipwrecks, Soiled Doves and Sundry Souls*, 2000.

Camfield, Tom. *Port Townsend, the City That Whiskey Built*, 2002.

Clark, Donald H. *Eighteen Men and a Horse: History of the Bloedel Donovan, Co.*, 1949.

Courtney, Al. *Sequim Pioneer Family Histories: Volume 1: 1850-1947*, Sequim Museum and Arts, 2000.

Courtney Al. *Sequim Pioneer Family Histories: Volume 2: 1850-1962*, Sequim Museum and Arts, 2001.

De Place, Eric and Stroming, Ahren. *Fifty Years of Oil Spills in Washington's Waters: What Can the Past Tell Us About the Future?"* Sightline.org, 2015.

Dietrich, William. "Who Won the Spotted Owl War," *Forest Magazine*, 2003.

Douglas, William O. "The Last Frontier in a Dark Forest: Forks,

Washington," in *A Vanishing America: The Life and Times of a Small Town*, 1964.

Ducceschi, Joan and Radke, Helen. *Olympic Leaders: The Life and Times of the Websters of Port Angeles*, 2003.

El Hult, Ruby. *The Untamed Olympics*, 1954.

Fletcher, Elizabeth "Bettine" Huelsdonk. *The Iron Man of Hoh, the Man, not the Myth*, 1979.

Fringer, Guy. *Administrative History of Olympic National Park*, 1990.

Graf, Fred William. *The Roosevelt Elk*, 1954.

Gustafson, Carl and Manis, Claire. *The Manis Mastodon Site: An Adventure in Prehistory*, 1979.

Kitchen, E.A. *Birds of the Olympics*, 1949.

Lauridsen, G.M. and Smith, A.A. *The Story of Port Angeles*, 1937.

Lawler, Andrew. "Pre-Clovis Mastodon Hunters Make a Point." *Science* Oct. 21, 2011: Vol. 334.

Mapes, Linda. *Breaking Ground: The Lower Elwha Klallam Tribe and the Unearthing of Tse-whit-zen Village*, 2009.

McCurdy, James G. *By Juan de Fuca's Strait*, 1937.

Morgan, Murray. *The Last Wilderness*, 1955.

Powell, Jay and Jensen, Vickie. *Quileute*, Seattle: University of Washington Press, 1976.

S.J. Clarke Publishing Co. *Washington, West of the Cascades Vol. II*, 1917.

Simpson, Peter. *Victorian Port Townsend*, 1961.

Simpson, Peter. *City of Dreams: A Guide to Port Townsend*, 1986.

Simpson, Peter and Hermanson, James. *Days That Are Gone* 1979.

Smith, LeRoy. *Pioneers of the Olympic Peninsula*, 1976.

Swan, James G. *The Northwest Coast* (Harper & Brothers, 1857; reprint, Seattle: University of Washington Press), 1972.

Swan, James G. *The Indians of Cape Flattery* (Smithsonian Institution, 1869; facsimile reproduction, Seattle: Shorey Book Store, 1972).

Thomas, Ned. *My Reaction*, 1994.

Vollenweider, Katherine. *Images of America; Sequim-Dungeness Valley*, Arcadia Publications, 2015.

Webster, E.B. *The Friendly Mountain*, 1917, revision by Annette Swan, 1921.

Webster, E.B. *Ferns of the Olympics: Nature's Lacework*, 1918.

Webster, E.B. *King of the Olympics: The Roosevelt Elk and Other Mammals of the Olympics*, 1920.

Webster, E.B. *Fishing in the Olympics*, 1923.

Welsh, William D. *A Brief Historical Sketch of Port Townsend*, 1941.

MEDIA OF THE NORTH OLYMPIC PENINSULA

Newspapers

Port Angeles/West End/ Forks

Model Commonwealth
Port Angeles Times
The Port Angeles Tribune
Port Angeles Herald
The Tribune-Times
Port Angeles Democrat
Democrat-Leader
Port Crescent Star
Port Crescent Leader
The People
People's Publishing Co.
The Dungeness-Beacon
Clallam Bay Record
Clallam Bay Press
The Republican
The Beaver Leader
Port Angeles Simoon
The Typhoon
The Daily Pop
Clallam County Courier
The Quillayute News
Quileute News
Quileute Chieftain
The Olympic
Olympic Leader
The Daily Leader

Port Angeles Evening News/
The Daily News/Peninsula
Daily News
The Bee
The (Second) Herald
Port Angeles Daily Herald
The Peninsula Free Press
Spruce
Forks Forum
Forks Forum and Peninsula
Herald
Shopping News/Chronicle
Sports Week
Realty Journal
Olympic Logger
Peninsula Business Journal
Olympic Peninsula
Homes-Land
Islander Homes-Land

Sequim

Dungeness-Beacon
The Sequim Press
Sequim Shopper
Jimmy Come Lately Gazette
Sequim Gazette
Sequim Sun
Sequim This Week

Port Townsend/Jefferson County

Port Townsend Register
The North-West
The Northern Light
The Message
Puget Sound Argus
Weekly Argus
The Cyclop
The Democratic Press
The Port Townsend Star
Port of Entry Times
Port Townsend Call
Morning Leader/Port
Townsend Leader/Port
Townsend and Jefferson
County Leader
Key City Monitor
City of Landes
The Evening Incident
Key City Graphic
The Herald
Port Townsend Daily
Democrat
Key City Mirror
Jefferson County Journal
Weekly Record
Jefferson County Herald
Port Townsend Tradesman
Quilcene Megaphone
Olympic Mining Record
Quilcene Queen
Irondale News
Hood Canal News

Radio stations

Port Angeles

KONP
KAPY
KKNW
KIKN
KSTI-FM
KZQM

Sequim
KSQM-FM

Forks
KVAC/KBDB/KFKB

Port Townsend
KPTZ

Public -Access TV

Port Angeles
Northland Cable
PNN

Port Townsend
PTTV

INDEX

S

Bill Lindstrom is a retired journalist with more than 55 years in the industry. He has been a sports reporter, sports editor, business editor, outdoor editor, managing editor, associate editor, and retired in 2013 after 21 years as city editor from *The Daily World* in Aberdeen, Wash. He served as local news editor for the *Peninsula Daily News* in Port Angeles from 1999-2001.

In addition to the *Daily World* and *PDN*, Lindstrom has worked at the Santa Ana, Calif. *Independent*, Sterling, Kan. *Bulletin*, Riverside, Calif. *Press Enterprise*, Santa Ana, Calif. *Register* (now Orange County), Olympia, Wash. *Daily Olympian*, St. George, Utah *Spectrum*, Roanoke Rapids, N.C. *Daily Herald* and Lake City, Fla. *Reporter*.

In 2014, he completed a 28-year project to publish his first book: *John Tornow: Villain or Victim?* It is a true story about a man suspected of killing his two twin nephews, igniting a 19-month manhunt before Tornow was killed in a shootout.

While conducting a book signing in Port Angeles in 2015, Lindstrom was approached by Brown M. Maloney and later commissioned to write this book.

Lindstrom, 76 in 2018, is single and lives in Olympia. He enjoys reading, traveling, and of course, writing.

CPSIA information can be obtained
at www.ICGtesting.com
Printed in the USA
BVHW082040161218
535485BV00001B/1/P